# CENSORSHIP AND THE PRESS, 1580–1720

# CONTENTS OF THE EDITION

VOLUME 1
General Introduction

Background 1557–1579
1580–1639
Edited by Cyndia Susan Clegg

VOLUME 2
1640–1660
Edited by Jason McElligott

VOLUME 3
1660–1695
Edited by Geoff Kemp

VOLUME 4
1696–1720
Edited by Mark Goldie and Geoff Kemp

Index

# CENSORSHIP AND THE PRESS, 1580–1720

General Editors
Geoff Kemp and Jason McElligott

Volume 3

1660–1695

*Edited by*
Geoff Kemp

LONDON AND NEW YORK

First published 2009 by Pickering & Chatto (Publishers) Limited

Published 2016 by Routledge
2 Park Square, Milton Park, Abingdon, Oxon OX14 4RN
711 Third Avenue, New York, NY 10017

*Routledge is an imprint of the Taylor & Francis Group, an informa business*

Copyright © Taylor & Francis 2009
Copyright © Editorial material Geoff Kemp 2009

All rights reserved. No part of this book may be reprinted or reproduced or utilised in any form or by any electronic, mechanical, or other means, now known or hereafter invented, including photocopying and recording, or in any information storage or retrieval system, without permission in writing from the publishers.

Notice:
Product or corporate names may be trademarks or registered trademarks, and are used only for identification and explanation without intent to infringe.

**BRITISH LIBRARY CATALOGUING IN PUBLICATION DATA**

Censorship and the press, 1580–1720.
1. Freedom of the press – England – History – 17th century. 2. Censorship – England – History – 17th century.
I. Kemp, Geoffrey. II. McElligott, Jason, 1972– III. Clegg, Cyndia Susan. IV. Goldie, Mark.
363.6'1'0942'09032-dc22

ISBN 13: 978-1-13875-150-7 (hbk) (vol-3)

*Typeset by Pickering & Chatto (Publishers) Limited*

# CONTENTS

Introduction   xi
Further Reading   xxix

**Restoration Restraint**   1
   Charles II, *A Proclamation for Calling in, and Suppressing of Two Books Written by John Milton ... And also a third Book ... by John Goodwin* (1660)   5
   Charles II, *Whereas Divers Scandalous Untruths and Treasonable Assertions ... in Several Books Commonly Called Almanacks and Prognostications* (1660)   8
   'Impeachment against Drake, for Publishing a Pamphlet, Intituled, "The Long Parliament Revived," &c.' (1660)   9
   Charles II, *A Proclamation for the Re-Printing, Publishing, and Using of a Book, Intituled, God and the King* (1662)   11
   'Printing and Printers' ('An Act for Preventing the Frequent Abuses in Printing Seditious, Treasonable and Unlicensed Books and Pamphlets') (1662)   13

**L'Estrange Takes Control**   21
   Roger L'Estrange, *Considerations and Proposals in Order to the Regulation of the Press* (1663)   23
   'LEstrange to bee Surveyor of the Printing Presse &c.' (1663)   50
   Roger L'Estrange, *Intelligencer*, 1 (1663)   52
   Letters from the Surveyor of the Press (1668)   56

**The Trial and Execution of John Twyn**   59
   *An Exact Narrative of the Tryal and Condemnation of John Twyn* (1664)   61

**Press Control and the Print Trade**   81
   [Richard Atkyns], *The Original and Growth of Printing* ([1660])   85
   *The London Printers Lamentation, or, The Press Opprest, and Over-Prest* ([1660])   89
   *A Brief Discourse concerning Printing and Printers* (1663)   96
   [John Seymour], *The Case of Libels* ([1677])   103

'The Company of Stationers against Seymour' (1678) — 106
*The Orders, Rules, and Ordinances ... of the Mystery or Art of Stationers of the City of London, for the Well Governing of that Society* (1678) — 109
*An Ordinance ... of the Mystery or Art of Stationers of the City of London* (1683) — 115
*A New Song in Praise of the Loyal Company of Stationers* (1684) — 118

**Heresy, Orthodoxy and the Press, 1666–76** — 121
  The Catching of Thomas Hobbes
    Parliamentary Examination of *Leviathan* (1666) — 125
    Letter Requesting Licence for Tract on *Heresie* (1668) — 126
    *Leviathan* Seized at the Press (1670) — 126
    Privy Council Inquiry into *Behemoth* (1679) — 127
  [Sir Charles Wolseley], *Liberty of Conscience upon its True and Proper Grounds Asserted and Vindicated* (1668) — 129
  Hugh Cressy, *Fanaticism Fanatically Imputed to the Catholick Church by Doctour Stillingfleet* (1672) — 134
  [Edward Hyde, Earl of Clarendon], *Animadversions upon a Book, Intituled, Fanaticism Fanatically Imputed to the Catholick Church* (1673) — 137
  [Herbert Croft], *The Naked Truth. Or, The True State of the Primitive Church* (1675) — 141
  Andrea Rivetus, Jr [Andrew Marvell], *Mr. Smirke; or, The Divine in Mode* (1676) — 143

**News, Libels and the Crown, 1670–80** — 151
  Charles II, *A Proclamation to Restrain the Spreading of False News, and Licentious Talking of Matters of State and Government* (1672) — 155
  Charles II, *A Proclamation to Restrain the Spreading of False News, and Licentious Talking of Matters of State and Government* (1674) — 157
  'Mr. Lestrange's Examination concerning "The Rehearsal Transposed", taken by Secretary Coventry, Jan. 23' (1673) — 159
  Charles II, 'A Proclamation for the Better Discovery of Seditious Libellers' and 'An Additional Proclamation concerning Coffee-Houses', *London Gazette* (1675/6) — 161
  'Whereas there have been lately Printed, and Published Several Seditious, and Scandalous Libels ...', *London Gazette* (1677/8) — 165
  'Joseph Leigh Citizen and Staconer of London maketh Oath ...' (1678) — 166

**Restoration Crisis, 1679–81** — 169
  Charles II, *A Proclamation for the Suppressing of Seditious and Treasonable Books and Pamphlets* (1679) — 173
  Charles II, *A Proclamation for Suppressing the Printing and Publishing Unlicensed News-Books, and Pamphlets of News* (1680) — 175

| | |
|---|---|
| *A Short, but Just Account of the Tryal of Benjamin Harris ... for Printing and Vending a late Seditious Book* (1679–80) | 177 |
| *An Impartial Account of the Tryal of Francis Smith ... for Printing and Publishing a late Book ... also of the Tryal of Jane Curtis ... for Publishing and Putting to Sale a Scandalous Libel* (1680) | 184 |
| *The Triall of Henry Carr, Gent, at the Guild-Hall of the City of London* (1681) | 190 |
| 'Articles of Impeachment of Sir William Scroggs' (1681) | 194 |
| **Arguments for Liberty of the Press, 1679–81** | 199 |
| [Charles Blount], *A Just Vindication of Learning: or, An Humble Address to the High Court of Parliament in Behalf of the Liberty of the Press* (1679) | 203 |
| William Lawrence, *Marriage by the Morall Law of God Vindicated against all Ceremonial Laws of Popes and Bishops* (1680) | 216 |
| William Denton, *An Apology for the Liberty of the Press* (1681) | 222 |
| **The Tory Reaction I** | 233 |
| Roger L'Estrange, *Observator in Question and Answer* (1681) | 237 |
| *A Ra-Ree Show* (1681) | 242 |
| Roger L'Estrange, *Notes upon Stephen College* (1681) | 246 |
| Roger L'Estrange, *Observator* (1683) | 249 |
| *L–gley C—s His Lamentation in New-Gate; Who Lies there in Danger of his Ears for Printing and Publishing Sedition and Treason* (1684) | 254 |
| *An Account of the Proceedings against Nathaniel Thomson, upon his Tryal at the Kings Bench-Bar Westminster* (1684) | 257 |
| **The Tory Reaction II** | 261 |
| *The Judgment and Decree of the University of Oxford Past in their Convocation July 21. 1683, against certain Pernicious Books and Damnable Doctrines* (1683) | 263 |
| Algernon Sidney, *The Very Copy of a Paper Delivered to the Sheriffs, upon the Scaffold on Tower-Hill* (1683) | 268 |
| John Northleigh, 'Introductory Remarks', in *The Triumph of our Monarchy, over the Plots and Principles of our Rebels and Republicans* (1685) | 272 |
| **Nonconformity as Sedition, 1683–5** | 279 |
| Thomas Delaune, *A Narrative of the Sufferings of Thomas Delaune, for Writing, Printing and Publishing a late Book* (1684) | 281 |
| 'Mr Baxter's Tryal' (1685), in Edmund Calamy, *An Abridgment of Mr. Baxter's History of His Life and Times* (1702) | 298 |
| **Censorship and Punishment under James II** | 303 |
| James II, *A Proclamation against Spreading of a Traiterous Declaration Published by James Duke of Monmouth* (1685) | 307 |

*The True Account of the Behaviour and Confession of William Disney Esq; Who was Tryed for High Treason* (1685)     309

*An Account of the Proceedings against Samuel Johnson: Who was Tryed at the Kings-Bench-Bar, Westminster, for High Misdemeanour* (1686) 312

*The Sentence of Samuel Johnson* (1686)     315

James II, *A Proclamation for Suppressing and Preventing Seditious and Unlicenced Books and Pamphlets* (1688)     317

*An Account of the Proceedings at Westminster-Hall ... Relating to the Tryal and Discharge of the Archbishop of Canterbury, the Bishop of S. Asaph, Bishop of Chichester, Bishop of Ely, Bishop of Bath and Wells, Bishop of Peterborough, and the Bishop of Bristol* (1688)     319

James VII, *A Proclamation Discharging the Importing, Vending, Dispersing, or Keeping Seditious Books and Pamphlets* (1688)     324

James II, *A Proclamation to Restrain the Spreading of False News* (1688)     326

James II, *A Proclamation ... Whereas the Prince of Orange and his Adherents ... have Contrived and Framed several Treasonable Papers and Declarations* (1688)     328

**Arguments against Censorship, 1689–90**     329

[Benedict Spinoza], 'In a Free Commonwealth it should be Lawful for Every Man to Think what he Will, and Speak what he Thinks' (1689)     333

Edmund Hickeringill, 'Of the Restraint of the Printing-Press' (1689)     340

[James Parkinson], *The Fire's Continued at Oxford: or, The Decree of the Convocation for Burning the Naked Gospel, Considered* (1690)     344

**The Printing Act in Question, 1692–3**     347

*Reasons Humbly Offered to be Considered before the Act for Printing be Renewed (unless with Alterations)* ([1693])     351

[Edmund Bohun], 'Reasons for Reviving the Act for Regulating the Press & Printing' (1693)     357

[James Harrington], *Reasons for Reviving and Continuing the Act for the Regulation of Printing* ([1693])     361

*Reasons Humbly Offered for the Liberty of Unlicens'd Printing. To which is Subjoin'd, The Just and True Character of Edmund Bohun, the Licenser of the Press* (1693)     365

*The Clauses chiefly Objected against in the Act 14o of Charles II. about Printing* ([1693])     389

**Suppressing Jacobitism**     391

William and Mary, *A Proclamation for the Better Discovery of Seditious Libellers* (1692)     395

*Animadversions upon that Proclamation of September 13. 1692. Entituled, for the Better Discovery of Seditious Libellers* (1692)     397

William Anderton, *True Copy of the Paper Delivered to the Sheriffs of
   London and Middlesex* (1693) 407
*An Account of the Conversation, Behaviour and Execution of William
   Anderton Printer, who was Condemned ... for High Treason* (1693) 410
**The Rejection of Licensing** 413
John Locke's Comments on the 1662 Printing Act ([1694–5]) 417
The Commons' Case against Renewing the Printing Act (1695) 422
'A Bill for the Regulation of Printing and Printing Presses' ([1695]) 425
'Remarks upon the Act Read in the House of Commons for Regulat-
   ing Printing and Printing Presses' ([1695]) 431
'Oxford Objections against Scheme of Printing Act' (1695) 433

Editorial Notes 437

# INTRODUCTION

The years 1660–95 represent a significant period in a significant era in censorship history. Not least, they reached from the birth to the death of legislation marking 'the culmination of over a century of Tudor and Stuart attempts to regulate the press', the 1662 Printing Act, the practical effect of whose final expiry in 1695 almost pales beside the symbolic importance the end of pre-publication censorship was accorded beyond its time and place by champions of freedom and constitutionalism.[1] It takes symbolic abstraction too far to see in these decades a transformation from a pre-modern to a modern orientation to censorship but, as with the accompanying paradigm of 'Restoration to Revolution', these were times of flux and change. This volume, like the others in this edition, is compiled in the belief that the changes, as well as many continuities, are best understood by appreciating the context within which they unfolded, revealed through the competing voices that articulated and animated them. The voices range from kings and philosophers to censors and printers, all engaged in contesting the parameters and purposes of the printing press and its control in the later seventeenth century. They speak through royal proclamations and parliamentary proceedings, letters and law suits, pamphlets and periodicals. That most of these sources were not only spoken but printed attests to the subject's importance as well as being, in some cases, evidence of both the effectiveness and limitations of early modern press censorship. This introduction provides a brief discussion of the significance of the period, the main contexts and themes relating to censorship and the press, and key developments during the years between 1660 and 1695.

## From Restoration to Liberation?

The value of access to early modern texts lies partly in the reminder that they were not addressed to us: that censorship was oriented towards the present, a more immediate future and also importantly towards the past. Restoration England found it hard to forget. The Act of Oblivion which Charles II urged on the Convention Parliament soon after his return in the spring of 1660 expressed the desire to 'bury all seeds of future discords' by expunging 'remembrance' of the conflicts of the previous twenty years.[2] It was a call for peace but in effect also a prelude to censorship, because the peace sought was the peace of silence that Charles I had tried and failed to maintain.[3] Restoration efforts to control the printing press confirmed and confounded these intentions, seeking to consign to oblivion books and ideas associated with the paper warfare that preceded and accompanied civil war, yet reviving the memory of past conflict in doing so. The causes and course of civil war far exceeded the bounds of print, not least as a war of three kingdoms beyond the London-centred print trade, but Restoration advocates of censorship like the licenser Roger L'Estrange insisted that the bond between an unrestrained press and societal disintegration had been proved in the crucible of the 1640s.[4] Charles II encouraged the passage of the 1662 Printing Act, which restricted presses and required books and pamphlets to be registered and licensed prior to printing, with the complaint that liberty of the press had been to blame for the 'late Rebellion'.[5] The loyalist warning cry down the decades would be 'forty-one is come again'; in England in 1641 it was paper bullets, not lead ones, which flew.

Yet before the end of the century the Printing Act and with it pre-publication press licensing had been rejected, for good as it transpired. To Sir William Blackstone, looking back from the second half of the eighteenth century, this was the moment when 'the press became properly free', while in the view of Lord Macaulay, a century further on, this 'emancipation of the press' did 'more for liberty and for civilisation than the Great Charter or the Bill of Rights'. Despite these encomiums, neither author was oblivious to the limitations behind the liberation. Blackstone wrote of the substantial difference between a 'theoretical' gain in law and the 'practical' expansion of freedom; Macaulay asked whether the legal and practical gain had any real theoretical impetus as it did not reflect a clearly-stated principle of press freedom but was driven by practical concerns such as trade monopolies.[6] In endeavouring to capture the longer transition as a 'moment', I would argue, the great lawyer and great historian simultaneously yet suggestively overstated and understated shifts in censorship practices and ideas across the period.

Such indeterminacy about the degree and nature of change is hard to avoid given not only the attempt to capture a complex reality but to do so through a concept – 'censorship' or, inversely, 'free expression' – itself subject to fluctuation across time and moral-political viewpoint. The seventeenth-century understanding of 'censorship' was primarily an association with the ancient Roman office charged with censuring morals and manners. If censorship is taken simply as a synonym for prior restraint then it can be argued, in the spirit of Blackstone and Macaulay but in the words of a more recent writer, that 'with the expiry of the Licensing Act, state censorship of the press ceased'.[7] However, if the term is taken in a wider sense to embrace all official censure or punishment oriented to controlling expression, in some ways a 'neo-Roman' view, then after 1695 censorship by state, law and even Church by no means ceased. Its continuing forms included the seizing of presses under warrant, post-publication punishments for seditious libel and other offences, parliamentary condemnation, and book burnings. Indeed, continuities from the Restoration are evoked by the 1660–95 period being book-ended (an apt term) by the seventeenth century's two executions of trade printers for treason – John Twyn in 1664 and William Anderton in 1693 – with England's last executed printer, John Matthews, following in 1719.

The rejection of prior restraint was not wholly drained of watershed status by such recurrences, however, any more than affinities with measures under Charles I or Cromwell deprive Restoration press control of its distinctiveness. It is customary to caution that the fall of licensing did not arise from a heroic campaign for free speech, nor did it give rise to 'absolute' freedom. However, its demise was not merely accidental. The retention of licensing after the Glorious Revolution sat uneasily with the rejection of the 'arbitrary and popish' regime that produced it, the effective elevation of Whig and tolerationist stances against it, and the obscuring of any clearly delineated orthodoxy on which it could rely. Liberty of the press was still a minority cause but by 1695 faith in licensing proved to have faltered too far to secure its salvation. Its dwindling allure even led ecclesiastical defenders of licensing to self-censor in seeking support, according to John Locke's ally in opposition John Freke, who told Locke the bishops were stressing copyright protections because 'they think property a very popular word, which Licencer is not'.[8] The Act's fall did not end censorship, any more than did the revolution, but it *did* end licensing in practice, and this proved the starting point for recasting the terms of debate such that liberty of the press, once treated as either anathema or aspiration, would come to be viewed as either accomplishment or enlarged aspiration. Regulating the press remained firmly on the parliamentary agenda after 1695, but after the rejection of bills in 1696 and 1698 the focus turned from content licensing towards registering presses and identifying their users through compulsory imprints. The basic principle of press freedom as the absence of pre-publication censorship was therefore eventually conceded and during the eighteenth century would become presumed central to the nation's liberties, not least influentially among the external observers of the European Enlightenment. The question for its advocates was still how to secure press freedom, but 'secure' now meant not only 'acquire' but 'protect' and make more certain.

## The Contexts of Censorship

Press freedom and censorship were only part of the issue. Attitudes towards the scope of liberty, conscientious expression and public deliberation were entwined with broader intellectual, political, religious and social developments during the period. The experience of restored monarchy, with reviving civil and religious tensions that led to the crisis of 1679–81 and culminated in the trauma of the 'Glorious' Revolution in 1688–9, constituted the larger-scale drama to which the press and its control was a sub-plot. The role of press censorship cannot adequately be grasped as a self-referential notion, distanced from the issues that made public expression appear a matter of critical importance to contemporaries. Most clearly of importance in the Restoration context were the causes evoked in Andrew Marvell's 1677 catch-cry against 'popery and arbitrary government': the partisan political and religious struggles which recurred around notions of rightful rule, representation and resistance, and over religious allegiance, church conformity and toleration, leading up to but also extending beyond the revolution of 1688–9. The years in which the press was busiest were predictably those of political crisis and change, with annual outputs of more than 2,000 titles in 1660, 1680 and 1689–90, as well as in 1695, a figure previously exceeded only in 1641–2 and 1648.[9]

The issue of liberty and control of the press was parasitical on these crises and disputes, in terms of the degree of importance accorded to curbing expression at any particular moment and in terms of the choice of arguments advanced to legitimate or challenge that control. Behind this ebb and flow, however, lay the general assumption that the press had power: as the quintessentially public form of communication, print was deemed liable to sway common opinion on controversial issues. This was more a matter of perception than proven 'media effects', but perceptions drove censorship policy and its application. Scholarly scepticism towards the importance of the press given seventeenth-century illiteracy or the vibrancy of oral and scribal communication therefore partly misses the point.[10] In fact literacy levels were reasonably high among groups who immediately concerned the authorities, with most male Londoners able to read and above-average literacy amongst the politically active or religiously nonconformist.[11] The vibrant oral culture also allowed the illiterate to share in the street-level diffusion of printed news and views. And while manuscript circulation was important, the levels of press output in the cauldron of the 1640s – the main empirical 'proof' underlying perceptions of press power – returned in the later seventeenth century, despite censorship. The annual average of titles in the 1640s was roughly equalled in 1677–95 – 1,778 to 1,730 – while the 1660–95 average of 1,439 was 40 per cent higher than across the same number of years to 1660. Only in 1666 did output drop to pre-1640 levels, London's great fire augmenting post-Restoration concord, real and enforced.[12] However, while such figures are important, so too was the influence on perceptions of contemporary claims of 3,000 unattached book trade workers tempted by illegal printing, or the estimate that 200,000 'Seditious Copies' circulated in the two years after the Restoration. In L'Estrange's view, exaggerated but influential, the nature of print was to be 'lying open, indifferently, to all', so whoever had mastery of the press, possessed dominion 'from the Top of Mankind to the Bottom'.[13]

The resulting presence of a blanket policy of pre-publication censorship is not the least of reasons for agreeing with Mark Goldie's observation that 'Restoration England was a persecuting society', even if the persecution of print was often directed at particular texts in particular crises.[14] The degree to which censorship was a defining condition of seventeenth-century discourse, the 'epic years of the English political intellect', has been much discussed.[15] Leo Strauss, Christopher Hill and Annabel Patterson in their different ways all urged 'reading between the lines' to account for a writing context of literary persecution.[16] More recent scholarship has tended to reject the paradigm of an 'era of persecution' and emphasized instead 'moments of persecution' tied to immediate priorities and pressures.[17] It has long been clear that Restoration censorship, and licensing in particular, was a blanket policy with many holes. While press output fell in the four years after the Printing Act's introduction, Fredrick Siebert estimated that across the years 1662–79 no more than 50 per cent of pamphlets carried a licence, and Don McKenzie calculated, on the basis of sources for his *Chronology and Calendar of Documents relating to the London Book Trade*, that less than 0.5 per cent of titles 1641–1700 were inquired into as suspect (400 out of 100,000).[18] However, it is important to avoid gravitating towards a false choice between the effects of censorship as wholly pervasive or as entirely negligible. The evidence confirms that censorship was not exhaustive but not that it was 'largely ineffective', unless we set aside questions about statistics and sources, ignore the pursuit of those hundreds of titles and discount 'chilling' effects on subsequent publishing and public debate. McKenzie acknowledged that 'many printers and booksellers were harassed, fined and imprisoned', and the *Chronology and Calendar*'s 1,636 pages document clear instances of censorship as well as the commercial restraints and disputes sometimes mistaken for censorship.[19] As noted earlier, given the printing and publishing of arguments against press control, logic as well as evidence supports a view that the press carried on in a persecutorial environment.

While context guided the incidence of suppression it also influenced the substance of attitudes and arguments applied to censorship, which were similarly informed by contemporary concerns and developments. Censorship's function was to silence disputes but disputes fed on division and Restoration England was deeply and increasingly divided on interwoven political and religious grounds. It is significant that enduring labels reflecting these cleavages – 'Whig', 'Tory', 'Dissenter' – became embedded in the nation's consciousness in the renewed paper warfare after 1679, when licensing lapsed. The press did not cause the crisis of 1679–81 but it articulated and organized division, and both this and the resulting backlash of suppression had longer-term ramifications for censorship: habituating the public to partisan debate, identifying liberty of the press as a (Whig) party cause and, conversely, suggesting that censorship could be a liability for any party out of power. A writer who later recalled that Charles II's Tory supporters had 'the Dominion of the Press' and persecuted Whigs 'for Printing without a License' had a counterpart in the Tory who protested at James Fraser's licensing of Whig books after the revolution (which included Locke's *Two Treatises* in 1689).[20]

As a context for discussion of censorship, however, the issue of political pluralism raised by the growth of party was throughout the period secondary to that of religious conformity and diversity. Arguments for free expression on the basis of religious toleration reflected the most frequent seventeenth-century motivation and were self-consciously distinct from overt claims for free political criticism or debate. The former emphasized a private sphere of conscientious expression, not engagement in deliberation on governance; in modern parlance it was 'liberal' not 'democratic'. Arguing for liberty of conscience therefore did not ordain political press freedom, yet extending free conscientious expression to the public medium of print made the already porous boundary more permeable, a political consequence that critics like L'Estrange were swift to emphasize. The 'Audacious Liberties of the Press', he declared, could not involve only private conscience but constituted a public act of appeal to the people, raising the question of whether sovereignty was in the king or the multitude, a question that over time the opponents of press censorship had to confront.[21] In this way, historical and intellectual context, print as a medium, a dialectic of tolerance and intolerance, and unintended consequences all contributed to outcomes important in themselves and in relation to subsequent developments, including the amalgam of individual rights and public purposes that is media freedom in liberal democracy.

The transition was a less-than-grand narrative, however. By definition, the realm of censorship was not an open field awaiting debate on its own principles but an often murky present in which paths to publication and suppression negotiated power relationships, partisan advantage and trade interests. Monarchs and ministers, parliamentarians and churchmen, printers and publishers, authors and censors – all had their own reasons to endorse or oppose censorship measures, sometimes both given changing circumstances. Printers, publishers and booksellers had a vested interest in the freedom to publish but as an organized trade had a stronger interest in maintaining a regulatory framework that limited competition and strengthened textual property, policed in part by its own trade body, the Company of Stationers. As the licensing framework combined censorship and trade regulation, the book trade had a strategic incentive to emphasize the dangers of print rather than their own interest in seeking its continuation. It was ironic that the conflating of censorship and trade issues helped bring down licensing in 1695, and with it much of the power of the stationers.

Censorship was also murky in practice, in the sense that we lack full knowledge of its day-to-day operation and in the sense that what we do know of its operation takes us outside the corridors of power, and any discussion of textual merit and demerit, to the darkened, early-morning streets of Restoration London, as the surveyor and messengers of the press, a constable and perhaps an informant printer lay in wait before a raid on an illicit press. Some light is shed on this underground world by items in this volume but the shadows meant that problems of efficient detection and policing remained amongst the mundane factors that contributed to the long-term failure of censorship. Those charged with the task could reap benefits, political and pecuniary, but it was not an easy job. L'Estrange complained repeatedly of a lack of power and resources, he and the press messenger Robert 'Robin Hog' Stephens were widely reviled, the vagaries of political power and religious orthodoxy were perilous, printers and publishers were determined and resilient, and beyond all this appeared the timeless paradox that censorship tends to increase interest and demand.

## Censorship, Press and Public Sphere

While much remains obscure at 'street level', the role of the press in the later seventeenth century has been illuminated and its importance acknowledged by recent scholarship, with a burgeoning number of books and articles directly addressing print culture and public discourse and other histories reflecting this heightened interest, Mark Knights's *Representation and Misrepresentation* being an example of the former and Tim Harris's *Restoration* of the latter.[22] It is noticeable, however, that the period's share in this broader historiographical turn towards the role of the press has not yet extended to the degree of scrutiny directed specifically at censorship in earlier periods.

Renewed interest in the post-Restoration decades and attention to the realm of public printed discourse have advanced in step over the past twenty years, the roots of both to some extent identifiable with 1989, when the tercentenary of the Glorious Revolution coincided with the publication in English of Jürgen Habermas's *Structural Transformation of the Public Sphere*.[23] While the anniversary spurred broad reflection on the nature of the Restoration, Habermas's sweeping analysis of the rise (and subsequent fall) of a realm of public political criticism amidst the diminishing practical and normative hold of censorship around the turn of the eighteenth century proved an inspiration to some early modernists, if an irritation to others. Where some saw bad history, scholarly exactitude sacrificed to a grand neo-Marxist schema, others saw behind the flaws a powerful heuristic allowing good history – detailed accounts of public, politics and press – to give and gain perspective within the larger framework of the long transition to democratic modernity.

One ironic outcome has been the number of studies not only confirming the existence of an 'early modern public sphere' but seeking to backdate it to the 1640s and even the 1530s, beyond a point Habermas himself thought was plausible.[24] The civil war period's opening up of political debate furnishes a strong case for a transitory public sphere, but Habermas's original dating to the period represented by the latter part of this volume and Volume 4 is acknowledged even by 'back-daters' as capturing the crucial formative years of a 'fully fledged' public sphere as 'a permanent feature of English public life'.[25] One of the significant features of the period covered by this volume, therefore, is that it reaches from the early Restoration censorial backlash that epitomizes the impermanence of previous public sphere incarnations to the threshold, at least, of the public sphere 'proper', where pre-publication censorship was rejected practically and normatively, and political periodicals and partisan debate persisted and expanded.

To a considerable extent the sequence maps on to the more venerable one charting the transition from censorship to liberty of the press, and to a certain extent the present historiography shares the tendency to bestride the 'high points', passing from the 1640s to post-1689, perhaps pausing at the Exclusion Crisis, rather as an alternative 'high persons' route passes from John Milton to John Locke, pausing at Andrew Marvell.[26] The study of censorship and the press in the later seventeenth century as a result presents an uneven terrain of insightful interventions and notable gaps. Many gaps are gradually in the process of being filled but relevant accounts covering the whole period are still lacking, the standard basic account remarkably still being part four of Fredrick Siebert's 1952 *Freedom of the Press in England*.[27] The later seventeenth century awaits the kind of extended, detailed attention of late afforded to the role of censorship in the earlier Stuart period and Interregnum.[28]

## The Path of Press Censorship

Post-Restoration England possessed an array of forms of press censorship and regulation: the licensing and registration system regularized by statute; common and statute law prosecutions for treason, seditious libel and misdemeanours; royal decrees and proclamations, along with prerogative licences and patents; the secretaries of state's enforcement powers of search and arrest; parliamentary orders to burn books and interrogate authors, printers and publishers; and powers of condemnation were also exercised by the Church of England, university authorities and local magistrates. This variety meant a weapon of censure or suppression was always potentially to hand, if also contributing to the sometimes haphazard character of enforcement. Virtually all the available measures had precedents in earlier times and to that extent censorship at the Restoration needed no restoration as such, because it had never really gone away. However, the provisions of the previous two decades, from the parliamentary printing ordinance of 14 June 1643, to which Milton's *Areopagitica* responded, through further printing acts in 1649 and 1653 to Cromwell's orders on the press in 1655, were deemed illegitimate by source. Equally, the main instrument for enforcing censorship under Charles I, the court of Star Chamber, had been abolished with the King's assent and widespread accord in 1641 and was not revived. The Restoration therefore required not a restoration but the reconstruction of a censorship system to the needs of a changed order in turbulent conditions.

Turbulence was manifest in the print conflict and attempts at censorship that preceded Charles II in May 1660, the Council of State in early April ordering the arrests of alleged agitators including both the royalist author Matthew Griffith and anti-royalist publisher Livewell Chapman.[29] A month later Samuel Pepys was reporting 'the happiest May-day that hath been many a year' as the Convention Parliament spread the news of Charles II's return by ordering his letters and declaration to be printed. According to Pepys, the Commons further ruled 'that all books whatever that are out against the Government of King, Lords, and Commons, should be brought into the House and burned'.[30] The order does not appear in the parliamentary record but suits the temper of the time. Within days of arriving in London on 29 May, the King secured an order in council against the printing in English of George Buchanan's *De Jure Regni* and *Rerum Scoticarum Historia* and soon afterwards he readily acceded to the Commons' request to issue a proclamation condemning works by John Milton and John Goodwin and ordering their prosecution. Charles also granted some authority to supervise the press by prerogative to the royalist writer John Berkenhead, whose imprimatur appeared on the trial account of the regicides in October, while the Commons independently moved to suppress works such as William Drake's *The Long Parliament Revived*.[31]

Over the next two years legislation followed to systematize the process of control. In June 1661 a new Treason Act confirmed the death sentence for compassing the king's death or diminution by speaking, writing or printing, its preamble recalling that the 'late troubles' had resulted in large measure from the 'multitude of seditious sermons, pamphlets and speeches, daily preached, printed and published'.[32] Then on 19 May 1662 the Restoration restraint of dissent took two large steps forward as royal assent was given to the Act of Uniformity and to the Printing Act, 'An Act for Preventing the Frequent Abuses in Printing Seditious, Treasonable, and Unlicensed Books and Pamphlets; and for Regulating

Printing Presses' (14 Car. II, c. 33).³³ The Printing Act largely followed previous models, regulating the number and location of presses and imposing a requirement for all works to be licensed before publication and entered in the registers of the Company of Stationers. Licensing powers were granted to a number of office holders and their deputies, the most important being the responsibility for 'affairs of state' accorded the secretaries of state, and authority over divinity, philosophy and science granted to the archbishop of Canterbury and bishop of London.³⁴

Some early uncertainty over the effectiveness and applicability of the provisions is suggested by the limitation of the Printing Act to two years, but it was renewed in 1664 (16 Car. II, c. 8) and for a longer term in 1665 (16&17 Car. II, c. 4). Parliament allowed the Act to lapse in the mounting crisis of 1679, leaving Charles II to reassert control by other means, but it was revived after his death in 1685 (1 Jac. II, c. 17) and renewed for a final time in 1693 (4 W. & M., c. 24) before its expiry in May 1695, with renewal rejected. The measure of effectiveness the Act did manage to attain, as well as a degree of distinctiveness and notoriety despite its debt to past models, was largely due to the zeal of the great Anglican loyalist censor and propagandist Roger L'Estrange, the 'bloodhound' of the press. Having earlier gained temporary authority in pursuing disloyal presses, L'Estrange was appointed surveyor of the press for life by Charles II in August 1663, also being granted a monopoly in publishing news.³⁵ Much of the responsibility for licensing and general enforcement devolved to L'Estrange and over the next fifteen years and beyond he built a reputation for persecuting the press that would remain unsurpassed, albeit unenvied. Knighted by James II, his service finally ended when imprisonment in December 1688 confirmed the ideological distance between the new regime and L'Estrange's high-Church, high-Tory politics.

In June 1663 L'Estrange had published *Considerations and Proposals in Order to the Regulation of the Press*, effectively his job application and just one of seventy-five titles he published, to which can be added 1,183 issues of his periodicals the *Newes*, *Intelligencer* and *Observator*.³⁶ This volume's interest is mainly his censorship activities but L'Estrange's own publication feats are clearly not irrelevant to the fate of the press and public debate during the period. As he declared in the first issue of the *Intelligencer*, the ideal was silence but given the unruliness of the press he was compelled to augment control with confutation.³⁷ This had a number of repercussions. Most obviously, going into print invited a continuation of any dispute, a dilemma so marked in L'Estrange's case that Charles II reportedly ordered him to desist in 1679 and as part of the wider silencing of newsbooks in 1682–3.³⁸ Second, the resulting dialectic could lead to some restating or refining of opposing arguments, or indeed a shift in the overall argument, such as when L'Estrange pressed the 'democratic' implications of religious claims for free expression. Third, going into print risked empowering readers, individually by appealing to them as judges and collectively by uniting them as a 'public'. L'Estrange animated Restoration censorship but his contribution could also cut across its purposes.

While *Considerations and Proposals* helped win L'Estrange his post, he did not gain approval for his full proposed range of mutilating and humiliating punishments. However, soon after appointment he was instrumental in the death of one offender, leading a raid on the premises of the printer John Twyn, then acting as a key witness against Twyn at his trial in February 1664. Twyn was convicted of printing *A Treatise of the Execution of Justice*, which attacked the 'bloody and oppressing' house of Stuart and called on the people to throw off the 'cruel yoke of this present Tyrant'. Being charged under the treason statute of Edward III, rather than the 1661 Act, made little difference to his punishment and he was executed and quartered. Twyn's trial coincided with those of the bookseller Thomas Brewster, printer Simon Dover and bookbinder Nathan Brooks, all three convicted of seditious libel and fined and pilloried for the *Speeches and Prayers* of the executed regicides.[39]

With these developments over 1660–4 the Restoration censorship regime asserted its powers and established its immediate target, the potential political challenge to restored monarchy. However, the Printing Act's stated target was 'heretical schismatical blasphemous seditious and treasonable Bookes Pamphlets and Papers', and the fate of censorship would be bound up with both religion and politics over the coming decades, intertwining concerns of orthodoxy, loyalty and stability. This was clear with 1664 also witnessing the pillorying of the Baptist minister Benjamin Keach for the allegedly seditious, heretical and 'Venomous' book *The Child's Instructor*, and in 1666 Thomas Hobbes's *Leviathan* was famously drawn into a parliamentary inquiry into atheistic and blasphemous literature.[40] The twin focus of censorship, drawing together politics and religion, was not matched in response, as noted earlier, with criticisms of its function dominated by arguments tied to liberty of conscience and toleration in religion. The use of print as a religious aid or even obligation, fostering the apprehension of God's truth in the face of priestly imposition, was the basis of arguments for liberty of the press throughout the period. In 1668 Sir Charles Wolseley argued that liberty of the press had helped the people realize 'there was not so much use of the clergy', in 1677 Andrew Marvell presented the attempt to strengthen press controls as evidence of the 'growth of popery', in 1681 William Denton augmented John Milton's anti-Catholic genealogy of licensing, in 1689 Edmund Hickeringill insisted that men must disobey the licensing law in order to obey God's law, in 1693 Charles Blount recalled 'popish' press suppression under Archbishop Laud, and amongst his other arguments John Locke complained that the Printing Act was overly 'ecclesiastical' and designed to protect 'Mother Church'.[41]

As the 1670s progressed the targets of censorship continued to be political and religious dissent, the King attempting to stifle the growth in news and debate over issues including religious indulgence and conflict with Parliament through proclamations threatening and supporting suppression. Control was sought both of printed material and the spoken word, not least in the coffee houses in which printed news was increasingly being debated, conjoining the twin forums of a Habermasian 'public sphere'. As concern at the court's absolutist and Catholic tendencies grew, Parliament itself became increasingly divided between the King's critics and supporters. The Earl of Shaftesbury's collaboration with Locke, *A Letter from a Person of Quality to his Friend in the Country*, was burnt by order of the House of Lords on 10 November 1675, and 1676–7 saw the upper house engaged in a large-scale inquiry into printed libels.[42] Among the targets was Andrew Marvell, who both argued against censorship and attracted its attention through prose tracts reiterating warnings of advancing tyranny in Church and state: *The Rehearsal Transpros'd* (1673), *Mr. Smirke* (1676), which reflected on the condemnation of Herbert Croft's *Naked Truth* in 1675–6, and *An Account of the Growth of Popery and Arbitrary Government*, which appeared a few months before Marvell's death in 1678. He was perhaps the central figure in the censorship story of this decade, and equal and opposite to L'Estrange in many ways.[43]

Marvell's final pamphlet was, as L'Estrange protested, an early shot in the paper warfare that was to accompany the crisis of Restoration government, battles being waged over the popish plot revelations, attempts to exclude the future James II, and more broadly over the policies and priorities of Charles II. This second paper war – the first being 1641–2 – was assisted by Parliament's failure to renew the Printing Act when it expired in May 1679, the loss of licensing requiring a turn by Charles's government towards stricter and harsher use of other methods of control, grounded in law and prerogative.[44] These included further use of proclamations, augmented by warrants to search out offending tracts and their printers, and backed by a controversial opinion sought from leading judges that the King could indeed suppress what he chose by proclamation. Increased use of the courts completed the task, and the corporal punishments meted out to writers, printers and publishers such as Benjamin Harris, Francis Smith and Henry Care in 1680 turned into capital retribution as the 'Tory reaction' gathered pace from 1681 with the executions of Stephen College and Algernon Sidney for treason linked to writing or publishing. Unlike his father, Charles II avoided the loss of London and control over its print trade, rebuilding order through the exercise of persecution and propaganda, the King's *Declaration* of 8 April 1681 drawing behind it a barrage of supportive royalist addresses.[45]

Initial support for James II bolstered by the return of licensing in 1685 saw a fall in printed disputes, but the reign's attempts to maintain control of public discourse were to become increasingly desperate as warnings of Catholic and arbitrary government revived and eventually overwhelmed the regime. As well as the return of Parliament and with it statutory censorship, James's succession saw further resort to treason law, with the printing of Monmouth's rebellious *Declaration* resulting in the execution of William Disney, and continuing harassment of the heterodox, with the convictions of Richard Baxter and Samuel Johnson for seditious libel.[46] These measures were, however, the prelude to a losing battle to silence opposition. The attempt to punish the seven bishops in 1688 for seditious libel proved a calamitous case of turning private (hence non-seditious) opposition into the real thing, feeding flames of printed news and speculation that James's proclamations were powerless to silence. The Printing Act proved less a protection for James than a shelter for the undermining of his religion and position, a 1689 catalogue listing 228 recent 'Discourses Published against Popery' by Anglicans and nonconformists. In December 1688, with James departed, the press of the royal printer was destroyed by the mob.[47]

As noted previously, the arrival of William of Orange brought no sudden transformation in the theory or practice of press control. The subject of censorship was not mentioned in the 1689 Bill of Rights, while licensing continued and was affirmed by the renewal of the Printing Act in 1693, the same year that fears of a Jacobite counter-revolution resulted in the execution of the printer William Anderton. Nonetheless, the context had changed, sapping some of censorship's presumption. L'Estrange lost his post, his high-Tory values lost their footing, and memory of the mid-century paper war lost some of its purchase as a justification for suppression. The politics of authors like Locke and Spinoza could be aired in the new space that opened up, the latter's arguments against censorship being translated and printed in 1689. The difficulty of clearly identifying or establishing political and religious orthodoxy after the revolution made licensing precarious, as the dismissal of the Tory licenser Edmund Bohun in 1692–3 demonstrated. And the 1689 Toleration Act was taken to signal a new latitude for religious expression, the exclusion of anti-Trinitarian publishing from its scope indicating a key censorship battleground over the next two decades: for and against deist and other rationalist books and pamphlets.

In these circumstances, the limits of licensing's effectiveness and legitimacy were becoming increasingly apparent. The Printing Act's renewal in 1693 was subjected to noticeably more scrutiny than in 1685, and when the Act once again lapsed in 1695 Parliament declined to renew it, partly due to the efforts of the 'College' associates Locke, Freke and the MP Edward Clarke. Attempts at revival or revision in subsequent months and years failed, and as the seventeenth century drew to a close England had turned away from a formal system of pre-publication censorship, if not post-publication action. The high-Church campaign against heretical books and pamphlets that now gathered pace, spearheaded by Francis Atterbury's 1696 *Letter to a Convocation Man* and contributing to the passing of the 1698 Blasphemy Act, is too easily taken as evidence of how little had changed; it was in fact a marker of concern at the perceived loss of control of communication with the fall of licensing, the gains of toleration and the ascendancy of low-Church leadership under William III.

The debate on press control therefore entered the eighteenth century with echoes of the mid-seventeenth century, as a conflict over the suppression of religious expression rather than as a direct challenge to the state's authority over political expression. At the same time, shifts were discernible which would inform the more secular concerns of subsequent decades: an emerging discourse of reason and rights, the gradual institutionalization of party combat in print, and the attempt, largely after the fact, to legitimate the loss of licensing by elevating liberty of the press to the status of a patriotic achievement, as the palladium of English liberties. Censorship would not be readily left behind, nor liberty of the press readily embraced, but 1660 and 1695 in their different ways were both watersheds, the flow between them a transitional period for press censorship.

## Notes

1. M. Treadwell, 'The Stationers and the Printing Acts at the End of the Seventeenth Century', in J. Barnard and D. F. McKenzie (eds), *The Cambridge History of the Book in Britain, Vol. IV, 1557–1695* (Cambridge: Cambridge University Press, 2002), pp. 755–76, on p. 755. The 1662 Act was based on Charles I's 1637 Star Chamber decree on printing but significantly carried parliamentary as well as royal authority and was more extensive in words and years, being 10 per cent longer in words and twenty-three years longer in force: see the headnote to Restoration Restraint, below. Its immediate predecessor, strictly speaking, was the 1649 Printing Act, from which it differed in important ways, notably in targeting both politics and religion where the 1649 Act addressed news and political criticism.
2. 12 Car. II, c. 11.
3. J. Scott, *England's Troubles* (Cambridge: Cambridge University Press, 2000), pp. 118–20.
4. G. Kemp, 'The Works of Roger L'Estrange', in A. Dunan-Page and B. Lynch (eds), *Roger L'Estrange and the Making of Restoration Culture* (Aldershot: Ashgate, 2008), pp. 181–223.
5. *CJ*, 8, p. 425.
6. W. Blackstone, *Commentaries on the Laws of England. Book the Fourth* (Oxford: Clarendon Press, 1769), pp. 152, 432; Thomas, Lord Macaulay, *History of England from the Accession of James II*, 4 vols (1848–61; London: Heron Books, 1967), vol. 4, pp. 124–5.
7. J. A. Downie, *Robert Harley and the Press: Propaganda and Public Opinion in the Age of Swift and Defoe* (Cambridge: Cambridge University Press, 1979), p. 1. The 1662 act, which in the seventeenth century was generally referred to as 'the act for regulating printing' or similar, began to be called the 'Licensing Act' in the second half of the following century. In recent times it has usually been labelled the Printing Act to recognize that its provisions extended beyond licensing.

# Introduction

xxv

8. John Freke and Edward Clarke to John Locke, 14 March 1695, in J. Locke, *The Correspondence of John Locke*, ed. E. S. De Beer, 8 vols (Oxford: Oxford University Press, 1976–89), vol. 5, p. 291.
9. J. Barnard and M. Bell, 'Annual Book Production 1475–1700', in Barnard and McKenzie (eds), *The Cambridge History of the Book*, pp. 779–84.
10. I. Atherton, 'The Press and Popular Political Opinion', in B. Coward (ed.), *A Companion to Stuart Britain* (Malden, MA: Blackwell, 2003), pp. 88–110.
11. David Cressy's well-known figure of 22 per cent illiteracy in early 1640s London, being based on signing ability, if anything underestimates basic reading ability: D. Cressy, *Literacy and the Social Order* (Cambridge: Cambridge University Press, 1980), p. 72; J. Barnard, 'Introduction', in Barnard and McKenzie (eds), *The Cambridge History of the Book*, pp. 1–25, on p. 18; K. Thomas, 'Literacy in Early Modern England', in G. Baumann (ed.), *The Written Word: Literacy in Transition* (Oxford: Oxford University Press, 1986), pp. 97–131, on pp. 103, 107. Keeble observes that Restoration nonconformists were one in ten of the total population but perhaps one in seven of the literate population: N. H. Keeble, *The Literary Culture of Nonconformity in Later Seventeenth-Century England* (Leicester: Leicester University Press, 1987), p. 138.
12. Barnard and Bell, 'Annual Book Production'. There were more than forty printing houses in London during the period, and perhaps 150 bookshops: A. Johns, 'Printing, Publishing and Reading in London, 1660–1720', in P. O'Brien, et al. (eds), *Urban Achievement in Early Modern Europe* (Cambridge: Cambridge University Press, 2001), pp. 264–83, on p. 265.
13. R. Atkyns, *Original and Growth of Printing* (London, 1664), sig. D4r; R. L'Estrange, *Truth and Loyalty Vindicated* (London, 1662), sig. A2v; R. L'Estrange, *The Case Put* (London, 1680), p. 7; R. L'Estrange, *A Short Answer to a Whole Litter of Libels* (London, 1680), pp. 13–14.
14. M. Goldie, 'The Theory of Religious Intolerance in Restoration England', in O. P. Grell, J. I. Israel and N. Tyacke (eds), *From Persecution to Toleration: The Glorious Revolution and Religion in England* (Oxford: Clarendon Press, 1990), pp. 331–68, on p. 331.
15. J. G. A. Pocock (ed.), *The Varieties of British Political Thought, 1500–1800* (Cambridge: Cambridge University Press, 1993) p. 7.
16. L. Strauss, *Persecution and the Art of Writing* (Glencoe, IL: Free Press, 1952); A. Patterson, *Censorship and Interpretation* (Madison, WI: University of Wisconsin Press, 1984); A. Patterson, *Reading between the Lines* (London: Routledge, 1993); C. Hill, 'Censorship and English Literature', in *Collected Essays of Christopher Hill*, 3 vols (Brighton: Harvester Press, 1985–6), vol. 1, pp. 32–71.
17. C. S. Clegg, *Press Censorship in Elizabethan England* (Cambridge: Cambridge University Press, 1997), pp. xi–xii, 4–5; D. Shuger, *Censorship and Cultural Sensibility* (Philadelphia, PA: University of Pennsylvania Press, 2006), pp. 1–2; K. Sharpe, *Remapping Early Modern England* (Cambridge: Cambridge University Press, 2000), pp. 46–7.
18. F. Siebert, *Freedom of the Press in England, 1476–1776* (Urbana, IL: University of Illinois Press, 1952), p. 243; D. F. McKenzie, 'Printing and Publishing 1557–1700: Constraints on the London Book Trades', in Barnard and McKenzie (eds), *The Cambridge History of the Book*, pp. 553–67, on p. 566.
19. D. F. McKenzie and M. Bell, *A Chronology and Calendar of Documents relating to the London Book Trade, 1641–1700*, 3 vols (Oxford: Oxford University Press, 2005).

20. R. Coke, *A Detection of the Court and State of England during the Four Last Reigns and the Inter-Regnum* (London, 1697), sig. A6v; E. Bohun, *The Diary and Autobiography of Edmund Bohun Esq.* (Beccles, Suffolk, 1853), pp. 82–4.
21. R. L'Estrange, *The Reformed Catholique: or, The True Protestant* (London, 1679), pp. 7, 12, 35; G. Kemp, 'L'Estrange and the Publishing Sphere', in J. McElligott (ed.), *Fear, Exclusion and Revolution: Roger Morrice and Britain in the 1680s* (Aldershot: Ashgate, 2006), pp. 67–90.
22. M. Knights, *Representation and Misrepresentation in Later Stuart Britain: Partisanship and Political Culture* (Oxford: Oxford University Press, 2005); T. Harris, *Restoration: Charles II and his Kingdoms* (London: Allen Lane, 2005). See also Further Reading, below.
23. J. Habermas, *The Structural Transformation of the Public Sphere* (1961; Cambridge: Polity Press, 1989); G. De Krey, 'Between Revolutions: Re-Appraising the Restoration in Britain', *History Compass*, 6:3 (2008), pp. 738–73.
24. J. Habermas, 'Further Reflections on the Public Sphere', in C. Calhoun, *Habermas and the Public Sphere* (Cambridge, MA: MIT Press, 1992), pp. 449, 465; P. Lake and S. Pincus, 'Rethinking the Public Sphere', in P. Lake and S. Pincus (eds), *The Politics of the Public Sphere in Early Modern England* (Manchester: Manchester University Press, 2007), pp. 1–30; J. Raymond, 'The Newspaper, Public Opinion and the Public Sphere in the Seventeenth Century', in J. Raymond (ed.), *News, Newspapers and Society in Early-Modern Britain* (London: F. Cass, 1999), pp. 109–40; D. Zaret, *Origins of Democratic Culture: Printing, Petitions, and the Public Sphere in Early-Modern England* (Princeton, NJ: Princeton University Press, 2000); A. Halasz, *The Marketplace of Print: Pamphlets and the Public Sphere in Early Modern England* (Cambridge: Cambridge University Press, 1997).
25. Lake and Pincus, 'Rethinking the Public Sphere', p. 13.
26. See, for example, Zaret's otherwise excellent *Origins of Democratic Culture*, p. 16; also R. W. T. Martin, *The Free and Open Press: The Founding of American Democratic Press Liberty, 1640–1800* (New York: New York University Press, 2001), p. 26; L. W. Levy, *Emergence of a Free Press* (Oxford: Oxford University Press, 1985), pp. 96–7, 101.
27. Apart from Siebert, there are several unsurpassed older accounts of particular events, as well as more recent accounts addressing print culture and, usefully if unevenly, censorship. For details see Further Reading, below.
28. Clegg, *Press Censorship in Elizabethan England*; C. S. Clegg, *Press Censorship in Jacobean England* (Cambridge: Cambridge University Press, 2001); C. S. Clegg, *Press Censorship in Caroline England* (Cambridge: Cambridge University Press, 2008); Shuger, *Censorship and Cultural Sensibility*; J. McElligott, *Royalism, Print and Censorship in Revolutionary England* (Woodbridge: Boydell Press, 2007).
29. 'Warrants of Council of State', *CSPD* (1659–60), pp. 561–75.
30. S. Pepys, *Diary*, 2 May 1660, www.pepysdiary.com/archive/1660/05/02/ [permalink, accessed 9 February 2009].
31. W. Kennett, *A Register and Chronicle Ecclesiastical and Civil* (London, 1728), p. 176 (7 June 1660); *CJ*, 8, p. 66 (16 June). For the proclamation (27 June) and condemnation of Drake, see texts in this volume.
32. 13 Car. II, c. 1: 'An Act for Safety and Preservation of His Majesties Person and Government against Treasonable and Seditious Practices and Attempts'.
33. *LJ*, 11, pp. 471–2.
34. *CJ*, 8, pp. 417, 435; *LJ*, 11, p. 469. For the provisions of the Act, see below, p. 13.

35. See below, p. 50.
36. See below, p. 23; Kemp, 'The Works of Roger L'Estrange'.
37. See below, p. 52.
38. *CSPD*, 10 August 1679.
39. See below, pp. 59–80.
40. On Keach, see *State Trials*, vol. 6, pp. 702–10; for Hobbes, see below, pp. 125–8.
41. See texts in this volume.
42. *LJ*, 13, p. 13; *HMC*, 9, Appendix, pp. 69–79.
43. On Marvell and censorship, see A. Patterson, 'Andrew Marvell: Living with Censorship', in A. Hadfield, *Literature and Censorship in Renaissance England* (Basingstoke: Palgrave, 2001), pp. 187–203; M. Dzelzainis, 'Andrew Marvell and the Restoration Literary Underground', *Seventeenth Century*, 22:2 (2007), pp. 395–410.
44. *CJ*, 9, pp. 582, 634.
45. Charles II, *His Majesties Declaration to all His Loving Subjects, Touching the Causes & Reasons that moved Him to Dissolve the Two Last Parliaments* (London, 1681); Knights, *Politics and Opinion in Crisis, 1678–81* (Cambridge: Cambridge University Press, 1994), pp. 317–29.
46. *CJ*, 9, pp. 729, 754; *LJ*, 14, p. 71.
47. E. Gee, *The Catalogue of all the Discourses Published against Popery, during the Reign of King James II. By the Members of the Church of England, and by the Non-Conformists* (London, 1689).

# FURTHER READING

Astbury, R., 'The Renewal of the Licensing Act in 1693, and its Lapse in 1695', *Library*, 5th series, 33 (1978), pp. 296–322.

Barnard, J., and D. F. McKenzie (eds), *The Cambridge History of the Book in Britain, Vol. IV, 1557–1695* (Cambridge: Cambridge University Press, 2002).

Crist, T., 'Government Control of the Press after the Expiration of the Printing Act in 1679', *Publishing History*, 5 (1979) pp. 49–77.

Dawson, N. M., 'The Death Throes of the Licensing Act and the "Funeral Pomp" of Queen Mary II, 1695', *Journal of Legal History*, 26 (2005), pp. 119–42.

Dzelzainis, M., 'Andrew Marvell and the Restoration Literary Underground', *Seventeenth Century*, 22:2 (2007), pp. 395–410.

Hamburger, P., 'The Development of the Law of Seditious Libel and Control of the Press', *Stanford Law Review*, 37 (1984–5), pp. 661–765.

Hinds, P., 'Roger L'Estrange, the Rye House Plot, and the Regulation of Political Discourse in Late-Seventeenth-Century London', *Library*, 3:1 (2002), pp. 3–31.

Joad R., 'The Newspaper, Public Opinion and the Public Sphere in the Seventeenth Century', in J. Raymond (ed), *News, Newspapers and Society in Early Modern Britain* (London: F. Cass, 1999), pp. 109–40.

Johns, A., 'Printing, Publishing and Reading in London, 1660–1720', in P. O'Brien, et al. (eds), *Urban Achievement in Early Modern Europe* (Cambridge: Cambridge University Press, 2001), pp. 264–83.

—, *The Nature of the Book* (Chicago, IL: University of Chicago Press, 1998).

Keeble, N. H., *The Literary Culture of Nonconformity in Later Seventeenth-Century England* (Leicester: Leicester University Press, 1987).

Kemp, G., 'L'Estrange and the Publishing Sphere', in J. McElligott (ed.), *Fear, Exclusion and Revolution: Roger Morrice and Britain in the 1680s* (Aldershot: Ashgate, 2006), pp. 67–90.

—, 'The Works of Roger L'Estrange', in A. Dunan-Page and B. Lynch (eds), *Roger L'Estrange and the Making of Restoration Culture* (Aldershot: Ashgate, 2008), pp. 181–223.

Knights, M., *Politics and Opinion in Crisis, 1678–81* (Cambridge: Cambridge University Press, 1994).

—, *Representation and Misrepresentation in Later Stuart Britain: Partisanship and Political Culture* (Oxford: Oxford University Press, 2005).

Levy, L., *The Emergence of a Free Press* (Oxford: Oxford University Press, 1985).

Locke, J., The Correspondence of John Locke, ed. E. S. De Beer, 8 vols (Oxford: Clarendon Press, 1979).

McDowell, P., *The Women of Grub Street: Press, Politics, and Gender in the London Literary Marketplace, 1678–1730* (Oxford: Clarendon Press, 1998).

McElligott, J., 'A New Model of Censorship', in J. McElligott (ed.), *Royalism, Print and Censorship in Revolutionary England* (Woodbridge: Boydell Press, 2007), pp. 210–27.

McKenzie, D. F., 'Printing and Publishing, 1557–1700: Constraints on the London Book Trades', in Barnard and McKenzie (eds), *The Cambridge History of the Book*, pp. 553–67.

McKenzie, D. F., and M. Bell, *A Chronology and Calendar of Documents relating to the London Book Trade, 1641–1700*, 3 vols (Oxford: Oxford University Press, 2005).

Monod, P., 'The Jacobite Press and English Censorship, 1689-1695', in E. Cruickshanks and E. Corp (eds), *The Stuart Court in Exile and the Jacobites* (London: Hambledon Press, 1995), pp. 125–42.

Nelson, C., and M. Seccombe, *British Newspapers and Periodicals, 1641–1700* (New York: Modern Language Association of America, 1987).

Pincus, S., '"Coffee Politicians does Create": Coffeehouses and Restoration Political Culture', *Journal of Modern History*, 77:4 (1995), pp. 807–34.

Raymond, J., *Pamphlets and Pamphleteering in Early Modern Britain* (Cambridge: Cambridge University Press, 2003).

Schwoerer, L. G., 'Press and Parliament in the Revolution of 1689', *Historical Journal*, 20 (1977), pp. 545–67.

—, 'Liberty of the Press and Public Opinion: 1660–1695', in J. R. Jones (ed.), *Liberty Secured? Britain Before and After 1688* (Stanford, CA: Stanford University Press, 1992), pp. 199–230.

—, *The Ingenious Mr. Henry Care, Restoration Publicist* (Baltimore, MD: Johns Hopkins University Press, 2001).

Siebert, F., *Freedom of the Press in England, 1476–1776* (Urbana, IL: University of Illinois Press, 1952).

Sutherland, J., *The Restoration Newspaper and its Development* (Cambridge: Cambridge University Press, 1986).

Thomas, D., *A Long Time Burning: The History of Literary Censorship in England* (London: Routledge & K. Paul, 1969).

Treadwell, M., 'The Stationers and the Printing Acts at the End of the Seventeenth Century', in Barnard and McKenzie (eds), *The Cambridge History of the Book*, pp. 755–76.

Walker, J., 'Censorship of the Press during the Reign of Charles II', *History*, 35 (1950), pp. 219–38.

Walker, R. B., 'The Newspaper Press in the Reign of William III', *Historical Journal*, 17 (1974), pp. 691–709.

Weber, H., *Paper Bullets: Print and Kingship under Charles II* (Lexington, KY: University Press of Kentucky, 1996).

# RESTORATION RESTRAINT

Charles II, *By the King. A Proclamation for Calling in, and Suppressing of Two Books Written by John Milton; the one Intituled, Johannis Miltoni Angli pro Populo Anglicano Defensio, contra Claudii Anonymi alias Salmasi, Defensionem Regiam; and the other in answer to a book Intituled, The Pourtraiture of his Sacred Majesty in his Solitude and Sufferings. And also a third Book Intituled, The Obstructors of Justice, Written by John Goodwin* (London: printed by John Bill and Christopher Barker, Printers to the Kings most Excellent Majesty, 13 August 1660). Wing, C3322; ESTC, R13189.

Charles II, *Charles R. Whereas Divers Scandalous Untruths and Treasonable Assertions against Our Person and Government have heretofore been Annually Dispersed, under Pretence of Predicting and Prognosticating Future Events, in Several Books Commonly Called Almanacks and Prognostications* ... (London: printed by John Bill and Christopher Barker, Printers to the Kings most Excellent Majesty, 12 September 1660). Wing, C3629; ESTC, R210800.

'Impeachment against Drake, for Publishing a Pamphlet, Intituled, "The Long Parliament Revived," &c.' (6 December 1660), *LJ*, 11, pp. 200–1.

Charles II, *By the King. A Proclamation for the Re-Printing, Publishing, and Using of a Book, Intituled, God and the King* (London: printed by John Bill and Christopher Barker, Printers to the Kings most Excellent Majesty, 5 December 1662). Wing, C3510; ESTC, R33281.

'Printing and Printers' ('An Act for Preventing the Frequent Abuses in Printing Seditious, Treasonable and Unlicensed Books and Pamphlets', 13&14 Car. II, c. 33, 10 June 1662), in *An Abridgment of the Statutes in Force and Use* (London: printed by John Bill and Christopher Barker, Printers to the Kings most Excellent Majesty, [February–March] 1663), pp. 173–80. Wing, E859B; ESTC, R11559.

The restored monarchy was acutely aware of paper warfare past and present, and King, Parliament, courts and restored Church contributed to the challenge of imposing order through condemnation, control and competing propaganda. Royal proclamations, parliamentary censure, legal and ecclesiastical proceedings and, most notably, the 1662 Printing Act sought to determine what the Restoration public might read.

Self-preservation, deterrence and revenge mingled in Charles II's early proclamation calling in John Milton's *Eikonklastes* (London, 1649) and *Pro Populo Angicano Defensio* (London, 1650), along with John Goodwin's *Hybristodikai*:

*The Obstructours of Justice* (London, 1649). The proclamation struck at regicide books a decade old but its use of the present perfect tense conveyed contemporary fears of their ability to undermine the son as they had the father's cause. The effect was slightly undermined by wording suggesting Goodwin's fault was defending Charles I, rather than defending the sentence passed on him. As the proclamation indicates, both writers were temporarily in hiding, and neither was to undergo the threatened trial.

Restoration concerns extended beyond the self-evidently political, reflected by the second proclamation here, aimed at astrological almanacs. Almanacs were immensely popular, being exploited for both commercial and political profit and prone to regulation on the same dual grounds. The Stationers' Company's fiercely-defended monopoly was one source of constraint, protecting an annual output that probably exceeded 300,000 copies, but the proclamation responded to a feared renewal of the 'astral republicanism' of pro-Parliament astrologers of the 1640s.[1] Their royalist opponents were led by George Wharton, whose reward was to be named licenser in the proclamation, an arrangement superseded by the Printing Act.

On 6 December 1660 the House of Lords heard the impeachment drawn up by the Commons against the merchant William Drake for writing *The Long Parliament Revived*. Drake's pamphlet, published in late October under the pseudonym Thomas Philips, reprinted the 1641 Act requiring Parliament's consent to its own dissolution and argued that the Long Parliament had not been dissolved, by itself or the King's death. On 17 November Drake was called to the bar of the Commons where he confessed to being the author and together with the printer James Cranford was committed to custody, although Cranford was soon released. On 20 November a report listed the book's offending passages, finding its conclusion to be that the Long Parliament 'being a lawful Parliament, This can be none'. The Commons declared the book seditious, ordered it to be publicly burnt, and appointed a committee to draw up the impeachment. On 12 December Drake was called to the Lords, where he apologized, saying he had not intended sedition. With dissolution looming, the Lords passed the case to the court of King's Bench, but there is no record of further proceedings.[2] In 1661 the new Treason Act (13 Car. II, c. 1) formally confirmed that the Long Parliament was dissolved.

Restoration press policy was not only about silencing but also using print to secure allegiance. Royal proclamations were themselves examples, in the case below from 1662 going further by instructing church and civil officers to ensure the teaching of the book *God and the King* while ordering the print trade to cap its price. *God and the King* was first published in 1615 and served as the Church of England's political catechism supported by a similar proclamation by James I.

It has usually been attributed to Richard Mocket, protégé of Archbishop George Abbot, although firm evidence is lacking.

The 1662 Printing Act (13&14 Car. II, c. 33), sometimes known as the Licensing Act, was the centrepiece of Restoration censorship, regulating the numbers and activities of those engaged in the print trade and enshrining the system of pre-publication licensing. It would remain in force until 1695, apart from a hiatus in 1679–85. The Act was enacted on 19 May 1662, taking effect from 10 June, and was itself printed for public consumption in an authorized abridgement from early 1663 under the heading 'Printers and Printing', as part of a collection of current statutes.[3] Another edition under the title *An Exact Abridgment* ... (London, 1663) confirmed the abridger to be the Gray's Inn lawyer William Hughes (*c.* 1587–*c.* 1663). Hughes mainly trimmed the Act's many repetitious phrases, although the preamble justifying the Act (printed below) was excised, and he also unfathomably omitted all reference to the licensing of divinity and philosophy by the archbishop of Canterbury and bishop of London in the second clause. The full text of the original Act appears in *Statutes of the Realm*, digitized on British History Online.[4]

The 1662 Act drew heavily on the Star Chamber Decree on printing of 11 July 1637, which in turn derived from the rather differently-worded decree in Star Chamber of 1586. However, the 1662 Act carried parliamentary as well as royal authority, and the full text of the Act, at about 5,920 words, was 500 words longer than the decree, with additions particularly in the licensing sections. Much of this was matter of detail and amplification but there were some revealing changes. One was the addition of 'heretical' to the decree's litany of 'seditious, schismatical or offensive'; another supplemented the injunction against anything scandalous to religion or Church with one ordering that no 'Doctrine or Opinion shall be asserted or maintained which is contrary to Christian Faith or the Doctrine or Discipline of the Church of England'. The decree's initial catch-all provision allowing further punishment for offences in Star Chamber or High Commission was deleted and not directly substituted in 1662, although a clause lower down provided for punishment in other courts of law. The 1662 Act did not, of course, preclude subsequent punishment under existing laws against treason, seditious libel, blasphemy and other offences.

The preamble of the 1662 Printing Act read:

> Whereas the well-government and regulating of Printers and Printing Presses is matter of Publique care and of great concernment especially considering that by the general licentiousnes of the late times many evil disposed persons have been encouraged to print and sell heretical schismatical blasphemous seditious and treasonable Bookes Pamphlets and Papers and still doe continue such theire unlawfull and exorbitant practice to the high dishonour of Almighty God the endangering the peace of these Kingdomes and raising a disaffection to His most Excellent Majesty and His Govern-

ment For prevention whereof no surer meanes can be advised then by reducing and limiting the number of Printing Presses and by ordering and setling the said Art or Mystery of Printing by Act of Parliament in manner as herein after is expressed. The Kings most Excellent Majesty by and with the Consent and Advise of the Lords Spiritual and Temporal & Commons in this present Parliament assembled doth therefore ordaine and enact And be it ordained and enacted by the Authority aforesaid That no person or persons whatsoever shall presume to print or cause to be printed either within this Realm of England or any other His Majesties Dominions or in the parts beyond the Seas any heretical seditious schismatical or offensive Bookes or Pamphlets wherein any Doctrine or Opinion shall be asserted or maintained which is contrary to Christian Faith or the Doctrine or Discipline of the Church of England or which shall or may tend or be to the scandall of Religion or the Church or the Government or Governors of the Church State or Common wealth or of any Corporation or particular person or persons whatsoever nor shall import publish sell or dispose any such Booke or Books or Pamphlets nor shall cause or procure any such to be published or put to sale or to be bound stitched or sowed togeather.

## Notes

1.  A. Johns, 'Printing, Publishing and Reading in London, 1660–1720', in P. O'Brien, et al. (eds), *Urban Achievement in Early Modern Europe* (Cambridge: Cambridge University Press, 2001), pp. 264–83, on p. 274; *ODNB*, 'William Lilly'.
2.  *CJ*, 8, pp. 186–7, 192–3; *LJ*, 11, pp. 200–1, 208, 217.
3.  *LJ*, 11, pp. 469, 472.
4.  See www.british-history.ac.uk/report.aspx?compid=47336 [accessed 3 March 2009].

Charles II, *By the King. A Proclamation for Calling in, and Suppressing of Two Books Written by John Milton; the one Intituled, Johannis Miltoni Angli pro Populo Anglicano Defensio, contra Claudii Anonymi alias Salmasi, Defensionem Regiam; and the other in answer to a book Intituled, The Pourtraiture of his Sacred Majesty in his Solitude and Sufferings. And also a third Book Intituled, The Obstructors of Justice, Written by John Goodwin* (London: printed by John Bill and Christopher Barker, Printers to the Kings most Excellent Majesty, 13 August 1660). Wing, C3322; ESTC, R13189.

By the King.

# A PROCLAMATION

For calling in, and suppressing of two Books written by *John Milton*; the one Intituled, *Johannis Miltoni Angli pro Populo Anglicano Defensio, contra Claudii Anonymi alias Salmasii, Defensionem Regiam*; and the other in answer to a Book Intituled, *The Pourtraicture of his Sacred Majesty in his Solitude and Sufferings*. And also a third Book Intituled, *The Obstructors of Justice*, written by *John Goodwin*.

CHARLES R.

Whereas John Milton, late of Westminster, in the County of Middlesex, hath Published in Print two several Books, The one Intituled, Johannis Miltoni Angli pro Populo Anglicano Defensio, contra Claudii Anonymi, aliàs Salmasii, Defensionem Regiam.[1] And the other in Answer to a Book Intituled, The Pourtraicture of his Sacred Majesty in his Solitude and Sufferings.[2] In both which are contained sundry Treasonable Passages against Us and Our Government, and most Impious endeavors to justifie the horrid and unmatchable Murther of Our late Dear Father, of Glorious Memory.

And whereas John Goodwin, late of Coleman Street, London, Clerk, hath also published in Print, a Book Intituled, The Obstructors of Justice,[3] written in defence of his said late Majesty. And wheras the said John Milton, and John Goodwin, are both fled, or so obscure themselves, that no endeavors used for their apprehension can take effect, whereby they might be brought to Legal Tryal, and deservedly receive condigne punishment for their Treasons and Offences.

Now to the end that Our good Subjects may not be corrupted in their Judgments, with such wicked and Traitrous principles, as are dispersed and scattered throughout the beforementioned Books, We, upon the motion of the Commons in Parliament now assembled, doe hereby streightly charge and Command, all and every Person and Persons whatsoever, who live in any City, Burrough, or Town Incorporate, within this our Kingdom of England, the Dominion of Wales, and Town of Berwick upon Tweed, in whose hands any of those Books are, or hereafter shall be, That they, upon pain of Our high Displeasure, and the consequence thereof, do forthwith, upon publication of this Our Command, or within Ten days immediately following, deliver, or cause the same to be delivered to the Mayor, Bayliffs, or other chief Officer or Magistrate, in any of the said Cities, Burroughs, or Towns Incorporate, where such person or persons so live; or, if living out of any City, Burrough, or Town Incorporate, then to the next Justice of Peace adjoyning to his or their dwelling, or place of abode; or if living in either of Our Universities, then to the Vice-Chancellor of that University where he or they do reside.

And in default of such voluntary delivery, which We do expect in observance of Our said Command, That then and after the time before limited, expired, the said Chief Magistrate of all and every the said Cities, Burroughs, or Towns Incorporate, the Justices of the Peace in their several Counties, and the Vice-Chancellors of Our said Universities respectively, are hereby Commanded to Seize and Take, all and every the Books aforesaid, in whose hands or possession soever they shall be found, and certifie the names of the Offenders unto Our Privy Councel.

And We do hereby also give special Charge and Command to the said Chief Magistrates, Justices of the Peace, and Vice-Chancellors respectively, That they cause the said Books which shall be so brought unto any of their hands, or seized or taken as aforesaid, by vertue of this Our Proclamation, to be delivered to the respective Sheriffs of those Counties where they respectively live, the first and next Assizes that shall after happen. And the said Sheriffs are hereby also required, in time of holding such Assizes, to cause the same to be publickly burnt by the hand of the Common Hangman.

And We do further streightly Charge and Command, That no man hereafter presume to Print, Vend, Sell, or Disperse any the aforesaid Books, upon pain of Our heavy Displeasure, and of such further Punishment, as for their presumption in that behalf, may any way be inflicted upon them by the Laws of this Realm.

> Given at Our Court at *Whitehall* the 13th day of *August*, in the Twelfth year of Our Reign, 1660.

*LONDON*, Printed by *John Bill* and *Christopher Barker*, Printers to the Kings most Excellent Majesty, 1660.

Charles II, *Charles R. Whereas Divers Scandalous Untruths and Treasonable Assertions against Our Person and Government have heretofore been Annually Dispersed, under Pretence of Predicting and Prognosticating Future Events, in Several Books Commonly Called Almanacks and Prognostications* ... (London: printed by John Bill and Christopher Barker, Printers to the Kings most Excellent Majesty, 12 September 1660). Wing, C3629; ESTC, R210800.

## Charles R.

Whereas divers Scandalous Untruths and Treasonable Assertions against OUR Person and Government have heretofore been Annually dispersed, under pretence of Predicting and Prognosticating future Events, in several Books commonly called *Almanacks* and *Prognostications*: OUR Will and Pleasure is, That no *Almanacks* or *Prognostications*, or any other Books of that nature, under what Name or Title soever, be Printed, Published or Dispersed, within OUR Kingdome of ENGLAND and Dominion of *WALES*, but such as shall be first Perused, Approved of, and Licenced by OUR Trusty and Wel-beloved GEORGE WHARTON[1] Esquire: And that all Writers of *Almanacks* and *Prognostications*, Printers, Book-sellers, and other Persons whatsoever herein concerned, do take special Notice of, and pay Obedience to this OUR Royal Command, as they will answer the contrary at their peril.

*Given at OUR Court at* White-hall *the 25. day of September, in the 12. Year of OUR Reign.*

## By His Majesties Command.

*Edw: Nicholas.*[2]

'Impeachment against Drake, for Publishing a Pamphlet, Intituled, "The Long Parliament Revived," &c.' (6 December 1660), *LJ*, 11, pp. 200–1.

DIE Jovis,6 Decembris ...

The Knights, Citizens, and Burgesses of the House of Commons, in the Name of themselves and all the Commons of *England*, do hereby declare, complain, and shew, against *William Drake*,[1] Citizen and Merchant of *London*;

That whereas this present Parliament, through the Blessing of God upon their Endeavours, and the incomparable Grace and Goodness of His Majesty's Royal Condescensions, have proved the happy Instruments of repairing the Breaches of this Kingdom, restoring the ancient Foundations, and passing many good and wholesome Laws for the Safety and Quiet of the People, and are daily preparing such others as may yet seem to be wanting:

Nevertheless, the said *William Drake*, in Contempt of His Majesty's Crown and Dignity, and of the Laws and Government of this Kingdom, and out of a wicked and malicious Intention to scandalize and subvert the Authority and Being of this present Parliament, and to raise and stir up Sedition and Division in this Kingdom, and against the Peace of our Sovereign Lord the King, hath lately, that is to say, upon or before the Fifteenth Day of *November* last, at *Westm*. in the County of *Middlesex*, written, printed, and published, in the Name of one *Thomas Phillips* Gentleman, a certain false, wicked, malicious, and seditious Pamphlet, intituled, *The Long Parliament revived; or, An Act for Continuation, and the not dissolving, the Long Parliament (called by King Charles the First in the Yeare 1640) but by an Act of Parliament; with undeniable Reasons, deduced from the said Act, to prove that that Parliament is not yet dissolved: Alsoe Mr. William Prinn his Five Arguments fully answered, whereby he endeavours to prove it to be dissolved by the King's Death, &c. By Thomas Phillips Gentleman, a sincere Lover of the King and Countrey.*

In which said scandalous and seditious Pamphlet, the said *William Drake*, amongst many other wicked Expressions, Clauses, and Assertions, therein contained, doth falsely, maliciously, and seditiously, affirm and declare,

Page 6. First, That all other Parliament have no legal Capacity, till this (meaning the Long Parliament, called in the Year 1640) be legally dissolved.

Page 14. Secondly, The Act (meaning the Act of Parliament to which the Title of the Pamphlet refers) is herein expressed, that by no other Way or Means but by an Act of Parliament it shall be dissolved; which being it cannot be done by the dead King, but may be done by the Successors, it ought to be so dissolved;

or else it must, and doth by virtue of this Act, still remain legally in full Being and Authority.

Page 17. Thirdly, How much it were to be wished, that the Legislative Authority might revert into that Channel (meaning the Long Parliament aforesaid) by which the Peace and Settlement of the Nation, through His Majesty's Gracious Influence, might durably, and without Question, be provided for and preserved.

Page 21. Fourthly, If that be a lawful Parliament (speaking of the Long Parliament aforesaid, which he elsewhere affirms to be in Being), then this can be none; nor no other, till this be legally dissolved.

All which Practices, for stirring up of Sedition, the Commons are ready to prove, not only by the general Scope of the said Book, but likewise by several Clauses therein contained, besides these before mentioned, and such other Proofs as the Cause, according to the Course of Parliament, shall require; and do pray, that the said *William Drake* may be put to answer all and every of the Premises; and that such Proceeding, Examination, Trial, Judgement, and exemplary Punishment, may be thereupon had and executed, as is agreeable to Law and Justice.

Charles II, *By the King. A Proclamation for the Re-Printing, Publishing, and Using of a Book, Intituled, God and the King* (London: printed by John Bill and Christopher Barker, Printers to the Kings most Excellent Majesty, 5 December 1662). Wing, C3510; ESTC. R33281.

By the King.

# A PROCLAMATION

For the Re-printing, Publishing, and Using of a Book,
Intituled, *God and the King*.

CHARLES R.

Whereas by the special Command of Our late Royal Grand-father, King James (of blessed memory) there was Compiled and Printed a Book or Treatise, Intituled, God and the King; or a Dialogue, Shewing that the King of England being Immediate under God, within his Dominions, doth rightfully claim whatsoever is required by the Oath of Allegiance:[1] which said Book or Treatise, being universally dispersed through these Realms and Dominions, did in those times (by the blessing of Almighty God) prove an effectual means, both for the instruction of the People in their Duty and Allegiance, and for avoiding the Penalties of the Laws and Statutes made and provided concerning the same. In respect whereof, and to the end Our loving Subjects may not be ignorant of, but rightly understand the said Duty, and the true meaning thereof, which by reason of the late times of Libertism and Distraction hath been by many too much neglected, and not duly considered, We have been graciously pleased to Direct, That the said Book or Treatise be forthwith re-printed and published. And Our further Will and Pleasure is, and We do by this Our Royal Proclamation (by and with the Advice of Our Privy Council) Will and Command all and every the Archbishops, Bishops, Mayors, Sheriffs, Bayliffs, and all other Officers and Ministers whatsoever within these Our Realms and Dominions, That they and every of them respectively, within their several Diocese, Limits, Liberties and Jurisdictions, do (by such ways and means, as they in their Wisdoms and Discretions shall think fit) advise and direct all School-masters and Teachers of the English and Latine Tongue, to teach their Scholars the said Book or Treatise, either in Latine or English, according to their respective capacities. And also, that it be recommended to all Masters of Families and Apprentices to have one of the said Books or Treatises, with advice to read and be instructed in the same, and the contents and true meaning thereof, thereby to enable themselves to understand and perform the said Oath, and avoid the Penalties of the Laws and Statutes made and provided against such as infringe or neglect the same. And for the better incouragement of Our Subjects in so good and necessary a work; We do by these presents straitly Charge and Command all Printers, Stationers and Booksellers, and all other persons whatsoever, That they or any of them do not at any time or times hereafter ask, take, or demand for the said Book or Treatise, above the price or sum of six pence of lawful money of England, as they tender Our pleasure, and will answer the contrary at their uttermost perils.

> Given at the Court at *Whitehall, December* the fifth, 1662. in the Fourteenth year of Our Reign.

> *GOD SAVE THE KING.*

*LONDON:* Printed by *John Bill* and *Christopher Barker*, Printers to the Kings most Excellent Majesty, 1662.

'Printing and Printers' ('An Act for Preventing the Frequent Abuses in Printing Seditious, Treasonable and Unlicensed Books and Pamphlets', 13&14 Car. II, c. 33, 10 June 1662), in *An Abridgment of the Statutes in Force and Use* (London: printed by John Bill and Christopher Barker, Printers to the Kings most Excellent Majesty, [February–March] 1663), pp. 173–80. Wing, E859B; ESTC, R11559.

## Printing and Printers.

I. Enacted, 14. *Car.* 2. *cap.* 33. No person whatsoever shall presume to print, or cause to be printed within the Kings Dominions, or beyond the Seas, any heretical, seditious, schismatical or offensive *Books* or *Pamphlets*, wherein any Doctrine shall be maintained, which is contrary to the *Christian Faith*, or the Doctrine or Discipline of the Church of *ENGLAND*, or may tend to the scandal of the Church, or the Government or Governors of the Church, State or Commonwealth, or any particular person; Nor import, sell, dispose, or procure to be published, or to be bound, stitched, or sowed together.

II. No person, *&c.* shall hereafter print, or cause to be printed any *Book* or *Pamphlet*, unless the same with all the Titles, Epistles, Preambles, Dedications, and other matters thereto annexed be entred first in the Book of the Register of the Company of *Stationers London* (except *Acts of Parliament, Proclamations*, appointed to be printed by warrant under the Kings Sign Manual, or one of his principal Secretaries) and unlesse the same Book, *&c.* and the matters thereunto annexed be first lawfully Licensed to be printed by such persons as shall be appointed to License the same, *viz.* All *Books* concerning the Common Laws, by the allowance of the Lord *Chancellor*, &c. Lord Chief Justices, and Lord Chief Baron, one or more of them, or by one or more of their appointments. All *Books* of *History* concerning the state of this Realm, or concerning the affairs of State, by the principal Secretaries, one or more of them; or by their, or one of their appointments. *Books* of *Honour* and *Arms* by the Earl Marshal, or by his appointment; Or by the three Kings of Arms, *Garter, Clarenceux*, and *Norroy*, or two of them, *Garter* to be one: All *Books* Imprinted, or Reprinted.

*Provided*; The *Chancellors* of the Universities shall License such *Books* as are to be Imprinted or Re-printed within the limits of the University, not medling with *Books* of the *Common Law*, or matters of State which belong to any particular persons without their consent. /

III. Every person and persons who shall be authorized to Licence the imprinting of Books, shall have a written Copy thereof; which said Copy shall be delivered to the Printer or Owner for the imprinting thereof; and after the imprinting thereof, shall entirely be returned to the Licencer to be kept in the publick Registries of the Lord Bishop of *Canter.* or *London*; or in the Office of the *Chancellor*, or *Vice-Chancellor* of either *Universities*; or with the Lord Keeper, Chief-Justices, Chief-Baron, Principal Secretaries, Earl Marshal, or King of Arms, of all such *Books* Licenced by them respectively. If it be an *English Book* to be Licensed, two Copies shall be delivered to the Licencer, one whereof shall be delivered back to the *Printer* or *Owner*, the other to be reserved as afore-said, to the end the Licencer may be secured, that it shall not be altered without his privity; And upon the Copy to be licensed, the Licencer shall testifie under his Hand, that there is not any thing therein contained which is contrary to the *Christian Faith*; or any of the matters, *&c.* in the first Clause of the *Act* contained; which *Licence* or *Approbation* shall be printed in the beginning of the Book, *&c.*

IV. Every Merchant and other person, *&c.* who shall hereafter import any *Book* or *Books* from any parts beyond the Seas into this Realm, shall import the same in the Port of *London* only, and not elsewhere without the Licence of the Arch-bishop of *Canterbury*, and Bishop of *London*, or one of them; and shall before the said Book or Books be delivered forth, or out of their hands, or exposed to sale, give a true Catalogue in writing of all and every such Book or Books, to the said Bishops, or one of them; and no Merchant or other person, *&c.* who shall import any Book or Books into the port afore-said, shall open any dry-fats, parcels, or other fardels[1] of Books; nor shall any searcher, or other Officer of the Custom-house, upon pain of losse of his place, suffer the same to passe, or to be delivered out of his hands or custody, before the said Bishops, or one of them, shall have appointed some Scholar, or learned Man, and one or more of the Company of Stationers be present at the opening to view the same; and if any heretical, seditious, scandalous, schismatical Book, or any part thereof, printed in *English* be found, they shall forthwith be brought to the said Bishops, or one of them, to the end the person, *&c.* who importeth, or cause the same to be imported, be proceeded against, as an offender against the Act, and such further course taken against such offensive Book or / Books, as by the said Bishops shall be thought fit for the suppressing of the same.

V. No person shall within this Kingdom, or elsewhere imprint, or cause to be imprinted, import, or cause to be imported into this Kingdom, or out of any the Kings Dominions, or any other parts beyond the Seas, any Books, Forms of blank Bils, or Indentures for any his Majesties Islands printed beyond the Seas, or elsewhere, which any person by virtue of any Letters-Patents granted, or by force of any entry thereof, duly made or to be made in the Register-book of the

Company of Stationers; or other Register afore-said, shall have the right, priviledge or authority solely to print without the consent of the owners of such Books, Copies, &c. nor shall bind, stitch, or put to sale any such Books, Form or Forms, without the like consent upon pain of forfeiture of the same; and upon further forfeiture of 6 s. 8 d. for every such Book, Form, &c. one moiety to the King, his Heirs, &c. the other to the owner, if he shall sue for the same within six moneths after such imprinting, importing, binding, &c. and for default of such suit by the owner, &c. the same moiety to the use of such person, as shall within one year next after such Offence committed sue for the same, to be recovered by action of Debt, &c. in any the Kings Courts of Record at *Westminister*, wherein no Essoin, &c. shall be allowed to the Defendant.

VI. Every person, &c. that shall hereafter print, or cause to be printed any Book, Ballad, Chart, or Pourtracture shall thereunto, or thereon set his own name, or shall declare the name of the Author thereof, if he be required by the Licencer, and by, and for whom such Books, Ballad, Chart, Pourtracture, &c. is or shall be printed, upon pain of forfeiture of all such Books, Ballads, Charts and Pourtractures, and other things printed contrary to the tenor of the Act: And the Presses, Letters, and instruments for printing thereof to be defaced and made unserviceable; and no person shall print, forge, put, or counterfeit, in or upon any Book, or Pamphlet, the name or mark of any other person, who shall have lawfull priviledge, or allowance of sole printing the same, without consent of the party so priviledged, upon pain of losse of all such Books, Pamphlets, &c. and shall be further proceeded against, as an offender against this Act.

VII. No Haberdasher of small-wares, Ironmonger, Chandler, Shop-keeper, or other person, not being licenced by the Bishop / of the Diocesse, nor having been seven years Apprentice to the Trade of a Bookseller, Printer or Bookbinder; nor being a Freeman of *London* by Patrimonial right, as Son of a Bookseller, Printer or Bookbinder, nor being a Member of the Company of Stationers, shall within *London*, or any other Market-Town, or elsewhere, receive, take, or buy, to barter, sell again, change or do away any Bibles, Testaments, Psalm Books, Common-prayer Books, Primmers, Abcees,[2] Licenced Almanacks, Grammars, School-Books, or other Book or Books, upon pain of forfeiture of the same.

VIII. No Merchant, Bookseller, or other person, shall Imprint, or cause to be Imprinted beyond the Seas, or Import, or knowingly assist, or consent to the Importation into this Kingdom, any English Book, or Books, or part of any Book which the greater part thereof is, or shall be English, or of the English Tongue; whether the same have been formerly printed, or not, upon pain of forfeiture of such Books, &c. and no Alien, or Forreigner shall bring in, or are suffered to sell here within the Realm, any Book or Books printed beyond the Seas, in any Language whatsoever, either by himself, or his Factor, except only such as be Free-printers, or Stationers of *London*, without the special Licence of the Bishops afore-said, or one of them, upon pain of forfeiture of such Books, so Imprinted, or sold contrary to the intent of the Act.

IX. No person, &c. within the City of *London*, or elswhere, shall Erect, or cause to be Erected, any Press or Printing-house, Vault, Cellar or Room for a Printing-house, or place to print in, unless he or they, who Erect such Presses, &c. shall first give notice to the Master or Wardens of the Company of Stationers, of the erecting of the same; and no Joyner, Carpenter, or other person shall make any Printing-presse; no Smith shall forge any Iron-work for a Printing-presse; No Founder shall cast any Letters which may be used for Printing, for any person whatsoever, nor shall any person, &c. bring or cause to be brought from beyond the Seas, any Letters Founded or Cast, nor buy any such Letters for Printing, Printing-presses, or other materials, belonging to Printing, unless he or they shall acquaint the Masters and Wardens of the Company of Stationers, or some of them, for whom the same Presses, Iron-works, or Letters, are to be made, Forged, Cast, or Imported, upon pain every offender, for such offence shall forfeit 5 *l*. one moiety to the King; &c. the other to the use of such persons, as shall sue for the same. /

X. For the time to come, no man shall be admitted to be a *Master-Printer*, till they who are now actual *Master-Printers*, shall be by death or otherwise reduced to the number of twenty, and from thenceforth the number of twenty shall be continued, and no more, beside the Kings Printers, and the Printers allowed for the Universities; and but four *Master-Founders* of Letters for Printers. The which *Master-Printers* and *Master-Founders* shall be appointed and allowed by the Bishops of *Canterbury* and *London* for the time being: And in case of death, or of forfeiture, or avoydance of any of their places and priviledges to Print by virtue of that *Act*, for any offence contrary to the same, or otherwise, the said Bishops for the time being, or one of them, shall and may appoint other persons to succeed and supply the places of such *Master-Printers* or *Founders*. And every person allowed, or permitted to have a Press or Printing-house before such allowance obtained, shall be bound with Surties to the King in the Kings Bench, or before Justices of Assize, or Justices of the Peace in their *Quarter-Sessions*, in 300 pound, not to Print, or suffer to be Imprinted in his house or Press, any Books whatsoever, but such as shall be lawfully Licensed.

XI. None of the *Master-Printers* to be allowed, shall keep above two Printing-presses at once, unless he hath been Master or upper Warden of the Company, who are allowed to keep three Presses and no more, unless for some great and special occasion for the publick, he have for a time leave of the said Bishops or one of them, to have the use of one or more above the number aforesaid, as their Lordships shall think fit.

XII. No *Printer* or *Printers* (except the *Kings Printers*) nor *Founder*, &c. of Letters for Printing, shall take or retain greater number of Apprentices than as followeth, *viz.* Every *Master-Printer*, and *Master-Founder* of Letters for Printing, if he hath been Master or Warden of his Company, three Apprentices and no more: Every Master and Founder that hath been of the Livery of his Company, two Apprentices: Every *Master-Printer* and *Founder* of the Yeomanry of his Company, one Apprentice, and no more, neither by Co-partnership, nor any other way whatsoever. Nor shall it be lawfull for any *Master-Printer*, or *Founder*, when one Apprentice is run away, or put away, to take another in his room, unless the Name of him or them so gone away, be raced out of the Hall-Book, and never admitted again. /

XIII. The severall Master-printers and Founders to be allowed, are to take care that all Journeymen-printers, and Journeymen-Founders of Letters for Printing, who are lawfully Free of the respective Mysteries, be set on work and employed in their respective Trades; and if any such, being of honest and good behaviour, and able in his Trade, do want employment, he shall repair to the said Master-printers and Founders respectively for the time being, who shall receive him, or them into work, if he hath not a Journeyman already, although the said Masters respectively with their Apprentices, be able without the help of such Journeyman, to discharge his own work; upon the pain of every such Master so refusing to receive such Journeyman of 5. pound, to be recovered by Bill, Plaint, *&c.* in any Court of Record, *&c.* wherein no essoin, *&c.* shall be allowed, one moity to the King, *&c.* the other to the Informer who will sue for the same within six moneths after the offence committed; and if any Journeyman shall refuse such employment, being offered by any Master-printer, or Founder, *&c.* or neglect it when they have undertaken it, shall suffer three moneths Imprisonment: and no Master-printer, or Master-Founder of Letters, shall employ to work either at the Case or Press, or otherwise about his Printing, any person, than only such as are Englishmen, and Freemen, or Apprentices to the said Trade of Printing, or Founding of Letters for Printing, respectively.

XIV. One or more of the Messengers of his Majesties Chamber, by Warrant under his Majesties *Sign Manual*, or under the Hands of his principall *Secretaries of State*, or the Master and Wardens of the Company of *Stationers*, with a Constable with them, shall have power to search all houses and Shops, where they shall know, or suspect any Books, or Papers to be Printed, Bound, or Stitched, especially Printing-houses, Book-sellers Shops and Warehouses, and Book binders houses and Shops, to view what is there Imprinting, Binding, *&c.* and to examine whether the same be Licenced; and demand a sight of the Licence; and if the Book imprinting, *&c.* shall not be Licenced, to seize upon so much thereof as shall be found imprinted, together with the Offenders, and to bring them before a *Justice* of the *Peace*, who may commit such Offenders to Prison till they shall be tryed, convicted or acquited for the said offences; and if the Searchers find any Papers, or Books, or part of Books unlicenced, which they suspect to contain / matters contrary to the Doctrine, or Discipline of the Church of *England*, or against the State or Government, then to seize upon such Book, *&c.* and to bring the same to the said Bishops for the time being, or one of them; or the Secretaries of State, or one of them, who shall take course for suppressing the same.

XV. All Printers of Books, Founders of Letters for Printing, and every other person, *&c.* working in the said Trades, who after 10 of *June* 1662. shall offend against the Act, or any clause or Article therein, and shall be convicted by verdict, confession or otherwise, shall for the first offence be disabled from exercising his respective Trade for three years, for the second offence shall for ever be disabled the said use and mystery of his said Trade and Mystery, and receive such further punishment by fine, imprisonment, or other corporal punishment not extending to life, as the Justices of the Courts of *Kings Bench*, or Justices of *Oyer* and *Terminer*, or Justices of *Assize* in their Circuits, or Justices of *Peace* in their *Quarter-Sessions* shall think fit to be inflicted upon on them.

XVI. Every Printer shall reserve three Copies of the best and largest Paper of every Book new Printed, or Re-printed with Additions, and shall before publick venting of the said Book, bring them to the Master of the Company of *Stationers*, and deliver them to him, one whereof shall be delivered to the Keeper of his Majesties Library, the other to be sent to the Vice-Chancellors of the two Universities respectively, for the use of the publick Libraries.

1. *Provided*, Nothing in the Act shall extend to the prejudicing of any the just rights and priviledges of the two Universities of this Realm, touching the Licensing, or Printing of Books in the Universities.

2. No search shall be made in the Houses of any of the Peers of the Realm, or any other person, *&c.* not being free of, or using any of the Trades in the Act mentioned, but by special Warrant from the King, or hand of one of the principal Secretaries, or for other Books, than such as are in Printing, or shall be Printed after 10 *June* 1662.

3. Not to extend to prohibit any Bookseller, who hath served seven years and is a Freeman of the Company of *Stationers*, from importing into the Realm any Books ready bound, not formerly prohibited, which have been Printed ten years before the importation. /

4. Not to be construed to prohibit any persons to sell Books or Papers, who have sold Books or Papers within *Westminster-Hall, Palace of Westminster*, or in any Shop within twenty yards of the great Gate of *Westminster-Hall*, before 20 *Novemb.* 1661, but that they may sell Books and Papers as they did before 1661, within the places aforesaid, but not elsewhere.

5. Not to extend to prejudice the just rights, or priviledges granted to his Majesty, or any his Royal Predecessors, to any person under his *Great Seal* or

otherwise, but that they may use such rights, &c. according to their respective grants.

6. Not to extend to prohibit *John Streater* Stationer,[3] from Printing Books, or Papers, but that he may still follow the Art and Mystery of Printing, as if this Act had never been made.

7. Not to extend to restrain the keeping and using of a Printing-press in the City of *York*, so as all Books of Divinity there Printed, be first Licenced by the Bishop of *York*, or such as he shall appoint, and all other Books respectively to whom the Licensing thereof shall appertain: and so as no Bibles be there Printed, nor other Book whereof the original Copy is belonging to the Company of *Stationers of London*, or any Member thereof.

This Act to continue in force two years, to commence from the 10. of *June 1662.* and no longer.

# L'ESTRANGE TAKES CONTROL

Roger L'Estrange, *Considerations and Proposals in Order to the Regulation of the Press* (London: printed by A.C., 3 June 1663). Wing, L1229; ESTC, R19523.

'LEstrange to bee Surveyor of the Printing Presse &c.' (15 August 1663). NA, SP 29/78/96.

Roger L'Estrange, *Intelligencer; Published for the Satisfaction and Information of the People. With Privilege*, 1 (London, printed by Richard Hodgkinson, living in Thames-street, over against Baynards Castle, 31 August 1663). N&S, 201/450; ESTC, P1749.

Letters from the Surveyor of the Press (1668). NA, SP 29/238/179.

The emergence of Roger L'Estrange as a pivotal figure in the Restoration press is charted in these four documents, which reflect his determination both to control and confute, to suppress and use print in the service of the King and Church.

L'Estrange's *Considerations and Proposals*, addressed to the King and Parliament and itself licensed on 28 May 1663 by George Stradling, chaplain to the Bishop of London, makes a case for reinforcing the censorship system introduced by the 1662 Printing Act. The Act was initially passed for two years and the subject had again become a topic of debate, as L'Estrange noted. He proposed coupling more stringent enforcement of pre-publication controls, particularly against unauthorized presses and distribution networks, with bloody punishment for publishing seditious tracts. A list of these was appended, featuring many Interregnum tracts such as Richard Baxter's *Holy Commonwealth*, Milton's *Tenure of Kings and Magistrates* and his sworn enemy Marchamont Nedham's *Mercurius Politicus* and *The Case of the Commonwealth Truly Stated*. L'Estrange claimed these 'old books' were among hundreds of thousands of seditious papers currently circulating. He listed as seditious positions the defence of Charles I's execution or denial of Charles II's title, all libels against the royal family, any discourse tending to stir up the people against the government, and any claim that the monarch could be judged by his people. Arguing that stationers and printers should not be entrusted with governing the press, he favoured appointing six surveyors of the press for differing categories of books. This proposal was not adopted but L'Estrange, who had been issued with a temporary warrant to seize illicit publications in February 1662, was himself confirmed in the post of surveyor two months after the publication of *Considerations and Proposals*.

Charles II's order of 15 August 1663 for a warrant empowering L'Estrange as 'Surveyour & Licencer' for life survives in the State Papers, endorsed with the above title on the reverse. Although initially limited in the types of books he could license, most of the licensing work of the secular authorities was subsequently delegated to L'Estrange. Alongside censorship powers, the warrant was important in awarding L'Estrange a 'sole Priviledge' of writing and publishing printed newsbooks, which within a month he exploited with the launch of the *Intelligencer*.

The first issue of the *Intelligencer* is often quoted for its warning of the dangers of giving 'the Multitude' printed news but is rarely read in its entirety, which allows a broader view of why and how L'Estrange took on the risk. The *Intelligencer* was published each Monday until 29 January 1666, with its companion paper, the *Newes, Published for Satisfaction and Information of the People*, appearing each Thursday over the same period. The creation of the official *Oxford Gazette*, later the *London Gazette*, in late 1665 led to L'Estrange ceasing publication, accepting a royal pension as compensation.

Insights into the life and work of the press surveyor are conveyed in two letters written in L'Estrange's fittingly frantic hand to his superiors in 1668. The first letter appeals for more resources, personal and professional, to Henry Bennet, Lord Arlington, who as secretary of state had oversight of control of the press. The second responded to Arlington's under-secretary Joseph Williamson, who had sent L'Estrange a number of suspect tracts for consideration. L'Estrange advised caution, although only to allow time to 'destroy offenders utterly'. It was Williamson, effectively the government's chief of intelligence in the 1660s, who terminated L'Estrange's *Intelligencer* and the relationship between the two men was not easy.

Roger L'Estrange, *Considerations and Proposals in Order to the Regulation of the Press* (London: printed by A.C., 3 June 1663). Wing, L1229; ESTC, R19523.

Considerations and Proposals
In Order to the
Regulation
OF THE
# PRESS:
*TOGETHER WITH*

Diverse *Instances* of *Treasonous*, and *Seditious Pamphlets*, Proving the *Necessity* thereof.

By
ROGER L'ESTRANGE.

LONDON, Printed by *A.C. June 3*ᵈ
*M. DC. LXIII* /

## TO THE
# KINGS
### Most Excellent
## MAJESTY.

*SIR,*

IT is not without some *Force* upon my *self*, that I have Resolv'd upon This *Dedication*; for I have no Ambition to appear *Pragmatical*, and to become the *Marque* of a *Peevish Faction:* But since my *Duty* will have it. Thus, I shall accompt all *Other Interests* as *Nothing* in Competition with my *Allegiance*. /

If Your Majesty shall vouchsafe to look *so far*, and *so low*, as into the *Ensuing Treatise*, You will find it, *Sir*, to be *Partly*, a *Deliberative Discourse* about the *Means* of *Regulating* the *Press*; (the matter being at This Instant under Publique Debate) and in *Part*, an *Extract* of certain *Treasonous*, and *Seditious Passages*, and *Positions*, which may serve to Evince the *Necessity* of That *Regulation*. The *Latter* of which, I do most Humbly Offer to Your *Royal Consideration*, not presuming in any Sort, to Concern *Your Majesty* in the *Former*.

In *This Extract*, is presented to *your Majesties view*; *First*, That *Spirit* of *Hypocrisie, Scandal, Malice, Errour*, and *Illusion*, that Actuated the *Late Rebellion*. *Secondly*, A *Manifestation* of the *same Spirit Reigning still*, and *working*, not only by the *same Means*, but in very many of the *same Persons*, and to the *same Ends*; That is, There is a *Combination*, and *Design* against Your *Sacred Life*, and *Dignity*, which is carryed on by the *same Arguments, Pretences, Wayes*, and *Instruments*, that *Ruin'd* Your *Royal*, and *Blessed Father*. / All which, I think my self *Bound*, not only in *Generals*, to *Declare*; but more *Particularly*, to *Trace*, and to *Discover* to Your *Majesty*, as a *Duty* which I owe both to *God*, and to my *Sovereign*.

The *first* part of the *Conspirators Work*, is to *disaffect* the *People* toward Your Majesties *Person* and *Government*; and their *next Business* is to *Encourage*, and *Carry on* those *Seditious Inclinations* into *Action*.

Touching the *Former; Scarce any one* Regicide *or* Traytor *has been brought to* Publique Justice, *since Your Majesties Blessed Return, whom either the* Pulpit *hath not* Canonized *for a* Saint, *or the* Press Recommended *for a* Patriot, *and* Martyr. (beside the *Arraignment* of the *Bench*, for the very *Formalityes* of their *Tryals*) What is the *Intent*, or what may be the *Effect* of Suggesting to the *People*, that there is no *Justice* to be found, either in Your *Cause*, or in Your *Courts*; (Both which are Struck at in the same Blow) is submitted humbly to Your Royal Wisdom. Nor is the Faction less Industrious to draw an *Odium* upon Your *Majesties Person*, and to *Perplex, Seduce*, and *Exasperate* the *Multitude*, / in Matters of *Religion*, and concerning the *Government* of the *Church*.

There have been *Printed*, and *Reprinted*, since Your Majesties Happy *Restauration*, not so few as a *Hundred Schismatical Pamphlets*, against *Bishops*, *Ceremonies*, and *Common-Prayer*: in many of which, Your Majesty is *Directly*, and in *All* of them *Implicitly*, *Charg'd* with an Inclination to *Popery*. The *Instruments* that Menage This Part of the Plot, are *Ejected Ministers, Booksellers*, and *Printers*: and it is believed, by men of Judgment, and Experience, in the Trade of the *Press*, that since *the late Act for Uniformity*, there have been Printed near *Thirty Thousand Copies of Farewel-Sermons*[1] (as they call them) in Defiance of the *Law*. *All which*, as they are now drawn together into one Binding, (to the Number of betwixt Thirty and Forty) and represented with *Figures*, do certainly make up one of the most *Audacious*, and *Dangerous Libels*, that hath been made Publique under any Government, and they are now Printing it in *Dutch* too, for the greater Honour of the *Scandal*. By These *Arts*, and *Practices*, the *Faction* works upon / the *Passions* and *Humours* of the *Common-People*; and when they shall have put *Mischief* into their *Hearts*, their *next Business* is to put *Swords* in their *Hands*, and to Engage them in a direct *Rebellion*: which *Intent* of theirs, together with the *Means* whereby they hope to *Execute* it, I shall humbly lay before Your Majesty in a few words.

That they *Propose*, and *Labour another Change*, appears, *First*; From the Recourse they have in almost all their *Schismatical Papers* to the **Obligation of the Covenant**;[2] which is no other, than *to Conjure the People under the Peyn of* Perjury, *to Treat* Your Majesty, *as the* Covenanters *did Your* Father; and (in a flat Contradiction to the Blessed Apostle) to pronounce, that *Hee that* (OBEYES) *shall receive to himself Damnation*. A *Second Proof* of their *Designe* may be drawn from their still pleading the **Continuance of the Long-Parliament;** & **the Sovereignty of the People**, which is but in Plain Terms, *to Disclayme Your Authority-Royal*, and to *Declare* to the World, that *they want nothing but* Another Opportunity *for* Another Rebellion. What may be the *Event* of *These* / *Libertyes*, belongs not to *Mee* to *divine*; but that *such Libertyes are taken*, I do, with great Reverence, presume to Enform Your Majesty: And further; that the *Visible Boldness*, and *Malice* of the *Faction*, seems not to be the *only Danger*; Diverse of the very *Instruments*, who are *Entrusted* with the *Care* of the Press, being both *Privy*, and *Tacitly Consenting* to the *Corruptions* of it; by virtue of which *Connivence*, many *Hundred-Thousands* of *Seditious Papers*, since your Majestyes Return, have passed *Unpunished*. And yet in This Prodigious *Licence*, and *Security* of *Libelling* Your Sacred *Majesty*, and the *Government*, let but any Paper be Printed that Touches upon the *Private Benefit* of some *Concerned Officer*; The *Author* of *That Paper* is sure to be *Retriv'd*, and *Handled* with sufficient *Severity*.

Finally; To present Your Majesty with some Common *Observations*: It is noted, *First*, as a very *Rare Thing*, for any *Presbyterian Pamphlet* to be *Seiz'd*, and *Suppressed*, unless by *Order* from *Above*. *Secondly*, It is observed of Those Offenders that are Discovered, that Generally the *Rich* have the Fortune / to *Come off*, and the *Poor* to *Suffer*: and *Thirdly*; that *scarce One of five, though under Custody, is ever brought to either of Your Majesties Principal Secretaryes of State*.

I have now Discharg'd my Soul both to *God*, and to Your *Majesty*; in what I take to be an *Honest*, and a *Neccessary Office*; and I have done it with *This Choice* before me, either to suffer the worst that *Malice*, or *Calumny* can cast upon me, or to Forfeit my *Duty*. I should not speak This but upon *Experience*, nor dare to mention it upon This Occasion, but that I think it highly Imports Your Majesty to know how *Dangerous* a Matter it is to Render you a *Publique Service*. To present Your Majesty with a Fresh Instance; I was lately Engaged as a *Commissioner*, in a *Publique Debate* on the behalf of the *Loyal Officers*; and for no other *Crime*, or *Provocation*, but for *Asserting the Profess'd Desires of the Whole Party*: A Certain Gentleman[3] took such a *Heat*, and *Confidence*, as Openly *to Charge me with Writing against Your Majesty*; *Affirming* withal, *that Your Majesty had Accused me for it to the Parliament,* / *and that my Lord Chancellor would Justifie it*: Since which time, it appears, not only that *Hee Himself* was the *first Person* that by a *Private Tale* had *Endeavoured to Exasperate my Lord Chancellor against Me;* but that being *called to Account by my Lords Order*, for so *Great*, and so *Injurious* a *Boldness*, both towards *Your Majesty*, and his *Lordship*, He desired God to Renounce him, if ever he spake the Words, (Although Delivered in the Face of *a Full Committee*.) If I were *Impudent* enough to trouble Your Majesty with a *Personal Character*, *His Familiar Discourses*, both concerning *your Sacred Majesty*, and *the Honourable House of Commons*, would afford matter for it; but let God witness for me, that I have *no Passion*, but for *your Majesties Service*, and for the *General Good* of Your *Loyal Subjects*: *Both which Interests*, I do humbly conceive to be very much *concern'd* in some *Provision*, that men may not suffer in their *Reputations*, for doing their *Duties*; and that *Those Persons* who have *Chearfully*, and *Honourably* passed through the *utmost extremities* / of a *Long* and *Barbarous Warr*, out of a sence of *Loyalty* to Your *Royal Father*, may not now at last, be stung to Death by the *Tongues* of *Tale-Bearers*, and *Slanderers* for being *Faithful* to Your *Majesty*. Which is the *Case* of *Many*, more Considerable then my Self, and among the *Rest* in *Particular* of

> Your *MAJESTIES*
> *Most Loyall and Obedient Subject*
> Roger L'Estrange. /

To the Right Honourable the
# LORDS
And, To the Honourable the
## COMMONS
Assembled in Parliament.

HAving been lately Employ'd,[4] to *Draw up* some *Proposals* touching *the Regulation of the Press*, and to *Search* for certain *Seditious Books*, and *Papers*: I think it Agreable both to my *Reason*, and *Duty*, that I *Dedicate* to your *Honours* some *Accompt* of my *Proceeding*; especially in This Juncture, when both / the *Danger*, and the *Remedy*, are the Subject of your *Present Care*. The *Drift*, and *Argument* of This Little Treatise, is Express'd in the *Title*. One Particular only was forgotten in the *Body* of the Discourse, which I must now Crave Leave to Insert in my *Dedication*; (i.e.) *An Additional Expedient for the Relief of Necessitous, and Supernumerary Printers*; Many of which would be well enough Content to *Quit* the *Trade*, and Betake themselves to *Other Employments*, upon Condition to be *Re-imburst* for their *Presses*, *Letter*, and *Printing-Materials*: and it is Computed that 4000 *l.* or thereabouts, would Buy off their *Stock*; for the *Raising* of which Sum, and so to be *Employ'd*, there occurrs This *Expedient*.

It is Credibly Reported, That there have been Printed at least *Ten*, or *Twelve Impressions* of a *Collection* Entituled, The *First*, *Second*, and *Third Volume of Farewel-Sermons*: (with the Figures of the Ejected Ministers) which is no *Other*, then an *Arraignment* of the *Law*, and a *Charge* of *Persecution*, against the *King*, and his *Parliament*.

Upon a Supposition of *Twelve Impressions*, (at a Thousand a piece, which is the Lowest) the *clear Profit*, beside the Charge of *Paper* and *Printing*, Comes to 3300 *l.* which Sum, being Impos'd as a Fine, upon *their Heads* for whom the Books were *Printed*, will defray a *Considerable Part* of the aforesaid *Charge*, and what is *wanting*, may be abundantly made up by the like Course upon the *Publishers* of *Other* Seditious Pamphlets, Keeping the Same Proportion betwixt the *Profit*, and the *Punishment*. /

Of the *Farewel-Sermons*, I Seiz'd the other day in *Quires*, to the Quantity of betwixt *Twenty* and *Thirty Ream* of Paper; and I Discovered likewise the Supposed Author of *Another Pamphlet*, Entituled (*A Short Survey of the Grand Case of the Ministry*,[5] &c.) Wherein is *Maintain'd*, in opposition to the Declarations Required by the Act of *Uniformity;* That in some Cases *It may be lawful to take Arms against the King* – *To take Arms by the Kings Authority, against his Person, or Those Commismissioned by Him* – And *that the Obligation of the Covenant is a Knot cut by the Sword of Authority, whilst it cannot be Loosed by Religious Rea-*

P. 21.
P. 22.
P. 23.

*son.* Concerning which, and many other Desperate Libels, if your Honours shall think fit to Descend into any Particular Enquiry, it may be made appear, that whereas not *One* of *Twenty* is *Now taken*, scarce *One* of a *Hundred* could *Scape*, if there were not *Connivence* (at least, if not *Corruption*) joyn'd to the *Craft* and *Wariness* of the *Faction.*

How the *World* will understand This *Freedome,* and *Confidence,* in a *Private Person,* I do not much Concern my Self: (provided that I offend not *Authority*) but the Question to *Me* seems *short,* and *easy, Whether it be Lawful, or not, for any Man that sees his Countrey in Danger, to Cry out TREASON?* and *Nothing Else* hath Extorted This *Singularity* of *Practice,* and *Address,* from

Your Honours
Most Dutiful Servant
Roger L'Estrange. /


Considerations and Proposals

In Order to the

# Regulation
OF THE
# PRESS.

I Think no man denyes the *Necessity* of Suppressing *Licentious* and *Unlawful Pamphlets,* and of *Regulating* the *Press;* but in what *manner,* and by what *means* This may be Effected, That's the Question. The Two Main-points are Printing and Publishing.

The Promoters,

The Instruments of setting the work afoot are These. The *Adviser, Author, Compiler, Writer, Correcter,* and the Persons *for* whom, and *by* whom; that is [to] say, the *Stationer* (commonly), and the *Printer.* To which may be Added, the *Letter-Founders,* and the *Smiths,* and *Joyners,* that work upon *Presses.*

and Publishers of Pamphlets.

The usual *Agents* for Publishing are the *Printers* themselves, *Stitchers, Binders, Stationers, Hawkers, Mercury-women, Pedlers, Ballad-singers, Posts, Carryers, Hackney-Coachmen, Boat-men,* and *Mariners.* Other Instruments may be likewise employ'd, against whom a General Provision will be sufficient. Hiding, and Concealing of unlawful / Books, is but in order to Publishing, and may be brought under the same Rule.

Touching the *Adviser, Author, Compiler, Writer,* and *Correcter,* their Practices are hard to be Retriv'd, unless the One Discover the Other.

This Discovery may be procur'd partly by a *Penalty* upon *refusing* to *Discover*, and partly by a *Reward*, to the *Discoverer*; but let both the *Penalty*, and the *Reward* be *Considerable*, and *Certain*: and let the *Obligation* of *Discovery* run quite Through, from the *first Mover* of the Mischief, to the *Last Disperser* of it. That is to say; *If any unlawful Book shall be found in the Possession of any of the Agents, or Instruments aforesaid, let the Person in whose possession it is found, be Reputed, and Punish'd as the Author of the said Book, unless he Produce the Person, or Persons, from whom he Receiv'd it; or else acquit himself by Oath, that he knows neither Directly, nor Indirectly, how it came into his Possession.*

A General Expedient in Order to Discovery.

Concerning the Confederacy of *Stationers*, and *Printers*, we shall speak anon: but the thing we are now upon, is, singly **Printing**, and what necessarily relates to it.

One great Evil is the *Multiplicity of Private Presses*, and Consequently of *Printers*, who for want of Publique, and warrantable employment, are forc'd either to play the Knaves in Corners, or to want Bread.

Multiplicity of Private Presses and Printers a great Evil. The Remedies are,

The *Remedy* is, to reduce all *Printers*, and *Presses*, that are now in Employment, to a *Limited Number*; and then to provide against Private Printing for the time to come, which may be done by the Means Following.

First; The *number of Printers* and *Presses* being resolv'd upon, let the Number of their *Journy-men*, and *Apprentices* be likewise *Limited:* and in like manner, the Number of *Master-Founders*, and of their *Journy-men*, and Their *Apprentices*; all which to be Allow'd of, and Approv'd by such Person or Persons, as shall be Authoris'd for that purpose; neither let any *Joyner*, *Carpenter*, or *Smith*, presume to work for, or upon any *Printing Press*, without such Allowance as aforesaid, according to the Direction of the late Act for Printing.[6] /

To Reduce, and Limit the Number,

Secondly, *Let all such* Printers, Letter-Founders, Joyners, Carpenters, *and* Smiths, *as shall hereafter be* Allow'd, *as aforesaid, be Respectively and severally Interrogated before their Admittance, in order to the Discovery of* Supernumerary Printers *and* Presses. *That is:*

And to discover the Super numeraries;

1. *Let the* Printers *be Question'd what* Private Presses *they have at any time wrought upon for so many years last past, and the time* When, *and* For, *and with* Whom: *and what* other Printers *and* Presses *they know of at Present, beside Those of the present Establishment.*

With the means of doing it.

2. *Let the* Founder *be also Examin'd, what* Letter *they have Furnish'd* since such a Time; When *and for* Whom, *and what* other Printers *&c.* – Ut Supra.[7]

3. *Let the* Joyners, Carpenters, *and* Smiths *be Question'd likewise what* Presses *they have* Erected, *or* Amended, *&c.* When, *and for* Whom? *and what* other Presses, Printers, *&c. – as before.*

And if after *such Examination it shall appear at any time within so many Months, that any Man has willfully* conceal'd, *or* Deny'd *the* Truth, *let him forfeit his Employment as a Person not fit to be Trusted, and let the Enformer be taken into* his Place *if he be capable of it, and desire it; or Else, let him be Rewarded some other way. The same course may be taken also concerning* English Printers *and* Presses *beyond the Seas.*

This may serve as to the Discovery of *Private Printers* and *Presses* already in Employment: Now to prevent underhand-dealing for the *Future*, and to Provide against certain *other Abuses* in such as are *Allow'd*.

**Let no Tradesmen but Printers use Printing-Presses.**

First; *Let a special care be taken of* Card-makers, Leather-Guiders, Flock-workers, *and* Quoyf-drawers;[8] *either by expressly inhibiting their use of such Presses, as may be apply'd to* Printing *of* Books, *or by tying them up to the same Termes, and Conditions with* Printers; *and let no* other Tradesman *whatsoever presume to make use of a* Printing-press, *but upon the* same conditions, *and under the* same Penalties *with* Printers. /

**Cautions for Securing and Regulating the Press.**

2ly. *Let no* Presse *or* Printing-House *be* Erected *or* Lett, *and let no* Joyner, Carpenter, Smith, *or* Letter-Founder *work for a* Printing-House, *without* notice (*according to the late Act*)

3ly. *Let no* Materialls *belonging to* Printing, *no* Letters ready founded, *or* cast, *be* Imported *or* Bought *without the* like notice, *and for* whom (*according to the late Act.*)

4ly. *Let every* Master-Printer *be* Bound *at least, if not* sworn, *not to* Print, cause *or* suffer *to be* Printed *in his* House, *or* Press, *any* Book *or* Books *without* Lawful Licence (*according to the late Act.*)

5ly. *Let no* Master-Printer *be Allow'd to keep a* Press *but in his own* Dwelling-House, *and let no* Printing-House *be permitted with a* Back-dore *to it.*

6ly. *Let every* Master-Printer *certifie what* Warehouses *he Keeps, and not Change them without giving Notice.*

7ly. *Let every* Master-Printer *set his Name to whatsoever he* Prints, *or causes to be* Printed (*according to the late Act.*)

8ly. *Let no* Printer *presume to put upon any Book, the* Title, Marque, *or* Vinnet[9] *of any other Person who has the Priviledge of Sole Printing the same, without the Consent of the Person so Priviledg'd (according to the late Act) and let no man presume to Print another mans Copy.*

9ly. *Let no* Printer *presume either to Re-Print, or Change the* Title *of any Book formerly Printed, without* Licence; *or to* Counterfeit *a* Licence, *or knowingly to put any mans Name to a Book as the* Author *of it, that was not so.*

10ly. *Let it be Penall to* Antedate *any Book; for by so doing, New Books will be shuffled among Old Ones to the Encrease of the Stock.*

11ly. *Let the* Price *of Books be Regulated.*

12ly. *Let no* Journy-man *be Employ'd without a* Certificate *from the Master where he wrought last.*

13ly. *Let no* Master *discharge a* Journy-man, *nor* Hee *Leave his* Master, *under 14 dayes Notice, unlesse by Consent.* /

14ly. *Let the Persons employ'd, be of* Known Integrity, *so near as may be*; *Free of the sayd Mysteries, and Able in their* Trades (*according to the late Act.*)

But if 60 Presses must be reduc'd to 20, what shall all those People do for a Livelyhood that wrought at the other 40? | Obj.

It is provided by the Late Act, that as many of them shall be employ'd as the Printers can find *Honest work* for, and a sufferance of more, is but a *Toleration* of the Rest to Print *Sedition*, so that the *Supernumeraryes* are in as ill a Condition *now*, as they will be *Then*; and yet something may be thought upon for their Relief. | Ans.

There have been divers *Treasonous and Seditious Pamphlets* printed since the *Act of Indemnity; as,* The Speeches of the Late King's Judges; Sir Henry Vane's (*Pretended*) Tryal; The Prodigies I *Part and* 2.[10] *and the Like. Let any of These Necessitous Persons, make known at whose Request, and for whose Behoofe These, or the Like Seditious Libells have been Printed, and they shall not only be Pardon'd for having had a hand in it Themselves, but the first Enformer shall upon Proof or Confession be Recommended to the first Vacancy whereof he is Capable in the New-Regulation, and the Next to the Second, and so successively: And moreover a Fine shall be set upon the Heads of the Delinquents, to be Employ'd toward the Maintenance of so many of the Indigent Printers as shall be Interpreted to Merit that Regard, by such Discovery.* | A Provision for Poor Printers.

Next to **Printing**, follows **Publishing** or **Dispersing**, which, in and about the Town, is commonly the work of *Printers, Stitchers, Binders, Stationers, Mercury-women, Hawkers, Pedlars,* and *Ballad Singers.* | Publishers and Dispersers about the Town

*Concerning* Printers, Stitchers, *and* Binders; *The* Penalty *may be* Double, *where the* Fault *is so: That is where the same Person (for Example) is found to be both* Printer *and* Disperser *of the same unlawful Books, he may be Punished in Both Capacities: of the Rest (the* Stationer *excepted) little needs be said but that they may be* Punishable, *and the* Penalty *Suited to the Quality of the* Offender. / | to be Punish'd

The most Dangerous People of all are the *Confederate Stationers*, and the breaking of That Knot would do the work alone. For the *Closer* Carriage of their business they have here in the Town, Their **Private Ware-Houses**, and **Receivers**. | The Stationers have their Private Warehouses, and Receivers.

*Let every* Stationer *certifie, what* Ware-Houses *he keeps, and not change them without giving notice.*

*Let the* Receivers *and* Concealers *of Unlawful, or Unlicens'd Books be Punish'd as the* Dispersers *of them, unless within 12 hours after such Receipt they give notice to* — *that they have such Quantityes of Books in their Custody, and to whom they belong.* | Receivers and Concealers to be Punish'd as Dispersers.

**The Stationers Agents for Dispersing their Books Abroad. Their wayes of Privy Correspondence and Concealment.**

They hold Intelligence *Abroad* by the means of *Posts, Carryers, Hackny-Coach-men, Boatmen,* and *Marriners:* and for fear of *Interceptions* they Correspond by *False Names,* and *Private Tokens*; so that if a *Letter,* or *Pacquet* miscarry, people may not know what to make on't. As for the Purpose; so many *Dozen* of *Gloves* stands for so many *Dozen* of *Books.* Such a *Marque* for such a *Price,* &c.

They enter in their *Day-Books,* only in General terms, such and such *Parcells of Books,* without naming *Particulars.*

**The means of Prevention & Discovery.**

1. *Let every* Stationer, *living in or about* London, *be oblig'd to keep a* Day-Book *of the* Particulars *of all the* Unlicens'd Books, *and* Papers, *which he sends, causes or allowes to be sent, by any of the* Messengers *above-mentioned, into any parts of his Majestyes Dominions; and let him Enter the* Names *likewise of the* Persons *to whom he sends them, under a* Penalty; *if either he be prov'd, to have kept a* False Book, *or to have* Corresponded *under a* False Name, *and let every* Stationer *elsewhere* (i.e. *within the Kingdom of* England, *and Dominion of* Wales) *be oblig'd to keep a* Day-Book *likewise, of what* Unlicens'd Books, *and* Papers, *he* Receives, *and from* whom, *upon the like Penalty.*

2. *Let no* Stationer *presume to send, cause or allow to be sent, either* by Land, *or* Water, *any* Dry-Fatts, Bales, Packs, Maunds, *or other* Fardells,[11] *or* Packquets *of* Printed Books, *or* Papers, *without* superscribing *them in such sort, that they / may be known to be* Books, *together with the* Names *of the Persons* from *whom they are* sent, *and* to *whom they are* Directed: *Under peyn of* Forfeiting *all Parcels of Books that are not so* superscrib'd, *or otherwise that are advertis'd under* False Names.

3. *Let every* Hackny-Coach-man, Carrier, Boatman, *or* Mariner, *that knowingly Transgresses in the* Private Conveighance *of such Letters or Packquets as aforesaid, be subjected to a Particular Penalty.*

*Concerning Books* Imported. *They must be* First Prepar'd beyond the {Seas;} Secondly, conveighed hither; *and* Thirdly, Received *and* Distributed here.

**An Expedient against Printing of English Books beyond the Seas;**

*Let the* English Printer, Vender, *or* Utterer *of any Books written in the* English Tongue, *or by an* English man, *in any* other Tongue *and Printed beyond the Seas, to the dishonour of his Majestie or of the Establish'd Government, be required to appear from beyond the Seas, by a Certain Day, and under such a Penalty; which if he Refuse, or wilfully fayl to do, Let it be made Penall for any Person Living within his Majestys Dominions, (after sufficient Notice of his such Contempt) to hold any further Correspondence with him, Either by Message, Letter, or otherwise, till he hath given satisfaction for his Offence.*

**and Importing and Disposing of them.**

*Let a General Penalty be layd upon the* Importers *of any* English Books, *whatsoever,* Printed beyond the Seas. *And so likewise upon the* Contracters, *for; the* Receivers, Concealers, *and* Dispersers *of, any Books whatsoever, Imported into This Realm, and Disposed of without due Authority. It rests now to be Consider'd.*

*First* What Books are to be supprest, *and* Secondly, Into what hands the Care of the Press is to be Committed.

*The Books to be supprest are as follows.* /

FIrst, All Printed Papers pressing *the Murther of the late King*.

Secondly, All Printed *Justifications* of that Execrable Act.

*Thirdly*, All Treatises Denying *His Majesties Title* to the *Crown* of *England*.

*Fourthly*, All Libels against the *Person* of His Sacred Majesty, His Blessed *Father*, or the *Royal Family*.

*Fifthly*, All Discourses manifestly tending to stirr up the People against the *Establish'd Government*.

*Sixthly*, All Positions Terminating in This Treasonous Conclusion, that, His *Majesty* may be *Arraign'd, Judg'd,* and *Executed,* by his *People*: such as are These Following.

*Coordination*, The *Sovereignty* of the *Two Houses*, or of the *House* of *Commons*; or of the *Diffusive Body* of the *People*, in Case of Necessity. The *Justification* of the *Warr* Rais'd in 1642. in the Name of *King* and *Parliament*. The *Defence* of the *Legality* and *Obligation* of the *Covenant*. The *Separation* of the *Kings Person* from His *Authority*. The *Denyal* of His Majesties *Power* in *Ecclesiastical Affairs*. The Mainteyning that the *Long-Parliament* is not yet *Dissolv'd*.

If it be objected that This Looks too farr Back; It may be Answer'd that *Persons* are Pardon'd, but not *Books*. But to more Particular Reasons for the Suppressing of *Old Pamphlets*.

*First;* It is (with Reverence) a Duty both from his Sacred Majesty and his Parliament, to the Honour, *and* Memory *of the* Late King, *to deliver the Reputation of That* Blessed Martyr, *from the Diabolical Calumnies, and Forgeries,* which are yet Extant against his Person, *and* Government. /

Secondly, *It is as much a Duty toward our* Present Sovereign, *of whose Royal* Family, *and* Person, *as much Ill is said, and Publish'd, as is possible for the Wit of Man to Utter, or for the Malice of Hell to Invent.*

Thirdly, *In Relation to* Political Ends, *and to the security of the* Publique, *they ought to be supprest: for they do not only Revile, and Slander his Majesties Royal Person, but many of them Disclaim his very* Title *to the* Crown; *and Others Subject his* Prerogative, *and Consequently his Sacred* Life *to the Sovereign Power of the* People; *and this is done too, with all the Advantages of a Pestilent and Artificial Imposture. Now why a* Pamphlet *should be Allow'd to Proclaim This Treason to the* World, *which but whispered in a* Corner *would certainly bring a* Man *to the Gallows, is not easily Comprehended.*

What Books, Libels, and Positions are to be suppressed, and

Reasons for the suppressing of old Pamphlets as well as new.

Fourthly, *It makes the* English Nation *cheap in the Eyes of the World, to find the* Bloud *and* Virtues *of the* Late King, *appear so little to be consider'd, beside the Hazardous Consequence of* Blasting *the* Royal Cause, *and of* Discouraging Loyalty *to Future Generations, by transmitting the whole Party of the* Royallists, *in so many Millions of virulent Libels, to Posterity, for a prostitute Rabble of* Villeins, *and* Traytours.

Fifthly, *Those Desperate Libells and Discourses do not only* Defame *the* Government, Encourage *and* Enrich *the* Faction, *and* Poyson *the* People; *but, while They are Permitted, Those* Stationers *and* Printers, *that would otherwise be* Honest, *are forced either to play the* Knaves *for Company, or to Break: for there's scarce any other Trading for them, but in That Trash. Their Customers will be supply'd, and if they ask for any of these Treasonous Books, they must either Furnish them, or Lose their Custom.*

Sixthly, *The same Reason that prohibits* New Pamphlets, *requires also the Suppressing of* Old *ones, (of the same Quality) for 'tis not the* Date, *that does the* Mischief, *but the* Matter, *and the* Number. *If they be /* Plausible, *and* Cunning *enough to* Deceive, *and then* Numerous *enough to* Spread, Buchanan, *and* Knox *will do the business as sure as* Baxter, *and* Calamy.[12] *Besides that in some Respects, the* Old Ones *have a great Advantage of the* New: *for being Written in times of* Freedom, *and Menag'd by great* Masters *of the Popular Stile, they speak* playner, *and strike* homer *to the* Capacity *and* Humour *of the* Multitude; *whereas they that write in the fear of a* Law, *are forc'd to cover their Meaning under* Ambiguities, *and* Hints, *to the greater Hazzard of the* Libeller, *than of the* Publique.

Seventhly, *They must be supprest, in Order to a Future Regulation: for otherwise 'tis but* Antedating New Books, *and making them pass for* Old *ones (which may be done with very little Hazzard of Detection) or else, as any Saleable Book grows scarse; 'tis but* Reprinting *it with a* false Date, *and by these* Additions, *and* Recruits, *a Stock of* Seditious Pamphlets *shall be kept in Motion, to the end of the world. In Fine, if they are not fit to be* Sold, *they are not fit to be* kept; *for a verbal Prohibition without an Actual Seizure will be rather an Advantage to the Private Trade, then a Hindrance; and bring Profit to the Factious Book-sellers and Printers, that have Copies ly upon their hands, by Enhansing the Prices.*

Having already set forth the Quality of those Pamphlets that ought to be suppress'd, together with the Necessity of Suppressing Old as well as New; It will now follow properly, that I give some Instances of both sorts upon the foregoing Subjects. /

# Instances of Treasonous and Seditious Pamphlets.

## *I*. Against the Life of the Late King.

*The Armies Remonstrance from* St. Albans, Nov. 16. 1648.[13]

We Propound that That Capital and Grand Author of our Troubles, the Person of the King, may be speedily brought to Justice, for the Treason, Bloud, and Mischief He is Guilty of.

*P.* 62.

*God's Delight in the Progress of the Upright.*

Have ye not sins enough of your own, but will ye wrap your selves up, in the Treachery, Murder, Bloud, Cruelty and Tyranny of others? *P.* 17. Set some of those Grand Malefactors a Mourning, (that have Caus'd the Kingdom to Mourn so many years in Garments Roll'd in Bloud) by the Execution of Justice, *&c. P.* 19.

Printed for *Thomas Brewster*, 1649. Delivered in a Sermon by *Thomas Brooks* before the Commons, *Dec.* 26, 1648.

## *II*. In Justification of Putting His Late Majesty to Death.

*The Speeches and Prayers of some of the Late King's Judges.*[14]

That men may see what it is to have an Interest in Christ in a Dying hour, and to be Faithful to his Cause.

I look upon it (**the Murther of the King**) as the most Noble and high Act of Justice that our Story can Parallel. *P.* 41. /

Printed 1660 Divers Impressions. The Publisher to the Reader. In a Personated Letter from *Cook* to a Friend.

*Mercurius Politicus.*[15]

That Heroick and most Noble Act of Justice, in Judging and Executing the Late King – An Act Agreeing with the Law of God, Consonant to the Laws of Men, and the Practices of all well order'd States and Kingdomes. *P.*784.

*Charles* the First was Executed a Tyrant, Traytor, Murtherer, and a Publique Enemy to the Nation *P.* 1032.

Printed by a Person now in Office and eminent employment, 1651.

## *III*. Against the Title of the Royal Family to the Crown of England.

*Mercurius Politicus.*

Playing the second Part of *Perkin Warbeck*,[16] who once Invaded the North after the same manner, with a Crew of *Scots* at his Heels, and had every Jot as good a Title as Himself, or as his Predecessor *Henry* the 7th.

*P.* 982.

P. 832.

We had a sufficient Reason to lay aside this Bastard Race of Usurpers and Pretenders, if it were for no other Cause, but the Meer Injustice and vanity of their Title.

P. 833.

We have cause to Cut off this Accursed Line of Tyranny, Bloud, and Usurpation.

*The False Brother.*[17]

Printed by Mr. *Baxters* Printer for *Fran. Tyton* 1651. one of his Majesties Servants, if he has not lately put off his place.
a A Foul and Treasonous piece, printed for Giles Calvert, 1652.
b Printed by Mr. Baxt. Printer for *Francis Tyton*, 1650.

The Parliament having wisely Chang'd the Government to a Common-wealth, and Cut off that hereditary Usurpation of Monarchy, which was never either justly Begun, or Continued. *P.* 34. /

ᵃ *The Rise, Reign, and Ruine of the House of* Stuarts.[18]

ᵇ *The true Pourtraiture of the Kings of* England.[19]

It is high time now to End that Line that was never either well Begun, or Directly Continued. P. 42.

*A Short Reply,* &c. *together with a Vindication of the Declaration of the Army of* England.[20]

Printed by one in Office and great Employment, for *Frank Tyton*, Aug. 16. 1650.
P. 24.

Touching the Right of This King's Inheritance, We affirm it not only to be none Originally, without the Consent of the Nation; but also, to be justly Forfeited, by his Own, and Father's Destructive Engagements against the Common-wealths and therefore we know not of any Duty, we Owe him more than to any other engaged Enemy of the Land.

---

*IV.* Treasonous, Malicious, and Scandalous Libels against the Person of his most Sacred Majesty and the Royal Family.

---

Printed for *Livewell Chapman*, 1660.
P. 2.

*Plain English.*[21]

What hope that the Reformed Religion will be protected and Maintained, by the Son, which was so Irreligiously betray'd by the Father?

1660. Since his Majesties Return.
P. 1.

*A Door of Hope.*

*C.S.* the Son of That Murtherer, is Proclaimed King of *England*, Whose Throne of Iniquity is built on the Bloud of Precious Saints and Martyrs. /

Printed by *Peter Cole*, 1648. The Author *Cook* the Regicide.

*The Case of King* Charles.[22]

The Murtherers of our Saviour were less Guilty than that Prince.

*An* English *Translation of the* Scottish *Declaration.*[23]

Let Justice and Reason blush, and Traytors and Murtherers, Parricides, and Patricides, put on white Garments, and Rejoyce as Innocent ones, if This Man (the late King) should escape the hands of Justice and Punishment.

An Implacable and Gangren'd Person.

A Butcher rather than a Prince of Bowels and Affection,

(Charles the 2ᵈ) the Son of a Bloudy Father, Heir to an Entayl'd Curse, more certain than to his Kingdom, Train'd up in Bloud, and one that never suck'd in any other Principles but Prerogative and Tyranny.

Printed by a person in Office and credit, for *Fran. Tyton*, 1650. P. 22.

P 13.

P. 19.

P. 23.

*The None-such* Charles.

(Charles the First) rather chose to submit to the Justice of an Axe in a Hangmans hand, than to sway a Scepter with Equity.

This Age knows what such a Tyrant was, in not feeling his force any more upon their Throats.

P. 167.

P. 169.

*A True State of the Case of the Common-Wealth.*[24]

That Accursed Interest; – a Family that God has cast out before us; – that has worn the marques and badges of Gods high displeasure for almost these Hundred years, *P.* 47. The Person of the young Pretender, is a son of Bloud, *&c. P.* 48. /

Printed 1654. by a person in Offices of great Trust and Benefit.

*Mercurius Britanicus.*[25]

If any man can bring any tale or tiding of a wilfull King, which hath gone astray these four years from his Parliament, with a Guilty Conscience, Bloudy Hands, a Heart full of broken Vowes and Protestations, *&c. P.* 825.

Printed by Mr. *Baxters* Printer. 1645.

---

*V.* Pamphlets tending manifestly to stir up the People against his Sacred Majesty, and the Establish'd Government.

---

*God's Loud Call.*[26]

Oh! Worm! Darest thou be so impudent to put thy self in Gods stead, to meddle with mens Consciences, and Lord it in Religious Concerns?

Printed by *Simon Dover*, 1661. *P.* 17.

*Smectymnuus Redivivus.*[27]

The Plastring or Palliating of these Rotten Members (*Bishops*) will be a greater Dishonour to the Nation and Church, than their Cutting off, and the Personal Acts of These Sons of *Belial*, being Conniv'd at, become National Sins.

Printed for *J. Rothwell*, 1660. Publish'd by Mr. *Thomas Manton*, since his Majesties Return. P. 58.

P. 66.

The Root of these Disorders, *(viz.* Popery, Superstition, Arminianism, and Prophaneness) proceedeth from the Bishops, and their Adherents (Whereof the *King* is One.)

Deliver'd by Mr. *Edmund Calamy.*

*A Sermon Preached at* Aldermanbury-*Church*, Dec. 28. 1662.[28]

The tongue of Man is not able to express the Misery of that Nation, where the Ark of God is Taken (*P.* 8.): and / the Ark of God is in This Instant in Danger of being Lost, (*P.*II.) We have lost our first Love to the Gospel, and to the Ordinances, (*ibid.*) Abundance of Priests and Jesuits are in the midst of us, and Popery preach'd amongst us. But where are our old *Eli's* now? our *Moses's?* our *Elijahs?* our *Uriahs?*

Printed by *Jo. Hayes,* 1662. The Author *Edw. Bagshaw.* P. 8.

*Animadversions upon the Bishop of* Worcesters *Letter.*[29]

We may lawfully refuse to submit unto such Impositions as God hath no where commanded.

1661. Begun by *Tho. Creek* for *Giles Calvert* and *Tho. Brewster,* and finish'd by the Order of *Calverts* wife, whilest her husband was a Prisoner for that very book. To the Reader. Printed for *Tho. Parkhurst,* 1662. Preached by *Thomas Watson,* calculated for *Corbet* and *Barkstead,* and Dated upon the very day whereon they were Executed, *Apr.* 19. 1662. P. 39. This Book was formerly condemned to be burnt by the Common Hangman, and Reprinted since his Majesties Return.

*The Year of Prodigies.*[30]

Amongst the Hellish rout of Prophane and ungodly men, let especially the Oppressors and Persecutors of the True Church look to themselves, when the hand of the Lord, in strange Signs and Wonders is lifted up among them; for – – The final overthrow of *Pharaoh* and the *Ægyptians* (those cruel Task-masters and Oppressors of the *Israelites*) did bear date not long after the Wonderfull and Prodigious Signs which the Lord had shewn in the midst of them.

*A Word of Comfort.*[31]

The Church of God appears in his Cause, and loseth Bloud in his Quarrel. (*P.* 8.)

Is not God upon the Threshold of his Temple, ready to fly? Are not the shadowes of the Evening stretched out? and may we not fear the Sun-setting of the Gospel? *P.* 30.

The Lord may let his Church be a while under Hatches, to punish her Security, and to awaken her out of her slumbering fits; yet surely the storm will not continue long. /

*A Dispute against the English-Popish Ceremonies.*[32]

Be not deceiv'd to think that they who so eagerly press this Course of Conformity, have any such end as Gods Glory, or the Good of his Church, and Profit of Religion. *P.* 9.

Let not the Pretence of Peace, and Unity, cool your fervour, or make you spare to oppose your selves, unto those Idle and Idolized Ceremonies, against which we dispute. *P.* 11.

# Instances of Pamphlets containing Treasonous and Seditious POSITIONS.

*VI.* The Three Estates are Co-ordinate, and the King one of the Three Estates.

*Baxters Holy Common-Wealth.*

The Soveraignty here among us is in King, Lords, and Commons. *P.* 72.

Printed for *Francis Tyton*, 1659.

*Parliament-Physick for a Sin-sick Nation.*[33]

The Government of England is a Mixt Monarchy, and Govern'd by the Major part of the Three Estates Assembled in Parliament.

P. 111.

*Ahabs Fall, with a Post-script to Dr. Fern.*[34]

The Houses are not only Requisite to the Acting of the Power of making Lawes, but Co-ordinate with his Majestie in the very Power of Acting. /

P. 42.

*VII.* The Soveraignty is in the Two Houses, in Case of Necessity.

*The Peoples Cause stated, in the (Pretended) Tryal of Sir Henry Vane.*[35]

1662.

The Delegates of the People in the House of Commons, and the Commissioners on the Kings Behalf in the House of Peers, concurring; do very far bind the King, if not wholly, – And when These cannot Agree, but break one from another, the Commons in Parliament. Assembled, are, *ex Officio*, the Keepers of the Libertys of the Nation, and Righteous Possessors, and Defenders of it against all Usurpers and Usurpations whatsoever.

P. 112.

P. 113.

*Observations upon his Majesties Answers, &c.*[36]

Parliaments may Judg of Publique Necessity without the King (if Deserted by the King) and are to be accompted, by Virtue of Representation, as the whole Body of the State.

P. 45.

*Right and Might well met.*[37]

Whensoever a King or other Superiour Authority creates an Inferiour, they Invest it with a Legitimacy of Magistratical Power to punish Themselves also, in Case they prove Evill-Doers. /

P. 7. *An.* 1648.

## VIII. The Power of the King is but Fiduciary; and the Duty of the Subjects but Conditional.

### *Jus Populi.*[38]

P. 1. *An.* 1644:

Princes Derive their Power and Prerogative from the People, and have their Investitures meerly for the Peoples Benefit.

### *Vindiciæ contra Tyrannos.*[39]

P. 120.
*An.* 1648.
P. 121.

If the Prince fail in his Promise, the People are Exempt from their Obedience, the Contract is made Voyd, and the right of Obligation is of no Force – It is therefore permitted to the Officers of a Kingdome, either All or some good Number of them to suppress a Tyrant.

1649.

### *The Tenure of Kings and Magistrates*[40] - - -

The Title.

- - - Proving that it is Lawful for any who have the Power, to call to Account a Tyrant, or wicked King, and after due Conviction to depose, and put him to Death, if the ordinary Magistrate have Neglected, or Deny'd to doe it.

## IX. The King is *Singulis Major, Universis Minor.*

March 13. 1647.

*A Declaration of the Lords and Commons touching the Four Bills.*[41]

It is the Kings Duty to pass all such Lawes, as Both / Houses shall Judg good for the Kingdom: Upon a supposition, that they are good, which by them are Judg'd such.

### *De Monarchiâ Absolutâ.*[42]

The Author
Edward Bagshaw, 1659.

Detrahere Indigno Magistratum etsi Privati non debeant; Populus tamen Universus quin possit, nemo, opinor, dubitabit.[43] *P.* 9.

### *Thorps Charge to the Grand-Jury at* York, March 20. 1648.[44]

Kings are Accountable to the People, I do not mean to the Diffused humours and fancyes of particular men in their single and natural Capacities; but to the People in their Politique Constitution, lawfully Assembled by their Representative. *P.* 3. 1649.

## X. The Kings Person may be Resisted but not His Authority.

### *Lex Rex.*[45]

Printed by a Person in Office and Employment. Octob. 7. 1644.

He that Resisteth the King, commanding in the Lord, Resisteth the Ordinance of God. But he who Resisteth the King, Commanding that which is against God, Resisteth no Ordinance of God; but an Ordinance of Sin and Sathan. *P.* 267. /

---

### XI. The King has no Power to Impose in Ecclesiastical Affairs.

---

*The Great Question.*[46]

I hold it utterly Unlawful for any Christian Magistrate to Impose the Use of Surplices in Preaching, Kneeling at the Sacrament, Set-Forms of Prayer, *&c.*

When once Humane Inventions become Impositions, and lay a Necessity upon that which God hath left Free; then may we lawfully Reject them, as Plants of Mans setting, and not of Gods owning.

1660. The Author *Edw. Bagshaw.*P. 2.

P. 51.

---

### XII. The Parliament of *November* 3ᵈ. 1640. is not yet Dissolv'd.

---

*The Peoples Cause Stated in the (Pretended) Tryall of Sir* Henry Vane.

1662.

How and when the Dissolution of the Long-Parliament (according to Law) hath been made, is yet Unascertain'd, and not particularly Declar'd: by reason whereof, (and by what hath been before shew'd) the state of the Case on the Subjects part, is much altered, as to the Matter of Right, and the Usurpation is now on the other hand. /

P. 111.

---

### XIII. The Warre Rais'd in 1642. in the Name of King and Parliament was Lawful.

---

*Baxters Holy Common-Wealth.*

I cannot see that I was mistaken in the main Cause, nor dare I repent of it, nor forbear the same, if it were to do again in the same State of things - And my Judgment tells me, that if I should do otherwise, I should be Guilty of Treason or Disloyalty against the Sovereign Power of the Land, and of Perfidiousness to the Common-Wealth.

Printed for *Francis Tyton*, 1659.

P. 486.

*The Form and Order of the Coronation of Charles the Second.*[47]

A King abusing his Power to the overthrow of Religion Lawes and Liberties – may be Controll'd and Oppos'd. This may serve to Justifie the Proceedings of this Kingdome against the Late King, who in an Hostile way set himself to overthrow Religion, Parliaments, Lawes, and Liberties.

1660. Since his Majesties Return. Preached by *Robert Dowgless*, at *Scoon, Jan.* 1. 1651. Pag. 10.

## XIV. The Covenant is Binding.

*A Phoenix: or, the Solemn League and Covenant.*[48]

Printed by *Tho. Creek* for *Giles Calvert, Tho. Brewster* and *Livewel Chapman,* since his Majesties Return.
A Sermon of Mr. *Calamys.* 1661. from the Presbyterian Ministers.

P. 13.

The breaking of our National Covenant is a Sin in Folio, a Sin of a high Nature – a greater sin, then a sin against a Commandement, or against an Ordinance, a sin not only of Disobedience, but of Perjury, a sin of Injustice / a spiritual Adultery, a sin of Sacriledge, a sin of great unkindness *P.* 138.

*Two Papers of Proposals.*[49]

The Covenant does undoubtedly Bind us to forbear our own Consent to those Luxuriances of Church-Government which we there Renounced, and for which no Divine Institution can be pretended.

*A Short Survey of the Grand Case,* &c.[50]

1663. Printed by *Henry Bridges.*

P. 21.

☞

A Treasonous Position.

Some say, the Terms are Dubious, if not false, it being indefinitely asserted. **It is not lawful to take Arms against the King on any Pretence whatsoever,** – Although *Our King is,* and *WE HOPE, EVER WILL BE,* so qualified, that in reference to *Him,* it *MAY* be true; yet it is not *Impossible* for a King *Regis Personam exuere;*[51] in *a Natural,* or *MORAL Madness,* or Phrensie, to turn Tyrant, yea Beast, Waiving his Royal Place, violently, extrajudicially, extramagisterially to assault his Subject, as *Saul* did *David:* In this Case, men think Nature doth Dictate it, and Scripture doth justifie a Man, *se defendendo vim vi repellere,*[52] to take Arms, though by rallying the Men of *Belial,*[53] not to *Resist,* yet to *Restreyn,* the King, and those who are Commissioned by him, until they make good their Retreat, and more safely run out of his reach.

As the *Presbyterians restreyn'd* the Late King.
P. 22.

To some it soundeth harsh to declare it **a Trayterous Position to take Arms by the Kings Authority, against the Kings Person, or those Commissioned by him** – for if some Ruffians should (which God defend) seize the Person of a King, he is a *Man,* from whom Commissions may be by fear extorted, whereby true Loyalty must be on their side, and Treason on the part of the Kings Council, Kindred, and Ministers of State, if Arming against his *Person,* by his *Authority* though on such a Pretence. /

P. 23.

The Convincing Demonstration that there lyes no Obligation on me, nor any other Person, from the Oath commonly called the Solemn League and Covenant, is a Knot cut by the Sword of Authority, whilst it cannot be loosed by Religious Reason.

P. 47.

We are Expectants of God's avengement of the Covenant now it hath been taken, – *We do not, cannot, will not Declare,* the Covenant doth not oblige me or any other person to endeavour *our* alteration of the Government in the Church.

I could add *More*, and *Worse* to the *Instances* already given, but these shall suffice for a Taste. The Question is now, By whom, *the Government and Oversight of the Press is to be undertaken*, and the *Contest* lyes at present betwixt the *Booksellers* and *Printers*, which although Concorporate by an Ancient Grant, are in this point become Competitors; and since they have divided Themselves, they shall be here likewise distinctly considered.

### *The* Stationers *are not to be entrusted with the care of the Press, for These following Reasons.*

First, They are both *Parties* and *Judges*; for diverse of them have brought up Servants to the Mystery of Printing which they still retein in Dependence: Others again are both *Printers* and *Stationers, Themselves*; so that they are Entrusted (effectually) to *search* for their *own Copies;* to *Destroy* their *own Interests;* to *Prosecute* their *own Agents*, and to *Punish Themselves:* for they are the Principal *Authors* of those Mischiefs which they pretend now to *Redress*, and the very *Persons* against whom the *Penalties* of this Intended Regulation are chiefly *Levell'd*.

2ly. It is not Adviseable to Rely upon the *Honesty* of People (if it may be Avoided) where That *Honesty* is to their *Loss:* Especially if they be such as have already given Proof that they prefer their *Private Gayn* before the / *Well-fare* of the *Publique:* which has been the Stationer's case throughout our Late Troubles, some few Excepted, whose Integrity deserves Encouragement.

3ly. In this Trust, they have not only the *Temptation* of *Profit*, to divert them from their Duty (a fair part of their stock lying in Seditious Ware) but the *Means* of *Transgressing* with great *Privacy*, and *Safety:* for, make *Them* Overseers of the *Press*, and the *Printers* become totally at *their Devotion*; so that the whole Trade passes through the fingers of their own Creatures, which, upon the matter, concludes rather in a *Combination*, then a *Remedy*.

4ly. It seems a little too much to *Reward* the *Abusers* of the Press with the Credit of *Superintending* it: upon a Confidence that They that *Destroy'd* the *Last King* for their *Benefit*, will now make it their businesse to *Preserve This* to their *Loss.*

5ly. It will cause a great *Disappointment* of *Searches*, when the Persons most concern'd shall have it in their Power to spoyl all, by *Notices, Partiality*, or *Delay.*

6ly. As the *Effectual Regulation* of the *Press* is not at all the *Stationers Interest,* so is it strongly to be suspected that it is as little their *Aym:* for *not One Person has been Fin'd, and but one Prosecuted,* (as is credibly Affirm'd) *since the Late Act,* notwithstanding so much Treason and Sedition Printed and disperst since That time.

*Reasons why the Stationers are not to be Entrusted with the Care of the Press.*

7[ly]. It is enjoyn'd by the Late Act that no Man shall be Admitted to be a Master-Printer, untill They who were at that time Actually Master-Printers, shall be by Death or otherwise reduc'd to the Number to Twenty: which Provision notwithstanding, Several Persons have since that time been suffer'd to set up *Masters*; which gives to understand that the reducing of the Presses to a *Limited Number* is not altogether the *Stationers Purpose*. /

## *The* Printers *are not to be Entrusted with the Government of the Press.*

Not the Printers,

First, All the Arguments already Objected against the *Stationers* hold good also against the *Printers*, but not fully so strong. That is, they are both *Partyes*, and *Judges*. *Self-ended*, (upon Experiment) under the *Temptation* of *Profit*. *Offenders* as well as the *Stationers*; and in all *Abuses* of the *Presse*, *confederate* with them. Beside, They will have the same Influence upon *Searches*; and they have probably as little *Stomack* to a *Regulation*, as the other. 'Tis true; the *Printers Interest* is not so *Great* as the *Stationers*; for where *Hee* gets (it may be) 20 or 25 in the 100 for *Printing* an Unlawful Book, the *Other Doubles*, nay many times, *Trebles* his Mony by *selling* it: Yet nevertheless the Printer's Benefit lyes at stake too.

2[dly]. It were a hard matter to Pick our *Twenty Master-Printers*, who are both *Free of the Trade*, of *Ability to Menage* it, and of *Integrity* to be *Entrusted* with it; Most of the *Honester* for being *impoverished* by the *Late Times*, & the great business of the Press being Engross'd by *Oliver's Creatures*.

although Incorporated;

But, They Propose to Undertake the Work upon Condition to be *Incorporate*. That is; *to be Disengaged from the Company of Stationers, and to be made a Society by Themselves*. It may be Answered that it would be with *Them*, as 'tis with *Other Incorporate Societies*: They would be True to the *Publique*, so far as stands with the *Particular Good* of the *Company*. But Evidently *Their Gain* lyes the *other* way: and for a State to Erect a *Corporation* that shall bring so great a *Danger* upon the *Publique*, and not one *Peny* into the *Treasury*, to Ballance the Hazzard, were a Proceeding not ordinary.

at giving Security.

But *they Offer to give Security*, and *to be Lyable to Fines*. Let That be done, Whether they be *Incorporate*, or *no*. *In case of Failer*, they'll be content to lose their *Priviledges*. What signifies That, but only a Stronger Obligation to a / Closer Confederacy? 'Tis True, The Printers in a Distinct and Regulated Society may do some good as to the General Business of Printing, and within the Sphere of that *Particular Profession*: but the *Question is Here*, how to *Prevent a Publique Mischief*, not how to *Promote* a *Private Trade*. But *are not Printers the fittest Instruments in Searches*? They are, without Dispute, *Necessary Assistants*, either for *Retrieving Conceal'd Pamphlets*, or for *Examination* of work in the *Mettle*, but whether it be either for the *Honour*, or *Safety*, of the *Publique*, to Place so great a

Trust in the Hands of Person of that *Quality*, and *Interest*, is submitted to better Judgments.

To Conclude; both *Printers*, and *Stationers*, under Colour of Offering a Service to the *Publique*, do Effectually but Design *One upon another*. The *Printers*, would beat down the *Book-selling* Trade, by Menaging the *Press* as Themselves please, and by working upon their *own Copies:* The *Stationers*, on the other side, They would Subject the *Printers* to be absolutely *Their Slaves*; which they have Effected in a Large Measure already, by so encreasing the Number, That the One Half must either play the *Knaves*, or *Starve*.

The *Expedient* for *This*, must be some way to Disengage the *Printers* for that Servile and Mercenary *Dependence* upon the *Stationers*, unto which they are at present subjected. The True State of the Business being as follows.

*The Dependence of the Printers upon the Stationers is Dangerous.*

First, The *Number* of *Master-Printers* is computed to be about 60. whereas 20. or 24. would Dispatch all the Honest work of the Nation.

2$^{dly}$. These *Sixty Master-Printers* have above 100 *Apprentices* (That is; at least 20 more then they ought to have by the Law.)

3$^{dly}$. There are, beside *Aliens*, and those that are Free of *other Trades*, at least 150 *Journy-Men*, of which Number, at least 30. are superfluous; to which 30. there will be added about 36. more, beside above 50. *Supernumerary Apprentices*, upon the Reduction of the *Master Printers* to 24. So that upon the whole Reckoning, there will be left a Matter / of 60. *Journy-men*, and 50. *Apprentices*, to Provide for, a part of which Charge might very reasonably be laid upon those that either Bound or Took any of the said Number, as Apprentices, contrary to the Limitation set by Authority.

These *Supernumerary Printers* were at first Introduced by the *Book-sellers*, as a sure way to bring them both to their *Prices*, and *Purposes*; for the Number being greater then could honestly Live upon the Trade, the *Printers* were Enforc'd either to Print *Treason*, or *Sedition*, if the *Stationer* Offered it, or to want *Lawful Work*, by which *Necessity* on the *one* side, and *Power* on the *other*, the Combination became exceeding Dangerous, and so it still Continues; but how to Dissolve it, whether by barely *Dis-incorporating* the *Company of Stationers*, and subjecting the *Printers* to Rules *apart*, and by *Themselves*; or by Making them *Two Distinct Companies*, I do not Meddle.

This only may be Offer'd, that in Case Those *Privileges* and *Benefits* should be Granted, to both *Stationers*, and *Printers*, which they themselves desire in point of *Trade*; yet in regard that *several Interests* are Concern'd, That of the *Kingdom* on the *one* side, and only That of the *Companies* on the *other*; It is but reason that there should be *several Super-intending Powers*, and that the *smaller Interest* should *give place*, and be *Subordinate* to the *Greater*: That is, The *Master*, and *Wardens*, to Menage the Business of their Respective *Trade*, but withall, to be

Subjected to some *Superior Officer*, that should over-took them *Both* on behalf of the *Publique*.

<small>Let the care of Printing be Committed to Six Surveighers of the Press.</small>

As the *Power* of *Licencing* Books, are by the Late Act vested in *several Persons*, with regard to the *several Subjects* Those Books treat of; so may there likewise be *several Agents* Authoris'd and Appointed for the Care of the Press, touching These *several Particulars*, under the *Name*, and *Title* of *Surveyors of the Press*: and every *distinct Surveyor* to keep himself strictly within the Limits of his *own Province*. As for Example. /

<small>One for Law.</small>

First, The *Lord Chancellour*, or *Lord Keeper* of the Greater Seal of *England* for the time being, the *Lords Chief Justices*, and *Lord Chief Baron* for the time being, or One or More of them, are specially Authoris'd to License, by *Themselves*, or by their *Substitutes*, all Books concerning the *Common Laws* of This Kingdom.

Let there be one Surveigher of the Press Constituted peculiarly for That Subject.

<small>Three for Divinity, Physique, &c. i.e. One for each University and the Third for London, &c.</small>

2$^{dly}$. All Books of *Divinity*, *Physique*, *Philosophy*, or whatsoever other *Science*, or *Art*, are to be License'd by the *Lord Archbishop* of *Canterbury*, and *Lord Bishop* of *London*, for the time being, or one of them, or by their, or one of Their Appointments, or by either one of the *Chancellours*, or *Vice-Chancellours* of either of the *Universities*, for the time being.

Let Three Other Surveighers of the Press be likewise Authorized for These Particulars.

<small>One for Heraldry, &c.</small>

3$^{dly}$. All Books concerning *Heraldry*, *Titles of Honour*, and *Arms*, or Concerning the *Office* of *Earl-Marshall*, are to be Licens'd by the *Earl-Marshall* for the time being; or in case there shall not then be an *Earl. Marshal*, by the *Three Kings of Arms* or any *Two* of them, whereof *Garter*[54] to be One.

This is to be the Subject of Another Surveigher's Care.

<small>and Another for State affairs, &c.</small>

4$^{thly}$. Books of *History*, *Politiques*, *State-Affairs*, and all other *Miscellanies*, or *Treatises*, not comprehended under the Powers before-mentioned, fall under the Jurisdiction of the *Principal Secretaries of State*, to be Allow'd by *Themselves*, or *one* of them, or by their, or one of their Appointments.

The Care of the Press concerning These Particulars may be another Surveighers Business. So that *six Persons may do the whole work*, with good *Order*, and *Security*. / Three *Substitutes* for the *Bishops*; and *Chancellours*, and *One* a piece for the *Rest*.

<small>For Encouragement there must be Benefit and Power.</small>

A word now touching the *Encouragements* of these Officers; and Then concerning *Penalties* to be Inflicted upon *Offenders*, and *Rewards* to be Granted to *Enformers*.

The *Inward Motive* to all *Publique* and *Honourable Actions* must be taken for granted, to be a Principle of *Loyalty*, and *Justice*: but the Question is here concerning *Outward Encouragements* to *This Particular Charge*. There must be *Benefit*, and *Power*. *Benefit*; that a man may Live *Honestly* upon the *Employment*: and *Power*; for the *Credit*, and *Execution* of the *Trust*.

The *Benefit* must arise *partly* from some *Certain*, and *standing Fee*; and in Part, from *Accessary*, and *Contingent Advantages*, which will be but *Few*, and *Small*, in Proportion to the *Trouble* and *Charge* of the *Employment*: for there must be, First; *A Constant Attendance*: and *a Dayly Labour* in hunting out, and over-looking *Books*, and *Presses*: and Secondly, A Continual *Expense*, in the Enterteynment of Instruments for *Discovery*, and *Intelligence*; which being deducted out of the Pittances of *Licences*, and *Forfeitures*, will leave the *Surveigher* a very *small Proportion* for his *Peyns*. The Employment being Troublesome and Chargeable.

The next thing is a *Power* to *Execute*; without which, the *Law is Dead*, and the *Officer Ridiculous*.

*Now concerning* Penalties *and* Rewards.

1. The *Gayn* of Printing some Books, is Ten times Greater, if they *Scape*, then the *Loss*, if they be *Taken*: so that the *Damage* bearing such a disproportion to the *Profit*, is rather an *Allurement* to Offend, then a *Discouragement*. The Inconvenience of small Penalties,

2. As the *Punishment* is too small, for the *Offender*; so is the *Reward* also, for the *Enformer*: for reckon the *Time*, *Trouble*, and *Money*, which it shall cost the *Prosecutour* to Recover his *Allotment*, he shall sit down at last a *Loser* by the Bargain: and more then That, he loses his *Credit*, and *Employment*, over and Above, as a *Betrayer* of his *Fellows*; / so great is the *Power* and *Confidence* of the *Delinquent Party*. and Rewards.

The way to help This, is, to *Augment* both the *Punishment*, and the *Reward*; and to Provide that the *Inflicting* of the *One*, and the *Obteyning* of the *Other*, may be both *Easie*, and *Certain*: for to Impose a *Penalty*, and to leave the way of *Raysing* it, so *Tedious*, and *Difficult*, as in This Case hitherto it is; amounts to no more then This: If the *Enformer* will *spend Ten Pound* 'tis possible he may *Recover Five*: and so the *Prosecuter* must *Impose a greater Penalty* upon *Himself*, then the *Law* does upon the *Offender*; or Else all comes to Nothing. Which in Cases of Publique Concern ought to be Deep upon the Delinquent and the Reward Certain and Considerable to the Enformer. An Expedient for the Quick and Easie getting of the Penalty.

An Expedient for this Inconvenience is highly Necessary; and Why *May not the Oath of One Credible Witness or More, before a Master of the Chancery, or a Justice of the Peace, serve for a Conviction.* Especially the Person Accused being Left at Liberty before such Oath taken, either to Appeal to the *Privy-Council*, or to abide the *Decision*.

Now to the several *Sorts* of *Penalties*, and to the *Application* of them.

**Penalties.**

The Ordinary *Penalties* I find to be *These*; *Death, Mutilation, Imprisonment, Banishment, Corporal Peyns, Disgrace, Pecuniary Mulcts:*[55] which Penalties are to be Apply'd with regard to the *Quality* of the *Offence*, and to the *Condition* of the *Delinquent*.

**Offences.**

The *Offence* is either *Blasphemy, Heresie, Schism, Treason, Sedition, Scandal*, or *Contempt of Authority*.

**Delinquents.**

The *Delinquents* are the *Advisers, Authors, Compilers, Writers, Printers, Correcters, Stitchers*, and *Binders* of unlawful Books and Pamphlets: together with all *Publishers, Dispersers* and *Concealers* of them in *General*: and all *Stationers, Posts, Hackny-Coachmen, Carryers, Boat-men, Mariners. Hawkers, Mercury-Women, Pedlers*, and *Ballad-Singers* so offending, in *Particular*. /

**Penalties of Disgrace,**

Penalties of *Disgrace* ordinarily in Practice are Many, and more may be Added.

*Pillory, Stocks, Whipping, Carting, Stigmatizing, Disablement to bear Office,* or *Testimony. Publique Recantation, standing under the Gallows with a Rope about the Neck, at a Publique Execution. Disfranchisement* (if Free-men) *Cashiering* (if Souldiers), *Degrading* (if Persons of Condition), Wearing some *Badge* of *Infamy*: Condemnation to *Work* either in *Mines, Plantations,* or *Houses of Correction*.

**Pecuniary Mulcts.**

Under the Head of *Pecuniary Mulcts*, are Comprehended, *Forfeitures, Confiscations, Loss of any Beneficial Office,* or *Employment, Incapacity* to *hold* or *enjoy* any: and Finally, all Damages accruing, and Impos'd, as a Punishment for some Offence.

Touching the *Other Penalties* before-mention'd, it suffices only to have Nam'd them, and so to Proceed to the *Application* of them, with respect to the *Crime*, and to the *Offender*.

The *Penalty* ought to bear Proportion to the *Malice*, and *Influence* of the *Offence*, but with respect to the *Offender* too: for the *same Punishment* (unless it be Death it self ) is not the *same Thing* to *several Persons*; and it may be proper enough to Punish *One Man* in his *Purse, Another* in his *Credit; a Third* in his *Body*, and All for the same Offence.

The *Grand Delinquents* are, the *Authors or Compilers*, (which I reckon as all One) the *Printers*, and *Stationers*.

**The Authors.**

For the *Authors*, nothing can be too *Severe*, that stands with *Humanity*, and *Conscience*. First, 'tis the Way to cut off the *Fountain* of our Troubles. 2$^{dly}$. There are not many of them in an Age, and so the *less work* to do.

**Printers and Stationers to be severely Punish'd.**

The *Printer*, and *Stationer*, come next, who beside the *Common Penalties* of *Mony*, Loss of *Copies*, or *Printing-Materials*, may be Subjected to These further *Punishments*.

Let them *Forfeit* the *Best Copy* they have, at the Choice of that *Surveigher* of the *Press*, under whose Cognisance the Offence lyes; the Profit whereof the said Officer shall / see Thus Distributed *One Third* to the *King, a Second* to the *Enformer*, reserving the *Remainder* to *himself*.

In some Cases, they may be condemn'd to wear some visible *Badge*, or *Marque* of *Ignominy*, as a *Halter* instead of a *Hat-band*, one Stocking *Blew*, and another *Red;* a *Blew Bonnet*[56] with a *Red T* or *S*. upon it, to Denote the Crime to be Either *Treason;* or *Sedition;* and if at any time, the Person so Condemn'd, shall be found without the said *Badge*, or *Marque*, During the time of his Obligation to wear it, let him Incurre some *further Penalty*, Provided only, that if within the said time, he shall discover and *seize*, or *cause* to be *Seized* any *Author, Printer*, or *Stationer*, Liable at the time of That *Discovery* and *Seizure* to be Proceeded against, for the Matter of *Treasonous*, or *Seditious* Pamphlets, the Offender aforesaid shall from the time of that Discovery be Discharg'd from wearing it any Longer.

This Proposal may seem *Phantastique* at first sight; but certainly *there are Many Men who had rather suffer any other Punishment then be made Publiquely Ridiculous*.

It is not Needful here to run through every Particular, and to Direct, in What *Manner*, and to What *Degree, These*, and *Other Offenders* in the like kind shall be *Punish'd*, so as to *Limit*, and *Appropriate*, the Punishment: but it shall suffice, having Specifi'd the several Sorts of *Offenders*, and *Offences*; to have laid down likewise the several *Species* of *Penalties*, Sortable to every Man's *Condition*, and *Crime*.

Concerning *Rewards*, something is said already, and I shall only Add for a Conclusion, that they are every jot as *Necessary* as *Punishments*; and ought to be *various*, according to the Several *Needs, Tempers*, and *Qualities* of the Persons upon whom they are to be *Conferr'd*. *Mony* is a *Reward* for *One; Honour* for *Another*: and *either* of these *Misplac'd*, would appear rather a *Mockery*, than a *Benefit*.

## 'LEstrange to bee Surveyor of the Printing Presse &c.' (15 August 1663). NA, SP 29/78/96.

[f. 180r]

# CHARLES R.

Whereas in contempt of Our Laws & authority many treasonous, Seditious, & unlicenc'd Pamphlets, Libells & Papers are dayly printed vended & dispersed by the obstinate & implacable Enemies of Our Royall person & Government, for redresse & remedy hereof, Our Will & Pleasure is That you prepare a Grant for Our Royall Signature for the erecting & constituting of an Office for the surveying of the Imprimery, & Printing Presses, & for the preventing of the inconveniences aforesd.[1] And it is Our Will & Pleasure, that you prepare a Grant for Our Royall Signature of y$^e$ sd Office unto Roger LEstrange Esq. of whose Loyalty & abilities Wee are well assured, & him to authorize & appoint to bee Our surveyour of all the Imprimery & Printed Pictures & alsoe of all Books & papers whatsoever hereafter to bee imprimted or reprinted, except Books concerning the Common Laws of this Realme or Books of History concerning the State of this Realme or any other Books concerning Affaires of State or concerning Heraldry, Titles of Honour & Armes or the Office of Earl Marshall or Books of Divinity / Physick Philosophy Arts & Sciences & such other books & papers as are granted by Our pres$^{nt}$ Patents to Our proper & peculiar Printers & usually claimed & imprinted by them by virtue of the sd pres$^{nt}$ Patents. To have & so hold the sd Office or Offices of Our sd Surveyour & Licencer for & during the terme of his naturall life to bee exersized by himselfe or his sufficient Deputie or Deputies w$^{ch}$ sd Deputy or Deputies are from time to time to bee approved by the late Arch Bishop of Canterbury & Lord Bp of London or one of them & by Our Principall Secretaries of State or either of them with a sole Priviledge of writing, printing & publishing all Narratives or relacions not exceeding two sheets of Paper & and all Advertisements, Mercuries, Diurnalls & books of Publick Intelligence.[2] And likewise of Printing or appointing to bee printed all Ballads, Maps, Charts, Portraictures & Pictures not formerly printed & all Breifs & Collections, Bills of Ladeing, Play-Bills, & Quacksalvers Bills,[3] & Customes & excise Bills, Post Office Bills, Auditors Bills, Ticquets & all formes or blanks of Bonds, Bills, Indentures & Warrants, with power to Search for & seize all / unlicensed Books & Papers & to seize & apprehend all Seditious treasonable, schismaticall, & scandalous books & papers & to seize & apprehend all & every the Offenders therein & to bring them before one of Our Principall Secretaries of State or the next Jus-

*'LEstrange to bee Surveyor of the Printing Presse'*   51

tice of Peace, to bee proceeded ag[st] according to Law, together with all other Priviledges & Powers necessary or conducting to Our Service in y[e] Premises. For w[ch] this shall bee your warrant, Given at Our Court at Whitehall the 15th day of August 1663 in the 15th year of Our reigne.

To our Attorney or Sollicitour Generall     By his Ma[ties]. Command   Henry Bennet.[4]

Roger L'Estrange, *Intelligencer; Published for the Satisfaction and Information of the People. With Privilege*, 1 (London, printed by Richard Hodgkinson, living in Thames-street, over against Baynards Castle, 31 August 1663). N&S, 201/450; ESTC, P1749.

THE

## INTELLIGENCER;

PUBLISHED

*For the Satisfaction and Information of the People.*

With Privilege.

Monday August 31. 1663.

## *THE INTRODUCTION*

*HIS Sacred Majesty* having been lately and graciously pleased to *Grant,* and *Commit* the *Priviledge* of *Publishing* all *Intelligence,* together with the *Survey,* and *Inspection* of the PRESSE, to *One* and the same *person*;[1] it may be good Discretion (I suppose) for the Person so entrusted to begin (as his first step toward the work) with some *Considerations,* and *Advertisements,* by way of *Preamble* and *Introduction* to the future *Order,* and *Settlement* of the *whole Affair.*

First, as to the point of *Printed Intelligence,*[2] I do declare myself, (As I hope I may, in a matter left so absolutely *Indifferent,*[3] whether *Any,* or *None*) that *supposing* the *Press* in / *Order;* the *People* in their right *Wits,* and NEWES, or *No Newes,* to be the *Question;* A *Publick Mercury*[4] should never have *My Vote*; because I think it makes the *Multitude* too *Familiar* with the *Actions,* and *Counsels* of their *Superiours*; too *Pragmaticall*[5] and *Censorious,* and gives them, not only an *Itch,* but a kind of *Colourable Right,*[6] and *Licence,* to be Meddling with the *Government.* All which (*supposing as* before *supposed*) does not yet hinder, but that in *This Juncture,* a *Paper* of *That Quality* may be both *Safe* and *Expedient*: Truly if I should say, *Necessary,* perhaps the Case would bear it, for certainly, there is not *anything* which at *This Instant* more Imports his *Majestie's Service,* and the *Publick,* then to *Redeem* the *Vulgar* from their *Former Mistakes,* and *Delusions,* and to *preserve* them from the *like* for *the time to come*: to both which purposes, the prudent Menage[7] of a *Gazett* may Contribute in a very high Degree: for, beside that it is *every bodies Money*, and (in truth) a good part of *most mens study*, and *Bus'ness*; tis none of the worst ways of *Address* to the *Genius*, and *Humour* of the *Common People*; whose *Affections* are much more capable of being *tuned*, and *wrought upon*, by convenient *Hints*, and *Touches*; in the *Shape*, and *Ayre* of a *Pamphlet*, then by the *strongest Reasons*, and *best Notions imaginable*, under any *other*, and more *sober Form whatsoever*. To which advantages of being *Popular*, and *Gratefull*,[8] must be added (as none of the least) that it is likewise *seasonable* and worth the *while*, were there no *other use* of it, then only to detect, and disappoint the *Malice* of those *scandalous* and *false Reports* which are daily *contrived*, and *Bruited*[9] against the *Government*.

So that upon the *Mayn*, I perceive the *Thing, Requisite*, and (for ought I can see yet *Once a week* may do the bus'ness, (for I intend to utter my *News*, by *Weight*, and not by *Measure*.) Yet if I shall find, when my *hand* is *In*, and after the *planting*, and *securing* of my *Correspondents*, that the *Matter* will fairly furnish *More*, without either *Incertainty, Repetition*, or *Impertinence*, I shall keep my self free to *double* at pleasure. / *One Book a Week* may be expected however; to be *Published* every *Thursday*, and *finished* upon the *Tuesday night*, leaving *Wednesday* entire for *the Printing it off*.[10]

The *Way*, as to the *Vent* that has been found most *Beneficial* to the *Master of* the *Book*, has been to *Cry*, and *Expose* it about the *Streets*, by *Mercuries*[11] and *Hawkers*; but whether *That Way* be so advisable in some *other respects*, may be a *Question*, for under Countenance of that Imployment, is carried on the *Private Trade* of *Treasonous*, and *Seditious Libels*, (nor, effectually, has any thing considerable been dispersed, against either *Church*, or *State*, without the *Aid*, and *Privity*[12] of this sort of *People*.) Wherefore, without ample *Assurance*, and *Security* against this *Inconvenience*, I shall adventure to steer *another Course*; which I only Mention, that in case of being put upon it, I may not hereafter be Charg'd with *Singularity*, and Caprice, for a proceeding wherein I am totally Governed by an *honest*, and *Conscientious Reason*, and *That* too, in a direct *opposition* to my *particular Profit*.

Touching the *prosecution* of the Work, I have already given my sense against *Repetitions*; which I *Dislike*, both in respect to the *Reader*, and to my *self*; for neither am I so good a *Husband*, as to *Vamp my Intelligence*,[13] nor so, *fowle* a *Dealer* as to make any man *pay twice* for the *same Commodity*. For the *Matter*, I shall endeavour to provide such, as may neither *tire the Reader*, nor *shame* the *Reporter*: and some care shall be taken too in point of *Order*, and *Coherence*; for the *whole*, as well as for the *Parts*, for the *Story*, as well as for the *Pamphlet*. Nor shall I give my self much peyne about the *Stile*; but let it e'en *prove* as it *sitts*, and *Lye* as it *Falls* (saving ever a *constant Reverence* to *Authority* and *Truth*,) Finally: after all this, if it happen at last, that I go less then my *Pretensions*, it shall content me that I *meant well*; and (at worst) that I have *Great Examples* for my *Comfort* and *Great Examples* for my *Excuse*.

A word now to the *second Branch* of my *Care* and *Duty*: / That is the *Survey* and *Inspection* of the *Press*.

I find it (in general) with the *Printers* as with their *Neighbors*, there are too *many* of the Trade to live one by another but more *particularly* I find them clogg'd with *three sorts* of people; *Forreigners*, persons not *Free* of the *Trade*, and *Separatists*[14] which I offer, to the end that when it shall be thought fit to *Retrench* the *Number*, the Reformation may begin *There*. In the mean time, to prevent mischief (as far as in *Me* lyes) and for *Their encouragement* that shall discover it, take These.

## ADVERTISEMENTS[15]

*Of Encouragement to the discovery of unlawful Printing.*

1. If any person can give Notice, and make Proofe of any *Printing Press, Erected* and *Being* in any *Private Place, Hole* or *Corner*,[16] Contrary to the Tenor of the Late Act of Parliament, for *the Regulating of Printing, and Printing-Presses*, let him repair with such Notice, and make Proofe of these to the *Surveyer* of the *Press* (at his Office at the *Gun* in *Ivy Lane*)[17] and he shall have *forty shillings* for his pains with what assurance of *secrecy* Himself shall desire.

2. If any such person as aforesaid shall discover to the said *Surveyor*, any seditious or unlawful Book to be upon such a Private Press Imprinting, and withall give his ayd to the seizing of the Copyes and the Offenders: his Reward shall be five Pounds.

3. For the Discovery and Proof of any thing Printing without *Authority*, or *Licence*, although in any Publique House,[18] Ten shillings.

4. For the discovery and Proofe of any seditious or unlawful Book to be sold or dispersed by any of the *Mercuryes*, or *Hawkers*, the Enformer shall have *Five shillings*. / But alas! *Discovery* signifies Little without *Punishment*: Wherefore it is of great Concern to provide that men may not thrive upon their *Transgressions*, and get ten times as much by a *Fault*, as they *Pay* for a *Composition*; which has been but too much a *Practice* of *Late* among the *Inferior Vi*[19] of the *Press*.

I had not spun my *Preamble* to This *Length*, but that *failing* of the News where upon I principally *depended*, and being not very good at *Quoyning*,[20] I chose rather to help out a sheet This way, then to break my *Word*, and deceive a *General Expectation*. But from hence, to

## Intelligence.

From *Coppenhagen Aug.* 8. 1663.

Upon the 2 Instant, we had here a Publique Thanksgiving, for the Detection of *Count Ulefelts* horrid Conspiracy:[21] and the day following, was Published his sentence, whereby (after being declared Traytor) he stands degraded from all his Offices, and Honours; and Condemn'd to have his Hand, and his Head cut off; his Body to be Quarter'd, and the Quarters to be placed upon the *Rampiers*;[22] his Own, and his Childrens Estates to be Confiscate; his Chief House to be demolished, and a Pillar to be Erected in the place of it, with a *Copper-Plate* upon the top, conteyning the *Exact* of the *Sentence*.

And now we talk of a *Conspiracy*, let me give ye the summe of what came to me lately by a very choice hand. /

*From* Amsterdam, *without Date.*

We are Advertis'd, that one, *Cobe,* and *Another* (by a false name) entred certain Goods in the *Custom House*, under the Notion of *Iron rodds* which being *suspected* and *search'd*, upon the *opening* prov'd to be *Pistols*, and *Carbines*, to the number of about a Thousand Armes. (*It is not Convenient to say any more of This at present; but it may be added, that the Presbyterians and Quakers have been observ'd to be more Busy and Confident of Late then ordinary, in several Quarters of the Kingdom.*) ...

## Letters from the Surveyor of the Press (1668). NA, SP 29/238/179.

[L'Estrange to Lord Arlington]

Apr: 22. 1668

(My Lord)

I have lost at least 40 Ounces of Blood, & stand at present confined to my chamber for a Fortnight, upon hazzard of my Life, by y<sup>e</sup> order of D<sup>r</sup> Willis.[1]

If this distemper may plead my excuse in not observing y<sup>r</sup> comand of my Attendance, it is well; If not, I'le wayte upon y<sup>r</sup> Lordshp in spight of all difficultys.

The Bearer of this Let<sup>r</sup> is a Gentleman whom I employ as my Agent, & will await your pleasure in any thing that commands his service. In y<sup>e</sup> busyness of y<sup>e</sup> Presse I have acted as far as my mony, credit, & Authority would carry mee; & y<sup>r</sup> Lordsp may remember that the last number I gave you, was for a warrant for those very Persons whom you have now in hold:[2] And if I had not brought them in, for their necks, long ere this, I would have been content to have forfeited my own.

The Law is so short, that unless the very Act of printing the very poynt in {the notice} be expressly proven, the Printer will come off. I do perswade my selfe the Government will find it a hard matter to reduce the Presse to that order I had brought it: And if I had been still allowed according to y<sup>e</sup> first in that of his Ma<sup>tyes</sup> Bounty, I would have kept it as clear as I had then made it. Not my Lord, that I ever made an Interest of His Ma<sup>tyes</sup> Service, or ever Designed it so. But I must confesse, I cannot but reflect upon my hard fortune with somewhat of Trouble, to see my selfe after 30 yeares assiduous, & unchangd able service,[3] & fidelity to the Crown, exposed at length either to want Bread, or live on y<sup>e</sup> object of a Common Charity. This I presume to speak nakedly as it is; & without any manner of Reproach, or insolence.

My Lord, I do not deserve to be blamed certainly, for using y<sup>e</sup> modest Liberty of an Honest man, & a Gentleman & I assure my selfe of a generous interpretation: Especially when y<sup>r</sup> Lordshpp shall duly consider to what degree I am punisht both in point of Honour, and Convenience.

I took freedom not long since to sollicit Mr Williamson[4] for his part more due of 25l. But he was pleased to remit y<sup>e</sup> matter to y<sup>r</sup> Lordsp. It would be a very personable favour in fine my Lord to appoynt mee a Reliefe. The last payment I had upon y<sup>r</sup> Lordsp's Accompt, was upon y<sup>e</sup> 15th of January 1666. And Mr Williamsons last payment was on Octob. 15. 1667.

I must now fashion it my selfe upon resolve to y̓ Lordsps good advice. And if there be any thing more in so worthless a thing as I am, may be made use of to you, I will most undoubtedly manifest my selfe to do, My Lord.

 Y̓ Honours most obedient & dutyfull servant
  Roger L'Estrange.


[L'Estrange to Joseph Williamson]
Apr: 24. 1668

I have perused all yᵉ Books & papers you sent mee, and marked ye passages which I find most lyable to censure: But till I see yᵉ examinations of wittnesses, & hear yᵉ circumstance of yᵉ proofes they are able to make, I can not make any judgment of yᵉ issue. I desire, the messengers that made yᵉ seizures, & yᵉ persons that made yᵉ discovery may be sent to mee, & I will then prepare such an Enformation as may serve for a Guide to yᵉ Kgs Counsell how to proceed.

 <u>Felo de se</u>. is undoubtedly Wallis his,[5] & I fear, a jury will not make much of it.

 the <u>Queryes</u>,[6] will punish most, because they reflect upon yᵉ pendence, & justice of ye present Parliment.

 <u>Omnia concessa in belo</u>,[7] although a vile pamphlet, is only lyable to ye same censure, with <u>Felo de se</u>, being a libele of yᵉ same quality.

 <u>The Poor Whores petition</u>.[8] I can fasten nothing upon, that a Jury will take notice of.

 <u>Liberty of Conscience</u>,[9] is a {discovery} I consider rather to be Answered than punish'd, unless as an unlicensed pamphlet.

 But yᵉ <u>saynts Freedom</u>,[10] which I sent you yesterday, has direct treason in it. And a little patience would have brought it home: But yᵉ Alarm is now so hott, that they all are upon their guard.

 I send you at present another Libell, which I pray keep private, & return it, because I am upon yᵉ quest of Wallis, who, as I heare has put himselfe into disguise. This <u>Roome for ye Cobbler</u>[11] is yᵉ damnedest thing has come out yet.

 You see too much of yᵉ Licensor of yᵉ Presse, and I do assure you, it is not every bodys worke so great is it. If yᵉ government was reserved, it might earn, & reward those that perform it.

 Give me leave more for my opinion in yᵉ case. If you cannot make fair of destroying those offenders utterly, I think they were better left alone, until an opportunity of making them sure, wᶜʰ I am confident you would not long wait for.

 Only this last Libell of yᵉ Cobblers I wish may be followed close & I will be as quick in it, as possible, so {henceforth} if you show it to yᵉ Ld Arlington, or to my Lord of Cant; let no words be spoken {any thing of} it, for what good I do in it might be by surprise.

I am yᵉ most humble servant. R LS.

# THE TRIAL AND EXECUTION OF JOHN TWYN

*An Exact Narrative of the Tryal and Condemnation of John Twyn, for Printing and Dispersing of a Treasonable Book* (London: printed by Thomas Mabb for Henry Brome at the Gun in Ivy-lane, 1664), pp. 2–5, 9–35, 73–7. Wing, E3668; ESTC, R15143.

Suppression and punishment became occupational hazards for many men and women in the book trade during the Restoration period but one printer paid the full penalty as the only member of the trade put to death under Charles II. This was the otherwise obscure nonconformist John Twyn, executed early in 1664 for printing a tract whose title alone was adjudged treasonable: *A Treatise of the Execution of Justice, wherein is Clearly Proved, that the Execution of Judgement and Justice, is as well the Peoples as the Magistrates Duty; and that if Magistrates Pervert Judgement, the People are Bound by the Law of God to Execute Judgement without them, and upon them*. Twyn was apprehended during the printing of the pamphlet in October 1663 and faced trial for treason the following February. The proceedings were recounted in print in *An Exact Narrative of the Tryal and Condemnation of John Twyn*, this account forming the basis for all later ones, including *State Trials*.

Twyn was in his mid-forties when executed, having been born around 1619 in Hertfordshire. In 1633 he was apprenticed to the London printer William Stansby and in 1640 he took up his freedom in the trade, later working in the king's printing house in Edinburgh, where he also married. By 1658 he had returned to London and by 1662 was widowed and caring for four small children. Operating from premises in Cloth Fair, he was involved in printing editions of the Bible and Hooker's *Ecclesiastical Polity* but also unspecified illicit work which led to his brief imprisonment early in the Restoration.[1] On 7 October 1663 his premises were raided and printed sheets of *A Treatise of the Execution of Justice* were seized. The *Treatise* subsequently circulated, although probably from another printing as surviving copies of the thirty-two-page pamphlet (Wing, T2095) differ slightly from seized pages held in the National Archives (NA, SP 29/88/76).

Details of the raid form the core of the trial narrative, providing fascinating insights into the practices of underground printers and their adversaries while also confirming how the 'fact' of printing was the only basis on which the jury was to determine guilt. The question of whether a tract's content was treasonable or seditious was deemed a matter of law, the province of the judges. Interestingly, Twyn was charged under the treason statute of 25 Edw. III, rather than the 1661 Act designed to protect Charles II (13 Car. II, c. 1), possibly because of the altered witness requirements of the latter, although either required finding printing to be an 'overt act' evidencing a treasonable intention. The issue was not mentioned in the court report, unlike the famous case of Algernon Sidney in 1683, the recollections of the judge Sir John Kelyng confirming that it was determined in private by the bench.[2]

The separation of the fact of printing from printed content also partly explains why only one of the *Treatise*'s offending passages was read out in court, the jury being told the rest were 'too Foul to be Repeated'. A brief summary of their treasonable import was instead provided, the chief justice Sir Robert Hyde nonetheless assuring the court that Twyn's crime was 'as High a Treason as can be Committed'. Thirteen passages were apparently listed in the indictment but this did not appear in the *Exact Narrative* or subsequent accounts. Their flavour can be deduced from the surviving version of the *Treatise*, which declared the godly duty of the people to oust the 'Bloody and Oppressing' house of Stuart: having suffered illegal taxes, episcopal tyranny and bloody war under Charles I they need not submit to the 'cruel yoke of this present Tyrant'.[3]

Twyn did not name the author of the *Treatise* and evidence for the later attribution to the rebel officer Captain Roger Jones is doubtful. The author of the *Exact Narrative* is also not known, although its preface, not included here, bears the marks of Roger L'Estrange's style, justifying publication as a deterrent to those involved in the current 'Insufferable Liberties of the Press'. Also omitted here is the account in the same pamphlet of the simultaneous trials for seditious libel of the bookseller Thomas Brewster, the printer Simon Dover and the bookbinder Nathan Brooks for *The Speeches and Prayers* of executed regicides (London, 1662) and, in Brewster's case, for *A Phenix, or, The Solemn League and Covenant* (London, 1662). The three were pilloried and fined, the preface to the *Exact Narrative* proposing that they thank the King's 'incomparable Clemency' for avoiding Twyn's fate, that of being hanged, disembowelled and quartered.

Notes
1. *ODNB*, 'John Twyn'.
2. J. Kelyng, *A Report of Divers Cases* (London, 1708), p. 23.
3. *A Treatise of the Execution of Justice*, pp. 15, 25.

*An Exact Narrative of the Tryal and Condemnation of John Twyn, for Printing and Dispersing of a Treasonable Book* (London: printed by Thomas Mabb for Henry Brome at the Gun in Ivy-lane, 1664), pp. 2–5, 9–35, 73–7. Wing, E3668; ESTC, R15143.

An Exact
# NARRATIVE
OF THE
Tryal and Condemnation
OF
# JOHN TWYN,
FOR
Printing and Dispersing of a
Treasonable Book,

At *Justice-hall* in the *Old-Bayly*.
*February* 20. in the Morning.

THE Court being set, Proclamation was made: *O Yes, All manner of Persons, that have any thing more to doe at this Sessions of the Peace and Sessions of* Oyer *and* Terminer, *held for the City of* London, *and Sessions of Goale Delivery, holden for the Citty of* London, *and County of* Middlesex, *draw near and give your attendance, for now the Court will proceed to the Pleas of the Crown of the said City and County.*

God save the King.    *Silence Commanded.*

*Clerk of the Peace.* Set *John Twyn*[1] to the Bar, (*who was set there accordingly.*)

   *Clerk   John Twyn,* Hold up thy hand.

   *Twyn*  I desire to understand the meaning of it; (*But being told he must hold up his hand in order to his Tryall, he held it up.*)

   *Clerk &c.   Thou standest Indicted in* London *by the Name of* John *Twyn late of* London *Stationer, for that thou as a false Traitor against the most Illustrious*

Charles *the second, by the grace of God, of* England, Scotland, France *and* Ireland, *King; Defender of the Faith, &c. Thy supream and natural Lord and Soveraign-, not having the feare of God in thine heart, nor weighing the Duty of the Allegiance, but being moved and seduced by the instigation of the Devill, and the cordiall Love, true Duty, and natural Obedience, which true and faithfull Subjects towards our Soveraign Lord the King, bear and of right ought to bear, altogether withdrawing, minding and with all thy force intending the Peace and common tranquility of this Kingdome to disturbe; and Sedition and Rebellion within these his Majesties Kingdomes to move, stir up, and procure; and discord between our said Soveraign and his subjects to make and move; The 27. day of* October *in the Year of the Reign of our said Soveraign Lord* Charls *the second, by the grace of God &c. the* 15th. *at the Parish of* St. Bartholmews *in the Ward of* Farrington *without* London *aforesaid, traiterously / didst compose, imagine, and intend the death and final destruction of our said Soveraign Lord the King, and the Ancient and Regal Government of this Kingdome of* England *to change, and subvert: And our said soveraign Lord the King of his Crown, and Regall Government to depose, and deprive; And these thy most wicked Treasons, and Traiterous imaginations to fulfill, thou the said* John *Twyn, the said 27. day of* October *in the year aforesaid, in the Parish and Ward aforesaid, advisedly, Devillishly and Maliciously didst declare, by Imprinting a certain Seditious, Poysonous and scandalous Book, Entituled,* A Treatise of the Execution of Justice, *&c.*

*In which said Book, amongst other things, thou the said* J. *Twyn, the 27th. day of* October *in the Year aforesaid, in the Parish and Ward aforesaid, falsely, maliciously and Traiterously didst imprint, &c.— Against the Duty of thy Allegiance, and the Statute in that case made and provided; and against the peace of our said Soveraign Lord the King, his Crown and Dignity.* What sayest thou, *John Twyn,* art thou *Guilty* of this *High Treason,* whereof thou standest indicted, or *Not Guilty?*

*Twyn.* I desire leave to speak a few words; My Lord, I am a very poore man: I have been in Prison severall Moneths—

*Cl.* Are you *Guilty,* or *not Guilty?*

*Twyn.* With all due submission to your Honours; I desire to speak a few words—

*Lord Chief Just. Hide,*[2] You must first plead to your Indictment, and then you may say what you will; That's the Rule of the Law; We receive no expostulations till you have pleaded to the Indictment, *Guilty* or *not Guilty.*

*Twyn.* I do not intend to answer to the Indictment, by what I shall now say; I am a poore man, have a Family / and three smal Children, I am ignorant of the Law, and have been kept prisoner divers moneths.—

*L. Hide* Pray plead to the Indictment; you shall be heard; say what you will afterwards.

*Twyn* I humbly thank you my Lord.

*Cl.* Are you *Guilty*, or *not Guilty*?

*Twyn.* I beseech you to allow me Councel, and some consideration; I desire it with all submission.

*L. Ch. Ju. Hide.* You must Plead first; then aske what you will.

*Cl.* Are you *Guilty* or *not Guilty*.

*Twyn. Not Guilty* of those Crimes.

*L. Ch. Ju. Hide.* God forbid you should.

*Cl.* How wilt thou be Tryed?

*Twyn* I desire to be Tryed in the presence of that God that is the searcher of all hearts, and the disposer of all things.

*L. Ch. Ju. Hide.* God Almighty is present here; there is no other Tryal by the Law of England, but by God, and the Peers; that is the Countrey; honest men. You shall have all your challenges, and all that's due to you, by the help of God; we are bound to be your Councel, to see you have no wrong; therefore put your self upon your Tryal, say how you will be Tryed.

*Twyn.* I desire to be Tried in the presence of God.

*L. Ch. Ju. Hide.* So you shall; God Almighty is present here; looks down, and beholds what we do here, and we shall answer severely if we do you any wrong. We are as carefull of our soules, as you can be of yours. You must answer in the words of the Law.

*Twyn.* By God, and the Countrey.

*Cl.* God send thee a good deliverance.

*L. Ch. Ju. Hide.* Now say what you will.

*Twyn.* I am a very poor man.

*L. Ch. Ju. Hide.* Nay, let me interrupt you thus farr, / what ere you speak in your defence to acquit your self of this Crime, that you may reserve till by and by; This is but an Arraignment, afterwards the Evidence for the King is to be heard, then make your defence; If you have any Witnesses on your part, let's know their names, we'le take care they shall come in. If I did not mistake; *you desired to have Councell*; Was That your request?

*Twyn.* Yes.

*L Ch. Ju. Hide.* Then I will tell you, we are bound to be of Councell with you, in point of *Law*; that is, the Court, my Brethren, and my Self, are to see that you suffer nothing for your want of knowledg, in matter of *Law*; I say, we are to be of Councell with you; But for this horrid Crime, (I will hope in Charity you are not Guilty of it, but if you are) it is the most Abominable and Barbarous Treason that ever I heard of, or any man else; The very *Title* of the *Book* (if there were no more) is as perfectly Treason as possibly can be: The whole book through; all that is read in the Indictment; not one Sentence, but is as absolute High Treason, as ever I yet heard of. A company of mad brains, under pretence of the Worship and Service of God to bring in all Villanies and Atheisme, (as is seen in that *Book*) what a horrid thing is this! But you shall have free liberty of defending your self. To the matter of *Fact*; whether it be *So* or *No*; in This case, the Law does not allow you Councel to Plead for you; but in matter of *Law*, We are of Councell with you, and it shall be our care to see that you have no wrong done you ...

[9]
*Cl.* Set *John Twin, Simon Dover, Thomas Brewster,* and *Nathan Brooks*[3] to the Barr.

 *Cl.* John *Twyn, Those men that you shall hear called, and Personally appear, must pass between our Soveraign Lord the King and you, upon Trial of your Life and Death; if you will challenge them, or any of them, you must do it when they come to the Book to be Sworn, before they be Sworn; And you that are for the Seditions and Offences, look to your challenges.*

 *Dover,* We desire we may have a Jury of *Book-sellers* and *Printers*; they being the men that only understand our businesse.

 *L, Hide,* There are those already that understand it as well as Book-sellers or *Printers*; besides, half the Jury are such,[4] and they are able to make the rest understand it, but you may challenge whom you will.

The Jury were,

| | |
|---|---|
| *William Samborne,* | *William Hall,* |
| *William Rutland,* | *John Williams,* |
| *Thomas Honylove,* | *James Flesher,* |
| *Robert Lucas,* | *Simon Waterson,* |
| *Robert Beversham,* | *Samuel Thomson,* |
| *Richard Royston,* | *Thomas Roycroft.* |

Who were severally Sworn by the Oath following /

*Cl. John Twyn,* Hold up thy hand, *You of the Jury look upon the Prisoner and hearken to his Cause, you shall understand that he stands Indicted in* London, *by the name of* John Twyn *late of* London, *Stationer;* (here the Indictment is read over again;) *Upon this Indictment he hath been Arraigned, and thereunto hath pleaded Not Guilty; and for his Tryal, hath put himself upon God and the Countrey, which Countrey you are: your charge is to inquire whether he be Guilty of the High Treason, in manner and forme as he stands Indicted, or not Guilty; if you finde him Guilty, you shall inquire what Goods and Chattels, Lands and Tenements he had at the time of committing the said Treason, or at any time sithence: If you finde him not Guilty, you shall inquire whether he fled for it; if you finde that he fled for it, you shall inquire of his good and Chattels, Lands and Tenements, as if you had found him* Guilty; *if you find him* not Guilty, *nor that he did fly for it, say so, and no more, and heare your Evidence. ... /*

Mr. Serjeant *Morton*.[5] May it please your Lordships, and you Gentlemen that are sworn of this Jury, I am of Councell with the King against *John Twyn*, the Prisoner here at Barr; who stands Indicted of a most Horrid, and Damnable Treason. It is, *The Compassing and Imagining the Death of the King, to deprive him of his Crown and Royal Government, and to Alter and Change the Antient Legal and Fundamental Government of this Kingdome*: which he has indeavoured to do and did intend to do, by Printing a Traiterous and Seditious Book, which in it self contains as many and as great Treasons as it was possible either for the Malice of the Devil or the Corrupt and Treasonable thoughts of Blood-thirsty Men to invent; It contains Treasons against the King in his own Royal Person; against his Government, both Ecclesiastical and Civil; full of Treasons, (as my Lord Chief Justice was pleased to observe to you) Treasons against the Queen, Scandals against all manner of Profession both in Church and Kingdom, of Magistracy, and Ministry: My Lord, there are in this Indictment *Thirteen* Paragraphs of that Treasonable Book Recited, and each of them contains as many Treasons, as there be lines in it; nay (My Lord) this Treasonable Book, it was intended to set a Flame in this Nation; to raise and stir up Rebellion in this Kingdom against the King and his Government. I shall observe to your Lordship, the *Time* when it was to be *Printed*: It was in the beginning of *October*, your Lordship knows, and I do not doubt but the Jury have heard, that there was a great and dangerous design in this Nation, set on foot by men of dangerous Principles, to Imbroyle this Nation in a *New Warr*, for the destruction of the King and his Government; It was Executed in part, as farr as Time and other Circumstance would give way and leave to the undertakers; (the 12. of *October* last) and my Lord, it was proved upon the Execution of a Commission of *Oyer* and *Terminer* at *York*, that / there was a Council here in *London*, that sat to prepare matter for an Universal Rebellion all *England* over; they sent their Agitators into the *North, West*, all parts; to give notice to their Party to be ready to Rise at a certain time; several dayes were appointed, but it seems they could not be ready till that 12th. of *Octob.* for *the Seditious Books that were to lead on that Design, and the Libels and Declarations could not be Printed before that day*;[6] and truely that had been Printed and Published too, if there had not been great Diligence used by the Kings Agents and Ministers, to take them just as they were preparing it. This Book, Gentlemen, doth contain a great deal of Scandal upon the Kings Government, dispersing False and Base Rumours, to the prejudice of it. It is a rule in my Lord *Cooke*, that *the dispersing of false and evil Rumours against the King and Government; and Libels upon Justices of the Kingdom; they are the forerunners of Rebellion.*[7]

We shall now go the *proof*; we shall prove that this Prisoner at the Bar, to Print this Book, had two Presses in one Roome; that he himself did work at one of those Presses, his Servants at the other, by his Command and in his presence: That he did Compose part of it: Print the sheets, Correct the Proofs, and Revise them all in his own house, which were corrected and brought back into the Workhouse by himself, in so short a time that they could not be carryed abroad to Correct, so that he must needs Correct them himself: That this Work was done in the Night time, (and it was proper, it was a deed of great darknesse and not fit indeed to see the light, and it was well it was strangled in the Birth, or else for ought I know we might by this time have been wallowing in our blood). We shall make it appear, that this man when Mr. *Le-Strange*[8] came to search his house, brake the Forms, conveyed away as many of the Sheets as he could from the Presse to other places; yet notwithstanding, Gods Providence was so great in the thing that he left there three or four sheets, which Mr. *Le Strange*, / then seized on, and many more within a little time after: And somewhat of the same matter, remained upon part of a Form of Letter, which his hast would not give him leave to break; When he was charged with it by Mr. *Le Strange*, he confessed that he had printed some sheets of this Seditious Book, and being demanded by Mr. *Le Strange*, what he thought of it? He told him, he thought *it was mettlesome stuff*; he had great joy in it, he confessed he had received money for printing of this; and much other matter, taken upon Examination before Mr. *Secretary*.[9] We shall call our Witnesses; I should have observed to you, that this man would have it done with all the privacy that could be, and to be done forthwith; there was great hast of it, about the beginning of *October* and the designe in the *North*, was upon the *Twelfth*, so that it was clearly intended for that Designe.

*Several Witnesses new sworn.*

*Joseph Walker*.[10] My Lord, whereas my Master is Indicted for Printing this Book—

*Lord Hide*. Your Master? Who is your Master?

*Walker* He at the Bar.

*L. Hide*. What say you of it?

*Walker* I desire to see the Book, [*it was shewed him*.] About the foure first pages of this Treatise I composed.

*L. Hide*. Who delivered it to you to compose?

*Walker*. My Master delivered the Copy to me.

*L. Hide*. What doe you mean by Composing?

*Walker*. Setting the Letters.

*L. Hide.* Well, and you set the letters to Print according to the Copy, and you had it of your Master, had you?

*Walker.* Yes my Lord; but all this Copy we did not print.

(*Part of the Copy in manuscript being shewed him, he said, he composed by that copy.*) /

*Serj. Morton.* How much did you Print?

*Walker.* About three sheets.

*Serj. Morton.* How many of those did your Mr. compose?

*Walker.* Truly Sir I cannot tell.

L. *Hide.* Did he compose one?

*Walker.* As to a whole one, I cannot say.

Mr. *Recorder.* Did he Compose the Title?

*Walker.* Here is no Title.

Mr. *Recorder.* No? Read the top.

*Wal.* A Treatise of the Execution, &c. (*He reads the Title.*)

*Recorder.* Did your Master Compose that?

*Walker.* No, I did.

L. *Hide.* Did your Master give you that to Compose?

*Walker.* Yes.

Serj. *Morton.* Who Composed the second, third, and fourth sheet?

*Walker.* I Composed some of them, but to particularize I cannot.

L. *Hide.* Who gave you what you did?

*Walker.* My Master.

L. *Hide.* Can you turn to any part of that you did Compose?

*Walker,* I cannot tell that.

L. *Hide.* You Composed you say foure pages; there are eight in a sheet, who composed the other of the same sheet?

*Walker.* I think my Master did.

L. *Hide.* At the same time and in the same room with you?

*Walker.* He wrought not in the same Room.

L. *Hide* After you had stampt the sheet, who did peruse, and over-read it, to see if it were right?

*Walker.* I carried them into the Kitchen and laid them down upon the Dresser by my Master.

L. *Hide.* Who compared them?

*Walker.* I know not.

L. *Hide.* Who brought them back to you? /

*Walker* My Master brought them into the Workhouse and laid them down.

L. *Hide.* Was there any body in the house that might Correct it?

*Walker.* Not that I saw.

L. *Hide.* When you had carried a sheet down, how long was it ere it was brought back again?

*Walker.* About an hour, or an hour and a half.

L. *Hide.* Was there any body in the house besides you and your Master?

*Walker.* There was my fellow Apprentice, and the Woman that keeps the House.

L. *Hide.* Were there no strangers there?

*Walker.* No my Lord.

Mr. *Rec.* Were they Printed in your Masters house?

*Walker.* Yes.

Serj. *Morton.* What room?

*Walker.* In the Press-room.

Serj. *Morton.* Did your Master work at the Presse about this work, any part of the time?

*Walker.* Yes, I saw him beat some sheets.

L. *Hide.* When you had printed one sheet, were there not some mistakes of the Letters to be mended?

*Walker.* Yes, there were *Literals*.[11]

L. *Hide.* Who made the Amendment?

*Walker.* Upon my Oath I cannot tell.

L. *Hide.* Do you believe it to be your Masters?

*Walker.* I cannot tell that.

L. *Hide.* Have you seen your Master write heretofore?

*Walker.* I have seen him write, but because I have heard of them that could counterfeit mens hands, I dare not swear it was his Writing.

L. *Hide.* Were the amendments that were brought back, like his hand? /

*Walker.* The Letters were something like them, but I cannot swear positively, that they were his.

L. *Hide.* No, that you cannot, unless you saw him write them; but was it like his hand?

*Walker.* It was not much unlike his hand.

Mr. *Recorder.* Did not your Master use to correct other works before this?

*Walker.* Yes.

Mr. *Recorder.* Then by the Oath that you have taken, were not the corrections of this Book like those of other corrections by his own hand?

*Walker.* I know not that.

Mr. *Record.* Did any body correct books in your house but your Master?

*Walker.* No Sir.

Serj. *Morton.* Did not you see your Master with Copie?

*Walker.* Yes he had Copy before him.

Serj. *Morton.* What time was this Printed? by night, or by day?

*Walker.* In the night time.

Serj. *Morton.* What directions did your Master give you about Printing it, did he direct any privacy?

*Walker.* He was not much desirous of that.

Mr. *Record.* At what time did you work about it?

*Walker.* In the morning, from two till four or five.

Serj. *Morton.* Pray Sir thus; were you in the house when Mr. *L'Estrange* came up?

*Walker.* Yes. ... /

Serj. *Morton.* What did your Master say when you told him Mr. *L'Estrange* was below?

*Walker.* Very few words, I cannot be positive in them.

Seri. *Morton.* To what purpose were they?

*Walker.* Hearing some body knock at the door, I went down into the Composing room, and looked through the window, and saw people; I imagined Mr. *L'Estrange* was there, and I told my Master, whereupon he said, *he was undone*, or to that effect. ...

Serj. *Morton.* Did not you by his direction break the Form[12] when Mr. *L'Estrange* came to search?

*Walker.* I brake one indeed.

Mr. Serj. *Morton.* What became of the other?

*Walker.* My fellow prentice brake it.

Mr. Serj. *Morton.* By whose direction?

*Walker.* I had no order for it, I brought it down and went to set it against a post, and it fell in peices.

Serj. *Morton.* Did you ask your Master who delivered him this Copy to Print?

*Walker* I did ask him two several times, but he made no answer. ... /

Serj. *Morton.* Was he not used to tell you the Authors of books that you printed?

*Walker.* The Authors he did not; but for whom they were printed he used to tell me: My Lord I humbly beg pardon for what I did, I was his Apprentice.

Lord *Hide.* How many sheets did you print?

*Walker.* Two Reams on a sheet, which makes 1000.

Lord *Hide.* The first page, being the *Title* of it, your Master brought to you to compose; At the same time when you were composing one part, your Master was composing another part of the same sheet in the next room, And part of it your Master did print as well as compose, I think you said this.

*Walker.* Yes.

Lord *Hide.* Likewise that the proofs were carried to him to overlook, and he brought them back within an hour or an hour and half after, and laid them down in the workhouse; and that you saw the hand of the amendments, but you cannot swear it was his, only you say, that it was not unlike it; and that he had corrected former sheets that you had printed, and that the hand with which he corrected others, and this, was alike; and that there was no stranger in the house to correct it.

*Walker.* Not that I saw.

Lord *Hide.* This is the substance of what you said.

*Walker.* Yes. ... /

Lord *Hide.* You did rise to work at two of the clock in the morning about it, and your Master said when you told him Mr. *L'Estrange* was below, that *he was undone.*

*Walker.* It was so my Lord.

Mr. *North.*[13] Mr. *L'Estrange,* Pray tell my Lord and the Jury of your taking this.

Mr. *L'Estrange.* My Lord I do remember that three or four daies or thereabouts before the twelfth of *October* last, I had notice of a Press that had been at work for several nights in *Cloth fair,*[14] and imployed a person to watch the house; who told me that they still gave over early in the morning, at day light, or soon after; At length, intelligence was brought me in these very words, That *now they were at it as hard as they could drive* (which was about four in the morning) I arose, went to one of the Kings Messengers, and desired him to take a Printer by the way, who did so, and I call'd up a Constable, and so went to *Twyn*s house, where we heard them at work: I knocked a matter of a quarter of an hour, and they would not open the door, so that I was fain to send for a Smith to force it; but they perceiving that, opened the door and let us in; there was a light when we came, but before the door was opened it was put out: when I was got up stairs, and a candle lighted, I found a form broken, (that is, the letters dispersed) only one corner of it standing intire, which was compared by a Printer that was there, with a corner of a page newly printed, and appear'd to be the same; This form was brought down out of the Press room into the composing room. As yet we could not find the whole Impression, but at last they were found thrown down a pair of back stairs, (I remember) they told me the Impression was *a thousand*: I asked him where he had the *copy?* he told me *he knew not: it was brought to him by an unknown hand*; I told him he must give an account of it; he told me at last *he had* *it from* Calverts *Maid*;[15] I ask'd him where the copy was, he told me *he could / not tell*, (when I speak of the *Copy*, I mean the *manuscript*) we searched near two hours and could not find it; and at length went thence to the Constables house in *Smithfield*, and staid there a while with the prisoner. I asked him (Mr. *Twyn* said I) who corrected this sheet? *Alas*, said he, *I have no skill in such things*; who revised it then? who fitted it for the Press? *Truely I had no body but my self; I read it over*; What thought you upon reading it? *Methoughts it was mettlesome stuffe, the man was a hot fiery man that wrote it*, but he knew no hurt in it.

Serj. *Morton.* When you had taken these sheets, were they wet, or not?

Mr. *L'Estrange.* They were not only wet, but half of them were imperfect, printed only on one side; missing the copy, I told him after he was carried to *Whitehall*, (Mr *Twyn* said I) it may possibly do you some good yet to bring forth this Copy, if you will be so ingenuous to produce the Copy, and discover the Author you may find mercy for your self, pray therefore get this copy, perchance I may make some use of it. After that, his servant, *Bazilla Winsor* brought out this part of the Copy. (*producing a sheet of the Manuscript in Court.*) ... / I asked Mr. *Twyn* further, How did you dispose of those sheets which you had printed, those several heaps whether are they gone? He told me he had delivered those sheets to Mistriss *Calverts* maid, at the Rose in *Smithfield*

Mr. *Record.* You say he told you Mistriss *Calverts* maid received them of him, Did you since speak with that maid.

Mr. *L'Estrange.* I was long in searching *Twyns* house and one of his Apprentices made his escape, and probably gave notice of it, for the night I went to Mistriss *Calverts* house, she and the maid too were fled, I have since taken the Mistress and she is now in custody, I have heard nothing of the maid since

J. *Keeling*.[16] *Twyn* owned to you that he had corrected some of the sheets, that he had read them, and said it was *mettlesome stuff*

Mr *L'Estrange.* I did ask him in the house of the Constable: Who corrected this? the Corrector must certainly know what it was. Said he, *I have no skill in correcting*. But when I speak of *correcting*, I mean who *revised* it, *overlooked* it for the Press; *I read it over*, sayes he.

*Twyn.* I never said such a word.

Mr. *L'Estrange.* He spake this in the presence of two or three here present; could you read over this Book, said I, and not know that it was not fit to be Printed? *I thought it was a hot fiery fellow, it was mettle or mettlesome stuff*, somewhat to that effect.

Serj. *Morton.* What did you hear him confess before Sir *Henry Bennet*?

Mr. *L'Estrange.* He owned the thing, that is, he acknowledged he had printed the sheet, I shewed there, and two other sheets of the same Treatise.

Serj. *Morton.* Did he acknowledge he corrected them.

Mr. *L'Estrange.* I know not whether before Sir *H. B.* he did, or no. /

Serj. *Morton*. What know you about money received by him.

Mr. *L'Estrange*. He said *Calverts* maid paid him 40 s. in part for that work.

*Twyn*. I said I had received money of *Calverts* maid for work I had done, but named not that.

### *Mr*. Dickenson[17] *Sworn*.

About the seventh day of *October*, it being *Wednesday* as I remember, about five a clock we attended *Mr. L'Estrange*, my self and others; we came to the house of the prisoner, in *Cloth-fair* and upon the backside of his house we stood listening a good while, and heard Presses a working; upon that, I came to the fore part, by *Mr. L'Estranges* order, and knocked, but none would answer, I took the Constables staff and knockt again, and none would answer yet; After that, *Mr. L'Estrange* knockt near half an hour and no body coming, he at last sent for a Smiths hammer to force it open. Afterwards, they came down, and opened the door. Then *Mr. L'Estrange*, and the *Printer* (Mr. *Mabb*)[18] went up stairs, I continued below with the Constable, and the Kings Messenger to observe whether any went in or out. After which, some sheets fell down on the other side of the house, meeting with one of them, and perceiving they had discovered the sheets they inquired after, I read some part of it, and finding what it was, I went up and found the sheets thrown behind the door; Mr. *Twyn* (said I) I wonder you would Print such a thing as this, you could not choose but know that it was very dangerous to do any such thing; he answered, that *He did not consider what it was*; questionless said I, you could not but know it was very dangerous, for when you revised it, you must needs know the sence of it, and think it was a dangerous business, what did you think of it? saies he *I thought he was a good smart angry fellow, it was mettlesome stuff*; or to that purpose. / This was the substance of our discourse: I did see some of the sheets Printed on one side, and some on both sides, the Form lay disordered, yet not so, but there was one corner of it yet remaining, and I having the sheet in my hand did compare them together; and to the best of my remembrance I do remember these very words, *Execution of Judgement, and Lord have*.

L *Hide*. Who did he say revised the Press?

*Dickenson*. He seemed to confess that he had corrected it himself, for when I urged it to him that he could not chuse but know the matter of it by reading it? truly saies he, *I thought he was an angry smart fellow, it was good mettlesome stuff indeed*.

Judge *Keeling*. The question asked by my Lord, is, whether he did confess he revised it, or whether you did collect it from his reply?

*Dickenson*. Truly by that answer I guessed he corrected it.

*Recorder*. Did he confess that he read it?

*Dickenson.* I put that question to him, and to the best of my remembrance he did not deny it.

L. *Hide.* To Mr. *L'Estrange* he confessed he read it over.

### Tho. Mabb *Sworn.*

My Lord I was with Mr. *L'Estrange* in this mans house, and being there, going up, we found the Press had been lately at work ... I went down, and below I found the two Formes, but broken, somewhat indeed was standing; whereof I took part in my hand, and read in the letters; Mr. Dickenson having the / sheets, he heard what I read, and looking on the sheet found them agree.

*Twyn.* What were the words that you read?

Mr. *Mabb.* The words were *Execution and Judgement, and Lord have*— There was a back pair of stairs out of his Press room, partly between his house and his neighbours, and in the hurry they had thrown the sheets down there, part fell behind the door, and part at the bottom. When I questioned him how many was done? he said five hundred, but I adjudged those I saw to be about seven hundred and fifty; looking again over the door I espied the remainder of the sheets about two hundred and fifty more, and I brought them together, and then he owned there was one thousand.

L. *Hide.* What else do you know?

Mr. *Mabb.* At the Constables house, I heard him use the words, that *it was mettlesome stuff*, and that *no body corrected it but himself*; said I, I wonder you would offer to do it, you could not compose it but you must understand it. Said he, *It was my bad fortune to meddle with it*; said I, You lost a Press but a little while since, I wonder you would do this; he seemed to be sorrowful. ... /

### Mr. Joseph Williamson[19] *Sworn.*

That which I can say, is, That I know this (*looking upon a paper*) to be my own hand writing, and to be the examination taken of this *Twyn*. I took it, and he owned it after it was written.

Serj. *Morton.* What was the substance of it?

L. *Hide.* What did he confess before Mr. *Secretary*? when he was examined.

Mr. *Williamson.* He said that the Copie of the Book was brought to him by one *Evans*, maid to Mistris *Calvert*, that for the *Author*, being asked if he knew him? he said he did not, and that he had seen the Copie of three sheets of the Book; that he had Printed only two of those sheets, a thousand exemplaries of each.

Serj. *Keeling.*[20] Did he confess that?

Mr. *Williamson.* Yes; and further, that he had delivered them to this *Evans* at the sign of the *Rose* in *Smithfield*;[21] that he himself had corrected those sheets he had Printed, and that he had read them after they were Printed: that for his pains and Printing of them, he had received fourty shillings in part, from this maid at the delivery of them, at the *Rose*, that the maid carried away those Exemplaries, from the *Rose*, and that he parted with her at the door.

Serj. *Morton.* I hope you observe Gentlemen; we have now done: we desire the Prisoner may give his answer to it, and then we shall make our reply.

L. *Hide.* What say you? you have heard the Witnesses and what is laid to your charge.

*Twyn.* I did never read a line of it in my life.

L. *Hide.* That's impossible, I'le tell you: first your own man, who set part, swears you did both Set and Print part of this Book your self; you gave him the title to Set, you composed one part of the Book, whilst he was Composing / another part; Is it possible you could Compose, and not read a line of it? He tells you further when the first Sheet was Printed, he brought it into the Kitchin, and laid it down, knew not of any one in the House but your self; About an hour, or an hour and a half after, you brought it back again Corrected, laid it down, and the hand that Corrected it, was not unlike your hand upon other Corrections of Books Pray Brother *Morton*, Let the Jury have Books, and Mr. *Lee* Read the Indictment, that they may see they agree.

Serj. *Morton.* I observed to you, there were *Thirteen* Treasonable Paragraphs, you shall find them marked out in the Margent.

L *Hide.* You shall see there are Treasons with a Witnesse, see the very Title.

Mr. *Lee.* (*Reads the Title of the Indictment*) 'A Treatise of the Execution of Justice; wherein is clearly proved, that the Execution of Judgment and Justice, is as well the Peoples as the Magistrates Duty, and if the Magistrates pervert Judgement, the People are bound by the Law of God to execute Judgement without them and upon them.'

L. *Hide.* That you gave to your man to set.

Mr. *Lee* reads, *It is one of the Scarlet Sins of this Nation, that the People suffer their Rulers*, &c.— The Particular Passages are too Impious to be Published, and indeed too Foul to be Repeated; but in Substance. Those mentioned in the Indictment, are as follows.

First, *The Supream Magistrate is made Accomptable to the People.*

Secondly, *The People are Rebelliously Incited, to take the Menage of the Government into their own Hands*

Thirdly, *They are Animated to take up Armes, not only against the Person of His Sacred Majesty; but likewise against the Royal Family.*

Fourthly, *They are Stirred up to a* Revolt (*in that very Term*) *as an Action Honourable, and Conscientious; making Publication* / *in the next Clause, of Encouragement to any Town, City, or County in the Three Nations to begin the Work.*

Fifthly, *The People are Laboured, not only to cast off their Allegiance to the King; but in Direct Terms to put His Sacred Majesty to Death* And to the purposes before mentioned tends the whole Scope of the Treatise.

Serj. *Morton.* You may judge of the rest, by this; we will not put you to any more expence of Time, there hath been sufficient Treason in that which you have read.

L. *Hide.* Now say what you will; but I must tell you, in those particulars that have been compared, there is as much Villanie and Slander, as is possible for the Devil, or man to invent: It is to destroy the King in his Person; to Rob him of the Love and Affections of His People; to Destroy the whole Family and all Government, Ecclesiastical and Civil: and this *Read* by your self, *Owned*, and *Caused* to be *Printed*.

*Twyn.* Except it was that sheet that Mr. *L'Estrange* read to me when I was taken, I never heard it before, nor read it.

L. *Hide.* Your man swears that you did *Set* and *Print* part of it; it's impossible to Compose and Set, but you must *Read* it; nay you did Examine and Correct the sheets; brought them up again; Mr. *L'strange* swears you confessed you read it over, it was *Mettlesome stuffe*; Mr. *Dickenson* sayes, you did not say you read it over, but he saying to you, it was impossible you should Set it and not Read it, You told him also *It was Mettlesome Stuffe*; You could not Judge it to be *Mettlesome Stuffe*, but you must read it; There is Mr. *Williamson* sayes that you confessed before Mr. Secretary *Bennet*, that you had seen three Sheets, Printed off two Sheets, Corrected those two Sheets; and after Printed, and delivered them; and that you had 40 s, in part of Payment; Besides this, when Mr. *L'Estrange* came first, you were up, (nay at two a Clock in the morning) when they came and knocked at the Door, they heard Presses going, you would make no / answer till they call'd a Smith with intent to force it open: when they came in, they found a Form brought out of the Printing Room, and broken all but one Corner: That taken up by a Printer, and compared with the Lines of the Printed Sheets, and found to agree. Some of the Sheets were Printed on one side only, the rest perfected, you threw them down Stairs, part into your Neighbours House; Said, *You were undone*, when you understood Mr. *L'Estrange* was there. What needed all this, but that you knew what you were doing? And did it purposely to do mischief?

*Twyn*, I did never Read, or hear a line of it, but when Mr L'Estrange read it when I was taken.

Judge *Keeling*, Was it printed at your House or no?

*Twyn*, I know not but that it might; not that I did it with my own hand.

Judge *Keeling*, The papers were found wet with you; who was in your House?

*Twyn*, My two Servants.

Judge *Keeling*, Did any set them at work but your self? did they work of their own heads?

*Twyn*, I did use to set them at work, but I did not set them on that particular work.

L. *Hide*, Have you any thing else to say? God forbid but you should be heard, but the Jury will not easily believe such denialls against so much Evidence.

Judge *Keeling*, Tell us to whom you carried this Copy to be Corrected?

*Twyn*, I know not who Corrected it.

L. *Hide*, If you have any thing to say, speak it, God forbid but you should have a full hearing, say what you will?

*Twyn*, I say I did not read it, nor heard it, till Mr. *L'Estrange* Read it.

L. *Hide*. Have you any thing else?

*Twyn*. It's possible I may upon Consideration.

L. *Hide*. We cannot spend all the day, I must let the Jury know they are not to take your Testimony. /

Serj. *Morton*. I am of Councel for the King; I shall reply if he will say no more.

Judge *Keeling*. You have heard your Charge, this is your time to make your Answer; if you do not speak now, you must not speak after; therefore if you have any thing to speak in your Justification, or witnesses to call, now is your time.

L. *Hide*. Let me give you this Caution, we cannot spend time in vain, we have other business before us, and it grows late, The best Councel I can give you is this; You said at first, that You desired to be Tryed in the presence of God; You are here in the presence of Almighty God, and I would to God you would have so much care of your Self, and do so much right to your Self, to declare the Truth, that there may be means of mercy to you. The best you can now do toward amends for this Wickednesse you have done, is by discovering the Authour of this Villainous Book; If not, you must not expect, and indeed God forbid that there should be any mercy towards you.

*Twyn*. I never knew the Author of it, nor who it was, nor whence it came, but as I told you.

L. *Hide*. Then we must not trouble our selves; Did you never see the hand before, with which this Copy was written?

*Twyn*. No.

L. *Hide*. I am very confident you would not then have been so mad, as to have taken such a Copy; A Copy fraught with such abominable Treason, and Lies; Abusing in the first place, the late King that is dead who was, I'le be bound to say it, as Virtuous, Religious, Pious, Mercifull, and Just a Prince as ever Reigned, and was as Villainously and Barbarously used by his Rebellious Subjects; Nay, you have not rested here, but have fallen upon this King, who has been Gentle and Mercifull, beyond all President; Since He came to the Crown, He has spared those that had forfeited their Lives, and all they had; And he has endeavoured to / Oblige all the rest of His People by Mildnesse and Clemency: And after all this for you to Publish so Horrid a Book; you can never make amends, God forgive you for it.

*Twyn.* I never knew what was in it.

L. *Hide.* You of the Jury, I will say only this, that in point of *Law*, in the first place, there is no doubt in the World by the *Law* of the Land, the Publishing such a Book as this, is as High a Treason as can be Committed; by this he has indeavoured to take away the Life of the King, and destroy the whol Family; and so consequently to deliver us up into the Hands of Forreigners and Strangers; It is a great blessing that we have the Royal Line amongst us. But I say there is no Question (and my Brothers will declare the same if you doubt it) that this Book is as fully Treason by the Old Statute; as much the Compassing and indeavouring the Death of the King, as possible; and he rests not there, but he incites the People to Rebellion, to Dethrone Him, to raise War; And the Publishing of this Book is all one and the same, as if he had raised an Army to do this; The Proofe is, that he *Set* part, *Printed* part, and Corrected it, by his own Confession, read it over, it was *mettlesome stuffe*; Confessed how many Sheets he Printed, the Reward and Recompence you took notice of it; and I presume no man among you can doubt but the Witnesses have spoken true, and for his Answer, you have nothing but his bare denyal, and so we shall leave it to You. ... /

*Cl.* Are you all agreed of your verdict?

*Jury* Yes.

*Cl.* Who shall say for you?

*Jury.* The Foreman.

*Cl.* Set *John Twyn* to the Bar, Look upon him my Masters; how say you, is he *Guilty* of the *High Treason* whereof he stands indicted, or *not guilty?*

*Foreman. Guilty.*

*Cl. of Newgate.* Look to him Keeper.

*Cl.* Hearken to your Verdict as the Court hath Recorded it; You say that *John Twyn* is *Guilty* of the *High Treason* whereof he stood indicted, and that at the time of committing the said Treason, or any time since, he had no goods, chattles, lands nor tenements to your knowledge, and so you say all.

*Jury.* Yes.

*Cl.* John Twyn, *Thou hast been arraigned for High Treason and thereunto hast pleaded Not Guilty, and for thy tryal hast put thy self upon God and the Country, and the Country hath found thee Guilty; what canst thou now say for thy self, why the Court should not proceed to Judgement, and thereupon Award Execution of Death against thee according to the Law?*

*Twyn.* I humbly beg mercy; I am a poor man, and have three small Children, I never read a word of it.

*L. Hide.* I'le tell you what you shall do; Ask mercy of them that can give it; that is of God and the King.

*Twyn.* I humbly beseech you to intercede with his Majesty for mercy.

*Cl. of Newgate.* Tye him up Executioner.

Cryer. *O yes, My Lords the Kings Justices command all manmer of persons to keep silence while Judgement is in giving, upon pain of Imprisonment.*

*L. Hide. John Twyn ... /* Yours is the most grievous and Highest Treason, and the most complicated of all wickedness that ever I knew; for you have as much as possibly lay in you, so reproached and reviled the King, the dead King, and his Posterity, on purpose to endeavour to root them out from off the face of the earth ... I will be so charitable to think you are misled. There's nothing that pretends to Religion that will avow or justifie the killing of Kings, but the *Jesuit* on the one side, and the *Sectary* on the other; indeed it is a desperate and dangerous Doctrine, fomented by divers of your temper, and it's high time some be made examples for it. I shall not spend my time in discourse to you to prepare you for death; I see a grave Person whose office it is, and I leave it to him. Do not think of any time here, make your peace with God, which must be done by confession, and by the discovery of those that are guilty of the same crime with you. God have mercy upon you; and if you so do he will have mercy upon you. But forasmuch as you *John Twyn* have been indicted of *High Treason*, you have put your self upon God and the Country, to try you; and the Country have found you guilty, therefore the Judgement of the Court is, and the Court doth Award. /

*That you be led back to the place from whence you came, and from thence to be drawn upon an Hurdle to the place of Execution, and there you shall be hanged by the Neck, and being alive shall be cut down, and your privy Members shall be cut off, your Entrails shall be taken out of your body, and you living, the same to be burnt before your eyes: your head to be cut off, your body to be divided into four quarters, and your head and quarters to be disposed of at the pleasure of the Kings Majesty. And the Lord have mercy upon your soul.*

*Twyn.* I most humbly befeeth your Lordship to remember my condition, and intercede for me.

*L. Hide.* I would not intercede for my own Father in this case, if he were alive. ...[22]

[73]

IN the *Interval,* betwixt the *Condemnation* and *Execution* of *John Twyn,* diverse Applications were made to him, in order both to his Temporal and Eternal Good; and in particular, Mr. *Weldon,* the *Ordinary* of *Newgate,*[23] spent much time and pains upon him, to convince him of that horrid Crime, for which he was to Suffer; Particularly pressing him to a *Confession* both of his *Offence*, and of the *Author* of that Treasonable Piece, for which he was to Die. His Answer was, *That it was not his Principle to betray the Authour; but it belong'd to others*: Whereupon Mr. *Ordinary* demanded of him, What it was, that could prevail with him, to undertake the Printing of it? He said, *He was a Poor man, that he had Received 40s. and the Promise of a Larger Summe, whereupon he undertooke it*; but who it was that made him that Promise, he would not discover. ... /

Being pressed to receive the *blessed Sacrament*, he return'd, that *he was not free to do it*; *He was against receiving according to the Forms of this Church; and he hoped, he might do well enough without it*; and in this temper he continued till he came to the Place of Execution; Where going up the *Ladder*, Mr. Sheriff told him, that if he had any thing to say, he should remember the cautions he had given him.

*Twyn.* I suppose this appearance of people doth expect that I should say something as to the matter I come here for. It is true, I come here Condemn'd as a *Traytor*, for *printing a book*, taken to be, and owned to be, and judged to be, *Scandalous* and *Seditious*.

Sir *R. Ford.*[24] And *Treasonable*, put that in too.

*Twyn.* For my own part, I can say this, I knew it not to be so, till I came to the Bar to be Tryed; I was surprized in the doing of it, both in the beginning, and at last, I was clear and free in my own thoughts as to intend any Sedition.

Sir *R. Ford.* I would not willingly interrupt a dying man; I told you before that you must not declare any thing in justification, or mitigation, of so foul a Crime; but if you had any thing to say that was for the disburthening of your own Conscience, or to give any good Admonitions to the people to beware of falling into the like Crime, you should be patiently heard: but I wonder you should go about to justifie your self in this, when you did confess both to my *brother* here, and my *self*, after Sentence, that That which was passed upon you, was just, and deserved.

*Twyn.* I do not say otherwise of it, but that it was just; but as to my ignorance of the matter of intending or imagining to foment and contrive any such thing tending to such ends, but barely for getting a little mony for my Family; I was as clear as the Child unborn of any other design knowingly, of any such thing, I do look upon it as a Surprizal; / First, I was Surprized in this matter, by reason of that dangerous sickness, and weakness I was in when it was brought; I received it with my own hands, but it was wrapt up in wast paper, and so I delivered it to my servant, he went on with it, and two or three dayes after, it was taken from me by those that came to search my house, who themselves told me they came upon information; so that it was a matter I was surprized with when it was brought in, by reason of my sickness and weakness, being unable to over look it ... [S]ome discovery was made by the confession of those that searched my house they came by information, not by chance: then when they had taken me, I did ingeniously acknowledge and confess who I had it of; and yet for all this, the searching after those persons concern'd was neglected that whole day; they were at home, and easie to be taken ... /

Sir. *R. Ford*. You shall not say that you are denied that *Christian Liberty* a dying man ought to have; We are not to suffer any reflections on this business; You had a fair tryal, I say we would not deprive you your Liberty of speaking, but do not abuse that Liberty that is given you, by spending your time impertinently, and fruitlesly, but if you have any thing further to offer to God, which is more for your good, go to that.

*Twyn.* I shall forbear to insist any further as to the Narration of that matter, I shall be very unwilling and tender of reflecting any thing upon the King, or the Government, or give offence to your Worships, any way.

Sir *R. Ford.* Nothing but that, shall offend us.

*Twyn.* I shall go to prayer.

Sir *R. Ford.* Do, do, we will joyn with you, and pray for you.

He continued in private *Prayer* on the *Ladder* some time.

Sir *R. Ford. Executioner*, do not turn him off, till he has given you a sign. ... /

Afterwards the Executioner comming down, Mr. *Twyn* told him the Signe should be by Moving his Foot ...

Then giving the Signe, the Executioner did his Office, and being cut Down, his Head was severed from his Body, and his body Divided into four Quarters, which are to be Disposed of as the King shall Assigne; *Since which time, his* Head *is placed over* Ludgate, *and his* Quarters *upon* Aldersgate, *and other Gates of the* City ...

# PRESS CONTROL AND THE PRINT TRADE

[Richard Atkyns], *The Original and Growth of Printing* ([London], [1660]). Wing, A4134; ESTC, R30711.

*The London Printers Lamentation, or, The Press Opprest, and Over-Prest* ([London], [1660]). Wing, L2906; ESTC, R207159.

*A Brief Discourse concerning Printing and Printers* (London: for a Society of Printers, 1663), pp. 1–4, 6–7, 9–13, 22–4. Wing, B4578; ESTC, R10943.

[John Seymour], *The Case of Libels* ([London], [20 March 1677]). Wing, C938B; ESTC, R173533.

'The Company of Stationers against Seymour' (1678), in *Modern Reports, or, Select Cases* (London, 1682), pp. 256–9. Wing, C5414; ESTC, R11074.

*The Orders, Rules, and Ordinances, Ordained, Devised and Made by the Master and Keepers or Wardens and Comminalty of the Mystery or Art of Stationers of the City of London, for the Well Governing of that Society* (London: for the Company of Stationers, 1678), pp. 19–25, 27–8. Wing, O403; ESTC, R11816.

*An Ordinance Ordained, Devised, and Made by the Master, and Keepers or Wardens, and Commonalty of the Mystery or Art of Stationers of the City of London* (London: for the Company of Stationers, 1683), title page, pp. 4–6. Wing, O411; ESTC, R216917.

*A New Song in Praise of the Loyal Company of Stationers, Who (after the general forfeit,) for their singular Loyalty, Obtain'd the First Charter of London, Anno 1684* (London: by N[athaniel] T[hompson], 1684). Wing, N761A; ESTC, R180967.

The impetus behind control of the press had two main sources: censorship and trade regulation, distinguishable in principle but often interwoven in practice and only partly disentangled by the copyright legislation of the eighteenth century. The texts in this section indicate how trade concerns intersected with the case for censorship, often with a central role for the Stationers' Company as both trade guild and enforcer of press regulation.

*The Original and Growth of Printing* by the former royalist officer Richard Atkyns (1615–77) was initially the 1660 broadside presented here, before expanding to a better-known thirty-two-page quarto pamphlet in 1664. Atkyns's skewed historical accounts of the press in England were damagingly influential as well as candidly self-serving in seeking to confirm royal control over the press as both public duty and private property, thereby reinforcing the patent for printing common law books awarded to his wife's father by James I, which Atkyns acquired. Text from the broadside resurfaced on pp. 2–9 of the 1664 pamphlet, which added responses to objections raised to the succinct earlier case, a spurious story of Henry VI and Archbishop Thomas Bourchier securing the production of books at Oxford in 1468 by funding the arrival of the printer Frederick Corsellis, making him a forerunner of Caxton and the press subject to royal censorship and ownership.

The anonymous *London Printers Lamentation* demonstrates how trade jealousies could be pursued alongside, or through, warnings of the chaotic and disloyal state of printing. The importance of press regulation to the safety of Church and state was held to be demonstrated by the contrast of pre-war order and post-1640 confusion, while old scores were revived by pointing to the links between the King's printers Christopher Barker and John Bill and anti-monarchical printing, both at the time of Charles I's execution and in their more recent use of Cromwell's printers, now disabled, Henry Hills and John Field.[1]

Past and present censorship harnessed to the service of trade rivalries was also a feature of the *Brief Discourse* published by a 'Society of Printers'. This was probably the same group who in 1660 petitioned the King for the separation of printers from the Stationers' Company as a new corporate body.[2] The petitioners declared the Company ineffectual in preventing the printing of sedition and heresy, and proposed that twelve printers should be given statutory powers of search and seizure. The *Brief Discourse* amplifies these points, arguing that the Company had been created for printers' benefit but was now dominated by publishers/booksellers lacking the inclination and inside knowledge needed to act effectively against underground and illegal printing.

John Seymour's printed broadside against the Stationers' Company, *The Case of Libels*, was mainly directed towards the limited audience of the House of Lords libels committee in early 1677. It probably circulated beyond the committee but the only known copy remains that in the Parliamentary Archives (HL/PO/JO/10/362, item 338, g1). Seymour was a royalist officer turned publisher who became embroiled in disputes with the Stationers' Company and particularly with Samuel Mearne, warden of the Company, over seditious publishing but also printing privileges (see 'The Company of Stationers against Seymour'). Mearne gave evidence that in 1668 Seymour had arranged the printing of two condemned tracts, the 'Advice to a Painter' by Andrew Marvell and Ralph Wallis's *Room for the Cobbler of Gloucester*. Seymour in turn supplied the Lords committee with lists of allegedly seditious positions from books he claimed Mearne was involved with: the ejected minister William Dyer's 'Sermons' (Dyer's *Christ's Famous Titles* had been reprinted in 1676) and Francis Osborne's *Works* (1673). *The Case of Libels* amplified the accusations against the Company and Mearne of being complicit in illegal printing while falsely promising reform to evade a *quo warranto*. Roger L'Estrange attested to the veracity of Seymour's account; given his antipathy to the Stationers' Company he may have been instrumental in devising it. Mearne replied in a submission to the committee, adding a paper of accusations against L'Estrange charging him with licensing for payment and favouring the 'fanatiques'.[3]

Seymour argued before the Lords libel committee that he had not printed sedition but only almanacs, claiming a patent from the Archbishop of Canterbury. This was the background to the wider dispute between Seymour and the Stationers' Company, leading to court in May–June 1678, printed as 'The Company of Stationers against Seymour', in which the company defended its claim to a monopoly by royal patent, originally from James I. As with other trade disputes the case had a censorship dimension in the court's rejection of the suggestion that in this post-Star Chamber era prerogative powers were a nullity and printing made common, as 'things that concern the Government, were never left to any mans liberty to print'. Judgement for the Stationers ruled that in the absence of a clear author, property in a work passed to the Crown for disposal.

The uneven contribution of the Stationers' Company to maintaining order in the book trade, with regard to both politics and property, was a recurrent concern, its authority being temporarily suspended by the Crown in 1663 and again in 1670. The much-delayed response was a set of *Orders, Rules, and Ordinances* endorsed by members and the government and printed in 1677–8. The document commits the Company to more strictly enforcing the 1662 Printing Act's limits on presses and printers, aiming to stamp out the 'Press in a hole', unlicensed printing and undisclosed knowledge of scandalous tracts.

The lapsing of the Printing Act from 1679 to 1685 created a breach in licensing whose dangerous implications were addressed by measures including heightened post-publication vigilance and a new *Ordinance* of the Stationers' Company relating to pre-publication registration. The *Ordinance*, while not reinstituting licensing as such, maintained that 'ancient usage' confirmed the continued requirement of pre-publication entry in the company registers. By identifying printer or publisher, it was anticipated the circulation of treasonable and seditious tracts could be punished and deterred.

The calling-in of corporate charters by Charles II led to the Stationers' Company being granted a new charter on 22 May 1684, replacing that granted in 1557. *A New Song in Praise of the Loyal Company of Stationers* was the ironical riposte of the printer and writer Nathaniel Thompson, whose *Choice Collections* of 'loyal songs' were enormously popular at this time.

Notes
1.   *CSPD*, 21 September 1660.

2. *CSPD*, undated, [November] 1660.
3. For an extended summary see *HMC*, 9, Appendix, pp. 69–79.

[Richard Atkyns], *The Original and Growth of Printing* ([London], [1660]). Wing, A4134; ESTC, R30711.

### The Original and Growth of PRINTING.

Concerning the Time of bringing this Excellent ART into *England*, and by whose Expence and Procurement it was brought; Modern Writers of good Reputation do most Erroniously agree together. Mr. *Stow*, in his *Survey* of *London*,[1] speaking of the 37th year of Henry the sixth his Reign, which was in 1459, saith, That the Noble Science of PRINTING was about this time found in *Germany* at *Mentz* by *John Guttenberg*[2] a Knight, And that *William Caxton* of *London* Mercer,[3] brought it into *England* about 1471. And first practised the same in the Abby of St. *Peter* at *Westminster*, With whom Sir *Rich. Baker* in his Chronicle[4] agrees throughout. And Mr. *Howell* in his *Historical Discourse* of *London* and *Westminster*,[5] agrees with both the former in the Time, Person, and Place in general; but more particularly declares the place in *Westminster* to be the Almonry there; And that *Islip* abbot of *Westminster* set up the first Press of Book-Printing that ever was in *England*.[6] These three famous Historians having filled the World with the supposed truth of this Assertion, (Although possibly it might arise through the mistake of the first Writer only, whose Memory I perfectly honour) makes it the harder Task upon me to undeceive the World again: Nor would I undertake this Work, but under a double notion; As I am a Friend to Truth, and so it is unfit to suffer one Man to be intituled to the worthy Achievements of another. And as a Friend to my self, not to lose one of my best Arguments of Intituling the King to this ART in his private Capacity.

Historians must of necessity take many things upon trust, they cannot with their own but with the Eyes of others see what things were done before they themselves were, *Bernardus non videt omnia*;[7] 'Tis not then impossible they should mistake. I shall now make it appear they have done so from their Own, as well as from other Arguments: Mr. *Stows* Expressions are very dubious, and the matter exprest very Improbable; He saith PRINTING was found in *Mentz*,[8] which presupposes it was practised some where else before, and lost: And further, That 'twas found in the Reign of *Henry* the sixth, in 1450. and not brought into *England* till Eleven years in the succeeding Reign of *Edward* the Fourth, being twelve years after, as if it had been lost again. If this be true, there was as little Rarity as Expedition in obtaining it, the age of twelve years time having intervened, and so indeed it might be the Act of a Mercer rather than a more eminent Person: But when I consider what great advantage the Kingdom in general receives by it, I could not but think a publick Person and a publick Purse must needs be concerned in so publick a Good. The more I Considered of this, the more inquisitive I was to find out the truth of it: At last, a Book came to my hands Printed at *Oxford*, in 1468.[9] which was three years before any of the recited Authors would allow it to be in *England*; which gave me some reward for my Curiosity, and encouragement to proceed further: And in prosecution of this Discovery, the same most worthy Person who trusted me with the aforesaid Book, did also present me with the Copy of a Record and Manuscript in *Lambeth-House*,[10] heretofore in his Custody, belonging to the See, (and not to any particular Arch-Bishop of *Canterbury*;) the Substance whereof was this, (though I hope, for publick satisfaction, the Record it self, in its due time, will appear.)

*Thomas Bourchier*,[11] Arch-Bishop of *Canterbury*, moved the then King *Henry* the Sixth, to use all possible means for procuring a Printing-Mold (for so 'twas there called) to be brought into this Kingdom; the King (a good Man, and much given to Works of this Nature) readily hearkned to the Motion; and taking private Advice, how to effect His Design, concluded it could not be brought about without great Secrecy, and a considerable Sum of Money given to such Person or Persons, as would draw off some of the Work-men from *Harlem* in *Holland*, where *John Guttenberg* had newly invented it, and was himself personally at Work: 'Twas Resolv'd, that less then one Thousand Marks would not produce the desir'd Effect: Towards which Sum, the said Arch-Bishop presented the King with Three Hundred Marks. The Money being now prepared, the Management of the Design was committed to Mr. *Robert Turnour*, who then was of the Robes to the King,[12] and a Person most in Favour with Him, of any of his Condition: Mr. *Turnour* took to his Assistance Mr. *Caxton*, a Citizen of good Abilities, who Trading much into *Holland*, might be a Creditable Pretence, as well for his going, as stay in the *Low-countries*: Mr. *Turnour* was in Disguise (his Beard and Hair shaven quite off) but Mr. *Caxton* appeared known and publick. They having received the said Sum of One Thousand Marks, went first to *Amsterdam*, then to *Leyden*, not daring to enter *Harlem* it self; for the Town was very jealous, having imprisoned and apprehended divers Persons, who came from other Parts for the same purpose: They staid till they had spent the whole One Thousand Marks in Gifts and Expences: So as the King was fain to send Five Hundred Marks more, Mr. *Turnour* having written to the King, that he had almost done his Work; a Bargain (as he said) being struck betwixt him and two *Hollanders*, for bringing off one of the Work-Men, who should sufficiently Discover and Teach this New Art: At last, with much ado, they got off one of the Under-Workmen, whose Name was *Frederick Corsellis*,[13] who late one Night stole from his Fellows in Disguise, into a Vessel prepared for that purpose; and so the Wind (favouring the Design) brought him safe to *London*.

'Twas not thought so prudent, to set him on Work at *London*, (but by the Arch-Bishops means, who had been Vice-Chancellor, and afterwards Chancellor of the University of *Oxford*,) *Corsellis* was carryed with a Guard to *Oxford*; which Guard constantly watch'd, to prevent *Corsellis* from any possible Escape, till he had made good his promise in Teaching how to Print: So that at *Oxford* Printing was first set up in *England*, which was before there was any Printing-Press, or Printer, in *France, Spain, Italy*, or *Germany*, (except the City of *Mentz*) which claims Seniority, as to Printing, even of *Harlem* it self, calling her City, *Urben Moguntinam Artis Typographicæ Inventricem primam*,[14] though 'tis known to be otherwise, that City gaining that Art by the Brother of one of the Workmen of *Harlem*, who had learnt it at Home of his Brother, and after set up for himself at *Mentz*.

This Press at *Oxford* was at least ten years before there was any Printing in *Europe* (except at *Harlem*, and *Mentz*) where also it was but new born. This Press at *Oxford*, was afterwards found inconvenient, to be the sole Printing-place of *England*, as being too far from *London*, and the Sea: Whereupon the King set up a Press at St. *Albans*, and another in the Abby of *Westminster*, where they Printed several Books of Divinity and Physick, for the King, (for Reasons best known to himself and Council) permitted then no Law-Books to be Printed; nor did any Printer Exercise that ART, but onely such as were the Kings sworn Servants; the King himself having the Price and Emolument for Printing Books.

Printing thus brought into *England*, was most Graciously Received by the King, and most Cordially Entertained by the Church, the Printers having the Honour to be sworn the Kings Servants, and the Favour to Lodge in the very Bosom of the Church; as in *Westminster,* St. *Albans, Oxford*, &c. By this means the ART grew so famous, that *Anno prim. Rich.*3.*cap.*9. when an Act of *Parliament* was made for Restraint of Aliens, from using any Handicrafts here, except as Servants to Natives, a special *Proviso* was inserted, that Strangers[15] might bring in Printed or Written Books, to sell at their pleasure, and Exercise the ART of Printing here, notwithstanding that Act: So that in the space of 40 or 50 years, by the special Industry and Indulgence of *Edward* the Fourth, *Edward* the Fifth, *Richard* the Third, *Henry* the Seventh, and *Henry* the Eighth, the *English* prov'd so good Proficients in *Printing*, and grew so numerous, as to furnish the Kingdom with Books; and so Skilful, as to *Print* them as well as any beyond the Seas, as appears by the Act of the 25 *Hen.* 8. *cap.* 15.[16] which Abrogates the said *Proviso* for that Reason. And it was further Enacted in the said Statute, That if any person bought Forreign books Bound, he should pay 6*s.*8*d. per* Book, *&c.*

But *Printing* became now so dangerous to the Commonwealth, That there were more Books Burnt in Ten years, then could be Printed in Twenty: So that it Concern'd the Prince altogether as much to Suppress the Abuse, as it did before to Obtain the Use of *Printing*; And had there not been a Reserve of Licensing such Books as should be *Printed* still remaining in the Crown, they might have published the wickedness of their own Imaginations with Authority. But Queen

*Elizabeth* at her very first Entrance to the Crown, finding so great Disorders in *Church* and *State*, by reason of the abuse in *Printing*, Secures in the first place the *Law* and the *Gospel*, of both which the Kings and Queens of *England* have Inherent Right as Heads of the Church, and Supream of the Law; and not onely in their publick, but private Capacity, as Proprietors; the Power and Signiory[17] of this, under Favour, cannot be severed from the Crown: The Kings being the Trustees of the People, who have formerly taken an Oath at their Coronation, *That they shall keep all the Lands, Honours, and Dignities, Rights, and Freedoms of the Crown of* England, *in all manner whole without any manner of minishment;*[18] *and the Right of the Crown, hurt, decay'd, or lost, to their Power shall call again into the Ancient Estate.* Which Oath, the said Queen kept inviolably, and liv'd the more quietly for it all the time of her Reign, and died in Peace. True it is, they may, and do gratifie their Friends and Servants, in giving them the Emoluments and Profits that arise from *Printing*; but the Power they cannot alienate from the Crown, without losing the most precious Stone out of their Diadem. To shew you one Example for all: The said Queen, the first Year of her Reign, grants by Patent the Priviledge of sole *Printing* all Books, that touch or concern the Common-Laws of *England*, to *Tottel*, a Servant to her Majesty, who kept it intire to his Death: After him, to one *Yestweirt*,[19] another Servant to Her Majesty: After him, to one *Weight* and *Norton*;[20] and after them, King *James* grants the same Priviledge to *More*, one of His Majesties Clerks of the Signet;[21] which Grant continues to this Day; and so for the Bible, the Statute-Laws, the Book of Common Prayer, Proclamations, as much as the Grammer, the Primmer,[22] &c., are all granted by Kings and Queens, not onely to gratifie their Friends and Servants, but to preserve the Regal Power and Authority on Foot, and these books, from being Corrupted.

*The London Printers Lamentation, or, The Press Opprest, and Over-Prest* ([London], [1660]). Wing, L2906; ESTC, R207159.

*The* London *Printers Lamentation, or, the Press opprest, and overprest.*

How Venerable and Worthily honoured in all Kingdomes and Common-wealths, the wonderfull and mysterious Invention, Utility and Dignity of Printing hath always been, can not be rationally contradicted, comparing it specially with the miserable condition and barbarousnesse of the Antients as well in the Eastern as the Western parts of the World, (as *Strabo de situ Orbis*,[1] write l.{5}) Who (as he saith) for the better conveying to Posterity the memorable Acts and Monuments of their present Times, conceived and contrived at first no better *medium*, than the Impression thereof with their fingers, or little sticks in Ashes or Sand, thinly dispersed and spread abroad in Vaults and Cells: But experience being the Mistresse of Art, some better Wits at length invented Knives and other Instruments for the Incision of Letters in Barks of Trees; Others, for the Graving or Carving of them in Stone; Others, with Pincers in Leaves of Lawrel, Fig-trees and other crassie leaves,[2] (as in *China*, and other parts of the Indies and Eastern Countries) impressed their Memorials in uncouth Characters: Since that, the use of Lead was brought in estimation for the Insculption[3] of words in a more convenient method. But (as the Adage is true, *Facile est inventis addere*,[4] and use tends every day more and more to perfection) the happy experiment, first of Parchment, and then of Paper was ingeniously found out, with the use of Canes, Pencils, Quils, and Inck of several sorts: Yet all this while the benefit accrewing by that Invention, tended no further, than to the composing of one single Manuscript at one time, by the labour and Inscription of one single Person: The rarity and paucity whereof hath caused such honour, reverence and Authority to be put upon the Antiquities of our Antcessors[5] as worthily they merit.

But at the length, this vast expence of Time and paines enforced mens wits (by a cogent necessity) to enquire into, and search out the more occult and secret Mysteries of Art, for their better convenience and communication of their Writings: And thereupon by the blessing of Almighty God, upon the study / and industry of *John Cuthenburge*,[6] the rare and incomparable mystery and Science of Printing of Books, was invented and practized at *Mentz* in *Germany*, above 200. years agone; And soon after that Art was brought over into *England* by one *William Caxton*, a Worshipfull Mercer of the famous City of *London*, and there put in use, with meritorious approbation of the Religious and Virtuous King *Henry* the sixth, and all the Estates of this Kingdome. Since which time (being about 220 years elapsed) that ingenious Mystery, splendour of Art, and Propagatrix of Knowledge hath been duely countenanced and encouraged with so much favour and respect of all our *English* Princes, that it is by laudable succession of time, arrived at that exquisite perfection, as we now see it in it self. For true is the Character of a Printer, to wit,

*Imprimit ille die, quantum non scribitur anno.*

In one dayes time a Printer will Print more,
Than one man Write could in a Year before.

To pretermit the honour and esteem placed upon it in particular by *Henry* the 8. and *Edward* the 6, and the Incorporation of the Stationers Company by Queen *Mary*, meerly and onely for her favour and respect to the Printers, and not to the Booksellers (albeit they were both in their several faculties then constituted in one day and Society, under one genericall and individual term of *Stationers*) Let us come to the Reign of the glorious Queen *Elizabeth* of ever blessed memory; And then we shall plainly and perspicuously discover her Majesties great love and Royal affection to Printing and Printers; who for the sake of them & it, so far descended from her Royal Thron as that her Highness not only made several gracious Grants unto them for better maintaining their poor, but also graciously recõmended (for the speciall encouragement and better subsistence of the Master Printers) the Regulation of that Mystery, and the Professors thereof, to the Right Honourable and Judicious, the Lords of her Majesties most Honourable Privy Council: Who 23. *June* 28. *Eliz*. made a memorable and noble Decree in the *Star Chamber*,[8] Confining the number of Master Printers in *England* to the number of twenty, to have the use and Exercise of Printing Houses for the time being; (besides her Majesties Printers, and the Printers allowed for the Universities;) Limitting and confining them within such an excellent Method and strict Regulation, as tended very much to the Peace and Security of the Church and State. But as the World waxeth / old as doth a Garment, and the corruptions and evill manners of Times and men grow daily to a greater maturity and ripeness in sin and wickednesse; And that all humane kinde are boldly inclined to rush through any forbidden mischief (like the old race of the Gyants, and the builders of *Babel*;) So in tract and processe of time, and specially in these later dayes (notwithstanding the severity and authority of that good Decree of the Queens time,) Printing and Printers about the year 1637. were grown to such a monstrous excesse and exorbitant disorder, that the prudent Limits, and Rules of that laudable Decree, were as much transgressed and infringed at that time, as the Kings-Bench Rules in *Southwark* have been extended and eloined in later dayes, for want of due execution of Justice.[9]

Wherefore by the speciall Command of our late Royal and most Illustrious King *Charls* of blessed memory, the Right Honourable *Thomas* Lord *Coventry*, Lord Keeper of the great Seale of *England*; The Lord Arch Bishop of *Canterbury*, his Grace, the Lord Bishop of *London*, Lord High Treasurer of *England*, the

Lords Cheif Justices, and the Lord Chief Baron, being sate together in Council in the *Star-Chamber* II. *July* 13. *Car.* And reviewing and maturely considering the said Decree and Ordinances of the Queens time; in very great Wisdome, Policy, and Prudence of State, thought fit and adjudged not onely to confirm the same, but also to make and subjoyn there to several usefull and convenient Additions and Supplements, as the reason of State, and the necessity of the times did then require. Which last Decree[10] with due renown to the memory of the makers thereof) was the best and most exquisite Form and Constitution for the good Government and regulation of the Press, that ever was pronounced, or can reasonably be contrived, to keep it in due order and regular Exercise.

But now may we well with sorrow cry out at this day, with the Comædian, *O Tempora, O mores!*[11] or, in another sense, with the Spouse in the Canticles, *Ca.2.v.15.*[12] *Take us the Foxes, the little Foxes, that spoile the Vines, for our Vines have tender Grapes.* Never was there such an honourable, ingenious and profitable Mystery and Science in the world so basely intruded upon, and disesteemed, so carelessy regarded, so unworthily subjected to infamy and disgrace, by being made so common, as Printing hath been since 1640. in the dayes of our miserable confusions and Calamities: Neither can it be repaired, or restored to its native worth and regular Constitution, so long as such horrid / Monstrosities and gibbous excrescences[13] are suffered to remain and tumour in that disorderly and confused Body, as now it existeth in it self.

The excessive number of Printing-houses and Master Printers, or such at least as use and exercise the faculty of Printing, (though some be *Book-sellers* onely by trade and education; and others are of other trades, not relative to Printing) is at present multiplied and encreased to above triple the number of twenty, constituted by that decree of the *Starre-chamber*: so that by means of that exorbitant and excessive number of above 60. Printing-houses in and about *London*, and the necessitous conditions of many of the Printers themselves, and the Imposition of others upon them (who if they will not adventure to print for them, what is unlawfull and offensive to the State and Government, (being treasonable and seditious, and most profitable for sale) shall not be imployed upon things lawfull and expedient) all the irregularities, inconveniences, and mischiefs, that can be imagined to be committed and done by the too much liberty and licenciousnesse of the Presse, have been and are occasioned at this day, and daily will (without some speedy remedy and restriction, for the better encouragement of the honest and ingenious Artists) be continued amongst us. How can it in reason be conceived to stand with the Royalty and Dignity of his most Excellent Majesty, (whom God Almighty prosper and preserve) or with the safety and security of his Kingdomes, to permit and suffer, either the fore-mentioned inconveniences for the future, or such notorious impieties and abhominable Indignities and Insolences, done and offered to his Majesties most Sacred Person and Estate, to go unpunished in the Actors thereof; who are neverthelesse in truth and reality his Majesties Printers; against whom there is just Cause of Complaint at this present. As for example, Mr. *Christopher Barker* and Mr. *John Bill*,[14] by their education and quality have little or no skill or experience in the Faculty and Art of Printing, as to the manual operation thereof, being never brought up in that Mystery: And the old Proverb is and will be true, to wit, *Senex Psittacus non capit ferulam*.[15] And albeit they are said and entitle themselves (by a very questionable and doubtfull Authority both in Law and Equity) to be his Majesties Printers; yet indeed are they but nominal and titular; for that the manual work and Impression itself, as well of the late Acts of Parliament, as also of his Majesties Proclamations, and other Royal / Acts of State, hath been actually performed by *Thomas Newcome, John Feild* and *Henry Hills*, printers:[16] Which three persons, to give them their proper Characters, have been the onely Instruments and Incendiaries against, and Enemies, to his sacred Majesty and his Friends, in their Stations and qualities, before and ever since the detestable and unparallell'd Murder of our blessed Soveraign his Royal Father, as far as the extent of the Presse could make them capable or extant.

Who Printed the pretended *Act of the Commons of* England *for the setting up an High Court of Justice, for the tryall of his Martyred Majesty in 1648?* Or, *The Acts for abolishing King-ship, and renouncing the Royall Line and Title of the* Stuarts? *Or, for the Declaring what Offences should be adjudged Treason? For taking the Engagement? for sale of Dean and Chapters Lands? for sale of the Kings, Queens, and Princes Goods and Lands; and the Fee-farme Rents? for sale of Delinquents Lands; or, the Proclamation of* 13. *of* September 1652. *After the fight at* WORCESTER, *offering, One Thousand pound to any person, to bring in his Majesties person? but only* John Feild, *Printer to the Parliament of* England (*and since by* Cromwell *was and is continued Printer to the University of* Cambridge!) *Omitting many other Treasonable Offences, and egregious Indignities done by him and* H. Hills *to the Royal Family, and good old Cause of the King and Kingdome, in all the late Tyrannicall Usurpation. Who Printed the Weekly* Intelligencer, *and* Mercurius Politicus, *with the* Cases of the Common-wealth stated, *and that* Interest will not lye, *for* Marchamont Nedham, *Gent, from* 1650. *till the blessed and assured hopes of his Majesties Restauration of Late, but* Thomas Newcome, *Printer, Dwelling over against* Baynards *Castle in* Thames-street! *And with what familiar Titles of honour did they salute His Majesty therein (we pray,) but of young* Tarquin,[17] *the son of the late* Tyrant, *the* Titular *King of Scots, the young* Pretender, *with an infinite more of the like treasonable extraction; which for brevitie-sake, and for that they are of* Miltons *strain, and so publiquely known, and were the weekly Trash and Trumpery of every Hawker, Pedlar, and Petty Carrier, we omit.*

But we cannot as yet pass-over his Majesties good friends, Hills *and* Feild (*take them* conjunctim *or* divisim:)[18] *What Zealots and Factors, (or blood-hounds and*

*Tarriers rather) they have been for that* abstract of *Traitors, Tyrants and Usurpers,* Oliver Cromwell, *his sonne* Richard, *and the pretended Committee of* Safety,[19] *in searching for, seazing and suppressing (as far as they could) all Books, Treatises, and Papers, asserting the Kings Right and Title to the Crown, or tending to / the Promotion of his Interest and Vindication of his Authority, the worst of his Majesties Enemies must necessarily, with shame and Detestation confesse! And is this all that hath been done by* Hills *and* Feild *to his Majesty onely, and his Royall Relations and Interests? No! Their Impieties and Insolences have mounted as high, as to become actuall and professed Traitors against the glorious Crown and Dignity of the* King of Kings, *blessed for ever: Have they not invaded and still do intrude upon his Majesties Royall Priviledge, Prærogative and Præeminence; And by the pusillanimous Cowardize and insignificant Compact of Mr.* Christopher Barker, *and another of his name,*[20] *and (not without probable suspicion,) by the consent and connivence of Mr.* John Bill *(though he was artificially defeated in his expectations of profit;) Have they not obtained, (and now keep in their actuall possession) the Manuscript Copy of the last Translation of the holy Bible in* English, *(attested with the hands of the Venerable and learned Translators in King* James *his time) ever since* 6 March 1655.[21] *And thereupon by colour of an unlawfull and enforced entrance in the* Stationers *Registry,*[22] *printed and published ever since for the most part in severall Editions of Bibles (consisting of great numbers) such egregious Blasphemies and damnable Errata's, as have corrupted the pure Fountain, and rendred Gods holy Word contemptible to multitudes of the people at home, and a* Ludibrium[23] *to all the Adversaries of our Religion? Have they not suffocated and suppressed all Books containing Pious and Religious Prayers and Devotions to be presented and offered to the blessed Trinity for the blessing of Heaven upon his Majesties Royall Person and Family, and the Church and State, by preventing and obstructing the Printing of the Common Prayer, Primars, and Psalters, contrary to the Statute of* 1.Q. Elizabeth c.2.[24] *and other good Laws and Ordinances, and the Ecclesiasticall Canons of the Church of* England; *unlesse that they contained Prayers for their late Protector! And are these small Offences to be past and pardoned, or such as shall deserve the favour of Indempnity and Oblivion? God forbid*!

*Impunitas peccati præbet ansam peccandi.*[25] The not punishing of offences, emboldeneth offenders to commit greater Enormities with brazen Browes,[26] as if they were incorrigible: And (as the Proverb saith) *He that saves a Thief from the Gallowes, shall first be robbed himself.* Is not the King as the breath of our nostrills, the anoynted of the Lord, his person sacred, his authority dreadfull? And is not all our present and future security and happinesse involved in his Majesties preservation and prosperity? And shall his Majesties most apparent and implacable enemies be cheifly entrusted in the great concernments of his State and Government, as *Newcome, Hills* and *Field* / are under his Titular Printers? God forbid. Are there not honest and well affected Printers in *London* sufficient &

able and willing to serve his Majesty; but his grandest adversaries must be pick'd out for his service? And the Printing for his Majesty managed at the House of that libidinous & professed Adulterer *H. Hills* in *Aldersgate-street*, one that for his Heresie in Religion (being an Anabaptist,) and his luxury in conversation (having hycritically confessed his fact in Print, and been imprisoned for his Adultery[27] with a Taylors Wife in *Black-friers*,) would scandalize a good Christian, and an honest man to be in his company. But it seemes the old confederacy compacted between *Barker, Hills*, and *Field*, (by the agitation of *Nedham*,) upon their conversion of the Copy of the Bible, cannot yet be forgotten; albeit it tend neversomuch to the dishonour, disparagement, and prejudice of his Majesties affaires? And therefore it is more than time (as is humbly conceived,) that as well the establishment of his Majesties office of Printer, as also the regulation of the number of Printers in *England* within good Rules and Limits, were speedily provided for and determined; and not any longer be carelesly and improvidently left and subjected to such extreme mischiefs, and fatal inconveniences. And moreover it is very fit to be taken into serious consideration, how much mischief, and sedition a Press at *New-England*,[28] may occasion and disperse in this Juncture of time, if the licenciousness thereof be connived at, and any longer tolerated; When as we daily see such ventilations of opinions, (inclining to factions and seditions) are the common Marchandize of the Press about the City of *London*: which to a sober Christian and Loyal Subject, are plainly destructive both of Church and State; which God for his glory, unite preserve and propagate in the old good Order and Government.

Having thus truly represented to publick view the Cause of our Lamentation, We will never despair of his Majesties seasonable and timely redress: Being humbly confident, that for want of Loyal and dutifull information presented to his Majesty, many Phanaticks, and disaffected persons to His Person and Government, (by a little counterfeit conversion and hypocritical subjection,) do continue and creep into his Majesties Service in many great places of trust and profit; who being dyed in grain in the principles of popular liberty, would willingly cast off his Majesties sacred Authority, and abandon his Person, as they did his Royal Fathers, if God for our sins / in Judgment, should permit them the least opportunity. *Quod malum infandum avertat Deus!*[29]

But briefly to conclude, we most humbly submit the necessity of our speedy reformation and redress, upon consideration of the many great miseries and calamities, that have hapned not only in *England, Scotland*, and *Ireland*; but also in *Germany, France*, the Netherlands, *Switzerland*, and other Countries and places, by the exorbitant and unlawfull exercise of Printing in modern times: Which, had the science and use thereof been known in the time of the grand profession of the *Donatist* and *Arian* Heresies,[30] would have immerged and drowned the whole World in a second Deluge of blood and confution to its utter destruction long time since. Yet however if our mystery be confined within fit and convenient bounds, and not permitted *transilire limites*,[31] it is and will be of singular use and convenience to his Majesty and his Dominion otherwise though the Art be so exquisite and excellent in it self, yet by Corruption and Depravation, it will become the more pernicious and perillous; As the strongest and richest Wine for want of good curing, will turne to the sharpest vinegar; and a little wound, or contusion neglected, will soon mortifie and corrupt it self to an immedicable Gangræn.

*Ignis abexiguo nascens, extinguitur undâ;*
*Sed postquàm crevit, volitantq; ad sydera flamme,*
*Vix putei, fontes, fluvij succurrere possunt.*

 *A little fire to quench is done with ease;*
 *But when it rages, and the flames encrease,*
 *Ponds, Fountaines, Rivers scarce can it surcease.*

The Application is easily inferr'd, in reference to the inconvenience of exorbitant and irregular Printing in general: And as for his Majesties titular Printers Mr. *Barker* and Mr. *Bill*, let them consider themselves, (as all other wise men will and must do,) under this trite and excellent Aphorisme, to wit, *Impossibile est, vel verè admodùm difficile, ut qui ipsa opera non tractant, peritè valeant judicare.*

 *Impossible, or very hard be't will,*
 *To judge a work well, wherein th'ave no skill.*

If a Presentment should be made of the matter of this complaint to any capable Inquest in this Kingdome, they would indorse it *Billa vera*, and not return it with an *Ignoramus*.[32]

 *All which is most humbly submitted to publick consideration, in*
 *hopes of Regulation and speedy Reformation.*

             GOD SAVE THE KING.

*A Brief Discourse concerning Printing and Printers* (London: for a Society of Printers, 1663), pp. 1–4, 6–7, 9–13, 22–4. Wing, B4578; ESTC, R10943.

A Brief
# DISCOURSE
Concerning
# PRINTING
AND
# PRINTERS.

Not to insist here, upon the time when, place where, and manner how *Printing* was invented; let it suffice to speak of the time of its bringing hither, the entertainment it had here, the progress it made, the abuses it hath suffered, and the encouragement (under favour) it ought to have among us.

*John Stow* in his *Annals*,[1] p.404. tells us, that it was brought into *England* by one *William Caxton* a Mercer of *London*, circa *Anno Dom.* 1471. which was the eleventh year of the Reign of *Edward the fourth.*

Hither being come, you may judge how the Learned / of that Age esteemed it, by the reception they gave it; not permitting it to take up its abode in common and ordinary houses, but receiving it into their Monasteries, as if they intended to make it a part of their own studies; which it seems they did for some time, it being practised not onely in the Abby of S. *Peter* in *Westminster*, but in that of S. *Austins* in *Canterbury*, S. *Albans*, and others.[2]

Thus it continued thirteen years, or thereabout, without any considerable improvement, as to *Englishmen*. And therefore (that such a Talent might no longer lie hidden as it were in a Napkin, but be employed for common good) in the first year of King *Richard the third*, in an Act of Parliament[3] made (amongst other things) for restraint of Aliens from using any Handy-crafts here (except as servants to Natives) a special Proviso was inserted, That strangers might bring Printed or Written Books to sell at their pleasure, and exercise the Art of Printing here, any thing in that Act to the contrary notwithstanding: and this done (as is intimated in the Preamble of the Act of 25 *H.* 8.[4] for repealing the said Proviso) not onely that the Kingdom might not want the benefit of so excellent an Invention, but that the Natives might thereby gain an insight into the same.

And *English-men* proving good proficients, in the space of thirty years they were grown so numerous, as to furnish the Kingdom with Books; and so skilfull, as to Print them as well as any beyond the Seas; as is attested by the said Act of 25 *H.* 8. which abrogates the said Proviso for that reason. And, the better to encourage and secure the Native Printers in the exercise of their new-acquired Faculty (as also the / Book Binders) it was in the said Statute further Enacted, that if any person bought forreign Books bound, he should pay 6s. -- 8d. per Book for every Book so bought: the like for any that bought any Printed Books of strangers, except in gross: with a Proviso against the inhansing the prices of Books, as in that Statute at large appears.

Thus we see that Printing was received into the Church in its infancie in this Nation; where having been nursed till it could creep abroad, the King and State took care of it when abroad: using strangers as Crutches to support it when weak, and securing it when strengthned, from being beaten with the same.

Printing being thus improved, and secured from forreign invasion, it continued for many years in the hands of *English-men* at large. But afterwards, in the 3[d] and 4th years of *Philip* and *Mary*, they were con-corporated together with Stationers, or Book-sellers, by the name of *The Company of Stationers*.[5] Which constitution, and concorporation, although it were without doubt made in favour of Printers, and for their encouragement and security (after the example of former Kings, as before is shewen) yet, where interest and prejudice swayes not, it will be judged rather destructive and mischievous then otherwise, by any that understand the case; at least, if perhaps it might conduce to their well-being then, when the Book-sellers were very few, and as inconsiderable, and so the Printers sufficient to hold the balance even, yea, to turn the scale with them; yet, the case being now much altered, the constitution ought, also to be changed: and Printers being (as aforesaid) freed from the intrusions of forreign Nations, should / not, in reason, be enslaved by the encroachments of Natives, nor suffer that which was intended for their benefit, to turn to their destruction; and so lose the fruition of the good designed by the several Lawes made in their favour, and without doubt intended by that Charter.

I say, now the case is altered: for whereas when the Grant was made, Book-sellers were very few, (as indeed they have been within mans memory) and those few not considerable (nor could they, in regard that all antient Books of worth were Printers Copies) now they are multiplied exceedingly (how much in so long a time, we may ghess by what we have seen in our short time:) and whereas at first they were but as an Appendix to the Printers, and (as cyphers) stood but to make up a number; now they are grown so bulkie and numerous (together with many of several other Trades that they have taken in) and so considerable withal, (being much enriched by Printers impoverishment, and chiefly built upon their ruines) that there is hardly one Printer to ten others that have a share in the Government of the Company; and those that have, either dare not stand for the Interest of Printing, for fear of losing a Work-Master;[6] or will not, because they have an interest among them; or if they do, it signifies nothing, in such a disparity of number. ...

[6]
Thus it was with Printers; and being thus, no marvel they are reduced to such a pass as they are. For whereas formerly (even in the last age) they were Aldermens fellows, and lived above the temptations of a necessitous condition; now (except one or two of the old stock, and a few others that raised themselves by the late times) they are so far from having considerable estates, that they can hardly subsist in credit to maintain their families. ... /

So that the Booksellers having engros'd almost all, it is become a question among them, whether a Printer ought to have any Copy or no: or if he have, they (keeping the Register)[7] will hardly enter it; or if they do, they and their accomplices will use all means to disparage it, if not down-right counterfeit it.

If it be said (as they commonly do) that they had not power to prevent or redress the irregularities of Printing, or to keep out intruders; it may be answered, That they had power (if they had not wanted something else) not to have done that themselves, which they could not help in others. But had they not power? how then could they demand or expect obedience? If Protection and Subjection are reciprocal,[8] they that cannot afford the one, ought not to exact the other.

But they may say what they will, we see and feel what they have done. And now I leave it to the consideration of all uninterested persons, whether those that for the time past have thus improved their opportunity of tyrannizing over Printers, ought to have the Government of them for the future, when the like opportunity cannot be wanting, as the constitution now is, they having gotten the start of them both as to number and estates. ...

[9]
Printing requires a more then ordinary inspection, because of the great influence it hath upon the Publike peace and safety, which is very much endangered by its irregularity, and which ought by all means possible to be preserved. Now by how much the more evil or danger there is in the miscarriage of a business, so much more care ought to be had in the management of that business: and the not due inspection of Printing being of such dangerous consequence, surely it ought to be committed to them that have the most perfect understanding thereof, and not to those that can pretend to no knowledge therein.

But to salve this, they say, We take Printers with us when we go to search; (whereby (by the way) they acknowledge their own insufficiencie.)

That frequent and diligent searching and over-looking of Printing-houses, is the onely way to keep Printing in order, I think cannot be denied. And since this cannot be done without Printers, why should not they onely be entrusted therewith? Again, in matters of great trust, it is not enough that a person skilled in the affairs entrusted, be employed therein; that person must also receive suitable countenance and encouragement in the discharge of his trust, or it may justly be feared his faithfulness will soon fail: and therefore the Law and Custom hath made provision in all like cases, to cut off such occasions, and to remove such temptations, the better to secure the end of the trust. And is the great trust of the oversight of the Press like to be well discharged, when they that are onely capable thereof must have no hand therein, but at the appointment of such / whose interest it is to keep both Printing and Printers in confusion and disorder? All men naturally as free Agents propound some benefit to arise from all their actions, which is the motive to their thorow and ready performance of such actions. But when they can propound no such end to themselves, they either do not act at all, or no further then they are forced; especially if it be so far from procuring benefit, that it brings mischief with it: as in our case, should Printers (as now constituted) use their utmost skill and care in discovering the abuses of the Press, the Stationers would have the credit and honour of it, and be reckoned the onely loyal and industrious men; and thereupon get new priviledges, together with the confirmation of their old; and the Printers so far from being benefited by it, that it would onely the better enable the Stationers to keep them under.

And truly the case being thus, here is not onely a temptation, but a ground for Printers (self-preservation being natural) to do the work either not at all, or but by halfs.

But to this it may be said, They may employ some certain Printer, giving him good encouragment, either to accompany them in their searches, or to go alone.

To which I anser: This were mercenary, and here would be place for bribing; and he that sees largest, should be the most spared, or the oftnest have pre-intelligence of searches, to evade them. And this would be far enough from answering the end of Regulation.

But then it may be objected, If ye would have neither Stationers, nor Stationers and Printer, nor Printer alone, who should be employed in the over-sight of Printing? /

*Answ.* I would have the over-sight of Printing committed to Printers onely; and not onely so, but to Printers as Printers, and not to Printers as Stationers.

Two reasons enforce this: the first respecting the prevention of Printing scandalous and mischievous Books; the other regarding the better Printing of all Books.

For the first, it hath been shewed already how ineffectual it is for any other but Artists to take the oversight of Printing, and how easily the inspection of strangers[9] may be eluded by any that have a minde to make a sinister use of that Art; and likewise how little better it is to call Printers to the assistance of others, since they are like to be but cold in their scrutiny, when their discoveries shall redound nothing to their own profit or reputation, but to the advantage of those that call them, whose hands will be thereby the more strengthned against them. It hath been shewed also how much less available it will be to employ a Mercenary in the case. So that Blasphemy against God, and Treason against the King; Errour and Heresie in the Church, and Faction and Sedition in the State, may still be (as it is and hath been) broached and fomented by the Press, for any thing to the contrary can be done by the present establishment, wherein they that onely have the capacity, have neither authority nor encouragement to discover and prevent such abuses; I mean, the Printers, who were they encouraged, as they are onely able, so they would be engaged both in Honour and Interest to be faithful in the discharge thereof. /

1. In honour: it would free them from the many clamours that lie against them. For at the first sight of any thing in print that is offensive, who is cryed out upon but the Printer, yea, all Printers, as if they were the most wretched of men! So that it is almost a shame to own that most noble Profession. Whereas indeed (as now) Printers are not Printers; that is, they have no power as a Society to rectifie disorders in Printing; and so bear the blame of that they cannot help. Besides, such enormities are generally committed by such as have irregularly crept into the exercise of the Art, in the want of a due establishment: neither do such transgressors ever want encouragers to begin, or chapmen[10] to vend such ware when finished, among the Stationers.

2. It would be for the interest of Printers to keep their Faculty in due order, since it would both prevent their damage, and procure them again: both which concern Printers in this case. ... /

For, if Stationers have obtained so many and great favours upon the account of Printing (which yet they have not in any measure been able to manage to the promoting of the Kings interest) much more shall the Artists themselves finde favour with his Majesty, when they shall be in a capacity to give testimony of their abilities, usefulness and diligence in that service, and the preservation of the peace of the Kingdom, wherein the well management of their Art is so much concerned.

Again, as it is the onely effectual way for the prevention or discovery of evil and mischievous Books; so also to procure the well doing of all Books. ...

[22]
Yea, Printing puts Books into every mans hand, whereby though we cannot practise all things, we may try all things. Now the Divine cannot pin anothers Faith upon his sleeve, and lead him implicitely, because the Bible is at hand, whereby a man may try whether what he saith be so or no. Nor can the Lawyer deviate in a cause, but he may be discerned by a quick eye, by reason of that light which shines round about us in Books of that Faculty. Neither can the Physitian prescribe at random, without being discover'd by the same means.

And whereas formerly the common people were entertained with feigned Traditions of the Legendaries, in stead of those Divine Oracles of the Old and New Testament; and with like fabulous stories of Giants, &c. in stead of real Histories: now they have not onely the Bible, but Expositions thereof, / bringing it in to their capacities, for their spiritual use and comfort; and the civil transactions of former times lively represented, whereby they may imitate the good, and shun the evil, and furnish themselves with Notions and Discourses sutable to rational Creatures. And all this by the benefit of Printing.

Yea, by this the Church of *Rome* hath received such a wound, as she will never be able to cure: for upon its discovery, such a light hath broken forth, that many Kingdoms and Countries that formerly had no other glimpse but what proceeded from her Dark Lanthorn, have hence received so great Illumination, that they finde just occasion to forsake her, notwithstanding her pretended Infallibility.

By this also our modern Pretenders of new lights, are discovered to be onely Revivers of old Errours; we having hereby the Ecclesiastical Histories of all former Ages, wherein we finde the Founders of those Follies and Impieties wherein these ape them.

To conclude, having given you the opinions of the Learned concerning Printing and Printers, let us wade a little into the discovery of the usage both it and they finde in other Countries. How it fares with them in *France*, the Stationers themselves inform us, in a Paper called, *The humble Remonstrance of the Company of Stationers*, signed by one *Henry Parker* Esq;[11] who saith, That *France especially favours that Profession and Trade of men*, (meaning Printers;) *for there they are above Mechanicks, and live in the Suburbs of Learning.* And a little before, speaking of *Europe*: *The more civil* (saith he) *a place is, the more regard it hath to Printing.* When he proceeds to commend the Papists, as well where the Inquisition is not, as where it is, for / their strict Regulation of Printing, whereby their Church is better fortified, and the Artists more encouraged then ours. Nor are Printers without extraordinary priviledges in most transmarine parts, as in *Italy, France, Spain, &c.* where (as if they were Church-men) they are exempted from those ordinary Taxes and Duties whereunto the rest of the people are liable. Nay, so great a respect have the Kings of *France* for this Art, that for many years they have maintained the practice of it in their own Royal Palace of the *Louvre*, at *Paris*; allowing the Artists a subsistence sutable to their eminent place, and generous employment: and in *Spain* it is mostly exercised in Monasteries and Religious Houses to this day, as it was here at its first arrival among us, as we have shewn in the beginning.

Neither is it to be forgotten, that those two great Monarchs, the one of *France*, the other of *Spain*, seemed to conceive themselves not sufficiently illustrious, unless they had eminently concerned themselves in the encouragement of this Art; and therefore they took upon them the Patronage of those famous Bibles in several Oriental Tongues, which pass under their great Names to this day.

*FINIS.*

[John Seymour], *The Case of Libels* ([London], [20 March 1677]).
Wing, C938B; ESTC, R173533.

### The CASE of LIBELS

*Whereas the Company of* Stationers, *being charg'd with the want either of Care or Integrity, in the preventing, Discovering or Suppressing of Treasonous, Seditious and scandalous Libels, have thought fit (with pretense of singular Zeal to the Publick) to discharge themselves by calumnious hint and reflections upon other People, the Truth of the Case is here set forth, and dutifully submitted to Authority.*

BY an Order of Council of *August* 19. 1670. a *Quo Warranto*[1] was directed against the *Stationers* Charter; And Sept. 20. following, upon Mr. *L'Estranges* Report to His Majesty in Council, that the Company had agreed upon certain By-Laws[2] for the better Government of their Members, a stop was put to the Proceeding.

The Danger (as they thought) being over; Notwithstanding divers express Commands from His Majesty under the Hand of a Secretary of State, requiring them to dispatch their By-Laws; and continual Instances from Mr. *L'Estrange* in His Majesties Name, by word of mouth, to the same purpose, they put off the Business above Six Years, without coming to a Conclusion.

The Motive to the stop of the *Quo Warranto*, was an Order of the *Stationers* Table[3] of *September* 15th. 1670. wherein they agree, that every Member of the Company shall be bound in a Recognizance to his Majesty, not to Print, Bind, or Publish any Unlicensed Book or Pamphlet.

Being afterwards pressed to put this Vote in Execution, they betook themselves to a Debate upon a Proposal of a new Charter, with further Power over their Members, and passed a Vote upon it *Aug.* 15. 1671.

In pursuance of this Vote, they addressed themselves to His Majesties Sollicitor General (the now Lord Chief Justice of the *Common Pleas*,)[4] who gave his Opinion under his Hand for a new Charter, *Aug.* 22. 1671. and the Company submitted to it.

Hereupon His Majesty Commanded Mr. *L'Estrange* to signifie His Gracious Pleasure to the Company, that He would renew their Charter; with further Powers, and an addition of Benefits and Priviledges to the Company.

Upon which signification, the Company passed a Vote *Octob.* 26. 1671. in acknowledgement of His Majesties Favour, and acceptance of His Royal Promise of a new Charter; these several Votes being attested by the Clerk of the Company, and ready to be produced.

From 1671. to this present 1676. they have only shifted, and delayd, without finishing any thing; till the last Summer Mr. Secretary *Williamson* requiring them in His Majesties Name to make an end, or to answer for their further Contempt before the King and Council, strictly charging Mr. *L'Estrange* to demand their asset to such Proposals as He should offer them for the better Government of their Members, and to make a Report thereupon. Pursuant to which Order, He deliverd to the Companies Table such an Expedient, as would hardly admit of any Exception, either to the Legality or Sufficiency of it: So that they pass'd a Vote *July* 14. 1676. that it should be the first thing taken into debate the next General Court.

But it was still put off, till Mr. Secretary *Williamson* sent for the Master and Wardens, and told them positively, that they should be call'd to account before the King and Council for their Contempt: Upon this they promis'd fair, and Mr. *L'Estrange* press'd them to call a Court, and finish; and forthwith to present the Project of the By-Law to the Judges.

A Court being call'd, He told them; *Gentlemen, this business has hung so many Years, and the King will be trifled no longer; The Parliament is at hand, and if this* By-Law *be not confirm'd before their meeting, we shall be pester'd with Libels and the blame will lie at your dore.*

Upon this, a Leading Man[5] at the Table started up, and cry'd out, *This is Mr. L'Estranges humour, He has a mind to make the Company Slaves, 'Faith I'le be none of them: He talks to Us of the King,* &c, Mr. *L'Estrange* hereupon told the Company, that He would make a Report of this to the King and Council, and stay no longer to see an affront put upon his Commission; and offering to depart, several of the Members stood up, and desired that the Passion and Indiscretion of one man, might not be taken for the sense of the Table; and that they believed the Company would very readily comply with what was propounded.

It is now considerable, that the Exception was not to the By-Law in gross, but to the reading of it to every Free-man upon the taking of his Oath, and the delivering of a Printed Copy to be set up in the Houses of all their Members: For being sworn to observe all the By-Laws of the Company already made, or which hereafter shall be made, they might pretend ignorance, if it had been only enter'd into the Bulk of their other By-Laws, without being detected of breaking their Oath.

The matter was urg'd so far, that a day was appointed for the final dispatch; which day being past, and Mr. *L'Estrange* receiving no account of what they had done, (which they promised he should,) he sent to the Master to know the issue of that Meeting; and his answer was, that truly they had done nothing, for they had not met at all; for one of their Members (the Person who before oppos'd it at the Table) though he knew the express business of that day, and though a Court was fairly summon'd, and himself sent to for the Key of their Common Hall, he refus'd to send it, and kept them out when they were ready to attend.[6] Since this time, they say they have lodg'd the By-Law in question in the hands of the Lord Chief Justice *Rainsford*,[7] and that it is the same which was agreed upon; but they gave no notice to Mr. *L'Estrange* when it was carried, (according to their promise) so that whether it be the same or not, he knows not.

It is humbly desired, that this Proceeding, though it be constructively the Act of the Company, may yet be understood to be only the Power of a Factious and Prevailing Party in it; whose Interest it is, for the Press to be at Liberty: And consequently they make it their Business to hinder the Regulation of it. How far they have obstructed it under the Notion of the Company, appears sufficiently already.

The next step must be to a Consideration of the Methods, and Practices of some particular, and principal Persons in the said Company: Where many times men of Loyal Principles, are through Weakness, or Necessity, involved in a Common Crime with the Seditious. As for Instance When a Libel is abroad, every man imploys his Book-seller to get it for him; and if he refuse, he loses his Custom; by which means the Innocent come to be punished for the faults of the Guilty. Under this Qualification will be found several persons, of whom use must be made to prove these following Particulars, if it shall be required.

1 That several of the Chief men of the Company do both Sell, and Connive at many of those Libells, which they are Commanded to Search for, and Discover.

2 That they give Notice beforehand of a Search to be made.

3 That upon Informations, they do sometime put off Searching, till things may be removed out of the way.

4 They do commonly prosecute the Discoverer of a Libel, and leave the Principal free; so that Printers dare not reveal any thing for fear of being undone. As in the Case of a Journy-man-printer,[8] who was only a Press-man, and Printed off without reading it, what another Composed by the order of his Master. This Journey-man Discover'd the Woman that brought it to the Press, and carry'd away the Printed Sheets, and he recovered at least a 1000 Copies; and did further Services, for which he received a Reward from a Secretary of State: And yet though the Company were ordered to Prosecute the Woman at Common Law, because she would not discover the Author; they Indicted the Journey-man-printer, and never meddled with the Woman, or Master of the Printing-house.

5 They Vilify the Authority of a Secretaryes Warrant, and him that Executes it: And one of them taking notice of a Printer that waited often upon a Secretary of State, though by his command and appointment, in order to a Discovery; tax'd the Printer publickly at the Hall Table, for applying him thither, and charged him to go no more. And it is confidently said, that a greater contempt hath been lately upon an Order of Council.

## 'The Company of Stationers against Seymour' (1678), in *Modern Reports, or, Select Cases* (London, 1682), pp. 256–9. Wing, C5414; ESTC, R11074.

### The Company of *Stationers* against *Seymour*.

The Company brought an Action of Debt against Seymour for printing Gadbury's Almanacks[1] without their leave. Upon a special Verdict found, the question was, Whether the Letters Patents whereby the Company of Stationers had granted to them the sole printing of Almanacks, were good or not. The Jury found the Stat. of 13 & 14 Car. 2. concerning Printing. They found a Patent made by King James of the same Priviledge to the Company, in which a former Patent of Queen Elizabeths was recited; and they found the Letters Patents of the King that now is. Then they found that the Defendant had printed an Almanack, which they found in his verbis & figuris:[2] and that the said Almanack had all the essential parts of the Almanack, that is printed before the Book of Common Prayer: but that it has some other additions, such as are usual in common Almanacks, &c.[3]

Pemberton.[4] The King may by Law grant the sole-printing of Almanacks. The Art of Printing is altogether of another consideration in the eye of the Law, than other Trades and Mysteries are; the Press is a late Invention. But the Exorbitancies and Licentiousness thereof has ever since it was first found out been under the care and restraint of the Magistrate. For great Mischiefs and Disorder would ensue / to the Common-wealth, if it were under no Regulation: and it has therefore always been thought fit to be under the Inspection and Controul of the Government. And the Stat. 14 Car. 2. recites that it is a matter of publique Care. In England it has from time to time been under the Kings own Regulation, so that no Book could lawfully be printed without an Imprimatur granted by some that derive authority from him to Licence Books. But the question here is not, Whether the King may by Law grant the sole-Printing of all Books; but of any, and of what sort of Books? the sole-printing of Law-Books is not now in question; that seemed to be a point of some difficulty, because of the large extent of such a Patent, and the uncertainty of determining what should be accounted a Law-Book, and what not. And yet such a Patent has been allowed to be good by a Judgment in the House of Peers.[5]

When Sir Orlando Bridgeman[6] was Chief Justice in this Court, there was a question raised concerning the validity of a Grant of the sole-printing of any particular Book, with a Prohibition to all others to print the same, how far it should stand good against them that claim a Property in the Copy paramount to the Kings Grant? and Opinions were divided upon the Point. But the Defendant in our Case makes no Title to the Copy; only he pretends a nullity in our Patent. The Book which this Defendant has printed, has no certain Author:[7] and then, according to the Rule of our Law, the King has the property; and by consequence may grant his Property to the Company.

Cur. There is no difference in any material part bewixt this Almanack and that that is put in the Rubrick of the Common-Prayer. Now the Almanack that is before the Common-Prayer, proceeds from a publick Constitution; it was first setled by the Nicene Council,[8] is established by the Canons of the Church, and is under the Government of the Archbishop of Canterbury. So that Almanacks may be accounted Prerogative Copies. Those particular Almanacks, that are made yearly, are but applications of the general Rules there laid down for the moveable Feasts for ever, to every particular year. And without doubt, this may be granted by the King. This is a stronger Case than that of Law-Books, which has been mentioned. The Lords in the Resolution of that Case relyed upon this, That / Printing was a new Invention, and therefore every man could not by the Common Law have a liberty of printing Law-Books. And since Printing has been invented, and is become a common Trade, so much of it as has been kept inclosed, never was made common: but matters of State, and things that concern the Government, were never left to any mans liberty to print that would. And particularly the sole Printing of Law-Books has been formerly granted in other Reigns. Though Printing be a new Invention, yet the use and benefit of it is only for men to publish their Works with more ease than they could before: Men had some other way to publish their Thoughts before Printing came in; and forasmuch as Printing has always been under the Care of the Government since it was first set on foot, we may well presume that the former way was so too. Queen Elizabeth, King James, and King Charles the First, granted such Patents as these; and the Law has a great respect to common usage. We ought to be guided in our Opinions by the Judgment of the House of Peers; which is express in the point: the ultimate resort of Law and Justice being to them. There is no particular Author of an Almanack: and then by the Rule of our Law, the King has the Property in the Copy. Those additions of Prognostications and other things that are common in Almanacks, do not alter the Case; no more than if a man should claim a property in another mans Copy, by reason of some inconsiderable additions of his own. Accordingly Judgment was given for the Plaintiffs, nisi causa,[9] &c.

*The Orders, Rules, and Ordinances, Ordained, Devised and Made by the Master and Keepers or Wardens and Comminalty of the Mystery or Art of Stationers of the City of London, for the Well Governing of that Society* (London: for the Company of Stationers, 1678), pp. 19–25, 27–8. Wing, O403; ESTC, R11816.

# THE
# ORDERS,
# RULES
## AND
# ORDINANCES,

Ordained, Devised and Made by the
Master and Keepers or Wardens and
Comminalty of the Mystery or Art of

# STATIONERS
## OF
## The City of LONDON,

for the well Governing of that Society.

[19]
AND whereas since the making of the late Act of Parliament made in his new Majesties Reign, intituled, An Act for preventing the frequent abuses in Printing Seditious, Treasonable and unlicensed Books and Pamphlets, and for regulating of Printing and Printing-presses, several members of the said Society have Erected Presses contrary to the said Act, and therewithall have printed several seditious, treasonable, schismatical, scandalous and unlicensed Books and Pamphlets, to the great Scandal of the said Company, and the Government thereof: For the future prevention whereof, It is hereby Ordained, That no Member of this Company shall hereafter Erect or cause to be Erected, any Press or Presses for Printing, or any Printing-house or Printing-houses; nor shall knowingly Demise or Lett,[1] or suffer to be held or used any House, Vault or Cellar, or other Room whatsoever, for a Printing-house or place to print in, unless he or they

who Erect such Press or Presses, Printing-house or Printing-houses, or shall so knowingly demise or lett such Houses, Cellar, Vault or Room, or suffer the same to be used, shall first give Notice to the Master and Wardens of the said Society, or one of them, of the Erecting such Presse or Presses, Printing-house or Printing-houses, or of such Demise, or suffering to work or Print, upon pain of forfeiting the summe of Ten pounds for every Offence to be committed contrary to any of the Clauses of this Ordinance, and Forty shillings a day during every day that the same shall continue, to be paid to the Master and Keepers or Wardens and Commonalty of the Mystery or Art of Stationers of the City of London, to the use of the Poor of the said Company. /

AND also it is further Ordained, That no Member or Members of the said Society, shall at any time from henceforth erect, or cause or procure or suffer to be erected any private Press or Presses, commonly called A Press in a hole, nor shall countenance, assist or contribute towards the erecting or setting up of any such private Presse or Presses, or shall knowingly accommodate, furnish, or supply any such private Presse or Presses, with Paper or any other materials for Printing, or contribute towards the same, or pay or contribute towards the payment of any Wages, Sallary or Hire, to any person or persons, for the working at any private Presse or Presses, or towards the payment of any Rent or Reward for any House or place where such private Presse or Presses shall be Erected and set up, or connive at or conceal any such Presse or Presses, House or Houses, place or places, or the Name or Names of any such person or persons that shall erect or cause to be erected, or contribute towards the erecting, furnishing, supplying, working at, or preparing work for any such private Presse or Presses, or shall willingly and knowingly buy, barter, or contract for any Impression or part of any Impression, of any Book or Books, or part of Book, Pamphlet or Paper; or knowingly bind, stitch, put together for sale, publish, dispose, or disperse any Book, Pamphlet or Paper, which shall be Imprinted at any such private Presse or Presses, upon pain that every Member in any of the said cases offending, shall be lyable to be disfranchised for such Offence, or to pay to the Master and Keepers or Wardens and Comminalty[2] of the Mystery of Art of Stationers of the City of London, such reasonable Fine, not exceeding Fifty pounds, as the Master, Wardens and Assistants of the said Company, or the major part of them in a Court of Assistants, shall Impose upon him for such his Offence. And for the better discovery of all such private Printing-presses, commonly called Presses in Holes, it is further Ordained, That every person and persons that shall discover any such private Printing-presse to the Master and Wardens of the said Society, or either of them, shall have the summ of Five pounds, or what more the Master or Wardens shall think fit, as a Reward for such his Service, to be paid to him out of the common Stock of the said Society, by the said Master or Wardens, or one of them, and shall be allowed in their or any of their Accompts. /

AND it is likewise further Ordained, That no member or members of the said Society, shall imploy either to work at the Case or Presse, or otherwise about his Printing, any Journeyman-Printer, Freeman or Foreigner, or other person whatsoever, that shall have offended in any of the cases mentioned in the Two last before-mentioned Ordinances, for the space of Three months next after due proof thereof made, either by Confession or otherwise, to the Court of Assistants of the said Society, and notice thereof given to the several Master-Printers of the said Society, without License from the Master or Wardens of the said Society first had and obtained; Upon pain that every Member so offending after Notice given as aforesaid, shall forfeit and pay to the Master and Keepers or Wardens and Comminalty of the Mystery or Art of Stationers of the City of London, the summe of Ten shillings for every month that he or they shall Imploy such Offender or Offenders as aforesaid.

AND it is likewise further Ordained, That no member or members of the said Society, shall knowingly permit or suffer his Apprentice or Apprentices, or Covenant-servants,[3] at any time to work at any Presse or Presses, any matter or thing whatsoever prohibited by the said Act of Parliament, and the before-mentioned Two Ordinances: and that if any such Master-Printer shall at any time discover or know that any of his Apprentices or Covenant-servants shall offend in any of the said Cases, That then such Master-Printer shall cause such Apprentice or Apprentices, or Covenant-servants, forthwith to be brought to the Chamberlain of the City of London for the time being, and make complaint of all such his and their Offences, to the end that such Offender and Offenders may be punished according to the ancient custom of the said City,[4] Upon pain that every Master-Printer not effectually putting in Execution this Ordinance, or faintly prosecuting the same, shall forfeit and pay to the Master and Keepers or Wardens and Comminalty of the Mystery or Art of Stationers of the City of London, the summe of Forty shillings.

AND it is also Ordained, That no Master-Printer, or other Printer or Workman, being a member of this Society, shall teach, direct or instruct any person or persons whatsoever, other than his or their own Legitimate

Son or Sons, in this Art or Mystery of / Printing, who is not actually bound as an Apprentice to some lawful authorized Printer; Upon pain that every person so offending, shall forfeit and pay to the Master and Keepers or Wardens and Commonalty of the Mystery or Art of Stationers of the City of London, the summe of Five pounds.

AND also it is hereby further Ordained, That no member or members of the said Society, shall hereafter Erect or set up, or cause to be erected or set up, or countenance, or contribute to the Erecting or setting up of any Printing-presse or Presses, for any new Printing-house or Houses, or shall supply or furnish the same with any Materials for Printing, untill the now Legal Master-Printers and their Printing-houses be reduced according to the direction of the aforesaid late Act of Parliament, Upon pain of forfeiting the summe of Fifty pounds for every such Offence, and Twenty pounds a month for every month that the same shall continue, to be paid to the Master and Keepers or Wardens and Commonalty of the Mystery or Art of Stationers of the City of London.

AND it is also hereby further Ordained, That if any Journey-man Printer, or other person, being a member of the said Society, shall work at any private illegal Press, and not discover the same within Two days after such working as aforesaid, to be Master and Wardens of the said Society, or any of them, or shall knowingly work at or upon the Printing of any seditious or scandalous Book, Pamphlet or Paper, or any other Book or Books, or part of any Book or Books imprinted wrongfully and without leave or Assignment of the lawful Owner, the sole printing whereof lawfully belonging to the said Society, or to any other person or persons, or shall knowingly bind, stitch, or sow together any such Book or Books, That then such Journey-man Printer, or other person as aforesaid, their or any of their Widows, shall not in any wise be admitted a Pensioner to the said Society ... /

The By-Law to be Read at the Administring of the Free-mans Oath,[5] and a Printed Copy thereof to be delivered to every Member of the said Company dealing in the *Stationers* Trade.

IT IS hereby Ordained, that no Member or Members of this Company shall hereafter knowingly Imprint or cause to be Imprinted any Book, Pamphlet, Portraicture, Picture or Paper whereunto the Law requires a License, without such License as by the Law is directed for the Imprinting of the same.

AND in Case any Member as aforesaid shall henceforth know of the Imprinting, Binding, Stitching, Publishing or Dispersing of any such Book, Pamphlet, Portraicture, Picture or Paper as aforesaid, such Member or Members as aforesaid, shall from time to time disclose the same unto the Master or Wardens of the said Company within Three dayes after the knowledge of such Offence committed, together with the Name or Names of / such Person or Persons so offending; Which said Master or Wardens upon such Information given, shall cause the same to be entred in a Book hereafter mentioned, within six dayes after such Information received, upon pain that every Person offending in either or any of these Cases, and having a part in the English Stock of this Company,[6] the Profits of such part of his Stock for one year shall be sequestred, and paid into the hands of the Master and Keepers, or Wardens and Comminalty of the Mystery or Art of Stationers of the City of London, to the use of the Poor or the said Corporation: Unless the Master, Wardens and Assistants, with the Consent of Roger L'Estrange Esq; or such Persons as hereafter shall have the like Power concerning the Press committed to them, as he now hath, upon hearing of the matter, shall according to the nature of the Offence think fit to mitigate the same.

AND, if any Person or Persons having no part in the English Stock of this Company, shall offend in either or any of the Cases aforesaid, Then such Person or Persons shall forfeit and pay to the Master and Keepers or Wardens and Comminalty of the Mystery or Art of Stationers of the City of London, to the use of the Poor of the said Corporation, the summe of Ten pounds; Unless the Master, Wardens and Assistants, with the Consent of the said Roger L'Estrange Esq; or of such Persons as shall succeed him in his Authority and Power as aforesaid, upon hearing of the Matter shall according to the Nature of the Offence think fit to mitigate the same. ...

AND, if any Printer shall offend herein, such Printer shall not for One year next following such Offence, nor after One year expired without the Consent of the Master, Wardens and / Assistants be employed in the doing of any work for or belonging to the English Stock of this Company.

AND be it further Ordained, That for the Future shall be kept by the Clerk of this Company, two Books; In one of which shall be fairly written such Informations given to the Master or Wardens as aforesaid; and in the other shall be fairly written, what Seditious, Scandalous, Treasonable and unlicensed Books and Pamphlets shall be seiz'd, and Discoveries thereof made, together with the Number of them, and the Persons from whom they were seiz'd: which Books shall be shewen to Roger L'Estrange Esq; when he shall think fit ...

[27]
ALL which Orders, Rules, Ordinances and Oaths, in manner and form aforesaid made, Wee the said Lord Chancellor of *England*, and Lord Chief Justices of either Bench, have seen, perused and Examined, and in Order to the preventing and avoiding of the Penalty inflicted by / the aforesaid Statute upon the Execution of Ordinances not approved, as by the said Act is directed, (And as far forth as by Law we may) we do approve, ratifie and confirm. In Witness whereof, to these Presents, We the said Lord Chancellor of *England*, and Lord Chief Justices of either Benches, have hereunto subscribed our Names, and set our Seals, the Second day of *February*, in the Thirtieth Year of the Reign of our Sovereign Lord *Charles* the Second, by the Grace of God King of *England, Scotland, France* and *Ireland, Defender of the Faith, &c, Annoq; Dom. 1677.*
  *H. Finch, C.*
  *Ri. Rainsford.*
  *Fra. North.*[7]

FINIS.

*An Ordinance Ordained, Devised, and Made by the Master, and Keepers or Wardens, and Commonalty of the Mystery or Art of Stationers of the City of London* (London: for the Company of Stationers, 1683), title page, pp. 4–6. Wing, O411; ESTC, R216917.

AN
# ORDINANCE
Ordained, Devised, and Made
BY THE
Master, and Keepers or Wardens,
and Commonalty of the MYSTERY
or Art of
## STATIONERS
OF THE
## CITY
OF
## LONDON

For the Well Governing of
that SOCIETY

LONDON:
Printed for the Company of *Stationers*. 1683 / ...

[4]

*At an* Assembly *of the Master, and Keepers or Wardens, and Commonalty of the Mystery or Art of* STATIONERS *of the City of* LONDON, *held at their Common Hall in the Parish of St.* Martin Ludgate,[1] *in the Ward of* Farringdon within London, *on* Wednesday *the Sixth day of* December, Anno Dom. *One Thousand Six Hundred Eighty and Two, For the well-governing of the Members of this Company, the Law and Ordinance hereafter mentioned, was then made, enacted, and ordained by the Master, and Keepers or Wardens, and Commonalty of the Mystery or Art of* STATIONERS *of the City of* LONDON, *in manner and form following,* viz.

**Whereas**, It hath been the Ancient Usage of the Members of this Company, for the Printer or Printers, Publisher or Publishers of all Books, Pamphlets, Ballads, and Papers (except what are granted by Letters Pattents under the Great Seal of England) to Enter into the Publick Register-Book of this Company, remaining with the Clerk of this Company for the time being, in his or their own Name or Names, All Books, Pamphlets, Ballads, and Papers whatsoever, by him or them to be Printed or Published, before the same Book, Pamphlet, Ballad, or Paper is begun to be Printed, To the end that the Printer or Publisher thereof may / be known, to justifie whatsoever shall be therein contained, and have no Excuse for the Printing or Publishing thereof, which Usage this Company now taking into their Consideration, do think that the due Observation thereof may be a means to prevent the Printing and Publishing of Treasonable, Seditious, and Scandalous Books, Pamphlets, Libels, and Papers, or Discover the Printers or Publishers thereof.

**It is therefore Ordained**, That all and every Member or Members of this Company shall before the Printing or reprinting of any Book, Pamphlet, Ballad, or Paper (except what are granted under the Great Seal of *England* as aforesaid) in his own Person cause to be Entred into the Register-Book of this Company (remaining in the Custody of the Clerk of this Company, paying the usual Fees for the Entring thereof) in his and their own Name and Names in words at length, the Title of all & every Book, Pamphlet, and Paper, that he or they shall hereafter Print or Publish, or cause to be Printed or Published. And to which Entry he or they shall set and subscribe his and their respective Name and Names, upon pain of / forfeiting to the Master and Keepers or Wardens, and Commonalty of the Mystery or Art of *Stationers* of the City of *London*, Twenty pounds; to be by them Recovered by Action of Debt, to their own Use.

Which said Ordinance in manner and form aforesaid, made at the Request of the said Master and Keepers or Wardens, and Commonalty of the Mystery or Art of *Stationers* of the City of *London*, by the Authority and Vertue of the said Act of Parliament made in the Nineteenth Year of the said King *Henry* the Seventh,[2] and for the preventing of the Penalty inflicted by the aforesaid Statute upon the Execution of Ordinances not approved, as by the said Act is directed (as far forth as by Law we may) *We* the said Lord Keeper, and Lords Chief Justices of either Benches,[3] do Approve, Ratifie, and Confirm. *In Witness* whereof, We the said Lord Keeper, and Lords Chief Justices of either Benches, have hereunto subscribed our Names, and set our Seals the said Tenth day of *February*, in the Five and Thirtieth Year of the Reign of our Sovereign Lord *Charles* the Second, by the Grace of God of *England, Scotland, France,* and *Ireland*, King, Defender of the Faith, &c. *Annoq; Dom.* 1682.[4]

*F. North,* C. S.

*Edm. Saunders.*

*Fr. Pemberton.*[5]

*A New Song in Praise of the Loyal Company of Stationers, Who (after the general forfeit,) for their singular Loyalty, Obtain'd the First Charter of London, Anno 1684* (London: by N[athaniel] T[hompson], 1684). Wing, N761A; ESTC, R180967.

## A New SONG,

In Praise of the Loyal Company of

## STATIONERS,

Who (after the general forfeit,) for Their singular Loyalty, obtain'd the first
CHARTER of *LONDON*, June 1684.[1]

To the Tune of, *Winchester Wedding*.

1.

IN *London* was such a Quarter,
   The like was never known,
About the forfeited CHARTER
   Betwixt the *Court* and the *Town*;
The Masters went crouding before,
   The Prentices i'th' Rear did fall,
There were ten thousand and more,
   Attended to lead up the Brawl:
*Kit* Arm'd with a Fork and a Spade,
   And *Bob* with a Shovel and Fork,
But *Tender* was for a surrender,[2]
   And now it began to work.

2.

Quoth *Willy* what lose the CHARTER?
   I'll sooner lose my Head;
Quoth *Robin* I'll die a Martyr
   Before that shall ever be said:
Quoth *John* you may shut up your Shopping
   Your CHARTER was all your Shield,
For every Sea-man of *Wapping*,
   May be Freeman now of the *Guield*;[3]

Quoth a *Butcher*; the Beggerly *French*
  Will out of our Mouths eat the Bread;
But the *Weaver*, he cock'd up his Beaver,
  And valiantly march'd at the Head.

       3.

But *Stationers Hall* so Loyal,
  The CHARTER by which they meet,
The gift of his Ancesters Royal,
  Did humbly lay at His Feet:[4]
Whose Suit he so far befriendeth,
  Their Liberties know no bound,
Their CHARTER her wings extendeth
  through *London*, and many miles round.
And now from the *Bigot* and *Whig*,
  (To distinguish the good men, and true)
The Table is purg'd, and the Rabble
  With the Members excluded withdrew.[5]

      4.

With limping *Dick*, the *Zealous*,
  Went doating yea, and nay,
And squinting *Jack* so Jealous.
  Lest Loyalty got the day.
With these *Jack Thumb* was reckon'd,
  And hungry *Will* of the wood;
And I *rank* the first, and the second,
  And *George* that will never be good.
And thus they did trip it along,
  Whilst *William* led up the Brawl,
But *Jonny* did storm above any,
  To be turn'd out of the Hall.

      5.

*Jack* gave his right hand to *Harry*,
  Who now his place had lost,
And swore if the day they carry,
  The *Loyal* shou'd pay for the Rest.
But *Robin* who made a tryal,
  And found how the Jig wou'd go,
Resolv'd to change sides, and be Loyal,
  But all the *Dissenters* said no;

Thus whilst to the CHARTER or Law,
    They would no obedience yield,
The glory was still *True Tory*,
    Is Master of the Field.

6.

Now to the *Stationers* Honour,
    The CHARTER is on Record;
Great *CHARLES* the Bountiful *Donor*,
    Their Franchises has restor'd;
To whose everlasting Glory,
    Thy Honour will still redound;
That they are the first in story,
    Who *London's* CHARTER did found;
Then to the brave Founder a Health,
    Who first did our Freedom create,
A Bumper to *CHARLES*; to the *Rumper*
    A Halter, and *Armstrong*'s Fate.[6]

Printed by *N. T.* at the entrance into the *Old-Spring-Garden,* 1684.

# HERESY, ORTHODOXY AND THE PRESS, 1666-76

The Catching of Thomas Hobbes:
   The Parliamentary Examination of *Leviathan* (16-17 October 1666), *CJ*, 8, p. 636.
   Letter Requesting Licence for Tract on *Heresie* (30 June 1668). NA, SP 29/242/79.
   *Leviathan* Seized at the Press (September-October 1670). NA, SP 29/279/95 and 95(1).
   Privy Council Inquiry into *Behemoth* (5 September 1679). NA, PC 2/68.

[Sir Charles Wolseley], *Liberty of Conscience upon its True and Proper Grounds Asserted and Vindicated. Proving, that no Prince, nor State, ought by Force to Compel Men to Any Part of the Doctrine, Worship, or Discipline of the Gospel. To which is added, the Second Part, viz. Liberty of Conscience, the Magistrates Interest; or, To Grant Liberty of Conscience to Persons of Different Persuasions in Matters of Religion, is the Great Interest of all Kingdoms and States, and particularly of England; Asserted and Proved*, 2nd edn (London, 1668), pp. 52, 57, 61-2, 67-70. Wing, W3311; ESTC, R10045.

Hugh Cressy, *Fanaticism Fanatically Imputed to the Catholick Church by Doctour Stillingfleet: And the Imputation Refuted and Retorted by S.C. a Catholick O.S.B.* ([?Douai], 1672), unnumbered sig., pp. 92-4, 96-9. Wing, C6898; ESTC, R1090.

[Edward Hyde, Earl of Clarendon], *Animadversions upon a Book, Intituled, Fanaticism Fanatically Imputed to the Catholick Church* (London: R. Royston, Bookseller to His Most Sacred Majesty, 29 November 1673), pp. 1-7, 16, 103-6. Wing, C4414; ESTC, R19554.

[Herbert Croft], *The Naked Truth. Or, The True State of the Primitive Church. By an Humble Moderator* (s.n., 1675), preface. ESTC, R9033

Andrea Rivetus, Jr [Andrew Marvell], *Mr. Smirke; or, The Divine in Mode: Being Certain Annotations, upon the Animadversions of The Naked Truth. Together with a Short Historical Essay, concerning General Councils, Creeds, and Impositions, in Matters of Religion* ([London], April 1676), pp. 1-5, 7-10, 13, 76. ESTC, R214932.

Restoration censorship had the dual, frequently inseparable, preoccupations of political and religious dissent, with heresy and heterodoxy subject to suppression in their own right and viewed as indissolubly linked to instability in the state. The main targets for the guardians of Church orthodoxy were Roman Catholicism, Protestant nonconformism, Anglican deviationism and a generalized atheism much alleged if little professed. All are represented in this section. It was around such doctrinal and ecclesiological conflict, rather more than political criticism or outright sedition, that censorship mainly revolved in the period, and from disputes over the needs of religious conscience and community arguments both for and against censorship arose.

Thomas Hobbes (1588–1679) defended censorship in *Leviathan* in 1651 then spent much of the rest of his life living with its spectre, his own writings facing condemnation as heretical and subversive. This was not straightforwardly the biter bit because Hobbes's elevation of the magistrate's authority also represented the diminution of Church power and the separation of censorship on grounds of public security from suppression of divergent religious opinion for its own sake. This did not prevent Hobbes's ideas being a target, however, with four instances represented here. The first was the move to examine *Leviathan* as part of Parliament's action against atheism and blasphemy in 1666, although no further proceedings ensued. Around this time Hobbes completed a manuscript on the law of heresy partly intended to exculpate his own views; the second item is a letter he wrote to the secretary of state Joseph Williamson in 1668 in an effort to secure a licence for publication. The licence was not granted, Hobbes's views only appearing posthumously in *An Historical Narration Concerning Heresy* (1680). The third item features the testimony of printer John Redmayne after a foiled underground attempt to print *Leviathan* in 1670; there is no convincing evidence of Hobbes's own involvement. Item four relates to Hobbes's history of the civil wars, best known under the title *Behemoth*, which appeared in print late in 1679. The Privy Council minutes transcribed here show that Hobbes was asked about its appearance with a view to prosecution alongside other libels of the time, the ninety-one-year-old writer replying that it was published without his authority. No further action was taken; within three months Hobbes was dead.

Sir Charles Wolseley (1629/30–1714) was an adviser to Cromwell whose Interregnum support for the claims of individual conscience found renewed expression in the debate on Protestant toleration that emerged in the late 1660s, the 'Clarendon Code' of enforced uniformity coming into question as the Conventicle Act faced renewal in 1668 (with Clarendon himself in exile). In 1668 Wolseley issued one pamphlet emphasizing the magistrate's duty to respect liberty of conscience and another stressing his interest in doing so, the two then being published together under the title above. The extension of the argument to liberty of the press came at the end of the second part and appeared something of an afterthought, perhaps prompted by contemporary reports of a clampdown on Huguenot printing in Catholic France. Wolseley's argument was based less on a direct appeal to conscience than on the search for religious truth and the association of press control with Rome, drawing on Lord Herbert of Cherbury's

1648 *Life and Raigne* of Henry VIII for Cardinal Wolsey's purported warning to the Pope of the religious liberties wrought by printing.

Criticism of Romish constraints on conscience coupled with suppression of Romish writings was the direction dictated by the Church of England's *via media*, leading Catholic writers to criticize the application if not the principle of censorship. When Edward Stillingfleet in 1671 challenged his adversaries to go into print and so meet in 'the open field' the Catholic convert Hugh Cressy pointed to censorship as the obstacle, his *Fanaticism Fanatically Imputed* (1672) eventually emerging from a foreign press. Stillingfleet later claimed he had a catalogue by him listing 200 popish books printed in English; certainly he managed to generate numerous printed responses from Catholic writers.[1] Cressy, a Benedictine monk, argued that Stillingfleet's claims for individual judgement and preoccupation with Rome opened the way to fanatics and truly seditious publications; he also pointed out that his opponent lacked a licence. He was in turn answered by the exiled Earl of Clarendon, who had been a Tew Circle acquaintance of Cressy. Clarendon expressed concern at a general press licentiousness manifested in the descent to published polemical exchanges, in his preface recalling the Marprelate press and also Thomas Nashe as its scurrilous but necessary antagonist. Clarendon's book, licensed by Thomas Tomkyns for the Archbishop of Canterbury, appeared in further editions in 1674 and in 1685. Cressy replied, excusing going into print by the elusiveness of his erstwhile friend, in *An Epistle Apologetical of S.C. to a Person of Honour* in 1674, the year of Clarendon's death.

The case of Herbert Croft's *Naked Truth* (1675) was notable for Andrew Marvell's intervention in *Mr. Smirke* (1676) but also for the way the condemnation of a bishop's writings seemed to confirm the unworkability of identifying and enforcing orthodoxy in Church policy and doctrine. Croft (1603–91), the Bishop of Hereford, issued his tract without a licence, as he acknowledged in his preface and as Marvell recounted, intending its call for comprehension to circulate among MPs. Parliament being dissolved he attempted to withdraw the work but it was printed and circulated, drawing calls for its suppression from the churchmen Francis Turner and Philip Fell, the latter observing that 'several things therein contained are as contrary to the known Laws as his Printing without Licence confestly was'.[2] The *Naked Truth* was subsequently investigated as part of a parliamentary clampdown on the press in early 1677.

Andrew Marvell (1621–78) had already inveighed against coercive conformity and clerical censorship as its prop in *The Rehearsal Transpros'd* (1672), which had itself been seized at the press but was rescued by the King's apparent appreciation of its support for his policy of indulgence. In *Mr. Smirke* Marvell defended Bishop Croft against the future bishop Francis Turner, blaming the campaign for burning the book on the 'Monopoly of Printing Pernicious Discourses' enjoyed by the 'Licensed Clergy', complaining that 'we seem to have got an Expurgatory Press, though not an Index, and the most Religious Truth must be expung'd and suppressed in order to the false and secular interest of some of the clergy'. He devoted some attention to the circumstances of *Naked Truth*'s unauthorized printing: the main source of this information. *The Naked Truth* and *Mr. Smirke* were both investigated in 1676–7 in an attempt to identify those behind their publication. Nathaniel Ponder was committed in 1676 for publishing Marvell's work and his fellow bookseller Thomas Sawbridge and the printer Henry Bruges, who along with Francis Smith was suspected of producing *Naked Truth*, were also later questioned.[3] However, both Croft and Marvell avoided punishment. Evidence on the case was presented to the Lords committee on libels in March 1677 as a new bill against unlicensed printing was being introduced into the Lords but in April Parliament was dissolved before the bill could progress through the Commons.[4] Marvell would include the bill in his evidence of 'impending tyranny' later in the year in *An Account of the Growth of Popery and Arbitrary Government*.[5]

Notes
1. E. Stillingfleet, *A Discourse concerning the Idolatry Practised in the Church of Rome* (London, 1671), sig. a2r; E. Stillingfleet, *An Answer to Several Late Treatises* (London, 1673), p. 73.
2. P. Fell, *Lex Talionis* (London, 1676), p. 1.
3. *CSPD*, 10 May 1676.
4. PA, HL/PO/JO/10/362, item 338, g2; Bell, *Calendar*, vol. 2, pp. 145–7.
5. A. Marvell, *An Account of the Growth of Popery and Arbitrary Government* (London, 1677), p. 86.

## The Parliamentary Examination of *Leviathan* (16–17 October 1666), *CJ*, 8, p. 636.

*Die Martis*, 16 *Octobris*, 18 *Car*. IIdi.

### Atheism, &c.

A BILL against Atheism, Profaneness, and Swearing, was read the Second time.[1]

*Resolved*, &c. That the Bill be committed to [list of names], and all the Gentlemen of the House that are of the Long Robe: And all the Members of this House that shall come, are to have Voices:[2] And they are to meet To-morrow at Two of the Clock in the Afternoon, in the Exchequer Chamber; and to look into the former Laws concerning this Matter; and to repeal what they find necessary to be repealed; and reduce them all into one Law, if they can; and provide for the effectual Execution of it: And that it be referred to this Committee to prepare and bring in a Bill for the better Observation of the Lord's Day: And to send for Persons, Papers, and Records.

*Die Mercurii*, 17 *Octobris*, 18 *Car*. IIdi.

### Atheism, &c.

ORDERED, That the Committee to which the Bill against Atheism and Profaneness is committed, be impowered to receive Information touching such Books as tend to Atheism, Blasphemy, or Profaneness, or against the Essence or Attributes of God; and, in particular, the Book published in the Name of one *White*;[3] and the Book of Mr. *Hobbs*, called *The Leviathan*;[4] and to report the Matter, with their Opinions, to the House.

### Regulating the Press.

*Ordered*, That a Committee be appointed to inspect the Act for regulating the Press; and to consider, Wherein it is defective; and bring in a Bill for supplying the Defects,[5] and for putting the Act in effectual Execution: And also to inquire, Whether there be any illegal Patent, or any Abuse, in the licensing or stopping the lawful Printing of Books:

And that it be referred to [names]. And they are to meet on *Friday* next, at Two of the Clock in the Afternoon, in the Speaker's Chamber: And to send for Persons, Papers, and Records.

## Letter Requesting Licence for Tract on *Heresie* (30 June 1668). NA, SP 29/242/79.

[Hobbes to Williamson, 1668]

To my much honoured frend
Mr. Williamson[6]
[f. 88]
Sir

 I have sent you sealed here the book I spake to you of. The words which you mislike are in the last page but one, w$^{ch}$ is the 12th page of the tract concerning Heresie,[7] and they are these.

> Some man may perhaps ask whether nobody was condemned and burnt for Heresie during the time of the High Commission. I have heard there were. But they who approve such executions may peradventure know better grounds for them then I doe. But those grounds are very well worthy to be enquired after.

They may be left out without trouble to the rest that goes before and after. I see no cause of exception against them, and desire to have them stand but if the rest cannot be licensed whilst these $^{words}$ are in, you may put them out.

 Our going out of towne is appointed on Monday, therefore I pray you let me have this againe licensed or not licensed before Sunday night.

  Sr I am your most humble servant
   Thomas Hobbes
    June the 30th. 1668

## *Leviathan* Seized at the Press (September–October 1670). NA, SP 29/279/95 and 95(1).

[Mearne to Williamson, 1670]

Sr

If y̆ Leviathan should be called for this enclosed may serve for y̆ present. Y̆ printer is gon & I am in great hast & just Leasure enough to subscribe my selfe

    Sr Your most humble servant

      Sam: Mearne[8]

        Councell chamber close Oct: 19


September 28th, 1670[9]

There came to my house Mr Leak master of the Company of Stationers with Warden Roper, accompanied with Mr Norton[10] and Mr Mearne, who found at my house printing a book intituled Hobbs Leviathan, and there seized on two sheets, the Thursday sennight[11] following they round again and took away my press, and demanded where the residue of the sheets were, which I told them, were thirty eight more, & were all seized upon. They likewise demanded of me who I printed this book for, I told them for Mr John Williams, who had it (he said) from Mr Andrew Crook,[12] with his order to print.

    Subscribed by me

      John Redmayne[13]

        printer

## Privy Council Inquiry into *Behemoth* (5 September 1679). NA, PC 2/68.

[Privy Council minutes]

[364]
At the Councill Chamber
in Whitehall 5th September 1679

Present
Marquis of Worcester
Earle of Radnor
Visct. Fauconberg
Lord Russell
Lord Cheif Justice North
Mr. Secty: Coventry
Sr. Thomas Chicheley

The Printers of Libells to be inquired at &c.

Wheras a booke entituled The History of the Civill Warrs of England, supposed to be writ by Mr. Hobbs, hath lately come forth in print,[14] And that severall notorious Bookes and Libells tending to the Defamation and Disturbance of the Governmt. have also been lately printed and published. It is this day Ordered by their Lo$^{ps}$. that Roger L'Estrange Esq$^{re}$. Surveyor of the Presse, do make strict enquiry after the Printers of the said Bookes, and Libells, and to return the names of such Printers as he shall so Discover to this Boord, that direction may be given for their being prosecuted according to Law ... /

Mr. Hobbs about his Booke[15]

Mr. Hobbs being by their Lo$^{ps}$. order, writ unto, touching a Booke entituled The History of the Civil Warrs of England, did own the writing therof, But that he had forbidden the printing of it, and sends letters to testifie the truth therof.

[Sir Charles Wolseley], *Liberty of Conscience upon its True and Proper Grounds Asserted and Vindicated. Proving, that no Prince, nor State, ought by Force to Compel Men to Any Part of the Doctrine, Worship, or Discipline of the Gospel. To which is added, the Second Part, viz. Liberty of Conscience, the Magistrates Interest; or, To Grant Liberty of Conscience to Persons of Different Persuasions in Matters of Religion, is the Great Interest of all Kingdoms and States, and particularly of England; Asserted and Proved*, 2nd edn (London, 1668), pp. 52, 57, 61–2, 67–70. Wing, W3311; ESTC, R10045.

# LIBERTY
## OF
# CONSCIENCE

Upon its true and proper Grounds
ASSERTED & VINDICATED ...

To which is added, The SECOND PART
*VIZ.*

## Liberty of Conscience,
### The Magistrates Interest ...

The *Second Edition*.

[52]
# LIBERTY of CONSCIENCE,

The Magistrates Interest:[1]

OR,

To grant *Liberty of Conscience* to persons of *different perswasions* in matters of *Religion*, is the great Interest of all Kingdoms and States, and particularly of *England*; Asserted and proved.

HAving thus far considered those things, which do most immediately reflect upon the Magistrates Duty, in allowing a due Liberty to each mans Conscience, We will in the next place consider, how far his Interest engages him this way. That 'tis the great Interest of all Protestant States, and particularly of *England*, To give Liberty to men of differing Apprehensions in the *Protestant Religion*, is evident; if we consider, That a Prince or State, by imposing the Principles of any one party in Religion, makes himself of that party, and engages all the rest against him. 'Tis no way prudent for a *Prince*, when his Subjects consist of many differing Judgments, to resolve to have them all of one mind, (a thing impracticable) or else to be their declared Enemy and Persecutor; 'tis a ready way to interrupt his own quiet and repose, without any other effect: for he will never by force and violence unite them in one Opinion, those differences will rather be fomented, and all animosities arising thereupon, and men rather fixed and confirmed by such Persecution, than any way removed from their Principles by it. 'Tis not the having several parties in Religion under a State, that is in it self dangerous, but 'tis the persecuting of them that makes them so. ...

[57]
The punishing men meerly for following the pure dictates of Conscience, is no doubt the true cause of many National miseries; And a State should be careful to avoid this, as they would preserve their own Safety and Welfare. If we look into that which naturally occasioneth several Opinions in Religion, 'tis that which a Prince should for his own Interest highly encourage, and that is Knowledge; for no doubt, as Knowledge encreaseth, it expatiates it self into variety of Thoughts and Principles; and as it enlargeth all other Sciences, so Religion. Knowledge is the Glory of a Nation, and that by which all matters of Concern to it, as War, Trade, Policy, and every thing else is highly enlarged. 'Tis the high Honour of a Prince to Govern a Wise and a Knowing People, as well as a Great People; 'Tis an impotent piece of Policy, and equally destructive to all publick Interest, to say *Subjects must be kept ignorant*, as to say, *They must be kept poor*. They are Maximes only fitted for a Tyrant, and such who only govern for themselves, and calculate

all Interests, as they concenter in their own, and by so doing, make themselves their own Idols. ...

[61]
Liberty of Conscience is the great means to diffuse / Gospel-knowledge in divine things, and that's the best and surest way to bar out Popery, and lock the door upon it for ever. Ignorance is the great and only preparative for implicite subjection. *Christendom* cannot (I dare say) afford an instance that ever any State or People, where Divine-Knowledge by Liberty of Conscience, and a Liberty for the Gospel was once spread, were in the least danger of turning Apostates to *Popery*, but have grown daily more and more into a detestation of it, and generally almost every man amongst them carrying a Weapon in his understanding to defend the *Protestant* Cause. ...

[67]
Two things are with much earnestness usually Objected against the grant of Liberty;

First
*That it is unbecoming the Zeal and Concern a Magistrate should have for the Truth of Religion, to give Liberty to anything but what he thinks to be so, and that such a Lukewarmness, as Liberty to several Opinions supposeth, does no way become him.*

Secondly.
*That giving Liberty to men of several Opinions, is the way to propagate and encrease them, and is of great danger to a State.*

For the First.
It is very fit that the Magistrate should espouse what he thinks to be the Truth, and keep himself to the strict practice of it, and use all lawful means to posses others with it; let him use all the means Christ and the Apostles used to convince and covert men; but let him not lay violent hands upon mens persons, because he cannot satisfie their understandings ...

Tolerating men has no more in it, than forcing men; 'tis only a Negative favour, there is nothing Affirmative in it; a Magistrate will never be charged with Lukewarmness in Religion, that makes use of all Gospel-means to promote Truth, and that he may do, and yet never violate the due Liberty of any man's Conscience. ... /

For the second Objection.

*That giving liberty to several parties, encreaseth them, and makes them dangerous to a State.*

First, 'Tis very fit, that wheresoever you will suppose errors to be sprung up, all the means Christ hath appointed for that end, should be used to suppress them, and reclaim men from them; let their mouths / be stopped with sound Doctrine, and spiritual Censures; the onely Question is about the use of the Temporal-power in such things: And experience tell us, That since the World began to this day, Principles and Opinions in the mind were never extinguished by the punishing the body; That old saying verifies it,

*Sanguis Martyrum, semem Ecclesiæ*,[2]

Nay, there is nothing under the Sun to promote an Opinion in Religion, like making men suffer for it; the constancy and courage of men in suffering for an Opinion, will sooner perswade men to it, than all the Discourses and Sermons in the World. ...

Consider the giving the Liberty under these two heads.

First, The giving of it to several Opinions and Parties, where they are already actually existing,

And secondly, The giving liberty so, as will occasion and produce such Parties and Opinions.

For the first, Where there are several Parties in Religion already in being, and diffused all over a Nation, as the Case is with us, there is no way to secure them, but to indulge them, for they are by their number outgrown the political part of persecution.

For the second Consideration of Liberty, the giving it so, as will naturally produce several Principles and Opinions in men, he that would prevent that, must give no Liberty to the Protestant Religion, must not let the Bible be read by the Vulgar: There is no way to keep out several Opinions in Religion, but an implicite ignorant subjection to an imposed Infallibility, and to do as the *Turks* do, who will not have any Learning or Discourse amongst them of Religion, for that very Reason, because they will have no Religion but *Mahomet*, nor no learning but the *Alcoran*; such policy, to murder mens Souls, is hatched in Hell. /

The very Art of *Printing* was at the first thought dangerous, because it was looked on as a thing like to introduce several Opinions in Religion. Cardinal *Woolsey*,[3] in a Letter of his to the Pope, hath this passage about it; *That his Holiness could not be ignorant what divers effects the new Invention of* Printing *had produced; for as it had brought in and restored Books and Learning, so together it hath been the occasion of these Sects and Schisms which daily appeared in the World, but chiefly in* Germany, *where men begin now to call in question the present faith and tenants of the Church, and to examine how far Religion is departed from its primitive Institution. And that which particularly was most to be lamented, they had exhorted Lay and ordinary men to read the Scriptures, and to pray in their Vulgar tongue. That, if this were sufferered, besides all other dangers, the common people at last might come to believe that there was not so much use of the Clergie; for if men were perswaded once they could make their own way to God, and that Prayers in their native and ordinary language might pierce Heaven, as well as in Latine, How much would the Authority of the Masse fall? how prejudicial might this prove unto all our Ecclesiastical Orders?* Lord *Herberts* Hist. of *Hen.* 8.[4]

Liberty of Conscience lies as naturally necessary to a *Protestant* State as Imposition to a *Popish* State; he must be a good Artist that can find a right middle-way between these two. 'Tis the glory of *Protestant-*States to have much of the knowledge of God amongst them, and that variety of mens Opinions, about some less weighty and more obscure matters of Religion, as it much tends to discovery of the Truth of them, so it no way breaks the Bond of *Protestant* Union, where men generally agree in the same Rule of Religion, and in all the chief and necessary Fundamentals of Salvation. Liberty of Conscience in such States, as it is their true and genuine Interest, and without which they will but deny themselves those advantages they might otherwise arrive at; so with the forementioned *Boundaries,* can never prove hurtful or dangerous, there being always a just distinction to be made between those who desire only to serve God, and such who pretend that, to become injurious to men. And thus we have seen, that not only Religion but Reason, not only Duty but Interest, do invocate Princes and States in this particular: To whom it may fitly be said in the words of the Psalmist, *Be wise now therefore, O ye Kings; and be instructed, O ye Judges of the Earth.*[5]

FINIS.

Hugh Cressy, *Fanaticism Fanatically Imputed to the Catholick Church by Doctour Stillingfleet: And the Imputation Refuted and Retorted by S.C. a Catholick O.S.B.* ([?Douai], 1672), unnumbered sig., pp. 92–4, 96–9. Wing, C6898; ESTC, R1090.

# FANATICISM
## Fanatically
### imputed

*To the Reader.*
 THE report is very current that Doctour Stillingfleet wonders, and even complains that, having made a generall formall *Challenge to Catholicks to come openly into the field against him*[1] being ready with Weapons in his hand, he cannot yet have the contentment to give further proof of his Skill and courage against them. But surely it is not for the Doctours credit to make such a Complaint, when the world knows how all passages into *the field* are stoppd and even walled up, I will not say, by himself, yet at least by his Partizans; how *Stationers* apprehend greater danger in publishing *Answers* to his *Book*, then any *Books* of Sedition or *Treason*; and how during the space of a few months since his last *Book* saw the light, *Searches* into *Presses* have been more sollicitously exact, and more frequent dayly and hourly, then they have / been all the years taken together since his *Majesties Restauration*, *Inquisitors* searching into every hole, turning over every small paper, and rigorously examining both Maisters and Servants whether any thing has been written against *Doctour Stillingfleet*.
 How securely now may the Doctor triumph, and as oft as he pleases, multiply his *Challenges* of *Defiance* against *Catholick Adversaries* so bound hand and foot ... / Not one word falls from his tongue or pen to give his now Prelats warning of their danger from Presbyterians, Independents, Latitudinarians and other Sects, though all these conspiring against them had held their Necks so many years of late under their feet.[2]
 But nothing can be more ridiculous to those Sectaries (nor truly more deserving detestation from all loyall Subjects) then to see the same *Sectaries quondam* friend[3] *Doctour Stillingfleet* zealously pretending a care of the Safety of his *Majesty* and the *State* against the seditious writings and / practises of ill-principled Subjects, and at the same time, as if he thought the world by vertue of the *Act of Oblivion* had quite forgott the last twenty years troubles, naming none but Catholicks as such ill-principled Subjects, who yet alone among all Dissenters

from the English Church had all of them unanimously adhered to his Majesty, and for his Majesties sake had defended also the said Church against the *Doctor* and his *Brethren in evill*, the Sectaries. ... /

It is a sad thing therefore that not one *Protestant* will open his eyes, and give warning of the dangerous proceedings of their *Champion*. Now whether that task and duty deserted by them, has not been efficaciously enough undertaken and performed by the *Authour* of the following *Treatise*, I leave to all indifferent *Judges* to determine. They are also hereby entreated to impute the *delay* of this *Answer* to the true cause above mentioned ...

[92]
Yet all this will not discourage us from endeavouring at least, to justify that the *Doctour* and his *Churches* are *meer Fanaticks*.[4] This we confidently pronounce, and to make this good we will not, as he has done, exemplify in the Writings or *actions* of a few persons culld out, with an intention to baffle, affront and revile them, but we will demonstrate upon his own grounds and *Principles*, that the very nature and *Essence* of his *Churches* and *Religion*, is *pure putid Fanaticism*.

90.[5] Now a demonstrable proof of this the *Doctour* himself affords us in the 13. and 15. *Principles* at the end of his *Book*. His words are these: *Such a particular way of Revelation being made choice of by God (for the means of making known his Will in order to the happines of Mankind) as Writing, we may / justly say, that it is repugnant to the nature of the Design, and the Wisdom and Goodnes of God to give infallible assurance to persons in Writing his Will for the benefit of Mankind, if those Writings may not be understood by all Persons who sincerely endeavour to know the meaning of them in all such things as are necessary for their Salvation.* And consequently, *there can be no necessity supposed of any infallible Society of men, either to attest or explain those Writings among Christians.*

91. What is this now but *Fanaticism* in the heighth of the *Notion* signified by the word, to make every *Christian Soberly enquiring* into Scripture to be his own *Teacher* in *all necessary Points of Faith* (and it is no matter what becoms of *unnecessary Points*) and to be a competent *Judge* of the true sence of *Scripture* in them: all this without any regard to all *Externall Authority infallible*, or *fallible* either; for an *infallible* one being unnecessary, what necessity can there be of a *fallible Authority*, which none is or can be bound to *Believe*? If it be *Fanaticism* to attend to and believe certain pretended *Illuminations, Inspirations* and *Revelations* concerning particular / matters, perhaps of no great importance, with a refusall to submitt them to any *Externall Authority*: what is it to ground his whole *Religion* upon his own fancy, enquiring into the true sense of *Divine Revelation*? ...

[96]
94. Now though the Doctour takes upon him, and is generally conceived by others to be a *Champion of the Church of England*, yet perhaps it would be rashnes in me from his warrant alone to affirme that the Church of England (that Church, I mean which is established by publick Authority) does now at last ground her Faith on such a Fanatick Principle, as the Doctour in her name has layd: For then it might / indeed be truly sayd, that the New Faith of the Church of England, is the very Faith of New England.[6] The Doctour, how learned soeuer otherwise, he is but a Neophit[7] in this Church: and therefore all he says not to be swallowed presently without examining: if he wrong the Church of England, I am unwilling to wrong her with him.

95. And one particular thing which I have observed from his Book, makes me suspect that my Lords the Bishops will not avow this Principle imposed by him on them, which is, that his Book wants an *Imprimatur*.[8] Now if an Approbation was either not demanded by him, or being demanded was refused him: it seems strange that against order and Publick command it should be permitted to be so dispersed without any Controll. But the truth is, there is a great Mistery of late in that *Formality* of *Approbations*: for some Books want an *Imprimatur* for the Reader, which was not wanting to the Printer. Perhaps the Doctours virulence against poore Catholicks was so highly approved by the grave *Censor Librorum*,[9] that rather then it should be hindred from / doing mischief to them, he was content the *Principles* also should passe: which utterly destroy the foundations of his own Church. This may seeme more probable, because in like manner a Licence is given to the Printer for a Book of Sermons,[10] in one of which, composed entirely of Lying Invectives against Catholicks, and by a most horrible calumny imputing the Pouder Treason[11] to the Preaching of Catholick Religion, there is this passage becoming a Preacher of the Gospell; *I wish that the Lawes against these Foxes (the Papists) might be put in execution, as they were anciently against Wolves.* Nothing but an utter extermination of Catholicks, it seems, will content the charitable Preacher, who seems to intimate also, that in his Judgment it is fitt a price should be sett on every Catholicks head as formerly on Wolves, to be payed to his murderer. Such a Sermon as this the Printer is licenced to print; but he who gave it, being ashamed that his Approbation of so barbarous a piece should appeare to the world, has given order that his Licence should be concealed.

96. What judgment therefore in this / regard, to make of the Doctours Book, truly I cannot determine. Only this I may say, That if Prelaticall Protestants do allow him for their Champion, and approve the Grounds of his Religion, it is one of the most Signall Victories that in any Age has been gained by a single Doctour over a whole Church, the Governours whereof will be forced to acknowledge that they have no Authority to teach truth, or condemn Errours; that all the people (formerly under them) are becom *Prophets*, and that all their Articles, Constitutions, and Ordonances have been composed and enjoyned by an usurped Authority. ...

[Edward Hyde, Earl of Clarendon], *Animadversions upon a Book, Intituled, Fanaticism Fanatically Imputed to the Catholick Church* (London: R. Royston, Bookseller to His Most Sacred Majesty, 29 November 1673), pp. 1–7, 16, 103–6. Wing, C4414; ESTC, R19554.

# ANIMADVERSIONS

Upon a Book, Intituled,

## FANATICISM
## FANATICALLY
Imputed to the Catholick Church

IT was the wish, not the hope of the most excellent *Lord Bacon* in his never enough admired *Advancement of Learning*,[1] that good Books had the quality or faculty of *Moses's* Rod, that being become a Serpent, eat up, and devoured the other Serpents, which were produced by the Rods of the Sorcerers or Magicians: The number was so great in his time of / idle, and impertinent, and Seditious Books, and the number of the Readers who were delighted with them was likewise so great, that Books of Learning, weight and importance found little countenance, and few Men at leisure to peruse them, and he saw no remedy, but by such a miracle: What would that great and discerning Person think, if he had lived in these days, when the licence of writing, and publishing light and scandalous Books of all Arguments, without any rules or limits of modesty is grown the Epidemical disease of the Nation, and a reproach to the Government, in the violation of the Laws, the contempt of the Magistrate, and the general contagion that is spread abroad, and threatens the very peace of the Kingdom, at least disturbs the sober conversation of it? The spirit of *Martin Marprelate*,[2] which hath for so many years been expired, or extinguished, is revived with greater insolence, and improved, and heightned as well against the State, as the Church in a petulancy of language, in a style so new, and unbecoming Men of honest education, that the gravest arguments in Divinity it self, and Texts of the Sacred Scripture are handled in a manner, and fashion, and with such vain and / Comical expressions, as have not used to be admitted in the lightest arguments, or in sober and chast mirth. The important and vital parts of Government, the dignity of the Laws established, and even the Person of the King himself, and the greatest Magistrates are arraigned, censured, and inveighed against in such a bitterness of words, with terms so reproachful, as have not been ever used in good company; and as if the *English* tongue were too narrow to comprehend all the Ribaldry and filthiness of their thoughts and inventions, they coin new words of contempt and indignation, and make use of a Dialect never heard of, but in the company of Ruffians, and the lowest and most debauch'd of the People, which for wit sake they apply to their vile purposes; so that this extravagance (if not timely suppressed) doth really seem to threaten, not only a general corruption of manners, but of the purity, and integrity of the Language, and of the good humor, and good nature, and modest conversation of the Nation; and upon this occasion I cannot but lament the want of that caution and prudence which was heretofore observed, when this unruly Spirit first broke out in the time of *Martin Marprelate*, who had / a contribution of Jests, and Scoffs, and Comical inventions brought to him, by all the party who desired to expose the Church and the Government of it, to the contempt and scorn of the loose and rude People. It was not thought worthy of any serious Man to enter into the lists with such adversaries, or to take notice of their Pamphlets, but Men of the same Classis,[3] of the same rankness of Wit and fancy, and of honester principles were the Champions in that quarrel. *Thom. Nash*[4] was as well known an Author in those days, as *Martin*, who with Pamphlets of the same kind, and size, with the same pert *Buffoonry*, and with more salt and cleanliness, rendred that libellous, and seditious crew so contemptible, ridiculous, and odious, that in a short time they vanished, and were no more heard of. What was urged or insinuated by any Men of discretion and understanding, that might make any impression upon sober, unwary, and misinformed Men, was carefully and learnedly answered by Persons assigned to that purpose, that the Church, or the State might not undergoe any prejudice by want of seasonable advice, without mingling any of the others froth or dregs in their compositions, which they left to the chastisement / of those who could as dexterously manage the same weapons, and were fitter for their company: And methinks grave and serious men, or they who ought to be grave and serious, should be afraid of imitating such adversaries in their licence and excesses, lest they should get into a scoffing vein, which they should not easily shake off, or lose their credit with worthy Men, for dishonouring the cause they maintain ironically.

 A man will hardly be thought provident enough, or solicitous for his own peace, and credit, who having discovered this unruly frantick disease, will expose himself to the malignity thereof, by approaching so near the company of those angry Wasps, and Hornets, who are like to be willing to take any opportunity to be revenged upon a Person, who hath presumed to be offended with their manner of writing, and in the same instant, submitted his own to their censure, which is like to be liable to as many exceptions of weakness and impertinence: To which I shall only say, that whatever other faults they shall discover in this short writing of mine, they shall not find the same of which I complain; I shall give no body ill words, / nor provoke them by contemning their Persons; and I chuse rather to be at their mercy, than not to endeavour the best way I can to divert men from that indecent way of reviling each other; and instead of answering Arguments, to traduce the Persons who urge them. Truth is of so tender, and delicate a constitution, that it is defiled by rude handling; and hath advantage enough to encounter and conquer its adversaries, by the vigour of its own beauty, without aspersing the deformity of the other, farther than unavoidable reason makes it manifest: I shall not interpose in those Arguments, which are now most agitated in that scurrilous style that I complain of, but chuse to take upon me to make Animadversions upon a Book lately published, at least lately come to my sight, Intituled, *Fanaticism Fanatically imputed to the Church of* England, *by Doctor* Stillingfleet, *and the imputation Refuted and Retorted by* S. C.[5] The Author whereof professes himself an avowed Enemy to the Church of *England*, and would be thought as much an enemy to the foul custom introduced into the Controversies concerning it, and the liberty men assume to deride Religion instead of vindicating it; to wound the profession, by a petulant / and scornful mention of the Professors; and by expressions full of pride and vanity, and destructive to peace and government: and yet how contrary soever this way of writing is to his practice and inclination; he hath some jealousie of himself, that upon the insupportable provocation he hath received, some phrases of bitterness may have scaped his Pen, which he doth believe he hath very good authority not to make any excuse for, and there being such plenty of that noisom Gall[6] scattered throughout his whole discourse, it will be but just to take a view of his provocation, and whether his revenge be no more than proportionable to the occasion, and then whether the imputation be not rather confidently retorted, than reasonably refuted; and whether in the endeavoring the one or the other, the bounds and limits of all modesty and civility are not so far transgressed, that the Author is liable to just censure. ...

[16]
[I] shall make no excuse for not affixing my name to what I write, which I do purposely decline, not by the example of S.C. but by the assurance I have, that the publishing my name would be so far from bringing any advantage to the cause for which I am solicitous, that it would rather increase and propagate the prejudice that is against it.[7] I do therefore provide a more natural countenance to support it; and which legally will supply the defect of the name, by having it Licensed by lawful Authority,[8] without which it shall never be published. ...

[103]
Methinks Mr. *Cressy* seems to imitate the example of angry women, who think it lawful to give worse words than they receive, which is the natural progress of choler; he provokes first the Doctor by reproaching him with the number of *Fanaticks* amongst us, to tell him, that there is *Fanaticism* likewise in many of their Church, and so mentions the Visions and Revelations, and Miracles in many persons of great esteem amongst them, and by those pertinent instances puts him into / great wrath: and he again to be revenged on him will no longer be contented that we have too many *Fanaticks* in the Church; but will prove that the very *nature* and *essence* of *our Church it self* and *our Religion* is *pure putid-Fanaticism* ... And from this charge upon the Church, without any one instance he falls again upon the *Presbyterians* and *Hugonots of France*, and reckons up some of the opinions they hold, and maintain, and then says (*pag.* 94.) *That he must take the boldness to tell him*; (a great boldness indeed) *that the Doctor himself does hold the same, and if he denies it, it is because he is ignorant of what passes in his own mind* ... /

Yet after all this he is compelled to confess, with perhaps, *That it would be rashness in him to affirm that the Church of* England *doth ground her faith upon such a Fanatick principle, as the Doctor lays; and if the Doctor wrongs the Church of* England, *he* (good man) *is unwilling to wrong her with him*: And in this fit of good nature he makes a kind of an Apology for the Bishops, who may be deceived themselves in the Doctors principles, by the negligence that is used in licensing Books to the Press, or rather the Doctors virulence against poor *Catholicks* was so highly approved by the grave *Censor Librorum*, that rather than it should be hindred from doing mischief to them, he was content that the *Principles also* should pass, which utterly destroy the / foundations of his own Church, and so concludes with some instances of the perfunctory care that is taken in the licensing Books. The *Church of England* cannot but be now secure, when a *Benedictine Monk* is so vigilant as to stand Sentinel, that she may receive no prejudice from her own Children, and he doth very well to put the Bishops in mind, that they may be more solicitous what Books are suffered to be printed, who have no less obligation upon them, to look that no lewd *seditious Books* are sold, as that none such may be printed; And if this kind advertisement of Mr. *Cressy* hath that operation upon the Magistrates of all sorts, both the Printers and Sellers, and it may be the Buyers of the multitude of *Popish Books*, which are every day vented with as much freedom as the *Book of Common-Prayer*, they of his own Religion will have new cause to celebrate his prudence, and acknowledge the great advantage he hath brought to their *cause*, by his *pen*, as he hath to their *persons* by his *modesty* and his *manners*.

[Herbert Croft], *The Naked Truth. Or, The True State of the Primitive Church. By an Humble Moderator* (s.n., 1675), preface. ESTC, R9033

TO THE
Lords and Commons
Assembled in PARLIAMENT.

*MY Lords and Noble Gentlemen*, You have fully expressed your Zeal to God and his Church, in making Laws for Unity in Faith, and Uniformity in Discipline; for, as our Saviour said, *A Kingdom divided against it self cannot stand;* so the same may certainly be said of a Church, the reason being the same for both: And I call the Searcher of all hearts, the God of life and death, to witness, that I would most readily, yea most joyfully sacrifice all I have in this world, my life and all, that all *Non-Conformists* were reduced to our Church. But it falls out most sadly that your Laws have not the desired effect, our Church is more and more divided; such is the perverse nature of man, *Niti in Vetitum*,[1] obstinately to oppose Authority, especially when they can pretend the colour of Religion and Conscience; this carries so great an applause among the Vulgar (still envious at Superiors) that it is, as it were Nuts to an Ape, sweeter to them than any other thing this world affords: for the enjoyment of this, they will endure any thing, imprisonment, loss of goods, yea sometime of life also. And this is it which mainly nourishes our Divisions, gives great advantage to the growth of Popery, and threatens the total ruine of our Church. Many who were formerly very zealous for our Church, seeing these our sad divisions, and not seeing those of the *Roman* Church, nor their gross Superstitions (which their Priests conceal till they have got men fast) are easily seduced by their preten'ed Unity, and daily fall from us. This makes my heart to bleed, and my soul with anguish ready to expire, rather than live to see that dismal day of relapse into their manifold Idolatries. Wherefore I humbled my Soul before God in fasting and prayer, begging daily the assistance of his holy Spirit, to direct me to some healing Salve for these our bleeding Wounds: and therefore I have some reason to believe, that what is contained in these following Papers, comes from the great goodness of God, who never fails those who seek him in humility and sincerity both, which I am confident I have done; and this I am sure of, that no worldly designs have moved me to this, but have often tempted me to give it over; I am also sure, that there is nothing contained therein, which is contrary to the known Laws of the Land: in this only I confess I have transgressed, in putting it forth without Licence; and for this I beg of God and you, as *Naaman* did of *Elisha*,[2] *In this thing the Lord and you pardon your Servant*; and I hope you will say unto me as *Elisha* did unto *Naaman, Go in peace*: and I farther hope, this shall not cast such a prejudice upon it, as to make you cast it by, or read it with disgust. I do not expect you should approve any thing upon the account of my seeking God in this, but upon my Reasons alledged; nor do I expect that upon my Reasons you should approve all: yet I beseech you seriously consider all, and God of his infinite goodness direct you to that which may make for the Unity of our Church, by yielding to weak Ones (if not wilful Ones also) as far as your Reason and Conscience will permit: sure you cannot so loath all condescension, as not to loath more and detest Papal confusion, which certainly comes on apace by our division; and of two Evils, both Reason and Religion require us to chuse the less. Now doubtless you cannot think condescension (if evil at all, sure not) so evil as Papal Idolatry; and that Papistry is Idolatry, is so clearly proved by our Learned Dr. *Stillingfleet*,[3] as it were lost labour to say more of it. Condescension may seem in some respects imprudent, but whether in this conjuncture of affairs imprudent, I beseech you again consider well. The Wisest men have changed their Counsels and Resolves upon second thoughts, much more upon experience, and approaching evils not at first discovered. It is a common thing with Princes when they find their main enemies power encrease much, to make peace with lesser enemies, on conditions never before to be endured; Self-preservation being the prime Principle in all Creatures rational and irrational, springing from Nature it self, it should in nature and reason over-ballance any other consideration; and whatever is done to this end, if not sinfully done, must needs be wisely done. I most humbly beseech the All-wise God, and sole giver of wisdom, to pour down his Holy and Wise Spirit upon you. *Amen.*

Andrea Rivetus, Jr [Andrew Marvell], *Mr. Smirke; or, The Divine in Mode: Being Certain Annotations, upon the Animadversions of The Naked Truth. Together with a Short Historical Essay, concerning General Councils, Creeds, and Impositions, in Matters of Religion* ([London], April 1676), pp. 1–5, 7–10, 13, 76. ESTC, R214932.

Mr. SMIRKE;
OR, THE
## DIVINE in MODE:

IT hath been the Good Nature (and Politicians will have it the Wisdom) of most Governours to entertain the people with Publick Recreations; and therefore to encourage such as could best contribute to their Divertisement. And hence doubtless it is, that our Ecclesiastical Governours also (who as they yield to none for Prudence, so in good Humor they exceed all others,) have not disdained of late years to afford the Laity no inconsiderable Pastime. Yea so great hath been their condescension that, rather then faile, they have carried on the Merriment by men of their own Faculty, who might otherwise by the gravity of their Calling, have claimed an exemption from such Offices. They have Ordained from time to time several of the most Ingenious and Pregnant of their Clergy to supply the Press continually with new Books of ridiculous and facetious argument. Wherein divers of them have succeeded even to admiration: in so much that by the reading thereof, the ancient Sobriety and Seriousness of the *English* Nation hath been in some good measure discussed and worn out of fashion. Yet, though the Clergy have hereby manifested that nothing comes amiss to them, and particularly, that when they give their minds to it, no sort of men are more proper or capable to make sport for Spectators; it hath so happened by the rewards and Promotions bestowed upon those who have labour'd in this Province, that many others in hopes of the like Preferment, although otherwise by their Parts, their Complexion and Education unfitted for this Jocular Divinity, have in order to it wholly neglected the more weighty cares of their Function. And from hence it proceeds, that to the no small scandal and disreputation of our Church, a great *Arcanum* of their State[1] hath been discovered and divulged: That, albeit Wit be not / Inconsistent and incompatible with a Clergy-man, yet neither is it inseparable from them. So that it is of concernment to my Lords the Bishops henceforward to repress those of 'em who have no Wit from Writing, and to take care that even those that have, do husband it better, as not knowing to what exigency they may be reduced: But however that they the Bishops be not too forward in Licensing and perfixing their venerable Names to such Pamphlets. For admitting, though I am not too positive in it, that our Episcopacy is of Apostolical Right, yet we do not find that among all those gifts then given to men, that which we call Wit is enumerated: nor yet among those qualifications requisite to a Bishop. And therefore should they out of Complacency for an Author, or Delight in the Argument, or Facility of their Judgements approve of a dull Book, their own understandings will be answerable, and irreverent people, that cannot distinguish, will be ready to think that such of them differ from men of Wit, not only in Degree, but in Order. For all are not of my mind, who could never see any one elevated to that Dignity, but I presently conceived a greater opinion of his Wit then ever I had formerly. But some do not stick[2] to affirm that even they, the Bishops, come by theirs not by Inspiration, not by Teaching, but even as the poor Laity do sometimes light upon it, by a good Mother. Which has occasioned the homely Scotch Proverb that, *An Ounce of Mother Wit is worth a Pound of Clergy*.[3] And as they come by it as do other men, so they possesse it on the same condition. That they cannot transmit it by breathing, touching, or any natural *Effluvium*[4] to other persons, not so much as to their most Domestic Chaplain, or to the closest Residentiary.[5] That the King himself, who is no less the Spring of That, then he is the Fountain of Honour, yet has never used the Dubbing or Creating of Witts as a Flower of his Prerogative: much less can the Ecclesiastical Power conferre it with the same case as they do the Holy Orders. That whatsoever they can do of that kind is, at uttermost, to impower men by their authority and commission, no otherwise then in the Licensing of Midwives or Physitians. But that as to their collating of any internal talent or ability, they could never pretend to it, their grants and their prohibitions are alike invalid, and they can neither capacitate one man to be Witty, nor hinder another from being so, further then as the Press is at their Devotion, which if it be the Case, they cannot be too circumspect in their management, and should be very exquisite,[6] seeing this way of writing is found so necessary, in making choice of fit Instruments. The Churches credit is more interested in an Ecclesiatical Droll then in a Lay Chancellor. It is no small trust that is reposed in him[7] to whom the / Bishop shall commit: *Omne & omnimodum suum Ingenium tam Temporale quam Spirituale*:[8] And, however it goes with Excommunication, they should take good heed to what manner of person they delegate the Keys of Laughter. It is not every man that is qualified to sustain the Dignity of the Churches Jester: and, should they take as exact a scrutiny of them as of the Non-conformists thorow their Diocesses, the number would appear inconsiderable upon this Easter Visitation.[9] Before men be admitted to so important an employment, it were fit they underwent a severe Examination; and that it might appear, first, whether they have any Sense:

for without that how can any man pretend, and yet they do, to be ingenious? Then, whether they have any Modesty: for without that they can only be scurrilous and impudent. Next, whether any Truth: for true Jests are those that do the greatest execution. And Lastly, it were not amiss that they gave some account too of their Christianity: for the world has always hitherto been so uncivil as to expect somthing of that from the Clergy; in the design and stile even of their lightest and most uncanonical Writings. And though I am no rigid Imposer of a Discipline of mine own devising, yet had any thing of this nature entered in to the minds of other men, it is not impossible that a late Pamphlet, published by Authority and proclaimed by the Gazette, *Animadversions upon a late Pamphlet, entituled the* Naked Truth, *or, the true state of the Primitive Church*,[10] might have been spared.

That Book so called *The Naked Truth*,[11] is a Treatise, that, were it not for this its Opposer, needs no commendation: being writ with that Evidence and Demonstration of Spirit, that all sober men cannot but give their Assent and Consent to it, unasked. It is a Book of that kind, that no Christian scarce can peruse it without wishing himself had been the Author, and almost imagining that he is so: the Conceptions therein being of so Eternal an Idea, that every man finds it to be but the Copy of an Original in his own Mind, and though he never read it till now, wonders it could be so long before he remembred it. Neither, although there be a time when as they say all truths are not to be spoken, could there ever have come forth any thing more seasonable. When the sickly Nation had been so long indisposed and knew not the Remedy, but (having Taken so many things, that rather did it harm then good,) only longed for some Moderation, and as soon as it had tasted this, seemed to it self sensibly to recover. When their Representatives in Parliament had been of late so frequent in consultations of this nature, and they the Physitians of the Nation, were ready to have received any wholsome advice for the Cure of our Malady: It appears moreover plainly that the Author is Judicious, Learned, Conscientious, a sincere Protestant, and / a true Son, If not a Father, of the Church of *England*. For the rest,[12] the Book cannot be free from the imperfections incident to all humane indeavours, but those so small, and guarded every where with so much Modesty, that it seems here was none left for the Animadverter, who might otherwise have blush'd to reproach him. But some there were that thought Holy Church was concerned in it, and that no true born Son of our Mother of *England* but ought to have it in detestation. Not only the Churches but the Coffee-Houses rung against it, they itinerated like Excise-spyes from one house to another, and some of the Morning and Evening Chaplains burnt their lips with perpetual discoursing it out of reputation, and loading the Author, whoever he were, with all contempt, malice and obloquy. Nor could this suffice them, but a lasting Pillar of Infamy must be erected to eternize his Crime and his Punishment. There must be an answer to him, in Print, and that not according to the ordinary rules of civility, or in the sober way of arguing Controversie, but with the utmost extremity of Jeere, Disdain, and Indignation: and happy the man whose lot it should be to be deputed to that performance. It was Shrove-Tuesday with them, and, not having yet forgot their Boyes-play, they had set up this Cock, and would have been content some of them to have ventur'd their Coffee-Farthings, yea their Easter-Pence by advance, to have a sting at him.[13] But there was this close youth who treads alwayes upon the heels of Ecclesiastical Preferment,[14] but hath come nearer the heels of *the Naked Truth* then were for his service, that rather by favour then any tolerable sufficiency carried away this employment, as he hath done many others from them. So that being the man pitched upon, he took up an unfortunate resolution that he would be Witty. Infortunate I say, and no less Criminal: for I dare aver that never any person was more manifestly guilty of the sin against Nature. But however to write a Book of that virulence, and at such a season was very improper: even in the Holy time of Lent when, whether upon the Sacred account, it behoved him rather to have subjugated and mortified the swelling of his passions or whether upon the Political reason, he might well have forborn his young Wit, as but newly Pigg'd or Calv'd, in order to the growth of the yearly summer provisions. Yet to work he fell, not omitting first to Sum himself up in the whole wardrobe of his Function; as well because his Wit consisting wholly in his Dresse, he would (and 'twas his concernment to) have it all about him: as to the end that being huff'd up in all his Ecclesiastical fluster,[15] he might appear more formidable, and in the pride of his Heart and Habit out-*boniface* an *Humble Moderator*.[16] So that there was more to do in equipping of Mr. *Smirke* then there is about *Doriman*,[17] and the *Divine in Mode* might have / vyed with Sir *Fopling Flutter*.[18] The Vestry and the Tiring-Roome[19] were both exhausted, and 'tis hard to say whether there went more attendants toward the Composing of Himself, or of his Pamphlet. Being thus drest up, at last forth he comes in Print. No Poet either the First or the Third day could be more concern'd, and his little Party, like men hired for the purpose, had posted themselves at every corner to feigne a more numerous applause: but clap'd out of time, and disturb'd the whole Company.

### *Annotations upon his Animadversions on the Title, Dedication, &c.*

AT first bolt in his *Animadversions on the Title, the Dedication, and the Epistle to the Reader*, he denounces sentence before inquiry but against the Book it self, forgetting already his subject, so early his brain circulates; and saith, that, *Having perused the Book thorowly he is abundantly satisfied not only from his* Stile, *which is something Enthusiastick* (his speech bewrays him) *but from his* matter and Principles *if he stick to any, that the Author is a borderer upon Fanaticisme and does not know it*. Even as the Animadverter is upon Wit and Reason; for I have heard that

Borderers[20] for the most part, are at the greatest distance, and the most irreconcilable. What the *Stile* is of a *Title*, and what the *Principles* of a *Dedication and Epistle* to the Reader (for these, *if any*, the Animadverter ought here to have stuck to) it's indeed a weighty disquisition fit for a man of his Talent. But I have read them over, and so have others of better judgement, and find every sentence therein poised with so much reverence, humility, and judicious Piety, that from an humane pen (allowing the Reader any tolerable share too of Humanity) I know not what more could have been expected. And as to the Matter, it seems to be but a Paraphrase upon the *Principles* of the Song of the Angels; *Glory to God on high, on Earth Peace, Good Will toward men.* If to speak at that rate, and upon such a subject, with so good an intention, be to have an Enthusiastick *Stile* or *Fanatical Principles*, it is the first crime of which I should be glad to be guilty. What in the mean time shall we say to these men, who out of a perverse jealousy they have of the Non-conformists, run, which few wise men do into the contrary extreme, affixing such odious names to every word or thing that is sober and serious, that with their good will they would render it impracticable for men even to discourse pertinently concerning Religion or Christianity? Put it upon this short issue: If the stile of the Epistle before the *Naked Truth* be Enthusiastick and Fanatical, the stile of the Animadverter is presumed, and so allowed of, as Spiritual, Divine, and Canonical. ...

[7]
But in this next Paragraph the Animadverter seems to have out-shot himself, that not content with having passed his own Ecclesiastical Censure upon the Author, he forges too in his mind a sentence of the Lords and Commons assembled in Parliament, who, *he Believes* and *'tis probable,* would have doom'd the Book to be burnt by the Hang-man. In this he hath meddled beyond his last: but it is some mens property: yet neither is it so likely they would have done it, at the same time when they were about passing an Act for the easing all Protestant dissenters from Penalties, had he vouch'd for the / Convocation, his Belief, or his probability might have been of more value.[21]

But what has he to do, (yet they have a singular itch to it) with Parliament business: or how can so thin a scull comprehend or divine the results of the Wisdom of the Nation? Unless he can, as in the Epilogue,

*Legion his name, a People in a Man,*

And, instead of Sir *Fopling Flutter*, he Mr. *Smirke*.

*Be Knight oth'-Shire and represent them all.*[22]

Who knows indeed but he may, by some new and extraordinary Writ, have been summon'd upon the Emergency of this Book, to Represent in his peculiar person the whole Representative? Yet by his leave, though he be so, he ought not to

Undertake before he be Assembled. I know indeed he may have had some late Precedents for it, and for some years continuance, from men too of his own Professions. And if therefore he should Undertake, and to give a good Tax for it, Yet what security can he have himself, but that there may rise such a Contest between the Lords and Commons within him, that, before they can agree about this Judicial Proceedings against the Book, it may be thought fit to Prorogue him.

The Crimes indeed are hainous, and if the Man and Book be guilty, may when time comes, furnish special matter for an Impeachment. That *he has made a breach upon their Glorious Act of Unniformity, Violated their Act, their most necessary Act* (the Animadverter hath reason by this time to say to) *against Printing without a License*: and I suppose he reserves another for aggravation in due times, the Act against seditious Conventicles. For these three are all of a piece,[23] and yet are the several Pieces of the Animadverters Armour: and are indeed no less, nor no more than necessary: For considering how empty of late the Church Magazines have been of that Spiritual Armour, which the Apostle found sufficient against the assaults of whatsoever enemy, even of Satan; what could men in all humane reason do less, then to furnish such of the Clergy as wanted, with these Weapons of another Warfare? But, although these Acts were the true effects of the Prudence and Piety of that season, yet it is possible (but who can provide for all cases?) that, if there have not already, there may arise thereby in a short time some notable inconvenience. For suppose that Truth should one day or other come to be Truth and every man a Lyer (I mean of the humor of this *Parliamentum Indoctum*,[24] this single Representativer, this Animadverter) you see there is no more to be said, as the Case stands at present, but Executioner do your Office. Nor therefore can it ever enter into my mind, as to that Act particularly of Printing, that the Law-givers could thereby intend to allow any man a promiscuous Licenciousness, and Monopoly of Printing Pernicious Discourses, / tending to sow and increase dissension thorow the Land (of which there is but too large a crop already;) as neither of Prohibiting Books dictated by Christian meekness and charity for the promoting of Truth and Peace among us, and reconciling our Differences; no nor even of such as are writ to take out the Blots of Printing-Inke, and wipe off the Aspersions which divers of the Licensed Clergy cast upon mens private Reputations: and yet this is the use to which the Law is somtimes applyed. And this Animadverter, who could never have any rational confidence or pretence to the Press or Print, but by an unlucky *English* saying men have, or by the Text-Letters of his *Imprimatur*, arraignes this worthy Author for Printing without Allowance, as if it were a sin against the Eleventh Commandment. Though a *Samaritan* perhaps may not practise Physick without a Licence, yet must a Priest and a Levite *alwayes pass by on the other side* and if one of them, in an Age, *pour Oyle and Wine into the Wounds* of our Church (instead of Tearing them Wider,) must he be Cited for it into the Spiritual Court and incurre all Penalties?[25] This high Charge made me the more curious to inquire particularly how that Book *The Naked Truth* was published, which the Animadverter himself pretends to have got a sight of with some difficulty. And I am credibly informed that the Author caused four hundred of them and no more to be Printed against the last Session but one of Parliament.[26] For nothing is more usual then to Print and present to them Proposals of Revenue, Matters of Trade, or any thing of Publick Convenience; and sometimes Cases and Petitions, and this, which the Animadverter calls the Authors Dedication, is his *humble Petition to the Lords and Commons assembled in Parliament*: And understanding the Parliament inclined to a Temper in Religion, he prepar'd these for the Speakers of both Houses and as many of the Members as those could furnish. But that, the Parliament rising just as the Book was delivering out and before it could be presented, the Author gave speedy order to suppress it till another Session. Some covetous Printer in the mean time getting a Copy, surreptitiously Reprinted it, and so it flew abroad without the Authors knowledge, and against his direction. So that it was not his, but the Printers fault to have put so great an obligation upon the publick. Yet because the Author has in his own Copyes, out of his unspeakable Tenderness and Modesty begg'd pardon of the Lords and Commons, in his Petition, for transgressing their Act against Printing without a Licence, this *Indoctum Parliamentum* mistaking the Petition as addressed to himself, will not grant it, but insults over the Author and upbraids him the rather as a desperate offender, *that sins on* he saith, goes on still in his wickedness, and hath done it *against his own Conscience*. Now truly if this were a sin it were a sin of the first Impression. /

And the Author appears so constant to the Church of *England*, and to its Liturgy in particular, that, having confessed four hundred times *with an humble, lowly, penitent, and obedient heart*, I doubt not but in assisting a Divine Service he hath frequently since that received Absolution. It is something strange that to publish a good Book is a sin, and an ill one a vertue; and that while one comes out with Authority; the other may not have a Dispensation. So that we seem to have got an Expurgatory Press, though not an Index,[27] and the most Religious Truth must be expung'd and suppressed in order to the false and secular interest of some of the Clergy. So much wiser are they grown by process of time then the Obsolete Apostle that said, *We can do nothing against the Truth*.[28] But this hath been of late years the practice of these single Representers of the Church of *England*, to render those Peccadilloes against God as few and inconsiderable as may be, but to make the sins against themselves as many as possible, and there to be all hainous and unpardonable. In so much that if we of the Laity would but study our Self-Preservation, and learn of them to be as true to our separate interest as these men are to theirs, we ought not to wish them any new Power for the future, but after very mature deliberation. Forasmuch as every such Act does but serve, as some of them use it, to make the good people of *England* walk in peril of their Souls, to multiply sin and abomination thorow the Land, and by ingaging mens minds under spiritual Bondage, to lead them Canonically on into Temporal slavery. Whereas the Laity are commonly more temperate and merciful (I might say more discreet) in the exercising of any Authority they are intrusted with, and what Power they have, they will not wear it thred bare: so that if I were to commit a fault for my life, (as suppose by Printing this without a License) I would chuse to sin against good Mr. *Oldenburg*.[29] ...

[13]
Notwithstanding that he writes forsooth in defence of the Church of *England*; and *against so vile a Cause*, as he stiles it, and under the Publick Patronage. Which is most disingenuously done, as on other accounts, so in respect of my Lord Bishop of *London*,[30] whom he has left in the lurch to justify another mans Follyes with his Authority. But however that venerable Person, who has for Learning, Candor, and Piety, as he does for Dignity also, outstripp'd his Age and his Fellows, have been drawn in to License what certainly he cannot approve of, it was but his First Fruits, and a piece of early liberality, as is usual, upon his new Promotion, and I am given to understand that, for the Animadverters sake, it is like to be the last that he will allow of that nature. ...

[76]
But to the Judicious and Serious Reader, to whom I wish any thing I have said, may have given no unwelcom entertainment, I shall only so far justify my self, that I thought it no less concerned me to vindicate the Laity from the Impositions that the *Few* would force upon them, then him to defend those Impositions on behalf of the Clergy. And moreover I judged my self most proper for the work, it not being fit that so slight a Pamphlet as his should be answered by any Man of great abilities. For the rest I take *the Naked Truth* to have been part of that effect which Reverend Mr. *Hooker* foretold *Pref.* to *Ecl. Policy*.[31] p. 10. The *time will come when Three words, uttered with Charity and Meekness, shall receive a far more blessed reward, then Three thousand Volumes writen with disdainful sharpness of Wit*. And I shall conclude with him in his close. *I trust in the Almighty that with us Contentions are now at the highest float, and that the day will come (for what cause is there of Dispair) when the Passions of former enmity being allaid, men shall with ten times redoubled tokens of unsainedly reconciled Love, shew themselves each to other the same which* Joseph *and the Brethren of* Joseph *were at the time of their Enterview in Egypt*.[32] And upon this condition, *let my Book also* (yea my self if it were needful) *be burnt by the hand of the*, Animadverter.

FINIS.

# NEWS, LIBELS AND THE CROWN, 1670-80

Charles II, *By the King. A Proclamation to Restrain the Spreading of False News, and Licentious Talking of Matters of State and Government* (London: printed by the Assigns of John Bill and Christopher Barker, 12 June 1672). Wing, C3581; ESTC, R21853.

Charles II, *By the King. A Proclamation to Restrain the Spreading of False News, and Licentious Talking of Matters of State and Government* (London: printed by the Assigns of John Bill and Christopher Barker, 2 May 1674). Wing, C3583; ESTC, R37629.

'Mr. Lestrange's Examination concerning "The Rehearsal Transposed [sic]", taken by Secretary Coventry, Jan. 23' (1673), in *Report on the Manuscripts of the late Allan George Finch, Esq.*, 4 vols (London: HM Stationery Office, 1913–65), vol. 2, pp. 9–10.

Charles II, 'A Proclamation for the Better Discovery of Seditious Libellers' (7 January 1676) and 'An Additional Proclamation concerning Coffee-Houses' (8 January 1676), *London Gazette*, 1059 (London: printed by Tho. Newcomb in the Savoy, 10–13 January 1675/6). ESTC, P1830.

'Whereas there have been lately Printed, and Published Several Seditious, and Scandalous Libels ...', *London Gazette*, 1288 (London: printed by Tho. Newcomb in the Savoy, 21–5 March 1677/8), p. 2. ESTC, P1830.

'Joseph Leigh Citizen and Staćoner of London maketh Oath ...' (26 March 1678). NA, SP 29/402/143.

The growth of news and public discussion in the early 1670s alarmed Charles II and his government, as the perceived growth of 'popery and arbitrary government' was increasingly to alarm Andrew Marvell and others as the decade wore on. The Crown's response included repeated proclamations seeking to recruit public support against the mischiefs of the press and bolster pre- and post-publication measures. Marvell's pamphlets, meanwhile, aligned censorship efforts with impending popery and tyranny, making them a prime target for what they criticized. The pursuit of the elusive author and his work provides insights into the experience shared by others who questioned the Anglican royalist direction of government policy. An example was *A Letter From a Person of Quality, to his Friend in the Country*, reflecting the views of John Locke and the Earl of Shaftesbury, which was ordered to be burnt as a 'dangerous Book' by the House of

Lords on 8 November 1675. Others were condemned by the Lords committee on libels which met from February to April 1677.[1]

The royal proclamation of 12 June 1672 testified to increasing concerns over the circulation of news and political discussion, as a general phenomenon but particularly in the heated circumstances following the King's twin declarations in March of religious indulgence and war on the Dutch. The proclamation also reflected the burgeoning partnership of published information and coffee-house discussion, drawing on the 1661 Treason Act in its attempt to curtail publication and conversation deemed damaging to king and state, and emphasizing the roles of writers and speakers rather than print as such.

Proclamations tended to follow familiar patterns, in the second example here extending to copying the 1672 title, but each also had a specific context and concerns. By spring 1674 these included the criticisms gathering pace against the Catholic and absolutist leanings of the court, exacerbated by the recent prorogation of Parliament and, as the proclamation mentions, rumours of its dissolution. Pamphleteers stirred controversy over the prorogation's stifling of parliamentary debate on issues ranging from recusancy and the Duke of York's Catholic marriage to the failings of government ministers. As in 1672 it was against the ensuing 'common and ordinary discourses' that the proclamation was aimed.

The background to the publishing of Andrew Marvell's *Rehearsal Transpros'd* is well documented but the testimony of Roger L'Estrange remains a fascinating instance of the censor endeavouring to save the King from himself in executing press policy. The book's seizure by the Stationers' Company warden Sam Mearne, the royal support for its publication and L'Estrange's efforts at damage limitation all emerged in the examination by the secretary of state Sir Henry Coventry. L'Estrange well knew the value of propaganda but could not share Charles's conviction that the anonymous author had 'done him right'. Ironically L'Estrange's licensing of the book was in 1677 laid before the Lords libels committee by Mearne as evidence that L'Estrange falsely granted royal approval for books and sided with the fanatics.[2] Two copies of the account of the examination are known, with the most-used version that in *HMC*, 7 (1879). The variant copy used here derives from the *HMC* report on the Finch papers now held at Hertfordshire Record Office; recent inquiry suggests the original is missing. Amongst other variations, this version spells correctly the name of the bookseller Nathaniel Ponder, although it miswrites Marvell's title as 'Transposed' instead of 'Transpros'd'.

Proclamations were printed as broadsheets for public display as well as being amplified through publication in the official *London Gazette*, as were the two further examples here. The first proclamation in the *Gazette* of 10–13 January 1676 was more direct than the previous examples in naming the press as its target, although both 1676 proclamations took an indirect route to curbing its effects: one seeking to entice informers to expose the producers of unlicensed news and comment, the other dealing with the licensing of coffee-houses, but adding the demand for a recognizance of £500 against allowing scandalous books and papers concerning government onto the premises.

Marvell's name appears repeatedly in the annals of 1670s censorship, although the author's identity was frequently the matter under inquiry. The notice in the *London Gazette* of 21–5 March 1678 was typical of advertisements promising rewards for information revealing authors or others involved in illicit works, in this case *An Account of the Growth of Popery and Arbitrary Government in England* (1677) and *A Seasonable Argument to Perswade all the Grand Juries in England, to Petition for a New Parliament. Or a List of the Principal Labourers in the Great Design of Popery and Arbitrary Power* ('Amsterdam', 1677). Marvell was responsible for both but avoided being identified sufficiently for punishment. He died in August after falling ill.

The affidavit of the stationer Joseph Leigh, taken at the time of the *London Gazette*'s call for information, described the abortive attempts in the previous two months to locate and interrupt the press that had been printing *An Account of the Growth of Popery*. The difficulties of enforcing press control were evident in Leigh's testimony on the unreliability of paid informers. Historians have often used the lengthy summary of the document in *CSPD* but this omits various details, some puzzlingly, such as the name of the 'black man', Lloyd, brought into the affair. Little is known of Leigh himself – he is not included in Plomer's *Dictionary* – but he appears to have mainly published medical and alchemical works before becoming a warden of the Stationers' Company, when he was among officers granted a warrant to search for seditious and unlicensed tracts.[3]

Notes
1. *LJ*, 13, p. 13; *HMC*, 9, Part II, Appendix, pp. 69–79.
2. PA, HL/PO/JO/10/362, item 338, g6.
3. *CSPD*, 1 February 1675; H. R. Plomer, *A Dictionary of the Booksellers and Printers who were at work in England, Scotland and Ireland from 1668 to 1725* (London: Bibliographical Society, 1922).

Charles II, *By the King. A Proclamation to Restrain the Spreading of False News, and Licentious Talking of Matters of State and Government* (London: printed by the Assigns of John Bill and Christopher Barker, 12 June 1672). Wing, C3581; ESTC, R21853.

By the King.
### A PROCLAMATION
To Restrain the Spreading of False News, and Licentious Talking
OF
## Matters of State and Government.

CHARLES R.

WHereas by the antient Laws and Statutes of this Realm, great and heavy Penalties are Inflicted upon all such as shall be found to be spreaders of false News, or promoters of any Malicious Slanders and Calumnies in their ordinary and common Discourses, and by a late Statute[1] made in the Thirteenth year of His Majesties Reign, Whosoever shall Utter or Publish any words or things to Incite and Stir up the People to hatred or dislike of the Person of His Majesty, or the Establisht Government, is thereby made uncapable of holding any Office or Imployment whatsoever, either in Church or State. Notwithstanding all which Laws and Statutes, there have been of late more bold and Licentious Discourses then formerly; and men have assumed to themselves a liberty, not onely in Coffee-houses, but in other Places and Meetings, both publick and private, to censure and defame the Proceedings of State, by speaking all of things they understand not, and endeavouring to create and nourish / universal Jealousie and Dissatisfaction in the minds of all His Majesties good Subjects: His Majesty considering therefore that Offences of this nature, cannot proceed from want or ignorance of Laws to Restrain and Punish them, but must of necessity proceed from the restless Malice of some, whose Seditious ends and aims are already too well known, or from the careless demeanour of others, who presume too much upon His Majesties accustomed Clemency and Goodness, Hath thought fit by Advice of His Council, to Publish this His Royal Proclamation; And both hereby forewarn, and straightly Command all His Loving Subjects, of what state or condition soever they be, from the highest to the lowest, That they presume not henceforth by

Writing or Speaking, to Utter or Publish any False News or Reports, or to intermeddle with the Affairs of State and Government, or with the persons of any his Majesties Counsellours or Ministers, in their common and ordinary Discourses, as they will answer the contrary at their utmost perils. And because all bold and irreverent Speeches touching matters of this high nature are punishable, not onely in the Speakers, but in the Hearers also, unless they do speedily reveal the same unto some of His Majesties Privy Council, or some other His Majesties Judges or Justices of the Peace within the space of Four and twenty hours next after such words spoken. Therefore that all men may be left without excuse, who shall not hereafter contain themselves within that modest and dutiful Regard which becomes them, His Majesty doth further Declare, That he will proceed with all Severity, against all manner of persons who shall use any bold or unlawful Speeches of this nature, or be present at any Coffee-house, or other publick or private Meeting where such Speeches are used, without Revealing the same in due time, His Majesty being resolved to Suppress this unlawful and undutiful kind of Discourse, by a most Strict and Exemplary Punishment of all such Offenders as shall be hereafter discovered.

Given at Our Court at *Whitehall*, the 12th day of *June*, in the 24th year of Our Reign. 1672.

## God save the King.

In the *SAVOY*,
Printed by the Assigns of *John Bill* and *Christopher Barker*, Printers to the Kings most Excellent Majesty. 1672.

Charles II, *By the King. A Proclamation to Restrain the Spreading of False News, and Licentious Talking of Matters of State and Government* (London: printed by the Assigns of John Bill and Christopher Barker, 2 May 1674). Wing, C3583; ESTC, R37629.

By the King.
## A PROCLAMATION
To Restrain the Spreading of False News, and Licentious talking of Matters
OF
State and Government.

CHARLES R.
WHereas of late many persons ill affected to the Government have assumed to themselves a Liberty in their ordinary Discourses to censure and defame the Proceedings of State, whereby they endeavour to create and nourish in the minds of His Majesties good Subjects an evil opinion of things they understand not; And further to promote their Seditious ends, they do daily invent false News, and spread the same abroad amongst the People, to the great scandal of His Majesties Government: Whereof his Majesty taking notice, and in particular of that very false Report of an intention to dissolve this present Parliament, which hath not been under deliberation, His Majesty seeing no cause to change His resolutions taken touching their meeting: His Majesty therefore looks upon the Spreaders of that Report as persons Seditiously inclined and ill affected to His Service; And considering that by the Laws of this Realm great and heavy penalties are to be inflicted upon all such as shall be found to be Spreaders of false News, or promoters of any Malicious Calumnies against the State by their ordinary and common Discourses, to stir up dislike in the People of His Majesties Person and the established Government,[1] whereof His Majesty is sensible the persons offending are not ignorant. / and heavy penalties are to be inflicted upon all such as shall be found to be Spreaders of false News, or promoters of any Malicious Calumnies against the State by their ordinary and common Discourses, to stir up dislike in the People of His Majesties Person and the established Government, whereof His Majesty is sensible the persons offending are not ignorant. Nevertheless, that all men may be left without excuse who shall not hereafter contain

themselves within that modest and dutiful regard which they ought, His Majesty hath thought fit, by the advice of His Council, to publish this His Royal Proclamation, And doth hereby forewarn and straightly Command all His Loving Subjects of what state or condition soever they be, from the Highest to the Lowest, that they presume not henceforth by any Writing or Speaking to utter or publish any false News or Reports, or to intermeddle with the Affairs of State and Government, or with the persons of any of His Majesties Counsellors or Ministers, in their common and ordinary Discourses, as they will answer the contrary at their utmost perils. And whereas all bold and irreverent speeches touching matters of this high nature are punishable not onely in the Speakers but the Hearers also, unless they do speedily Reveal the same unto some of His Majesties Privy Council, or some other His Majesties Judges or Justices of the Peace; His Majesty doth hereby further Declare, that he will proceed with all severity not onely against such persons as shall use any bold and unlawful speeches of this nature, but also against those persons who shall be present where such speeches are used, without Revealing the same in due time, His Majesty being resolved to Suppress this Unlawfull and Undutifull kind of Discourse, by a most strict and exemplary Punishment of all such Offenders as shall hereafter be Discovered.

Given at Our Court at *Whitehall*, the Second day of *May*, 1674. in the Six and twentieth year of Our Reign.

## God save the King.

*LONDON*,
Printed by the Assigns of *John Bill* and *Christopher Barker*, Printers to the Kings most Excellent Majesty. 1674.

'Mr. Lestrange's Examination concerning "The Rehearsal Transposed [*sic*]", taken by Secretary Coventry, Jan. 23' (1673), in *Report on the Manuscripts of the late Allan George Finch, Esq.*, 4 vols (London: HM Stationery Office, 1913–65), vol. 2, pp. 9–10.

Declares he never heard of the book till the first impression was distributed. One Brome, a bookseller,[1] told him it was printed for Ponder,[2] 'who owned the thing and said that if the book were questioned, there were those would justify and bring him off.' Two sheets of a second impression being seized at the press by Mr. Mearn,[3] one of the Wardens of the Stationers' Company, Ponder came to L'Estrange and told him that the Earl of Anglesey[4] desired to speak with him. They went together to the Earl's house in Drury Lane, who spoke to the examinate in these or the like words:– 'Look you, Mr. L'Estrange, there is a book come out (the Rehearsal transposed) I presume you have seen it. I have spoken to his Majesty about it and the King says he will not have it supprest, for Parker[5] has done him wrong, and this man has done him right – Pray give Mr. Ponder your licence to it that it may not be printed from him.'[6] To this the examinate replied that since it was the King's pleasure he would not meddle, but that there were things in it not fit to be licensed, as '*the Roman Emperor's receiving a dagger*, p. 244, and *the wisdom of the King and Parliament exposed*, p. 310.' His Lordship took the book from Ponder and having looked at those places agreed that they were better out than in, advising / him to alter them, but let the body of the discourse remain. Examinate answered that he 'did not love to tamper with other men's copies without the privity and allowance of the author,' to which his Lordship replied that he knew nothing of the author, but thought the alterations might be made. After leaving the Earl, Ponder desired the examinate to give him a note to the printers, 'what direction his Lordship had given him from his Majesty concerning this book,' which he did accordingly.

'The next work was to read over the book, in order to a licence,' which was done in Ponder's presence, and the examinate 'changed and struck out several sharp reflections upon Bishop Laud[7] and Dr. Parker, and others also of a more general prospect,' after which he gave his licence, which being signed by a warden of the Company, was delivered to the clerk to enter. The clerk refused to do this, on which the examinate wrote to him, at the instance of Ponder, to know his reason, declaring that he, this examinate, 'disliked the thing as much as anybody, but that being over-ruled himself, he expected the Company's officers should likewise conform.' Ponder then told him that Lord Anglesey had sent for one of the Wardens and the clerk and threatened to bring the matter before the King and Council. Examinate and Ponder went again to the Earl, who was ill of the gout, and his Lordship after discoursing on the methods of the Stationers' Company, directed a more particular enquiry as to the point in question, and at examinate's request wrote a letter which is annexed to this examination.[8]

L'Estrange says, moreover, that the book was not printed according to the emendations of this copy licensed by him 'and so in equity not imputable to the licensor,' and the first licence being withdrawn, a second was desired by Ponder 'upon another title-page,' which was granted expressly with condition of using the corrected copy, which Ponder promised faithfully to do. *Signed* Roger L'Estrange.

Charles II, 'A Proclamation for the Better Discovery of Seditious Libellers' (7 January 1676) and 'An Additional Proclamation concerning Coffee-Houses' (8 January 1676), *London Gazette*, 1059 (London: printed by Tho. Newcomb in the Savoy, 10–13 January 1675/6). ESTC, P1830.

## The London Gazette.
### Published by Authority.

From Monday January 10. to Thursday January 13. 1675.

A Proclamation for the better Discovery of Seditious Libellers.

CHARLES R.

WHereas divers malicious and disaffected persons do daily devise and publish, as well by Writing, as Printing, sundry false, infamous, and scandalous Libells, endeavouring thereby, not only to traduce and reproach the Ecclesiastical and Temporal Government of this Kingdom, and the publick Ministers of the same, but also to stir up and dispose the minds of His Majesties Subjects to Sedition and Rebellion; for the discovery of such wicked Offenders, and to the intent that they may receive the severest Punishments which by the Laws of this Kingdom may be inflicted upon them, His Majesty (with the advice of His Privy Council) doth by this His Royal Proclamation Publish and Declare, That if any person or persons shall discover and make known to either of His Majesties Principal Secretaries of State,[1] or to any Justice of Peace, the person or persons to whom any such Libell, at any time since the last Act of General Pardon,[2] hath been, or shall hereafter be brought, and by him or them received, in order to Print or Transcribe the same, or the Place where such Libell shall be Printing or Transcribing, whereby the same shall happen to be seized; Or the person or persons by whom any such Libell at any time since the said Act hath been, or shall hereafter be Printed or, Transcribed; Or shall discover and make known to either of the said Principal Secretaries, or to any Justice of Peace, any private printing Press kept and used for Imprinting unlicensed Pamphlets or Books by an person or persons whatsoever; He or they making every such Discovery shall have and receive as a Reward from His Majesty, the Sum of Twenty pounds. And His Majesty doth further hereby Publish and Declare, That if any person or persons shall discover and make known to either of the said Principal Secretaries, or to a Justice of the Peace, the Author of any such Libell, which at any time since the said Act of General Pardon hath been, or shall hereafter be devised and made; Or the persons or person who at any time since the said Act have, or hath handed or brought, or shall hereafter hand or bring any such Libel to the Press, or to any person or persons in order to Print the same; He or they making such Discovery, shall receive and have from His Majesty, the Sum of Fifty pounds: And to the end that the person or persons making such Discovery, may without any charge or attendance, immediately after the same made, receive the respective Rewards hereby proposed, His Majesty doth by this His Royal Proclamation, require the Lord High Treasurer of *England*, or the Commissioners of the Treasury for the time being, that he or they do satisfie and pay the said respective Sums to the person or persons making such Discovery, without any delay or abatement whatsoever. And His Majesty doth hereby strictly charge and command all and every His Justices of the Peace, to whom such Discovery shall be made, that he or they with all possible speed do give notice thereof to His Majesty, or to one of His said Principal Secretaries, to the end that the said Libells may be suppressed, and the parties offending may be effectually prosecuted.

Given at Our Court at *Whitehall* this Seventh day of *January* 1675. In the Seven and twentieth Year of Our Reign.

## An Additional Proclamation concerning Coffee-houses.

CHARLES R.

WHereas His Majesty by His Royal Proclamation bearing date the *29th* day of *December* last, upon the Reasons therein contained, did Command and Require all manner of persons, from and after the Tenth day of this instant *January*, to forbear to Sell or Utter by Retail (to be spent within their respective Houses any Coffee, Chocolate, Tea or Sherbett, and did give directions to His Justices of the Peace, and the Chief Magistrates (within their respective Counties, Cities and Towns Corporate) not to grant any new Licenses to that purpose, and to revoke Licenses formerly granted. And whereas since the issuing forth of the said Proclamation, several Retailers of the said Liquors, by their humble Petition on the behalf of themselves and other Retailers, did humbly Represent to His Majesty, That there are great quantities of Coffee and Tea at present in their hands, for which the Duties are already paid; besides what are already Shipped in parts beyond the Seas for *England*, and cannot be Remanded without great loss to the Owners thereof. And further, thereby, (confessing the former Miscarriages and Abuses committed in such Coffee-Houses, and expressing their true sorrow for the same, and promising their utmost Care and Endeavour to prevent the like, for such time as they shall be permitted to Retail the said Liquors in their respective Houses) did humbly beseech His Majesty, That he would be Graciously pleased to give them some further time for the Vending of the said Commodities which would otherwise lie upon their hands. And did further Offer, That if they might be permitted to continue to Retail the said Liquors (within their Respective Houses) they would not onely take the Oaths of Allegiance and Supremacy, but also enter into Recognizances to His Majesty respectively, at the Sessions of the Peace to be holden in the respective Counties, Cities and Liberties where their Houses are, to be Conditioned in the Form hereunder expressed: His Majesty taking the Premises into His Princely Consideration, out of His Royal Compassion, and to prevent the Loss and Prejudice which might accrue to the said Retailers, so far forth as may consist with the Peace and Security of the Government, Doth by this His Royal Proclamation (with the advice of His Privy Council) Declare his Royal Pleasure to be, That all and every the Retailers of the Liquors aforesaid, which at the time of the Date of His said former Proclamation, did Sell by Retail the Liquors aforesaid, or any of them, shall have Permission to Utter and Sell by Retail the said respective Liquors, in their respective Houses, until the Four and twentieth day of *June* next; They and every of them respectively entring into a Recognizance of the Penalty of Five hundred pounds to His Majesty, before the Justices of the Peace, or Chief Magistrates, at their respective Sessions of the Peace, Conditioned in the Form hereunder written, and then and there taking the said Oaths of Allegiance and Supremacy. And His Majesty doth hereby Order and Declare, That His respective Justices of the Peace and others having Authority by the Statute in that behalf, to grant Licences, do not (upon the account onely of the said former Proclamation) before that time, Recall the Licenses formerly Granted: And where any Licenses now are, or before that time shall be expired, they do according to the Rules mentioned in the said Act of Parliament; and upon performance of what is hereby Required, Grant Licences to the said respective Retailers, which may continue in Force until the said Twenty fourth of *June* next, and no longer.

    Given at our Court at *Whitehall*, the Eighth day of *January*, in the Seven and twentieth Year of Our Reign 1675.

## The Form of the CONDITION.

*THe Condition of this Recognizance is such, That if the above-bound* A. B. *shall at all times hereafter, so long as he shall be Permitted or Licensed to Sell and Retail Coffee, Chocolate and Tea, use his utmost endeavour to prevent and hinder all Scandalous Papers, Books or Libels concerning the Government, or the Publick Ministers thereof, from being brought into his House or to be there Read, Perus'd or Divulg'd; and to prevent and hinder all and every person or persons from declaring uttering and divulging in his said House all manner of False / or Scandalous Reports of the Government, or any the Ministers thereof: And in case any such Papers, Books, or Libels, shall be brought into his said House, and there openly Read, Perus'd or*

*Divulg'd,* or in case any such False or Scandalous Reports shall be there openly declared, utter'd or divulg'd, if the said A.B. shall within Two dayes respectively next ensuring, give Information thereof to one of His Majesties Principal Secretaries of State, or to some one of His Majesties Justices of the Peace, then this Recognizance to be void, &c.

'Whereas there have been lately Printed, and Published Several Seditious, and Scandalous Libels ...', *London Gazette*, 1288 (London: printed by Tho. Newcomb in the Savoy, 21–5 March 1677/8), p. 2. ESTC, P1830.

W*Hereas there have been lately Printed, and Published several Seditious, and Scandalous Libels against the Proceedings of Both Houses of Parliament, and other His Majesties Courts of Justice, to the Dishonour of His Majesties Government, and the Hazard of the Publick Peace: These are to give Notice, That what Person soever shall Discover unto one of the Secretaries of State, the Printer, Publisher, Author, or Hander to the Press of any of the said Libels, so that full Evidence may be made thereof to a Jury, without mentioning the Informer; especially one Libel, Intituled,* An Account of the Growth of Popery, &c.[1] *And another call'd,* A Seasonable Argument to all the Grand Juries, &c.[2] *the Discoverer shall be rewarded as follows: He shall have Fifty Pounds for such Discovery, as aforesaid, of the Printer, or the Publisher of it from the Press; and for the Hander of it to the Press One hundred Pounds. And if it fall out that the Discoverer be a Master, or a Journyman-Printer, he shall be Authorized (in case of tracing the Proof up to the Author) to Set up a Printing-House for himself; and no Agent either in the Printing, Publishing, or Dispersing of the said Libels, shall be Punished for so doing, in case he shall contribute toward the Discovery of the Author of any such Libel.*

## 'Joseph Leigh Citizen and Staĉoner of London maketh Oath ...' (26 March 1678). NA, SP 29/402/143.

[f. 192]

Joseph Leigh[1] Citizen and Staĉoner of London maketh Oath that about January last One William Paxton being his former acquaintance and a scrivenor in Southwark came to his house and desired to speak with him at the Kings Head Tavern, in S$^t$ Johns Streete, where accordingly this Depon$^{t2}$ went and there found with him one — Webb and after some discourse they told this depon$^t$ of a Private Presse, and spoke with greate sence of the Publick danger of such Evils whereupon they appointed to meet this depon$^t$ the next morning, And that then they would be more pticular with him, And being met at the time and place appointed they then told this Depon$^t$ that the Presse was Erected at one Cartwrights, and then gave him Very distinct descriptions of the house, which was found true, when y$^e$ same Presse was seized.

Soon after this, Came forth a Book Entituled An Account of the Growth of Popery &c.[3] whereupon this Depon$^t$ had Recourse to the said Paxton & Webb thinking them fitt to doe service in discovering of the Presse which Printed it. They thereupon Readily Engaged to doe their Utmost and Paxton would something say that they could not only go within a few houses of it but to the particular house as easy as to any Rooms in Mathew Fowlers house[4] & Webb likewise told him he doubted not but to find another Presse of Cartwrights Printing of Primers to which the Depon$^t$ Replyed, Let me have this first, and you have your money for it, And then wee will after that to which Paxton Replyed, it's best or to that purpose.

Neverthelesse Execution after frequent meetings was not don Paxton Excusing of it that they left off worke for a while because of the taking of the Press at Mortlake, Afterwards when a fix't day was neare at hand Paxton comes & tells this Depon$^t$ / That they had by some Casualty broke the Spindle of the Presse and that they could not be at work soe soone, But a little while afterwards he came & said that they were furnish't but were not yet setled into work Principally by their feare to stir yet; But brought a Black man into this Depon$^{ts}$ Company for one of them which had wrought at ye Presse[5] And took this Depon$^t$ aside & told him he should give him money whereupon this Deponent ask't him what was fitt, he told him that he could not give him lesse than Ten shillings, soe this Depon$^t$ gave $^{Paxton}$ Ten Shillings to give him, and once or twice more he gave him money. Paxton told him his Name was Lloyd, At another time Paxton brought another (who this Depon$^t$ thinks was named Haynes) as another workeman he gave him noe money for he perceived he was drunk or Rather fainedly soe,[6] and Very Crafty.

Paxton after about a weekes absence & this Depon[t] seekeing of him, met by appointmt on Wednesday the 13th of this March, and amongst other discourses Paxton told this Depon[t] that Harrington was in this businesse of the Growth of Popery, And further that he would goe lodge that night where the Printing house was that he might be sure not to be mistaken, And that this Depon[t] might be Ready at an howers warneing But this Depon[t] had not heard from him since to [that] purpose

And this Depon[t] further saith that Paxton & Webb came to him about five or six weekes agoe being Saturday & told him they would shew him ye Printing house he went with them & they shewed him a house on Bednal Greene[7] they went by it and when they were past it Webb said he heard y[e] Noise of the Presse but Paxton said it could not be for they would not goe to work till the Thursday followeing Only it was a Silke Weaver they had put in the front to Damp the Noise for they intended to worke below stairs / And he desired that they would not goe till Thursday and then they would be fix't. But this Depon[t] with the Warden of the Company of Staçoners & some others went on Munday followeing, and search't strictly, but found noe footesteps of Printing having been there, nor any preparations for one to be there, Afterwards Paxton in further discourse speakeing of his own accord to this Depon[t] of this Traine of Men said they are Printing, and Dollaring, and the Bibell and all,[8] And this Depon[t] saith further that he did heretofore find by discourse with M[rs] Whyte in Newgate (who is now Condemned for Clipping & Coyning) that the Private Printers and Coyners were mutually knowne Each to other.

26. die Martij 1678                                                             Joseph Leigh
corā me Mgrō C
Miles Cooke[9]

# RESTORATION CRISIS, 1679-81

Charles II, *By the King. A Proclamation for the Suppressing of Seditious and Treasonable Books and Pamphlets* (London: printed by John Bill, Thomas Newcomb, and Henry Hills, Printers to the Kings most Excellent Majesty, 31 October 1679). Wing, C3514; ESTC, R33283.

Charles II, *A Proclamation for Suppressing the Printing and Publishing Unlicensed News-Books, and Pamphlets of News* (London: printed by John Bill, Thomas Newcomb, and Henry Hills, Printers to the Kings most Excellent Majesty, 12 May 1680). Wing, C3428; ESTC, R35883.

*A Short, but Just Account of the Tryal of Benjamin Harris, upon an Information brought against him for Printing and Vending a late Seditious Book called An Appeal from the Country to the City, for the Preservation of His Majesties Person, Liberty, Property, and the Protestant Religion* (London, February 1679-80). Wing, S3565; ESTC, R18707.

*An Impartial Account of the Tryal of Francis Smith upon an Information brought against him for Printing and Publishing a late Book commonly known by the Name of Tom Ticklefoot, &c. As also of the Tryal of Jane Curtis, upon an Information brought against her for Publishing and Putting to Sale a Scandalous Libel, called A Satyr upon Injustice: Or Scroggs upon Scroggs* ([London], February 1680). Wing, S4026; ESTC, R12969.

*The Triall of Henry Carr, Gent, at the Guild-Hall of the City of London, the 2d. Day of July, 1680* (London: printed by I.G. for R. Taylor near Stationers-Hall, [February] 1681), pp. 1-2, 14, 20-4, 26. Wing, T2190; ESTC, R2771.

'Articles of Impeachment of Sir William Scroggs' (3 January 1681), *CJ*, 9, pp. 697-9.

The escalation of the perceived 'growth of popery and arbitrary government' into popish plot and exclusion crisis was accompanied by the lapse of the Printing Act in May 1679 when not renewed by a Parliament divided and preoccupied then truncated by dissolution. The crown moved to fill the void by having royal powers authorizing search and seizure backed by a legal opinion solicited in the Privy Council from leading judges and counsel. The ruling in late October asserted a prerogative and common law authority for the king to act against seditious libel or any tract deemed dangerous to public peace. Among its most ardent advocates was Lord Chief Justice Sir William Scroggs, who was under fire from the press after the acquittal in his court of the alleged Catholic conspirator Sir George Wakeman. In the last week of October Scroggs declared in a printed speech that 'the Law wants not power to punish a Libellous and Licentious Press, nor I a Resolution to execute it'. His view that the King could prevent printing and publishing what he chose by proclamation was later recalled by his fellow judge Sir William Atkyns, the objection that this usurped a function of Parliament becoming a key complaint in the Commons counter-attack in late 1680.[1] The stage was set for the contest of Scroggs and the press, forming a crucial dimension of the deeper restoration crisis.

The message of royal power over print was spread in the proclamation of 31 October 1679, four days after delivery of the judges' ruling. Its similarities to the 1676 proclamation show how the ruling was taken to confirm, not create, such authority in pursuit of public peace, with the message purposely delivered as such. The urgency and directness of the command to seize presses and persons was nonetheless discernible, and became apparent in enforcement, with the October ruling taken as the expression of a major legitimating source in subsequent court proceedings.

The October 1679 ruling did not extend to pre-publication licensing but a further report of the judges to the Privy Council on 5 May 1680, announced in the *London Gazette* of 3–6 May, gave the view that 'His Majesty may by Law Prohibit the Printing and Publishing of all News-Books and Pamphlets of News whatsoever, not Licensed by His Majesties Authority, as manifestly tending to the Breach of the Peace, and disturbance of the Kingdom'. The *Gazette* soon afterwards carried the proclamation reproduced here, forbidding all printed news unless licensed by the king's authority. This reduced the field temporarily to the *Gazette* itself. The proclamation was dated 12 May at Whitehall but emerged in print on 17 May and carried this date in the *Gazette*.

Benjamin Harris appeared in court before Scroggs on 5 February 1680 charged with publishing a seditious book, *An Appeal from the Country to the City, for the Preservation of His Majesties Person, Liberty, Property, and the Protestant Religion* (1679). Harris's periodical *Domestick Intelligence* had been irritating the authorities since it began the previous July and indeed his arrest may have been linked to critical remarks about Scroggs in the issue of 20 January.[2] The *Appeal*, probably written by Charles Blount, circulated in pamphlet form and as folio sheets, both from unknown sources: Harris denied involvement in its printing.[3] It exploited popish plot fears to promote the King's illegitimate son James, Duke of Monmouth, at the expense of his uncle, the Duke of York, accompanied by warnings of 'Troops of Papists' ravishing wives and daughters, dashing children's brains out and cutting Protestant throats. Monmouth's reliance on the people was taken to ensure 'the Worse the Title, the Better the King', which along with protests at limiting parliaments was fixed on by the prosecution. Chief Justice

Scroggs and the London recorder George Jeffreys, who led the prosecution, were keenly aware this was a trial of strength in the public eye, in their opening and closing remarks censuring the vociferous 'multitude' present. Doubts over the applicable law were dismissed by Scroggs on the basis of the judges' ruling the previous October, and he castigated the jury for their qualified verdict, which excited the crowd in gesturing towards the possibility that Harris was 'guilty' only of selling the book innocently. The jury had not been allowed to retire with a copy of the pamphlet, nor was Harris permitted to address them. The bookseller was pilloried, fined £500 and imprisoned when unable to pay; Scroggs said he wanted him publicly whipped.[4] Harris recovered to claim fame as publisher of America's first newspaper, the single issue of *Publick Occurrences* in 1690.

In Harris's case, Scroggs observed that only Francis Smith was equally factious. Smith's turn for trial came two days later, on 7 February, on a charge of publishing a scandalous pamphlet critical of Scroggs's role in the Wakeman case entitled *Some Observations upon the Late Tryals of Sir George Wakeman, Corker and Marshal, &c. By Tom Tickle-Foot the Taborer, Late Clerk to Justice Clodpate.* Jeffreys noted that Smith's trial was being taken in shorthand and would soon itself enter public discourse, which was accomplished with the help of the printed account, to which was appended a summary of the trial of Jane Curtis for the satire *Scroggs upon Scroggs*. Smith, who faced repeated arrests and punishments in 1679–81, did not appear personally, his wife Eleanor telling the court he was too ill. Jeffreys said Scroggs had 'been libelled and reproached with as base a Book as ever was written against any Magistrate'. Smith's punishment was unclear, his trial judge inviting an appeal to Scroggs's mercy, although like Harris he was in prison when the new Parliament began to review the trials late in 1680. He was later to publish the tract which contributed to Stephen College's execution in 1681.

The prolific Whig writer Henry Care (sometimes 'Carr') produced the violently anti-Catholic *Weekly Pacquet of Advice from Rome* from December 1679 to mid-1683, with intermittent government interruption. In July 1680 Care appeared before Scroggs charged with having maliciously and unlawfully written and had published the issue of 1 August 1679, which depicted a Catholic physician (the recently-acquitted Wakeman) making justice deaf and blind. The content clearly prompted the prosecution although Scroggs also made the offence the mere fact of issuing news without royal licence, emphasizing the judges' ruling made two months previously (which as confirmation of prior law presumably could apply to a paper predating the ruling). Care's *Weekly Pacquet* had already been called in during 1679 on this basis, an attempted ban recalled in the impeachment of Scroggs. Evidence in the 1680 trial centred on proving the words were Care's, Scroggs remarking that one author found was worth twenty printers, as well as dismissing defence caveats about malicious intention, and complaining of interventions by the 'rabble' present. Care was found guilty but sentencing, deferred to October, was not followed through. The printed account took a further four months, appearing with an imprimatur dated 18 February 1681 that recalled a warrant to publish granted to the shorthand writer John Combe by the House of Lords on 28 October. This required Combe to obtain the approval of the trial judge, although by February this was hardly feasible.[5] The title page advertised an appended narrative of the treason trial against the 'popish midwife' Elizabeth Cellier. On being acquitted the previous June, Cellier had published *Malice Defeated* in vindication, only to be convicted of publishing a scandalous libel and jailed in September.

The October 1679 ruling and its application loomed large in the abuses charged on the judges when the Commons launched its inquiry into the alleged subversion of the law in late 1680. Sir Francis Winnington, who had been Care's counsel, accused them of substituting their private opinion for the judgement of Parliament in the matter of printing.[6] The main target was Scroggs, the Lord Chief Justice's concerted struggle to quash a critical press featuring in the articles of impeachment read in the Commons on 3 January 1681. The ban on publishing without prior authority, the large fines meted out, and the resulting imprisonment of Harris, Smith and Care among others, were taken to assume a power belonging to Parliament, to assist popery and to revive Star Chamber excesses. On 5 January the Commons moved to proceed with Scroggs's impeachment, sending the articles to the Lords, and to investigate the accusations against other judges, although neither process was concluded, the King proroguing Parliament on 10 January and in April ensuring the strategic retirement of Scroggs on a generous pension.[7]

Notes
1. William Scroggs, *The Lord Chief Justice Scroggs His Speech* (London, 1679), p. 4; *Grey's Debates*, vol. 9 (London, 1769), p. 308.
2. The *Protestant (Domestick) Intelligence*, 57, 20 January 1679/80. The paper, retitled due to the competing *True Domestick Intelligence*, urged those who had been 'oppressed' by Scroggs to come forward.
3. *ODNB*, 'Benjamin Harris'.
4. *CJ*, 9, p. 689.
5. *LJ*, 13, pp. 626–7.
6. *Parliamentary Debates*, vol. 2 (London, 1741), p. 3.
7. *CJ*, 9, p. 700; *ODNB*.

Charles II, *By the King. A Proclamation for the Suppressing of Seditious and Treasonable Books and Pamphlets* (London: printed by John Bill, Thomas Newcomb, and Henry Hills, Printers to the Kings most Excellent Majesty, 31 October 1679). Wing, C3514; ESTC, R33283.

## By the King.
## A PROCLAMATION
For the Suppressing of Seditious and Treasonable Books and Pamphlets.

CHARLES R.

WHereas divers Malicious and Evil disposed persons have of late Printed and Published many Seditious and Treasonable Books and Pamphlets, endeavouring thereby to dispose the minds of His Majesties Subjects to Sedition and Rebellion; and also Infamous Libels reflecting upon particular Persons, to the great Scandal of His Majesties Government: For the Suppressing whereof, His Majesty (with the Advice of His Privy Council) doth by this His Royal Proclamation strictly enjoyn and Command all and every His Judges, Justices of the Peace, Mayors, and other Magistrates, to cause all Seditious and Scandalous Books and Pamphlets whatsoever, being Libels against the Government, or against any Publick or Private Person whatsoever, to be Seized on, and the Makers, Printers, Sellers, or Publishers of the same, to be Apprehended and Committed to Prison, to the end they may be Proceeded against, and Punished according to Law. And to promote the Discovery of such wicked Offenders, His Majesty doth further by this His Royal Proclamation Publish / and Declare, That if any person or persons shall within the space of One year next ensuing, Discover or make known to His Majesties Privy Council, or either of His Majesties Principal Secretaries of State, or to the Lord Chief Justice, or any other the Judges of His Majesties Court of Kings-Bench, the Author or Printer of any Seditious and Treasonable Book or Pamphlet, every such Discoverer shall immediately after the Conviction of the Offender, have and receive from His Majesty the Reward of Fourty pounds of Lawful English Money; And to that end His Majesty doth hereby Require the Commissioners of His Treasury, or High Treasurer of England for the time being, to pay the same accordingly, without any delay or abatement whatsoever. And His Majesty is further pleased to Declare and Assure, That His Gracious Pardon shall be granted to any Hawker, or Disposer of any such Books or Pamphlets, who shall make Discovery of the Bookseller or Printer from whom he or they received the same; and likewise to any Bookseller or Printer of any such Books or Pamphlets, who shall Discover and make known the Authours thereof. And lastly His Majesty doth strictly Charge and Command all Officers and Persons whatsoever, to take notice of this His Royal Proclamation, and to be Aiding and Assisting in all things requisite for the Suppressing of the said Libels, and the Discovery and Apprehension of the Offenders, upon pain of being Proceeded against as Contemners of His Majesties Royal Authority, in a Matter of so great Concernment to the Publick.

Given at Our Court at *Whitehall* the One and thirtieth day of *October* 1679. In the One and thirtieth year of Our Reign.

## God save the King.

*LONDON.*
Printed by *John Bill*, *Thomas Newcomb*, and *Henry Hills*, Printers to the Kings most Excellent Majesty. 1679.

Charles II, *A Proclamation for Suppressing the Printing and Publishing Unlicensed News-Books, and Pamphlets of News* (London: printed by John Bill, Thomas Newcomb, and Henry Hills, Printers to the Kings most Excellent Majesty, 12 May 1680). Wing, C3428; ESTC, R35883.

## By the King.
## A PROCLAMATION
For Suppressing the Printing and Publishing Unlicensed News-Books, and Pamphlets of News.

CHARLES R.

WHereas it is of great Importance to the State, That all News Printed and Published to the People, as well concerning Foreign, as Domestick Affairs, should be agreeable to Truth, or at least Warranted by good Intelligence, that the minds of His Majesties Subjects may not be disturbed, or amused by Lies or vain Reports, which are many times raised on purpose to Scandalize the Government, or for other indirect Ends; And whereas of late many Evil-disposed Persons have made it a common Practice to Print and Publish Pamphlets of News, without License or Authority, and therein have vended to His Majesties People, all the idle and malicious Reports that they could Collect or Invent, contrary to Law; The continuance whereof would in a short time endanger the Peace of the Kingdom, the same manifestly tending thereto, as has been declared by all His Majesties Judges unanimously:[1] His Majesty therefore considering the great Mischief that may ensue upon such Licencious and Illegal Practices, if not timely prevented, hath thought fit by this His Royal Proclamation (with the Advice of His Privy Council) strictly to Prohibit and Forbid all Persons whatsoever to Print or Publish any News-Books, or Pamphlets of News not Licensed by His Majesties Authority. And to the intent all Offenders may know their Danger, and desist from any further Proceedings of this kind, His Majesty is Graciously pleased hereby to Declare, That they shall be proceeded against according to the utmost Severity of the Law: And for that purpose, His Majesty doth hereby Will and Command all His Judges, Justices of Peace, and all other His Officers and Ministers of Justice whatsoever, That they take effectual Care, that all such as shall Offend in the Premisses, be proceeded against, and punished according to their Demerits.

Given at Our Court at *Whitehall* this 12ᵗʰ day of *May*,[2] in the Two and thirtieth year of Our Reign.

## God save the King.

*London*, Printed by *John Bill*, *Thomas Newcomb*, and *Henry Hills*, Printers to the Kings most Excellent Majesty. 1680.

*A Short, but Just Account of the Tryal of Benjamin Harris, upon an Information brought against him for Printing and Vending a late Seditious Book called An Appeal from the Country to the City, for the Preservation of His Majesties Person, Liberty, Property, and the Protestant Religion* (London, February 1679–80). Wing, S3565; ESTC, R18707.

## A SHORT
## BUT
## JUST ACCOUNT
## OF THE
# TRYAL
## OF
## Benjamin Harris,
### UPON AN
## INFORMATION

Brought against him
For Printing and Vending a late Seditious Book called

## An Appeal from the Country

To the CITY,

For the Preservation of His Majesties Person, Liberty, Property,

### AND THE

## Protestant Religion,

On Thursday, the fifth of this Instant *February*, at the *Guildhall* in the City of *London*, There was an Information exhibited by the King's Council before my Lord Chief Justice *Scroggs*,[1] against *Benjamin Harris*[2] Bookseller to this purpose, *viz*. That He the said *Benjamin Harris*, did maliciously and designedly to scandalize the King and Government, cause to be printed, and sold, a late seditious Book called, An *Appeal* from the Country to the City, for the preservation of His Majesties Person, Liberty, Property, and the Protestant Religion;[3] and after it was read, *Mr. Recorder*[4] made a speech to the Jury, and the whole Court, to this effect.

Gentlemen,
I *Hope, This being a matter to be tryed in the* City *of* London, *Persons coming here in great Multitudes, come to blush rather than to give incouragement to it; and if we can give Your Lordship, and this Jury satisfaction that this Person is guilty of the offence, according as it is laid in the Information, I hope that both you, and all others that shall hear it, (for I perceive there is a great expectation this day from this cause,) I hope, I say, You will all abominate any man that shall offer at any such like thing. Indeed we live in an age where all sort of Faction and Rebellion is countenanced, Magistrates reviled, and scandalized by some persons, who think they have Authority so to do. It is just like such another kind of Religion, which some have now of late taken up, that rather than they will be thought to turn Phanaticks, they will turn plain Atheists, and others, who scorn to be either downright Rebels. This Book is as base a piece as ever was contrived in Hell, either by Papists, or the blackest Rebel that ever was: It seems to carry with it a fine Character, and has a figure of all plausible obedience to the Crown, to wit,* an Appeal, *&c*. For the preservation of His Majestie's Person, Liberty, Property, and the Protestant Religion. *But if any of you have seen it, I hope you will be so far from giving any countenance to it, as that you will, with me, think, 'tis so far from tending well to the Government, that it is only designed to rake up all Sedition and Rebellion, and the very worst of all Rebellion. I must confess, I would rather have believed that it was only the sake of lucre made him do what he did, for that would have somewhat extenuated his Crime, if he had not read it first; but then to go, and have it Printed, and exposed to sale, &c. this is a great aggravation,* /
*If the same sort of Insinuation had been used towards any private Tradesman, as hath been offered to the* KING *and Magistrates, I believe there is no man but would say, That e're this time he might have hid his head.*
*But Dissemblances of Pretences for the sake of the Protestant Religion now adays in his Shop will pass well enough, and Persons can tell you there how far you may go from hence to* Rome *with safety; and after they have blackened their mouths with Tobacco and Smoke, and do not rail against the Church and the Government, they are looked upon strait as no Protestants.*

*But still as to this Person, the farther to urge it, by way of aggravation upon him, he could vauntingly make his Boasts, when it was put home to him. Why he would venture to do such things, &c? That he had above a Thousand Persons who would stand by him in whatsoever he did.*

Lord Chief Justice. There was hardly ever any Book more pernicious to set us together by the Ears than this, nor any thing a greater Incendiary; One can hardly write a worse—

Says he, 'We in the Country have done our parts, in Choosing; for the generality, good Members to serve in Parliament; but if (as our Two last Parliaments were) they must be Dissolved, or Prorogued, whenever they come to redress the Grievances of the Subject, we may be pitied, but not blamed. If the Plot takes effect, (as in all probability it will) our Parliaments are not then to be Condemned, for that their not being suffered to Sit occasioned it.'

So that here is a sly way of casting it upon the KING Himself. And if it be not down-right Treason, I am sure, it is just upon the heels of it. 'Tis a most abominable Piece.

*Then were called the Witnesses, to prove that the Books were Sold in his Shop, and after they were all Sworn, first of all Mrs.* Grover, *a Printer's Wife,*[5] *stood up, who confessed she had half a dozen of them, but not of him; for he was either gone out, or not in the way, but she had them of his Man.*

*Then stood up one* Mary Darby,[6] *and she said, She had four of them.*

*After her, Mr.* Benjamin Tooke,[7] *at the* Ship *in St.* Paul's Churchyard *Bookseller, was Examined, who said he saw several Quires of them in the Shop. And being asked by Mr.* Harris, *How he knew they were all those Books? He answered, That he turned over a great many of them, and found them all the same.* /

Mr. Recorder. My Lord, he was so mighty zealous of this Book, of so great importance, no doubt, to his Party, that for fear he should be disappointed in time, he gave somewhat to hasten it.

Mr. Recorder. Call— the Printer's Man, and swear him. (*Who stood up, and was sworn.*)

Mr. Recorder. What did Mr. *Harris* give you, ha?

Printer's Man. He laid me down Six-pence.

Lord Chief Justice. And what, that was for hastening the Book, was it not?

Printer's Man. I cannot tell Sir, not I, but he gave me Six-pence.

Mr. Recorder. And what, did you do it in the Day-time, was you not at it in the Night?

Printer's Man. Yes, I was upon it in the Night.

Mr. Recorder. Ay, it was a deed of darkness, and so fit for Night-work.

*Mr. Serjeant Strode.*[8] My Lord, If it can be made out to your Lordship and this Jury, that he designed maliciously to scandalize the KING and the Government by it, we must acquiesce, but that, my Lord, he absolutely denies; but seeing it running up and down the Town, he gets some of them, and suffers them to lie up and down in his Shop, and this only as a common thing to get money, so that we suppose it may not lie within the Information, because it does not intentionally scandalize the KING and the Government.

*Mr. Williams.*[9] He in his Trade sold this Book, and that we admit; but, my Lord, it is a material part of the Information, that it was done with a malicious design *&c.* and we do not take it so, but for the other matter we submit to it.

*Lord Chief Justice.* Then you do admit, that he did sell some of these Books.

*Mr. Williams.* We do, my Lord, that he did sell one.

*Mr. Ollibear.*[10] My Lord, this Book was publickly sold in other Book sellers Shops before we had it, and so we thought in a way of Trade, we might do the like; but as soon as ever we heard there was any thing ill in the Book, we supprest the selling of it.

*Mr. Serjeant Strode.* They say, my Lord, the Printer had Six-pence given him by Mr. *Harris* — Friend, does not he come, and give you some money at other times? have you never had any of him before?

*Printer's Man.* No, Sir, I never Printed any thing for him before.

*Mr. Serjeant Strode.* Was not this Printed before you saw it?

*Printer.* Not to my knowledge.

*Mr. Serjeant Strode.* Pray ask the first Witness. Was not this in Print before you saw it in his Shop?

*Mrs. Grover.* Yes, my Lord.

*Mr. Williams.* My Lord, he is a man of other Principles than to do such things. /

*Mr. Lord Chief Just.* There is scarce any but *Smith*,[11] that is so Factious a Seller of Books, as *Harris*: All your *Domestick-Intelligences* are so; for which, you know, you have forfeited your Recognizance[12] almost in every Book.

*A Neighbour was called by Mr.* Williams, *to give an Account of Mr.* Harris.

*Neighb.* My Lord, I have known him about a Twelve-Month; and I have always looked upon him, to be a fair Conditioned, Quiet, Peaceable Man: He is, and has been so Reputed among his Neighbours. And I have never seen any thing from him, but what was very Quiet and Peaceable.

*Mr. Recorder.* A Book-Seller, that causes a Factious Book to be Printed, or Re-printed, if it was Printed before, is a Factious Fellow.

*Lord Chief Just.* You say right.

Mr. *Goodall* (another Neighbour of Mr. *Harris's*) said, upon his being asked, If he were acquainted with him? and, If he were wont to Oppose, or to Scandalize the KING or Government? That he never heard such a like thing of him.

Mr. *Recorder.* I presume, that none of these do stand by him, in any such thing: But he, being advertised of it, and being asked, *Why he would offer to Expose to Sale such a Book as this*? He answered and said, *That he had a Thousand Persons, that would Stand by him.*

*Call* Robert Stevens.[13]

*Lord Chief Just.* What can you say?

*Rob. Stephens.* My Lord, I have seen this Book several times in his Shop, and others too: And I have asked him, *Why he would so publickly Vend them*? (I did not indeed Buy one of them my self, but I caused a Man to Buy one for me) and he said, *He had several Thousands to Stand by him*: and he is accounted an *Anabaptist*. He said so before the *Masters* and *Wardens* of the *Company*; who questioned him, why he sold such Scandalous Things? and he said, *He had several Thousands to Stand by him.* /

*Then spake the* Lord Chief Justice *to this Purpose.*

Because my *Brother* shall be satisfyed with the Opinion of all the Judges of *England*, what this Offence is, which they would insinuate, as if the meer Selling of such a Book, was no Offence. 'Tis not long since, that all the Judges met, by the *King's* Command; as they did sometime before too: and they both Times declared unanimously, That all Persons, that do Write, or Print, or Sell any Pamphlet; that is either Scandalous to Publick, or Private Persons; such Books may be seized, and the Person punished by Law: That all Books, which are Scandalous to the Government, may be seized; and all Persons so Exposing them, may be Punished. And further; That all Writers of News, though not Scandalous, Seditious, nor Reflective upon the Government, or the State; yet if they are Writers (as there are few others) of False-News, they are Indictable, and Punishable upon that Account.[14]

So that, your Hopes of any thing of that kind, will be vain; for all the Judges have declared this Offence, at the Common-Law, to be Punishable in the Seller, though in the way of his Trade: The Books may be seized, and the Person punished.

As for this Book, in particular; You can hardly read a more base, and pernitious Book, to put us all into a Flame: It gives you such Incitements, and such base Incouragements, with such Reflections upon all sorts of Persons, (for I have Read it upon this Account) that I think, there can scarce be a worse made. He would set up another Man, that has no Title, to the Crown: For (sayes he) *the*

*Greatest Danger accruing to your Persons, as well as to the whole Kingdom, upon the KING's untimely Death, will proceed from a Confusion, and want of some Eminent and Interested Person, whom you may trust, to Lead you up against a* French and Popish *Army: For which purpose, no Person is fitter, than his Grace, the Duke of* Monmouth;[15] *as well for Quality, Courage, and Conduct, as for that his Life and Fortune depends upon the same Bottom with Yours. He will stand by You; and therefore, You ought to stand by him. And remember the Old Rule is,* He who hath the worst Title, ever makes the best KING; *as being Constrained by a Gracious Government, to supply what he wants in Title: That instead of,* GOD and my Right; *his Motto may be,* GOD and my People. He sayes, *Such a one would make a better KING; / for, as you see, the Worse the Title, the Better the KING. A KING, with a Bad Title, makes a Better KING, than he that hath a Good One; for, he shall be obliged to Comply with, and will humour the People, for want of a Title.* A Thing, which is of the basest Nature, that can be: And yet this Man must give Money, to hasten the Printing of such a Book; and he had several Quires of them in his Shop. Except the Writer of it, there cannot be a worse Man in the World; who, for Trival Profit, will neglect the Peace and Quiet of his Country, and set us all together by the Ears, for a Groat. And, Mr. *Harris*, if you expect any thing in this World, of this kind of Favour, you must find out the Author; for he must be a Rebellious, and a Villainous Traytor: For, though he seems to inveigh against *Popery*, it is only to be a Rebel. And certainly, he has rejected all the Laws of *God*, and all Obedience that Man requires; and prophaned all Holy Writ. He is some Body, whose Fortune does not suit with his Condition; and who, because he is not at ease and quiet himself, will let no Body else be so neither.

You have nothing more to do, but to give your Verdict: } *Speaking to the* Jury, *who presently with-drew.*

If there be any thing in Law, let me know it; because you go out.

Then one of the Jury asked my Lord, if they might not have the Book with them, which was there in the Court, and it was answered in the Negative.

Before the Jury went out, Mr. *Harris* would fain have spoke to them for himself, but it was not permitted him.

*Then, after a little while tarrying, they returned to the Bar.*

And being, as is usual, asked if they were agreed on their Verdict, and who should speak for them; they answered yes, and appointed their Foreman, who said He was guilty of selling the Book.

At which there was a very great and Clamorous Shout.

Lord Chief Justice said, that was not their business, they were only to determine whither barely Guilty, or not Guilty.

The Recorder would have had them given their Verdict by the Poll, but they all unanimously Cryed out, they were all Agreed, and then the Foreman gave the

Verdict again, Guilty. / Mr. Recorder then prayed, that he being for the King, Mr. *Harris* might stand Committed; who was thereupon presently delivered to a Tippstaff to be carryed to the Kings Bench.[16]

Mr. *Harris* earnestly beseeched his Lordship, that he might be sent to any other Prison, and named *Newgate* three or four times, but it was not granted him: Thereupon he said, I hope God will give me Patience to go through it.

Then my Lord Chief Justice spake to the Jury to this Effect.

I am sorry you gave Countenance to this Cause so much, as to stir from the Bar, when the Evidence was so full, and when I told you plainly, not only my Opinion, but likewise that of all the Judges of *England*, that selling this Book was an Offence at the Common Law, for which they ought to be punished: and yet with your Scruples, you give the Party (with their Hollows, and Shoutings) to take Advantage; though you did mean upon the matter, the same thing then, you do now: Yet you see, upon every little occasion, when a thing shall seem to thwart the Government, how ready they are to send up their loud Hollowings. It was not so prudently done as might have been done.

We had need look about us, for if at such a time, and for such a base Book, such Clamorous Noises shall be made, what shall become of us? Our Lives and Fortunes are at stake. Would I knew some of those Shouters, I would make them know, I would punish them: I am Incensed in the behalf of the Government, and of all our Lives and Fortunes, that such shall go unpunished.

*An Impartial Account of the Tryal of Francis Smith upon an Information brought against him for Printing and Publishing a late Book commonly known by the Name of Tom Ticklefoot, &c. As also of the Tryal of Jane Curtis, upon an Information brought against her for Publishing and Putting to Sale a Scandalous Libel, called A Satyr upon Injustice: Or Scroggs upon Scroggs* ([London], February 1680). Wing, S4026; ESTC, R12969.

An

Impartial Account

OF THE

# TRYAL

OF

FRANCIS SMITH, &c.

On *Saturday* the seventh of this *Instant February*, 16⁷⁹⁄₈₀ at the *Guildhall*, in the *City of London*, there was an Information between our Soveraign Lord the *KING*, and *Francis Smith* Bookseller,[1] brought before *Mr. Justice Jones*,[2] one of the *Judges* of the *Kings Bench*; and after the *Jury* was sworn, Mr. *Holt*[3] began after this manner:

*Mr. Holt.* May it please your Lordship, here is an Information preferred in behalf of the *KING* against *Francis Smith*, Bookseller, and it sets forth, that, after Sir *George Wakeman, Will. Marshall, Will. Rumley*, and *James Corker*, were indicted and tryed on the 18th. of *July*, 1679.[4] for divers *High Treasons* at the Sessions-house in the *Old-Baily*, before Sir *James Edwards*, then Lord Mayor of *London*, and the Lord Chief Justice *Scroggs*, and others, the Defendant, *Francis Smith*, published a scandalous Libel, relating to the late Tryals, which was intituled, *Some Observations upon the late Tryal*, &c.[5] the words are particularly set forth in the Information; to which the Defendant pleads not guilty; but if we prove it upon him, you of the Jury are to find for the King; and if you find he is not guilty, you are to say so, and no more, &c. Then *Mr. Recorder*[6] spake to this effect:

*Mr. Recorder.* My Lord, I am of Council against the Defendant for the King, who stands informed against for a very great Offence: the Information particularly sets forth, that whereas some certain persons were indicted at the

Sessions-house in the *Old-Baily* before the then Lord Mayor, Sir *James Edwards*, and other persons then in commission of *Oyer* and *Terminer*, and *Gaol-delivery* for that place, and particularly, my *Lord Chief Justice Scroggs*, and after the Tryal was over, and the persons thereupon acquitted, there was a Book, which is mentioned in the Information, printed and published, and it is a Book that is known by the name of *Tom Ticklefoot*; / a very abusive thing; but persons now being to grow wonderful witty in the beginning of their Books, in hopes to insnare people to read them, and to prevail upon them so far as to make them believe there is somewhat extraordinary by the title. You see, malice finds out all the waies in the world to insnare and gain upon the people; to so bad an Age are we come.

But I confess, it is the second time ever since I had the fortune or happiness to know this City of *London*, that I have known such expectations, as have been upon two Causes in this place: the first was but two daies ago,[7] the second is at this time, wherein is truly, a sort of countenance, I am afraid, too much given by persons that dare pretend to be no other sort of Protestants, but can impudently outface all sort of Governours. Now, as all persons ought to abhor and detest that damnable Doctrine, that men hope to be Saints in another world, because they may commit Murders in this; so this ought too as much to be condemned by all Protestants as the other, that men shall endeavour to rebel, and be factious in this world, that so they may be reckoned good Subjects: the One are as far from being good Saints, as the Others from being good Subjects. I take this occasion to speak all this before your Lordship, and this Court, because I hope the City of *London* will never be corrupted by the base insinuating of some idle busie-bodies in it. Men, who cannot, or will not be pleased, because (forsooth) every thing does not go according to their mind and fancy; and though by no means they will allow the *POPE* to be *Infallible*, yet every factious fellow will expect, that every one should pay him that tribute as *Infallibly*, as if he were the only fit person to give Measures to *Government* and *Governours*.

When we come to have extraordinary cases and persons, extraordinary occasions ought to be taken to inflict due and just punishments upon them.

And when they shall dare to come to disparage *great men* that act by *Supreme Authority*, men that act by their *Consciences*, and because they cannot be steered by the humours of these sort of people, therefore they must be looked upon as *Papists*, or at least, as *bribed*, because they cannot comply with that base humour which some sort of persons have.

I take notice of this to your *Lordship*, because one that is intrusted in as great a place for the welfare of this Nation, as any whosoever, is extreamly concerned in the affair of this day; I mean, the *Lord Chief Justice* of the *King's Bench*,[8] who, being assisted with / several other Judges, because, as far forth as it did appear to him, did deliver the sense of the whole Court, who, for acting according to his Conscience, and as he ought to do, hath been *libelled* and *reproached* with as base a *Book* as ever was written against any Magistrate whatsoever: If such things as this shall be permitted, then there will be an end of your *Lordships* sitting here, or any where else, or of any other that shall act as a Magistrate ought to act, and that shall not be afraid to do his duty. But such is the happiness of this *City*, in this *Jury*, that, I must confess, I receive so much the greater satisfaction that it comes before them: for as I know the men to be men of Loyalty and Affection to the Government, and will be so just to him, that if they do not find him guilty of the matter of the Information, they will acquit him; so, on the other side, they will not think themselves to be awed by a *multitude*, or inslaved by private insinuations, to debauch their consciences, either in respect to God above, or to the King, his Vicegerent here on Earth; therefore observe your duty to both, that you may render to *Cæsar* the things that be *Cæsars*, as well as to God, the things that are God's.[9]

Now as the *KING* is God's Vicegerent, so is every Magistrate the *King's* Vicegerent in that particular.

I would not take up so much of your *Lordships* time, but that I see this is a matter of great expectation: and I know that every word is taken in short-hand, to be commented upon as persons humors shall steer them. I do think, as being the *Mouth* of the *City* of *London*, it is my duty to speak thus much, that I hope, nay, I may dare confidently affirm, that the Generality of the City of *London*, all good men, and men of abilities &c. Are for the KING, and the Government, as it is now established by Law.

(*At which there was a general hem through the Court.*)

Having said thus much against this person *Mr. Francis Smith*, I must say, that if the way of common report were evidence enough to convict a man, he would be convicted without any more adoe, but such is the happiness of our Lawes, that they expect testimony, besides common fame.

I would rather a great deal it might be a caution to *Mr. Smith*, if there had not ben many before, and that he could not be convicted, and the Evidence not plain in proof against him.

Well, he printed this Book in the name of another person, one *Mrs. Brewster*,[10] he sold several of them in Quires to several people, and *Mrs. Brewster* questioning wherefore he should put / her name to this Book, truly, he said, he intended no harm to her, for he was resolved to save her harmless, and this we will prove to you; and likewise that several Books have been taken in his shop, and he justifying himself in what he had done, and his further resolution to expose them still to sale: and if we shall prove this to you, there will be an end of all sort of Justice, if in case that you, who are the only means of bringing men to justice, will not contribute to have justice executed where it ought to be; none can be legally punished, unless they be legally convicted; and I doubt not your honesty and loyalty, but that you will do your part by conviction, and by justice too.

Against all Libellers, I am sure, there is Law enough, and every honest man will endeavour to have it put in execution against them, as far forth as it lies in his way. I hope the generality of those that are here, do come to shew an abhorrency against this person informed against, and not to give any countenance to such base actions.

*Mr. Williams.*[11] Council for the Defendant. My Lord, the Libel is sufficiently infamous, we must needs own, and I do not come to justify the thing, neither *Mr. Smith* my Client, nor any body else that shall be guilty of it: The question is, whether he be guilty of, *&c.* as it is laid in the Information.

*Mr. Recorder.* Sir do you admit the *Record*?

*Mr. Justice Jones.* If you do not admit it, you must call in your witnesses, and prove what you can.

> *Whereupon* Rob. Stephens, Anne Brewster, *and* Margaret Clark[12] *were called into Court, and stood up behind the Jury.*

*Mr. Williams.* Sir, If you will give me leave, you shall hear what we will admit.

*Mr. Recorder.* Come, come, Sir, if you do not admit the *Record*, we will have none of your Anticipations.

*Mr. Williams.* What call you your speech but Anticipation?

My Lord, the poor man, my Client, is a lanquishing, sick, and dying man, and one that is almost ruined, if any submission will serve the turn, he will give all the submission that is fit for a man to give: all that we say is this, that he did not order this to be Printed, as it is laid in the Information. – But I think we may admit –

*Mr. Fettiplace* said, (who was Council on the same side) he had no such order given him by his Client, as to admit the Record.

Then they were just going on to swear the witnesses, but / Mr. Justice *Jones* said, *It would be very well if they would admit,* &c. *Defendant come to submission.*

*Mr. Recorder.* Ay, that is your best way, for it would be a great means to testifie that your submission is really intended as a submission; but if it be to prepare you to think that you are innocent, then we will not have your submission – And I am for a sinners Repentance with all my heart.

*Mr. Justice Jones.* If your Client be willing to submit, let the *KING* have a Verdict in Law, and then he will find my Lord Chief Justice *Scroggs* full of pity and compassion; and if I can see any signs of Repentance, I will promise you to intercede to my Lord for him.

*Mr. Williams.* One that came from my Client told me, that if he had offended, he would submit to any thing: and now here is his wife come.

*Mr. Justice Jones.* I would save him if I can, if he will throw himself into mercy.

Well, what do you say, *Mrs.* for your Husband?

*Mrs. Smith.*[13] My Lord, my Husband is very sick and weak, and is not able to come himself, or else he would have done it; but I asked Mr. *Williams* if it were not best to submit to the Court.

Mr. *Justice Jones.* Are you content to own it shall be so?

*Mrs. Smith.* I leave it to the Gentlemen, my Council, I shall acquiesce in what they think fitting.

Mr. *Williams.* Then I presume to admit the *Record.*

Mr. *Justice Jones.* (*Speaking to the Jury.*) Then you are to find for the *KING.* 'Tis the Cause of the *KING*, although only my Lord Chief Justice be concerned. 'Tis a high scandal, a great scandal against a great Officer and Magistrate of the *KING.* I will say nothing more to aggravate the offence at this time, because I would invite Repentance in all persons that have offended in this, or the like cases.

> *Then the Jury, being asked whether they were agreed on their Verdict, said yes, and chusing their Fore-man to speak for them, he gave the Verdict, guilty.*

Mr. *Justice Jones.* Well, Mistress, you have done very well, if, now you for your Husband came here to make a publick acknowledgement of his guiltiness, hereafter he shall go, and ingeniously make submission to my Lord, I know he is a person of that pitty and compassion, that he loves no mans ruine, but / delights rather in the universal welfare of all people; and I promise this, that I will be an intercessor to my Lord in your Husbands behalf.

Mr. *Recorder.* And as far forth as I can contribute to it, I will do the same.

*Then came on the Tryal of* Jane Curtis,[14] *Wife of* Langley Curtis, *for Publishing and Selling a Seditious Libel, called,* A Satyr upon Injustice: *Or* Scroggs upon Scroggs.[15]

*Mr Holt.* May it please Your Lordship, and Gentlemen of the Jury, here is an Information brought against *Jane Curtis*, and it sets forth, that the defendant did publish and put to sale a seditious Libel against my Lord Chief Justice *Scroggs*, the Defendant pleads not Guilty, if we prove it upon her, you are to find for the KING, and if not you are to say so, and no more.

Mr. *Williams* said (who was a Council for the Defendant) he would admit the Record, whereupon they proceeded no further to tryal, but the woman being called, she said,

*Mrs. Curtis.* I was ignorant in the matter, and knew no such thing, my Lord, my Husband, and please your Lordship was in the Country a hundred miles off of me, in *Lincolnshire.*

*Mr. Justice Jones.* You did it ignorantly, and simply, without any malice, and I suppose, you are heartily sorry for it. You see your Neighbour there Mrs. *Smith*, hath shewed good discretion in the behalf of her Husband; she has ingeniously declared that he shall come and make submission, and if I find you as submissive, and as sorry for what you have done, I may do the like for you.

*Mrs Curtis.* In any thing that I have done, I know not myself Guilty, and if I am, I beg your Lordships pardon with all my heart, my Lord, or anybodies else.

*Mr. Justice Jones.* I know you will find mercy from my Lord *Chief Justice*, and therefore go and make your submission.

Then the Jury proceeded to give their verdict, and there Foreman said, Guilty.[16]

*The Triall of Henry Carr, Gent, at the Guild-Hall of the City of London, the 2d. Day of July, 1680* (London: printed by I.G. for R. Taylor near Stationers-Hall, [February] 1681), pp. 1–2, 14, 20–4, 26. Wing, T2190; ESTC, R2771.

Recorder.[1]

THIS Person[2] among others, intending to Scandalize the Government, hath caused a Book to be published, which I have here in my Hand, called, *The Weekly Packet of Advice from Rome*,[3] there are some Papers besides what are bound up together, that are continued on, which, my Lord, would not be amiss for us that are of the Kings Counsel to take notice of, not only for the *Juries* Satisfaction, but likewise for the Satisfaction of this great Auditory, some whereof I know come to pick *Advantage*, and to know whether or no Rascals may not have Liberty to print what they please. Now all the Judges of *England* having been met together,[4] to know whether any Person whatsoever may expose to the publick Knowledge any manner of Intelligence, or any matter whatsoever that concerns the Publick? They gave it in as their Resolution, that no Person whatsoever could expose to the publick Knowledge any thing that concerned the Affairs of the Publick without Licence from the King, or from such Persons as he thought fit to entrust with that Affair. But such is the Age that we live in, that a man that hath Wit enough for to libell any Man in the Government, thinks he hath Licence enough to expose that Man to publick Knowledge also. And they do it under specious Pretences, because they think that any man may be exposed to the publick Censure, that they can either call a *Papist*, or / but *popishly* affected, and that man is either the one or the other, that is not agreeable to every Rascally Humour that some People affect. I acknowledge, my Lord, that any man that will in a Legal Manner endeavour to suppress *Popery*, ought to be encouraged in his Endeavour, to the utmost, but if in Case any man will be transported with Zeal, because he is of a Party, and under pretence of endeavouring to Suppress *Popery*, should support a *Party*, that man ought to be detected. The Author of this Pacquet of *Advice from Rome*, or the Publisher of it, Mr. *Carr*, that is now the Defendant, he thinks he can scratch the Itch of the *Age*, and that he may Libel any man concerned in the Government, if he can but call him a *Papist* or *popishly* affected; let a man be never so honest, let a man be never so much for the Support of that Religion that every honest Man ought to Support, that is, the *Protestant Religion* as it is Established by Law, without going to *Rome* or *Amsterdam* for Assistance. I will not mention the Persons that are concerned in it, but I will *apply* my self wholly to this matter, that it is the Opinion of all the Judges of *England*, that it is the Law of the Land, that no Person should offer to expose to publick Knowledge any thing that concerns the Government without the Kings immediate Licence. Now we are to try whether this Person exposed this thing to public Knowledge, and that is matter, Gentlemen, that you are to trie. The other is the Business of the Court, we are to say whether, if we prove the Fact, this man is guilty of Punishment, and no doubt the Justice of the Nation will punish him. But when I see so many swarm about me, I am willing to hear what Proof there is.

Sir *Francis Winnington*,[5] I am of Counsel for the Defendant, I only offer it to your Lordship, that the Information may be proved. ....

[14]
Sir. *F.W.* ... Now, my Lord, I say, I must submit it to your Lordship, I say, that as to the causing it to be Printed, or the causing it to be Published, or that this individual Paragraph was writ by him in Order to its being Printed or published, my Lord, I say, there is but remote and conjectual Evidence, and an angry *Papist* might contrive this way to have an Innocent *Protestant* found guilty.

*People.* Hem —

*L.C.J.*[6] You see what a Case we are in, Gentlemen, You see what a sort of People we are got among. Go on Sir *Francis.*

Sir *F.W.* With your Lordships leave, I have one thing to put to your Lordship. The Information sayes, *false, illicite, & malitiose.* I know there are some things that do imply Malice in themselves. Truly, my Lord, I am upon a tender Point, and know not how to express my self. I say, supposing it should fall out, that this Man writ this Book, and he might have some little extravagancies in his Head in writing, whether this Man did it maliciously to scandalize the Government, as the *Information* says, is a Question. Truely, my Lord, there is many an indiscreet Act a man may be guilty of, that cannot be called a malitious Act; and that is the second thing, there must be Evidence that this Man did it maliciously, or that he did it with a design to scandalize the Government. If you be of Opinion, that it is otherwise, that is, in your Lordships Breast, we are of the Negative, and we say, we can't prove a Negative. But if you find him Innocent, I suppose there will be no Cause to complain of him afterwards, for he had no Malice in his Heart. ...

[20]
*L.C.J.* Really, Gentlemen, I thought not that this had been a Cause of that Moment, that now I find it. For their very *Disturbance* hath *altered* it from Mr. *Carr's,* to a publick concern.[7] The noise which they make, this way that these People use, that with their shouts and noise attend the cause, hath *quite spoiled it.* As in the Case of *Harris.*[8] But those People that did then attend him, leave following him in a Goal, *for Five Hundred Pounds,* which may be five shillings a piece had discharged him of, if they had been as free of their purses as they are of their noises and acclamations: So that in Truth, they are only violent against

the Government whilest they can make shouts and noises, but if it come once to deliver a man from a penal sum they will let him rott in Goal.[9] ... [T]hey prove themselves / hereby, Enemies to the *Government*, and false to that *Interest*, and *Men* that they seem to espouse; that come only here to affront a *Court of Justice* with their Shouts and Noises. ... And, let them know, it hath turned this mans Cause, into a publick Cause, because, here are People that do espouse it, and the Government is hereby concerned much more than by any one Action that this *Carr* could have done. I have said so much the more of this, that I might shew you to what a sad Cause this is brought, from what at first it was. For, if it had past without such a noise, as you see how they express themselves, I should not have thought much matter in it, and though, you had convicted him, I should have thought a better / *Sentence* might have served the turn: but, *they have undone Carr, if you find him guilty,* and so, it's like to prove, when ever there is a popular attendence upon publick Causes that concern the Government. ...

The Question is, whether he was the Author, or Publisher of this. You hear, he is thought the Author, but say his Councel, it is not plain, and that is true. But, it seems by their own Witnesses, to any mans Understanding, that they look't upon him as the Author. But then, is he the Author, and Publisher of this particular Book? I had rather, Mr. *Carr*, with all his Faults about him, and his Hummers, should go away with applause, and have him found not guilty, than do him wrong in one Circumstance: for, I come to try Causes according to the truth of Fact, I come not to plead on one side or another. Not to Condemn Men that are Innocent; nor, to acquit them, if they be guilty. Now, it remaines for you to consider, *what Proofs you have, as to this particular Book,* against which, the Information lies. And that's the Printer himself,[10] who is one of the best sorts of Evidence that can be hand: for, you very well know, that Evidences of Fact, are to be expected according to the nature of the thing. ... /

*As* for those Words, *Illicite, malitiose,* unlawfull; for that I must recite what Mr. *Recorder* told you of at first, what all the Judges of *England* have declared under their hands. The words, I remember are these, when by the Kings Command, we were to give in our Opinion, what was to be done in point of the regulation of the Press. We did all subscribe, that to Print, or Publish any *News-Books* or *Pamphlets of News* whatsoever, is illegal; that, it is a manifest intent to the Breach of the Peace, and they may be proceeded against by Law for an illegal thing. Suppose now, that this thing is not scandalous, what then. If there had been no reflection in this Book at all, yet, it is *illicite*, and the Author ought to be convicted for it. And that is for a publick notice to all People, and especially, *Printers*, and *Booksellers*, that they ought to Print no Book, or Pamphlet of News whatsoever, without Authority. So as he is to be convicted for it as a thing *illicite* done, not having Authority. *And* I will assure you, if you find any of those Papers,

I shall be more merciful in the Consideration of their Punishment, if it be inoffencive. But, if so be they will undertake to Print News foolishly, they ought to Be punished, and shall be punished, if they do it without *A*uthority, though, there is nothing reflecting on the Government; as an unlawful thing. The reason is plain. So fond are Men in these Days, that when they will deny their Children a penny for Bread, they will lay it out for a Pamphlet. *A*nd it did so swarm, and the Temptations were so great, that no man could keep two pence in his Pocket / because of the News. But still, they never repented of laying out their Mony, till they found, there was nothing against the Government. This is not worth a Farthing, there is nothing of Treason in it, we will not give a Farthing for it. Therefore this Book, if it be made by him to be published, it is unlawful, whether it be malitious or not. ...

[26]
The Jury went from the Bar, and nigh an hour after returned, and brought him in guilty.[11]

  *L.C.J.* You have done like honest Men.

## 'Articles of Impeachment of Sir William Scroggs' (3 January 1681), *CJ*, 9, pp. 697–9.

*IMPRIMIS*, That he the said Sir *William Scroggs*, then being Chief Justice of the Court of King's Bench, hath traiterously and wickedly endeavoured to subvert the fundamental Laws, and the established Religion and Government of this Kingdom of *England*; and, instead thereof, to introduce Popery, and Arbitrary and Tyrannical Government against Law; which he has declared by divers traiterous and wicked Words, Opinions, Judgments, Practices, and Actions.

2ly, That he the said Sir *William Scroggs*, in *Trinity* Term last, being then Chief Justice of the said Court; and having taken an Oath duly to administer Justice according to the Laws and Statutes of this Realm; in pursuance of his said traiterous Purposes, did, together with the rest of the Justices of the same Court, several Days before the End of the said Term, in an arbitrary Manner, discharge the Grand Jury, which then served for the Hundred of *Oswaldston* in the County of *Middlesex*, before they had made their Presentments, or had found several Bills of Indictment, which were then before them ... By which sudden and illegal Discharge of the said Jury, the Course of Justice was stopped maliciously and designedly; the Presentments of many Papists and other Offenders were obstructed; and, in particular, a Bill of Indictment against *James* Duke of *Yorke*, for absenting himself from Church, which was then before them, was prevented from being proceeded upon.

3dly, That, whereas one *Henry Carr*[1] had, for some time before, published every Week a certain Book, intituled, "The weekly Pacquet of Advice from *Rome*, or, The History of Popery;" wherein the Superstitions and Cheats of the Church of *Rome*, were from time to time exposed; he the said Sir *William Scroggs*, then Chief Justice of the Court of King's Bench, together with the other Judges of the said Court, before any legal Conviction of the said *Carr* of any Crime, did, in the same *Trinity* Term, in a most illegal and arbitrary manner, make, and cause to be entered, a certain Rule of that Court against the Printing of the said Book, in *haec verba*,[2] /

"*Dies Mercurii, proxime post Tres Septimanas Sanctæ Trinitatis, Anno 32 IIdt Regis.*

"*Ordinatum est, quod Liber, intitulat*, The Weekly Pacquet of Advice from *Rome*, or the History of Popery, *non ulterius imprimatur vel publicetur per aliquam Personam quamcunque*;

*Per Cur.*"[3]

And did cause the said *Carr*, and divers Printers, and other Persons, to be served with the same: Which said Rule, and other Proceedings, were most apparently contrary to all Justice, in condemning not only what had been written, without hearing the Parties, but also all that might for the future be written on that Subject; a manifest Countenancing of Popery, and Discouragement of Protestants; an open Invasion upon the Right of the Subject, and encroaching and assuming to themselves a Legislative Power and Authority.

4thly, That he the said Sir *William Scroggs*, since he was made Chief Justice of the King's Bench, hath, together with the other Judges of the said Court, most notoriously departed from all Rules of Justice and Equality, in the Imposition of Fines upon Persons convicted of Misdemeanors in the said Court; and particularly, in the Term of *Easter* last past, did openly declare in the said Court, in the case of one *Jessop*,[4] who was convicted of publishing false News, and was then to be fined, That he would have Regard to Persons, and their Principles, in the imposing of Fines; and would set a Fine of Five hundred Pounds on One Person for the same Offence, for the which he would not fine another One hundred Pounds: And, according to his said unjust and arbitrary Declaration, he the said Sir *William Scroggs*, together with the said other Justices, did then impose a Fine of One hundred Pounds upon the said *Jessop*, although the said *Jessop* had before that Time procured one *Hewett* to be convicted as Author of the said false News; and afterwards, in the same Term, did fine the said *Hewett*, upon his said Conviction, only Five Marks: Nor hath the said Sir *William Scroggs*, together with the other Judges of the said Court, had any Regard to the Nature of the Offences, or the Ability of the Persons, in the imposing of Fines, but have been manifestly partial and favourable to Papists, and Persons affected to and promoting the Popish Interest, in this time of imminent Danger from them; and, at the same time, have most severely and grievously oppressed his Majesty's Protestant Subjects; as will appear upon view of the several Records of Fines set in the said Court: By which arbitrary, unjust, and partial Proceedings, many of his Majesty's Liege People have been ruined, and Popery countenanced, under Colour of Justice; and all the Mischiefs and Excesses of the Court of Star Chamber, by Act of Parliament suppressed, have been again, in direct Opposition to the said Law, introduced.

5thly, That he, the said Sir *William Scroggs*, for the further Accomplishing of his said traiterous and wicked Purposes, and designing to subject the Persons, as well as the Estates, of his Majesty's Liege People, to his lawless Will and Pleasure, hath frequently refused to accept of Bail, though the same were sufficient, and legally tendered unto him by many Persons, accused before him only of such Crimes, for which, by Law, Bail ought to have been taken; and divers of the said Persons being only accused of Offences against himself; declaring, at the same time, That he refused Bail, and committed them to Gaol, only to put them to

Charges; and using such furious Threats, as were to the Terror of his Majesty's Subjects; and such scandalous Expressions, as were a Dishonour to the Government, and to the Dignity of his Office: And particularly, That he, the said Sir *William Scroggs* did, in the Year One Thousand Six hundred Seventy-and-nine, commit and detain in Prison, in such unlawful Manner, among others, *Henry Carr, George Broome, Edward Berry, Benjamin Harris, Francis Smith* senior, *Francis Smith* Junior, and *Jane Curtis*, Citizens of *London*:[5] Which Proceedings of the said Sir *William Scroggs* are a high Breach of the Liberty of the Subject, destructive to the fundamental Laws of this Realm, contrary to the Petition of Right, and other Statutes; and do manifestly tend to the Introducing of arbitrary Power.

6thly, That he the said Sir *William Scroggs*, in farther Oppression of his Majesty's Liege People, hath, since his being made Chief Justice of the said Court of King's Bench, in an arbitrary manner, granted divers general Warrants for attaching the Persons, and seizing the Goods of his Majesty's Subjects, not named or described particularly in the said Warrants ...

7thly, Whereas there hath been a horrid and damnable Plot, contrived and carried on by the Papists, for the Murdering of the King, the Subversion of the Laws and Government of the Kingdom, and for the Destruction of the Protestant Religion in the same; all which the said Sir *William Scroggs* well knew, having himself not only tried, but given Judgment, against several of the Offenders; neverthless he, the said Sir *William Scroggs* did, at divers Times and Places, as well sitting in Court, as otherwise, openly defame and scandalize several of [the] Witnesses, who had proved the said Treasons against divers of the said Conspirators, and had given Evidence against divers other Persons, who were then untried; and did endeavour to disparage their Evidence, and take off their Credit; whereby, as much as in him lay, he did traiterously and wickedly suppress and stifle the Discovery of the said Popish Plot, and encourage the Conspirators to proceed in the same, to the great and apparent Danger of his Majesty's most sacred Life, and of the well-established Government and Religion of this Realm of *England*.

8thly, Whereas the said Sir *William Scroggs*, being advanced to be Chief Justice of the Court of King's Bench, ought by a sober, grave, and virtuous Conversation, to have given a good Example to the King's Liege People, and to demean himself answerable to the Dignity of so eminent a Station; yet the said Sir *William Scroggs*, on the contrary, by his frequent and notorious Excesses and Debaucheries, and his profane and atheistical Discourses, doth daily affront Almighty God, dishonour his Majesty, give Countenance and Encouragement to all Manner of Vice and Wickedness, and bring the highest Scandal on the publick Justice of the Kingdom.

All which Words, Opinions, and Actions of the said Sir *William Scroggs*, were by him spoken and done traiterously, wickedly, falsly, and maliciously, to alienate the Hearts of the King's Subjects from his Majesty, and to set a Division between him and them, and to subvert the fundamental Laws, and the established Religion and Government of this Kingdom, and to introduce Popery and an Arbitrary and Tyrannical Government; and contrary to his own Knowledge, and the known Laws of the Realm of *England*: And thereby he, the said Sir *William Scroggs*, hath not only broken his own Oath, but also, as far as in him lay, hath broken the King's Oath to his People, whereof he the said Sir *William Scroggs*, representing his Majesty in so high an Office of Justice, had the Custody: For which the said Commons do impeach him the said Sir *William Scroggs* of the High Treason against our Sovereign Lord the King, and his Crown and Dignity, and other the high Crimes and Misdemeanors aforesaid. ...

# ARGUMENTS FOR LIBERTY OF THE PRESS, 1679–81

[Charles Blount], *A Just Vindication of Learning: or, An Humble Address to the High Court of Parliament in Behalf of the Liberty of the Press*, by Philopatris (London, April 1679). Wing, B3307; ESTC, R16824.

William Lawrence, *Marriage by the Morall Law of God Vindicated against all Ceremonial Laws of Popes and Bishops* ([London], 1680), pp. 162–7. Wing, L690; ESTC, R7113.

William Denton, *An Apology for the Liberty of the Press*, appended to Denton, *Jus Caesaris et Ecclesiae vere dictae* (London: for the Author, and are to be sold by John Kersey and Henry Faythorn, at the Rose in St. Paul's Church-Yard, 1681). Wing, D1066; ESTC, R203695.

The centrality of the press to the crisis of 1679–81 was mainly manifested in news-centred polemics and their punishment but more extended arguments for liberty of the press also appeared in print at this time, of a kind not really seen since Milton's *Areopagitica* in 1644. The first of these, Charles Blount's *Just Vindication of Learning*, drew heavily on *Areopagitica* in making its case around the time renewal of the Printing Act was under consideration in early 1679. The other two examples included here followed over the next two years, penned by the former royal physician William Denton and the former Cromwellian lawyer William Lawrence. None had any clear immediate impact but all three reflected as well as informed contemporary concerns about the role of the press, and Blount, in particular, would play an important part in challenging censorship in subsequent years.

Charles Blount's *A Just Vindication of Learning*, like its model *Areopagitica*, carried a prefatory address to Parliament, being intended to influence consideration of the renewal of the 1662 Printing Act, whose expiry with the session was raised in the Commons on 2 April 1679. On 22 April the committee considering expiring laws was empowered to send 'as well for licensed as unlicensed books' but Parliament was prorogued on 27 May without the Act being renewed.[1] To what extent the *Just Vindication* hit its mark is unclear, although it has been credited with striking 'a responsive chord', and Blount would later return to the cause to further effect.[2]

Blount (1654–93) came from a gentry family whose shared inclination towards political and spiritual questioning led Charles in 1678 to membership of the Whig Green Ribbon Club and authorship of *Anima Mundi*, a work of soul-searching condemned by the Bishop of London and subsequently burnt.[3] Blount appears to have sent Hobbes a copy, along with a letter saying he had read Hobbes's 'Treatise of Heresie in Manuscript' and alluding to clerical condemnation of books.[4] Blount would again experience the condemnation of his work following the publication of *An Appeal from the Country to the City* (see Restoration Crisis, above). The differing pro-inquiry and anti-Catholic impulses of these separate suppressed works together animated the *Just Vindication*, with its warning that under a popish government 'the Priest rides the Soul, and the Prince the Body' owing to the 'Laicks Ignorance and Servitude', for the removal of which 'there hath never been discover'd any better expedient among men, than that of the Liberty of the Press' (by which was meant absence of pre-publication licensing). The tract was listed as 'Milton's Ghost' in Wood's *Athenae Oxoniensis* and Blount openly acknowledged Milton's influence in tracing the genealogy of licensing as 'an old Relique of Popery', while also silently borrowing several of *Areopagitica*'s literary flourishes elsewhere.[5] However, he diverged from Milton notably in his argument for the ability of an uncensored press to secure accountability in the public interest, through what Tindal and Locke would later term the law of reputation. Blount may have influenced John Locke's 1695 criticisms of licensing, one echo being the insistence on having the same freedom to write as to speak. *A Just Vindication of Learning* was reprinted in 1695, and was bound as part of Blount's *Miscellaneous Works* of that year.

Blount, Milton and William Lawrence shared a concern with the laws on the press and, curiously, also the laws on marriage. Lawrence (*c.* 1613–82), a lawyer who had been a minor judge and MP in the 1650s, brought the two together most directly in his *Marriage by the Morall Law of God Vindicated*, with ecclesiastical control of the press seen as a means of obscuring the true content of law, human and divine. The broader contention of the book was that sexual congress rather than ceremony made marriage by moral law – *contactus, non contractus, facit matrimonium* – the implication being that Charles II's illegitimate son James, Duke of Monmouth, was lawful successor. The work gained the interest of Shaftesbury and Locke – who loaned his copy to James Tyrrell – while also attracting the attention of others markedly less sympathetic.[6] The book ended suddenly with a small but dramatic notice advising readers that a raid on the press had forced the printer and author to break off their work. It appears to have been notified to the secretary of state's office in 1681, by which time the concluding part had been published as *The Right of Primogeniture* and was reported as being present 'in all the great sectaries' libraries', although the outcome of any further investigation is unclear." Lawrence died six months later, having also opposed censorship in another 1681 tract, *The Two Great Questions*; all his published works appeared in the last two years of his life. The excerpt from *Marriage by the Morall Law* included here deals with Lawrence's view that historically control of the press has allowed the bishops to define laws governing heresy and Church discipline to the exclusion of truthful dissent. He moves on to a more general argument rebutting possible objections to liberty of the press, extending the discussion from spiritual to temporal benefits, and recalling his own difficulties in acquiring a licence for a printed petition.

William Denton (c. 1605–91), unlike Blount, Lawrence, or indeed Milton, was a royal servant, being a court physician under Charles I and Charles II, although he embraced the 1688–9 revolution and followed the path from anti-popery to liberty of the press trodden by those other writers. His *Apology for the Liberty of the Press* appeared as an appendix, separately paginated, to the large work *Jus Caesaris*, in which Milton's *Treatise of Civil Power in Ecclesiastical Causes* provided the starting point for an Erastian denial of churches being independent societies as opposed to a united (and originally democratic) national body bound and governed by legislature and king. The *Apology for the Liberty of the Press* makes less eclectic use of Milton, drawing on *Areopagitica* for its history of papal censorship but also going direct to Milton's source, Paolo Sarpi, and updating both with references to the papal *Index* of 1659 and its successor in 1667. Denton also adapts some of Milton's imagery in minor yet interesting ways. For instance, 'confuting by dint of Reason is the only Cornish Hug that can lay flat' was Milton with added 'reason', and Denton urged post-publication watchfulness by the 'state' alone rather than Milton's 'church and state'. In a preface to *Jus Caesaris* Denton mentioned that the truths he had previously published had 'galled some', suggesting a personal as well as political and ecclesiological background to the postscript on the press.

Notes

1. *CJ*, 9, pp. 582, 600, 634.
2. T. Crist, 'Government Control of the Press after the Expiration of the Printing Act in 1679', *Publishing History*, 5 (1979) pp. 49–77, on p. 50.
3. *Observator*, 290 (14 February 1683); *ODNB*.
4. T. Hobbes, *The Correspondence of Thomas Hobbes*, ed. N. Malcolm, 2 vols (Oxford: Clarendon Press, 1994) vol. 2, pp. 759–63.
5. A. Wood, *Athenae Oxoniensis*, 4 vols (London: Rivington, 1813–20), vol. 4, p. 55. See also G. Sensabaugh, *That Grand Whig Milton* (Stanford, CA: Stanford University Press, 1952), pp. 61, 204–5.

6. J. Locke, *The Correspondence of John Locke*, ed. E. S. De Beer, 8 vols (Oxford: Oxford University Press, 1976–89), vol. 5, p. 292.
7. *CSPD*, 7 September 1681.

[Charles Blount], *A Just Vindication of Learning: or, An Humble Address to the High Court of Parliament in Behalf of the Liberty of the Press, by Philopatris* (London, April 1679). Wing, B3307; ESTC, R16824.

# A Just Vindication OF LEARNING:

OR,

An Humble Address to the
High Court of

# PARLIAMENT

In behalf of the

## Liberty of the Press,

By *Philopatris*.

# PROEM.

May it please you, my Lords and Gentlemen,
THis *Session of Parliament*[1] *is of such high Importance to these parts of the World, that Heaven seems to have committed the Universal Fate of Christendom to Your disposal; from whose Proceedings, both* France, Spain, Germany, Holland, *and this part of the Universe, must take their Measures: Nor will it be a Vanity in me to affirm the same thing of You, which heretofore* Tacitus *did of the* Battavi,[2] 'Who in the time of the *Romans (saith he)* were able to confer a Victory upon whatever Party they adhered to'.

*The* Parliaments *of* England *have ever been Formidable to their Neighbours, but You above all others seem to have been reserv'd by Providence, for those Great and Weighty Affairs which are now in Agitation as well at home as abroad, and for which purpose You are here Convened. You only are able to cast out that Angel of Darkness, with his many Legions, who is at this time endeavouring to destroy our best of Kings and Governments: You only are able to Center this reeling Kingdom, which staggers and groans under the Plurisie of Popery, and which (if not now prevented) may in time attaint and corrupt the whole mass of* English *Bloud: You only are able to preserve that so necessary Religion, and Sacred Property of our* British *Isle, by continuing (as there now is) a Protestant Head, upon a Protestant Body; without / which, our Prince would be no other than a Father-in law to his People, and they Sons-in-law to him: besides, the incoherence would be as great and disagreeable, as to behold a black* Indian *Head, annex'd unto a white Body. Neither would such a conjunction be more Unnatural; than Inconvenient, since He that is arbitrary over the Soul, as in Popery, hath ever a co-equal power over the Body and the Estate; which is evident from the examples of* France, Spain, *and other Popish Governments, where the Priest rides the Soul, and the Prince the Body (a Tyranny as disagreable to our Gracious Soveraign's Nature to impose upon us, as it would be insupportable for our* English *Spirits to bear.)*

*Now the Original of these Popish Villanies (as I humbly conceive) proceeds not more from their Sacerdotal Malice and Interest, than from their Laicks Ignorance and Servitude; without which, their Clergy would at the best be rendred but like Wolves without Teeth. Wherefore to devest their Priests of this power of doing ill, nothing would be more conducive than the propagating of Wisdom and Knowledge amongst the populace; since as Ignorance renders men obedient and susceptible of the meanest Slavery, so doth its contrary put all men upon their Guard:* Omnes enim nos sumus, aut corvi qui lacerant, aut cadavera quæ lacerantur.[3] *Now for the more speedy effecting hereof, there hath never been discover'd any better expedient amongst men, than that of the* Liberty of the Press, *whereby whoever opposes the Publick Interest, are exposed and rendred odious to the people: as on the contrary, they who merit well of their Country, are ever recorded with immortal Honour to posterity. So that if Fame and Ambition (as all generous Souls must acknowledge) have so / great an influence over the minds of active men, what can be more reasonable, what can be more serviceable to the World, than that which hurries men into a necessity either of acting Virtuously, or of forfeiting their so-much-desired Honour for ever? and such I take to be the consequence of a* Free Press. *From which consideration, since the late Act which laid that severe restraint upon* Printing, *is so near Expiring*,[4] *my humble Address to Your Lordships, and to You Gentlemen of the House of Commons, is, that before You proceed to the Continuation of any thing of that Nature, You would condescend so far to look down upon these ensuing Arguments, against any such Inquisition or Embargo upon Science, wherein You may happily find some Reasons, which (though not founded upon private ends, like those of our Adversaries) may yet prove sufficiently satisfactory to all, but that* Deadweight *of Interest which opposes us; and will not be converted, for that it is not for its Interest so to be.*

*This, My Lords and Gentlemen, is all from him who would Sacrifice his Life and Fortune for his King and Country, coveting no other Title of Honour whereby to be distinguished, than that of*

Philopatris.[5] /

# A JUST VINDICATION
## OF
# LEARNING,
## AND THE
## Liberty of the PRESS.

ALL civilized People, as well Ancient as Modern, have ever had that veneration and deference for Learning, that almost no Nation, dis-engaged from Barbarism, wants its publick Donations either of magnificent Structures, or plentiful Revenues, for the encouragement of Literature and Learned men. Such Patrons and Admirers of Learning were the *Heroes* of old, that they seem to contend about nothing more, than to excell in their Liberality to the *Muses:* Thus we see *Alexander the Great* presented *Aristotle* with 800 Talents, also *Xenocrates* the Philosopher with 50 Talents;[6] *Antiochus* likewise presented his Physician *Theombrotus* with 60000 Crowns; *Homer* for his Works receiv'd a thousand pieces of Silver from the *Candiots*;[7] nor did that suffice, but Cities must fall together by the ears for the honour of his Birth: so liberal were the Ancients to all manner of Science; nor have our Modern Benefactors been inferiour to them, as our / two famous Universities may testifie to Posterity. Yet notwithstanding all these Encouragements, Learning hath of late years met with an obstruction in many

Pl. Alex

places, which suppresses it from flourishing or increasing, in spight of all its other helps, and that is, the *Inquisition upon the Press*, which prohibits any Book from coming forth without an *Imprimatur*; an old Relique of Popery, only necessary for the concealing of such defects of Government, which of right ought to be discover'd and amended. However, as our Government is not sick of the same Distemper, so need we not the same Cure, but rather the contrary: for as an ill face cannot be too closely masqued, so neither can a good one be too much exposed.

That Books are of great use to a Government, is evident, First, for that they are the only Records of Time, which excite us to imitate the past Glories of our Ancestors: 2ly. we owe our manner or form of Divine Worship to Books alone: 3ly. we owe our Philosophy, or contemplation of God in his Works, to the same cause. For mens Natural Abilities, like Natural Plants, need pruning by Study: thus we see that Histories make men wise; Poets, witty; Mathematicks, subtle; Natural Philosophy, deep; Moral Philosophy, grave; Logick and Rhetorick, able to dispute; all which Excellencies are to be acquired only from Books: since no Vocal Learning is so effectual for Instruction, as Reading; for that written discourses are better digested, and support themselves better on their own weight, than words disguised by the manner of expression, cadence or gesture, which corrupt the simplicity of things; when also the suddenness / of Pronunciation allow not the Audience time sufficient to reflect upon what was said. Moreover, Books flatter much less, and have more universal precepts, than Discourse; which generally affects Complaisance, and gaining the Hearers good will: Particularly in Morality, where great persons are better instructed, and more plainly reprehended for their faults by Books, than by Discourses: Books being therefore in the main so useful to Humain Society; I cannot but herein agree with Mr. *Milton*, and say, that (unless it be effected with great Caution) You had almost as good kill a Man, as a good Book; for he that kills a Man, kills but a Reasonable Creature, Gods Image: Whereas he that destroys a good Book, kills Reason it self, which is as it were the very Eye of God.[8]

Having thus demonstrated how much the World owes to Learning and Books; let me not be altogether unmindful of *Faust* and *Guttenburg*, the promoters of both; who by their Ingenuity discovered and made known to the World that Profound Art of Printing, which hath made Learning not only Easie, but Cheap; since now any person may accommodate himself with a good moderate Library at the same Price, as heretofore *Plato* payed for three Books of *Philolaus* the *Pythagorian*,[9] viz. Three Hundred Pounds. This was the Invention wherewith *Cardan* upbraided the Ancients, saying, *Antiquitas nihil par habet*.[10] Nay, *Thuanus* goes higher, when speaking of the Inventors of this Art, he saith, *Quibus plus debet Christianus orbis, quám cuiquam fortissimorum belli ducum ab propagatos fines patria unquam debuit.*[11] And / truly so we do; but still provided, that the

Gell. *lib.* 5. ch. 17.

Subt. *lib.* 17.

Hist. *lib.* 25.

Inquisition upon it be removed, without which, this Art design'd at first for the service of the Publick, will prove useful to none but the Licenser. Therefore in opposition to any such Restraint, I shall here demonstrat the unreasonableness of any such License or *Imprimatur*.[12]

1. From the Ancient usage as well of the *Greeks*, as *Romans*, who were both highly Eminent for Learning; and whom in this particular we need not be ashamed to imitate: We do not find amongst the *Greeks*, that their *Vetus Comædia*[13] (which was so much censured for Libelling and Traducing men by Name, as to be prohibited Acting on the Stage) was ever supprest from being read; but rather the contrary; for that *Plato* himself recommended the Reading of *Aristophanes* (the loosest of all those old Comædians) to his Royal Scholar *Dyonisius*.[14] Neither do we read any where, that either *Epicurus* or that Libertine School of *Cyrene*, or what the *Cynick*[15] Impudence utter'd, with many other Sects and Opinions, which tended to Voluptuousness, and the denying of a Providence, were ever prohibited or question'd. Also amongst the *Latines*, we find *Lucretius* versifying his *Epicurean* Tenents to *Memnius*, without any molestation, and had the honour to be published a second time by *Cicero*[16] the great Father of the Commonwealth, although he himself disputes against that same Opinion in his own Writings. Neither do we read of any Decree against the Satyrical sharpness of *Lucilius*, *Catullus*, or *Flaccus*.[17] Likewise in matters of State, the Story of *Titus Livius*, though it extoll'd / and magnify'd *Pompey's* party, was not ther[efore] suppress'd by *Octavins Cæsar*[18] of the other Faction. Nay even in the times of Christianity, unless they were plain invectives against Christianity, as those of *Porphyrius* and *Proclus*,[19] they met with no interdict till about the year 400. in a *Carthaginian* Council,[20] wherein Bishops themselves were forbid to read the Books of Gentiles, but Heresies they might read: Whereas others long before them, scrupled more the Books of Hereticks, than of Gentiles. And that the Primitive Councils and Bishops were used only to declare what Books were not commendable, passing no further censure, but leaving to each ones Conscience to read, or to lay by, till after the year 800. is already observed by Father *Paul*, that great unmasker of the *Trentine* Council:[21] After which time, the unsatiable Popes engross'd more and more every day, till *Martin* the 5th. by his Bull, not only prohibited, but was the first that Excommunicated the Reading of Hæretical Books; For about that time, *Wicklif* and *Huss*[22] growing formidable, were they who first drove the Papal Court to a stricter policy of prohibiting: Which Course *Leo* the 10*th*.[23] and his Successors followed, until the Council of *Trent* and the *Spanish* Inquisition engendering together, produced these two Monsters, an *Index Expurgatorius*, and a *Licenser*,[24] When they enacted, that no Book, Pamphlet, or Paper should be Printed, till it were Approved and Licensed under the hands of two or three Gluttenous Fryers: So that in fine, there was

never any such Inquisition upon Learning known in the World, till *Slavery supplanted Liberty, and Interest Religion.*[25] /

2. It is the greatest Affront and Discouragement that can be offer'd to Learning and Learned men: For so far to distrust the Judgment and Honesty of one who hath but a common repute in Learning (having never yet offended) as not to count him fit to Print his mind, without a Tutor or Examiner, least he should drop a Scism or something of corruption, is the greatest displeasure and indignity to a free and knowing spirit, that can be put upon him. What advantage is it to be a Man, over it is to be a Boy at School, if we have only 'scap'd the Ferula, to come under the Fescu of an *Imprimatur?*[26] When a man Writes to the World,[27] he summons up all his Reason and Deliberation to assist him; he Searches, Meditates, is industrious in Consulting and Conferring with his Judicious Friends; after all which, he takes himself to be inform'd in what he Writes, as well as any that writ before; if in this the most consummate act of his fidelity and ripeness, no years, no industry, no former proof of his Abilities, can bring him to the state of Maturity, as not to be still distrusted, unless he carry all his considerate diligence, all his midnight watchings and expense of *Palladian* Oyl,[28] to the hasty view of an *Unleasured Licenser*, perhaps much his Younger, perhaps much his Inferior in Judgment, perhaps one who never knew the Labour of Book-writing, or perhaps one altogether ignorant of that Art or Science whereof the Author Treats. When if he be not repuls'd or slighted, must appear in Print like a Puny[29] with his Guardian, and his Censors Hand on the back of his Title,[30] to be his Bail and Surety that he is no Idiot or Seducer: This / cannot but be a derogation to the Author and to the Book, as well as to the priviledge and dignity of Learning. And what if the Author shall be of so Copious a Fancy, as to have many things well worth the adding, come into his Mind after Licensing, while the Book is yet under the Press, which frequently happens even to the best of Writers, and that perhaps a dozen times in one Book? The Printer dares not go beyond his Licensed Copy; so often then must the Author trudge to his Leavegiver, that those his new Insertions may be view'd; and many a Journey will he make 'ere that *Licenser*, (for it must be the same man,) can either be found, or be found at Leisure; in the mean while, either the Press must stand still, which is no small Damage, or the Author lose his most Correct Thoughts, and so send forth his Book Imperfect. How can any man esteem himself Doctor enough to Teach with Authority in his own Book, when he himself and all that he Writes must submit to the jurisdiction and censure of another?

3. 'Tis a great prejudice even to the Book it self, to come out under the partiality and ignorant approbation of a *Licenser*: Every Acute Reader upon the first sight of a Pedantick *License*, will be apt to misinterpret the word (*Imprimatur*) and think it signifies no more, but that, this Book is foolish enough to be Printed; when seeing it comes out under the wardship of another, he will

be apt to say, I know nothing of the *Licenser*, but that I have his own hand for his arrogance; who shall warrant me his Judgment? The State, Sir, replyes the *Stationer;* But hath a quick return, The State shall be my Governours, / but not my Criticks; they may be mistaken in the choice of a *Licenser*, as easily as this *Licenser* in the choice of an Author: Whereunto he might also add from my Lord *Bacon, That such Authorized Books are but the Language of the Times.*[31] For though a *Licenser* should happen to be more then ordinary Judicious, which will be a great hazard in the next succession; yet his very Office and Commission enjoyns him to let pass nothing but what is Vulgarly received already. Nay, if the work of any Deceased Author, though never so Famous in his Life time, come to their hand for License to be Printed or Reprinted; if there be found in the Book any one Opinion that thwarts the *Licenser's* Humour, whether it be of a Vacuum, Motion, Air,[32] or never so inconsiderable a Subject; the sense of that great man shall to all Posterity be lost, out of the presumptuous Rashness of a pedantick *Licenser*. So that if these things be not seriously and timely resented by them who have the remedy in their power; but that *Licensers* are permitted to gnaw out the choicest periods of exquisite Books, and to commit such a Treacherous Fraud against the Orphan remainders of the worthiest men after death, the more sorrow will belong to that helpless race of men, whose misfortune it is to have Understanding. Henceforth let no man care to learn, or care to be more than worldly wise; for certainly in higher matters to be ignorant and slothful, to be a common stedfast Dunce, will be the only pleasant life, and only in request.

4 It is not only a reflection upon Books and particular men, but it is likewise an undervaluing and / vilifying of the whole Nation: I cannot set so small value for all the Invention, the Art, the Wit, the grave and solid Judgment which is in *England*, as to imagine that it can be comprehended in any 20 Capacities,[33] how good soever much less than it should not pass except their Superintendence be over it, except it be sifted and strained with their Strainers, and that it should be uncurrant without their Manual Stamp:[34] Truth and Understanding are not such Wares as to be Monopolized and Traded in Tickets, Statutes and Standards. We must not think to make a Staple Commodity of all the knowledge in the Land, to Mark and License it like our Broad-cloath and Woolpacks: What is it but a servitude, like that imposed by the *Philistines*, not to be allow'd the Sharpning of our own Axes, but we must repair from all quarters to twenty Licensing Forges?[35] Had any one written and divulged Erroneous things, and scandalous to an Honest Life, mis-using and forfeiting the esteem had of his reason amongst men; if after conviction, this only censure were adjudged him, that he should never henceforth Write but under the Authority of an Examiner; this could not be apprehended less then a disgraceful punishment. Whence, to include the whole Nation, and those that never yet thus offended, under such diffident and suspectful Prohibition, renders it no less then a National disparagement; and

so much the more, seeing Debtors and Delinquents may walk abroad without a Keeper, but inoffensive Books must not stir forth without a visible Jaylor in their Title: Nor is it a less reproach to the Commonalty; since, if we be jealous over them, / as that we dare not trust them with an *English* Pamphlet: What do we but censure them for a giddy, vicious, unthinking crowd; in such a sick estate of discretion, as to be able to take nothing down, but through the Pipe of a *Licenser*. Now that this proceeds from the care or love of the Commonalty, we cannot pretend; since in those Popish places where the Laity are most hated and despised, the same strictness and severity is used over them.

5. It reflects upon our Church and Clergy, of whose labours we should hope better, and of the proficiency which their Flock reaps by them; then after all this Light of the Gospel, all this continual Preaching, they should be still frequented with such an un-principled, un-edify'd and Laick rabble,[36] as that the Whiff of every new Pamphlet should stagger them out of their Catechism and Christian walking. This may have much reason to stagger and to discourage the Ministers, when such a low conceit is had of all their Exhortations, and the benefiting of their Hearers, as that they are not thought fit to be turned loose to three Sheets of Paper, without a License; that all the Sermons, all the Lectures Preached, Printed and Vented in such numbers and such Volumes, should not be Armour sufficient against one single Enchyridion Unlicensed:[37] I am confident that a Kingdom governed by the rules of Justice and Fortitude, or a Church built and founded upon the rock of Faith and true Knowledge, cannot be so Pusillanimous.[38] That all freedom of Writing should be thus restrained with the proud curb of an *Imprimatur*, must needs administer cause of doubt, and discouragement / to all Learned and Religious men, who may justly suspect the Reason and Power of that cause which durst not stand a Tryal of Skill. Every Author Writes either Truth or Falshood; If he Writes Truth, why should he be oppressed or stifled? And if he delivers what is False, let him be confuted by Answer, whereunto every Author is subject; since no cause ever suffered by being answered, only by Fire and Faggot.[39] That Liberty is the Nursery of Science, appears in that there is nothing hath so much clouded and discouraged the *Italian* Wits, as their *Inquisition*; which restraining all manner of Philosophick freedom, hath for these many years produced nothing but obsequious flattery: In which Country the Famous *Galileo*[40] was oppressed under the *Inquisitions* Tyranny, for thinking otherwise in Astronomy, then the *Dominican* and *Franciscan* Licensers thought.

6. This Licensing of Books is one of the most dangerous and mischeivous Monopolies and Oppressions our Government is subject to: Since, put the Case we were under an evil Prince,[41] ( as now we are under a good one) he paying this *Licenser* his Stipend, might influence him so far, as to make him License all Books against the Interest of the Subject, or to the Defamation of any publick Spirited Lords or Commoners; and to prohibit only such Books as are in the

Vindication of such persons who are for the Liberty and Property of the Subject: For that 'tis ever the Interest of a *Licenser*, above all, to regard the Favour of his Prince. (though to the prejudice and almost ruine of his Country.) Who payes him his / Wages? His Prince. Who hath the disposal of all Places and Offices of Preferment? His Prince, Then who should he study to please, right or wrong, but his Prince and Pay-master? that is, if he be such as most *Licensers* are, low-spirited men, who consider nothing but their own present Interest. Why should I not have the same freedom to write, as to speak?[42] If I speak any thing that is evil, I am lyable to be punish'd, but yet I am never examined before I speak what I am about to say: So let not my Book be Censured by one Interested man alone in private, till it hath tryed the publick Test; and then if there be any thing ill in it, I am ready to answer for it. Why must no Writing, either in the behalf of such great matters, as Liberty, Property, and Religion, or in the behalf of such small trifles, as Funeral Tickets, Play-house Bills, City Mercuries, Hackney-Coach Bills, Quack-Doctors Bills, and the like, be Printed without a License? Is it for that the Subject of these Bills or Tickets are dangerous to the Government? or rather, that this Monopoly would be injured in its Prerogative, if the least Word or Letter be Printed without paying Toll to this *Licenser*. Heaven grant that in time, there be not the same Restraint and Monopoly over Wity Discourse, as there is now over Ingenuous Writing:[43] Since by the same reason, the Royal Jester may demand a Spell of Money for every Jest that is broken in Discourse, as well as the *Licenser* doth expect a reward for every Ingenious Piece or Jest, that is Printed in Books: When with more Gravity then Wit, having with great Study and Labour, Corrected some such dangerous / Author as *Thomas a Thumbis*;[44] he from his Learned Grammatical Pen, which casts no Ink without *Latin*, drops forth that Lordly word *IMPRIMATUR*; either because he judged no Vulgar Tongue was worthy to express so pure a Conceit; or rather perhaps, for that our *English*, (the Language of men, ever famous and bold in the Atcheivements of Liberty,) will not easily find servile Letters enough to spell such an Arbitrary Presumptuous word, as is that of *IMPRIMATUR*.

7. This trouble of Licensing doth very much prejudice and injure the very *Licensers* themselves in the Calling of their Ministry, if they will discharge that Office as they ought; because of necessity they must neglect either the one duty or the other.

8. It robs us of that great Argument we make use of against the *Mahometans*;[45] and what is worse, Popish Religion, *viz*. That Ignorance is the Mother of their Devotions; since how can We justly brand their Religions, for being founded meerly upon their Laicks Ignorance; when we in the like manner discountenance Knowledge our selves? How can we upbraid Papists for not daring to permit their Common people to read the Bible, when we do the same thing in effect, by tying all persons up to one mans Exposition and Interpretation of

the same, *viz.* the *Licenser's*; who will not permit any Exposition to come forth that thwarts his own particular Judgment. I am confident, that if the *Turk* or the *Pope*, could be assured to make all men Expound the *Alcoran* and Scriptures according to the sense of the *Mufti* and / *Conclave*,[46] they would neither of them be against the Common peoples reading them; so that we all three aim at one & the same thing, only by different ways; and that is our mistake: For let their falshoods use what artifice they can; yet we do in a manner Libel our own Truth, when by Licensing and Prohibiting, fearing each Book, and the shaking of each Leaf, we distrust her own strength: Let her and Falshood grapple; who ever knew Truth put to the worst in a free and open Encounter? Her confuting is the best and surest oppressing,[47] when it leaves all standers by no room no doubt. *The punishing of Wits enhaunces their Authority, and forbidden Writing is thought to be a certain spark of Truth that flyes up in the Faces of them who seeks to tread it out.*[48] When a man hath been working at the hardest Labour in the deep Mines of Knowledge, and hath furnisht himself out in all Equipage, drawn forth his Reasons as it were in Battail-array; scatterd and defeated all objections in his way, summons his Adversary into the Field, offers him the advantage of Wind and Sun if he pleases, only that he might try the matter by dint of Argument; for his opponent then to Sculk & lie in Ambuscade, to keep a narrow Bridge of Licensing, where the Challenger should pass; this, though it be courage enough in a Souldier, is but Weakness and Cowardice in the Wars of Truth. For Truth needs no Policies, no Stratagems, no Licensings to render her Victorious; these are only the shifts and defences that Error uses against her power:[49] So that if it once come to Prohibiting, there is nothing more likely to be Prohibited then Truth it self, even the very Bible; as we may / see it is by the first Inventors of this Monopoly. To justifie the Suppression of Books, some may Cite the Burning of those *Ephesian* Books[50] by St. *Paul's* Converts; but that agrees not with our Case, for there it was not the Magistrate, but the Owners of the Books themselves who burnt them in remorse.

9. And Lastly, Give me leave to tell you, that Licensing and Persecution of Conscience are two Sisters that ever go hand in hand together, being both founded upon one and the same Principle: Therefore to Asperse the one, permit me to Defame the other. Now although I allow no indifferency to those Religions whose Principles destroy Government, nor those Religions that Teach ill Life (both which Errors the Papists are guilty of.) *Yet I cannot but wish, that all men would use one another so gently and so charitably, that no violent Compulsion should introduce Hypocrisy, and render Sincerity as well troublesome as unsafe.*[51] It would be hard measure for any man to blame that Chyrurgion[52] who refused to cut off a mans Head only to Cure a Wart or Pimple upon his Chin or Cheek: Now the Case is altogether the same, and we may as well decree a Wart to be Mortal, as a various Opinion in *re alioqui non necessariâ*[53] to be Capital and

Damnable. I would fain know why is not any Vicious Habit as bad or worse, then a False Opinion? Why are we so zealous against those we call Non-conformists, or Hereticks, and yet at the same time dear Friends with Drunkards, Fornicators, Swearers, Intemperate and Idle Persons?[54] I am certain that a Drunkard is as contrary to God, and lives as contrary to the Laws of Christianity as any Heretick; and I am also sure that I know what Drunkenness is, but I am not sure that such an Opinion is Heresie, nor would any man else be so dogmatical in these matters, did he not mistake confidence for certainty.[55] Faction and Heresie were things unknown in the World, till the increase of Interest, and abatement of Christian Simplicity; when the Churches Fortune grew better, her Sons worse, and her Fathers worst of all.[56] Why should I hate men because their Understandings have not been brought up like mine, have not had the same Masters, have not met with the same the Books, nor the same Company, or have not the / same Interest, or are not so Wise, or are much Wiser, and therefore do not determine their School-questions to the sense of my Sect or Interest? I think they are in an Error, but they believe me to be in the wrong; If they Erre, they do it not through Obstinacy, but Ignorance; and if God affords them his Patience, why should we not lend them ours? It was nobly and bravely answered (for a Heathen) of *Tamberlain* the Great;[57] who (when his High Priest desired him to reduce all that part of the World to one Religion) replyed: 'No, I will not; for that how (saith he) do I know but the same God, who hath delighted himself so much with the variety of all other things, as appears in Men, Beasts, Birds, Fish, Trees, Herbs, Flowers, *&c.* May not also delight himself as much in variety of Worship? Therefore I will punish none but such as deny either a God or his Providence, and him will I put to death'. Certainly 'tis very unreasonable for men to press and pretend every Opinion in matters of Religion, as necessary in so high a degree, that if they spoke Truth, or indeed two of them in 500 Sects, which are now in the World (and for ought I know there may be 5000.) it is 500. to one but every man is Damn'd; for every Sect Damns all but it self, and yet that is Damn'd of 499. and it is excellent Fortune then if that escape. All Wise Princes heretofore, till they were overborn with Faction, gave Toleration to different Sects, whose Opinions did not disturb the publick Interest:[58] And not without reason; for that being restrained and made miserable, mutually endears the discontented Party, and so begets more hearty and dangerous Confederations against the oppressing Government.

Now how unreasonable soever such kind of Persecutions may appear to all tender hearted Christians; yet if once a License prevails (when men shall not be permitted to justifie their Innocence to the World) 'tis greatly to be fear'd that these mischiefs, and worse then these (if possible) will be the consequence of it. Having therefore thus plainly and at large demonstrated the inconveniences of a Licensing Press, give me leave to write upon the square, and shew you the /

Objections of our Adversaries, which without wrong to their cause, may be justly comprehended under one head, and that is this.

*Objection*, If (say they) a Restraint be not laid upon Printing, and some Supervisors assigned over the Press; how then can we be secured from Libells against the King, the Church, the State, and private men? As also from Popish Books of all sorts? Now this I take to be the only Material Objection, wherewith they can have any shew of a pretence to baffle and obstruct our design.

To which I *Answer*: First, that to expect any assurance that no such Books shall be written, is more then Mortal man can give; since we see that during this late Act, and should there be even a *Spanish* Inquisition erected amongst us; yet there are some Authors and some Printers so bold, that the one to vent his Humour, and the other for the Lucre of Money, would Write and Print such Books in spite of the strictest enquiry, and in defiance of the severest Penalty; And these are the Authors that are most dangerous, and also most incorrigable, being persons however that are more likely to be silence'd by Liberty then by Restraint: For experience hath already shew'd, that all such Acts will prove uneffectual to them. Secondly, supposing any such Authors are taken and discovered; why, we need no other new Laws for the punishing of them ( I humbly conceive) then what are already in force: As for example, if any Audacious Villain shall Publish Treason, he is already lyable to suffer as a Traytor; or if he Writes Scandalous Reflections upon the Government, I presume he is by the present Laws of the Land subject to a Fine and Imprisonment. Again if he publishes any Atheism, Heresie or Schism, he is lyable to an Excommunication, and to be proceeded against accordingly in the Spiritual Court: Or if in his Writing he Defames any particular person he is obnoxious to a *Scandala Magnatum*[59] if he be a Peer; and to an Action upon the Case for Slander, if he be a Commoner. And last of all for Popish Books, *Quære* whether there be not *Statutes* already in force for the abolishing them, made 3 and 4 of *Ed.* 6.[60] For although this *Statute* was / once repealed by the 1 *M.* 2. yet that of the 1 *M.* 2. was likewise afterwards repealed by the 1 *Jac.* 28. So that I cannot apprehend wherein we have need of any other new Law of this nature, unless it be to preserve to the poor Book-sellers their just and undoubted property of their Copies, which is their House and Land, they having the same Title for the one, as we have for the other.

## POSTSCRIPT.

H*Aving thus therefore my Lords and Gentlemen tendred to your serious consideration these few reasons against any such Inquisition upon the Press, I shall presume to offer but this one Proposal to Your Judgment, and so conclude, viz. That if these fore-mentioned Arguments prove so unneffectual, as that your Prudence shall think* *fit to take some further care, about the regulating of the Press; then if it be Enacted, that any Book may be Printed without a License, provided that the Printers and the Authors Name, or at least the Printers be Registred whether or no this will not have all the good, but none of the bad Consequence of a* Licenser? *And that those which otherwise come forth, if they be found Mischeivous and Libellous, shall be committed to the Flames, as also the Author to Condigne Punishment but in this as in all other things I most humbly submit my self to Your Supream Wisdom and Judicature.*

FINIS.

William Lawrence, *Marriage by the Morall Law of God Vindicated against all Ceremonial Laws of Popes and Bishops* ([London], 1680), pp. 162–7. Wing, L690; ESTC, R7113.

*They corrupt the Press, both as to Scripture and Law, and interdict Protestants to write against Papists, or answer them.*

*Coke* 3. part 40.[1] saith, *There was a Statute supposed to be made,* 5. R. 2.[2] *That Commissions should be by the Lord Chancellor made, and directed to Sheriffs and others, to Arrest such as should be Certified into the* Chancery *by the Bishops and Prelates, Masters of Divinity, to be Preachers of Heresies, and notorious Errors, their Fautors,*[3] *Maintainers, and Abetters, and to hold them in strong Prison, until they will justifie themselves to the Law of the Holy Church.* By colour of this supposed Act certain Persons that held Images were not to be worship'd, *&c.* were holden in strong Prison, until they (to redeem their vexation) miserably yielded before these Masters of Divinity to take an Oath, and did swear to worship Images, which was against the Moral and Eternal Law of Almighty God. We have said (by colour of the supposed Statute, *&c.*) not only in respect of the said Opinion, but in respect also, that the said supposed Act, was in truth never any Act of Parliament, though it was Entred in the Rolls of Parliament; for that the Commons never gave their consent thereunto. And therefore in the next Parliament, the Commons prefer'd[4] a Bill reciting the said supposed Act, and constantly affirmed that they never assented thereto, and therefore desired that the supposed Statute might be aniented,[5] and declared void. For they protested, that it was never their intent to be justified, and to bind themselves and their Successors to Prelates, more then their Ancestors had done in times past: And hereunto the King gave his Royal Assent in these words, *Ypleist au Roy.*[6] And mark well the manner of the penning the Act: for feeling the Commons did not assent thereunto, the words of the Act are, *It is Ordained and Assented in this present Parliament, That,* &c. And so it was, being but by the King and the Lords.

It is to be known, that of ancient time, when any Acts of Parliament were made, to the end the same might be published, and understood, / especially before the use of Printing came into *England,* the Acts of Parliament were ingrossed into Parchment, and bundled up together with a Writ in the King's name, under the great Seal, to the Sheriff of every County, sometime in *Latine,* and sometime in *French,* to command the Sheriff to proclaim the said Statutes within his Bailwick, as well within Liberties,[7] as without. And this was the course of Parliamentary Proceedings, before Printing came in use in *England,* and yet it continued after we had the Print, till the Reign of *H.* 7.

Now at the Parliament holden in 5. R. 2⁸ *John Braibrook*⁹ Bishop of *London* being Lord Chancellor of *England*, caused the said Ordinance of the King and Lords to be inserted into the Parliamentary Writ of Proclamation to be proclaimed amongst the Acts of Parliament: which Writ I have seen, the purclose¹⁰ of which Writ, after the recital of the Acts directed to the Sheriff of N.¹¹ in these words, *Nos volentes dictas concordias, sive ordinationes in omnibus & singulis suis Articulis inviolabiter observari, tibi præcipimus quod prædictas concordias, sive ordinationes in locis infra Balivam tuam, ubi melius expedire volueris, tam infra libertates, quam extra, Publice Proclamari, & teneri facias juxta formam Prænotatam, Teste Rege apud* Westm. 26. Maij. Anno Regni Regis R. 2. 5.¹² But in the Parliamentary Proclamation of the Acts passed in *Anno* 6. R. 2. the said Act of the 6. R. 2. whereby the said supposed Act of 5. R. 2. was declared to be void, is omitted: and afterwards the said supposed Act of 5.R.2. was continually Printed, and the said Act of 6. R. 2. hath been by the Prelates ever from time to time kept from the Print.¹³ What *English* Protestant can read this without horror? what? doth he not observe it? why 'tis that Counterfeit Act of Parliament. 5. R. 2. 1382. whereby Bishops usurp to be Judges of the Souls and Consciences of Protestants, and to put them in strong Prison till they conform and submit to the will of the Bishop, 'tis that Counterfeit Act whereby they usurp to be Judges of Heresie, and to make Protestants Hereticks when they please; 'tis that Counterfeit Act whereby they have compell'd the Subjects to swear to worship their Idols; 'tis that Counterfeit Act whereby they have dragged so many Pious Martyrs to the Stake, and burnt them, filling the whole Land with fiery Furnaces;¹⁴ 'tis that Counterfeit Act by which the Bishops have usurped Power to destroy Religion, Liberty, Propriety, and Lives of all Protestant Subjects at their pleasure; 'tis that Counterfeit Act which was never assented to, but disclaimed, detested, abrogated, and declared null and void by the House of Commons. 6.R.2. *Anno* 1382. and hath been yet most presumptuously caused to be printed as a valid Act by the Bishops being Masters of the Press; and the true Act of Abrogation 6.R.2. Whereon all the Subject hath depends, most wickedly suppress'd, and never Printed. /

*Coke* 2. *Part. Fol.* 584.¹⁵ saith, And here is to be observed how the Statute of 35. *E.* 1.¹⁶ hath been dealt with since the 17*th.* of *E.* 3. for in an Act of that Year, a branch of the Statute of 35. *E.* 1. was recited, That forbad any thing should be attempted or brought into the Realm, which should tend to blemish the King's Prerogative, or in prejudice of his Lords and Commons, which is now wholy omitted;¹⁷ and *Fol.* 585. he saith, Note in the Roll of Parliament of the Statute of 38. *E.* 3. *Cap.* 1. of *Provisors*,¹⁸ there are more sharp and biting words against the Pope then in Print, a Mystery often in use, but not to be known of all men;¹⁹ from which examples it is manifest, that this came by the Fraud of the Bishops, who before Printing, were Masters of the Authentick Copies of the Laws appointed for promulgation; and since Printing, are Masters of the Press, to interdict and publish what they will.

*Accipe nunc horum insidias & Crimine ab uno,
Disce omnes.*[20]

These few Frauds are discover'd in Print against the Interdictors of Printers, which discovery they would likewise have interdicted if they had been able, for these latter Books of my Lord *Coke* were prohibited to be Printed,[21] and got out in the late time of Troubles: but by these it is clear, which were only spoken *obiter*,[22] and without any inquisition after them, that all they are guilty of are not discover'd, and that to give either Spiritual or Temporal Judges Power to interdict the Press, is to give them Power to have what Law, what Gospel, what Text, what Translation, what Canonical, what Apocryphal,[23] what Scripture, what Act of Parliament, what Common Law, what Statute, what Religion, what Justice, what Liberty, and what Slavery they please.

Besides which Power of Fraud and Forgery destructive to all Truth, these further mischeifs follow all interdictions of the Press, but I shall first answer such Objections as are made against the Liberty of it.

First, *If Liberty of the Press should be permitted, Enemies would have it equal with Friends, Papists with Protestants, Hereticks with Orthodox.*

Secondly, *They would Print Blasphemy, Idolatry, Treason, Rebellion, Uncleanness, Calumny, Reviling, Derision, and all manner of Heresie.*

To the First is answer'd, (1.) That it is impossible to exclude Enemies and Papists from Printing, they being possess'd of so many Transmarine Presses,[24] whence they can with far greater advantage vent their matters, then from any Presses in *England*. (2.) Admit they could be excluded, yet in prudence they ought not, but are more necessary to be admitted then Friends; for those whom we use to call Friends, are *pessimum inimicorum genus Adulantes*,[25] the worst kind of Enemies, Flatterers, who flatter and sooth us up in our Vices, and destroy us, but any truth / of our Faults we shall never hear but from Enemies. *Plutarch* therefore calls an *Enemy, a School-Master which costs us nothing.*[26]

2. As to the matters of Blasphemy, Idolatry, or Uncleanness; neither Enemy or Friend will so far dishonour themselves, or their Cause, as to Print them openly, for it is against their interest; As to Treason or Rebellion, who that hath an Enemy, doth not desire to know beforehand, wherein the strength of his Cause, as well as of his Forces lies; and to have the War Proclaimed in Print before it begin, that he may the better provide against. Besides, if there were but a Law made, that nothing shall be printed, without the names of the Author and Printer, with their Additions and Designations: And that all Crimes against the publick, committed by Printing, should be punished by Indictment according to Law; and all injuries to private persons, should be reparable by the parties

injured, on their Actions according to Damage: Who would dare make himself guilty of a publick Crime, or private Injury in Print, to which he had set his name?

3. As to matters of Heresie, such as by accident become dangerous to public safety, the prudence of the Legislators, may, where they find cause, prohibit them, both Press and Pulpit; but not in the Thoughts and Consciences of Men: As in the end of the Wars of *Germany*, between the *Lutherans* and *Catholicks* it was Enacted, mutually on both sides on pain of death, *That no* Catholick *should Preach against the* Lutheran *Doctrine, or* Lutheran *against the* Catholick; *but both should enjoy the liberty of their own Consciences to themselves.*[27] This agreement was here made, otherwise those bloody Wars would never have ended, without a total destruction of one of the Parties.

And likewise such a Law were here much more necessary, between dissentient Protestants, who were Brethren, then it was between the *Lutherans* and *Catholicks*, who were mortal Enemies; That no dissentient *Protestant* should Print or Preach publickly, on any point of Ceremonial dissentiency, or other matter not necessary to Salvation, except in such matters as are particularly allowed by Supream Authority, to exclude Popery; there being Field-room enough in the Moral Law of God, to exercise gifts in Preaching; and matters which have the promise of this life, and of that to come; and no cause for any to complain, who have liberty likewise of Conscience to use what *Protestant* Ceremonies, and Form of Worship they will to themselves, though they have not power to compel the Consciences of others, who are dissentients. But if *Protestants* are tolerated to Print or Preach against one another, this is the thing the Papist would have, and knows will in the end make them both a prey to himself.

But though *Protestants* ought not to preach one against another, yet the juncture of Affairs being not at present in great *Britain*, as before / mention'd in *Germany*, and an appearance of War Plotted by the *Papist*, rather to begin than end with the *Protestant*, the Bishops ought not to be suffer'd to interdict either Press or Pulpit to the *Protestants* against them.

To come at length to the further mischiefs insuing the Interdiction of the Press; any Interdiction of the Press (except in Cases before mention'd) either to Friend or Enemy, is a dishonour to the *Protestant* Religion, as if it dared not suffer it self to be disputed, or to meet an Enemy in the open field; whereas in truth, it is not *Protestancy* but *Episcopacy*. 'Tis not the Moral Law which is the *Protestant* Law, but the Ceremonial which is the *Popish* Law, which dares not encounter the shock of an Enemy: And 'tis Fiction and not Truth, Vice and not Vertue, which fears either Press or Pasquil.[28]

2. The Foreign Presses being impossible to be interdicted to the *Papist*, if the *English* are interdicted to the *Protestant*, he is thereby silenced, and prohibited to answer the *Papist*, let him preach what he pleaseth.

3. By Interdiction, the profit of the *English* Protestant Print-houses will be transported to Foreign Papists; which will be a great discouragement to so necessary a Trade in *England*, and prejudice to the Protestant Religion, and Policy.

4. The Interdiction of the Press will multiply the greater evil of Libels and Lampoons.

It increases unlearned Sects and Heresies, who if drawn to Print would either not be able to form their Doctrine in Principles or Positions; or if they were, they would appear so absurd as would be fit to imploy boys to laugh at, rather than Doctors to confute: Such were *Mahomet's*, whose *Alchoran*[29] is not therefore suffered to be Printed, or Translated.

5. It causes the more dangerous way of spreading Heresies, both learned and unlearned, to be neglected how to prevent, which is the secret creeping into private Houses, leading Captive silly Women, with whom they walk like the Pestilence in the dark;[30] whereas if they appeared in Print or publick Preaching, they might be known where they are, and opposed.

6. It stops the truth of all intelligence,[31] which is so invaluable a Treasure, and difficult to be got into the Gates of Princes.[32]

7. A free Press is the pulse of the Body politic, from which is impossible for the wisest State-Physician to discern, or prevent the public Distempers, unless it is suffer'd to beat free without a Ligature.

8. It stops all just causes of complaint, and appeal of the Subject to the King and Parliament, against Judges and great Officers, both Spiritual and Temporal. It was my own ill fortune to be pickt Sheriff[33] / of a County, which enforced me to draw a Petition to be presented to the King and Parliament; desiring some remedy against the old Popish Oath, continued to be imposed on Sheriffs; wherein they swear to destroy the Protestant Religion, under the name of *Lollary*;[34] and likewise to be relieved against the extortions of Officers of the *Exchequer*, on Sheriffs: which not knowing how otherwise conveniently to Address, I appointed the Messenger to get a License to Print; which he tried to do, but though there was nothing in it but Humility and Truth; as who dare present otherwise to the Legislative Power? The Licenser Swore *He would not License it for Five Hundred Guinneys*, whereby it could not be done.

9. It stops all presentments by the People to the King and Parliament of public grievances, in regard the extent of the Three Kingdoms[35] is great, and remote; and therefore neither fit nor possible, multitudes should come so far to present Petitions in person; and if not done in person, there are so many Papists, and Foreign Agents, and their favourers in the way, as may, and do often intercept from the King's knowledg, the humble applications of his Protestant Subjects, as is easie to do, when perhaps comprised only in one sheet of Paper. To avoid therefore the stifling of all just complaints of the Subjects, and the ill consequences which have been too often occasioned thereby, of presenting Petitions

by Tumults and Armies: It is far more safe and equal, that the Press should be open to the People in all public Addresses to Supream Authority; it being many times a sufficient satisfaction to them, if they understand that the King and Parliament do but vouchsafe to hear their complaints and desires, though they think it not fit to grant them: And a Child will often times awe his Enemies from harming him, if he do but threaten them he will tell his Father, where they know he hath that liberty given him.

10. It appears by experience, That the Liberty of the Press in *Holland*, and other Foreign States, where permitted, not only bring no inconveniences, but very great benefits and advantages to the People. ...

William Denton, *An Apology for the Liberty of the Press, appended to Denton, Jus Caesaris et Ecclesiae vere dictae* (London: for the Author, and are to be sold by John Kersey and Henry Faythorn, at the Rose in St. Paul's Church-Yard, 1681). Wing, D1066; ESTC, R203695.

AN

# APOLOGY

FOR THE

LIBERTY

OF THE

# PRESS.

THough I cannot with truth aver, that stealing out in Print, *sine permissu superiorum*,[1] is as justifiable as stealing a Nap,[2] or stealing away from Company at pleasure, yet I hope it is not to be numbred *inter graviora delicta*:[3] And that I may with much truth say, that to padlock the Press is but a new Trick or Tyranny, rather devised by those whom for shame we cannot own for pious in their Lives, or orthodox in their Doctrines, and indeed, whom it is a reproach to imitate. A *Romish Practice*, or at best but a new *Canonical Slight*,[4] (unknown to the first and purest Men and Times) forged in and crept out of the *Saincted Inquisition* by the *Holy Fathers* thereof, who to shew their wonderful zeal to Religion and divine Truths, have put the *Bible* it self in the *Front*, or first rank of *prohibited Books*,[5] and so corrupted the Fathers by their Additions and Substractions, that those of their Inquisitory Editions can no otherwise be esteemed the true Off-spring of their Natural Fathers, then *Theseus*'s Ship could be called his Ship, after it had so often been hack'd and hewed, patch'd and mended, that there was scarce a whole Rib or Plank that did remain the same that it was when it was first built, which because it still kept the same form, though little of the old matter, did still retain the Name of *Theseus* his Ship.[6] Tho' *Christians* have no other *divine Rule or Authority* without them warrantable to one another, as a common Ground or Rule, (either for holy Living, or determination of Controversies in matters of Religion) unto which all ought to submit but the *Scriptures*, nor any other Evidence or Patent, to make out their title or claim to *Heaven* and *heavenly* things, nor unto their *great Gospel-Priviledges*, but the *Scriptures*; yet so just and tender have the heretical Fathers of all Christendom, the Popes been, that contrary to all express *Apostolical Commands*, by their *Indices Expurgatorii*, (whereof there are seven, if not more extant)[7] in the very front of prohibited Books placed the Bible, forbidding it to be printed or read in any vulgar Tongue printed or written, (and they account all Languages *vulgar* but *Latin, Greek, Hebrew, Chaldaick, Syriack, Aithiopick,*[8] *Persian, Arabick*) as may be seen in the fifth general Rule in the *Index* printed at *Madrid*, 1667.[9] viz. *Cum experientia docuerit ex permissione sacrorum Bibliorum lingua vulgari plus inde ob hominum / temeritatem, ignorantiam aut malitiam detrimenti quam utilitatis oriri, prohibentur Biblia lingua vulgari extantia cum omnibus eorum partibus impressis aut manuscriptis: pariter Summaria & Compendia quamvis Historica eorundem Bibliorum aut Librorum Sacræ Scripturæ Idiomate aut lingua vulgari: non tamen clausulæ, sententiæ, aut capita, quæ libris Catholicorum hæc explicantium & citantium inseruntur.*[10]

By this holy *Inquisition* also these men (so wise are they in their Generation) have endeavoured to appropriate and monopolize unto themselves the whole power of the Press, and as much as in them lyes, to *cajole* the secular power thereof, (and not without grand reason of State Ecclesiastick;)[11] for they have been so dexterous at it, that they have already expunged the ancient Authors and Councils of all that makes for *temporal Authority: Ab initio non fuit sic.*[12] The matter of Fact stands thus; the reasonableness of the Practice shall follow.

In the primitive Church *Heretical Books* were examined and declared to be such by the *Councils*, but not prohibited by them, nor by the *Pope*, but by the *Prince*.[13] The *first Council* of *Nice* condemned the *Heretical* Doctrine of *Arius*; but *Constantine* the *Emperor* did forbid his Books by *Imperial Law*.[14] The *Second Council* of *Constantinople* did declare *Eunomias* to be an Heretick; but the *Emperor Arcadius* did prohibit the Books of the *Eunomians* and *Maniches* by a Law, which is in the *Theodosian Code*.[15] The *third Council* of *Ephesus* declared *Nestorius* to be an *Heretick*, and his Books were forbidden by a Law of *Theodosius*, which is in the *body* of the *Civil Laws*.[16] The *fourth Council* of *Chalcedon* condemned the *Eutychians*, and their Books were forbidden by a Law of the *Emperor Martian*,[17] which is in the same aforesaid Book; and in *Spain* the King *Ricaredus* those of the *Arrians*.[18] This was the manner of the *Church*, until the year 800. since which Times the *Popes* of *Rome* have by Usurpation declared divers Writers to be *Hereticks* and *heretical*, that will not subscribe to the Canons of that *Conventicle of Trent*.[19]

But all this while the *Press* was not guarded, nor *Transcribing* forbidden, but left free: Books only, and those but few censured and prohibited until after the year 1200. and then also but sparingly, until about the time of *Wickliff Husse*, and *Jerome* of *Praghe*,[20] which was about 1371. in the days of *Edw*. 3d. *Rich*. 2d. and *Pope Martin* 5th. who by his *Bull*[21] excommunicated all Sects of *Hereticks* in their esteem, especially *Wicklefists* and *Hussites*, and had recourse also unto a stricter *Guardianship* of the *Press*, and also to *Excommunication*, nay to *Fire* and

*Fagot* also against them and their Books; and good reason and high time it was so to do, for that their Doctrines touched to the quick the Reformation of the *Heretical Doctrines*, and lewd practices of the *Court of Rome*; and therefore that faithless and jugling *Council* of *Constance*[22] in a time of Schism did condemn them, their *Books and Bones,[24] (though *Wickliffe* had been quiet in his Grave above 40 *years* before) causing them to be taken up, burned, and their Ashes to be thrown into the River, such was their rancour of heart; since which Times the *Popes* succeeding have made it their grand Concern to prosecute the same design, which is still on foot at this very day, *viz.* to lay Foundations to maintain, and make great the *Authority* of the *Court of Rome*, by depriving men of *knowledge, which is absolutely necessary to defend themselves from Abuses, Usurpations, and Delusions*, with which the *Court of Rome* is full fraught. And therefore *Paul* 4th. caused an *Index* to be composed, which being perfected *Anno* 1659.[25] was so severe and strict, that there scarcely remained a Book to be read, if rightly observed; for that therein many Authors and / Books were condemned, which for 1, 2, or 300 *years* had usually been read by the *Romanists*, with the privity and without the Contradiction of the *Popes* then ruling; and amongst the Modern, some of those which were Printed in *Italy*, even in *Rome* it self, with approbation of the *Inquisition*, and allowed also by the *Brief* of the *Pope himself*, are forbidden, as *Erasmus* on the *New Testament*, which *Leo* 10*th*. having read, approved by his *Brief*, dated the *tenth* day of *September*, One thousand five hundred and eighteen.[26]

*Counted to be 200 Volumes by Aineas, Sylisius, and Jo. Cocleus, in his Book de Historia Hussitarum.[23]

But which is most considerable as to the main of my intent and purpose is to shew, that where the *Hogen Mogen Pontiff* (not unlike the chief *Mufty*)[27] doth domineer, there the very bowels of orthodox and sound Books, (*wherein the Authority of Kings and Civil Magistrates is defended* from the *Usurpations* of the Clergy, and in which the Hypocrisies and Tyrannies of the *Clergie* are manifested) are hellishly raked into, purged, prohibited, and condemned with strange Cruelties; and which is yet more abominable, this is done under the *colour of Faith and Religion*, by which the people under that very pretence of Religion, are miserably cheated and deluded. A greater mystery of Iniquity was never broached, then to *use Religion so dirtily*, as under pretence thereof, to make men, as much as in them lyes, insensible, nay brutish, by keeping them from the knowledge, and consequently from the *love* of the *truth*. What is this less then *Antichristian*, and like men *abominable, disobedient, and to every good work reprobate*, and to sit as God in the Temple of God,[28] (as *Judex vivorum & mortuorum*)[29] working *after the working of Satan with all power and deceivableness of unrighteousness*?

But though the *Court* of *Rome* hath assumed to it self to prohibit Books, whether they concerned *Religion* or other Matters, yet before these latter years they have not been so impudent as to dare to say, that the *Prince* also hath not power to forbid Books. *Cardinal Baronius*[30] was the *first* that spake that boldly, but was not seconded by any a long time after; but he in the beginning of the year 1605. printing the 11*th*. Tome of his *Ecclesiastical Annals*, libelled therein the *Monarchy* of *Sicily* with much bitterness, and against many *Kings* of *Arragon*, and especially against *King Ferdinand* the *Catholick*, and the Progenitors of the Fathers side of him who then reigned; which Book coming to *Naples* and *Millan*, were prohibited by the King's Officers;[31] whereof the Cardinal having notice, made a bitter Invective against those Officers unto the *Colledge of Cardinals*, assembled in the *vacancy* of the *See* of *Clement* the 8*th*. for that in so doing they had forsooth laid hands on Ecclesiastical Authority. And afterwards when *Paul* the 5*th*. was chosen *Pope*, he wrote unto the *King* of Spain the 13*th*. of *June* the same year,[32] wherein amongst other things he concluded, that to the *Pope only* did belong the approving of Books of all kinds, much more Ecclesiastical ones. Notwithstanding the *King* of *Spain* was so wise as to abett and continue the Prohibition of his Officers; at which the *Cardinal* was so netled, that he could not contain himself; but printing his 12*th*. *Tome*, 1607. he inserted a Discourse, stigmatizing that Prohibition as abominable and impious, affirming that Princes do it, because the Books *rebuke their unjust acts*, and that it was to take out of *St. Peter's hands*, and putting into the *Prince's*, one of the Keys[33] given him by *Christ*, *viz*. the Key of knowledge, to discern good Customs from bad. But the *King of Spain* (maugre[34] his virulent Tongue and Pen) was so far from recalling the said Prohibition of his Ministers, that after long patience, *viz*. in the year 1610. he published an *Edict* in Print all the World over,[35] wherein he condemned and forbade the Book in such grave and apt terms, that he gave *Baronius* a *Rowland* for his *Oliver*.[36] Could there / be a higher Affront or Indignity offered to *temporal Majesty*, then for a foreign haughty *Prelate* to send into a *Prince's Dominions*, a Book in Print against him and his Government, and to justifie it to be lawful so to do, and that under *colour of Religion,* and the Authority of *Christ* given to *St. Peter*, when God and the wisest World doth know that there never was any such donation, and that it was unlawful for the Prince to withstand and prohibit it? *Deus bone!*[37] What will not proud *Prelates* attempt, *per fas nefasq*;[38] if their Copyhold of *Ecclesiastical Jurisdiction* or *Ecclesiastical Liberty* be but touched? It hath been long since observed by the judicious and worthy *Servite Padre Paulo,*[39] to be plain by all Histories, that Ecclesiastical Jurisdiction and Liberty hath occasioned all the Disputes and Differences which have happened between his *Holiness* and other *Princes* in these latter Ages.

Thus far only to shew how, when, by whom, and wherefore this politick piece of prudence of guarding the Press hath been invented and practised. And farther to shew, that *Baronius* chargeth the like Usurpation on temporal Majesty for ends that are not good, when in truth the *Pope* and his *Minorite*[40] *Priests* and *Friars* are much more guilty of that crime, denying it to temporal Princes, that they themselves only may rule uncontroulably from *Dan* to *Beersheba*,[41] from one end of the Earth to the other. *Divine Truths* and *right Reason* are more universal, and of more force and vertue then all the Councils that ever were, or ever will be, and ought more to be had in reverence and esteem, and ought to be obeyed, from what point of the Compass soever they come, or from what Pen soever they flow, and ought to have no restraint or prohibition put upon them, which would give them check at least, if not check-mate. For that such Prohibition would discourage Learning, and hinder Discoveries, and put a damp upon searching and inquisitive Brains and Abilities, and impeach that natural Right and Liberty, which belongs to every Individual. And thus to stifle and mortifie Reason and Truths is the worst of all Murders; for that by such Prohibitions many Truths may be lost, which may be an irrecoverable loss not unto particular persons only, but to whole Nations and Kingdoms; for if nothing must be printed but by the leave of some grand *Dominican Inquisitor* or chief *Mufty*, what Truth or Religion can we have other then that in *Trentine Creed* or *Mahumetan Alcoran*?[42] Falsest Seducers! God himself never created men, nor never gave talents of Reason or Judgment, subject and captivate unto the Reason and Judgment of others, but hath endued and trusted every man with his own proper talent of Reason to make his own choice, according to which only he shall be judged at the Judgment of the great Day. There would but little work be left for *Priests* and Preaching, if Law, Compulsion, and such Prohibitions should take place, and impose Doctrines, which ought to be governed only by demonstration of Reason, and by perswasive means. What wisdom can there be to choose or refuse? or what praise or dispraise, reward or punishment, can equally be distributed by doing, or not doing good or evil, without full knowledge of good and evil, and that left to our own free choice? What more ordinary then to have one Error exploded by another? and for the Fathers themselves to endeavour to confute that for Heresie or Error, which is the more orthodox Opinion, and for the Popes (whom *Hen*. the 8*th*. was often pleased in Drollery to call his *Vicars of Hell*) to disagree among themselves, even about this or that Translation of the Bible it self, witness that of *Sixtus Quintus*, and of *Clement* the 8*th*.[43] Did not *Arminius* fall into those Opinions now denominated by his Name, by undertaking to confute an *Anonymus* / Discourse written at *Delf*?[44] The Story of Dr. *Reignolds* and his Brother,[45] converting each other from *Protestant* to *Papist*, and from *Papist* to *Protestant*, by disputing to convince each other, is fresh and memorable.

Again, Are all Licensers *Apostolical*, endued with the Spirit of *Truth* and *Infallibility*, and without *Biasses*? Are the Fathers Inquisitors, and all other Licensers, more learned, more judicious, more honest, or endued with a greater measure of the Spirit of Truth and Grace, then all those that write? Is it honest, or just, to use subtleties to deprive wise men of any Advantages for greater knowledge, or for saving their souls, for fear fools and ill men should make ill use of what is written or printed? *Veritas non quærit Angulos; Truth* needs no such Artificers:[46]

besides, it is but a pitiful shift to guard one Avenew, and leave others round about unguarded. Why should we walk contrary to the Prescript of God and Nature, by curtalling the means of knowing and distinguishing *Truth* from *Error*? The Ingenuity of *Truth* requires it not; and it is but a sad piece of prudence to put such an affront upon Learning and learned men, for fear some *Truth* should rise up in judgment against some that manage Designs and Ends that are not good: moreover, it is marvellous difficult to fit a rigorous Law without offence to God, that must equally respect good and evil, as a Law of this nature and import doth; and nothing doth more easily bring a Law into dis-use, then the impossibility, or great difficulty in keeping it, and the great rigour in punishing the transgressors, especially when the same good end may be obtained, by ordaining only things neccessary, and moderate punishments. The *Gospel* it self was at first a *Schism* or *Heresie* both to *Jew* and *Gentile*, and yet was spread all the World over by Preaching before ever it was written or printed: of such efficacy are *divine Truths*, that first or last prevail they will; so that in truth perhaps there was not much more wisdom in the first Contrivers of this Trick, then was in *Will. Fessy*, who in spite to a Warrenner, would set open the Warren-Gates, that his Conies might all run away; or rather in that other Tony in the Fable, who thought to impound the Rooks by shutting the Park-Gate only.[47] What advantage, I pray, was it to *Martin* the 5*th*. and his *Council* of *Constance*, that they condemned the Doctrines of *Wickliffe*, and *Husse* their *Books*? Are they not more believed now than then? I do not mean such Doctrines as they falsified and foisted in, which were none of theirs, as *Deus debet obedire Diabolo*, &c.[48] Or what Advantage got *Leo* the 10*th*. by condemning *Luther* and his Books?[49] Or what Advantage was it to *Pope Paul* the 5*th*. or to his Cause, that he prohibited a *Treatise of Gerson's*, (that had been printed above 100 years before) and many other Books by Name then printed, and all other Writings which *should be made* against his Interdict against the *Venetians*?[50] O! much many ways. First, It had the Fate of all such dishonourable and disingenuous Practices; Effects contrary to expectation, *viz.* that the most understanding persons did from such a practice conclude, that Reason could not stand, nor be on their side, who would not suffer the Reasons on both sides to be made manifest, and come to the *Lydius lapis*,[51] the Test of right Reason. It was also judged marvellous strange, that all Writings which might be made were prohibited, which was to prejudge before they knew or could understand, (as if endued with the Spirit of *Pithon*[52] or of Prophecy) they did foresee that men could write nothing on their side, that could abide the touch, or the light; or else that they were such Plenipotentiaries, as that they had full Authority to extinguish indifferently the good with the evil. Preposterous ways! and therefore that wise Republick[53] deem'd it more / for their honour and justification, and advantage, not to imitate his Holiness, nor the Advisoes of his sacred Conclave, in that which they reprehended in them; and therefore they permitted to print and read who would, that thereby *appealing unto all the World, all the World might see on their part* that nothing was palliated, or disguised, and that they did not distrust the judgment of the Universe on what they had done; and this was done like a State full of Gravity, and full of Wisdom.

Full contrary did those *magnificent Cardinals, Bellarmine, Baronius,* and *Colonna* act,[54] whilst they imployed all their Wits and Learning, not only to blot out those Hand-writings that were, and would have made against them, but by pitiful Sophistry and Querks to raise a dust or mist in the minds of their Readers by their own Writings, to disguise and obscure the *Truth,* that it might not be discovered, nor ever come clearly to the Test; and what honour they atchieved thereby, Historians are full, and such Fates commonly attend such pitiful Policies and Practices.

The truth is, every Government is, or ought to be such, as to be above all little dirty Intrigues; and this is no great one, *Nitimur in vetitum,* Books like *Poma Adami,*[55] the more forbidden, the more desired; it being ever suspected in such Cases, that some Truths lye therein hidden, which if discovered, would fly in the faces of such Opponents, as subtlely endeavour to trample them under foot; besides, such licensed Books are but the language of the present Times, and have their Vicissitudes and alternate Fates.[56] We have experienced it in our own days and times; when Episcopacy was to be pulled up root and branch, then forsooth all Presses ought to be open and free; it was the Peoples Birth-right and priviledge, and the dawning of the day of Truth appearing, after the *Sun had gone down upon our Prophets, and the day had been dark over them* for some years past.[57] But no sooner had they unmitred the Prelates, and minced Episcopacy as small as Herbs to the Pot, that every Priest might be a Prelate in his several Parish, under another title and vizard, but that the old Acts were new broacht, and trumpt up again, and the freedom of the Press must be beleaguered with a Committee, forsooth, of Examinations, and a Commission of twenty, and learning to her old Barnacles again.[58] This device was first set on foot by *Antichristian mystery,* and design to smother *Light* and *Truth,* that the Contrivers might the more cleverly set up the Kingdom of Antichrist, in *Cimerian darkness of ignorance,*[59] and if it were possible to hinder all reformations of their Lives and Doctrines, and to insinuate and establish Falshood. *Turkish policy*! To uphold their *Alcoran,* they prohibit Learning and Printing, worthy of *Romish* not *Protestant* Imitation; *Protestants* need it not; *Truth,* (which is their Shield and Buckler) is as strong as the Almighty; *Magna enim veritas & prævalebit:*[60] Who ever knew her put to the worse? Let *Truth* and *Error* enter like fair Combatants and Wrestlers into the Lists; confuting by dint of Reason is the only *Cornish Hug*[61] that can lay flat. It is *Error,* not *Truth,* that stands in need of such lame Crutches; write that write will, Licensing or not Licensing may make Truth more or less visible or diffusive, but not less victorious; *Contraria juxta se posita magis elucescunt. Rectum*

*March 2. 1642.*

*est Index sui & obliqui*;[62] the crookedness of Error will the more appear, if once brought to the light and true Rule: Why are we then so *be-Jesuited*, seeing by locking up the Press *Truth* is much more likely to be supprest then Falshood and Error? The great and usual Clamour and Out-cry against the Liberty of the Press is, that it encourageth *Libellers* against Kingdoms, States, and men in Authority. If they characterize and represent falsly, it is then a / Libel, and a Crime to be, and may be punished by the Judges. If *they despise Dominion, and wrongfully speak evil of Dignities, quâ tales*, it is a Crime of the same nature. But if publication or declaration of Truths shall be esteemed Libels, there's no Law, no Logick, nor yet Divinity for that. Nay, it is derogatory even to the God of Truth; *Go tell Judah of her sins, and Israel of her transgression*. If *Ahab and his Fathers house trouble Israel*, it's no crime for *Elijah to tell him so*; nor in *Nathan* to say unto *David, Thou art the man.*[63] And the *prophane Prophets of Israel must be prophesied against*. All Governments were instituted by God for the good of the governed, and it is not Libelling to tell them so. Forbidding publication of Books, without an *Imprimatur* first obtained, is to make the Licensers Judges of all Truths and Opinions; and it's odds that they will let nothing pass, but what is calculated and fitted to their own Interest, and the *Interest* and *Genius* of the *present Times*. And is not this a Crime of the same nature with the *Indices expurgatorii*, which all honest, wise and pious men abhor. It is at best but an oblique Art, servant only to *Times, Parties* and *Interests*, destructive to Learning and Ingenuity, to suppress Monuments of Reason used by their Adversaries, on whose side happily *Truth* is. The more noble and warrantable way is to abandon all such little and disingenuous Tricks and Devices, and labour by all holy means and endeavours to suppress Vice. To punish and discountenance sin and sinners, is more glorious before God and man, then to padlock Presses; it being a shrewd sign that *Truth* is not on their side, that suppress the adverse Reasons. *Truth* is able to justifie it self, and acquire its own glory and reward of Ingenuity, and Christian Simplicity, when suppressing or expunging betrays, that we either distrust God for the maintenance of his own Truths, or that we distrust the Cause, or our selves, or our Abilities. It is one thing to stifle Books in the womb,[64] before ever they are permitted to see light, or that before they are either known or understood, and that perhaps by one single person, who happily may be much less learned, honest, or orthodox then the Author; and another thing to condemn both Author and Book, when examined, and found faulty and erroneous: For it is most just and reasonable, that all and every State should consider how Books as well as men do behave themselves, and punish or not punish accordingly;[65] accordingly one – *Carter* a Printer[66] suffered in Queen *Elizabeths* days.

§. Consider matter of Fact, by looking a little back. Although it was early foretold that *Antichrist* would come, nay that many *Antichrists* were already come, yet until after the 800*th*. year, about which time the *Eastern Empire* divided from the *Western*, there were not many *Hereticks* found in the Western parts for 300 *years* after. But after the *year* 1100 by reason of the continual Jars[67] which for 50 *years* before had been between the *Popes* and the *Emperors*, which continued unto the year 1200. with frequent Wars, there did arise many *Hereticks*, (as the *Popes* were pleased to call them, by as good *Logick* as the *Lion* is fabled to call the Foxes Ears, *Horns*) whose most common *Heresies* were against the *Pope's usurped Authorities*, over *Clergie* and *Laity*. This moved the Popes and their Conclaves, for Ends not good, to establish the two Religious Orders of *St. Francis* and *St. Dominick*,[68] (pure *Fanaticks*) which were soon filled with the most zealous and learned Persons that that Age could afford, altogether devoted to the maintaining of the *Court of Rome*, and the Authority of the *Pope*; to which two Orders the care of the Inquisition newly erected was committed, and what hath / followed since is obvious to every intelligent man, which soon spawned the first sanguinary Law against Hereticks, by the help of the *Emperor Frederick the* 2*d*. 1244. imposing *fire on Hereticks*.[69]

§. But before this we had no Charm nor Lock upon the Press; no Purgatory for Books; no *Limbus Patrum*[70] for their Authors; we had no proper, real and propitiatory Sacrifice in the Mass for the living and the dead, nor dry or demi-Communions; no *Conventicle* at *Trent*; no new Creed with 12 new Articles either of *Trent* or of *Johannes Baptista Posa*,[71] a *Spanish Jesuit*, never heard of before, newly printed, newly come forth; no blotting out of the second Commandment; no dividing of the tenth Commandment into two, to amuse and cheat the People; no Doctrine of Infallibility, nor yet of Probability; no Penance Sacramental; no Satisfaction; no Sacramental Confession, as now used; no *Hurtado*; no *Filliucius*; no *Bauny*; no *Lessius*; no *Escobar*;[72] no *Jesuits Morals*; no power to depose Kings; no dissolving Oaths of Allegiance; no Gunpowder-Treasons, and an Iliad[73] more of such damnable Errors and Heresies. I conclude therefore that it bears no shew, that forbidding men to write tends to any good end, but really to the end to conceal the Truth, and to shew it to the World only under a Mask, or some deceitful Light.

I shall conclude with this Observation concerning Printing it self, That in the days of *Luther*, and Troubles of *Germany*, about *Religion* and Vices of the *Clergie*, it was suggested unto *Clement the* 7*th*. that the occasion of them all was from the *new Invention of Printing*,[74] scarce 80 *years* found out, and now not possible to be suppressed; which though it had brought to light many Books and much Learning, yet they found that in this short time it had made a great discovery of their *Arcana Imperii*,[75] their jugling Arts and Legerdemains, much to their prejudice, (which whilst the *Laity* were kept ignorant of, all went for currant on their side) and imputed thereto all the Troubles of *Germany*, about

By *Faust* and *Guttenburg*

those *Centum gravamina*,[76] then complained of; for that now men being better enlightned by *printed Books*, began to call in question the present Faith, and Tenets of the *Church* of *Rome*, and to examine how far Religion was departed from its *primitive Institution and Purity*. Among which one great Crime was, that the *Laity* and vulgar sort of men were taught and exhorted to *read the Scriptures*, and pray every one in their own native Language: A great Crime, I confess, and much to be dreaded; for if this were permitted to pass for currant Doctrine, the Vulgar would quickly discover their Cheats and Usurpations, and believe that the *Clergie* had abused and *cheated* them hitherto. For if men were once perswaded, that they could make their own way and court to God by their *own prayers and addresses* in their own Tongues, which they understood, and that they would be heard, and be more prevalent in Heaven, than mumbled in *Latin*, without understanding what they prayed for, it would certainly bring Contempt on the *Mass* and *Mass-Priests*, on *Pardons* and *Pardon-mongers*, on *auricular Confession* and *Confessors*, and on the *power* of the *Keys*, and in sum would impeach all Ecclesiastical Jurisdiction, which (by *Sinister Artifices*) had been got and kept secret by the *Clergie* for many generations.

For without all doubt, the keeping of these and the like Mysteries, (rather of Iniquity than) of Religion, wickedly obtained, and as wickedly kept in the hands of Priests only, (*participes Criminis*, parties to their Cheats)[77] have given that esteem the Priests now have amongst the *Romanists* through many Ages to this very day. /

Now since Printing hath made such Discoveries of such Mysteries of Iniquity, and brought to light the more pure Word and Doctrine, so that their Traditions, their Indulgences, their false Glosses, and their other like Trumperies, could not prevail as formerly, *Romish Craft* sought out other pestilent Inventions to maintain their Impieties, whereof *padlocking the Press* was not the least, to keep the Laity ignorant. And though they could not wholly suppress Printing, yet in *Romish* Territories they ordained, that no Book should be printed without an *Imprimatur* first obtained from some *Inquisitor*, or some such like *Myrmidon*,[78] digging deep to hide their Counsels from all the Laity, and to stifle any Light or Truth, that was not suitable to their deeds of Darkness; hence hath proceeded the obstructions of many Truths fit to be made common, but have not been able to appear in the light but by stealth: Instead thereof they now set up *heathen Philosophy and Metaphysicks* against *Scripture*, to make good their mysterious Juglings, disputing and reasoning more out of them than out of holy Writ. Thus they set up Learning (or rather quirks of Learning) against Learning, and old musty Traditions of former Times, and such obscure passages as needed their Interpretations and Explanations, and all to keep the *Laity* in suspence between fear and controversal Juglings and Equivocations: Nay, they rather have recourse to Tropes and Allegories, (where none are needful) if not to *Cabala*[79] it self than allow that all the parts of Religious Worship, (tho' never so clear and plain to every Understanding, as to fall easily within common Understandings) should be without their Explications or Expositions; so that they cannot monopolize the Mysteries of their Church-Government so closely and wholly within their Ecclesiastick Circle, but discoveries are made of their *Cheats*.

These things well weighed and considered, the Conclusion is natural, that it bears no shew, that forbidding men to write tends to any good end, but really to the end to conceal the *Truth*, and to shew it to the World in *Mascarata*,[80] or some deceitful Light only.

# THE TORY REACTION I

Roger L'Estrange, *Observator in Question and Answer*, 1 (London: H. Brome, 13 April 1681). N&S, 458.1001; ESTC, P1869.

*A Ra-Ree Show* (London: B.T., and Sold at his Shop in Pauls Church-Yard, 1681). Wing, C5226A; ESTC, R36037.

Roger L'Estrange, *Notes upon Stephen College* (London: Joanna Brome, at the Gun at the West-End of St. Pauls Church-Yard, 1681), pp. 10–14, 43–5. Wing, L1281; ESTC, R7200.

Roger L'Estrange, *Observator*, 325 (London: Joanna Brome, 23 April 1683). N&S, 458.1325; ESTC, P1869.

*L–gley C—s His Lamentation in New-Gate; Who Lies there in Danger of his Ears for Printing and Publishing Sedition and Treason, for this Five Years Last Past. A Song* (London: J. Dean, Bookseller in Cranborn-Street, in Leicester-Fields, near Newport-House, 1684). Wing, N673; ESTC, R42983.

*An Account of the Proceedings against Nathaniel Thomson, upon his Tryal at the Kings Bench-Bar Westminster, who was Tried, and Found Guilty on Wednesday the 26$^{th}$ of November 1684. For Printing a Dangerous and Seditious Libel, Intitled the Prodigal Return'd Home, Asserting the Popes Supremacy in Ecclesiastical Affaires, &c.* (London: A. Banks, 1684). Wing, A349; ESTC, R209740.

Ascendancy over the press became an important ambition of the loyalist counter-attack that gained pace following Charles II's removal of Parliament to Oxford and then into limbo in early 1681. This produced continued efforts to clamp down on opposition propaganda, extending to execution for treason in the case of Stephen College in 1681, but also a propaganda effort led by the King's own ten-page *Declaration* of 8 April and fed by loyal addresses, pamphlets and periodicals, notably L'Estrange's *Observator*. Aspects of the strategy of control augmented by confutation between 1681 and 1685 are represented here and in the next section.

Roger L'Estrange launched his *Observator* on 13 April 1681 with the salvo: 'Tis the Press that has made 'um Mad, and the Press must set 'um Right again'. The often-quoted remark, in itself a foretaste of First Amendment as much as Gulag, is given its context here in the first number of the epic Tory periodical, which was to continue over six years and 931 issues, under slightly varying titles.

L'Estrange's dual commitments to confutation and control had shifted towards the former as burgeoning Tory use of the press coincided with the depletion of his powers as surveyor of the press following the lapse of the Printing Act. The *Observator* became L'Estrange's greatest achievement, arguing the case against dissent and for absolute monarchy but always intended to supplement not displace censorship, regularly identifying likely candidates for suppression, which L'Estrange continued to pursue in deed as well as word.

The conviction of Stephen College in 1681 has been called the show trial that 'heralded the crushing of the whigs'.[1] The printed ballad *A Ra-Ree Show* was taken as evidence of the treasonous inclination of the 'protestant joiner', as endorser of the lyric and originator of the accompanying illustration. College was arrested and in July tried in London, but a Whig jury returned an ignoramus verdict. A second trial was held in Oxford, where a conviction was secured, with the *Ra-Ree Show* part of the wider case against College, who was executed on 31 August. One reader wrote on the copy in the Huntington Library: 'A most scandalous libell agt ye Government, for wch & othr things Colledge was justly executed', with the word 'justly' interpolated to confirm the point. Francis Smith was fined and pilloried for his part in having the *Ra-Ree Show* printed. College had become a popular source of satirical ballads in 1679-81, with Scroggs, the Duke of York and ultimately the King among the targets, and Whig leaders like Shaftesbury among his supporters. The 'ra-ree show' was a satirical label for the rare entertainment orchestrated by the King to gull the 'freeborn fools', dominate the representative, and deliver all to Rome. College's later Whig martyrdom was assisted by the publication of *A True Copy of the Dying Words of Mr. Stephen College*, published by his wife Edith.

L'Estrange foresaw the danger of College gaining posthumous support and moved quickly to forestall it by issuing his *Notes upon College*, in which he defended the conviction using College's testimony in the trial and also in his *Dying Words*. Among other evidence L'Estrange considered the production of the *Ra-Ree Show*, reflected in the excerpts here. He noted that College's protestations of ignorance about the author or printer of the verses did not extend to directly denying a role in designing the accompanying cartoon. Furthermore, L'Estrange claimed to have a manuscript of College's final speech, which he said matched the handwriting behind the *Ra-Ree Show*. A second edition of the *Notes upon College* was published in the same year (Wing, L1282).

The Tory reaction did not guarantee press freedom for anyone, including its own. L'Estrange faced attempts to suppress the *Observator* from enemies and his own side, for whom his populist approach and incitement of opponents were very mixed blessings. In 1683, *Observator* number 325 provided an unusual instance of L'Estrange arguing for (his) liberty of the press in the face of the latest such attempt. Amongst earlier instances, the King at one point in 1680, so pre-*Observator*, reportedly ordered L'Estrange 'to forbear writing such papers as tend to division', and on the day of College's execution a Whig rearguard action saw the *Observator*'s publisher Joanna Brome presented to the London grand jury for promoting popery and sedition, alongside Nathaniel Thompson for the *Loyal Protestant* and Benjamin Took for *Heraclitus Ridens*.[2] In 1683 Brome was again presented, for the *Observator* of 14 April (no. 319), this time being charged with publishing news without prior authority, the messenger of the press Robert Stephens having personally bought a copy from her.[3] Stephens, L'Estrange's erstwhile assistant turned enemy, had been seeking to build a case for some weeks, even conspiring to set up an illicit opposition paper to convince the authorities that the *Observator* stirred rather than silenced dispute.[4] The *Observator* no. 325 provided L'Estrange's response to the accusations.

L'Estrange declared in the *Observator* that his age's Prynne, Burton and Bastwick were Care, Curtis and Harris.[5] Despite the title of the mocking ballad *L–gley C—s His Lamentation in New-Gate*, Langley Curtis was not in danger of losing his ears, like Prynne, but like his fellow Whig writer-publishers and along with his wife Jane he had indeed been tangling with the authorities for 'Five Years last past', as the title claimed. In 1679 he and Care had been called to account for their *Weekly Pacquet*, Curtis being released on a bond of £200 that was several times in jeopardy. He also published *Julian the Apostate* (1682), for which the author Samuel Johnson spent four years in jail after being convicted of seditious libel.[6] The ballad refers to the aftermath of Curtis's court appearance in December 1683 for *The Night-Walker of Bloomsbury*, a broadsheet dialogue envisioning the ghost of the executed Lord Russell walking abroad, for which Curtis was committed to Newgate and one of his hawkers ordered to be whipped. On 21 April 1684 Curtis was fined and pilloried.[7] His spell in Newgate was marked by the *Lamentation*, which followed the Tory publisher James Dean's similar *Coll. Sidney's Lamentation* the previous year and celebrates a more general crushing of the Whigs. The ballad, headed by staves of music, was printed on the verso of another scurrilous song, *A New Miracle or Dr. Nomans Safe Return* (Wing, N673).

The Tory reaction also did not protect its own when Nathaniel Thompson veered over the line from Toryism to Catholicism, as the printed account recording his conviction for producing a seditious libel on 26 November 1684 shows. The offending work was *The Prodigal Return'd Home*, a substantial anti-Protestant book written following the conversion of its anonymous author, the ejected Cambridge fellow E. Lydiott. Thompson had a turbulent career after arriving in London from Dublin as a printer in the late 1660s, later branching into publishing and writing. He was investigated during the House of Lords inquiry into anti-court libels in 1677[8] before becoming a more overtly pro-court propagandist, mainly through the *Loyal Protestant Intelligence*, although this did not end his troubles. 'Popish Nat' was fined and pilloried on 20 June 1682 for tracts claiming Sir Edmund Berry Godfrey was a suicide not murder victim, and in the preface to *A Choice Collection of 120 Loyal Songs* (1684), Thompson rued 'having seldom less than 3, or 4 Indictments at a Sessions against Me'. A prominent publisher of Catholic works under James II, he died in 1687. The publisher of the 1684 trial account, 'A. Banks', was presumably Alexander Banks, his fellow printer and co-defendant.

Notes
1. M. Goldie, 'Danby, the Bishops and the Whigs,' in T. Harris, P. Seaward and M. Goldie (eds), *The Politics of Religion in Restoration England* (Oxford: Basil Blackwell, 1990), pp. 75–100, on p. 99.
2. *CSPD*, 10 August 1680; R. L'Estrange, *Dissenters Sayings, The Second Part* (London, 1681), preface (no sig.).
3. *Observator*, 323; *CSPD*, 16 April 1683. For details of the Observator's publishing history, see G. Kemp, 'The Works of Roger L'Estrange', in A. Dunan-Page and B. Lynch (eds), *Roger L'Estrange and the Making of Restoration Culture* (Aldershot: Ashgate, 2008), pp. 181–223.
4. *CSPD*, 14 March 1683, 8 June 1683.
5. *Observator*, 188 (August 1682).
6. See below, pp. 304–5.
7. Old Bailey Proceedings, 12–14 December 1683, p. 4; J. Sutherland, *The Restoration Newspaper and its Development* (Cambridge: Cambridge University Press, 1986), p. 202.
8. *HMC*, 9, Appendix, pp. 69, 73.

Roger L'Estrange, *Observator in Question and Answer*, 1 (London: H. Brome, 13 April 1681). N&S, 458.1001; ESTC, P1869.

# THE OBSERVATOR,

## In QUESTION and ANSWER

### Wednesday, April 13. 1681.

Q. *WEll! They are so.*[1] *But do you think now to bring 'um to their Wits again with a* Pamphlet?

A. Come, Come, 'Tis the *Press* that has made 'um *Mad*, and the *Press* must set 'um *Right* again. The Distemper is Epidemical; and there's no way in the world, but by *Printing*, to convey the *Remedy* to the *Disease*.

Q. *But what is it that you call a* Remedy?

A. The *Removing* of the *Cause*. That is to say, the *Undeceiving* of the *People*: for they are well enough Disposed, of themselves, to be Orderly, and Obedient; if they were not misled by *Ill Principles*, and Hair'd and Juggled[2] out of their Senses with so many Frightful *Stories* and *Impostures*:

Q. *Well! To be Plain and Short; You call your self the* Observator: *What is it now that you intend for the Subject of your* Observations?

A. Take it in few words then. My business is, to encounter the *Faction*,[3] and to Vindicate the *Government*, to detect their *Forgeries*, to lay open the Rankness of their *Caumnies*, and *Malice*; to Refute their *Seditious Doctrines*; to expose their *Hypocrisy* and the *bloudy Design* that is carry'd on, under the Name, and Semblance, of *Religion*; And, in short, to lift up the Cloke of the *True Protestant* (as he Christens himself) and to shew the People, the *Jesuite* that lies skulking under it.

Q. *Shall the* Observator *be a* Weekly Paper, *or How*?

A. No, No; but oftner, or seldomer, as I see Occasion.[4]

Q. *Pray favour me a word: When you speak of a* True Protestant, *don't you mean a* Dissenting Protestant?

A. Yes, I do: For your *Assenting* and *Consenting Protestant* (you must know) is a *Christian*.

Q. *And is not a* Dissenting Protestant *a* Christian *too*?

A. Peradventure, he *is* one; peradventure, *not*: For a Dissenter has his Name from his *Disagreement*, not from his *Perswasion*.

Q. *What is a Dissenter then?*

*A.* 'Tis Impossible to say either what a *Dissenter IS*, or what he is *NOT*. For he's a *NOTHING*; that may yet come to be *ANY thing*. He may be a *Christian*; or he may be a *Turk*:[5] But you'l find the best account of him in his *Name*. *A DISSENTER, is one that thinks OTHERWISE*. That is to say, let the *Magistrate* think what he pleases, the *Dissenter* will be sure to be of *another Opinion*. A *Dissenter* is not of *This*, or of *That*, or of *Any Religion*; but *A Member Politique of an Incorporate Faction*:[6] or Otherwise; A *Protestant Fault-Finder* in a *Christian Commonwealth*.

*Q. Well! but tho' a* Dissenter *may be* any thing; *A* Dissenting Protestant *yet tells ye* what *he Is*.

*A.* He does so, he tells ye that he *is a Negative*: an *Anti-Protester*; One that *Protests AGAINST*, but not *FOR* any thing.

*Q. Ay: but so long as he opposes the* Corruptions *of the Church of* Rome.

*A*. Well: And so he does the *Rites*, and *Constitutions* of the Church of *England* too. As a *Protestant*, he does the *former*; and the *Other* as a *Dissenter*.

Q. *But is there no* Uniting *of These* Dissenters?

*A*. You shall as soon make the Winds blow the same way, from all the Points of the Compasss.

*Q. There are* Good *and* Bad, *of* all Opinions, *there's no doubt on't*: *But do you think it fayr, to Condemn* a whole Party *for some* Ill men *in't?*

*A*. No, by no means: The *Party* is neither the *Worse*, for having *Ill* men in it, nor the *Better*, for *Good*: For whatever the *Members* are, the *Party* is a *Confederacy*; as being a *Combination* against the *Law*.

*Q. But a man may* Mean honestly, *and yet perhaps ly under some* Mistake. *Can any man help his Opinion?*

*A*. A man may *Mean well*, and *Do Ill*: he may shed *Innocent Bloud*, and *think he does God good Service*. 'Tis True: A man cannot help *Thinking*; but he may help *Doing*: He is *Excusable* for a *Private* Mistake, for That's an Error only to *himself*; but when it comes once to an *Overt Act*, 'tis an *Usurpation* upon the *Magistrate*, and there's no Plea for't.

*Q. You have no kindnesse, I perceive, for a* Dissenting Protestant; *but what do you think of a bare* Protestant *without any* Adjunct?

*A*. I do look upon *Such* a *Protestant* to be a kind of an *Adjective Noun-Substantive*; it requires something to be joyn'd with it, to shew its Signification. By *Protestancy* in *General* is commonly understood a *Separation* of Christians from the Communion of the Church of *Rome*: But to *Oppose Errors*, on the *One hand*, is not Sufficient, without keeping our selves *Clear* of Corruptions, on the *Other*. Now it was the *Reformation*, not the *Protestation*, that Setled us upon a true *Medium* betwixt the two *Extremes*.

*Q. So that you look upon the* Protestation, *and the* Reformation,[7] *it seems, as two several things.*

*A.* Very right; But in such a manner only, that the *Former*, by Gods Providence, made way for the *Other*.

*Q. But are not all* Protestants *Members of the* Reformed Religion?

*A.* Take notice, *First*, that the *Name* came Originally from the *Protestation* in 1529 against the *Decree of Spires*,[8] and that the *Lutheran Protestants* and *Ours* of the Church of *England*, are not of the *Same Communion*. Now *Secondly*, if you take *Protestants* in the *Latitude* with our *Dissenters*, they are not so much a *Religion*, as a *Party*; and whoever takes this Body of *Dissenters* for *Members* of the *Reformed Religion*, sets up a *Reformation* of a *hundred and fifty Colours*, and as many *Heresies*. The *Anabaptists, Brownists, Antinomians, Familists, &c.* do all of them set up for *Dissenting Protestants*; but God forbid we should ever enter these *People* upon the Roll of the *Reformation*.

Q. Well! *But what do you think of* Protestant Smith *and* Protestant Harris?[9]

A. Just as I do of *Protestant Muncer*; and *Protestant / Phifer*,[10] a Brace of Protestants that cost the Empire 150000 Lives: and our own *Pretended Protestants* too, of Later Date, have cost *This Nation little lesse*.

Q. *Ay: But these are men of quite another Temper: Do not you see how zealous they are for the Preservation of the* King's Person, *the* Government, *and the* Protestant Religion?

*A.* I *See* well enough what they *Say*, and I *know* what they *do*. Consider, *First*, that they are Profess'd *Anabaptists*: *Smith* no less then a *pretended Prophet*;[11] and the *Other*, a kind of a *Wet Enthusiast*. Secondly; 'tis the very *Doctrine* of the *Sect* to root out *Magistracy*, Cancel *Humans Laws*; *Kill*, and take *Possession*; and *wash their Feet with the Bloud of the Ungodly*; and where ever they have set Footing, they have *Practic'd* what they *Taught*. Are not these likely men now, to help out a *King*, and a *Religion*, at a dead list? If you would be further satisfy'd in the Truth of things, reade *Sleidan, Spanhemius, Gastius, Hortensius, Bullinger, Pontanus*, The *Dipper dipp'd, Bayly's Disswasive, Pagets Heresiography, &c.*[12] *Hortensius* tells ye, how *Jack of Leydens Successor*[13] murthered his Wife, to make way to his Daughter, P. 74. and after that, cut a girls throat, for fear she should tell Tales. *Gastius* tells us of a Fellow that cut off his brothers Head, as by Impulse, and then cry'd, *The Will of God is fulfilled, lib.* I. Pa 12.[14] *Jack of Leyden* started up from Supper *to do some business* (he said) *which the Father had commanded him*, and cut off a Soldiers Head; and afterwards cut off his Wives Head in the *Marketplace. Sleydans Comment. Lib.* 10.[15]

Q. You will not make the Protestant-Mercury[16] to be an Anabaptist too, will ye?

*A.* If you do make him *any thing*, I'le make him *That*. But in one word, they are *Facitous* and *Necesitous*; and consequently, the fittest Instruments in the world, for the Promoting of a *Sedition*. First, as they are *Principled* for't; and then, in respect of their *Condition*; for they are every man of them under the

Lash of the Law, and Retainers to Prisons; So that in their *Fortunes* they can hardly be *worse*. Insomuch, that it is a common thing for them to lend a Name to the countenancing of a Libel which no body else dares own.

Q. *Well! but let them be as* poor, *and* malicious *as* Devils, *so long as they have neither* Brains, *nor* Interest, *what hurt can their Papers do?*

A. The Intelligences, you must know, that bear their *Names*, are not of *their Composing*, but the Dictates of a *Faction*, and the Venom of a Club of *Commonwealths-men* instill'd into those Papers.

Q. *These are* Words, *all this while, without* Proofs; *Can you show us particularly where the Venom lies?*

A. It is the business of every Sheet they Publish, to Affront the *Government*, the *Kings Authority*, and *Administration*; the *Privy-Council*; the *Church, Bench, Juries, Witnesses*; All *Officers, Ecclesiastical, Military*, and *Civil*: And no matter for *Truth* or *Honesty*, when a *Forg'd Relation* will serve their turn. 'Tis a common thing with them, to get half a dozen *Schismaticall* Hands to a *Petition*, or *Address* in a corner, and then call it, the sense of the Nation: and when all's done, they are not above twenty Persons, that make all this Clutter in the Kingdom.

Q. But to what End do they all this?

A. To make the Government *Odious*, and *Contemptible*; to magnifie their own Party; and fright the People out of their *Allegeance*, by *Counterfeit Letters, Reports*, and *false Musters*, as if the sober and considerable part of the Nation were all on their side.

Q. *We are in Common Charity to allow, for* Errors, *and* Misreports, *and not presently to make an Act of* Malice, *and* Design, *out of every* Mistake. *Can you shew me any of these* Counterfeits, *and* Impostures *that you speak of? These* Cheats *upon the* People, *and* Affronts *upon the* Government?

A. Yes, yes; Abundantly. And I'le give you Instances immediately upon every point you'l ask me: Only This note, by the way; That let them be *Mistakes*, or *Contrivances*, or what you will, they all run Unanimously *against* the Government, without so much as one Syllable in *favour* of it: Which makes the matter desperately suspitious.

Q. Let me see then, in the First place where any Affront *is put upon the* Government.

A. *Some Persons* (Says Smiths Prot. Int. N. 7.)[17] *in* Norwich, *&c. who have a greater stock of* Confidence *and* Malice, *then* Wisdom, *and* Honesty, *are so far transported with* Zeal *to serve the* Devil, *or his* Emissaries *the* Papists, *that they are now Prosecuting several* Dissenting Protestants *upon* Stat. 35. Eliz. &c.[18] (And so the Protestant-Mercury, N. 15)[19] *Some People at* Norwich, *are playing the* Devil *for* Godsake: *several honest, peaceable*, Protestant Dissenters, *having been troubled for not coming to* Church, *or having been Present at* Religious Meetings, &c. Now what greater *Affront* can there be to *Government*, then This language, *First*, from an *Anabaptist* that is a *Professed Enemy* to *all Government*; and *Secondly*, from a *Private Person*, Bare-fac'd, to arraign a *Solemn Law*: A *Law* of this *Antiquity*; a *Law* of Queen *Elizabeth's*, (a Princess so much Celebrated by our *Dissenters themselves* for her *Piety, Good Government*, and *Moderation*;) a *Law* which, upon Experience, has been found so *Necessary*, that the bare *Relaxing* of it, cost the *Life* of a *Prince*, the *Bloud* of *two or three hundred thousand* of his *Subjects*, and a *Twenty-year-Rebellion*? To say nothing of the dangerous Consequence of making it *Unsafe* for *Magistrates* to discharge their Duties, for fear of *Outrages*, and *Libells*.

Q. *Well*! *But what have you to say now to the* Kings Authority, *his* Administration, *and his* Privy Council.

A. *Smith* (in his *Vox Populi*, P. 13.) saith, that *the King is oblig'd to pass or Confirm those Laws his People shall Chuse*.[20] at which rate, if they shall tender him a Bill for the *Deposing* of himself, he is bound to *agree* to't. *Secondly*, in the same Page, he *Denies the Kings Power of Proroguing or Dissolving Parliaments*: which is an *Essential of Government* it self, under what Form soever, and he's no longer a *King, without it*. And then for his *Administration*, P. I. the *Anabaptist* charges upon his Majesty *those many surprising and astonishing Prorogations, and Dissolutions* (as he has worded his Meaning) *to be procur'd by the Papists*. And then, P. 15. he wounds both the *King*, and his *Council*, at a Blow; in falling upon *those that make the King break his Coronation-Oath*; arraigning his *Council*[21] in the *First* place, and the *King himself* in the *Second*; and that for no less then the breach of *Oath*, and *Faith*. – Wee'l talk out the rest at our next Meeting.

*London*, Printed for *H.Brome*, at the Gun in S.*Pauls* Church-yard.

*A Ra-Ree Show* (London: B.T., and Sold at his Shop in Pauls Church-Yard, 1681). Wing, C5226A; ESTC, R36037.

# A RA-REE SHOW.

*To the Tune of* I am a Senceless Thing.

*Leviathan.*[1]
COme hither, *Topham*,[2] come, with a hey, with a hey,
Bring a Pipe and a Drum, with a ho,
   Where e're about I go,
   Attend my *Ra-ree show*,
With a hey, Trany nony nony no.

*Topham.*
That monstrous Foul *Beast*, with a hey, with a hey,
Has *Houses Twain* in's Chest, with a ho,
   O *Cooper, Hughs* and *Snow*,[3]
   Stop Thief with *Ra-ree Show*,
With a hey, Trany nony nony no.

For if he should escape, with a hey, with a hey,
With *Halifaxes Trap*[4] with a ho,
   He'd carry good *Dom. Com.*[5]
   Unto the Pope of *Rome*,
With a hey, Trany nony nony no.

*Levi.*
Be quiet ye Dull Tools, with a hey, with a hey,
As other Free-born Fools with a ho,
   Do not all Gaping stand,
   To see my *Slight* of *Hand?*
With a hey, Trany nony nony no.

'Tis not to *Rome* that I, with a hey, with a hey,
Lugg about my *Trumpery*, with a ho,
   But *Oxford, York, Carlile*,[6]

And round about the *Isle*,
With a hey, Trany nony nony no.

But if *they* would come out, with a hey, with a hey,
Let them first make a Vote, with a ho,
   To yield up all they have,
   And *Tower Lords*[7] to save,
With a hey, Trany nony nony no.

    *Top.*
Now that is very hard, with a hey, with a hey,
Thou art worse than *Cut-nose Guard*, with a ho,
   And *Clifford, Danby, Hide,*
   *Hallifax*[8] does all outride,
With a hey, Trany nony nony no.

Holy Ghost in Bagg of Cloak, with a hey, with a hey,
Quaking King in hollow Oak, with a ho,
   And *Rosamond* in Bower,[9]
   All Badges are of Power,
With a hey, Trany nony nony no.

And Popularity, with a hey, with a hey,
Adds Power to Majesty, with a ho,
   But *Dom. Com.* in little Ease,
   Will all the World Displease,[10]
With a hey, Trany nony nony no.

    *Levi.*
Let 'um hate so they fear, with a hey, with a hey,
Curst Fox has the best Chear, with a ho,
   Two States in *Blind-house* pent,[11]
   Make brave strong Government,
With a hey, Trany nony nony no.

    *Top.*
But Child of Heathen *Hobbs*,[12] with a hey, with a hey,
Remember old *Dry Bobbs*,[13] with a ho,
   For fleecing *Englands* Flocks,
   Long Fed with Bits and Knocks,
With a hey, Trany nony nony no.

    *Levi.*
What's past, is not to come, with a hey, with a hey,
Now Safe is *David's* Bum, with a ho,

Then hey for *Oxford* ho,
Strong Government, *Ra-ree show*,
With a hey, Trany nony nony no.

*Ra-ree Show* is Resoul'd, with a hey, with a hey,
This is worse than Disoul'd, with a ho,
    May the mighty weight at's back
    Make's Lecherous Loyns[14] to crack,
With a hey, Trany nony nony no.

Me-thinks he seems to Stagger, with a hey, with a hey,
Who but now did so Swagger, with a ho,
    Gods-Fish he's Stuck i'th' Mire,
    And all the Fat's i'th' Fire,[15]
With a hey, Trany nony nony no.

Help *Cooper, Hughs*, and *Snow*, with a hey, with a hey,
To pull down *Ra-ree Show*, with a ho,
    So, So, the Gyant's down,
    Let's *Masters* out of *Pound*,[16]
With a hey, Trany nony nony no.

And now you have freed the Nation, with a hey, with a hey,
Cram in the *Convocation*, with a ho,
    With *Pensioners* all and Some,
    Into this *Chest* of *Rome*,[17]
With a hey, Trany nony nony no.

And thrust in *six* and *Twenty*, with a hey, with a hey,
With *Not Guilty*, good plenty, with a ho,
    And hout them hence away,
    To *Cologne* or *Breda*,[18]
With a hey, Trany nony nony no.

Ha-loo the *Hunts* begun, with a hey, with a hey,
Like Father, Like Son,[19] with a ho,
    *Ra-ree Show* in *French*-Lap,
    Is gone to take a Nap,
    And *Successor* has the Clap,[20]
With a hey, Trany nony nony no.

**London**, Printed for *B. T.* and Sold at his Shop in *Pauls* Church-yard: For the good of the Publick, 1681.

Reproduced by permission of the Huntington Library, San Marino, California.
Shelfmark Rare Books 135850.

Roger L'Estrange, *Notes upon Stephen College* (London: Joanna Brome, at the Gun at the West-End of St. Pauls Church-Yard, 1681), pp. 10–14, 43–6. Wing, L1281; ESTC, R7200.

[10]
§. 4. The Libellous Pictures, and Particularly the Raree Show prov'd to be Colleges.

MY Lord, (says College) *as to the Papers Charg'd*[1] *upon me to be mine, I declare I know not of them.* Tryal. pag. 74. *I cannot deny but that they were in my House; but that I was the* Author *or did take them in, is as great a Mistake as ever was made.* Ibid. *I know nothing of the* Printing *of them, nor was I the* Author *of them.* Ibid. *I do declare I know nothing of the* Original, *the* Printer, *nor the* Author. p. 75. There's a great deal more of this stuff in the *Tryal*, to the same purpose; but I shall lay no hold of any thing he says in his *Defence*, save where he *Confesses*: But it will be allow'd, I hope, that some weight might be laid upon what he delivers in that which is publish'd under the Title of *A True Copy of the Dying Words of Mr.* Stephen College, *left in Writing under his own hand, and confirmed by him at the time of Execution,* Aug. 31. 1681. *at* Oxford, *Publish'd by his own Relations, and Printed for* Edith College.[2] ... /

He was Interrogated in the Castle[3] some few days before he suffer'd, whether he did not with his own hand draw the design for the Ballad of *A Raree-Show*? and whether *that very Draught* was not taken with the other Prints, in his *House*? His Answer was that *he was neither the* Author *of the Verses or Ballad, nor did he know either the* Author, *or the* Printer. And then for the *Design*,[4] he bad them *shew it* (knowing it to be lost) *and he would own it, if it were his.*

Now to expound this Riddle, 'tis probable he did not know the *Author*, nor the *Printer*; and yet it is clear that the *first design* was of his *drawing*; and by him accommodated to the *Verses*, without so much as knowing who was the *Poet*. He might possibly deliver that Draught also to have it *Cut*, without knowing the *Graver*;[5] as it is certain that he did deliver the *Verses* to be *Printed*, though perhaps without knowing the *Printer*. And this does evidently appear from the Testimony of the *Printer himself.*[6] /

The *Printer* confesses and declares upon the sight of one of the Papers found at *Colleges*, that it was wrought at *his Press*; that he did it for *Franck Smith*,[7] who told him that it was a *Merry, Joking thing*, but a *Truth*, which Corresponds with the Evidence, that *College* said it was *as true as that Gods in Heaven.* The Printer informs likewise, that *Francis Smith*, upon the reading of the Staves[8] to him *Expounded* them; (but without the *Picture*) and told him that there was a *Captain* with a *Pack at his back*, and that was the *King*; and that He in the *Mire* was the *King*; and that He with the *Two Faces* was the *King* again; and that it was a *Merry Jocose thing, and had been sung before several Lords at Oxford*:[9] Which Particularities do punctually agree with the Evidence against *College*, from whom undoubtedly *Franck Smith* receiv'd the *Manuscript*; and *College*, it seems told *Smith* no more upon this occasion, than what he had told before to other People. The Book-seller, I find, knew well enough what he did too, being very earnest with the Printer not to discover his *Name*, but to say that *he had the Copy from a Gentleman, to him unknown;* adding moreover these words, (*A body may be Troubled about it, but there's no treason in it.*)

Now after all that is said, lest it should be suggested that there's no positive Proof yet against *College*, that he had any thing to do with this Libell, we shall now put that Question out of all dispute. There was a Paper of *Colleges Intercepted*, which upon Examination he utterly *deny'd* at *first*; but finding himself *Discover'd*, he *Confess'd* in. This was some few days before his Execution. The Paper here intended, was the *Speech*, word for word, that was Printed for *Edith College*, which being show'd to the Joyner, he acknowledg'd it to be *of his own Hand-writing*; and so is the *Manuscript* also of the *Raree-Show* / from whence that Ballad was Printed; and I have the *Original* at this Instant by me, to satisfie any man that shall make a doubt whether or no it was of *Colleges Writing*. Besides that, he sung the Ballad in several places, and particularly at Sir *Philip Matthews's*,[10] at *Southcot*, as divers Persons of Credit are ready to attest: And by the token that Sir *Philip* charg'd him to *forbear, for he would not suffer any such thing in his House*; or to this effect.

I cannot but deplore the Infatuated blindness of this Unhappy Creature, that should now at his last Extremity, instead of discharging his soul by a publique and sincere Repentance, be troubling of his head with Shifts and Reservations, as if he were contriving how to cast a mist before the Eyes of God and Man; and in a case so open too, that half an eye sees thorow it. ...

[43]
We shall now as briefly as may be, apply matter of *Fact* to the Capital parts of his *Charge*. The *Designing* of the Sculpture[11] to his *Raree-Show* is prov'd upon him so point blank, that he himself had not the face to deny it: And *that Draught* made him as *Guilty of*, and as *Answerable for the Malicious intent of it*, as if the *Ballad* had been originally his *own*: His *Publishing* of it was a *further* Aggravation of the Crime; and the Pleasure he took in *Singing* it up and down (as he did to several eminent Persons of quality) and in *Exposing* it, made all that was in it his own too. In that *Doggrel Copy* there is Chalk'd out the very Train of the whole *Conspiracy*; and so plainly too, that it will not bear any other Construction: ...

[45]
The Faction did, without dispute, flatter themselves that they should find Friends, even in the Parliament it self, to Authorize them in their Enterprize; (but they were egregiously mistaken it seems in their measures.) And they grounded their Hopes upon the Interest they had made in most places of the Kingdom to secure an Election for their turn. This Prospect and Confidence does most notoriously appear in the contrivance of the *Raree-Show*, which in truth looks liker a Song of *Triumph*, as for a thing *already* done, then a bare *Project* and *Exhortation* toward the doing of it: Insomuch that they have in this Ballad delineated the very *Scheme* of their Intentions. It is a thing very remarkable too, that the same Pulse beats still in all their Pamphlets of Appeal to the Multitude; which speaks them clearly to be animated with the same souls, and directed to the same end. As *Vox Patriae*[12] for the purpose, (among forty others.) What is it, but under the Notion of *Petitions* and *Addresses*, in the name of the People of *England*, a certain *Compendium* of Instructions toward the Forming and carrying on of a *Conspiracy?* This Libel lays out the very Model of the Plot, for which *College* was / *Try'd, Condemn'd,* and *Executed*. ...

Roger L'Estrange, *Observator*, 325 (London: Joanna Brome, 23 April 1683). N&S, 458.1325; ESTC, P1869.

## The Observator

*The State of* Stephens'es *Case; and an* Essay *at his* Character. *His scandals upon the* Secretary, *the* Attorny-Generall, *and Other* Great Persons above. *This* Observator *humbly recommended to the Consideration of* Publique Justice.

Munday, April 23. 1683.

TRIMMER. *One Tale's Good 'till Anothers Told.* And I do Assure ye, 'tis the *Crack*[1] all over the *Town*, that *Stephens*[2] *will Carry't*. Why prethee consider it well. First, the *Observator* is Represented as a **Scandalous Libell**.[3] 2ly. *Publish'd without* **Lawful Authority**. 3ly, There's the *Order, Command,* and *Encouragement* of a **Secretary of State, Mr Attorney Generall**,[4] and **Other Great Men above**. Pray will you speak to These Points, *Briefly,* and *Plainly* now.

*OBSERVATOR.* As *Briefly* as I *can*; and as *Plainly* as ever any man spake to *any thing. First,* Though that *Foul-Mouth'd Fool himself*; and the *Seditious Gang* that he *Herds* with (for 'tis no longer the **Devill** in the **hoggs**,[5] but the **hogg** in the **Devills**) Though *They* I say, run **Bellowing** up and down against it, as a **Scandalous Paper**; there is not yet so much as the Least *Glance* in the *Indictment*, of an *Exception* to the Matter of the Paper: But Mrs *Brome* is barely *Prosecuted*, for **Printing** or **Causing to be Printed**, and for **Publishing** the 319th *Observator,*[6] without **Lawfull Authority**. So that the Quality of the Paper is no part of the Question. Wherefore **Stephens'es** *Councell* will not for the Honour of the *Court*, and of *Publique Justice*; and for the *Shame* of *Good People*, pretend to Wheedle the *Jury*, with any *Stories*, that *'tis an* **Enflaming Paper**; that *it keeps up* **Animosities**, and breeds **Dissention** and **Mis-understandings** *among his Majesties Liege-People*; (or any of This *Paltry Stuff*:) for 'tis not the Point, in any wise, whether it be **So** or **Not**; But *This* is the *Single Question*. (All other dashes of *Dawbing,*[7] and *Insinuation* apart.) Had *she*, or *Had she* not, a **Legall** *Authority* for the *Publishing* of it? And *all Other Consideration* is utterly *Forreign* to this *Case.*

*Trim.* Well! And by *What* **Authority** now does she Cause it to be *Printed*, and *Published*?

*Obs.* Now y'are *upon't.* She *Publishes This* Paper by the *same Authority,* that all *Other Members* of the Company of *Stationers,* Publish their *Books* and *Papers* where they do not Invade **Propriety.**[8] There are no *Licencers appointed,*[9] for *Printers,* and *Booksellers,* in *Ordinary Cases,* to *Repair* to: So that they *must,* either *Print,* or *Publish,* without *License,* where there is no *License* to be had, or else neither *Print* nor *Publish* at all; that is to say, in *English,* they must **give over their Trade.** So that as Matters stand at present, Every man *Prints* and *Publishes* what he pleases himself, without any Further *Legall Restraint* upon him, then that he becomes *Answerable* at his *Perill* for the *matter* of the *Book* or *Paper* that he *Prints* or *Publishes.* So that here's no more **Law** in *this Case,* against Mrs *Brome,*[10] for *this Paper,* then there is against **Every** *Member of the Company of Stationers* for what He *Prints* and *Publishes*: And then one can hardly Imagine a *Bolder Usurpation* upon the *Common Liberty* of the *Subject* then is *Attempted* by that *Insolent Rascall* upon *Mrs Brome* in *this Instance.* For the *Freedom* of *Every Individuall* in that *Society* lies *Expos'd* upon the *same Reason*: And 'tis but **His** *Picking* and *Chusing* at *pleasure,* where they lye **All Equally** at *Mercy*: In which Case, he has no more to do, to put *Mony* in his Pocket, then to look about him, and cry **Bleed you Rogues, or I'le Indict ye.**

*Trim.* Does he not wear the *Kings Livery*?[11]

*Obs.* And is he not the *Scandall* of it? And of the *Government* too? that only *suffer* him because they do not *know* him. How often has this *Glavering Fellow* come to Mee for *Notes* against *Care, Curtis, Starkey,*[12] and *Others* of that *Gang,* upon pretence forsooth to make use of such and such Passages out of their *Papers* in *Evidence against* them; I gave him Those *Instances* that would certainly have *reach'd 'em*; but the *Devil-a-bit*[13] I ever heard of them *more*; nor can I Imagine, what *became* of them, unless they were *Improv'd* to raise the *Price* of the *Market.* Did not I tell him where he should find that *Libell* of **Treason in Grain,** for which *Sam. Harris* was *Arraign'd*?[14] Did not I *Name* the *Person* to him that *had* it; and give him *Directions* how to *Manage* That Affair? (which *Directions,* if he had pursu'd, the *Devil himself* could never have Slipt the *Noose*): But this Coxcomb runs upon his *Head,* with his *Brains* in his *Heels*: So that betwixt the **fool** on the *One* side, and the **Knave** on the *Other,* it came to *Nothing* in the *Conclusion.* Am not I able to *prove,* that he was told where *Hunt*[15] was, &c? In One word; his *Conversation* is almost wholly among the *Known,* and most *Malicious Enemies* of the *Church,* and of the *Crown*; and he is (to use a *Term of Law*) **spew'd** out of *All Companies,* that have a *regard* to *any Principles* either of *Duty, Sobriety,* or *Good Manners.* Besides, that it is *Notoriously Known* even where he is *Forc'd* to take any man up, or to *Hunt* after any man that is of the *Seditious Leaven,*[16] how *Officiously* and *Heartily* he Employs the Little Interest he has, to bring him *off* again; But if he happen to Stumble upon a Person of *Another Principle* that has play'd the *Fool*, there's no *Mercy* with him.

*Trim.* Well! I could Wish this *Breach* were *Piec'd-up* again; when all is done. **This Fellow is a Usefull Instrument.**[17]

*Obs.* Go thy ways *Old Trimmer!* Thou wil't be *Damn'd* with *This Labell* out of thy Mouth (For King and Parliament.) Piec'd dost thou Call it? As if thou wert to make *One Centaure* of us; And 'tis Forty to One *Stephens* should be the Man too, and the *Observator* the Beast. Why it is so *Mean*, so *Nasty*, and so *Scandalous* a Wretch, I would turn away a *Lacquey* that should but Descend to drink a pot of Ale with him. But now let me shew you the **Usefullness of such an Instrument as** *This*. He gets ye some *Seditious Pamphlet* or other, (as he is **told**) and away presently to *Court* with it; And *This* Hee calls a **Discovery**; There, he goes *Grinning* about, *My Lord, have you seen the Book I took? Sir, have You seen the Libell that I Seiz'd? By God*, Tom, *I'le Mawl these Rogues before I have done with 'em*; And what's / this *Mighty Bus'ness* at last; but some *Common street-Libell*, that **Neglect** and **Impunity** had *Encourag'd* to walk **Barefac'd**; and every *Porter* in the Street could have done the *same Service*. In short, he has not the **Brains** to do the bus'ness he pretends to. And then for his **honesty**, he gets ye a *Warrant*, and away with that to a *Coffee-House*; where the Business is *Immediately Buzz'd* about from One to Another, 'till at last, 'tis in Every bodys Mouth, who was the *Authour*, the *Printer*, or *Publisher* of such or such a *Pamphlet*: and that the *Messenger of the Press* has a *Warrant* for him: How This comes to Pass, I know not, but 'tis an *Admirable way* of giving notice to any man to be *gone*, without the Charge of a *Penny-Post*. But in one word; whoever Compares *Stephens* with other of the *Kings Messengers*, upon the *Effectual Execution* of their *Warrants*, (where there is any thing of *Address* or *Industry* requir'd for the *Discovery* and *Apprehension* of the *Person*) shall find the *Proportion* of above *Five* to *One against* him: And so here's more then enough sayd to the **Instrument**. But now to the **Authority** again of *Mrs Bromes* **Publishing** the *Observator*. Either her *Authority's Good*, (as I sayd before:) Or every Person of the *Company*, that *Prints* & *Publishes*, is *Liable* to the same *Indictment*.

*Trim.* Nay pray hold. Does not the *Kings Proclamation*[18] **Prohibit Printing and Publishing** of **Books**, without **His Majesties Authority?**

*Obs.* No. Not of *Books*, in *Generall*; but only of *Books*, and *Papers* of **News**, and **Intelligence**. So that you must either make *This INDIVIDUAL Paper*, to be a *Paper* of **News**; (which has not One *Word* of *News* in't) or else, the *Proclamation* has nothing to do with *This Paper*. Nor has the *Law Directed* any *Authority* for the *Licensing* of a Paper of *This Quality*.

*Trim.* But what if this should be found at last to be a Paper of News?

*Obs.* What if a **Man** shall be found to be a **Woman**? Our **Ignoramus-Days** are *gone*,[19] *Trimmer*; when men would *see* things *Invisible*; and yet at the same time, not *Distinguish* betwixt *Light* and *Darkness*. How long has it been **News**, I prethee, to *Reply* upon *Libells*? How long has it been **News**, to Assert the *Principles* of *Duty*, and *Obedience*; and the *Rights* of *Sovereign Power*, and of an *Imperiall Prince*? How long has it been **News**; when the *Honour*, and *Authority* of the *Crown*, and of the *Church* are *Openly Attacqu'd* and *Defam'd*, in **Printed Libells**, to *Defend* the *Government* in **Printed Replies**? But what is it now, that you call **His Majesties Authority**? (Even Admitting this 319*th Observator* to be a *Paper* of **News**) I have the *Kings Broad-Seal* for't, (which I take to be a *Sufficient Authority*) in these very words. **We do by These Presents Give and Grant unto Roger L'Estrange, & his Assigns, the sole Privilege of Writing, Printing, & Publishing All** Mercuries, Diurnals, and **Books** of Publique Intelligence, &c.[20] And I have at This Day an *Annuall Consideration* for my *Patent-Right* in the *Gazette*.[21] So that *News*, or no *News*, 'tis all a Case to *Joanna Brome*. And *in fine*, the Cause lies within This Compass.

If it be not a **News-Paper**, it *needs no License*: If it **Be a News Paper**, here's the **Broad-Seal** (of *Aug.* 22. 1663.) for my *Authority*: Beside (as I told ye the Other day) that the Paper is constantly sent to the Offices of the Secretaries of State[22] befor it is *Publish'd*.

*Trim.* Well! But he has done no more then he had *Order* for, from the **Secretary**, and the **Attorny Generall**, and **Other Great Men above**. He has told this to severall People; and I believe, to Mr *Tanner* (the Clark of the Peace)[23] among the rest; and upon a Motion of Mrs *Bromes*, in the Court, *Mr Recorder*[24] gave to *Understand*, that the *Attorny Generall* was Concern'd in the *Proceeding*.

*Obs.* Mr *Recorder* (let me tell ye) was *misenform'd*; for upon Signifying to Mr *Attorny* what *Use* that *Jugling Knave Stephens*, had made of *his Name*, and *Authority*, he was pleas'd to tell the Gentleman that *Stephens was an Idle Fellow, and Wish'd him to Acquaint the Recorder; that he knew nothing of the Bus'ness, gave no such* **Order***, and had nothing to do in't.* So that according to your hint, Mr *Recorder* had this *Enformation*, probably, from the *Clark of the Peace*, if not from *Stephens himself*. You must know further, that *Stephens* being *Charg'd* the Same day *Publickly* in the *Street* for an **Impudent Lying Villain***, to Cover his Rogueries with the* **Pretended Authorities** *of the Kings Councell*; when the *Attorny General Disclaim'd* any *Order*, or *Privity*, in the *bus'ness*; the *Sneaking Rascal* Clapt his Tayle between his Legs, and went Sniv'ling *away, denying that ever he had Pretended any Authority, either from the* Secretary, *or the* Attorny; And so betook himself to a Couple of *Known Criminalls* against the Government, for *Instructions*, how to Manage his *After-Game*: But I presume, it will appear at last, that he us'd the *Names* of the *Secretary*, & the *Attorny-General*, for a *Shooing-Horn*, to *Draw-on Mr Tanner*, into the *Cause*. Shall a *Little Knave* run the Risque of his *Ears* for the *Forgery* of a *Name* to a *Bond*; and shall this *Audacious Falsifyer Forge* an *Order* of *Secretary of State*, and of the *Kings Attorny-Generall, GRATIS*?

*Trim.* But if you can Blow it off, there's no hurt done.

*Obs.* Is it *Nothing* with you then, for *Mee* to be *Publish'd* all over the *Kingdom*, in *Ten Thousand News-Letters* as a *Rogue*, that the *Kings Ministers* & *Councel*, have Order'd to be *Prosecuted* as a *Libeller*? Is it *Nothing* again, for **Those Ministers** and **Councell**, to be Represented as the *Drivers-on*, & *Abettors* of so *Barbarous*, and *Unjust* a *Proceeding* against *Me*?

*Trim.* You'l go too far, before you think on't.

*Obs.* Nay 'faith *Trimmer*, I'le go *thorough* with it *Now*, before I *leave* it, and *cast off* that same *Cumbersome Modesty*, now at **last**, for the *Preservation* of my **Credit**; which (like a *Consciencious Fool*) I have *Cherish'd thus long*, to the *Ruine* of my **Fortune**. Is it *nothing* do ye think to Start a *President* of *this Quality*, at *this Season*; to set the whole Nation a *Gaping* after the *Issue* of it? The *Friends* of the *Government* on the *One* side; the *Enemies* of it on the *Other*: the *Kings* and the *Churches Cause* in the *Middle*; and *Blind Fortune* Throwing up *Cross* or *Pile*,[25] which of the *Two* shall *Carry't*. If it goes for *Stephens* the *Verdict* speaks as loud as a *Proclamation, Turn ROGUES and PROSPER.*

*Trim.* So that all Depends upon *your Observator.*

*Obs.* Very much I assure ye, upon the **Example**; for though it be a *Particular Case*, 'tis a *Publique Question*: And what do you think people would say on't, if they should see this *Profligate Knave Supported* against the *Government*, by the *Faction*, (which they are now *Labouring* all that is in 'em to do) and *L'Estrange Abandon'd*, as a *Sacrifice* to the *Faction*, by the *Government*. But my *Injuries* are *Redress'd*, so soon as they are made *known*; And **That's the Principal End of this Observator.**

*London*, Printed for *Joanna Brome* at the Gun in S.Pauls Church-yard.

*L-gley C—s His Lamentation in New-Gate; Who Lies there in Danger of his Ears for Printing and Publishing Sedition and Treason, for this Five Years Last Past. A Song* (London: J. Dean, Bookseller in Cranborn-Street, in Leicester-Fields, near Newport-House, 1684). Wing, N673; ESTC, R42983.

## L-GLEY C—S
### His Lamentation in *New-Gate*;

Who lies there in danger of his Ears for Printing and Publishing Sedition and Treason, for this Five Years last past.           A SONG.

I.

COme Whigs out of fashion, of me take compassion,
   my Ears are in danger, my case may be yours;
Long, long have I reigned disturbing the Nation,
   now, now am made Captive to the higher Powers:
With Pacquet[1] & Pamphlets, abus'd *Church & Chaplets*,[2]
   with *C—s* Damn'd *Courants*[3] did abuse the *King* so,
*That none can defend us, till* Tyburn *befriend us,*
   *and send us a Hunting for* Tapskie *below*.[4]

II.

The loss of our Charter, and *Colledge* the Martyr,[5]
   his Flayls are all seiz'd, and our Arms made a prey;
We have lost *Ignoramus*,[6] both *Jew*, *Turk*, and *Tartar*,
   no Plots nor Caballs to recover the Day:
Since *Tony*[7] left squinting, our Cause has been sinking,
   and our Party for *Tyburn* advancing you know;
*There's none can defend us, till* Tyburn *befriend us,*
   *and send us a Hunting for* Essex[8] *below*.

III.

The Law for a Livery, will put me i'th Pillory,
   a damn'd hard Wooden Ruff for a Saint of the Cause;[9]
Had a Tory my place, I wou'd flear[10] and look merrily,
   with hardened Brick-batts I'de pelt him with blows.
When my Head peepeth thorough, the *Tories* will *hollow*,
   at poor *L–gley C—'s* cry *O Raree Show*;[11]

*Now none will defend us, till* Tyburn *befriend us,*
   *and send us a Hunting for* Russel[12] *below.*

### IV.

Poor *Colly* was Whipt too, for stretching an oath or so,
   and Damn'd *Tory Rutland*,[13] too hard for us all;
These dayly misfortunes will all our Designs undoe,
   would his *Fountain*-Tavern[14] wou'd sink, burn, or fall,
But alas I am Gailed,[15] and must not be bailed,
   as we serv'd the Papists, must we be serv'd so?
*There's none will defend us, till* Ketch *does befriend us,*
   *and send us a Hunting for* Walcot[16] *below.*

### V.

Wou'd I were with *Patience*, I'de keep in his Stations,
   and save both my Ears,[17] for the Doctor may want,
I fear they'l be crapt if I live till next Sessions,
   then *Prance*[18] for his Swearing, may sweat and look blank,
But after a Coller, oft cometh a Halter,
   my Neck like my Ears are in danger, you know,
*There's none can defend us, till* Ketch *doth befriend us,*
   *and send us a Hunting for* Sidney[19] *below.*

### VI.

Poor *A—ld* is Pounded, for Lying Confounded,
   by *Wooster*, which he did most basely defame:
Poor *Giles* he was Pillar'd, 'cause *A—ld* was wounded,
   tho' by his own hands, Sir, in *Jack-an-Apes-Lane*;
Now *Giles*[20] he is Bailed, and *A—ld* is Goaled,
   there may lie and Rot too, for ought that we know:
*There's none will defend us, till* Ketch *doth befriend us,*
   *and send us all head-long toth'* Old Rump[21] *below.*

### VII.

*Mowbery* and *Balderen*, Swore more like Fiends, then men,
   they both have been perjur'd ten thousand times o're:
They had but one Wife, and she still lay between them,
   they being our Saints, tho' she cou'd be no Whore;[22]
*Dangerfield* Swore too, all forts of Oaths, black and blew,
   tho' he had been Carted, and Pillar'd before;
Yet they still escaped,[23] tho' worse no Hell raked,
   Then why may not I, that can Rebel no more?

### VIII.

Yet that fortunate Hour, they got out of the Tower,
    both *Wildman* and *Trenchard*, Old *Charlton*[24] and all:
I may find Friends too, tho' *Jefferies*[25] lookt sower,
    and Pardon perhaps, when I come to *White-hall*;
Guineys five Thousand too, (for Printing of Treason)
    like some for Ploting; a kind Recompence; due,
While others for Loyalty, in the Goal dayly Dye,
    I'le into the Country, and live like a Prince.


Printed for *J. Dean*, Bookseller in *Cranborn-street*, in *Leicester-Fields*, near *Newport-House*, 1684.

*An Account of the Proceedings against Nathaniel Thomson, upon his Tryal at the Kings Bench-Bar Westminster, who was Tried, and Found Guilty on Wednesday the 26<sup>th</sup> of November 1684. For Printing a Dangerous and Seditious Libel, Intitled the Prodigal Return'd Home, Asserting the Popes Supremacy in Ecclesiastical Affaires, &c.* (London: A. Banks, 1684). Wing, A349; ESTC, R209740.

AN
ACCOUNT
OF THE
# PROCEEDINGS
AGAINST
## Nathaniel Thomson,
UPON HIS
# TRYAL
AT THE
KINGS Bench-Bar
Westminster,

*Who was Tryed, and found Guilty on* Wednesday *the* 26th *of* November 1684. *For Printing a Dangerous and Seditious* LIBEL, *Intitled the* PRODIGAL RETURN'D HOME, *asserting the* POPES *Supremacy in Ecclesiastical Affaires*, &c.

THE House of *Nathaniel Thompson* the Printer,[1] upon Information, that divers Seditious Books or Papers, were Printed by him: And especially, a Book Intituled the *Prodigal returned home*;[2] asserting the Popes Supremacy in Ecclesiastical Affairs being searched, *&c.* A considerable quantity of those Books, were found and seized by Mr. *Stephens*[3] Messenger to the Press; as likewise, a Book known by the name of *Doleman* about Succession,[4] whereupon Mr. *Thomson* by virtue of a Warrant, being taken into Custody, after some Examination was Committed to *Newgate*, Bail not being accepted, in a case of such a dangerous consequence; notwithstanding, he moved by his Counsel at the *Kings-Bench* Bar, for a *Habeas*

*Corpus*, which after some difficulty he obtained, and was thereupon removed *Corpus cum Causa*,[5] to the *Kings-Bench*, and charged with an Indictment of Trespass and Misdemeanours, for Printing the said Seditious and dangerous Libel; upon which, the Tryal come on upon *Nisi prius*,[6] on the 26*th* of *November* 1684. when as the Council for the King, after the Juries being Impanell'd, and sworn, opened the Case, Informing the Jurors that *Nathaniel Thomson* the Defendant, stood Indicted, for Printing a Seditious and dangerous Book or Libel, asserting the Pope's Supremacy above the Kings, in order to withdraw His Majesties Subjects from their Allegiance, and to bring a scandal upon the Established Government *&c.* and that divers of the said Books, Intitled the *Prodigal returned home*, had been found in his House, that he had been noted for a Person, who had accustomed himself to Print and disperse Libells *&c.* which accordingly would appear to them upon Evidence, to this effect, the Indictment being opened, the Witnesses were called and sworn when, as Mr. *Stephens* gave / Evidence, that being Informed by one *Alexander Banks*,[7] not long before in Service with Mr. *Thomson*, that several ill Books seditious and dangerous to the Government, had been Printed by his Master, and that many had been dispos'd, and that himself had help'd to Compose part of a Book, called the *Prodigal returned home*, and that he doubted not, if search was speedily made, some part of them might be found in the House, he on the 21*th* of *October* last, taking to his assistance one Mr. *Clinch* a Constable, and suddenly entring the House, found several of those Books in Quires,[8] and that he found another seditious Book, in the hands of Mr. *Thomsons* Maid servant, which she had taken from her Mistriss, further urging, that he had formerly Printed and Published the Appeal, and the Libellous Pamphlet Intitled the Noble Peers Speech, *&c.*[9] and that Mr. *Thomson* since his confinement, had confessed he had Printed Three Hundred of the Books, for which he was brought upon his Tryal, but that he had done them for a gentle Man, that was to carry them beyond the Seas, not designing to disperse them in *England*, and that he had named the Author, but his name he could not well remember: The Evidence having proceeded thus far against the Prisoner, *Alexander Banks* was Examined, and demanded whether he had not Composed part of the Book in question, who with many abrupt stammerings, endeavoured to deny it, although he had formerly sworn it, and his Examination taken by Mr. Recorder,[10] produced, for which willfull Retraction, being sharply reproved, Mr. *Clinch* the Constable was Examined, who confirmed all that Mr. *Stephens* had sworn, in relation to the finding the Books in the House of Mr. *Thomson*, adding, that meeting with Mrs. *Thomson*,[11] and perceiving her to hold something slyly behind her, he demanded what it was, to which she replied nothing, but he pressing her to see it, her Maid took it out of her hand, and went about to escape with it, but was taken, and the Book seized, which imported matter of very evil consequence.

Notwithstanding, the Evidence being thus full, that the Jurors might the better understand the malicious design of the Libel, divers Paragraphs on which the Prosecution was grounded, were Read, Importing, that the Proselites of the Reformed Churches, by reason of the Heresie they embraced, were not capable of Salvation, and that St. *Peter* being once appointed Head of the Church, the Pope as his Successor, derived this Power from him, and that all Ecclesiastical dignities must of necessity hold of him and the Bishops &c. ought to be of his Constituting, Insinuating how *Gregory* the Great,[12] had the whole Power of Ecclesiastical Affaires in his hands, and that Christian Princes intermedled not therein, when he sent St. *Augustine*[13] and his *Monks* into this Nation, who Established the *Romish* Religion, and subjected the Ecclesiasticks to the Sea of Rome, In fine, it altogether appeared to justifie the *Romish* Religion, and plead for the Popes Supremacy, magnifying the Pontifical Prelates, and justifying them in their Usurpation, and unlawful claime.

To this the Prisoners Council made reply, that he hoped what had been proved, would not extend to make his Client guilty of publishing the Books (which he could not deny were ill and not justifiable) for as much as it did not appear, he had exposed any of them to fail, to which it was replied, that he had confessed he had Printed them, and it could not be Imagined he designed them for wast Paper, or to dispose of to any other end, than to disperse them, or that they might be dispersed, and that such things were of ill consequence, nor had this been the first Libel the Prisoner had Printed, as had appeared upon Evidence, when little or no other defence being made, the Right Honourable the Lord Chief Justice,[14] gave the Charge, fully summing up the Evidence and minding them especially, of what the Prisoner had voluntarily confessed, laying open the dangerous effects such Libells might produce; declaring, than upon the Evident proof they had before them, and the confession of the Prisoner which had been sworn, they could no less then find him Guilty, where upon laying their Heads together, without going from the Bar, they gave in their Verdict, that *Nathaniel Thomson* was Guilty of the Trespass, &c. And continued in order, to receive the Judgment of the Court.

*LONDON*, Printed for *A. Banks*, 1684.

# THE TORY REACTION II

*The Judgment and Decree of the University of Oxford Past in their Convocation July 21. 1683, against certain Pernicious Books and Damnable Doctrines Destructive to the Sacred Persons of Princes, their State and Government, and of all Humane Society* (Oxford: printed at the Theater, July 1683). Wing, O891; ESTC, R14238.

Algernon Sidney, *The Very Copy of a Paper Delivered to the Sheriffs, upon the Scaffold on Tower-Hill, On Friday, Decemb. 7. 1683. By Algernoon Sidney, Esq; Before his Execution there* (London: R[obert] H[orn], J[ohn] B[aker] and J[ohn] R[edmayne] and are to be sold by Walter Davis in Amen Corner, 1683). Wing, S3766; ESTC, R12869.

John Northleigh, 'Introductory Remarks', in *The Triumph of our Monarchy, over the Plots and Principles of our Rebels and Republicans, Being Remarks on their Most Eminent Libels* (London: Benj. Tooke at the Ship in St. Paul's Church-Yard, July 1685), sigs B–C4. Wing, N1305; ESTC, R10284.

The Tory reaction gained further impetus after the uncovering of the Rye House plot in June 1683, with the trials of Lord William Russell and Algernon Sidney supplemented by renewed attacks on writings held to reveal and spread rebellious and republican ideas.

The Oxford convocation's 1683 *Judgment and Decree* was the closest the Restoration period came to a papal *Index* in its formal listing of 32 books and 27 'damnable doctrines', targeting Whigs, Dissenters, Jesuits (Bellarmine and Parsons) and Thomas Hobbes. It gained further official sanction through Charles II's message of support and thanks, having earlier gained the unanimous assent of 250 Oxford dons meeting in convocation, marginalizing any voice of dissent.[1] The loyal dons then contributed loud 'hums' of approval as the condemned books were burnt outside the Bodleian Library.[2] The list had been compiled within weeks of the Rye House plot revelations, its swift drafting helped by ready acquaintance with offending works on the part of the Professor of Divinity William Jane, who had been Bishop Compton's licensing chaplain and preached to Parliament against 'dayly Libels, and Defamations against the Government'.[3] Passed in Latin in convocation, it was translated and printed to instruct a wider audience. A further edition was printed at Dublin (Wing, O892). The *Decree* was itself burnt in 1710 after the Sacheverell trial (see Volume 4 of this edition).

Algernon Sidney's conviction and execution in November–December was notoriously secured by Lord Chief Justice Jeffreys's insistence that manuscript drafts found in his room constituted an 'overt act' proving Sidney's treasonous intent. During his trial Sidney insisted he had never printed or circulated his writings so could not be held to have intended to stir unrest, but this was taken to be irrelevant to the issue of whether they confirmed his guilty mind. In the printed *Humble Petition of Algernoon Sidney*, addressed to the King, Sidney argued that the papers were 'private thoughts' on an old book (Sir Robert Filmer's *Patriarcha*) and not 'fit for the Press', so could not fall under the treason statute 25 Edw. III, but this had been overruled by 'the Violence of the L.C.J.' Sidney's *Discourses concerning Government* were eventually published in 1698. Within days of his execution on 7 December 1683 printed copies were circulating of *The Very Copy of a Paper Delivered to the Sheriffs, upon the Scaffold*, in which he claimed a right to reply publicly to Filmer's ideas. A further edition appeared as *Colonel Sidney's Speech, Delivered to the Sheriff on the Scaffold* (Wing, S3765), apparently pirated from the version authorized by the sheriffs. Copies of the *Paper* were also printed at Dublin.

At the close of Charles II's reign, the writer, physician and lawyer John Northleigh (1656–1705) attempted his own *Index* or *Judgment* by reflecting at length on republican books of the previous five years in *The Triumph of Our Monarchy*. He added sweeping protests about the rebellious press in the work's 'Introductory Remarks', reproduced here, together with reflections on the response by loyalist writers like himself and L'Estrange. The whole book of nearly 800 pages devoted chapters to the anonymous *Brief History of the Succession* (1681; usually attributed to John Somers), *Plato Redivivus* (1681; by Henry Neville), Thomas Hunt's *Postscript for Rectifying some Mistakes in some of the Inferior Clergy* (1682); Samuel Johnson's *Julian the Apostate* (1682) and 'Mr. Sidney's Papers', for which Northleigh relied on the glimpses provided by accounts of Sidney's case. By the time he completed the book in early 1685 Charles II had died so a dedicatory epistle to James II was added, along with a commendatory verse by John Dryden lauding Northleigh and the new King, and an advertisement stating that most of the tract had been printed before the Printing Act was revived (on 2 July). Wing lists a second 1685 edition (N1306) although this is only a variant collation, certain pages being repeated. A second edition appeared in 1699 under the title *Remarks upon the most Eminent of our Antimonarchical Authors and their Writings* (Wing, R949), without Northleigh's name (or his dedication to James II).

Notes
1. See below, p. 330.
2. R.A. Beddard, 'Tory Oxford', in N. Tyacke (ed.), *The History of the University of Oxford, vol. 4: Seventeenth-Century Oxford* (Oxford: Clarendon Press, 1997), pp. 863–905, on p. 896.
3. W. Jane, *A Sermon Preached on the Day of the Publick Fast* (London, 1679), p. 49.

*The Judgment and Decree of the University of Oxford Past in their Convocation July 21. 1683, against certain Pernicious Books and Damnable Doctrines Destructive to the Sacred Persons of Princes, their State and Government, and of all Humane Society* (Oxford: printed at the Theater, July 1683). Wing, O891; ESTC, R14238.

### The JUDGMENT and DECREE
#### OF
### The UNIVERSITY of OXFORD
Past in their Convocation July 21. 1683.

ALtho the barbarous Assassination lately enterpriz'd[1] against the person of his Sacred Majestie and his Royall Brother, engage all our thoughts to reflect with utmost detestation and abhorrence of that execrable Villany, hateful to God and Man; and pay our due acknowledgments to the Divine Providence which by extraordinary methods brought it to pass, that the breath of our nostrils the Anointed of the Lord is not taken in the pit which was prepared for him: and that under his shadow we continue to live, and enjoy the Blessings of his Government: Yet notwithstanding we find it to be a necessary duty at this time to search into and lay open those impious Doctrines, which having of late been / studiously disseminated, gave rise and growth to those nefarious attemts: and pass upon them our solemn public Censure and Decree of condemnation.

Therefore to the honor of the holy and undivided Trinity, the preservation of Catholic truth in the Church: and that the King's Majestie may be secur'd from the attemts of open and bloudy enimies, and the machinations of Traiterous Heretics and Schismatics: We the Vice-Chancellor, Doctors, Proctors, and Masters Regent and not Regent[2] met in Convocation in the accustom'd manner, time and place, on Saturday the 21 of July in the Year 1683. concerning certain Propositions contained in diverse Books and Writings published in English, and also in the Latin tongue repugnant to the holy Scriptures, Decrees of Councils, Writings of the Fathers, the Faith and Profession of the Primitive Church: and also destructive of the Kingly Government, the safety of his Majestie's Person, the Public Peace, the Laws of Nature, and bonds of humane Society: By our Unanimous assent and consent, have Decreed and Determin'd in manner and form following.

*Proposition* 1. All Civil Autority is derived originally from the People.

2. There is a mutual compact, tacit or express, between a Prince and his Subjects; and that if he perform not his duty, they are discharg'd from theirs. /

3. That if lawful Governors become Tyrants, or govern otherwise then by the laws of God and man they ought to do, they forfeit the right they had unto their Government.

*Lex Rex.*[3] *Buchanan de Jure Regni.*[4] *Vindiciæ contra tyrannos.*[5] *Bellarmine de Conciliis, de Pontifice.*[6] *Milton, Goodwin.*[7] *Baxter H.C.*[8]

4. The Soveraignty of *England* is in the three Estates, *viz.* King, Lords, and Commons. The King has but a coordinate power and may be overruled by the other two.

*Lex Rex. Hunton of a limited and mix'd Monarchy.*[9] *Baxter H.C. Polit. Catech.*[10]

5. Birthright and proximity of bloud give no title to rule or Government, and it is lawful to preclude the next heir from his Right of Succession to the Crown.

*Lex Rex. Hunt's Postcript.*[11] *Doleman.*[12] *History of Succession.*[13] *Julian the Apostate.*[14] *Mene Tekel.*[15]

6. It is lawful for Subjects without the consent and against the command of the Supreme Magistrate to enter into leagues, covenants and associations, for defence of themselves and their religion.

*Solemn League and Covenant,*[16] *Late Association.*[17]

7. Self-preservation is the fundamental law of nature, and supersedes the obligation of all others, whenever they stand in competition with it.

*Hobbes de Cive. Leviathan.*[18]

8. The doctrine of the Gospel concerning patient suffering of injuries, is not inconsistent with violent resisting of the higher powers in case of persecution for religion.

*Lex Rex. Julian Apostat. Apolog. Relat.*[19] /

9. There lies no obligation upon Christians to passive obedience, when the prince commands any thing against the laws of our Country; and the primitive Christians chose rather to die then resist, because Christianity was not yet setled by the laws of the Empire.

*Julian Apostate.*

10. Possession and strength give a right to govern, and success in a cause or enterprise proclaims it to be lawful and just; to pursue it is to comply with the will of God, because it is to follow the conduct of his providence.

*Hobbes. Owen's Sermon*[20] *before the Regicides Jan.* 31. 1648. *Baxter, Jenkin's Petition*[21] *Octob.* 1651.

11. In the state of nature there is no difference between good and evil, right and wrong; the state of nature is a state of war, in which every man hath a right to all things.

12. The foundation of Civil Autority is this natural right, which is not given, but left to the Supreme Magistrate upon mens entring into societies, and not only a foreign Invader but a domestic Rebel puts himself again into a state of nature, to be proceeded against not as a subject but an enemy: and consequently acquires by his rebellion the same right over the life of his Prince, as the Prince for the most heinous crimes has over the life of his own Subjects.

13. Every man after his entring into a society retains a right of defending himself against force, and cannot transfer that right to the Commonwealth, when he consents to that union whereby a Commonwealth is made; and in case a great many men together have already resisted the Commonwealth, for which every one of them expecteth death, they have liberty / then to joyn together to assist and defend one another. Their bearing of arms subsequent to the first breach of their duty, tho it be to maintain what they have don, is no new unjust act, and if it be only to defend their persons, is not unjust at all.

14. An Oath superadds no obligation to pact, and a pact obliges no further than it is credited: and consequently if a Prince gives any indication that he does not believe the promises of fealty and allegiance made by any of his subjects, they are thereby freed from their subjection, and notwithstanding their pacts and oaths may lawfully rebel against, and destroy their Soveraign.

*Hobbes de Cive. Leviathan.*

15. If a People that by oath and duty are oblig'd to a Soveraign shall sinfully dispossess him, and contrary to their Covenants chuse, and convenant with another; they may be obliged by their latter Covenant notwithstanding their former.

*Baxter H. C.*

16. All oaths are unlawful, and contrary to the word of God.

*Quakers.*[22]

17. An Oath obliges not in the sense of the Imposer, but the takers.

*Sheriffs case.*[23]

18. Dominion is founded in grace.

19. The powers of this world are usurpations upon the Prerogative of Jesus Christ, and it is the duty of God's People to destroy them in order to the setting Christ upon his throne.

*Fifth-Monarchy men.*[24] /

20. The Presbyterian Government is the Scepter of Christ's Kingdom, to which Kings as well as others are bound to submit; and the King's Supremacy in Ecclesiastical affairs asserted by the Church of England is injurious to Christ, the sole King and Head of his Church.

*Altare Damascenum.*[25] *Apolog. relat. Hist. Indulgen.*[26] *Cartwright.*[27] *Travers.*[28]

21. It is not lawful for Superiors to impose any thing in the worship of God that is not antecedently necessary.

22. The duty of not offending a weak brother is inconsistent with all human Autority of making Laws concerning indifferent things.
*Protestant Reconciler.*[29]

23. Wicked Kings and Tyrants ought to be put to death, and if the Judges and inferior Magistrates will not do their office, the power of the sword devolves to the People; if the major part of the People refuse to exercise this power, then the Ministers may excommunicate such a King, after which it is lawful for any of the Subjects to kill him, as the People did *Athaliah*, and *Jehu Jezabel.*
*Buchanan, Knox, Goodman, Gilby,*[30] *Jesuits.*

24. After the sealing of the Scripture Canon, the people of God in all ages are to expect new Revelations for a rule of their actions, [a]and it is lawful for a private man, having an inward motion from God, to kill a Tyrant[b].
[a]*Quakers and other Enthusiasts.* [b]*Goodman.*[31]

25. The example of *Phineas* is to us instead of a Command; for what God has commanded or approved in one age, must needs oblige in all.
*Goodman. Knox. Napthali.*[32] /

26. King Charles the first was lawfully put to death, and his murtherers were the blessed instruments of Gods glory in their Generation.
*Milton. Goodwin. Owen.*

27. King Charles the first made war upon his Parliament; and in such a case the King may not only be resisted, but he ceaseth to be King.
*Baxter.*

We decree, judge and declare all and every of these Propositions to be false, seditious and impious; and most of them to be also Heretical and Blasphemous, infamous to Christian Religion, and destructive of all Government in Church and State.

We farther decree that the Books which contain the foresaid propositions and impious Doctrines, are fitted to deprave good manners; corrupt the minds of unwary men, stir up seditions and tumults, overthrow States and Kingdoms, and lead to Rebellion, murther of Princes, and Atheism it self: and therefore we interdict all members of the University from the reading the said Books, under the penalties in the Statutes exprest.

We also order the before recited Books to be publicly burnt, by the hand of our Marshal in the court of our Scholes. /

Likewise we order that in perpetual memory hereof, these our decrees shall be entered into the Registry of our Convocation, and that copies of them being communicated to the several Colleges and Halls within this University, they be there publicly affixt in the Libraries, Refectories, or other fit places, where they may be seen and read of all.

Lastly we command and strictly enjoyn all and singular Readers, Tutors, Catechists and others to whom the care and trust of institution of youth is committed, that they diligently instruct and ground their Scholars in that most necessary Doctrine which in a manner is the Badge and character of the Church of England, of submitting to every Ordinance of man for the Lords sake, whether it be to the King as supreme, or unto Governors as unto them that are sent by him, for the punishment of evil doers, and for the praise of them that do well: Teaching that this submission and obedience is to be clear, absolute and without exception of any State or order of men: Also that all supplications, Prayers, Intercessions and giving of thanks be made for all men, for the King and all that are in Autority, that we may lead a quiet and peaceable life in all godliness and honesty; for this is good and acceptable in the sight of God our Savior. And in especial manner that they press and oblige / them humbly to offer their most ardent and daily Prayers at the Throne of Grace for the preservation of our Sovereign Lord King Charles from the attemts of open violence, and secret Machinations of perfidious Traitors: that he the Defender of the faith, being safe under the defence of the most High, may continue his reign on Earth, till he exchange it for that of a late and happy Immortality.

*FINIS.*

Algernon Sidney, *The Very Copy of a Paper Delivered to the Sheriffs, upon the Scaffold on Tower-Hill, On Friday, Decemb. 7. 1683. By Algernoon Sidney, Esq; Before his Execution there* (London: by R[obert] H[orn], J[ohn] B[aker] and J[ohn] R[edmayne] and are to be sold by Walter Davis in Amen Corner, 1683). Wing, S3766; ESTC, R12869.

The Very COPY of a

# PAPER

Delivered to the

## SHERIFFS,

Upon the Scaffold on *Tower-hill*, on *Friday Decemb.* 7. 1683.

### By Algernoon Sidney, Esq;

Before his Execution there.

*Men, Brethren, and Fathers; Friends, Countrymen, and Strangers*;

IT May be expected that I should now say some Great matters unto you, but the Rigour of the Season, and the Infirmities of my Age,[1] encreased by a close Imprisonment of above Five months, doth not permit me.

Moreover, we live in an Age that maketh Truth pass for Treason: I dare not say any thing contrary unto it, and the Ears of those that are about me will probably be found too tender to hear it. My Tryal and Condemnation doth sufficiently evidence this.

*West, Rumsey*, and *Keyling*,[2] who were brought to prove the Plot, said no more of me, than that they knew me not; and some others equally unknown unto me, had used my Name, and that of some others, to give a little Reputation unto their Designs. The Lord *Howard*[3] is too infamous by his Life, and the many Perjuries not to be denyed, or rather sworn by himself, to deserve mention; and being a single Witness would be of no value, though he had been of unblemished Credit, or had not seen and confessed that the Crimes committed by him would be pardoned only for committing more; and even the Pardon promised could not be obtained till the Drudgery of Swearing was over.

This being laid aside, the whole matter is reduced to the Papers said to be found in my Closet[4] by the Kings Officers, without any other Proof of their being written by me, than what is taken from suppositions upon the similitude of an Hand that is easily counterfeited, and which hath been lately declared in the Lady *Car*'s Case[5] to be no Lawful Evidence in Criminal Causes.

But if I had been seen to write them, the matter / would not be much altered. They plainly appear to relate unto a large Treatise written long since in answer to *Filmer*'s Book,[6] which by all intelligent Men is thought to be grounded upon wicked Principles, equally pernicious unto Magistrates and People.

If he might publish unto the World his Opinion, That all Men are born under a necessity derived from the Laws of God and Nature, to submit unto an Absolute Kingly Government, which could be restrained by no Law, or Oath; and that he that hath the Power, whether he came unto it by Creation, Election, Inheritance, Usurpation, or any other way had the Right; and none must Oppose his Will, but the Persons and Estates of his Subjects must be indispensably subject unto it; I know not why I might not have published my Opinion to the contrary, without the breach of any Law I have yet known.

I might as freely as he, publickly have declared my Thoughts, and the Reasons upon which they were grounded, and I persuaded to believe, That God had left Nations unto the Liberty of setting up such Governments as best pleased themselves.

That Magistrates were set up for the good of Nations, not Nations for the honour or glory of Magistrates.

That the Right and Power of Magistrates in every Country, was that which the Laws of that Country made it to be.

That those Laws were to be observed, and the Oaths taken by them, having the force of a Contract between Magistrate and People, could not be Violated without danger of dissolving the whole Fabrick.

That Usurpation could give no Right, and the most dangerous of all Enemies unto Kings were they, who raising their Power to an Exorbitant Height, allowed unto Usurpers all the Rights belonging unto it.

That such Usurpations being seldom Compassed without the Slaughter of the Reigning Person, or Family, the worst of all Villanies was thereby rewarded with the most Glorious Privileges.

That if such Doctrines were received, they would stir up men to the Destruction of Princes with more Violence than all the Passions that have hitherto raged in the Hearts of the most Unruly.

That none could be Safe, if such a Reward were proposed unto any that could destroy them.

That few would be so gentle as to spare even the Best, if by their destruction a Wild Usurper could become God's Anointed; and by the most execrable Wickedness invest himself, with that Divine Character.

This is the Scope of the whole Treatise; the Writer gives such Reasons as at present did occur unto him, to prove it. This seems to agree with the Doctrines of the most Reverenced Authors of all Times, Nations and Religions. The best and wisest of Kings have ever acknowleged it. The present King of *France* hath declared that Kings have that happy want of Power, that they can do nothing contrary unto the Laws of their Country, and grounds his Quarrel with the King of *Spain, Anno.* 1667. upon that Principle. King *James*[7] in his Speech to the Parliament *Anno.* 1603. doth in the highest degree assert it: The Scripture seems to declare it. If nevertheless the Writer was mistaken, he might have been refuted by Law, Reason and Scripture; and no Man for such matters was ever otherwise punished, than by being made to see his Errour; and it hath not (as I think) been ever known that they had been referred to the Judgment of a Jury, composed of Men utterly unable to comprehend them.

But there was little of this in my Case; the extravagance of my Prosecutors goes higher: the above-mentioned Treatise was never finished, nor could be in many years, and most probably would never have been. So much as is of it was Written long since,[8] never reviewed nor shewn unto any Man; and the fiftieth part of it was produced, and not the tenth of that offered to be read. That which was never known unto those who are said to have Conspired with me, was said to be intended to stir up the People in Prosecution of the Designs of those Conspirators.

When nothing of particular Application unto Time, Place, or Person could be found in it, (as hath ever been done by those who endeavour'd to raise Insurrections) all was supplied by *Innuendo's*.

Whatsoever is said of the Expulsion of *Tarquin*; the Insurrection against *Nero*; The Slaughter of *Caligula*, or *Domitian*; The Translation of the Crown of *France* from *Meroveus* his Race unto *Pepin*; and from his Descendants unto *Hugh Capet*, and the like, applied by *Innuendo* unto the King.[9]

They have not considered, that if such Acts of State be not good, there is not a King in the World that has any Title to the Crown he bears; nor can have any, unless he could deduce his Pedigree from the Eldest Son of *Noah*, and shew that the Succession had still continued in the Eldest of the Eldest Line,[10] and been so deduced to him.

Every one may see what advantage this would be to all the Kings of the World; and whether that failing, it were not better for them to acknowledge they had received their Crowns by the Consent of Willing Nations; or to have no better Title unto them than Usurpation and Violence, which by the same ways may be taken from them. /

But I was long since told that I must Dye, or the Plot must Dye.

Least the means of destroying the best Protestants in *England* should fail, the Bench must be filled with such as had been Blemishes to the Bar.[11]

None but such as these would have Advised with the King's Council, of the means of bringing a Man to death; Suffered a Jury to be packed by the King's

Solicitors, and the Under-Sheriff; Admit of Jury-men who are not Freeholders; Receive such Evidence as is above mentioned; Refuse a Copy of an Indictment, or to Suffer the Statute of 46 *Ed. 3.*[12] to be read, that doth expresly Enact, It should in no Case be denied unto any Man upon any occasion whatsoever; Overrule the most important Points of Law without hearing. And whereas the Stat. 25 *Ed. 3.*[13] upon which they said I should be Tried, doth Reserve unto the Parliament all Constructions to be made in Points of Treason, They could assume unto themselves not only a Power to make Constructions, but such Constructions as neither agree with Law, Reason, or Common Sence.

By these means I am brought to this Place. The Lord forgive these Practices, and avert the Evils that threaten the Nation from them. The Lord Sanctifie these my Sufferings unto me; and though I fall as a Sacrifice unto Idols, suffer not Idolatry to be Established in this Land. Bless thy People, and Save them. Defend thy own Cause, and Defend those that Defend it. Stir up such as are Faint; Direct those that are Willing; Confirm those that Waver; Give Wisdom and Integrity unto all. Order all things so as may most redound unto thine own Glory. Grant that I may Dye glorifying Thee for all thy Mercies; and that at the last Thou hast permitted me to be Singled out as a Witness of thy Truth; and even by the Confession of my Opposers, for that OLD CAUSE[14] in which I was from my Youth engaged, and for which Thou hast Often and Wonderfully declared thy Self.

We do Appoint *Robert Horn*, *John Baker*, and *John Redmayne*, to Print this Paper, and that none other do Presume to Print the same.

*Peter Daniel.*
*Sam. Dashwood.*[15]

John Northleigh, 'Introductory Remarks', in *The Triumph of our Monarchy, over the Plots and Principles of our Rebels and Republicans, Being Remarks on their Most Eminent Libels* (London: Benj. Tooke at the Ship in St. Paul's Church-Yard, July 1685), sigs B–C4. Wing, N1305; ESTC, R10284.

Introductory Remarks.

*FEW Persons amongst the mighty numbers that have writ, shall condemn* more the Vanity *of Writing; tho' I hope as few have used it less in* Vain: *The first Design of my putting Pen to Paper, was only to correct the Licentiousness of Paper and Pen, and to supply with a timely animadversion, the Expiration of a temporary Act;*[1] *'twas Time sure, 'twas high Time for every Loyal Heart to use his Ink, when they had almost scribled us all into Blood; and to weeld his Pen in the defence of the Government, when the Knife was at our Throats, and their Swords drawn: I know the weakness of the dint of Argument against the power of Steel: And the Impertinence of persuasion where the Law can Compel; but since the Pen has the power of provoking a Rebellion, and that experienced, 'tis as warrantable an experiment to turn its Point; and make the same Wand to lay the Devil that it raises; and since the* Laws *were almost silenced / only with their threatning* Arms: *'Twas time to animate the dead Letter: To make it know its force and exert its power; and to strengthen a Government: That seem'd but too weak for its self, and unhappily distrusted its own security; And that to this purpose the power of the Pen has not been ineffectual, will appear from these subsequent Observations; Which the comfortable success will better justify, than their prosperous Rebellion could have been made again Just; and which I'le assure you now 'tis some Comfort to observe: Especially to those that were so bold as to be concerned, that dared to stem the torrent of Schism and Sedition, when 'twas but a dangerous Duty; and embarqu'd with the Government, in a storm; when the Waves rose and raged horribly, and the* gathering of the People, was like the noise of many Waters.[2]

It is observable that upon the first dissolution of the Westminster Parliament,[3] *that which might be as well called the* healing one; *whose sober debates had superseded the fallen unadvisedness of the subsequent: closed the wounds of an Intestine War, cemented the Government of Church and State; Compact, and firm; for about twenty years; beyond what the force of Rebellion / could devide; or Plot and Treachery undermine; That Parliament which they Libelled, Publisht for Pensionary;*[4] *only because it would not take pay of the People, where perhaps, they would have been truly paid: That Parliament which with regret they call the* long:[5] *And all honest Hearts resent as too* short; *whose unhappy dissolution rivall'd almost the fatality of the late perpetual sitting; whose Prudent Progress gave some probability of sounding a Plot: which others inconsiderate rashness hath left without a bottom; if not beyond belief or Foundation, by* proceedings unwarrantable *and bold*. 'Tis *observable, I say, that then the Serpent of Sedition, that like the Primitive one was curst in the Restoration, forc't to creep on its Belly, and crawle upon the Dust, began first to raise its Venom'd head; and with audacious Libels, spit its Poyson in the very face of Majesty: We know we had Plots before, and that* Oats[6] *his too; not as a Discoverer, but as prime Rebel, and Conspirator; not as an informer of Popish ones but a Ring-leader of a Republican: we know we had then too our* Tongues *that were hanged for* Treason; *as well as those that could since get Traytors Hang'd: yet still midst all those unsuccessful / attempts to Rebel, Sedition never grew so much and succeeded, that blessed Interval of near twenty years quiet, tho' oft endeavoured to be interrupted, never afforded so much* Treason *from the Press, as for the last* five *years has been Publisht in their Prints; Libels lookt as if they had been Licensed for a* Lustrum;[7] *and as if the temporary Printing Act had expired seasonably, 'twas never* resolved *amongst all their* Orders *to be revived; 'twas opposed even when moved, unanimously, that* Treason *too might be Publisht with a* Nemine contradicente;[8] *'twas presumed, I suppose, the better Pen-men were their own; and I grant them the more pestilent; that could spread their Contagion as fast as the Plague, and to the Monarchy as mortal; for almost* five *years the Distemper was Epidemick; and the State* Empericks[9] *had poysoned the body Politick almost beyond the Antidote of true Medicine and Art, it Sympathis'd with Pestilence in the Natural, almost incurable; reigned most populously in Towns and Cities; and turned every Corporation into a politick* Pest-House: *Appeals*, vox Patriæ,[10] *Liberties of* England; *Fundamental Rights, were exposed in Capital Letters upon every Stall; and that dedicated to Representatives; / and some Penn'd by them too; for the Information of the People; or in a less preposterous Phrase for their Confusion; Sedition seemed to be countenanced with suffrages, and seconded, as they thought, with the supream power of the Nation. They expected Treason should have been enacted for Law; and Laws repealed that had declared* High Treason. *'Tis almost preposterous and incredible, tho' unhappily too true, that more Sedition was fomented from the* discovery of this Popish Plot, *than all the* Jesuits *in Hell could have raised, while yet* undiscovered, *we forged out one anothers ruin from the very deliverance; and to fall with harder fate the less to be lamented; by our selves, and just escapt the* storm *we strove to perish more miserably in the* Port. *Such was the state of affairs, when some of our Loyal Hearts first ventured to stem the Tide, the fierce influx of an Impetuous Rebellion; that like a true torrent came rolling on with noise and clamor; and threatned ruin from afar: The first that opposed the Great* Goliahs[11] *of their Cause, that defyed too even the Armies of the living God; and the strength of his Anointed; was he who from his Youth had serv'd the Crown, with his Pen as well as / his Sword; and before him too did their* Dagon[12] *fall; one whom they had designed formerly for a Victim, when they sacrificed, their Prince; whom Providence reserved for their Scourge, and for which since some of them have publickly curst its dispensation, Libelled him in their Emblematical Representations, (in which, I confess, they neither spared their King) breaking his Halter like a Dog, and running for his Life and Neck; and that by the very same hands of Villains that had forfeited their own to the Government, and were afterward faster noosed.*[13]

How Zealous *were our* Popular Patriots *against the least animadversion that was made on the most audacious Libel, and even Judges themselvs arraigned, for daring to execute those Laws, the meanest villain, could daily dare to violate: How curious to enquire for the least accusation against the worthy Person above described, and only because he dared to do his duty; when 'twas dangerous to do so: It was a pretty sort of expedient, tho the most absurd Politicks, for the countenancing of the* Popish-Plot, *to bring every one concerned in it, that would not swallow the whole Mass of it raw, crude and undigested; and that before / they had cook'd it up with* Narrative *too; while their* Protestant *rashness at the same time precipitated them but into a* Romish *Doctrin, of Resignation to their Senate instead of a Church, and believing their house of* Commons *with a Faith implicite; yet this was all done too, and this Gentleman whose Writings only declared him a little scrupulous in matters of belief; (when even by the most credulous in all Ages, it has been allowed to doubt; and by the Great* Des Cartes[14] *the wisest Philosopher as a step to the knowledg of the Truth.) Him 'twas expedient to* Metamorphose, *with the power of an Oath; which was then Omnipotent, from an avowd* Protestant, *into a profest* Papist:[15] *I use that poetical Expression, because they might as well have sworn him through all the transformations of* Ovid,[16] *into* Bull, Bear; *or* Dragon, *born a profest Son of the Church, conformed through all his Life, to all its Ceremonies; a Champion for her with his Pen, and with it a publisht Enemy to* Rome, *even in his own Works; having about him Eyes, Nose, Ears: And from Head to Foot all the true shapes of a* Protestant Humane Creature; *but the Spell of* Affidavit *beyond that of* Circe, *turned Him all into the Beast of /* Babylon;[17] *all his Hair vanisht into a shaven Crown; The Whore came riding on his very back, and the fleecy Cowl of Priests came tumbling o're his Shoulders; and the* Common-Prayer *he held in his Hand, ran all into red Letters, and the* Mass-book: *His being a* Papist, *and a* Priest, *was as much credited as the Plot it self; and might have had the Resolution of the* House of Commons *to the point of his Religion as well as the truth of the Conspiracy; not a Member but was well satisfyed of his Apostacy, and could Menace him in Publick with a* Topham *or a* Tyburn.[18] *And he the first Instance, that under a Government yet establisht, a Religion then Laboured for with Zeal, who for Writing in the defence of both, was forc't to fly for his security*[19] *and Preservation, tho as publickly cleared from the perjur'd Accusation, before his King, before his Council, as good Judges at least as the Credulous* Commons; *these careful* Patriots *being often abused by their*

*Country-men, for whom they were so Zealous; Oaths, Affidavits, and that* Cloud of Witnesses, *had almost obscured the* light *of Reason and Understanding.*

Another Worthy Person,[20] *tho' unknown, that at the same time blest our Land with / the Benefit of his Pen, while with the bounteous river he hid his head; whose Ingenious Dialogues only Corrected their sawcy Libels; with a smile and with a pleasant reproof of their Falshoods made them feel the smartness of his Truth: Him they Libelled too for* Popish, Mercenary, Pensioner to the Party: *So Zealous were they for the subverting of the Government, that they could damn all that did but dare to assert it; Break the very Laws of society in their Censures; and what they could not prove with their* Affidavits *condemn upon Presumption.*

*With what sawcy; Petulant Animadversions did they treat the Dean of* Paul's *Sermon of Separation;*[21] *A piece penn'd with that Judgment and Moderation, that it was only envyed for being so; commended and applauded by the Pen, even of one of their most virulent Scriblers, that had engaged Himself for the vilifying of the Church, in which he was Christned; and fighting against the Banner of his Christ, for which he had vowed himself a Souldier;*[22] *And with the subtile Insinuation of righting of her Prelates, wrong'd and abused her whole Hierachy; yet such an one could allow that peaceable and pious piece, to be without exception; / but what Reason could not resist, must be baffled by a* Buffoon, *and a Pen employed to Burlesque the very* Bible, *rather than want an answer to the* Text; *and the sacred service of the Church, prophaned with the tropes of* Trinkets, *and the Metaphor of an Hobby-horse; tho upon other Occasions she can be transformed into the more terrible beast of the* Revelations: *The Author was Anonymous,*[23] *and so escap't the thanks of the House; but what ever were the scurrilous Animadversions on the foresaid, and the like Ingenious, Loyal, and elaborate pieces; 'tis observable they had so much Influence on some of our blindest Zealots as to open their eyes, brought some of their Villanies to* light, *that had been so long transacted in the* dark, *and drove the Faction to stand a little at bay, that had ran the Nation almost out of her Wits; coold their brutal Zeal down into Humane Sense, acquainted them with what was truly Religious, and heartily Loyal, instead of a devout* Phrensy *and a mistaken* Loyalty.

*All that I can arrogate to my self, is but what I shall always be proud of, of having done my Duty, and that to my Soveraing, as well as his Subjects, in a seasonable Animadversion / on as damnable a piece of* Treason, *as ever was brooded by the most perjur'd heads that ever; hatcht a Rebellion: That specious pretext of an Association,*[24] *That* Covenant *to Rebel against the Life and Honor of their Prince, with Scripture warranty; and in the fear* of God; *tho' the very* Text *tells them,* touch not mine Anointed; *And next to fearing their God, follows* honouring *their King. I cannot say I was Instrumental in the following Abhorrences; but hope the God of Heaven, blest my poor endeavours*[25] *so far as to encourage but an Abomination of the draught of* Hell, *which I hope too, I there represented as black as the Devil that*

Vid. Hunts Postscript.

Vid. Mischief of Imposition.

*contriv'd it, or to give it its true Colour, almost in its own blackness; my foreboding thought shewed me in it like a Glass, all the Villanies and Treasons that have since succeeded, tho' not prospered; The very Scheam and Embryo of this teeming Plot; The very* Metaphor *of the* Trojan *horse that carryed Fire and Sword in its Belly, brought within the Walls of our House of* Commons, *as they themselves assure us; I am sure as unhappily as that within those of* Troy *by almost pulling them down, and exposing the whole Kingdom to the flame; and that too by the / treachery of as false a* Sinon[26] *of our Age; as great a Renegado to Prince and People; and whom they too had saved from being Justly sacrificed, only for their ruin, and destruction; And that I have done in spight of those Censures, I have laboured under of having been* Mercenary *and set a* Work *of having been more* Zealous *than* Wise: *As an Anonimous Scribbler*[27] *has been pleased to represent to the World; but I thank my Stars that have envolved me with the fate of the Government, and when ever that can't stand, I desire to fall; but the puny pedantick Soul shall know, I can give him a prefatory Animadversion for his* Postscript Reflexion. *As to my being Mercenary, whoever condemn me for that, are as Ignorant in their Censures, as unreasonable; for I did for the Prevention even of that very Callumny decline the taking of a single Penny; the least sort of gratuity, for any Copy, or single Letter; that in the plain, Litteral Sense, I might be said to serve the Government for nought; I thank my God that has allowed me that Competency, that I can write with pure Affection, and not for Bread, with the sense of my Soul; not of my Belly: Tho' it has appeared on Evidence, that the great Patron of their Cause / kept open entertainment for the pampering Sedition; and feeding the flames of Rebellion with the very sops of his Table; discommending there the most virulent Satyrs, only because not bold enough in expressive Treason; but too* little *favouring Rebellion.*[28] *And as for the Presumption of my being set a work, of which they have accused me too in their Prints, that's more false than it is truly malicious; the villains thought none bold enough of himself to defend the Government, when they could with so much Impudence invade it, I was so far from being instigated by Persuasion, that even my own acquaintance, my most familiar Friends, were unconsulted; and my Person at this very time unknown to any single Person of that Court Party they would have me to serve, I urgd this to let them know the falseness of their sordid Suggestions, and the real truths of their most malicious falsehoods, and moreover and above, all, the goodness and equity of that Cause, I shall ever defend, and that more willingly with all my dearest blood, than one drop of Ink; that Persons refusing profit or, emolument, without application for interest or preferment, discourag'd, disgusted, and hardly dealt with, even by some of those seats of Literature, where they say / the Doctrine is nothing but absolute Dominion; and the best of teaching Tyrany, tho indeed, nothing but the solid Seminaries of true learning and Loyalty.*

---

Marginalia:
- Vid. *Proceedings at the Old-Bayly.*
- Vid. *Postscript to the History of the Association.*
- Vid. *Settles Recantation.*

*But to satisfy such; themselves, and their Treasons,* set me a work,[29] *both black enough to have exasperated the dullest Soul; And even a Dumb Son would break into Speech, to see the* Father *of his* Countrey *ready to be slain.* ... /

*But if the wretch has the Confidence, to survive his Conviction; can he call it now* Begg'd, *when the* Gentleman[30] *at whose door 'twas laid, there powerful Patriot, their deifyed darling, has appeared since the very Devil of Rebellion, double dyed in Treasons, designed Murders of the Royal Line, and intended Massacre of the best of People; and that beyond the Contradiction of Impudence it self; Having transcribed all that Rebellious Scheam into the graphical Plan of his Conspiracy; raised upon it Foundations, an Insurrection as sure as Plot and Treachery could contrive; the train laid, the match ready, and only because his* Fauxes *were not so forward to give Fire,*[31] *burns with indignation at the dulness of his own miscreants, that unlike the true Machival Assassin, did not dare to dispatch quickly, but tamely sufferd villanies to miscarry for want of Courage, / and his being* failed, *Conscious of his undiscovered guilt, and bigg with* acted *Treason, seeks for safety where 'twas only left, in flight, flies to a* forreign, *what he designed to set up at home, A* Rebellious Republick;[32] *seals his hatred to the Government there with his latest breath, and his last Will; and leaves for a Legacy the success of his Conspiracy; that's* Blood, *and* Slavery, *to his kind Countrymen for creating him a* Patriot.

*Vid.* Truly the Gentleman is very sharp, and his sharpness had been Commendable, had any been found guilty, of framing or abetting the Paper.

*I thank him kindly for his Bit and Knock, which had their Villanies succeeded the one would scarce have been a Morsel of Bread, the other a good thump with a Stone, or their* sanctifyed Flayle; *but there was none found* guilty of framing *it; nor indeed like to be, when the* Jury[33] *themselves were* associated *against the Government, and transcribed the very Crime of their Criminal into practice; That Jury who by an early Anticipation of his Guilt, might perhaps have saved the blood of some, their own Darlings, before it had been so deeply tainted with the Venom of that old Serpent; whom now his / fallen Angels Curst too for Concomitancy: and in their dying words, as the Author of their Ruin, That Jury that might have prevented the danger of the Kings Life, only by exposing that of a* Traytors, *and of whose Royal Blood they must have been guilty by Consequence, had the villany not been blasted by Providence, and are now only Innocent by a miracle, and without Repentance still guilty. And I have that Charity to believe that the subsequent discoveries, have given some of them a sight and sence too, of their error; that they were only blinded with an* Ignoramus, *because in the* Dark; *and that they are satisfyed the God of Heaven has brought now the Contrivance of Hell to* Light: *And yet for a little Animadversion on these, amongst whom some I hope are ready to condemn themselves, the Reflecter represents me as* furious, ignorant, uncharitable; *but with what face can he urge that none* abetted *the Paper, unless with such an one as his own Conscience must fly in, who himself* abetts *it as far (as the popular Pedant, is*

Postscript.

*pleased to call it)* the Peccant part,[34] *that is, the cunning Knave would adhere to Treason, as far he could without Hanging; But was not the* Paper abetted *at the very Bar, and / that by* Bernadiston;[35] *that shamm'd off that Treason on the Parliament, as he would have done since the Plot it self on the* Abhorrers: *And for which we have Reason to thank him, and not his House of* Commons, *It could not have been believed that such a thing could have been offered in such an Honorable Assembly, had it not been kindly insinuated by their Civil Interrogatories; but then the Gentleman would have us believe for the sake of his Innocent Jury. They never heard of or saw the thing, till Printed by the Loyal Stationers with the Covenant,* Jigg by Joul,[36] *(as his clumsy Phrases have it) but did ever a more malicious Ass forge such falsehood in the face of the Sun, against Evidence as clear as the Lamp of Heaven it self: When the same to a syllable was all read to them in open Court, the same that himself insists to be Printed*[37] *in Collums with the Covenant?...*

Vid. Proceedings of the Old-Bayly. p. 14, 15.

# NONCONFORMITY AS SEDITION, 1683–5

Thomas Delaune, *A Narrative of the Sufferings of Thomas Delaune, for Writing, Printing and Publishing a late Book, called, A Plea for the Nonconformists* ([London]: for the Author, 1684). Wing, D892; ESTC, R18432.

'Mr Baxter's Tryal' (1685), in Edmund Calamy, *An Abridgment of Mr. Baxter's History of His Life and Times. With an Account of many others of those Worthy Ministers who were Ejected ... And a Continuation of their History, till the Year 1691* (London, 1702), pp. 616–20. ESTC, T109211.

The campaign against Whig and republican publishing was accompanied by continuing harassment of nonconformists accused of comparable disloyalty to the unity of religious and political orthodoxy. L'Estrange was not alone in believing that every Protestant nonconformist was effectively a republican. Two cases are included in this section, the first from late in Charles II's reign, the other coming to court at the beginning of James II's reign. Each involves a famous figure, although Richard Baxter was targeted because of his existing fame, whereas Thomas Delaune gained celebrity through the tragic circumstances of his conviction and death and their later exhumation by Daniel Defoe.

The sufferings of Thomas Delaune have long been amongst the best-known instances of religious intolerance under the later Stuarts, their notoriety based on the death in prison not only of Delaune but of his wife and two children, and on the frequent later reprinting of his fatal writings and testimony, Defoe contributing a lengthy preface to editions from 1706. In censorship terms, however, Delaune's crime was publishing dissent not being a Dissenter, and his *Narrative* offers a fascinating first-hand view of the miserable anxiety of a writer caught up in the process of press control. The Baptist minister's pamphlet *A Plea for the Non-Conformists* (1684) responded to the churchman Benjamin Calamy's *A Discourse about a Scrupulous Conscience* (1683), whose dedication to Lord Chief Justice Jeffreys did not bode well for Delaune's later appeal to Calamy to intercede in the Christian spirit of free discussion. The *Plea* was interrupted at the press on 29 November 1683 and Delaune was charged at the Old Bailey the following January with scandalizing the common prayer book, provoking contempt of the king, and stirring sedition and rebellion. The pamphlet was ordered to be burnt and its author fined 100 marks and committed to Newgate until paid. With no one ready to pay the fine, a reticence both John Tutchin and Defoe found remarkable, and presumably no family income, Delaune's wife and children joined him in jail and all died during 1684–5. The *Plea* and *Narrative* were reprinted together in 1704, with Defoe's long preface in 1706, and several times afterwards.

Richard Baxter's writings were frequently a target for censorship and censure, partly for their own sake but equally for the high profile of their author as a figurehead of nonconformity. Baxter (1615–91) generated plenty of targets with his prolific lifetime output of around 130 books, declaring his commitment to 'Preach by the Press to many thousands, and for many years after I am dead' and opposing the 'resisters of the publication of the Word of God'.[1] His *Holy Commonwealth* (1659) was among the books ordered burnt in 1683 by the Oxford *Decree*, although in 1670 he had recanted its publication, if not all its arguments. On 28 February 1685 Baxter was arrested and on 18 May was brought before Lord Chief Justice Jeffreys to face charges of seditious libel for having written and recently published passages deemed critical of the bishops and therefore the Crown in *A Paraphrase on the New Testament* (1685). Baxter believed his long-standing foe Roger L'Estrange had picked out the passages for indictment and certainly L'Estrange proclaimed in the *Observator* that he was right to act as 'General Censor' in protecting the multitude against the poison of this 'Book of Common Use'.[2] Baxter was convicted, fined 500 marks and imprisoned pending payment; he remained in jail until his fine was remitted on 24 November 1686. The trial was notorious for the abuse of Baxter by Jeffreys, although admittedly the sources of the *State Trials* account were sympathetic to Baxter, with contributions from his supporters informing the account reproduced here from Edmund Calamy's *Life* of Baxter.

Notes
1. R. Baxter, *A Christian Directory* (London, 1673), sig. A3v, p. 60; *ODNB*.
2. *Observator*, 3:8 (25 February, 1685).

Thomas Delaune, *A Narrative of the Sufferings of Thomas Delaune, for Writing, Printing and Publishing a late Book, called, A Plea for the Nonconformists* ([London]: for the Author, 1684). Wing, D892; ESTC, R18432.

A
NARRATIVE
OF THE
SUFFERINGS
OF
*THOMAS DELAUNE*, &c.

SIR,[1] I am concern'd to acquaint you with my Case; and because possibly some affairs that are more considerable to you, may have Diverted you from any inquiry, respecting a Prisoner (whose complyance to you made him so) I will give you a brief account of the whole, and intreat you to give me some Resolution to some certain things which I shall propose; which if fairly Resolv'd, will in my Opinion prove a considerable step to convince a great many *Scrupulous Consciences*,[2] or else give a check to Pulpit and Press-Chalenges; and mollify the hearts of such as so ruinously and severely prosecute them for such Scruples as are invincible by any other medium then what you direct to, *viz.* Our only RULE of Faith, the BIBLE.

*My Case is briefly Thus.*

On the Twenty-ninth of *November* last,[3] late in the Evening, I was Apprehended by one *Robert Stephens* a Messenger to the Press; And by him carried before Sr. *Thomas Jenner*, now Recorder of *London*, who asked me divers Questions, the most Material of which are mentioned in the following Letter sent afterwards to him: By the same / Recorder I was sent to the Compter in *Wood-street*,[4] where I had most wretched Accomodation; I was turn'd in amongst the Common-side *Prisoners*, where a hard Bench was my *Bed*, and two Bricks my *Pillow*; and not suffered to see some of my Acquaintance that were Prisoners there, as Dissenters.

Next Morning Mr. *Stephens* got me call'd to the Lodge, and to his praise be it spoken, narrowly search'd me for Papers, but found none for his purpose, and so left me to be turned in again; but a little while after I was sent by a fresh Warrant to *Newgate*. The Copy of which follows.

*To the Keeper of* Newgate *or his Deputy.*

London ss.

You are hereby required to receive into your Custody the Body of *Thomas Delaune, and him safely keep, untill he shall be Delivered by due Course of Law; for that it appeared before me, by his own Confession, that he is the* Author *and* Penman *of a certain Pamphlet Entituled* A Plea for the Nonconformists,[5] *and hath caused many hundred Sheets thereof to be Printed, wherein are contained several Seditious and dangerous matters against the Government, and for that he refused to find Sureties to appear at the next Sessions of the Peace, to be held for the* City *of* London *at the* Old Bayly, *and to be of the good behaviour in the mean time, and for your so doing this shall be your Warrant. Given under my Hand and Seal, this XXXth day of* November. Anno Caroli Secundi nunc Angl, &c. 35. Annoq. Dom. 1683.[6]

Tho. Jenner, *Record.*

Ex a per A. Nicolas.[7]

By vertue of that warrant I was committed to *Newgate*, and Lodg'd amongst Felons, whose horrid Company made a perfect representation of that horrible place which you describe when you mention Hell. But after two days and nights, without any Refreshment, the unusualness of that society and place having impaird my health, / the constitution of which at the best is very Tender, and Crazy; but I am now in the Press-yard,[8] a place of some sobriety, tho still a Prison.

Some few days after, I sent the following Letter to Sr. *Thomas Jenner*, and on the Eighth of *December* by my Wife another to you, the words of the former were these.

*To Sr. Thomas Jenner Knight, Recorder of* London.

Sr. *You know I was Committed Prisoner first to the Compter in* Woodstreet, *then to* Newgate, *by your warrant. In my Mittimus[9] tis said that I refused to give Bail, which is a mistake, for being asked by you whether I would give Bail then? I said I could not, it being so late at Night, when I had no opportunity to send to such as would Bail me, and being askt whether I would give Bail the next Morning? I said I knew not whether I could or not, because I was not certain whether such to whom I might have made Application, would do it or not: This was no Sullenness, nor Obstinacy in me, but what my Real apprehensions then were. Some Friends of mine, Freemen of this* City, *went afterwards to be my Bail, but they were told you were not at home. They made thereupon an application to Sr.* William Turner,[10] *who referd them to you.*

It is said in the Warrant that I confessed I was the Author *of a Libel, Entituled* A Plea for the Nonconformists; *wherein are contained things dangerous to the*

Government, *which thus much and no further, is true: I confessed before you that I delivered a Manuscript of my own writing to one* John How,[11] *with that Title, in order to be Printed, and that if the Print agreed with the Manuscript I would own it, otherwise I could not, because the misplacing of a Stop, the misprinting of a Letter, or Syllable, or some other Erratas of the Press, would alter the sence, even to contradiction of what was intended to be discussed; which was not, as my Indictment words it, (in a form of aggravating terms) but in order to a plain disquisition of such things as Dr.* Calamy *from* Pulpit *and* Press, *invited Dissenters to inquire into, as you may see in his Book called* A Discourse of a Scrupulous Conscience.[12] *There is / nothing of matters Relating to the Civil State, in what I am Charg'd with, for I am not concern'd with that, but if the Guide's of the Church (as. Dr.* Calamy *calls the Benific'd men of the Church of* England) *will make publick Chalenges, they should receive Objections without punishing the Objectors, whose (Supposed) Crime is only for obeying them; and that you know* Sr. *is disagreeable to Justice.*

*If any thing I have done falls within the Lash of* English *Laws,* Fiat Justitia.[13] *But I am satisfy'd I have done nothing in this point unbecoming an honest Subject, a Scholar, a Gentleman, and which is worth all, a Christian. I Commit the whole matter, with Respect to this Dispute, to that Supream Legislator, who is without Exception just, and who will judge all that are Subordinate to him, which is all from Sr. your Servant*

Thomas Delaune.

*To Dr.* Benjamin Calamy, *These.*

Sr. *In your Printed Sermon, Intituled* Scrupulous Conscience; *you know you gave a fair invitation to such as differ from you, to examine what each party* (viz. Conformists *and* Nonconformists) *say for themselves, with respect to the Rites and Ceremonys which the Guides of the Church impose on their Members, and by Penal Laws upon their* Protestant *fellow Subjects, the Nonconformists: Without doubt your call to such, pre-supposed a Reply, by which you expected that there may be either an Opportunity given to you and your Brethren, to Rectifie what Scrupulous Consciences Misunderstand, or that there may be some Relaxation procured of the severity they undergo, if their Dissent appears to be warranted by that only Rule of Faith which Dr.* Stillingfleet[14] *and other Eminent Conformists Call the* BIBLE.

*If you did not expect an Answer, or thought that none (for fear of the Act of Uniformity,* &c.) *would make any return to your Call, what can a man of Reason judge, but that it was a Florid Declamation, or a Triumphant Harangue, a meer mockery and ensnareing of poor* Scrupulous Consciences, *when they must be so muzled that they must not Exhibit the Causes of / their Doubts. Sir you know that 'tis unequal to Gag the Respondent, when the Oponents mouth is at liberty; or to Manacle the assaulted, when the Challenger Flourishes a Menacing Sword.*

*Upon that publick Call of yours, I adventured to examine (with the most diligent search I could make) what each of the said parties say for themselves, and this not out of any Litigious principle (that* Pruritus Disputandi)[15] *now too fatally grown Epidemical; but to give such as are Concern'd occasion, to investigate these disputed matters to the very foundation, to the clearing up of truth in a juncture when it can never be more Seasonable. What was digested, was intended to be sent you in a Manuscript with some modest Inferences and inquiries, but upon Recollection I judged it would more answer your End,* viz. *Publick Information, to have such Arguments, as are producible by the Dissenters, as Publick as the Invitation you gave them from Pulpit and Press: It being equal that the Answer should be as spreading as the Objections.*

*I am far from the Vanity of pretending to be your Competitor in the faculties of the Schools;*[16] *I cannot judge of them any otherwise then as unserviceable to* Christian Religion, *unless Tinctured with that Grace Derivative only from the Sanctifier of all Gifts, which I hope you partake of.*

*I am one of the meanest of the Flock, yet not below the regards of the Sheep herd of Souls, who is no Respecter of Persons, and whose Example such as call themselves his* Ambassadors *ought to follow. And therefore though some who pin their faith upon Canonical Sleevs,*[17] *may censure me, for opposing (or if I may use a Millitary metaphor, taking up the Gantlet against a man of your figure) yet I can take up my satisfaction in this, that it was not Pride, nor a popular Itch, much less the love of a Prison, influenced me to become an Answerer of your* Scrupulous Consciences.

*I could heartily wish (as a mercy to these Nations) that all Religious Differences were Composed by Evangelical Rules, and that all who own the Name of Christ, would serve him with one heart, and with one soul, and not tear each other to pieces, which by consequence must expose them as a Prey to such as gape for their Destruction. /*

*If the Sanctions of Christ in the Old and New Testament ought to regulate the modes of his Worship, and that we are under an indispensible Obligation to Obey that* Magna Charta *of Heaven, then let us either quit the name of Christians, or act according to the Supream Law-givers unrepealable Statutes, quite exploding what's undeniably borrowed from the* Pompilian *or* Pontifical Canons.[18]

*Some Sheets have been Printed off, of what I intended to present to you, but the* Messenger *of the* Press *interupted the procedure, and got me Committed to* Newgate *where I am now confined. There is nothing done, nor was intended to be done, but a fair Examination of those things your Sermon invited to, which I had thought (if termed Criminal) should fall rather with in the Cognizance of Divines, then the men of Law. For methinks the Pandects*[19] *should not be the Oracles of Religion; and that temporal Statutes should be so Civil as to give precedency to the sacred Records.*

*'Tis possible that inquirers into Religion will look upon it, as a preposterous proceeding, and disagreeable to the Nature of the* Christian Faith, *to force doubting persons by penaltyes to Embrace it; for that can never make them good Converts, but Hypocrites. May they not say that tis a horrid disparagement to the self-evidencing Light of the Gospel, if it cannot stop the mouths of the Gain-sayers any other way then by the Rigid Executions of Acts of State? I cannot find that Christ or his Disciples ever* Church-cursed *or* Newgated Scrupulous Consciences *to Conformity.*

*My Confinement is for accepting your invitation to hear both sides, and I appeal to you, whether it be Candid to punish me for Obeying a Guide of the Church? I look upon you* (in honour) *Obliged to procure my Sheets* (yet unfinished) *a publick Pasport, and to me my Liberty: else I must conclude it unfair, and that if the Irresistible Logick of Goals grows Al-a-mode,*[20] *it will make the Reformation some pretend to, suspected to be very little Meritorious of that Name.*

*Religion is a Sacred thing, and has been most horribly abused by Such as have superadded their own inventions, or those Traditional Popperies, received from our Deceiv'd and Superstitious / Ancestors. I am satisfied, you as well as Dr.* Stillingfleet *will own* (or ther's no debating with you) *that the* Scripture *is our only Rule of Faith. If so, pray let your Scrupulous Consciences be won to Conformity, by that. All Men are not of Equal Capacity to apprehend things doubtfull, for if they had been so, there had been no necesity of* Preachers; *and the Methods of convincing Men, is as plainly lay'd down in the* Bible *as any thing there, viz. By plain demonstrative Arguments, meek and winning Perswasions, not the Sylogisms of* Prisons Pillories, &c.

*I Beseech you in the fear of God, and as you will answer it to our great Lord and Master* Jesus Christ, *that without respect to any other end then the good of Souls (as the profession you take Obliges you to) that you would Treat* Scupulous Consciences *as you would be dealt withal your self: If they have no reason for their* Dissent, *and will without ground suffer* Imprisonments, *with all the Ruinous Concomitants of so dismal a Circumstance; tis certain that* Bedlam[21] *is more fit for them, then such places of* Confinement *as are appointed for men in their wits; and by consequence tis pity to be so severe with such Simpletons. But if you will allow them any* Modicum *of Reason, then I appeal to all the Guid's of the Church, whether it be not more consonant to the precepts of our* Soveraign Legislator,[22] *to confine them by his* Rules, *rather then by such Coercive methods which his* Majesty *judg'd Ineffectual in his Declaration of indulgence* March 1672?

*As* Truth *seeks no Corners nor Suborners, and as* Real Beauty *will not be beholden to the Artificial daubings of a* Pencil, *so the* Christian Religion *(where professed in its naked Simplicity) needs no other argument to beget* Proselites *then its own Lovely and Illustrious* Features, *altogether plain, honest, and every way Amiable, voyd of all Meretricious Gawdery,*[23] *or that Majestical Pomp which pleases only the External Sense.*

*I have no malignity against any Person whatsoever, much less against your Church, or any of its Members; all I desire is, that* Scrupulous Consciences, *who trouble not the peace of the* Nation, *should be dealt withal* (at least) *as weak Brethren, / according to* Rom. 14. 1.[24] *and not Ruin'd by Penaltys for not Swallowing whats imposed under the notion of* Decency and Order, *tho Excentrick*[25] *to the Scheme we have of it in our only* Rule of Faith. Sr. *I intreat you to excuse this Trouble from a Stranger who would fain be convinced by something more like* Divinity *then* Negate,[26] *where any Message from you shall be welcome, to*

*Your Humble Servant*
Thomas Delaune.

From the *Press-yard*
*Newgate* the 8*th* of
*December*. 1683.

To this Letter, Delivered by my Wife, I received an Answer to this effect, *That if I had been* Imprisoned *upon the account of* Answering *your* Book, *you would do me any kindness that became you*: But not hearing from you, I sent the following Letter by my Wife.[27] ... /

January the 9th 1683.

Reverend Sir.
*What you once and again preached and then printed, respecting a* Doubtful Conscience, *has loudly enough call'd all such as were Dissatisfy'd about some* Rites and Ceremonys, *to Examine the Reasons on both sides.*

*Others being silent I obey'd you in that particular, not meerly to wrangle (for the Encounter is unequal, betwixt a Man so Eminent as you are, and so mean a Person as I am) but that an occassion may be given, in compliance to what you desired to conclude Controversys of this nature*

*If meerly for such Obedience I must be punished I know not how, nor in what manner, is there not a new way of conquering* (Scrupulous Consciences) *unheard of in the Holy Scriptures, Started by some certain Ringleaders?*

*I purposed from Holy Writ and approved Writers, to Examine / what we ought to judg of these things. From that light of our paths, found that Lanthorn,* psal. 119. 105.[28] *I gathered some Reasons against those various and multiplied Errours which have crept into the Church.*

*For that only thing am I brought to a* Prison, *where there is nothing amiable.*

*Whether Arguments of that kind will prevaile to prove the Suppositions in your* Sermon, *Let the Supream Judg Determine.*

*Or whether any of the doubting persons can that way be compelled into the Spiritual Sheep-fold,* judg you?

*Theres nothing against the* Kings Majesty, *nothing about the* Civil Government, *nothing against the* Peace *of this* Monarchy, *there asserted.*

*The only dispute is about the original of* Rites *and* Ceremonys, *and of some things which under a shew of Truth, though not Righteously, are charged upon Doubting persons.*

*What the* Court *will do with me I know not, the will of the Supreme Father be done. Inward and outward peace in this, and Everlasting Peace in the World to come, to all such as worship the Saviour of mankind according to his word, is Pray'd for, by.*

THO. DELAUNE.

*I Desire you to Return me some Answer becoming a Divine, by my Beloved Wife,*[29] *as you have promised.*

To this Letter you answered by word of Mouth to my Wife, (for I had no answer in writing,) that you lookt upon your self *Unconcerned*, as not being mention'd in the sheets you saw with the *Recorder*: To satisfy which doubt I sent you a Third Letter, with the First sheet of the *Book* I am imprison'd for; which was a plain Demonstration that it was an answer to your *Call*, you know the Letter was thus.

January the 14th. 1683.

Sir,

*Whereas, in Answer to my two Letters you said to my Wife, / that my Papers no way concern'd you*, viz. *Such as I am indicted for; To satisfy you, with respect to that matter, I here send you the first Sheet, and leave you to consider, whether in pure generousity you are not oblig'd to procure a Prisoner (whose Obedience to you made him so) his liberty. I am Sir.*

*your humble servant,*<br>THO. DELAUNE.

I appeal to your Consience, whether I had not some reason to expect some return to these Applications?

But I had none to any purpose, and that too but in a few words by my wife: I had some thoughts that you would have performed the Office of a Divine, in visiting me in my place of Confinement; either to Argue me out of my *Doubts*, which your promis'd SCRIPTURE and REASON, not *a Mittimus* and *Newgate* could easily do. To the former I can yeild – To the latter, it seems, I must – This is a severe kind of Logick, and will probably dispute me out of this World, as it did Mr. *Bampfield* and Mr. *Ralphson*[30] lately, who were my dear and excellent Companions in Trouble – and whose absence I cannot but bemoan, as having lost in them a Society that was truly pious, truly sweet, and truly amiable: But I hope the God of mercy will supply the want, by a more immediate influence of Comfort, then what can be obtained at second hand.

On the tenth of *December* two Bills were found against Mr. *Ralphson* and me, by the *Grand-jury* of *London*, whose Names are as followeth.

| | |
|---|---|
| *Tho. Vernon.* | *Josias Ewth.* |
| *Tho. Goddard.* | *John Paine.* |
| *Will. Gore.* | *William Fazakerly.* |
| *Will. Wills.* | *Jos. Sparrow.* |
| *Rand. Manning.* | *Joh. Reendal.* |
| *John Martin.* | *David Pool.* |
| *Richard Hows.* | *Ri. Beauchamp.* |
| *Tho. Hodges.* | *Rob. Minories.* |
| *Joseph Woolhead.* / | |

On the 13*th* day of the same Month, we were called to the *Sessions-House* in the *Old-Bayly*; And then our Indictments were read in *English*, to which we pleaded not Guilty. We desired Copies of the said Indictments, and time to make our Defence till next Sessions; which the Court after some pause granted. The substance of the Indictment against me was thus – *Iuratores pro Domino Rege supar Sacram suum presentant quod.* Tho Delaune *nuper Delondon Gener ligeare su,* &c., *In plain English thus, as to the material part of it.*

*The Jurors for our Lord the* King, *upon their* Oath *Present, that* Thomas Delanne *late of* London Gent. *Not regarding his due* Allegeance, *but contriving and intending to disquiet and disturb the peace and common Tranquillity of this Kingdom of* England, *&c. To bring the said Lord the* King *into the greatest hate and contempt of his Subjects – Machinating and farther intending to move stir up and procure* Sedition *and* Rebellion, *and to disparage and Scandalize the Book of* Common Prayer, &c.

*On the* 30*th day of* November *in the* 35*th of the* King, *at* London *in the parish of St.* Botolph without Bishops Gate, *in the Ward of* Bishops-Gate *aforesaid; by Force and Armes,* &c. *Unlawfully, Seditiously and Maliciously, did Write, Print, and Publish, and Caused to be Written, Printed and Published, a certain False, Seditious and Scandalous Libel, of and concerning the said Lord the King, and the Book of* Common Prayer, *aforesaid, Intituled* a Plea for the NONCONFORMISTS.

*In which said Libel are contained these false, Fictions, and Scandalous sentences following,* viz. 'The Church of *Rome* and *England* also, are great Transgressors, to presume to vary from Christs precept, in altering or adding to the form of words exprest by Christ, in this of *Luke.* for so they have done: They say *forgive us our trespasses, as we forgive them who trespass against us*; when there are nosuch words in Christ prayer, his words are, *forgive us our Sins or Debts, for we also forgive every one that is indebted to us*,[31] *and* (says the Indictment / again) in another part of the said Libell are contained these false, Fictions, Seditious, and scandalous Sentences following, *viz*. And may we not say that in these following particulars we do Symbolize with Idolatrous Rome herein? *First*, by injoining and imposing this (here the Indictment makes an *Innuendo viz*. Meaning the Book of Common Prayer aforesaid) as a set form as they do with penaltys, contrary to the Scripture. *Secondly*, by an often Repetition of the same form in the same exercise three or four times at least, *in so much*, that in Cathedrall Churches it is said or sung ten or twelve times a day, contrary to Christs Express words, that when we pray, we do not make vain Repetitions as the Heathens doe, for they think they shall be heard for their much Speaking. *Thirdly*, by injoyning the whole congregation, Men and Women, to repeat the same after the Priest, though no such Directions by Christ. Nay he forbids Women to pray or prophesie in the Church. *Fourthly*, in Singing this Prayer in the Cathedrals by Responses of People, without the least warrant from Christ for such Song-praying' (Then the Indictment ends with a fearfull Aggravation, that is) 'in contempt of the King, and to the evil and most pernicious example of all such other Dlinquents in the like case, and against the peace of the said Lord now King, his Crown and Dignity, *&c*.'

The Copy of the Indictment signed *Wagstaffe*.

On the 16*th* of *January* we were called again to the *Sessions-House*,[32] but there being some Tryals that prov'd very tedious, we were not brought on.

The next day we were called to the outter Bar, after the attendance of divers hours in a place not very lovely, and in the sharpest Winter that you have known, which I likely prov'd the original of that indisposition which carry'd my two friends beyond the Jurisdiction of *Sessions, Bale-Docks*,[33] or *Press-yards*, to a glorious mansion of rest. /

Then a Jury was sworn to pass upon us, whose names were.

| | |
|---|---|
| *James Wood.* | *Thomas Medcalf.* |
| *James Smith.* | *John Harbing.* |
| *Bernerd Mynn.* | *Samuel Seale.* |
| *Thomas Jenny.* | *Laurence Weld.* |
| *Kenelme Smith.* | *John Callow.* |
| *Matthew Walker.* | *Richard Johnson.* |

I desir'd my Indictment should be read in Latine, which was done. Then the Gentlemen of *Law*, aggravated things with there usual *Rethorick* – one of them, (I think the Attorney General)[34] was pleased to say that the Prisoner that stood there before (for Mr. *Ralphson* was try'd before me) did labour to undermine the state, and that man (meaning me) would undermine the Church: So that to Incence the Jury against us, he said, *heres* CHURCH *and* STATE *struck at*.

Which *Sr.* was very improbable to be true, for tis wonderful that any *Church* or *State* so potent as this is, should fear two such underminers, as that Extravagant *harangue* term'd us. For my part I cannot be righteously charged with any attempt against either, unless my obedience to you, be so: And then if I be guilty, you that tempted me to it, can never prove your self innocent.

Being desired to speak what I had to say for my self, I spoke the following words, which one that knew me took in Short-hand, though without my knowledge.

My Lord, *Last Sessions I pleaded not Guilty, that is not Guilty* Modo et forma,[35] *for I design'd not* vi et Armis,[36] *to raise* Rebellion, Sedition, &c. I detest such things; *he that Swears in that Respect against me, must be perjur'd – The instances in the Indictment relate to no such thing.* My Lord, *I pray you to trouble no Witnesses about me, I won't* prevaricate. *I have written some Papers Intituled* A Plea for the Nonconformists, *not Instigated by the feign'd formalitys in the Indictment; but it was at the Loud Chalenge of Dr.* Calamy, *one of the Kings Chaplains, in his Discourse about a* / Scrupulous Consciences, *Dedicated to your Lordship, wherein he called upon doubting Persons to examine what could be said on both sides, which I did; Now since publick Chalenges are made to be Answered; to punish me for Obeying a Guide of the Church*, is hard, very hard.

*I desire that the intire Paragraphs may be read, from which the* Crimes *Charged against me are infer'd. If fragments only be produced against* me, *from which* no perfect sence *can be deduced; I shall be unfairly dealt with: The Coherence of* Sence *in a* Continued Discourse, *not* Scraps *and* Broken-pieces *of* Sentences, *can demonstrate the* Scope *of an* Argument.

*If what I have written be True, 'tis no* Crime, *unless Truth be made a* Crime; *if false, let Dr*. Calamy, *or any of the Guides of your Church Confute me* (as he promised, *p*. 25. of his Sermon aforesaid) *by good Scripture and good Reason, then I'le submit. If the latter Method be not taken, (I must Repeat it)* 'tis very hard, *my Lord*, 'tis very hard.

Here the chief Justice[37] interupted me, addressing himself to the Jury, and *expounded that part of the Indictment which I excepted against*, saying, *it was only for forms sake, and that any breach of the peace in the sence of the Law, may be said to be* vi & Armis, *by force and arms, with some other expressions to that purpose* – To the Latter which I acknowledged, *he said, after a Torrent of Aggravations, Gentlemen, if you believe that man (pointing to me)* viz. *In what I had confessed in writing the* Nonconformists Plea, *you must find him Guilty*, viz. *of the whole Indictment*. And which they *readily did accordingly*.

The next day, (*viz.*) the 18*th*, I received my *Sentence*. The very same with Mr. *Ralphson, viz*. (As 'tis recorded.)[38] ...

'*Thomas Delaune*, Find 100 Marks, and to be kept Prisoner, / &c. (which *&c*. they interpret till he pay his Fine) and to find good Security for his good behaviour for one whole year after-wards, and that the said Books, and seditious Libels by him published, shall be burnt with *Fire, before the *Royal-Exchange* in *London*. And if he be discharged to pay * six Shillings.'

Signed *Wagstaffe*.

* not with water you must note.
* To the Hangman for the Faggots I suppose.

The Recorder asked me some questions then, (*viz.*) *Whether I was in Orders? I told him I was never in any Ecclesiastical Orders, nor never Preach'd among any People. That I was bred a Scholar, and had been a School-Master, and kept a Grammar School till forc'd from it by the present prosecutions*, &c.

The Court told both Mr. *Ralphson* and me, *that in respect to our Education, as Scholars, we should not be* Pillory'd, *though ('twas said) we deserv'd it*.

We were sent back to our place of Confinement, and the next *Execution day*, our Books were burnt, as the Sentence ordered it, WITH FIRE in the place aforesaid, and we continue here; but since I writ this, Mr. *Ralphson* had a Supersedeas[39] by *Death* to a *better place*.

Thus Sir, you have a series of my Circumstances; I will make no complaints of the usage I had, when forc'd, as aforesaid, to Lodge amongst a Rabble of wretches, whose society seem'd to me to be a Hell upon Earth, as before; nor of my other hardships, as Confinement, loss of Employment, loss of Health, &c. But if you have any sence of Humanity in you, you will Recollect your self, and procure me my Freedom, (being not able to pay the Fine) lost by obedience to your publick *Call*. Sir, I must tell you plainly, that you discover'd in your very dedication to Sr. *Gorge Jefferies*,[40] now chief Justice, a kind of Doubt, to say no more, Respecting your Cause.

You say there (P. 2. Ep. Ded.) *How many it* (viz. your Sermon) *will anger and displease, I am not at all concerned, and tho I may be thought by some ill advised in publishing such a Sermon, yet, every one* (\*) *will commend and justify my discretion in prefixing your name before it: For so great an awe have*\* *the Enemys of our Church and Government of your Loyalty and Fidelity to both, that they will* Not dare Loudly *to condemn what you are pleased to Protect, they will be justly* Affraid *of Quarrelling with me, when they know I have* Engaged *you on my side*.

* of your Mind.
* Meaning Protestant Dissenters.

From these Expressions I must conclude (If you are in earnest) that you care not how much you offend your weak Brother. The Apostle *Paul* was of another mind, *Rom*. 15. 1. &c. *We then that are strong, ought to bear the infirmitys of the weak, and not to please our selves; let every one of us please his Neighbour for his good to Edification*. Pray consider this, and what follows in the same Chapter: And I. *Cor*. 8. 12. *But when you sin so against the Brethren and wound their weak Consciences, ye sin against Christ*. ver. 13. *Wherefore if meat make my Brother to offend, I will eat no flesh while the World standeth, lest I make my Brother to offend*: And I *Thes*. 5. 14. the same Evangelical Doctor, exhorts you, *To Comfort the feeble minded, Support the weak, and to be patient toward all men*. And Gal. 6. 1. *To restore the faulty in the Spirit of Meekness*.

What a Superlative, *what a true Christian* Complyance is here! Worth the imitation of the Guides of your Church! This Apostle would rather make a perpetual fast from flesh, then offend his *Weak Brother*. And I am apt to think no flourishes of *Pulpit-Rhetorick* ever drop't from *him*, to grieve his *Weak Brethren*, and that he never shrouded his writings, or preachings, under the terrible Patronage of such men as you Represent Sr. *Gorge Jefferies* to be. I have a kind of fancy that your said Patron, now *Lord Chief Justice*, as he is a *Gentleman* in Eminent place, and of a piercing Judgement, Strong Memory, and of fluent Oratory, could not but look through the Superficial Addresses of that Dedication.

In the second place, a Man so dignified as he is, must certainly take it as an affront to his title of *Lord Chief Justice,* that you should say that men will be *Justly affraid* of quarrelling with you, when they know you have Engaged him on your side. That same word (Affraid) denotes a Champion-like Courage in you; that no body should dare to come near you; and withal, a Reflection on the justice of your Patron, that he will take your part *Right* or *Wrong*. As to the word (Quarrelling) I know no body that has assaulted you in any more perillous Attaque, then in Examining the Merits of the Cause as you Preached, and by the same Sermon (transfigur'd from the *Press*) invited men to do.

No Force and Arms were used against you by me, but Pen, Ink and a few Papers. The Indictment makes this a very formidable kind of Artillery. /

But to bring the matter a little closer, I must desire you will please to take notice of this Hainous Charge given in against me, and how made good in the Indictment, and how severely handled both by the Juryes and Court thereupon.

The charge, as you have heard, is for *intending to disturb the* Publick Peace, *To bring the King into the greatest* Hate *and* Contempt *of his* Subjects, *to stir up and procure* Sedition *and* Rebellion: a high and Heinous Charge indeed! But how is this made good? *viz.* By *my disparaging the Book of Common Prayer*. But how doth that appear? *Viz.* By *the force of Arms used Unlawfully, Seditiously, and Maliciously, to Write, Print and Publish a* Seditious *and* Scandalous Libel, *Concerning our Lord the King and the Book of Common Prayer, Intituled* A Plea for the Nonconformists. But wherein doth it appear by any thing which is writ in that Book, that this Hainous Charge is made good? *viz. By their pregnant instances, produced out of the Book expressed in the Indictment.*

The which therefore, since we must suppose they are the most Hainous and Dangerous passages to be found therein, and most proper and significant to make good the Charge, I shall for your information, and that you may the better judge how the Charge is proved against me, give you the intire paragraph out of which the instances were picked, which I must beg the justice of you to Read; & which I could not with all my Entreatys Obtain of the Court, tho so necessary (as you'l find) to come to the right sence, (and for greater Illustration, I shall distinguish the instances of the Indictment in a different Character) know therefore that I having (in the *Plea for the Nonconformists*) from *p.*14. at your desire, been giving an account what the *Nonconformists* Answer to that great Objection; that all things they scruple in the *Rites* and *Ceremonies* of the Church, are not *Popish Novelties*, but of Primitive *Antiquity*, (as you say) and having distinctly gone through most of them, giving their Reasons why they are not of *Primitive Antiquity*, but of *Popish Novelty*, and contain in the *Mass-Book* – This Objection came to be started, *p.*40. 'But what do you say to the Lords Prayer? must we forbear that too, because we find it in the *Mass-Book*; tho so publickly injoyn'd by Christ to use it, as a stinted form, *Luke* 11.2. That when we pray, we should say, Our Father, *&c*? To which the *Nonconformists* say, / that it is a great mistake to suppose that Christ hereby in this Scripture, has appointed this to be a set form, to be prayed by all in these prescript words, when we pray unto God, for then it would be unlawfull to use any other words, then these herein expressed, in our prayers, and that the Disciples and Apostles sinned in using other words in those their prayers we read of in Scripture, and so does the Church of *England*, in forming so many Collects and Prayers; And. *p.*41.42.'

Secondly, *The Church of* Rome *and* England *are great Transgressors, to presume to vary from Christ precepts, in altering or adding to the form of words expressed by Christ in this* 11 Luke. *For so they have done, they say,* Forgive us our Trespasses, as we forgive them who Trespass against us, *when there are no such words in Christs Prayer, his words are,* forgive us our Sins, our Debts opheilemata[41] for we also forgive every one that is Indebted to us. *Which, saith the Indictment, are false, fictious, and scandalous sentences, but it shews not wherein.* Indictment

'And also the Doxology, which is not in this Prayer in *Luke II.* (*viz. For thine is the Kingdom and the Power and the Glory for ever and ever*, Amen.) But you'l say, as to the Doxology, it is expressed by Christ at the end of the same prayer in his Sermon on the Mount, *Mat.*6. It is very True, it is so, where he delivers this prayer not as a set form, but a pattern of prayer: *After this manner Pray ye houto's*[42] – to this purpose, and which is an Explication of what he says, *Luke* 11.2. when you pray, *say*, Our Father *&c*. That is, *after this manner*, and which can only be a warrant to the; Church of *England*, or any other, to make such alterations Christ no more intending to tye the Disciple who desired to be instructed how to pray, to this form of words (nor any other Disciple) then he did the twelve Disciples when he sent them out to Preach with this word of Command, *Math.*10.7. *Preach, saying, The Kingdom of Heaven is at hand*; that they should thereby be tyed to those very words in their Preaching (and Preach nothing else) but as this was given as a Text or Theme to Preach by, so the other to pray by: The Disciple who proposes the question, *Vers. 1.* Desires that they may be taught to pray as *John* taught his Disciples; but such a / set form of Prayer we find not that *John* in his Teachings gave to his Disciples, neither do we find that any of Christ's Disciples or Apostles did pray this very prayer, to which our Expositors do agree.

'*Grotius*,[43] saith on *Luke* the 11.2. That Christ herein Teacheth us a Compendium of those things we are to pray for; at that time (saith he) they were not bound to the use of so may Words and Syllables: As also *Tertullian, Cyprian, Musculus, Cornelius Alapide*: and *Austin*[44] himself (upon the place) who saith *Liberum est*, it is free for us to ask the same thing in the Lords Prayer, *Aliis atque aliis verbis*,[45] sometime one way, and sometimes, another.

'Doth not *Paul* tell us expressly, he knew not what to pray for, but as the Spirit gave him utterance, *Rom*. 8. But he did know what to pray for if this was to be his prescript form.

'*Tertullian* saith, they prayed *Sine Monitore*, without a Monitor (or Common-Prayer-book) and *Socrates* tells us that among all the Christians of that age scarce two were to be found that used the same words in Prayer, *Chrysostom* on *Rom*. 8. *Homil*. 14. saith, With other gifts they had the gift of Prayer, which was also called the Spirit, but he who had the gift, did pray for the whole multitude, for that was Expedient unto the Church, & also did instruct others to Pray.

'And though we find neither Christ, nor his Apostles, impose this or any other form of Prayer to be used by us (but that we Pray in the Spirit, and Praise in the Spirits: and that God being a Spirit, seeketh and accepteth such worships) yet we find the Popes and their Councils imposing this and other Lyturgical forms.

'The Councell of *Toledo*, Anno. 618. Decreed in the Ninth *Canon*, that every day both in publick and private worship, none of the Clergy omit the Lords Prayers, under payn of Deposition; since (say they) Christ hath prescribed this, saying, When you pray say, Our Father, *&c*. And how formally and carnally, has the Pater-noster[46] been muttered over by the superstitious Papists, ever since.'

*And may we not enquire, whether in the following particulars we do not Symbolize with the Romish worship herein, which the Indictment injuriously words thus.* /

*And may we not say that in these following particulars (for may we not enquire whether in the following particulars) we do Symbolize with Idolatrous Rome herein*) 'For we do not Symbolize with the Romish herein,) (meaning) saith the indictment with an *Innuendo*) the Book of Common Prayer, whereas it only relates to the Lords prayer.[47]

First. *By enjoying and imposing this, as a set form, without the Sanction* of any sacred Text *to warrant* it, (which the Indictment words, contrary to the Scriptures)

Secondly. *By an often repetition of the same form in the same exercise, three or four times at least, insomuch that in Cathedral Services, it is said, or sung, ten or twelve times in a day, contrary to Christs express words, that when we pray we should not make vain repetitions as the Heathens do, for they think they shall be heard for their much speaking,* Mat. 6.7.

Thirdly. *By enjoyning the whole Congregation, both men and women, to repeat the same after the Priest, tho no such direction by Christ; nay he forbids women to pray, or Prophesie, in the Church,* I Cor. 14. 34. &c.

Fourthly. *In singing this prayer in Cathedralls by Responses of Priests and People, with musick, without the least Divine Authority for such Song-Praying.*

Which the indictment saith are fictious, seditious, and scandalous sentences (but shew not wherein,) Thus have you the whole paragraph and what is picked out of it, to make good the charge; whereby you will easely discern,

Whether I have done otherwise therein then given you at your Call, a true and modest account of the *Nonconformists Arguments*, why the Lords Prayer is not a stinted set form of Prayer as supposed, but a pattern to pray by, which is done by several Arguments, *viz.*     1 Query.

1. From the practices of both Churches, *Rome* and *England*, who have both altered and added to it, which they ought not to have done (no not so much as one Syllable) if so intended by Christ.

2ly, From the practises of the Antients, and Opinions of many Learned Commentators upon the place.

3ly, Because neither Christ not his Apostles have so injoyned and practised it as a stinted form.

4ly, Because the Church of *Rome*, without Scripture Authority, have so imposed, and practised it; and therefore are those Queries, Whether for us so to impose it with penaltys, and to make often Repetitions of it, with Responses of Priest and People, and to sing it with Musick, is not without Scripture warrant, and a Symbolizing with *Rome* therein? and where's the *Sedition, Rebellion*, breaking the *Publick peace* by *force*, and *Arms* in all this?

2ly, Whether the picking out part, and leaving out the greater part, Changing of words, and inverting of sence, is not most Injurious dealing? for what is it not, which may not be made of any mans sayings and writings, if such a liberty may be taken? For may it not with such a latitude be proved by Scripture, that there is no God, or any such Blasphemy or Immorality?     2 Query.

3ly, Whether the Grand Jury, in honesty and good Conscience, could find this Bill upon their Oaths, and the Petty Jury[48] cast me upon it, and the Court past Sentence upon me thereupon, without admitting the whole Paragraph to be Read, and Considered, as so was earnestly desired by me?     3 Query.

4ly, If this writing of mine, was only occasioned and drawn forth at your Call, as your Book evidenceth, and as declared to the Court; then doth not that hainous Charge of a Malicious and Seditious contriving, intending, / and Machinating *Sedition*, and *Rebellion*, and violating *Publick peace*, fall to the Ground?     4 Query.

5*ly*, If this part of the *Nonconformists Plea* be true, where is the Crime? Must I be made guilty, and punished for speaking the Truth? And if you were so satisfied, why did not you Interpose to prevent a precipitate Sentence and Verdict, and preserve an Innocent person? If it appear'd otherwise to you, Why did you not by word and writing endeavour my Conviction, and shew me my Error, and Mistake before the Sessions, that I might publickly, have owned and taken the Shame, as my three Letters with so much Importunity press't upon you; and that I was neither Obstinate, nor Incorrigible, you have againe and againe under my hand? And what an open Ear I had to receive conviction from Reason and Scripture, the Mediums you proposed to Treat a *Scrupulous Conscience* with, and thereby to have acquitted your self from being a Decoy to inveagle into the Snare, and then leave them, but wholy to reject both, and silently to suffer me to be crushed, is worse dealing, and less Charity then the Guides of the Church put forth in Q. *Marys* days, who failed not of Prison visits and endeavours, to convince the *Hereticks* (as they called them) before they were delivered to the Secular Powers for Destruction.

6. Query.

6*ly*, Whether from this Liberty that is taken in Indictments (as in Chancery Bills) to say the worst of things which may be said against any, and assign the matter of fact to prove it forreign thereto, yet that the Jurys finding the matter of fact, must render a man Guilty of the whole Indictment, both matter and form, seems very hard, and no other then turning Judgment into Wormwood and Hemlock,[49] and a bringing Legal proceeding, into great contempt?

For instance, if a man is charged in an Indictment that be contrary to his Allegiance, and not having the fear of God before his Eyes, but being moved by the Instigation of the Devil, did such a day, in such a place, bring the King into greatest Hate and Contempt amongst his Subjects, and did most Maliciously and Seditiously, &c. against the *Publice peace*, by force and Arms, Read a Chapter in the Bible in English before several People (which was Crime enough heretofore, however it is now) that the proving and confessing the matter of fact, (or any of the like nature as foreign from the Crimes urged, must according to our Court-proceedings, bring him in Guilty of the whole Indictment, in order to be sentenced accordingly.

But ought not a Jury before they bring in their verdict upon Oath, as they would acquit themselves of the horid sin of perjury, Examine and have sufficient proof to make good those Luxuriant Cut-throat forms? And whether such matter of fact, either by the Righteous Law of God and Man, can render a man Culpable of so Hainous a charge of *Malice, Sedition, Rebellion*, bringing the King into *Hatred* and *Contempt*, breaking the *Publick peace* by force and arms, before they make him Guilty thereof, and cause him to be punished for the same?

Thus *Sr.* you have a naked account of my Case, and if you Please, or any other of the Church Guides, to examine the respective Circumstances of it, or apply that soveraign Medium of good Scripture and good Reason to Convince me, you or they will satisfy the world that ye are honest Guides of the Church, and reduce many to your Communion, as well as

*Your humble Servant,*
Thomas De-Laune.

'Mr Baxter's Tryal' (1685), in Edmund Calamy, *An Abridgment of Mr. Baxter's History of His Life and Times. With an Account of many others of those Worthy Ministers who were Ejected ... And a Continuation of their History, till the Year 1691* (London, 1702), pp. 616–20. ESTC, T109211.

## Mr. Baxter's Tryal

In the Reign of King *James* the Second, which began *Feb.* 6. 168⅘. The same Methods were continu'd as had been us'd in his Brothers Time. On the 28th of *February*, Mr. *Baxter* was Committed to the *Kings-Bench* Prison, by my Lord Chief Justice *Jefferies*'s Warrant, for his Paraphrase on the New Testament, Printed a little before;[1] which was call'd a Scandalous and Seditious Book against the Government. On the 6th of *May*, which was the first Day of the Term, he appear'd in *Westminster* Hall,[2] and an Information was ordered to be drawn up against him. *May* the 14th, He Pleaded not Guilty to the Information. *May* the 18th, he being much Indispos'd, mov'd that he might have farther Time given him for his Tryal, but it was deny'd him. He mov'd for It by his Council; but *Jeffreys* cries out in a Passion, *I will not give him a Minutes Time more to save his Life. We have had* (says he) *to do with other sorts of Persons, but now we have a Saint to deal with; and I know how to deal with Saints as well as Sinners. Yonder* (says he) *stands OATS in the Pillory* (as he actually did at that very Time in the New Palace-Yard;)[3] *and he says he suffers for the Truth, and so says* Baxter; *but if* Baxter *did but stand on the side of the Pillory with him, I would say Two of the greatest Rogues and Rascals in the Kingdom stood there.*

On *May* the 30th, in the Afternoon, He was brought to his Tryal, before the Lord Chief Justice *Jeffreys* at *Guild Hall.* Sir *Henry Ashhurst*,[4] who could not forsake his own, and his Fathers Friend, stood by him all the while. Mr. Baxter came first into Court, and with all the Mask of Serenity and Composure, waited for the coming of the Lord Chief Justice, who appear'd quickly after with great Indignation in his Face. He no sooner sate down, then a short Cause was Call'd and Try'd: After which the Clerk began to read the Title of / another Cause. *You Blockhead you* (says *Jeffreys*) *the next Cause is between* RICHARD BAXTER *and the King.* Upon which Mr. *Baxter*'s Cause was Call'd. The Passages mention'd in the Information, were his Paraphrase on *Mat.* 5. 19. *Mark* 3. 6. *Mark* 9. 39. *Mark* 11. 31. *Mark* 12. 38,39,40. *Luke* 10.2. *John* 11.57. and *Acts* 15.2. These Passages were pickt out by Sir *Roger L'Estrange*,[5] and some of his Companions. And a certain Noted Clergy-man (who shall be nameless) put into the Hands of his Enemies some Accusations out of *Rom.* 13, &c. as against the King, to touch his Life, but no use was made of them. The great Charge was, that in these several Passages he reflected on the Prelates of the Church of *England*, and so was Guilty of Seditions, *&c.* The Kings Counsel open'd the Information at large with its Aggravations. Mr. *Wallop*, Mr. *Williams*, Mr. *Rotherham*, Mr. *Atwood*, and Mr. *Phipps*, were Mr. *Baxter*'s Counsel, and had been Feed by Sir *Henry Ashhurst*. Mr. *Wallop*[6] said, that he conceiv'd the Matter depending being a Point of Doctrine, it ought to be referr'd to the Bishop his Ordinary: But if not, he humbly conceiv'd the Doctrine was Innocent, and Justifiable, setting aside the Innuendo's, for which there was no Colour, there being no Antecedent to refer them to (*i.e.* no Bishop or Clergy of the Church of England nam'd.) He said the Book Accus'd, *i.e.* the Comment on the New Testament, contain'd many Eternal Truths: But they who drew the Information were the Libellers, in applying to the Prelates of the Church of *England*, those severe Things which were written concerning some Prelates, who deserv'd the Characters which he gave. My Lord (says he) I humbly conceive the Bishops Mr. *Baxter* speaks of,[7] as your Lordship if you have read Church History must confess, were the Plagues of the Church, and of the World. Mr. *Wallop*, says the Lord Chief Justice, *I observe you are in all these dirty Causes, and were it not for you Gentlemen of the Long Robe, who should have more Wit and Honesty, that support and hold up these Factious Knaves by the Chin, we should not be at the Pass we are.* My Lord, says Mr. Wallop, I humbly Conceive, that the / Passages Accus'd are natural Deductions from the Text. *You humbly Conceive*, says JEFFREYS, *and I humbly Conceive: Swear him, Swear him.*[8] My Lord says he, under Favour, I am Counsel for the Defendant, and if I understand either *Latin* or *English*,[9] the Information now bro't against Mr. *Baxter* upon so slight a ground, is a greater Reflection upon the Church of *England*, than any Thing contain'd in the Book he's Accus'd for. Says *Jeffreys* to him, *Sometimes you humbly Conceive, and sometimes you are very Positive: You talk of your Skill in Church History, and of your Understanding* Latin *and* English: *I think I understand something of them as well as you; but in short must tell you, that if you don't understand your Duty better, shall teach it you.* Upon which Mr. Wallop *sate down.*

Mr *Rotheram*[10] urg'd that if Mr. *Baxter*'s Book had sharp Reflections upon the Church of *Rome*, by Name, but spake well of the Prelates of the Church of *England*, it was to be presum'd that the sharp Reflections were intended only against the Prelates of the Church of *Rome*. The Lord Chief Justice said, *Baxter* was *an Enemy to the Name and Thing, the Office and Persons of Bishops*. Rotheram added, that *Baxter* frequently attended Divine Service, went to the Sacrament and perswaded others to do so too, as was certainly and publickly known, and had in the very Book so charg'd, spoken very moderately and honourably of the Bishops of the Church of *England*. Mr. *Baxter* added, my Lord, I have been so moderate with Respect to the Church of *England*, that I have incurr'd the Censure of many of the *Dissenters* upon that Account. BAXTER *for Bishops*, says JEFFREYS. *That's a merry Conceit indeed. Turn to it, turn to it*. Upon this *Rotheram* turn'd to a Place where 'tis said, *That great Respect is due to those truly call'd to be Bishops among us*: Or to that Purpose: *Ay* saith *Jeffreys, This is your* Presbyterian *Cant; truly call'd to be Bishops*, that is himself and such Rascals call'd to be Bishops of *Kidderminster*,[11] and other such Places. *Bishops set apart by such Factious, Sniveling* Presbyterians *as himself: A* Kidderminster *Bishop he means. According to the saying of a late Learned / Authour; and every Parish shall maintain, a Tithe Pig Metropolitan.*[12] Mr. *Baxter* beginning to speak again; says he to him, *Richard, Richard, dost thou think we'll hear thee Poison the Court*, &c. *Richard thou art an Old Fellow*,[13] *an Old Knave; thou hast Written Books eno' to Load a Cart, every one as full of Sedition (I might say Treason) as an Egg is full of Meat.*[14] *Hadst thou been Whipp'd out of thy Writing Trade Forty Years ago, it had been Happy. Thou pretendest to be a Preacher of the Gospel of Peace, and thou hast one Foot in the Grave, 'tis Time for thee to begin to think what Account thou intendest to give. But leave thee to thy Self, and I see thou'lt go on as thou hast begun, but by the Grace of God, Ile look after thee. I know thou hast a mighty Party, and I see a great many of the Brotherhood in Corners, waiting to see what will become of their mighty Donne*,[15] *and a Doctor of the Party* (looking to Dr. Bates)[16] *at your Elbow, but by the Grace of Almighty God I'le Crush you all.* Mr. *Rotheram* sitting down, Mr. *Attwood*[17] began to shew, that not one of the Passages mention'd in the Information ought to be strain'd to that Sense, which was put upon them by the Innuendo's; they being more natural when taken in a milder Sense: Nor could any one of them be apply'd to the Prelates of the Church of *England*, without a very forc'd Construction. To Evidence this, he would have read some of the Text; but *Jeffreys* cry'd out, *You shan't draw me into a Conventicle with your Annotations, nor your Sniveling Parson neither*. My Lord says *Attwood*, I conceive this to be expressly within *Roswell's* Case,[18] lately before your Lordship. *You conceive*, says Jeffreys, *you conceive amiss: It is not*, My Lord, says Mr. *Attwood*, that I may use the best Authority, permit me to repeat your Lordships own Words in that Case. No, *you shan't*, says he. You need not speak, for you are an Authour already; tho' you Speak and Write impertinently. Says *Attwood*, I can't help that my Lord, if my Talent be no better; but it is my Duty to do my best for my Client. *Jeffreys* thereupon went on, inveighing against what *Attwood* had Publish'd: And *Attwood* justify'd it to be in Defence of the *English* Constitution; declaring that he never disown'd any Thing he had / Written.[19] *Jeffreys* several Times order'd him to sit down; but he still went on. My Lords, says he, I have Matter of Law to offer for my Client; and he proceeded to Cite several Cases wherein it had been adjudged that Words ought to be taken in the milder Sense, and not to be strain'd by Innuendo's. *Well*, says Jeffreys when he had done, *You have had your say*. Mr. *Williams*, and Mr. *Phipps* said nothing, for they saw 'twas to no Purpose. At length says Mr. *Baxter* himself, my Lord, I think I can clearly Answer all that is laid to my Charge, and I shall do it briefly: The Summ is contain'd in these few Papers, to which I shall add a little by Testimony. But he would not hear a Word. At length the Chief Justice summ'd up the Matter in a long and fulsome Harangue. *'Tis notoriously known* (says he) *there has been a Design to ruine the King and the Nation. The Old Game has been renew'd: And this has been the main Incendiary. He's as Modest now as can be: But Time was, when no Man was so ready* at Bind your King in Chains, and your Nobles in Fetters of Iron: And to your Tents O Israel.[20] *Gentlemen, for Gods sake don't let us be gull'd twice in an Age,* &c. And when he concluded, He told the Jury, that if they in their Consciences believ'd he meant the Bishops and Clergy of the Church of *England*, in the Passages which the Information referr'd to, they must find him Guilty: And he could mean no Man else. If not, they must find him not Guilty. When he had done says Mr. *Baxter* to him, Do's your Lordship think any Jury will pretend to pass a Verdict upon me upon such a Tryal? *I'le Warrant you,* Mr. *Baxter* say he; *don't you Trouble your self about that.* The Jury immediately laid their Heads together at the Bar, and found him *Guilty.* He had Subpæna'd several Clergymen, who appear'd in Court, but were of no use to him, thro' the Violence of the Chief Justice. The Trial being over, Sir *Henry Ashhurst* led Mr. Baxter thro' the Crowd, (I mention it to his Honour) and convey'd him away in his Coach.

On *June* the 29th following, He had Judgment given against Him. He was Fin'd 500 marks; to be in Prison till he paid it; and be bound to his good Behaviour for Seven Years.

# CENSORSHIP AND PUNISHMENT UNDER JAMES II

James II, *By the King, A Proclamation against Spreading of a Traiterous Declaration Published by James Duke of Monmouth* (London: printed by the Assigns of John Bill Deceas'd; and by Henry Hills, and Thomas Newcomb, Printers to the Kings most Excellent Majesty, 15 June 1685). Wing, J310; ESTC, R226084.

*The True Account of the Behaviour and Confession of William Disney Esq; Who was Tryed for High Treason by the Kings Especial Commission of Oyer and Terminer, held at the Marshalsea in Southwark, on Thursday the 25th of June, 1685* (London: printed by George Croom, at the Sign of the Blue-Ball in Thames-street, over against Baynard's-Castle, 1685). Wing, T2344; ESTC, R6085.

*An Account of the Proceedings against Samuel Johnson: Who was Tryed at the Kings-Bench-Bar, Westminster, for High Misdemeanour: And Found Guilty of Writing and Publishing Two Seditious and Scandalous Libels against the Government, on Monday the 21th of June. 1686* (London: A.M., 21 June 1686). Wing, A351; ESTC, R402.

*The Sentence of Samuel Johnson, at the King's-Bench-Barr at Westminster* (London: printed by D. Mallet, next Door to Mr. Shipton's Coffee-House near Fleet-Bridge, 17 November 1686). Wing, S2554A; ESTC, R214822.

James II, *By the King, A Proclamation for Suppressing and Preventing Seditious and Unlicenced Books and Pamphlets* (London: printed by Charles Bill, Henry Hills, and Thomas Newcomb, Printers to the King's most Excellent Majesty, 10 February 1688). Wing, J348; ESTC, R18650.

*An Account of the Proceedings at Westminster-Hall, on the 29th, and 30th. of June 1688. Relating to the Tryal and Discharge of the Archbishop of Canterbury, the Bishop of S. Asaph, Bishop of Chichester, Bishop of Ely, Bishop of Bath and Wells, Bishop of Peterborough, and the Bishop of Bristol* ([London], 1688). Wing, A363; ESTC, R18992.

James VII, *A Proclamation Discharging the Importing, Vending, Dispersing, or Keeping Seditious Books and Pamphlets* (Edinburgh: printed by the Heir of Andrew Anderson, Printer to His most Sacred Majesty, 15 August 1688). Wing, S1770; ESTC, R183452.

James II, *By the King, A Proclamation to Restrain the Spreading of False News* (London: printed by Charles Bill, Henry Hills, and Thomas Newcomb, Printers to the King's most Excellent Majesty, 26 October 1688). Wing, J372; ESTC, R223048.

James II, *By the King, A Proclamation ... Whereas the Prince of Orange and his Adherents ... have Contrived and Framed several Treasonable Papers and Declarations ...*

(London: printed by Charles Bill, Henry Hills, and Thomas Newcomb, Printers to the King's most Excellent Majesty, 2 November 1688). Wing, J263; ESTC, R222838.

James II and VII's reign was marked by efforts to protect his increasingly uneasy hold on power by controlling printed debate and expressions of opposition. At the beginning and end of the reign he found himself attempting to suppress the message of armed opponents, successfully in 1685 with the execution of the printer of Monmouth's *Declaration*, less so in 1688. In between, control of printed discourse was pursued through the renewal of the Printing Act on 2 July 1685 (for seven years from 24 June: 1 Jac. II, c. 17), repeated proclamations on the press, and trials including those of Richard Baxter (see above) and Samuel Johnson. However, these and accompanying measures also generated opposition, none more so than the misguided attempt in the final year of the reign to apply to the seven bishops the charge of seditious libel.

The eight-page *Declaration of James Duke of Monmouth* appeared with Monmouth at Lyme Regis on 11 June 1685, was circulating in London by 13 June, and was 'answered' two days later with the short proclamation reproduced below, declaring as a traitor anyone who published or distributed the *Declaration*, or who possessed it without revealing the fact. The proclamation was issued on the same day the Commons concurred with the Lords in ordering the *Declaration* burnt, this being mentioned in the text.[1] The rebellion itself was suppressed within a month, with Monmouth executed on 15 July.

The Monmouth *Declaration* was probably written by Robert Ferguson but it was his fellow plotter William Disney who was apprehended on 15 June and executed a fortnight later for his part in issuing the tract. The *True Account of the Behaviour and Confession of William Disney* describes the midnight raid that woke Disney and revealed a press and printed sheets of the *Declaration*. Publication of the *True Account* was authorized by L'Estrange, recently knighted for his censorship work and given warrants to examine suspects, although a full resumption of his powers awaited the royal assent for the revived Printing Act a few days later. The tract contains what little is known of Disney's trial by special commission on 25 June, when he was convicted of printing a treasonable tract. Disney himself was an obscure figure, emerging in Whig politics in the exclusion crisis and being examined in 1680 over his attempts to show that Monmouth was legitimate, with the secretary of state Leoline Jenkins taking the view that Disney was employed by others.[2] He was not known to have experience in printing, although it has been suggested he worked on the *Declaration* with the Quaker publisher John Brickhurst.[3]

Samuel Johnson (1649–1703) was chaplain to Lord Russell until the latter's execution in 1683 and was twice tried and punished for writing and publishing sedition, first under Charles II and then under James II. His humiliating punishment in 1686, requiring degradation as a clergyman, sealed his Whig reputation as a living martyr against a tyrannical anti-Protestant regime. Johnson had gained fame and notoriety with his 1682 pamphlet *Julian the Apostate*, which proposed that a Catholic successor might be opposed as the fourth-century pagan emperor Julian had been resisted. He was investigated and harried and finally in November 1683 was tried and convicted of seditious libel, the tract burnt and the author left languishing in prison for failing to pay his 500 marks fine. 'Julian' Johnson continued to agitate against James, however, and on 21 June 1686 he was tried for a further libel, *A Humble and Hearty Address to all the Protestants in the Present Army*, and its companion paper, which urged soldiers to resist the invasion of the nation's religion and rights. It was claimed that around 20,000 copies were distributed. One interesting if fruitless defence pursued in the trial, referred to in *An Account of the Proceedings against Samuel Johnson*, was to question the charge of publication given that Johnson did not disseminate the tract – indeed, the copies were delivered for distribution in a nailed-up box.[4]

Johnson's move for an arrest of judgement following his conviction only resulted in his further condemnation, recounted here in *The Sentence of Samuel Johnson* along with the confirmation of the original sentence: to pay 500 marks, stand in the pillory and be whipped from Newgate to Tyburn. A clergyman would normally have been immune from the humiliation of pillory and whip but on 20 November 1686 Johnson was degraded from the ministry and declared a layman by a Church court, and two days later beaten more than 300 times with a knotted whip. In 1689 the House of Commons investigated the trial and sentence, reversing the judgement and declaring the sentence illegal and cruel.[5]

Attempts to enforce the Printing Act continued at the start of what proved to be King James's final year with *A Proclamation for Suppressing and Preventing Seditious and Unlicenced Books and Pamphlets*, which enjoined officials to take stricter action against offenders. The proclamation was particularly directed at the street level trade in pamphlets, targeting the hawkers and sellers.

In June 1688, the trial of the seven bishops represented a doubly impolitic attempt to apply the law of seditious libel, both because it was applied to Anglican bishops by a Catholic monarch and because there was no published libel on which to mount a plausible case that they stirred sedition. The bishops pointed out that they did not print the petition they presented to James against the reading of his declaration of indulgence, and it is seldom noted that the jury reached a not guilty verdict based on both the fact of publication and question of seditious intent. This had the immediate effect of undermining the King as well as a longer-term impact, being appealed to as a precedent a century later in reforming libel law. The trial narrative printed for common consumption and reproduced here refers to the dispute over use of the term 'publishing' and the way it almost proved decisive but for Heneage Finch, the bishops' own counsel, interrupting the summing-up. This led to extended discussion of the lawfulness of the *Declaration* and dispensing power which might not otherwise have occurred. The account was reprinted as an eight-page quarto at Edinburgh in 1689 (Wing, A364), which has supplied several words unreadable in the early lines of the London edition.

Royal fears of the destabilizing impact of print beyond the London hub were confirmed in this proclamation from Edinburgh *Discharging the Importing, Vending, Dispersing, or Keeping Seditious Books and Pamphlets*. It expressed concern at the importing of books printed overseas, and listed condemned titles seen as having particular currency in Scotland, including Buchanan's *De Jure Regni* and Rutherford's *Lex, Rex*, as well as the 1680 Sanquhar declaration and others. The proclamation was to be read at market crosses across the kingdom, as well as in churches, ordering the submission and destruction of all copies of the listed tracts.

By October 1688 the need to quell spreading news and discussion had become more urgent given an awareness of the 'intended Invasion' revealed by this royal *Proclamation to Restrain the Spreading of False News*. It followed previous practice, complaining of both spoken and published reports, and warning that production and reception were culpable. The Williamite landing was less than a fortnight away but Edmund Bohun remarked that the proclamation only 'increased the Aversion men then generally had for the Government'.[6]

William of Orange's invasion was armed with propaganda, the ground prepared by publishing a declaration from The Hague for smuggled circulation in England. On arriving in the West Country William almost immediately had a printing press operating at Exeter to generate copies of his main declaration. The proclamation these papers prompted was James's desperate counter-shot, warning of the punishments attending publishing or dispersing any Williamite papers, although this time, according to Bohun, its effect was only to alert a wider public to the existence and significance of the declarations.[7]

Notes
1. *LJ*, 14, pp. 41–3.
2. *CSPD*, 26–30 April, 1680.
3. *ODNB*, 'William Disney'.
4. *ODNB*. See also *State Trials*, vol. 11, pp. 1339–54.
5. *CJ*, 10, p. 193.
6. E. Bohun, *The History of the Desertion* (London, 1689), p. 26.
7. Ibid., p. 35.

James II, *By the King, A Proclamation against Spreading of a Traiterous Declaration Published by James Duke of Monmouth* (London: printed by the Assigns of John Bill Deceas'd; and by Henry Hills, and Thomas Newcomb, Printers to the Kings most Excellent Majesty, 15 June 1685). Wing, J310; ESTC, R226084.

By the King,

# A PROCLAMATION

Against Spreading of a Traiterous Declaration Published by *James* Duke of *Monmouth*.

JAMES R.

WHereas James Duke of Monmouth,[1] in order to Excite and Stir up Our Subjects to Joyn with him, in a Rebellion against Us, hath lately by his Rebellious Emissaries, Published and Dispersed a most Vile and Traiterous Paper, against Us and Our Government, Entituled, The Declaration of James Duke of Monmouth, and the Noblemen, Gentlemen, and others now in Arms for Defence and Vindication of the Protestant Religion, and of the Laws, Rights, and Priviledges of England, from the Invasion made upon them, and for Delivering the Kingdom, from the Usurpation and Tyranny of Us, by the Name of James Duke of York;[2] which Paper Our Lords Spiritual and Temporal, Assembled in Parliament, have Justly Condemned to be Burnt by the Hands of the Common Hangman, as Containing the Highest of Treasons, which the utmost Malice of Our most Implacable Enemies could falsly Contrive against Us: We out of Our Princely Grace and Tenderness to Our Subjects, lest any of them through Ignorance of the Danger, they will inevitably incur thereby, may be misled to Receive and Entertain the said Traiterous Paper, or to Publish the same to others their Fellow Subjects, have thought fit with the Advice of Our Privy Council, hereby to give Notice thereof, to all Our Loving Subjects, and do hereby strictly Charge and Command all Our Lieutenants, Deputy-Lieutenants, Sheriffs, Justices of the Peace, Mayors, Bayliffs, Headboroughs, High-Constables, Petty-Constables,[3] and all other Our Officers Military and Civil, and all and every Our Loving Subjects within this Our Realm of England, Dominion of Wales, and Town of Berwick upon Tweed, that they Apprehend and Cause to be Apprehended, all and every

Person and Persons, who shall Publish, Disperse, or Entertain, without Discovery thereof to the next Justice of the Peace, the said Traiterous Paper, to the End they may be Proceeded against as Traytors to Us Our Crown and Dignity, as they will Answer the Contrary at their Peril.

Given Our Court at *Whitehall* the Fifteenth Day of *June*, 1685. In the First Year of Our Reign.

## God save the King.

*LONDON*, Printed by the Assigns of *John Bill* deceas'd: And by *Henry Hills*, and *Thomas Newcomb*, Printers to the Kings Most Excellent Majesty. 1685.

***The True Account of the Behaviour and Confession of William Disney Esq; Who was Tryed for High Treason by the Kings Especial Commission of Oyer and Terminer, held at the Marshalsea in Southwark, on Thursday the 25<sup>th</sup> of June, 1685*** (London: printed by George Croom, at the Sign of the Blue-Ball in Thames-street, over against Baynard's-Castle, 1685). Wing, T2344; ESTC, R6085.

The True ACCOUNT
OF THE
Behaviour and Confession
OF
William Disney, Esq;
Who was Tryed for
HIGH TREASON

ON *Thursday June* the 25th. 1685. *William Disney*, Esquire; being Indited of High Treason,[1] for Printing and Publishing a most Vile and Trayterous Paper against His most Sacred MAJESTY and Government: Intituled *The Declaration of* James *Duke* of Monmouth, *and the Noble-Men, Gentlemen, and others now in Arms*, &c.

*The* Messenger *deposed*, That having a Warrant for the Apprehending of *William Disney*, Esquire; he took some Files of Musqueteers,[2] and Two or Three Gentlemen to his Assistance; when approaching to the / House of one *Tyrrel* a Gardiner in the Parish of *Lambeth*, on *Monday June* 15th. 1685. between Twelve and One of the Clock in the Morning, he broke into the Appartment of *Disney's*, where entering his Chamber, he found the Prisoner in his shirt, who craved his Breeches, but the Messenger replyed no, saying, if he had a Night-gown he might put it on: Immediately after, viewing his Breeches, there was found a Dagger in his pocket, also some other things, likewise a brace of Pistols, and a great Hanger in the nature of a Scymeter.[3]

His Maid *Mary Allett* was supposed to be in Bed with him, by reason her Cloaths were upon his Bed: His Daughter[4] about Eleven years of Age, or thereabouts, was in another part of the Room a Bed alone: The Messenger farther deposed, that getting into the Printing-House, he there found the Forms (as Printers call them) of the Trayterous Declaration in the Printing-Room, there being by computation about 750 of them Printed on one side, and about Five of the said Trayterous Declarations perfect.[5] Upon the Messengers questioning how they came there? he pretended Ignorance.

The Evidence appearing very plain, and he having nothing to say for himself, was found guilty of High Treason, Sentenced to be Drawn, Hanged, and Quartered; which was accordingly done, at *Kennington Common*, in the County of *Surrey*, on *Monday* the 29*th*. of *June*, 1685. and his Quarters set upon the City Gates.

## A True and full account given by the Minister of St. *George*,[6] concerning the Behaviour, and last dying Speeches of *William Disney*, Esq; *June*, 29*th*. 1685.

BEtween Nine and Ten of the Clock in the Morning, I was sent for by the High Sheriff of *Surrey*, to officiate as Ordinary[7] at the Execution of the Prisoner at the *Marshalsea*; before he was brought out, a neighbouring Minister and I (upon the Sheriffs motion) went into the Room where he was; when the Reverend Parson (having seen him the Night before) askt him whether he had considered of those things which he had formerly offered him, and did very pathitically press him that he would give Glory to God by a full and ingenuous Confession of his Crime, intimating to him the fatal consequences that might have followed if he had perfected that evil work: How many Mens Lives might have been lost in the quarrel; whose blood / he was so far guilty of, as he contributed to the increase of the Rebellion, by his Printing the Trayterous paper (or words to the same effect.) To which the Prisoner answered (with some signs of discontent) to this purpose: That he hoped, (he speaking to the Minister) did not come to press him to burden himself now: That he had nothing to say that might bring any person into trouble, and his time was short, so he desired not to be troubled about any such matters; so that few words passed e're we parted; finding him resolved not to make any discovery, I only told him I did intend to meet him at the place of Execution, and he thanked me.

When he came to the Gallows and was in the Cart, I came to him and asked him, how he desired to improve those few moments of his Life that were yet to come? He answered in Prayer: I asked, will you pray for your self, or shall I pray for you? He answered, I will pray, and desire you to pray for me. Whilst the Executioner was preparing the Rope, I shewed him the *Bible*, saying Sir, what comfortable Sentence do you remember out of this word of God for your present use? He answered, *Jesus Christ came into the World to save Sinners*, of whom I am chief:[8] And then he proceeded in general terms to acknowledge himself a great Sinner against God; but affirmed that he had made his peace with God, that he had confessed his Sins with humility and fervency, and had begged Gods pardon; and did not doubt but God had for the merits of his Son *Jesus Christ* pardoned all his Sins, and he was now under very comfortable hopes that he should soon be happy, not upon the account of his own merits, but the merits of *Jesus Christ*. I told him this was very good, if his hopes were well grounded: He replied, his hopes were grounded on the Scriptures, which assured him that *Christ* dyed to save Sinners. Whereupon I recounted to him some other Gracious promises of God to true Penitents, as that of *Ezechiel, If the Wicked man turneth away from his wickedness, and doth that which is lawful and right, he shall save his Soul alive,* &c.[9] After which he made his Address to God in Prayer, That he would forgive him all his Sins, and sanctify this his affliction to him; and prayed to God to bless the King, that he may be merciful and kind to his Subjects, as well as just to his Enemies. He farther observed how Gracious God was to him in giving him this admonition (as he called it) for God might have taken him off by some sudden death, or deprived him of his Senses, and then (he said) it must have been worse with me, but now God hath given me time to bethink my self: So that though the dolour[10] and the shame of this death having so many Spectators (upon whom he looked) may somwhat / discompose me, yet I have peace and comfort within. Afterwards he desired me to pray with him, which I did briefly according to his mind and present example: And closing with the Lords Prayer, he answered every Petition deliberately, and calmly. He declared that he lived in and did now dy in the Communion of the Church of *England*, were[11] he repeated again in these words, *The Protestant Church of England*. After Prayer, I asked him whether we should Sing some part of a *Psalm?* he answered, no: Then I asked him whether he had any thing more to do or say? he answered, I have nothing more but to return you thanks for your care of me. And I pray God bless you and hear your Prayers for me, and mine for you, and our Saviour *Christ* for us both: And so I left him going to his long home.

*This according to the best recollection of my thoughts, is the Sum, and as near as I can remember, the words that passed between Mr.* Disney *and me*

ANDREW WESTON.

*An Account of the Proceedings against Samuel Johnson: Who was Tryed at the Kings-Bench-Bar, Westminster, for High Misdemeanour: And Found Guilty of Writing and Publishing Two Seditious and Scandalous Libels against the Government, on Monday the 21th of June. 1686* (London: A.M., 21 June 1686). Wing, A351; ESTC, R402.

AN ACCOUNT

OF THE

# PROCEEDINGS

AGAINST

## Samuel Johnson:

Who was Tryed at the Kings-Bench-Bar, *Westminster*, For High Misdemeanour: And found Guilty of Writing and Publishing Two Seditious and Scandalous L I B E L S against the Government, on *Monday* the 21*th*. of *June*. 1686.

S*Amuel Johnson* having been Arraigned, upon an Information, for high Misdemeanours, in Writing, Printing, and Publishing two Scandalous and Seditious Libels, *&c*. And thereto pleading No*t Guilty*; was, by a Rule of Court, brought again to the Court of *Kings-Bench, Westminster*; on *Monday, June* the 21*th*. in Order to take his Tryal: When, as a *Jury* of Knights and Gentlemen of the County of *Surry*, being Sworn, the Information was read; the Substance of which was, That he, the Prisoner, had, in the Parish of St. *George's Southwark*, on the 25*th*. of *May*, in the Second Year of his Majesties Reign, maliciously and designedly Published two Pernicious, Scandalous, and Seditious Libels, to raise and stir up Sedition and Rebellion in his Majesties Liege-Subjects, *&c*. The Title of One being, *A Humble and Hearty Address to all the Protestants in the Present Army*. And the Other, *Viz. The Opinion is this, That Resistance may be used, in case our Religion and Rights should be Invaded.*[1] Both of which were therein specified at large; tending to withdraw them from their Duty and Allegiance, and to excite and stir up the Souldiers, *&c*. to Mutiny and Rebellion, *&c*.[2] After this, the Information was, by the King's Council, opened to the *Jury*, as to the Nature and Circumstances, together with the evil Consequences that might attend such bold and dangerous Attempts: which being rendered largely and exactly as to the Particulars mentioned in the said Information, wherewith the Prisoner was Charged, they proceeded to call their Witnesses to prove the Fact.

And *First*, Mr. *Belamy*, at the *Three Brushes*[3] in *Southwark*, being Sworn, gave Evidence, That coming acquainted, sometime since, with the Prisoner; and about a Fortnight before *Whitsuntide* last, discoursing with him, the second of these Libels was mentioned; and soon after, he sent him a Box with some Rheams of them in it, to be dispersed; and gave him notice, that he had a second Paper in the Press; and withal, a Caution not to Publish those he had sent before, till he had received that which proved to be the former Libel before mentioned. And further, That about six or eight Months before that, the Prisoner had sent him other Libels to dispose; and being shewed the Libels mentioned, in the Information, he deposed they were the same that had been sent him. His Man likewise gave Evidence, That he had received a Box nailed up, but could give no account of what was in it, as to Particulars.

*Ann Whitny*, sometimes Servant to the Prisoner, being Sworn, gave Evidence, That by her Master's or Mistresses Direction, she was not certain which, / she took a Porter, and caused him to carry a Box, wherein one of the Libels mentioned (*Viz.* the second) was inclosed to Mr. *Belamy*; and that she had, by the like Order, carried other Papers loose, some of which were the *Address*, &c. And being asked by the Prisoner, how she knew that; her reply was, That she knew it, insomuch that she had read the Title, and very well remembred it.

The Porter that carried the Box gave Evidence, that the Maid had hired him to carry a Box to the Three Brushes, and that she went with him, and paid him according to Agreement, and that he took it up in *Spittle-fields*.[4] After this, the Messenger who searched the Prisoner's Lodging with the Right Honourable the Earl of *Sunderland*'s Warrant,[5] being Sworn, gave Evidence, That he found a Paper in Writing upon a Table or Shelf, which appeared in Court to be part of the Copy, or the same with the Paper, Intituled, *The Opinion*, &c. He Swearing upon Sight thereof, that it was the same he found in the Prisoner's Lodging: Then was the Book of the Vestry, or Parish Affairs of St. *Pauls Covent-Garden* produced; wherein the Prisoner sometimes past had given an Acquittance for Money received, as an Assistant Curate, &c. which being compared with the Paper, seemed not to differ in the Hand; but no other Evidence appeared in that Case, than that the Book had been always kept in the Vestry, and for the most part under Lock and Key; and it being put to the Prisoner, he did not greatly deny it: when, for a further Confirmation, *John Darby* a Printer, and his Wife,[6] were Sworn; the former deposing, That he had Printed a Book for the Prisoner from the Manuscript, and that Hand was very like that of the Libel produced in Court, but he had never seen him write, and therefore could not be positive that that Manuscript was his own Hand: As for his Wife, her Evidence was, That the Prisoner paying her some Money, she had given him an Acquittance,[7] but that, as she conceived, he wrote all but her Name; for going up Stairs, he soon returned with an Acquittance, which she Subscribed. One Mrs. *Culeford* and her Husband, who appeared to be concerned in the management of the Libels, were called, but the former only appeared, and an Information being exhibited against her, she pleaded, *Not Guilty*. This being what materially was given in Evidence for the King, the Prisoner had leave to make his Defence; who after some Discourse, not pertinent to the matter, alledged, That he had been confined, and had not had opportunity to prepare for his Defence, as not having leave to go to his Council: To which the Court replied, that he had leave upon the Motion made on his behalf, to send for Council, and that they ought not to be refused coming to him: Then he urged several other frivolous matters; which being over-ruled by the Court, he proceeded to intimate, that he hoped, that seeing he was Indicted for a Seditious and Scandalous Libel, *&c.* the *Jury* would consider whether those Papers they had heard read, were so or no; but was told, that the *Jury* ought to consider it only as to the Matter of Fact, whether he was Guilty of Writing or Publishing them, *&c.* and that the rest lay in the breast of the Court to consider: Thereupon he urged, that though they might be sent, yet it was no Publication, as it was laid in the Indictment, because the Box was nailed. But being fully answered in that point, and loose Papers appearing likewise to be sent, the Council for the King summed up their Evidence to the *Jury*, none appearing on the behalf of the Prisoner. After which the Court gave the Charge, putting the Prisoner, as well as the *Jury*, in mind of the great Mischief that such Libels might occasion: And minded him likewise, that it was within a small matter of High Treason, and might have been raised to that degree, were not the Laws, and those who managed them, tender of Life, *&c.* After the Charge was given, the *Jury* withdrew, and returning within a quarter of an hour, brought in the Prisoner Guilty of the high Misdemeanour.

*The Sentence of Samuel Johnson, at the King's-Bench-Barr at Westminster* (London: printed by D. Mallet, next Door to Mr. Shipton's Coffee-House near Fleet-Bridge, 17 November 1686). Wing, S2554A; ESTC, R214822.

THE
# SENTENCE
OF
Samuel Johnson,

*Samuel Johnson*, having been Tryed and Convicted the last *Term*, for a *High-Misdemeanor* in writing the above-mentioned *LIBELS*; and being Convicted thereupon, he was (by Rule of Court) brought down to Receieve his Sentence,[1] which is as followeth, *viz.*

After Mr. *Attorney General*[2] had moved for Judgment, Mr. *Johnson* told the Court that he had moved for an Arrest of Judgment, / forasmuch as he had several Exceptions to make, all of which, he urged in his own Defence, using several Evading and Extenuating Arguments, whereby to make the Court believe that he intended no Evil in the Consequence of his Writing; but to teach the Army their Duty to God and their Prince, and how they ought to behave themselves as they were English Men, with many other weak Arguments, all which prevailed nothing with the Court, but rather aggravated his Crime: In that he used some Texts of *Scripture* in way of Comparison, which he would have insinuated to be his Meaning in the intent of the said *LIBELS*; and that he had said nothing but what was Lawful to say.

But the Court told him that his Exceptions were but a kind of a Paraphrase, which did much aggravate his Crime, more than any way excuse him; and that he did abuse the *Scriptures*, yea, and himself too, in making such Scriptural Exceptions; and that it was a Crime of very Evil Consequence, that one in his Station should offer to be Guilty of so Heinous an offence, that did tend so much to incite and stir up the King's Subjects to Rebellion against him; and that he should pretend to Write to the Souldiers who are under a Command, and dare not Rebell; therefore it must be meant of others, yea, the main strength of it, *viz.* His intention in the *LIBELS* was against the King himself, and desired him to consider of what bad Example it was to others; and the great abuse of Religion, and a discredit to the Clergy of this Kingdome, *&c.* with many other aggravating Circumstances: All which, the Court said deserved very great Punishment; the more, in that the offence was Committed by such an Author, who should have been a Credit to Religion, and to all the Professors of it; and that his Fault was so apparent to the World, that no one could be so stupid, but to be sensible of it: Telling him also, that he should be degraded from his Ministerial Function and Preferment,[3] which the Court was very sorry for, &c. Yet must pronounce this following Sentence.

And that is,

That he pay a Fine of Five Hundred Marks.

And that he stand in the *Pillory* three times, *viz.* On *Monday* next in the *Pallace Yard* at *Westminster*; and on the *Wednesday* following at *Charing-Cross*; and on the *Monday* after that, at the *Royal-Exchange* in *Cornhill*.

And to be whipt from *Newgate* to *Tyburn*, and to stand Committed till all be performed, &c.

James II, *By the King, A Proclamation for Suppressing and Preventing Seditious and Unlicenced Books and Pamphlets* (London: printed by Charles Bill, Henry Hills, and Thomas Newcomb, Printers to the King's most Excellent Majesty, 10 February 1688). Wing, J348; ESTC, R18650.

# By the King,
# A PROCLAMATION
For Suppressing and Preventing Seditious and Unlicenced Books and Pamphlets.

JAMES R.

WHereas in and by an Act of Parliament made in the Fourteenth year of the Reign of Our late Dearest Brother King Charles the Second, Entituled, An Act for preventing Abuses in Printing Seditious, Treasonable, and Unlicensed Books and Pamphlets, and for Regulating of Printing and Printing-Presses, (which said Act is, by another Statute or Act of Parliament made in the First Year of Our Reign Revived and Continued)[1] It is amongst other things Enacted, That no person or persons whatsoever, not being Licensed in that behalf by the Lord Bishop of the Diocess, nor having been Seven Years Apprentice to the Trade of Bookseller, Printer, or Bookbinder, nor being a Freeman of the City of London by a Patrimonial Right, as Son of a Bookseller, Printer, or Bookbinder, nor being a Member of the Company of Stationers of London, shall, within the City or Suburbs of London, or any other Market-Town, or elsewhere, receive, take, or buy, to barter, sell again, change, or do away any Book or Books whatsoever, upon pain of Forfeiture of the same. And whereas of late several Persons not being qualified by the said Act, and particularly great numbers of loose and disorderly people commonly called Hawkers and Pedlers of Books, have taken upon them to receive or buy several Unlicensed, Seditions, and many times, Treasonable Books and Pamphlets, framed and contrived by malicious persons on purpose to amuse and disturb the minds of Our loving Subjects, or for other evil or indirect ends and purposes, and have carried, sold, and dispersed the same about the Streets, and in other places of Publick resort, and also in Coffee-Houses, Taverns and private Families, to the great abuse and scandal of Our Royal

State and Government, and in open and manifest Breach and Contempt of Our Laws. We therefore considering the great Mischief that doth ensue upon such Licentious and Illegal Practices, and being Resolved effectually to provide against the like Mischiefs for the future, are pleased by this Our Royal Proclamation, by and with the Advice of Our Privy Council, to Command and Require that the said Act be put in Execution, and duly and strictly observed and kept: And We do also streightly Prohibit and Forewarn, That from henceforth no person or persons commonly called Hawkers, or Pedlers of Books, or any other person or persons whatsoever not being qualified as aforesaid to buy or sell Books, do or shall presume to go about the Streets, or from House to House, to Sell, or Expose to Sale any manner of Book or Books, Pamphlet or Pamphlets whatsoever, nor do or shall by any ways or means whatsoever Buy or Sell, or Expose to Sale any manner of Books or Pamphlets whatsoever, contrary to the purport and true meaning of the said Act of Parliament, under such Pains, Penalties and Forfeitures as by the said Act are Provided, and upon pain of incurring such further Punishments as by the utmost Rigour of the Laws, and by Our Prerogative Royal may be inflicted on such Offenders for their Contempt of this Our Royal Commandment: Hereby strictly Charging and Commanding all Judges, Justices of the Peace, Mayors, Sheriffs, Bayliffs, Constables, and all other Our Officers and Ministers; as also the Master and Wardens of the said Company of Stationers now and for the time being, and all other Our Subjects whom it shall or may concern, That they and every of them do from time to time use their and every of their best and utmost Powers, Skills and Endeavours respectively, for the utter Suppressing and Preventing of the Printing and Publishing of all such Unlawful Books and Pamphlets aforesaid, and for Prosecuting, Punishing, and utterly Suppressing all and every person and persons offending in the Premisses, according to the utmost Rigour of the Law, and Our Royal intent and meaning herein Declared, as they Our said Officers and Subjects do tender Our Pleasure, and will answer the contrary.

Given at Our Court at *Whitehall* the Tenth day of *February* 1687/8.
In the Fourth Year of Our Reign.

# GOD SAVE THE KING.

*An Account of the Proceedings at Westminster-Hall, on the 29th, and 30th. of June 1688. Relating to the Tryal and Discharge of the Archbishop of Canterbury, the Bishop of S. Asaph, Bishop of Chichester, Bishop of Ely, Bishop of Bath and Wells, Bishop of Peterborough, and the Bishop of Bristol* ([London], 1688). Wing, A363; ESTC, R18992.


An Account of the Proceedings at *Westminster-Hall*, on the 29th, and 30th. of *June*, 1688. Relating to the *Tryal* and *Discharge* of the Archbishop of *Canterbury*, the Bishop of S.*Asaph*, Bishop of *Chichester*, Bishop of *Ely*, Bishop of *Bath* and *Wells*, Bishop of *Peterborough*, and the Bishop of *Bristol*.

THE Indictment when read, was very much excepted against, on the account of its Form, in that it did not mention all the Petition they were Indicted for; there was not either the Title of it expressing to whom it was directed (*Viz. To the Kings*[1] *Most Excellent Majesty*, was omitted,) and the prayer afterwards (*We therefore Pray*, &c.) was not there; which being closely pursued by the Bishops Council,[2] seemed to invalidate the whole business. Then it was not and could not be proved by the Kings Council, that the Bishops presented the Petition to the King. They had in the Court[3] the Original, and subpoena'd some of the Arch-Bishops and Bishops Chaplains, Servants, and others, to prove their hands, which was not done very clearly upon most of them; all the proof of the Kings Council had for the presenting the Petition to His Majesty, did not directly prove it upon them: The most it amounted to, was either that the King told them he had it from the said Bishops; or, that my Lord Chancellor did ask them; if it were theirs (when they were summon'd before the King and Council,) and that they then express'd an aversness to own it; saying before the King, that if His Majesty did insist on it, and that it should not be improved to their disadvantage, or produc'd in evidence against them, that they would be plain, and leave it to His Majesty. Upon this the Bishops Council had some reflexions which my Lord Chief Justice[4] told them he must not hear. But this did not amount to a full proof of the point. Then the Bishops Council did greatly insist upon the Indictment being laid in a wrong County; for it was proved upon Oath, that the Arch-Bishop[5] was not out of his House for a very considerable time before he was summon'd to the King in Council. Now what was alledg'd against them. was done at *Lambeth*,[6] and therefore in *Surrey* the Indictment ought to have been laid, which seem'd much to affect them. After this, the Bishops Council objected against the term *Publishing*; whereas what was said to be done by them, was in the privatest way that could be, and given only to the King, which caus'd a long debate between both Parties, of things requisite to denominate a *Publication*, all did still appear favourable on the Bishops side: and here things were going to a conclusion, and the Judg was entered upon summing up the Evidence; but Mr. *Finch*,[7] (one of the Bishops Council) interrupted my Lord Chief Justice, saying, there was one material Evidence remaining: Whereupon, my Lord desisted, tho with some seeming dissatisfaction to the rest of the Bishops Council: For the Judg was going on very favourably for the Bishops Cause; some of the Bishops importun'd my Lord Chief Justice to proceed, but he would not: And so it brought on more discourse about the former subjects, and occasion'd the sending for my Lord President,[8] who came into Court after it had stayed an hour for him: The evidence that he gave upon Oath, could not fully prove the delivery of the Petition to the King by the Bishops. When before, for the proof of this, the Sollicitor[9] did very greatly importune some Witness for the King, (that had upon Oath deliver'd, what they knew about this matter, which was as aforesaid) by putting to them very intricate questions; my Lord Chief Justice reproved him, saying, it was not to be suffer'd; adding, that if he went on thus, he would let the Bishops Council loose on him.

After these things, my L.C.J. ask'd the Bishops Council, what else they had to plead; whereupon they proceeded to that part of the Indictment that calld the Bishops Petition *A Scandalous Seditious Libel*, &c. which occasion'd very great, solemn and most pleasing debates, For, hereupon they entered into and discuss'd the lawfulness of the Declaration and the Dispensing Power, which were harang'd by every one of the Bishops Council in most brisk, home[10] and admirable Speeches, for the space of three hours, shewing the Declaration to be against and contrary to Law, which no Power could dispence with or abrogate, but that which made it, (*viz.* a Parliament) and that the Ecclesiastical Laws had the same foundation as the Civil, and could be therefore no more dispens'd with. That the Declaration did evacuate the Laws for Sabbath-breaking, Fornication, *&c.* and let loose the reins to the most extravagant Sects and licentious Practices; and that all Laws might be dispensed with, as well as some: That the Bishops were sworn to maintain the Ecclesiastical Laws; and in representing the Case thus to His Majesty they had done both as the Law directed them, and according to *Prudence, Honour*, and *Conscience*. There were hereupon publickly read several Acts of Parliament, Records of the Tower, and Parliament Records; among which, one Act of Parliament was observeable; that gave the King Power to dispence with a Law for a stated time: So that what Dispensing Power he ever had, was both given and bounded by Parliament. From what they produc'd out of the Parliament Records and otherwise, they greatly confirm'd what was said in the Petition, of the Dispensing Power, having been often declared illegal in

Parliament, and particularly in the years 62, and 72, and in the beginning of His Majesties Reign, which was in 85, when the Parliament declar'd the Popish Officers could not be dispens'd with; but that it was contrary to Law to do so, tho they were willing by Act of Parliament to indemnifie such as His Majesty should nominate, &c. And they shew'd how the like Dispensing Power upon the same occasion was accounted illegal in 62, and 72, both by Parliament and the King himself, who offered the Seal to be tore off, and gave the testimony of his disowning such a Dispensing Power. To which the Sollicitors chief Answer was, that the King then lack'd Money, and that such Acts as aforesaid (whatever they might say) did confirm, not give the King's Dispensing Power. In short, the Bishops Council behav'd themselves in this weighty matter with a great deal of gallantry and plainness, nowise inferior to most mens expectations and desires. The chief of the managers for the King, was the Sollicitor *W. Williams*,[11] who as was apprehended, did no great wonders for invalidating the foregoing Arguments He was very hot and earnest (if not passionate) in proving it a / Libel; saying, It would be so, tho it were done by them to redress a certain grievance: Whereupon, my L.C.J. asking what course then they should take, or what they should do in such circumstances; he answered, *Acquiesce.* (which occasion'd a very great Hiss over the Court) He added farther to prove it Libellous; the insinuating Expressions of gaining the Populace, by saying, 'It was not for want of due tenderness to Dissenters, in relation to whom, we are willing to come to such a temper, as shall be thought fit, when that matter shall be consider'd and settled in Parliament and Convocation.' In Convocation, said he, what's the meaning of that? But here my L.C.J. gave him a check, and restrain'd what he seem'd greatly dispos'd to vent against it. There was not very much said by the rest of the Kings Council, at least, nothing more considerable than his. The King's Attorney General was pretty moderate; Sir *Barth. Shores*[12] spoke a little, but was presently silenc'd, (in the vacancy of stay for my Lord President, my L.C.J. said to Sir *Barth. Shores*, Now Sir *Bartholomew*, we have time to hear your Speeches) Serjeant *Baldock*'s Argument[13] against the Bishops, was chiefly upon their refusing, the King requiring such a slender matter so easily to be done; for they were not enjoyn'd to read, but only to send about and disperse it: Yet this they would not do. It concluded with the Kings Council.

Then my Lord Chief Justice summing up the business, was favourable to the Bishops in the former part of the Tryal, and could not say the matter of Fact was fully proved upon them, but was inclin'd to make the Petition a Libel; because of its accusing the King of Flaws in Government. He said but little to oppose what had been brought by the Bishops Council against the Declaration and Dispensing Power. After him spoke Judg *Holloway*,[14] and very much in the Bishops behalf, giving it as his judgment, that it could not be a Libel, being done from a conviction of Conscience by such Persons in such an humble modest manner.

Then Judg-*Powel*[15] spoke to the same effect, giving it as his opinion that it could not be a Libel, being the only way to redress themselves: He had also some smart expressions to confirm what the Bishops Council had urged against the Declaration and Dispensing Power: So that Judg *Powell* gave his opinion also in favour of the Bishops. Then Judg *Allibon*[16] standing up, professed he would not meddle with the Dispensing Power (tho it had been so much canvass'd and pleaded against) but would only speak to the business of the Paper being a Libel; and he did accordingly, urging it to be so, not barely because it was a Petition: For, said he, Any one under grievance may Petition His Majesty, but not about affairs of Government,[17] for that would tend to very bad consequences, and promote Discontents or worse in the Nation. Nor (as he added) can the pretended fairness, as to the manner of it, be an excuse; for the more it hath that way, so much the worse; and so concluded it in his sense a Libel. But urging a Precedent to confirm what he had said, he was partly mistaken in it, as Judg *Powell* and the Bishops Council shew'd him, and he himself acknowledged.

Then the Court broke up, the Jury went together, and the Bishops with all the privacy they could, to their respective Abodes; but wherever the People met with them, they huzza'd and humm'd them in a great abundance. There was a prodigious full Court and Hall, a very great many of the Peers and Nobility present, and also the Bishop of *Chester*, of whom they took no kind of notice: The Bishop of *Rochester*[18] did not meet with much better regard.

The Jury sate up all night, tho they were very soon unanimous in their Verdict, which they prudently resolved to give in open Court; and accordingly, next day about Nine or Ten they brought them in

*Not Guilty.*

### The Names of the Lord Bishops COUNSELLORS.

Sir *Francis Pemberton*.  Mr. *Pollixfin*.
Sir *Creswell Levins*.     Mr. *Treby*.
Sir *Robert Sawyer*.       Mr. *Summers*.[19]
Mr. *Finch*.

### The Names of the JURY Sworn.

Sir *Roger Langly* of *Westminster*.
Sir *William Hill* of *Tedington*.
*Robert Jennings* of *Hayes*, Esquire.
*Thomas Harriot* of *Islington*, Esquire.
*Jeoffry Nightingale* of S. *Giles Cripplegate*, Esq;
*William Withers* of the same, Esquire.

*William Avery* of *Enfield,* Esquire.
*Thomas Austin* of *South-Myms,* Esquire.
*Nicholas Grice* of *Neston,* Esquire.
*Michael Arnold* of *Westminister,* Esquire.
*Thomas Done* of *S. Giles in the Fields,* Esquire.
*Richard Shoreditch* of *Ickenham, Esquire*

FINIS.

James VII, *A Proclamation Discharging the Importing, Vending, Dispersing, or Keeping Seditious Books and Pamphlets* (Edinburgh: printed by the Heir of Andrew Anderson, Printer to His most Sacred Majesty, 15 August 1688). Wing, S1770; ESTC, R183452.

## A PROCLAMATION
*Discharging the Importing, Vending, Dispersing, or Keeping Seditious Books and Pamphlets.*

JAMES by the Grace of GOD, King of Great-Britain, France and Ireland, Defender of the Faith. To      Macers[1] of Our Privy Council, Messengers at Arms, Our Sheriffs in that part, conjunctly and severally, specially constitute, Greeting: Forasmuch as we being informed, that there are many Impious and Scandalous Books and Pamphlets printed in Holland, and elsewhere, Inciting Our Subjects to Murder and Assassination, as well as Rebellion, to the great reproach of the Christian-Religion, and the ruine of all Humane Society; in which also Our Government, and the Actions of Our Royal Predecessors, and Our own, are represented as Cruel, Barbarous, and Tyrannical, and all such as have Served and Obeyed Us, are railed at as Enemies to GOD, and their Native Country: Notwithstanding of the great Care We have always taken to Tollerate all different Perswasions, and the Clemency We have shown in Pardoning the greatest Criminals; Which Books are brought Home into this Kingdom, and Vended, and Spread here; and We being most desirous, on this, as on all other Occasions, to prevent any of Our Subjects being brought into a Snare. We have thought fit hereby to Intimat, and make Known, that if any of Our Subjects shall hereafter bring Home, Vend or Sell, Disperse or Lend any of the Books underwritten, viz. All Translations of Buchanan de Jure Regni, Lex Rex, Jus Populi, Nephtali,[2] The Cup of cold Water, The Scots Mist,[3] The Appologetical Relation, Mene Techel, The Hynd set loose,[4] The treasonable Proclamations issued out at Sanquhar, and these issued out by the late Duke of Monmouth, and the late Earl of Argile,[5] or any other Books that are, or shall be hereafter Written or Printed defending these Treasonable and Seditious Principles, they shall be lyable as if they were Authors of the saids Books; and all other Our Subjects are hereby Commanded to bring in any of the saids Books they have, and deliver them into any Privy Counsellor, Sheriff, Baillie of Regality, or Bailliaries, or their Deputs, or any Magistrats of Burrows,[6] to be transmitted by them to the Clerks of Our Privy Council, to the end the same may be destroyed, with Certification, that whoever (except Privy Counsellors) shall be found to have any of the saids Books, and not to have delivered them up, shall be fyned, for Our Use, in such a Penalty, as Our Council shall appoint, for each of the saids Books, that he or they have not delivered up. And appoints the saids Books and Pamphlets to be brought in betwixt and the Dyets[7] following, viz. these in the Town of Edinburgh, and Suburbs thereof, betwixt and the first Tuesday of September next to come, and all others within this Kingdom, betwixt and the first Tuesday of November next to come. And to the end Our Royal Pleasure in the Premisses may be made publick and known, Our Will is, and We Charge you strictly and Command, that incontinent, these Our Letters seen, ye pass to the Mercat-Cross of Edinburgh, and whole remanent Mercat-Crosses[8] of the Head-Burghs of the Shires of this Kingdom, and other places needful, and there in Our Name and Authority, make Publication of Our Royal Pleasure in the Premisses. And recommends to the Most Reverend the Arch-Bishops, and Right Reverend Bishops, to cause read this Our Royal Proclamation, in all the Pulpits of this Kingdom, upon some convenient Lords Day. in the Forenoon, immediately after Divine Service, that none pretend Ignorance.

Given under Our Signet at *Edinburgh* the Fifteenth day of *August*, One thousand six hundred eighty eight Years. And of Our Reign the Fourth Year.

*Per Actum Dominorum Secreti Concilii.*[9]

**GOD SAVE THE KING.**     WILL. PATERSON, *Cls. Sti. Concilii.*[10]

James II, *By the King, A Proclamation to Restrain the Spreading of False News* (London: printed by Charles Bill, Henry Hills, and Thomas Newcomb, Printers to the King's most Excellent Majesty, 26 October 1688). Wing, J372; ESTC, R223048.

By the King,
## A PROCLAMATION.
To Restrain the Spreading of *FALSE NEWS*.

JAMES R.

ALthough since Our Accession to the Crown, We have Graciously extended Our Royal Mercy and Clemency to Our Subjects by several General Pardons, one whereof was lately Published;[1] Yet We are sensible that divers evil disposed Persons, being not Reformed or wrought upon by such Our Grace and Favour, do, notwithstanding, make it their Business by Writing, Printing, or Speaking, to Defame Our Government with False and Seditious News and Reports, thereby intending to amuse Our loving Subjects, and as far as they are able, to create in them an universal Jealousie and Discontent, especially in this time of Publick Danger, threatned by the intended Invasion upon this Our Kingdom, and consequently to alienate the Hearts of such of Our loving Subjects from Us, who otherwise would readily yield unto Us that Aid and Assistance, which by their Natural Allegiance they are bound to do: And whereas by the Ancient Laws and Statutes of this Realm, great and heavy Penalties are inflicted upon all such as shall be found to be Spreaders of false News, or Promoters of any malicious Slanders and Calumnies, in their ordinary and common Discourses, or otherwise, and more especially upon such who shall utter or publish any Words or Things to incite and stir up the People to Hatred or Dislike of Our Person, or the Established Government: Notwithstanding which, there have been of late more bold and licentious Discourses than formerly, and Men have assumed to themselves a Liberty, not only in Coffee houses, but in other Places and Meetings, both publick and private, to Censure and Defame the Proceedings of State, by speaking evil of Things they understand not: We therefore considering that Offences of this nature proceed from the restless Malice of evil Persons, or from the careless Demeanour of others, who presume too much upon

Our accustomed Clemency and Goodness, have therefore thought fit by this Our Royal Proclamation, by and with the Advice of Our Privy Council, streightly to Forewarn and Command all Our Subjects, of what Estate or Condition they be, that they presume not henceforth, either by Writing, Printing or Speaking, to utter or publish any false News or Reports whatsoever, or to intermeddle with the Affairs of State or Government, or with the Persons of any of Our Counsellors or Ministers in their common and ordinary Discourses, as they will Answer the contrary at their utmost Perils.

And because all Bold and Irreverent Speeches touching matters of this high Nature, and all Malicious and False Reports tending to Sedition, or the Amusement of Our People, are punishable not only in the Speakers, but in the Bearers also, unless they do speedily reveal the same unto some of Our Privy Council, or some other of Our Judges or Justices of the Peace; Therefore that all Persons may be left without Excuse, who shall not hereafter contain themselves within that modest and dutiful regard which becomes them, We do further Declare, That We will proceed with all Severity and Rigour against all such Persons who shall be guilty of any such malicious and unlawful Practices by Writing, Printing, or other Publication of such false News and Reports, or who shall receive or hear the same, without revealing or giving Information thereof as aforesaid, in due time; We being resolved to suppress the said Enormities by a most strict and exemplary Punishment of all such Offenders as shall hereafter be discovered. And We do hereby streightly Charge and Command all and singular Our Judges, Justices of the Peace, Sheriffs, Mayors, Bayliffs, and all other Our Officers and Ministers whatsoever, to take effectual Care for the speedy Apprehension, Prosecution, and severe Punishment of all such Persons who shall at any time hereafter be found Offenders herein.

Given at Our Court at *Whitehall* the 26th day of *October*, 1688. In the Fourth Year of Our Reign.

## God save the King.

James II, *By the King, A Proclamation ... Whereas the Prince of Orange and his Adherents ... have Contrived and Framed several Treasonable Papers and Declarations ...* (London: printed by Charles Bill, Henry Hills, and Thomas Newcomb, Printers to the King's most Excellent Majesty, 2 November 1688). Wing, J263; ESTC, R222838.

## By the King,
## A PROCLAMATION.

JAMES R.

WHereas the Prince of Orange and his Adherents, who design forthwith to Invade Our Kingdoms, in order thereunto have contrived and framed several Treasonable Papers and Declarations,[1] hoping thereby to Seduce Our People, and (if it were possible) to corrupt Our Army, a very great Number whereof being Printed, several Persons are sent and employed to disperse the same throughout Our Kingdoms: And although all Persons (as well in Criminal as in other Cases) are bound to take notice of the Law at their Peril; Yet to the intent that none may think to escape due Punishment, or to excuse themselves when they shall be Detected, by pretending Ignorance of the nature of their Crime; We are Graciously pleased by this Our Royal Proclamation, Published by the Advice of Our Privy Council, to forewarn and admonish all Our Subjects, of what Degree or Duality soever, that they do not Publish, Disperse, Repeat or Hand about the said Treasonable Papers or Declarations, or any of them, or any other Paper or Papers of such like nature, nor presume to Read, Receive, Conceal or Keep the said Treasonable Papers or Declarations, or any of them, or any other Paper or Papers of such like nature, without Discovering and Revealing the same as speedily as may be, to some of Our Privy Council, or to some of Our Judges, Justices of the Peace or other Publick Magistrates, upon Peril of being Prosecuted according to the utmost Severity of Law.

Given at Our Court at *Whitehall* the 2d day of *November*, 1688. In the Fourth Year of Our Reign.

GOD SAVE THE KING

# ARGUMENTS AGAINST CENSORSHIP, 1689–90

[Benedict Spinoza], 'In a Free Commonwealth it should be Lawful for Every Man to Think what he Will, and Speak what he Thinks', in [Benedict Spinoza], *A Treatise Partly Theological, and Partly Political, containing some Few Discourses, to Prove that the Liberty of Philosophizing (that is Making Use of Natural Reason) may be Allow'd without any Prejudice to Piety, or to the Peace of any Common-Wealth, and that the Loss of Public Peace and Religion it self must Necessarily Follow, where such a Liberty of Reasoning is Taken Away* (London, 1689), ch. 20. Wing, S4985; ESTC, R21627.

Edmund Hickeringill, 'Of the Restraint of the Printing-Press', in *A Speech Without-Doors: or Some Modest Inquiries Humbly Proposed to the Right Honourable the Convention of Estates, Assembled at Westminster, Jan. 22. 1688/9, concerning, I. Bigotism, or Religious Madness, II. Tests, and the Present Test in Particular, III. Penal Laws in Matters of Religion, IV. The Necessity of Changing and Recanting our Opinions in Religion, V. Restraint of the Press* (London: printed by George Larkin, at the Two Swans without Bishopgate, 17 January 1689), section V, pp. 32–4. Wing, H1827; ESTC, R20396.

[James Parkinson], *The Fire's Continued at Oxford: or, The Decree of the Convocation for Burning the Naked Gospel, Considered* ([London], 30 August 1690). Wing, P494; ESTC, R1197.

The conflation of the Glorious Revolution and the end of licensing by the 'friends of liberty' of the late eighteenth century has long been recognized as an over-simplification. Freedom of expression was neither demanded nor secured by the revolutionists in 1688–9, apart from free speech in Parliament itself, although indirectly some latitude was gained through the passing of the 1689 Toleration Act. The Printing Act remained in force, if fraught in application. However, some saw in the changing times and the (temporary) easing of restrictions the moment to advance a case for press freedom, either personally in the case of Edmund Hickeringill and James Parkinson or indirectly in the case of the anonymous translator and publisher of Spinoza. This testified to a movement of ideas that would help seal the end of licensing over the next decade.

Spinoza's theological-political *Treatise*, with its concluding argument for freedom of thought and expression, was originally published in Amsterdam in Latin in 1670. Its radicalism quickly gained notoriety, earning it a place on the *Index* and leading Spinoza himself to oppose its translation into Dutch to avoid it being banned.[1] In England his ideas were criticized by More, Cudworth, Tenison and others and the *Treatise*'s only appearance in English before 1689 was via translated extracts from the discussion of miracles in chapter 6 of Charles Blount's *Miracles, No Violations of the Laws of Nature* (1683), a book which was quickly attacked for its Spinozism. In the turbulent but more tolerant context of 1689 an anonymous translation of the whole book appeared, the translator's preface challenging 'the Crape Gown and the Long Robe' to prove it contained doctrines any more damaging than those recently spread by churchmen and lawyers. Chapter 20, dealing with the freedom of expression, is reproduced here.

Edmund Hickeringill (c. 1631–1708) was a churchman of unconventional views which contributed to the belief in free expression conveyed in this excerpt from his *Speech Without-Doors* addressed to the 1689 convention. A Baptist and Quaker before becoming minister in Colchester, Hickeringill had attacked the censorship powers of L'Estrange in the 1670s while at the same time being critical of Marvell's tolerationist *Rehearsal Transpros'd*. His criticisms of episcopacy and ecclesiastical courts brought him into conflict with the Church hierarchy, and notably the Bishop of London Henry Compton, who eventually brought a charge of *scandalum magnatum* which led to Hickeringill in 1684 being made to recant the 'seditious principles' of his books.[2] In *Speech Without-Doors* he advanced a comprehensionist religious settlement before offering arguments against restraining the press in the final section. In the book's opening dedication to the convention Hickeringill excused the lack of an imprimatur, complaining that the present licensers would refuse authority to anything that threatened their interest and trade, a theme he returns to in the section on the press. The printer of the tract, George Larkin, had twenty years previously been involved in the underground production of Marvell's *Advice to a Painter*.[3]

James Parkinson (1653–1722) was possibly the only Whig who attended the Oxford convocation's 1683 condemnation of pernicious books, apparently being 'hissed out' before the decree was passed unanimously. The memory rankled, particularly as he was hounded out of his fellowship at Lincoln College as a 'rank stinking whigg' when convicted of uttering seditious words.[4] He campaigned for reinstatement, in part by publishing an account of his expulsion in 1689, following this by returning to the 1683 decree in *The Fire's Continued*, seeing its echo in the more recent condemnation of *The Naked Gospel*, by Arthur Bury, the rector of Exeter College. Parkinson pointed out that if the 'famous Judgment and Decree' had succeeded the revolution could not have occurred, recorded his own plight, and considered the arguments of Bury's tract. *The Naked Gospel* had been published in spring 1690 and discussed the damaging irrelevance of closely defining the doctrine of the Trinity, amongst other things. The book was ordered burnt on 19 August 1690 but the arguments it generated over the Trinity spurred continued controversy at Oxford and beyond for the next decade and more.

Notes
1. B. Spinoza, *Complete Works* (Indianapolis, IN: Hackett, 2002), Letter 44, p. 882.
2. *ODNB*.
3. See above, p. 82.
4. R. A. Beddard, 'Tory Oxford', in N. Tyacke (ed.), *History of the University of Oxford, vol. 4: Seventeenth-Century Oxford* (Oxford: Clarendon Press, 1997), pp. 863–905, on pp. 896–900.

[Benedict Spinoza], 'In a Free Commonwealth it should be Lawful for Every Man to Think what he Will, and Speak what he Thinks', in [Benedict Spinoza], *A Treatise Partly Theological, and Partly Political, containing some Few Discourses, to Prove that the Liberty of Philosophizing (that is Making Use of Natural Reason) may be Allow'd without any Prejudice to Piety, or to the Peace of any Common-Wealth, and that the Loss of Public Peace and Religion it self must Necessarily Follow, where such a Liberty of Reasoning is Taken Away* (London, 1689), ch. 20. Wing, S4985; ESTC, R21627.

# CHAP. XX.

*In a Free Commonwealth it should be lawful for every Man to think what he will, and speak what he thinks.*

WEre it as easie to command Mens Minds, as it is their Tongues, all Supreme Powers would reign securely, and no Government would be Violent or Tyrannical: For then every Man would live according to the Will of those in Supreme Power, and would think every thing true or false, good or evil, just or unjust, according to their Determinations and Decrees. But it is impossible, as we have observed in the beginning of the 17*th* Chapter,[1] that any Man's Mind or Thoughts should be in another Man's power; because no Man can transfer, or be compelled to transfer his natural Right of Reasoning and Judging of Things, upon any other Man: And therefore that Government is counted Tyrannical, which would reign over / Mens Minds; and Supreme Powers do their Subjects wrong, and deprive them of their just Right, when they command them to receive or reject, according to their Prescriptions, whatever they declare to be true or false; and positively appoint what Opinions and Notions Men in their Devotions shall have of God; which is a thing wholly in a Man's own power, and from which no Man, tho' he would, can part. I confess, a Man's Judgment may be so many ways prepossest, that tho it be not directly and absolutely in another Man's power, yet it may have such a dependence on him, as to be thought very much at his dispose; but in spite of all that Art can do, Men will abound in their own Sense, and there will for ever be as many diversities of Opinions, as there are of Palats:[2] Tho' *Moses*, not by Craft, but by Divine Power, had so prepossest the Minds of his People, that they believed he said and did all things by Divine Inspiration; yet he could not escape ill Reports and sinister Interpretations; much less then can other Monarchs. Were the thing possible, it might rather be done in Monarchical, than in Democratical Government, which is managed by an Assembly of all, or the greatest part of the People; and the Reason I think is obvious. /

Tho' Supreme Powers have right to all things, and are believed to be Interpreters both of Law and Religion; yet they could never keep Men from judging of things according to their Reason and Capacities, nor from being this or that way affected. They may indeed account all men Enemies who do not in all things absolutely think as they do; but we do not here dispute of their Power, but of what is most convenient and profitable. I grant, that Supreme Powers may Reign Tyrannically, and put Subjects to death for very slight Causes, if they please; but all Men will deny that this can be done with Reason or Prudence, because it will prove dangerous and destructive to the Government: Yea, it may be denied that Supreme Magistrates have absolute Power, and consequently have not absolute Right to do such things as these; because we have proved, that the Right of Supreme Magistrates is determined by their Power.[3] If then no Man can part with this Liberty of Judging and Thinking what he will, but every Man by the Sovereign Right of Nature is Master of his own Thoughts, Supreme Powers in any Commonwealth can never hope for Success, in prescribing to Men of different Opinions, Limits and Rules for what / they shall say: For if Wise-men cannot keep silence, much less can the ignorant Multitude hold their peace, it being all Mens Infirmity, tho' never so much Secresie be required, to make others privy to their Counsels: And therefore that Government is Violent, where every Man is deny'd the Liberty of saying and declaring what he thinks; and that Government is moderate and well ordered, where such a Liberty is allow'd. 'Tis true, and no Man can deny, but that Supreme Magistrates may be injur'd and offended by Words as well as Deeds; and tho' it be impossible wholly to take away this Liberty from Subjects, yet, on the other side, it will be pernicious to put no Restraint upon it: So that now my Business is to shew, how far this Liberty, without any danger to the Peace of the Commonwealth, or prejudice to the Right of Supreme Power, may and ought to be allow'd; which was, as I have hinted in the beginning of the 16*th* Chapter, my chief Intention and Design.

From the Fundamentals of Government which I have already explain'd, it clearly follows, That the ultimate End of Government is not to domineer, and keep Men in fear and Subjection; but to free Men from Terror, that every Man / may, as far as 'tis possible, live securely; that is, may still retain his natural Right of subsisting and acting without hurting himself, or any other person. I say, The End of Government is not to turn Rational Men into Beasts or walking Engines, but to suffer both their Souls and Bodies to do each their proper Duties, allowing them the free Use of Reason, that they may not by Hatred, Envy, Anger, or Deceit, become Enemies to one another: So that the End of Publick Government is indeed Liberty; and to the forming of a Commonwealth, it is absolutely necessary, that the Power of making Laws and Decrees should be either in all, in some, or in one single Person: For seeing in every Man's Opinion, tho' it be free, there is difference and variety, and every Man is apt to believe that he knows all things; 'tis impossible to make them all of one mind, or to agree in their Discourse. So that they can never live peaceably, unless every one part with his power of doing what his own Mind prompts him to. But tho' every one part with the power of doing what he pleases, yet he doth not part with his power of Reasoning and Judging; so that tho' he cannot without offence act or do any thing against the Decrees or Determinations / of the Supreme Powers; yet he may freely think, judge, and consequently speak; provided in what he simply speaks or teacheth, there be Reason, and no crafty malicious Design, through Hatred or Revenge, to make, by vertue of his own Authority, Innovation in the Commonwealth. For example, If a Man think a particular Law contrary to right Reason, and therefore fit to be repealed; yet if he submit his Opinion to the Judgment of the Supreme Power, (whose Right it is to make and repeal Laws) and in the mean time do nothing contrary to the Tenor of that Law, he deserves well of the Commonwealth; as doth every good Subject: But if, on the contrary, he speak against that Law purposely to accuse the Magistrate of Injustice, and to render him odious to the People; or if he seditiously endeavour to abrogate that Law, in spite of the Magistrate, he is a rebellious Disturber of the Publick Peace.

We see then upon what ground every Man, without prejudice to the Peace of the Commonwealth, or to the Right of Supreme Powers, may speak and teach what he thinks, if he leave them the power of regulating Mens Actions, and do nothing contrary to their Decrees, / tho' he sometimes do contrary to that which in his own Opinion and Judgment he thinks to be good; which notwithstanding he may with a good Conscience, yea ought to do, if he will be accounted a good Subject. For, as I have already shewn, Justice depends upon the Decrees of the Supreme Power, and no Man can be said to be Just, unless he live according to the known Laws. Piety, as I have declared in the preceding Chapter, chiefly consists in the practice of things which preserve the Peace and Tranquillity of the Commonwealth;[4] which cannot possibly be preserved, if every Man should live as he pleaseth: And therefore 'tis Impiety in any Subject, to act contrary to the Decrees of the Supreme Power; because, were it lawful for every Man so to do, the total Ruine of the Commonwealth must necessarily follow. No Man can be said to act against the Dictates of his own Reason, who submits to the Decrees of the Supreme Power; because every Man by the persuasions of his own Reason resolved to part with his Right of Living according to his own Will: And this is proved by practice; for in Councils compos'd of the Supreme or Subordinate Powers, it seldom happens that any thing is decreed or determin'd / by the universal Consent and general Vote of all the Members; yet the Results of those Counsels, whatever they be, are always accounted as much the Decrees of those who voted against, as of those that voted for them: So that by the very Principles of Government, we see, that without any wrong done to the Rights of Supreme Power, a Man may use the Liberty of his own Judgment: And 'tis very easie from the Fundamentals of Government, to determine what Opinions in a Commonwealth are to be accounted Seditious; namely, those which directly nullifie and destroy the Covenant, whereby every Man obliged himself to part with his Right of Living according to his own Will. For example, If any Man think the Supreme Power is subject to some other Power; that a Man ought not to perform his Promises; or, that it is lawful for every Man to live as he pleases: These, and the like Opinions, render a Man seditious, because they are directly repugnant to the foresaid Covenant; not barely because they are his Judgment and Opinion, but because such Opinions have in them a great deal of Crime and Guilt: For even by so thinking, a Man tacitly breaks all the Bonds of that Fidelity which he promised / to the Supreme Power. Therefore other Opinions, which contain no actual Breach of the Covenant, no Revenge, no Anger, *&c.* are not to be accounted Seditious, unless it be in a Commonwealth where Reason is depraved, and where ambitious and superstitious Men are grown to such a heighth, that they cannot endure those that are honest or ingenuous, but will have the People think their Authority greater than the Supreme Magistrate's. I do not deny, but that there may be some Opinions, which tho' they seem to intend nothing but simply to argue and judge, what is true, and what false; yet they may be very maliciously propounded and divulged: Of these we spoke in the 15*th*. Chapter, but so that Reason nevertheless should remain free. Lastly, If we seriously consider, that every Man's Fidelity to the Commonwealth, as his Faith towards God, ought to be judged and known only by his Works; namely, by Charity towards his Neighbour; we cannot doubt but that the best Commonwealths will give every Man the same Liberty of Reasoning, that they do of Believing. I confess, by such a Liberty some Inconveniences may sometimes happen: But what Wisdom and Prudence can prevent all Inconveniences? / He that by Laws thinks to prevent all, will sooner provoke then amend vicious Men. Inconveniences that cannot possibly be prevented or avoided, must be tolerated; we must bear with them, tho' we suffer by them. Of how many Mischiefs are Luxury, Drunkenness, Envy, and Covetousness the Cause? Yet these are tolerated, because tho' they be Vices, it is not in the power of Laws to restrain them. How much more then ought Liberty of Judgment to be allowed, which is truly a Vertue, and should not be supprest? No Inconveniences can arise from it, which may not, as I will prove, be avoided by the Authority of the Supreme Magistrate. Beside, this Liberty is very necessary to the Advancement of Arts and Sciences, in which the greatest proficiency is made by those men who have their Judgments free from preoccupation. But suppose mens mouths may be stopt, and so awed, that they shall not dare to utter any thing against the Determinations of the Supreme Power; yet 'tis still impossible to keep them from thinking what they please; and when men think ill of Magistrates, there breach of Faith soon follows; and nothing is to be expected in such a Commonwealth, but abominable Flattery, / Perfidy, and the destruction of all ingenious Arts. 'Tis not so easie a matter to keep men from talking; the greater care is taken to keep them silent, the more many times will they talk. Perhaps Covetous men, Flatterers, and meanspirited People, who place their chiefest Felicity in filling their Bags and their Bellies, may hold their Peace; but vertuous honest men, who have had Liberal Education, cannot be silent: Such is mens Nature, that nothing is a greater Vexation to them, than to see those Opinions, which they verily believe to be true, condemn'd; and themselves accounted wicked and sinful, for doing that which they think is their Duty both towards God and Man. This makes them detest the Laws, and count any seditious Attempts against the Magistrate lawful and just. In Laws against Opinions, wicked men are seldom concern'd; such Laws are commonly made, not to restrain bad, but to provoke good men; and cannot be defended without a great deal of danger to the Government: Such Laws are likewise useless; for men cannot obey Laws which condemn those Opinions they firmly believe to be true: And, on the other side, they who think those Opinions false, take the Laws that / condemn them, to be their Privileges; wherein they so triumph, that afterward the Magistrate, if he would, is not able to repeal them. Lastly, The making of such Laws hath often caused great Schisms in the Church; for if men did not hope with the general applause of the People to insult over their Adversaries, and get Preferment, by procuring the Magistrate to favour, and the Laws to countenance their Opinions, Learned Doctors would quickly leave their fierce Disputes, and bitter Contentions. Reason and daily Examples tell us, That Laws which command what every man must believe, and forbid speaking or writing against this or that Opinion, are commonly instituted to gratifie or give way to the Passions of those, who rather than endure a Baffle[5] from ingenious men, will with their stern and morose Authority turn the Peoples Zeal into Fury, and hound them on upon whom they please. But would it not be much better, to suppress the Anger and Rage of the Multitude, rather than make Laws against men that love Vertue and Learning, and bring the Commonwealth into such a Condition, that honest harmless men cannot live in it? What can be more mischievous to a Commonwealth, / than to send Honest men like Rogues into Banishment, only because they are of this or that Opinion, and cannot dissemble? Can any thing be more pernicious, than to treat Persons of a free ingenuous disposition like Enemies, and for no Crime or Wickedness put them to death, making the Scaffold, which frights none but Villains, a publick Theatre whereon innocent Persons give such Examples of Courage and Patience, as turn to the shame and reproach of the Supreme Magistrate's Majesty? They that know themselves to be honest, never fear Punishment, as the wicked do; neither will they by base whining Submissions and Recantations endeavour to avoid it: Their innocent Minds are not troubled with Guilt or Repentance; they do not think it shameful, but glorious, to die for Liberty and a good Cause. To whom can their Death be a Terror? The base ignorant Multitude know not why they suffer; honest men are their Friends, and none but seditious Persons their Enemies; and all but base Sycophants and Flatterers, are ready to follow their Example. That Faith and Honesty then may be in greater esteem, than Flattery and Dissimulation; that Supreme Magistrates may keep their Power, and not be forced to / yield to seditious Persons, Liberty of Judgment ought to be allowed, and men are so to be govern'd, that tho' they be of different and contrary Opinions, they may however live together in peace and amity. Without doubt this way of Governing is best, and subject to least Inconveniences, seeing it is most agreeable to Mens Nature: For in Democratical Government (which comes nearest to the State of Nature) all covenant to act, but not to reason and judge by common Consent; my meaning is, because all men cannot think the same things, they have agreed to make that a binding Law which had most Voices, reserving still a Power of repealing that Law, when they thought fit. And therefore where there is least Liberty allow'd of Judging, there men are farthest from their natural State, and the Government is full of Force and Violence. To make it evident, that from this Liberty can arise no Inconveniences which the Supreme Magistrate may not with ease avoid, and keep men of contrary Opinions from hurting one another, I need not go far for Examples. The City of *Amsterdam* hath, to the wonder of all the World, and its own great advantage, tasted the Fruits and Benefit of this Liberty; for in that flourishing / Commonwealth and famous City, men of all Nations and Religions live together in peace; and when they would trust any man with Goods or Money, they only desire to know whether he be rich or poor, or whether in his Dealing he be a man of his Word, or a cheating Knave; they never enquire of what Religion or Sect he is, neither is that regarded in any Court of Justice; there is no Sect so odious, but hath the Publick Magistrate's Protection, if they do no man wrong, live honestly, and give every one his Due. How great a Schism was there occasion'd not long since, by a Controversie in Religion, between the Remonstrants and Contraremonstrants?[6] And it appeared by many Examples, that Laws made to take away Disputes concerning Religion, did much more provoke than pacifie People, and made some take the greater Liberty. Schisms proceed not from the study of Truth, that Fountain of Meekness and Moderation; but from an imperious Humour of prescribing to others: And therefore they are rather to be counted Schismaticks, who damn other mens Writings, and stir up the waspish Multitude against them; than those that write to Learned men, and call nothing but Reason to / their aid: So that they are truly Disturbers of the Publick Peace, who in a Free Commonwealth would take away the Liberty of mens Judgments, which ought not to be supprest.

We have now shewn, *First*, That 'tis impossible to take away mens Liberty of speaking what they think: *Secondly*, That this Liberty may without prejudice to the Rights of Supreme Power be granted to every man, and that every man may use this Liberty, provided he design no Innovations in the Commonwealth, and act nothing against the known establish'd Laws thereof: *Thirdly*, That this Liberty, which every man may enjoy if he do not break the Publick Peace, can cause no Inconveniences which may not easily be restrained or remedied: *Fourthly*, That all men may make use of this Liberty without being guilty of any Impiety. *Fifthly*, That all Laws made concerning Opinions and Matters meerly speculative, are useless and unprofitable. *Sixthly*, and lastly, we have proved, That this Liberty may not only be allow'd, without any Danger to Publick Peace, Piety, and to the Right of Supreme Power; but ought to be granted for the Preservation of all these: For where there are Endeavours to take away / this Liberty, and men are arraigned only for Opinions, without examining whether they have any evil Intentions, there honest men are made Examples, and suffer a Martyrdom; which doth not at all terrifie but irritates and moves the People to Pity and Revenge. Learning and Arts decay, Faith is corrupted, Flatterers and perfidious Persons are countenanced, Adversaries triumph in having their Will, and prevailing on the Supreme Powers to embrace their Doctrine, which at last inclines them not only to undervalue, but usurp their Authority, boasting they are God's Elect, that their Power is from God, but the Magistrate's Authority only from men, and consequently, the Magistrate's Power subordinate to theirs; which absolutely destroys the very Being of all Commonwealths; and therefore, as I shew'd in the 18*th*. Chapter, a Commonwealths greatest Safety is to place Religion and Piety in the Practice of Justice and Charity, and to make things Sacred as much subject to Supreme Power, as things Civil, and to take cognizance of nothing but mens Actions, suffering every man to think what he will, and speak what he thinks.

I have now in this Treatise done what I design'd; and I do again sincerely profess, / That I have written nothing which I do not freely submit to the Examination and Judgment of the Supreme Powers of my Country: If they think any thing I have said, be contrary to the Laws or Publick Safety thereof, I recant it. I know my self a man subject to Errors; but my chiefest Care hath been to write nothing but what is consonant to Reason, to the Laws of my Country, and to the Rules of Piety and Good Manners.

*FINIS.*

Edmund Hickeringill, 'Of the Restraint of the Printing-Press', in *A Speech Without-Doors: or Some Modest Inquiries Humbly Proposed to the Right Honourable the Convention of Estates, Assembled at Westminster, Jan. 22. 1688/9, concerning, I. Bigotism, or Religious Madness, II. Tests, and the Present Test in Particular, III. Penal Laws in Matters of Religion, IV. The Necessity of Changing and Recanting our Opinions in Religion, V. Restraint of the Press* (London: printed by George Larkin, at the Two Swans without Bishopgate, 17 January 1689), section V, pp. 32–4. Wing, H1827; ESTC, R20396.

## SECT. V.

### *Of the Restraint of the* PRINTING-PRESS.

PRinting, though reckon'd amongst *the New Inventions*, is *now* become *an Old Trade* in *London*, and has *begot one or two* more Trades; the *Book-seller* and *Stationer*, which are all Incorporated into a *Body-Politick*; called, *The Company of Stationers*; no despicable *nor mean* Company (or Hall) in this splendid City; one *Stationer was enough* for a City, before *Printing* came up; and of *Book-sellers* there were none, but *Scriveners*.

But, *now* they are become the *Numerous Issue* of the Press; and enabled to make *By-Laws* for the Regulating their Trade; which is *their Lively-hood*: And the Question is, Whether it be reasonable and lawful to *hinder them of their Lively-hood*, of their Trade, under pretence of Publique-good, by *shutting up the Press*, and stopping their Trade, by *excluding all* that have not a Passe, (and some say you may *with as much reason* Exclude all men from the *Kings-High-Way*, the Birth-right of every *English-man*, or stop their Mouths and starve them) except they *bring a Passe* Sign'd by Sir *Roger*, the Bishops Chaplain,[1] *or the like*; to permit them to *Earn* their Livings?

There's an Act of Parliament[2] for it, you'll say, and for that Trick, I say, I'll determine nothing *positively* against it.

But, Acts of Parliament *are not like the Laws* of the *Medes and Persians*,[3] which cannot be *alter'd*. The *Ægyptian* Priests told *Herodotus* that the Sun had *chang'd it's course* four times within the last Preceding *Eleven thousand and* odd years; an *Æra*, as long before *Adam*, as since.[4]

But, if the *Sun* change it's course *sometimes*, and the *Moon often times*, and *Parliaments* change their Acts[5] *sometimes twice in Ten Years*, as afore-said; then surely *this Act for Restraint of the Press* (without the License of the Bishops Chaplain or Sir *Roger, &c.*) is not *immutable*.

The Arguments to keep the *Press-doors shut*, center all in this, That a Liberty thereof, *without the Pass of a License*, may prove pernicious *not only* to private men, but to *the Publique*, to the *Church*, to the *State*.

Libels will *fly about to wound* mens Reputations; and, which is a consideration of greater weight, The Church and State may thus be shot at, and wounded, and yet like shooting with *White Powder*,[6] the Wound is *felt*, but none knows *whence* the Bullets came.

This is an Inconvenience; but, *if this be all*, the Argument is *fallacious*: For, as in *other* Trades, things that are *rare, dear and hard to come by*, are the *readiest Commodity*; so also in the *Book-sellers* Trade, no Books vend *so nimbly*, as those that are sold (by *Stealth* as it were) and want *Imprimaturs*.

This *Restraint by Licensers* will not prevent the *flying Pamphlets* and Reputation-Wounders; we may well say, *it will not*, because by Experience 'tis found *it never did*. /

But, if the *By-Law already made by the Stationers Company*,[7] were Enacted by *Parliament*, with some *additions*, all the Inconveniencies of *Restraining the Press from Printing the best Books*, (because it is perhaps against the *Diana of Mr. Licenser*,[8] or the *Craft by which he gets his Wealth*) will be prevented; and all the *Reputation-Wounders* will be discovered, and without *further Proof*, brought to Condign Punishment: Namely, A Law, that every *Author*'s and *Printer*'s Name, and their several places of *Residence*, and the mans Name for whom they were *Printed*, and who *Publishes* and *Vends* them, be Printed in the *Title-Page* of every Book or Pamphlet; And that such *Printed Names* shall be a sufficient Evidence, as if under their own *Hand-Writing*; provided it be proved by *Witnesses and Writing*, that the Author gave *order* for it (and that the Printer (there named) did *really Print* the same:) And that it shall be *Felony*, (or some Crime or Punishment) to Print any Book or Pamphlet in other manner; or to Print *false Names*; Or with what other *Proviso's* the Wisdom of a Parliament shall think meet.

The Pope indeed *has some Reason* to Restrain all Printing, without his *Approbation License*, or *Instruction*; because it is very meet and right so to do; granting his Infallibility, An *Index Expurgatorius*[9] is a *necessary* and just *Consequence* thereof.

But, Church of *England, that disclaims all such Impudent pretence*; what Reason *can she give* to be the *only Door-keeper* to the Press, except she could also get an Act of *Parliament* that it shall not be *Lawful* hereafter for *God Almighty* to open any mans Understanding clearer, nor to give him *better Eyes* then the *Licenser*.

For, How many Excellent Books, both in *Divinity* and *Humanity*, are Suppress'd, *because they are excellent, and too good* to get an *Imprimatur*?

This made the Great Duke of *Buckingham*[10] *say*, That the Clergy have but *one Vote*; for the Inferiour Clergy generally think themselves notably *sharp-sighted* in Affairs, if they can but *look up to the Top* of the Church-Steeple, and see how *the Cock stands*;[11] and as the Wind blows, *many* of them sometimes *Conform themselves*.

Thus Haggards[12] listen to the Huntsmans *Halloo and Horn*, but seldome put their *Noses to the Ground* to examine the Scent; For which the Huntsman Whips them *smartly* sometimes, yet 'tis *all one*.

No men are greater Vassals then small Clergy-men, or at least *more Oppress'd* with unreasonable *Assents* and *Consents*, in spight of Mathematicks, and illegal Procurations, Synodals, &c.[13] even *when there is no Synod*, no Visitation, &c. yet (*poor Hearts*) they out with their Purse, and pay the Bishops Silver, and the Rich Arch-Deacons Silver, though some of them *Pawn the Pewter-Dish for it*; and yet for all this Vassallage, some of them does not so much as Whimper, Groan, nor Complain, nor Vote otherwise then (as the Word is *Ecchoed* amongst them) though at such a time as this, when a Parliament can help us.

Thus have I seen a *Step Mother* Whip the Child till it *Roar* again, and then take it up again and Whip it for *Roaring*; and then make it go down on its *Knees*, ask *Forgiveness*, *Kiss the Rod*; threatning to give it *twice as much* if it tell it's *Father*: But come on't what will, I will say – *God help*, the while.

Has *any man* in the World *any other or better* Commission to Preach, then what Christ gave his Disciples? (Mat. 28.19.) namely, *To go and teach*, and make all *Nations* Disciples by Baptizing them; and he will be *with such* to the end of the World; not with those Individual Apostles (who are *dead*) but their Successours (Lawfully ordain'd) to the end of the World. /

Let any *man show me a Reason* if he can, why a Presbyter *Lawfully ordain'd*, and therefore *Commissionated* by Christ to *Teach all Nations*, &c. should need *any other* License? And is not *teaching* in Print from the *Press*, the same or better, and of *more general* and universal *benefit* to all-men, and *all Nations*, then the *narrow Pulpit*, though it stand *aloft*?

And dare any Christian prefer the Words of an Act of Parliament, before the *Words of God* and our Lord Jesus, who has commanded all Men *to let their Light so shine before Men, that they may see their good Works*, (in Print, the most Excellent, Universal, and Charitable Good Works in the World, if they be agreeable to Holy Scripture, and right Reason) and glorifie their Father *which is in Heaven*,[14] without leave or License?

Does not our Law-Books say, That all Statutes are *Ipso facto*, Void, if against the *Common Law*, *(viz.* the Light of Reason, or Law of Nature) or against the *Law of God*?

But it is against the *Common Law* to take away, or Obstruct any Mans Trade or Birthright, *(as Printing is to many Men)* when the Publick, *the State and the Church*, and *every private* Man's Reputation, may be better and sufficiently Ensured by other Ways?

Is there not a Positive Law of Christ to all Christians, *not to hide their Talent in a Napkin*,[15] (though the Licensers for Self-Interest, will not give us an *Imprimatur* to improve it?)

Is there not a Plain-Law of Christ, That we should not put *our Light under a Bushel*,[16] but on a *Candlestick*, that all that come in may see the Light? The Liberty of the Pulpit, Bench or Press, are the *Golden Candlesticks*: the Self-ended *Imprimatur's* very Wooden Ones, (God knows) if this little Treatise cannot be Gain-said nor Confuted, but by the Goaler?[17]

Is there not a Positive Law of Christ; *Not to quench the Spirit*?[18] And shall any *Unchristian Law* quench it, for Self-ends, and because they are so mad as to shut their Eyes, and scorn to amend, or be cured by a charitable Hand, that is willing to do it for God's sake, and not for any other Fee?

Since then there is a *Positive Law* of Christ to let our Light so shine before men, that they may see our *Good and Charitable Works*, (in Print to chuse) that *Pater Noster* (which is in Heaven) *may be Glorified*; Then let us give to *Cæsar* the things that are *Cæsars*;[19] but let us not rob God, to give unto *Cæsar* the things that are Gods Peculiars and Property.

And what *Honest* Protestant would not think it much more Honour to be *Gods Advocate*, (in such a Book as this, (as little as it is,) Pleading *Gods Cause*, his Right and Sole Dominion over Consciences, than by Invading Liberty of Conscience (Gods Throne) to *arrive to the highest Preferments*, (the Effect of Favour (many times) or fore wilder Chance?)

And now have I done with the Five Chapters, which are all Uniform and of a Piece; there went but the Shears (or Sections) between them, for Methods sake. ...

[James Parkinson], *The Fire's Continued at Oxford: or, The Decree of the Convocation for Burning the Naked Gospel, Considered* ([London], 30 August 1690). Wing, P494; ESTC, R1197.

*The FIRE's continued at* OXFORD:
OR,
The Decree of the Convocation for burning *the Naked Gospel*, considered.

*In a Letter to a Person of Honour.*

*Honoured Sir,*
I Gave you in my last the state of the Controversy between the Bp. of *Exeter*, and the Rector and major part of the Fellows of *Exeter*-Colledg at *Oxford*,[1] as well as I could collect it from the Relations I could meet with, and from their Petition to her Majesty, before whom the Cause is depending. In the mean time, the *Gazette* will inform you, The University of *Oxford*, in Convocation held, *Aug.* 19. instant, has past their Judgment and Decree[2] against certain Propositions as Impious and Heretical, cited out of a certain infamous Libel – entituled, *The Naked Gospel*,[3] which (say they) impugn and destroy the chief Mysteries of our Faith, always held and maintained in the Catholick Church, and especially in the English. And in the Preface to their Decree, they say, it not only denies, but exposes to scorn that very Lord Jesus Christ, who is God blessed for ever.

Now, Sir, before I take into consideration the impious and heretical Propositions, give me leave to give you a short Summary of the Tendency and Design of the Book, and of the reputed Author's printing it at his own Charge, as I am inform'd by some that know him, for I do not know him my self, nor ever had any communication with him.

And first of the Author's Design in writing it. When the King had called a Convocation to reconcile (as was hoped) to the Church of *England*, the several Parties in this Kingdom, and to satisfy (if possible) the Consciences of those who differ from it, this Author was willing to contribute to so good a Work.[4] But because a direct Address might appear too great a boldness (as some that went that way afterward found) he conceiv'd that a clear stating the first Principles of the Gospel, would appear more suitable to so learned a Body, and useful toward enlargement of the Mind to a comprehensive Charity. He therefore got this Treatise printed, with design to steal a Copy of it into the Hand of every Member of the Convocation, without publishing it to the World. No sooner was the Impression finished, but he found the Hopes of the King, and the Generality of good Men disappointed, / by the rigour of the prevailing Party in the Convocation; and a great Noise made about this well-design'd Book, whereof some few Copies had gotten abroad. The Author hereupon made some Changes in the middle of the Book, leaving out such Passages as appeared most offensive; and of this Impression he communicated more Copies than he had done of the former. But now cometh out a stolen Impression[5] of the first Book made at *London*, by he knows not whom, which put it out of his power to dispose as he pleas'd, of a Book that was his own.

1. By Writing, and then by Printing and Altering, wholly at his own Cost. Thus it appears his Design was not to disturb the Peace of the Church, but to promote it.

2. The Design and Tendency of the Book, I will presume to whisper to you, (out of hearing of the Convocation) is such, as partly by reconciling Controversies, partly by distinguishing necessary Articles from those that are not necessary, and cutting off Disputes about the Modes and Niceties of things in gross necessary; by giving such a Scheme of Christian Religion as is clear and plain to vulgar Capacities, and apt to remove Doubts, and Fears, and Uncertainties, and to satisfy good Peoples Minds touching their being in the true way of Salvation, notwithstanding the many Differences and Disputes among conscientious Men, which they are either not able to determine, or not with full satisfaction to themselves; to turn Mens Minds from the study of Opinions, and Speculations, to Practical Piety, Devotion toward God and Christ, and Love toward all Christians of all Perswasions; in the mean time making Rents and Divisions, Heats and Animosities about Matters hardly determinable, to be dangerous and unbecoming sincere Christians. This Book, I say, having this Design and Tendency, were not People prejudiced against it by rash and presumptuous Decrees and Censures, might be of as great benefit to the World in general, and the Christian World in special, as perhaps any Book of that Subject that has been publish'd these hundred Years. When you have read the Book, I doubt not but you will be of my Mind. But for all that, I could have wished the Author had not, by some elegant Figures of Speech, either bordered upon Hyperbole's, or made his Mind less intelligible to common Readers, and laid himself more open to the Cavils of his fierce Enemies, (which he did not fear among so learned Men as our Convocation.)[6]

For, except the manner of expression, I make no question but your own Memory will suggest to you, that (as we say of the Holy Scriptures, they contain in one Bundle all those excellent Precepts and Instructions, which lie dispers'd, some in one, some in another of the Philosophers) so the *Naked Gospel* contains nothing but what is found by Parcels, in other eminent and allowed Authors, whom the *Oxford* Convocation dare not pass Sentence upon, tho' they have appear'd of late

Years presumptuous enough in that kind; witness their famous Judgment and Decree past in Convocation, *July* 21. 1683. declaring 27 Propositions *to be False, Seditious, and Impious; and most of them to be also Heretical and Blasphemous, infamous to Christian Religion, and destructive to all Government in Church and State.*[7] And this at such a time, when the Court solicited that Judgment for promoting their horrid Design of introducing Popery and Arbitrary Government into these Kingdoms, and rooting that pestilent Heresy of Protestantism out of all Nations; to which that *Oxford*-Decree was greatly serviceable. And had the Body of the People of *England* been thoroughly perswaded of the Truth, Equity, and Religion of that Decree in all the Propositions, we could never have had the happy cause of blessing God for delivering us from French Tyranny, and Popish Cruelty and Superstition, by the glorious Courage and Conduct of his Highness the Prince of *Orange*; nor could the Peers, and Representatives of the Nation in Convention, / have settl'd the Crown upon their most Excellent Majesties, *William* and *Mary*; but we had in all likelyhood been for ever enslaved to a bigotted Popish King, and the Lady of *Loretto*'s Heirs.[8] For it is observable, that the Vote of the Convention, which declared K. *James's* Throne vacant, was grounded upon his having broken the Contract between King and People. And that there is such a Contract, is the Proposition condemned as impious by the same Hand which now condemned the *N.G.*[9] At this time we see that those Bishops, and others, that have throughly digested the *Oxford*-Principles of Passive Obedience, and Non-resistance, can rather lose their Preferments, than swear Allegiance to our King and Queen. And since divers of the Clergy profess to swear to their Majesties as King and Queen *de Facto* only; Have we not reasonable grounds to suspect the Passive-Obedience-men of the Convocation to be such? And perhaps our Author may have somewhat more incurr'd their Enmity by his being (as I hear he is) a *de Jure* Liege-man, and did not join his Sufferage in that Decree.[10]

This burning Decree of the Convocation of *Oxford, July* 21, .83. brings fresh to my Mind the most unjust Expulsion of Mr. *Parkinson*[11] from that University, and consequently from his Fellowship in *Lincoln*-Colledge, whereby, and from his Pupils, he receiv'd about 120 *l. per Annum*; of all which he was depriv'd, without any Trial, about the very time of that Convocation, and for holding (as was pretended) some of those Propositions condemned by that Decree; and whilst he stood indicted for the same at the Assizes of *Oxford*, where, and at the King's-Bench *Westminster*, he was forced to give attendance for about three Years. And tho' he has been restor'd to the Liberty of the University, by the late Vice-Chancellor, now Bishop of *Bristol*;[12] yet to this Day he cannot procure restoration to his Fellowship, much less reparation of his great Damages sustain'd in the space of full seven Years. How does Dr. *H*—'s[13] Conscience suffer him to sleep while it is not done, since he was the chief Agent in that Expulsion![14]

# THE PRINTING ACT IN QUESTION, 1692–3

*Reasons Humbly Offered to be Considered before the Act for Printing be Renewed (unless with Alterations) viz. for Freedom of Trade in Lawful Books, and setting Severe Penalties on Scandalous and Seditious Books against the Government* ([London], [December 1692–January 1693]). Wing, R548A; ESTC, R217973.

[Edmund Bohun], 'Reasons for Reviving the Act for Regulating the Press & Printing' (December 1692–January 1693). Cambridge University Library, Sel.3.238 (334).

[James Harrington], *Reasons for Reviving and Continuing the Act for the Regulation of Printing* ([London], [January 1693]). Wing, R511; ESTC, R229650.

*Reasons Humbly Offered for the Liberty of Unlicens'd Printing. To which is Subjoin'd, The Just and True Character of Edmund Bohun, the Licenser of the Press* (London, c. 24 January 1693). Wing, B3313; ESTC, R17412.

*The Clauses chiefly Objected against in the Act 14o of Charles II. about Printing* ([London], [February 1693?]). Wing, C4597C; ESTC, R233924.

In 1692–3 the Printing Act once more came up for renewal, having been continued in 1685 from 24 June for seven years and to the end of the next session (1 Jac. II, c. 17). The Act was duly renewed in the session beginning in late 1692, although only for a shorter period and only after a more intensive discussion than previously inside and outside Parliament, aspects of which are presented here. On 1 December 1692 the Commons appointed a committee to consider expiring laws and on 23 December endorsed its recommendation to continue the Printing Act, ordering a bill to be brought in, which was eventually presented on 3 February 1693.[1] The bill on expiring laws passed both houses by 8 March but against considerable opposition to its press clause. The Commons divided 99 to 80 on whether to grant a second reading to the clause continuing the Printing Act and in the Lords there was a thwarted amendment allowing unlicensed publication if the names of author and printer were supplied, as well as one preventing searches of peers' houses. A protest was entered by eleven Lords, which criticized the Act 'Because it subjects all Learning and true Information to the arbitrary Will and Pleasure of a mercenary, and perhaps ignorant, Licenser; destroys the Properties of Authors in their Copies; and sets up many Monopolies'.[2] The Act was nonetheless continued for a year, dating from 13 February

1693, and to the end of the next session (4&5 Wm. & Mar., c. 24). It passed at a time of heightened concerns over print's ability to destabilize the new regime (see 'Suppressing Jacobitism', below).

A petition of printers and booksellers was received by the Commons on 17 February protesting that the Printing Act prevented free exercise of their trade.[3] The printed paper reproduced here, *Reasons Humbly Offered to be Considered*, was a forerunner of the petition, complaining that since 1662 the Act had allowed dominant stationers to monopolize lucrative patents and exclude the rest of the trade under the 'specious Colour' of preventing seditious and scandalous books. A *Supplement* to the paper also appeared (Wing, S6188A), accusing the master and wardens of the Stationers' Company of contriving to have the Act renewed in 1685 to serve their interests, and working with L'Estrange to obstruct publications, using phrasing at times reminiscent of Blount's *Just Vindication of Learning*. It acknowledged that L'Estrange had departed but complained that another of the same political persuasion was in post, pointing to the 1685 introduction to Filmer's *Patriarcha* written by Edmund Bohun, now licenser of the press.

Edmund Bohun (1645–99) had become licenser on 7 September 1692, but was peremptorily removed from the post on 24 January 1693, having been ordered into custody by the House of Commons on 20 January. The *Reasons* and *Supplement* therefore probably date from late December or early January. A manuscript defence of the Printing Act was also written around this time, at one or two points responding to the printers' *Reasons*. Bohun himself was the probable author, the manuscript *Reasons for Reviving the Act* being preserved within his collection of tracts and letters in Cambridge University Library. Bohun was from the start a controversial choice as licenser given his Tory and High Church leanings. He criticized his Whig predecessor James Fraser as 'a Scot by nation and inclination' who allowed the reprinting of traiterous books of the 1640s and attacks against divine right. Bohun's tenure was accordingly brief, ending when he was taken into custody on Parliament's orders on 20 January 1683 and dismissed the following day after licensing Charles Blount's *King William and Queen Mary Conquerors*.[4] In *Reasons for Reviving the Act*, themes advanced by loyalists like L'Estrange are echoed, particularly the contribution of paper war and liberty of the press to Charles I's downfall, and the revival of the spirit of faction in the present because of 'ill management' of the press and Printing Act. It argued that the licensing process could make clear what doctrines and positions were orthodox and what proscribed, although as licenser it was soon apparent that Bohun himself was not in a position to identify and prescribe orthodoxy.

A single-sheet defence of the Printing Act published in January 1693, *Reasons for Reviving and Continuing the Act* urged censorship and the protection of property in copies. It was probably the work of the young prosecution lawyer James Harrington (unrelated to his late namesake). Harrington had been a student at

Christ Church, Oxford, and went on to represent the university as a lawyer and as an advocate in printed controversy. In a 1691 tract he had defended the Oxford convocation's condemnation of the *Naked Gospel*, arguing that the resort to print proved Arthur Bury's intent to take 'Socinian' arguments beyond the purported readership of Oxford deans.[5] Harrington's *Reasons* defended the Printing Act in part by emphasizing considerations of copyright, privilege, piracy and imports relevant to contemporary disputes involving the Oxford University presses.

Consideration of the Printing Act in 1693 attracted the later seventeenth century's third adaptation of Milton's *Areopagitica*, following Charles Blount in 1679 and William Denton in 1680. This was *Reasons Humbly Offered for the Liberty of Unlicens'd Printing*, whose first part was signed with the date 17 January 1693. However, an account attacking Bohun's suspect Tory opinions, drawing quotations from his writings, was added as a postscript over the next few days as the licenser came under the investigation of Parliament. The first part provides a comparatively lengthy defence of liberty of the press, borrowing heavily from Milton, with some updating to attack Jacobite libels, and even signed 'J.M.' at the end. The pamphlet as a whole has often been attributed to Charles Blount but this seems untenable, for three main reasons: the second part attacks Blount's *King William and Queen Mary Conquerors*; Blount could more easily have reprinted the *Just Vindication of Learning* (as occurred posthumously in 1695); and internal evidence, indicated in notes below, confirms that the tract drew anew on *Areopagitica*, rather than following the *Just Vindication*. The twenty-page postscript attacked Bohun on the basis of his published opinions and performance as licenser, claiming that he promoted absolutist and popish works and the Jacobite cause, and was 'cronies' with L'Estrange in poisoning the kingdom. When the issue of the Printing Act re-emerged in 1695, John Locke informed Andrew Fletcher of Saltoun that he had just read *Reasons Humbly Offered for a Liberty of Unlicensed Printing* and advised that, although there was nothing 'extraordinary' in it, Fletcher should acquire a copy and pass it to Locke's parliamentary ally Lord Monmouth 'before the bill for printing comes up to the Lords house'.[6]

*The Clauses chiefly Objected against in the Act 14o of Charles II. about Printing* is dated 1685 by Wing, although the parallels between its objections and those voiced in 1693 in the Lords about trade concerns and house-searching suggest a closer affinity to the later than the earlier consideration of licensing's renewal. Further details of its production remain elusive, however.

Notes
1. *CJ*, 10, p. 762.
2. *CJ*, 10, p. 820; *LJ*, 15, p. 280.

3. *CJ*, 10, p. 817.
4. E. Bohun, *The Diary and Autobiography of Edmund Bohun* (Beccles: privately printed, 1853), pp. 82–4; *CJ*, 10, p. 786.
5. J. Harrington, *A Defence of the Proceedings* (London, 1691), p. 47.
6. *The Correspondence of John Locke*, ed. E. S. De Beer, 8 vols (Oxford: Clarendon Press, 1979), vol. 8, pp. 434–7, 'Addendum: additional letters', letter1854A, 1 March 1695.

***Reasons Humbly Offered to be Considered before the Act for Printing be Renewed (unless with Alterations) viz. for Freedom of Trade in Lawful Books, and setting Severe Penalties on Scandalous and Seditious Books against the Government*** ([London], [December 1692–January 1693]). Wing, R548A; ESTC, R217973.

***Reasons humbly offered to be considered before** the Act for Printing **be renewed (unless with Alterations)** viz. **for Freedom of Trade in Lawful Books, and setting severe Penalties on Scandalous and Seditious Books against the Government.***

THE Trade of Printing hath been an Ancient Manufacture of this Kingdom (and as such) fit to be Encouraged for the publick good; yet by that Act,[1] and the great Powers thereby given, or at least colourably thence taken, by the Masters and Wardens of the Stationers Company and other Patentees, to the very great Prejudice, and publick Damage of the Nation, by inhauncing[2] the Price of Books, and also to the Impoverishment of the generality of the Members of that Company, *viz.* Printers, Booksellers, Book-binders, Haberdashers and several other considerable Traders, who have been thereby restrained from the most beneficial part of their Ancient Trade and Right by their Apprenticeship.[3]

King *James* I. about the thirteenth Year of his Reign, granted to the Master, Wardens and Comminalty of the Mystery of Stationers, *London*, a Patent of Priviledge to Print, Utter and Sell all manner of Primers, Psalters, Psalms, Almanacks, and several other Books, for ever, with a Clause of Prohibition to all others;[4] therein also giving Power to the said Master, Wardens and Assistants to make By-Laws for the management of the said Patent; who have so effectually contrived their own Profit therein, that for thirty Years last past they have constantly divided above 12*l. per cent.* yearly, besides other frequent and more private Dividends, and extravagantly chargable Feastings, out of the Profits of the thus monopolized Trade (excluding the generality of the Members of that Company from any Benefit of the said Patent, though it was granted to the whole Body.)

In the year 1662. they did, by the Solicitation of Sir *R. Lestrange*,[5] obtain the said Act, under the specious Colour of *Preventing Seditious, Scandalous, and Treasonable Books,* &c.[6] which indeed was principally by them designed to support their intended Monopoly; for in a very short Time after they purchased into their Hands several other Patents, which they had set Agents on to beg of the then King: To purchase which Patents they have engag'd the Corporations

Inheritance,[7] and brought a Rent-charge thereon to almost 600*l. per ann.* to the very great Injury of the Corporation in general, to serve a particular End. And then confederating with other Patentees, Bibles and the generality of other Books of publick and general use were got into Patents, and that so comprehensive, that near seventy several Books were got into one Patent, and thereby advanced to above double the Price they were sold for before. And to secure their Monopoly from expiring, and to tye up the Crown therein from investing any others during that Time, they obtained two or three Patents for the same Books, to take place in Reversion almost to an hundred Years to come. Our own Printers being thus restrained, the greatest part of the Printing-trade was carried hence into *Holland, viz.* English Bibles, Common-Prayer Books, Testaments, Psalters, Grammars, Almanacks, and multitudes of other Books of general and perpetual use, and from thence exported to all our Foreign Plantations, *Ireland, Scotland*, and also hither, for the gain of above *cent. per cent.*[8] to the Traders therein.

Vast Quantities of these Books have been seized by these Patentees, who besides Seizure, did also prosecute the Persons in whose Hands they found them, by vertue of the said Act; and thereby extorted exorbitant Sums of Mony, beyond the Penalty of the said Act, they having taken Care to have the Penalty of their thus monopoliz'd Books ascertained by the said Act, the Penalty being 6*s.* 8*d. per* Book: But Seditious and Treasonable Books they were thereby only charged as an Offence against the said Act,[9] which was an Offence by other Laws before that Act, and will be so when it is expired. /

These Patentees, after having, as aforesaid, by Seizure amassed great numbers of these *Holland* printed Books, they on purpose forbear to furnish the Market with the same of their own Printing (all other Printers being by the said Act restrained from that part of Trade) have to a thus empty Market sold again the said seized Books; and have further reseized the very same Books themselves sold, and likewise prosecuted the Persons again in whose Hands they found them, extorting from them the Penalty of the said Act of 6 *s*, 8 *d.* to the utter Ruin of many considerable Merchants and other Traders. They having procured an Agent of their own (whom, for his Encouragement, they made Partner in this their Monopoly) to be made Messenger of the Press, under the specious Pretence of serving the Government in suppressing Seditious Books; which was only a Colour to carry on the Ends aforesaid.[10]

They joyned together, and bought three Horses, and sent the Clark and Beadle, the Servants of the Master and Wardens, and a Secretary's Messenger, to ride all *England* over, to seize on the Books in their Patents, which they alledged to be counterfeit; Who did seize accordingly, though on many of such as were of their own Printing: And after two or three Months Ravage they returned back, giving an Account to the said Master and Wardens, and the other Patentees, what Books, and from whom they had seized them. These Patentees sent Writs out of the *Exchequer* and *King's-bench* to prosecute the Persons from whom they had seized, upon the Penalty of the said Act (many of which) Books, thus seized, had been before sold by the Plaintiffs, in the Prosecution; and did force exorbitant Compositions.

Mr. *John Jekil* stood Trial[11] for about 25 Bibles, before Judge *Hales*, and was cast upon the said Act, and paid 6 s 8 d per Book for the Bible to one Patentee, and 6 s 8d. per Book for the Psalms to the other Patentees; though but one Book, yet thus divided, made two Penalties, Mr. *Jekil* paid about fifty Pounds Costs and Forfeitures. How many Times these Bibles had been seized before they came to Mr. *Jekil's* Hand, and how many times they have been sold and seized since is worthy consideration; and this practised under the Authority of that Act.

The Noise of Mr. *Jekil's* Judgment upon his Trial, coming abroad into the Countries, to the Knowledge of those prosecuted there, frighted them so that some came up to Town, and others sent to their Correspondents and Friends here, to compound with the Prosecutors at any Rate; whose Composition was usually 6 s 8 d per Book, and 40 or 50 Shillings for pretended Charge of Seizure and Prosecution: But if a Bible had the Common Prayer in it, then there were three times 6 s 8 d. Composition Mony, *viz.* Bible, Common Prayer and Psalms; how much of which hath come to the King (half being his due) the Records thereof in the *Exchequer* may shew.

It is suggested in the said Act, That the Trade of Printing is over-charged with Printers, and therefore fit to have their Number retrenched; which is Enacted accordingly thereby.

To which is humbly supposed, That if the Manufacture of Printing were left free, as other Trades, it would employ above double the number of Printers that are in *England*, and that on Lawful Work too. For, since the Year 1662. (when the Act was made) there have more English Bibles, and other English Books, been printed in *Holland*, by one *Athias* a Jew,[12] (among many other Printers there) than have been printed by any four Printers in *England* in that Time; which *Holland*-printed English Books have been merchandized to us, and to the King's Subjects in our Plantations abroad, which might have been so done from hence, had they been afforded here at the same reasonable Rates: Which they might have been had the Trade been free. Freedom of Printing here would soon produce a Manufacture to export as well to our Plantations as to those very Countries who now furnish us and them, whereby the King's Customs would be advanced by Paper imported and Books exported, the Merchant enrich'd, and the Printer and Bookbinder, and many other Trades employed, which by these Monopolies have been hitherto frustrated. These Books being prohibited are always imported by Stealth, so that the King is always defrauded in his Customes.

The Government of all the Printing in *England* (except the two Universities) is by the said Act vested into the Hands of the said Master and Wardens, who to gain the Universities also into their Hands have farmed the whole Printing in *Cambridge*:[13] And in the year 1688. did petition King *James* (under pretence to be enabled to suppress seditious Books, their old Stalking-horse) That they might, in his Majesty's Name prosecute the *Oxford*-printing by a *Quo Warranto*,[14] which being granted by the said King, the Master, / Wardens Assistants and the other Patentees did solicit *Father Peters*[15] and other such fit Instruments, to promote the same; And in return of this Service (besides Clusters of Guineas) they suffered their publik Ware-house-keeper, to propagate to Sale their Popish Books, which was notified to their Party all over the Nation, as a happy Omen of its speedy Conversion to the Catholick Faith, their Books were now freely printed and sold by the Governours of that Company at their Common Hall: Which Prosecution was carried on at the joynt Charge of these Patentees, who have since used other means to get the *Oxford* printing into their Hands; for about twelve Months since they did so far endear themselves to Dr. *Edwards* and Dr. *Aldrich*, one Vice-chancellor of *Oxford* last Year, the other this, to whom they gave Bond of many thousand Pounds Penalty to save them harmless in the disposessing the University's Printers,[16] and farming the same to these Patentees (who had kept down the Price of Books to one third of what these Patentees sold them at before) which the said Vice-chancellors did undertake and effect, though contrary to the general Inclination of that venerable Body, whereby above 35000 Bibles, and many thousands of other Books three quarters finished, were rendered waste Paper, And twenty or thirty Families, that for twelve or fourteen years last past have been maintained by this Manufacture in *Oxford*, are many of them now utterly ruined, to make way for present Sale of many Thousands of their formerly seized *Holland* printed Books, and for the rise of Books printed by these Patentees; which are already advanced one third Penny, and are threatned to be raised double, if the Act be renewed: Which *Holland* Books (by the renewal of the said Act) may be re-seized, and Prosecutions made again (though sold by these Patentees) as they formerly have done many times over.

They are now Zealous to get that Act renewed, that they may be enabled to continue these Practices, and to tax the Publick, as they have done for 30 years past. They have thus long taxed the Nation 1500 *l.* and upwards yearly, in the Almanack Trade only; and this is their aim in getting the Act renewed, they do thereby sell that for three Pence, which at one Penny would be a sufficient Trading Price, and sufficiently gainful. They do likewise discourage Authors, who, for Commenting or Expounding upon part of a Book, which is their Text (as they use the Term) must be constrained to pay them a Premium for it, or be forced to sell their Works to them, though but for one fourth of what others would give, if they had the freedom to Print them; which none will dare to do (if that Act be renewed.) Dr. *Hammond*, Mr. *Pool*,[17] and many other Reverend and Learned Authors have been compelled to pay them their extravagant Demands, for using the Bible Text to Comment upon (tho' but a small part thereof, as the Book of *Psalms*, &c.) The like practised upon *Virgil, Ovid, Terence*, &c. or any of the old Classick School-books which were got into their Patents; in some of which the sole Printing of 50 or 60 were contained.

By the said Act it is Enacted, That a Book being Licensed and Entred into the Register Book of the Company of Stationers, it is forbid to be Printed without the Owners License (who by Vertue of that Entry is Owner) under the Penalty of 6 s. 8 d. per Book; which Register hath (by the undue Practices of the Master and Wardens) been so ill kept, that many Entries have been unduly made; insomuch, that the true Proprietors both by Purchase, License and Entry, all duly made of several Books, which afterwards have been erased, or the Leaves wherein they were written, have been cut out, and undue Entries made to others who had no right; which is directly contrary to the plain words and meaning of the said Act; whereby the Owners have not only been defrauded of their Right, but also rendred liable to the Penalty of 6 s. 8 d. per Book, for all the Books they Printed, Sold or Bound. Many learned Authors have been defrauded of their Rights thereby, who, after many years Pains and Study, and afterwards by a bare Delivery of their Books to be Licensed or Transcribed, have been barred by surrepitious Entries made in the said Register (to instance in the Book called *Regula Placitandi*,[18] among many others, written by a learned Lawyer and worthy Member of this Parliament.) Wherefore, it is humbly represented whether the Irregularities, aforesaid, may not have rendred the Act impracticable to be executed, agreeable to Justice and Equity; and if the Act be renewed, if it may not establish a wrongful Possession, unless that Register be first duly rectified.

The Property of English Authors hath been always owned as Sacred among the Traders, and generally forborn, hitherto, to be invaded; but if any should invade such Properties, there is remedy, by Laws already made, and / no other were ever thought needful till 1662. The Works of *Homer, Hesiod, Horace, Ovid, Virgil, Cæsar, Lucan, Plautus, Tully, Florus, Curtius*, and Multitudes of other ancient Classick Authors, which were always free to all Printers and Booksellers to Print, before the making of the said Act; but since are got into Patents, and by that Act prohibited from being Printed, under the Penalty of 6 s. 8 d. per Book, to the inhansing the Prices, the hinderance of the Printer, and are only an encouragement for Foreigners to import upon us; which are the Grievances long endured, and now complained of; and humbly Prayed to be considered, before the Act for Printing be continued.

It is said, The Charter to the University of *Oxford*, for Printing of all manner of Books (which the Master, Wardens, &c. have now formed into their own Hands) is now proposed to be confirmed in Parliament:[19] Which Charter (if confirmed without a saving to every Man his particular Property) seems to defeat all particular Properties in Copies, both in respect to Booksellers and Authors, and makes the Owners liable to the Penalties in that Charter, which are very severe, besides the loss of their Property; the Patentees will agree the saving of Patent-books, peradventure, well enough; but will readily consent that particular Property may be gain'd into their Controle.

Till the year, 1662. it was not thought needful, by any precedent Parliament of *England*, to make an Act for to regulate or restrain Printing more than other Trades, neither doth that Act inflict any new Penalty for seditious Books, but leaves them to the former Laws. About the beginning of the Popish Plot, this Act was discontinued;[20] and Sir *Roger Lestrange*, Surveyor of the Press, and the Messenger of the Press, were both severely censured in Parliament, and that Act was not thought fit to be renewed till the late King *James*'s Reign; where Sir *Roger Lestrange*, being a Member of Parliament, got the said Act to be renewed.[21]

Now (if the Tables were turned) That scandalous and seditious Books, &c. were forbid, under the Penalty of 6 s. 8 d. or 100 l. per Book; and Books thus monopolized, by Patents, were left to the determination of the Law; it is humbly presumed, the Government would be much less pestered with them than heretofore; neither would there be need to charge the Government with two hundred Pound *per Annum* for a Surveyor of the Press, nor fifty Pound *per Annum* for a Messenger of the Press, as it was formerly to Sir *Roger Lestrange* (if it be not still done so to others.) If Books Mechanical, Mathematical, Trade, Cookery, Husbandry, Phisick, Surgery, Geography, and the like, were not required to be Licensed, the Bishops Chaplains would be so much the less disturbed from their Studies;[22] and it is humbly presumed the Government can scarcely be harmed thereby.

By that Act Printers are restrained from setting up their Trades, to which they served their Apprentiship; whereby Multitudes of them have been forced to go to *Holland* and other Countries, to work as Journy-men there, in Printing English Bibles and other English Books; vast numbers whereof, have been brought over into *England* by Merchants, for gain; one Merchant (among many others) importing near twenty thousand English Bibles yearly, besides vast quantities of our English Books, that were got into Patents, and restrained by the said Act, under the Penalty aforesaid.

All which Matters are humbly offered to be considered (before the said Act be renewed) by many hundreds of Traders in the said Manufacture, who by having freedom to follow their Trades on lawful Work, shall not be necessitated to betake themselves (for a Livelihood) to unlawful Work, as too many have been forced to do, or to turn Porters or some other servile Employments, which their Parents and Friends little dreamed of when they placed them Apprentices to their Trades.

*FINIS.*

## [Edmund Bohun], 'Reasons for Reviving the Act for Regulating the Press & Printing' (December 1692–January 1693). Cambridge University Library, Sel.3.238 (334).

It was One of Plato's Laws[1] in his work de Leg: That noe Writting should be published without the Approbation and consent of the supreame Magistrat, The reason of w$^{ch}$ is eternall, and is a thousand times more strong since the Inventing of Printing than it was before, when writing was only used, because of the Facility and cheapness, and celerity,[2] of dispersing all Papers – above what is possible by writing.

This has necessitated all the Nations about us to look well and severely to the Presse, well knowing noe Government can long continue in Peace, where this Terrible Engine is set at Liberty to force up the foundations of it, ag$^t$ w$^{ch}$ nothing can stand.

Yet fractious times and divided Nations are more liable to be disquieted and torn up by this Engine than those that are more quiet and united.

Before the Time of the reformation (viz. The yeare 1517)[3] Printers applied themselves wholly to the Printing the Ancient Manuscripts; or books written by the great Men of those times for the promoting Learning, the Printers being then Learned Men, and excellent Judges of Bookes, and the Art not Degenerated into a Mercenary Trade: And whilst this State of things continued noe body thought, nor had any reason to think of regulating the Press; But noe Sooner was the Reformation Sett on foot by Luther and others in Germany but the Press was imployed on both sides, till at Last it became Dubious for both parties whether it had done good or Hurt, and then both the parties in most places began to regulate and or restrain it.

What Terrible havock it made before this was done in Germany, the Netherlands, and France, during the holy League,[4] is well known to all Learned Men, and need not be spoken here. In England it was later brought in, and of slower growth, Yet it had its share too; some having been punished and others hanged in Queen Eliz. Times, for Printing Seditious Books; w$^{ch}$ with a Decree in the Star Chamber[5] soe well prevented the growth of this mischief that things were kept in tollerable order till about 1640, and it is well known the Calamities the Nation groaned under between that and 1660 were mostly promoted by a Lawless Liberty of the Presse, and without it could neither have been carried so high, spread soe farr or continued soe Long. /

The Parliament party encouraged it and Applauded it soe long as it promoted their designs, but when the Nation grew weary of the miseries of a Warr that threatned its utter ruine, and the Tide of Popular favour began to turn another

Way, then they saw plainly they must put a restraint upon the Presse, or it would as certainly ruine as it has raised them, and soe it was curbd by Ordinances of Parliament,[6] and a Surveyor or Lycenser of the Presse was appointed and soe it continued under Oliver Cromwell till the year 1658 or 1659 when it broke loose again & tore up all their Babel by the Foundation.

In the beginning of Charles the 2d his Reign this Act was made upon wise and mature considerations as appeareth by the Preamble,[7] and continued in Force till 1679 or thereabouts and in the disorder occasioned by the Popish Plott it broke loose again; and continued at Liberty till the first yeare of James the 2d. to the Ruine of many a Family, and the Losse of many a Life, wch might otherwise have been saved, not to mention the Hazard the Nation ran by exasperating the contending parties agt each other; so that by the time last mentioned all men saw the Necessity of Reviving it.

The ill management of it since that time hath done more harm to the Nation than can be recovered in many yeares if ever perfectly: Yet after all there are Some Men who are now pleading for the Liberty of the Press for ends and purposes that may be guessed at, tho not Spoken. As to what is said agt the Stationers Company I shall Leave them to answer for themselves and confine my self to what concerns the publick only.

As perhaps there was never any Nation divided into more factions than this of England is at this day, soe there was never any in wch the Factious were more Animated the One against the other. The Times are also overcast and threaten Us with an Invasion from abroad and Insurrection at home[8] and therefore of all other this Nation at this time is not be trusted to the Insinuations of Crafty, Passionate, imprudent and designing Men. They that mean well by mistake and they that mean ill upon design may equally promote Our ruine if good care be not taken.

Wee are not only opposed to the violence of Our Domestic Factions but also to the Frauds of the French Kings, and the Jesuites Emmisaries and Agents, soe that if the Presse were now free, all the Old, and all the New Factions, the French Kings / Ministers, and the Jesuites Emmisaries would play their parte in all Manner of Shapes upon Our Stage and to our Cost without doubt at long run.

Notwithstanding all the care that could be taken as yet and the Law to the Contrary Great quantities of Books and papers have since the Revolution been printed and dispersed about the Nation and wch is yett worse, they have not been sold but given away, to all Sorts of Men, and some of these of noe small Bulk or Price, wch showes that it is done by the Purse of the French, or by a publick Charge noe private person being able to bear soe great an expense as this is, and it is humbly conceived this consideration alone is enough to determine any man that is a freind to the present Government against the setting the Press at Liberty now, whatever he might think at another time.

For the present restraint cannot absolutely stop this Evil, yet it puts a great Curb upon it, and makes it much more difficult, than it will be when the Press shall be free and they may print what they please in the Publick presses.

But wee are told the Common Law will punish all Seditious and trayterous Papers?[9] True but then they will first be published and have done a great part of the Mischeif was intended by them. 2. The Authors and Printers will often not be found or hardly convicted, and the Booksellers and Printers will be in a fine Condition, when they shall neither print nor vend a book but w$^{th}$ the Hazard of their Lives and Estates: They are noe Judges of what is fitt and Lawfull, and may Justly and truly many times plead Ignorance, and it will oftentimes be very hard to Punish them in Instances that are Dammageable to the Governm$^t$; soe that if there were noe other Reason but this there ought to be a Licenser or Surveyor of the Presse to preserve well meaning but ignorant Men, and those that have little Leisure to read from being imposed upon to their Ruine.

As it is very reasonable that noe Printer or Bookseller, should claim a Right in any Authors work, without his expresse Consent, soe it is reasonable when he has obtained that by Purchase or free gift that his right should be ascertained to him and appeare upon Record, w$^{ch}$ cannot be if this Act is not revived, till another is made, and what is defective in this may afterwards be supplyed in another bill when the houses will have more Leisure than they can have now the year is so much advanced. /

What is objected concerning the ill keeping the Book at Station: hall,[10] is of noe force now, because there is another Register kept by the Licenser of all books Licensed, w$^{ch}$ in time to come will prevent those Abuses or at least detect them, and for time past Power may be given to the Licenser or some other fitt person, or Persons, who is not interested, to hear and Determine all differences between the Authors and booksellers and to settle them, and also to examine all the Pretended Rasures,[11] Leaves cut out and other Abuses in the Present Register.

The Last Grand Objection is that it will save the King £250 the year; supposed to be paid to the Licenser & Messenger of the Presse, w$^{ch}$ if true will be ill saved money.[12] It were more for their Ma$^{ties}$ Interest, that there were 2 or 3 Messengers of the Presse rather than to part with the Single One they now have to save £50 the yeare, And as to the Licenser or Surveyor of the Presse, There is noe Officer imployed by the Crown, w$^{ch}$ is not better paid considering his great Labour & Hazard, but if this will not be accepted the State may be eased of the Burthen by allowing him a competent Summe for each book that is printed, the Omission of w$^{ch}$ in the Act is One of the greatest Defects in it and a principal cause the Act has not had its full effect w$^{ch}$ might have otherwise been expected.

They move that 6$^s$:8$^d$ might be laid upon every seditious book[13] and perhaps the assigning that summe to the Licenser and Messenger of the Presse to make them the more Industrious to suppress them would goe neer to affect the Design, but then it must extend to all unlicensed Books.

The making the forfeit absolute if a Lycense be not produced and payable both by the Vendor and Printer upon pain of Imprisonment without any Prior Indictment, but with a Liberty of appeale as in the Conventicle Act.

The Want of Encouragement to the Lycenser and of a speedy conviction are the two causes this Act has not had all the effect that it might have had, but yet better a weak defence than none at all, and therefore it is hoped and humbly prayd that the Act may be revived in this present Session of Parliam$^t$ and that what is wanting may be supplyed in the next.

[James Harrington], *Reasons for Reviving and Continuing the Act for the Regulation of Printing* ([London], [January 1693]). Wing, R511; ESTC, R229650.

## REASONS
FOR
Reviving and Continuing the ACT
FOR THE
Regulation of PRINTING.

IT must be agreed, that the Press deserves and needs both *Encouragement* and *Restraint*; and Experience hath proved the Usefulness of this Law for both those Purposes.

The Design of the Act[1] is,

First, To prevent *Seditious, Blasphemous*, and *Treasonable* Books, the necessity of which Care in the present Age is as apparent, as 'twas in the former. The Preamble of this Act remains still too true to admit of a denyal: And the same, or the like Method for *Licensing*, and *punishing* of unlicens'd Books, hath been practised for near 100 Years past,[2] before and after the Reign of K. *James* I.

But until this legal Provision was made, in contempt of the repeated Orders of the King and Council, and other Courts, unlawful Pamphlets were daily Published;[3] and the number of them would probably still have increased, if this Law had not taken care, not only to impose and exact Penalties, but to restrain the number of Presses, and to forbid all private Ones, and to facilitate Searches during the Work, which afterwards for the most part are fruitless and vain, because in all probability the Libel hath then had its Vent, and the Author his end.

The Second Design and Intent of this Act is,

To *encourage* and *preserve Property* in Books to their Authors and their Assigns, and this by enjoyning Entries in a Publick Register,[4] (which is regularly and fairly kept), by Prohibiting the Importation of any Books from beyond the Seas which were Printed here before; and lastly, by ascertaining the rights of Copies to the Proprietors thereof; which Provisions almost in the very same words was Established, not only by Decrees in *Charles* I. time, and long before, but also by an Act of Parliament *Sept.* 29. 1649.[5]

This Law is not only convenient for Authors of the present and future Ages, but just even in respect of antient Copies, in which a legal Interest hath been acquired, and that at great Charges; and these Interests are become the Lively-hood and sole Estate of several Widows, Fatherless Children, and other whole Families.

The Mystery of Printing was first introduced into *England* at the Charge of the Crown,[6] and upon increase of the number of Artists, was Governed by direction of the King, or King and Council, and then by Decrees of the Star-Chamber, and then by Acts or Ordinances made in the late Times, and since the Restoration, by Act of Parliament. But Property in Publick or Private Copies, was always preserv'd entire and free, The Right and Interest of the Company of **Stationers**, in Books of Common and Publick Use, was lawfully Vested in them before the Reign of King *James* I. some of which Copies were purchased at great Expence from the *Crown*, some from private Persons, and others bequeathed to them by the then Proprietors, and great Stocks were expended and still are laid out to that purpose. They are now under Obligations of giving 200 *l. per Annum* to the Poor of the Trade, and this they have never failed in, and tho their Stocks have not yielded some years above 4 or 5 *per Cent*,[7] yet they have maintained several Families thereby every Year, who must necessarily Perish upon the loss of such Copies, and the failure of the Stock therein.

*Object.*[8] Printing is a *Manufacture*, and ought to be as free as any other Trade.

*Answ.* This was never a Free-Trade since its first Introduction, but always under Regulation; and infinite Inconveniences must ensue upon a licentious Use of it; and the Policy of all Ages from its first Practice in *England*, hath been to Govern it by Rules, and under Limits. As to Execution of the Act, in respect of Restraint, none were ever disabled to use the Art, unless in scandalous or unlawful Work; and if an universal Liberty were once permitted, such practice would quickly increase, and would be even beyond the Power of any Government to controle.

*Object.* Penalties have been exacted, and many Persons have been rigorously Prosecuted for Importation of Books from abroad.

*Answ.* It's true that Prohibited Books have been seized, and the small Penalties sometimes taken, but *lawfully, regularly, mildly*, and that only from incorrigible **Pirats**; and the Charge generally hath been greater than the Profit of such Prosecutions, through the smalness of the demanded Forfeitures. And the Case which was most complained of, was that of Mr. *Jekyl*, who Imported Foreign Prints, to the damage of English-men's Property; and that was adjudged by the Reverend the *L. C. J. Hales*, and this his Judgment did command a great submission to the Law almost ever since.[9]

*Object.* That Books may be had cheaper from *Holland*, and therefore not to be Prohibited, for the Subject may be supplied from thence with more ease, and the Customs advanced.

*Answ.* As to the Subject, the Stat. 25. *Hen.* VIII. remains still in force, by which the price of Books[10] may be settled and reformed as occasion doth or may require. And that the *Dutch* do in the trade of **Printing** Pirate upon us is no more than they do by most other Nations and they will always be able to do so, because their Hirelings fare worse, and work for less. But surely the **Workmen-Printers** in *London* have no reason to thank the Author of such an Objection: for an *English Printer* would be loth to change Conditions with any *Printer* in **Holland**. Then as to the Kings Customs being raised by such Importation of Foreign Prints, it must be agreed that 'twou'd encrease them some small trivial matter, but the gain would be so little, and the Balance so burthensome on the other side, that it is easily demonstrable to be no more than one Penny profit to the Crown for 5 *l.* loss to the *English* Subject: And it is to be hoped, That such an Increase of the Revenue will never be acceptable to their Majesties, or the Parliament.

And if it should be admitted. That if the right of those Copies which is vested in the Crown, and those that claim under it by **Charter** or **Patent** were made Publick, the Price of such Books might possibly be abated. Yet in those Prints which are of publick Consequence, the Exactness of the Impression ought chiefly to be regarded, and it is the Prudence of the Government to lodge this Trust in such Hands, as may take care not only of a moderate Price of those Books, but of a good and correct Edition of them; which, as it is performed with great Charge, so must it necessarily in some measure enhance the Value of the Books. Of this we have a clear Instance lately in Two *Mercenary* Fellows,[11] that were **Printers** to the **University** of Oxford. For when that Venerable Body thought it a work proper for them to wave their own Interest for the Publick good, and upon just expectation of correct Editions, had given way to the Printing many thousand Bibles, with design to abate the general Price of them in this Nation, at the loss of their own Private Advantage; they found that Bibles were not only Printed on ill Paper and *worse* Letter, and were scarce *legible* at first, and in a short time torn and worn out; but were *falsly* and *scandalously* set forth, with Omissions of many Material Passages, with the change of Negatives into Affirmatives, with many Thousand Faults and Errata's, to the great Prejudice of Religion, and the Dishonour of that Famous **University**. And when one of those Undertakers was charg'd with breach of Trust in Printing such a **Common-Prayer-Book** as could not be read, he fairly answered, '*That all Persons ought to have it by heart, and it was no matter whether it was read or not, so it was worn out in their hands*'. When this Answer was not fully satisfactory, and no Amendment was to be expected from a Man of those Principles. The **University** in general, and particularly most of the **Governors** thereof, thought it necessary for the Publick good and their own Honour, not to renew the Licence,[12] which was then determined, to those who had so plainly abus'd it, but generously to refuse such Endearments as were liberally offer'd to effect so base and scandalous a Design.

And at the same time it was the Prudence of that Body not to encourage a Monopoly, by granting that Licence to the King's Printers, who had a concurrent Right of Printing Bibles with the University; but to the Company of Stationers,[13] who claim'd no right in this kind, but under the University, and would be obliged in Interest to under-sell the King's Printers. The like effectual Care was expresly taken in the Agreement for moderating the Price of Bibles for the future; for imploying of all the Families formerly maintain'd by Printing in the University; for buying off all the imperfect Books of the former Undertakers, though *fraudulently* and *surreptitiously* begun: Insomuch that no Colour of Exception to the Agreement, either in point of Right or Honour, or indeed Favour was left, but the open denial of many of the Article of it, which as soon as read carry in them a Confutation of the Charge. And certain it is, That those Calumnies will gain credit only with those that have not the happiness to know the Character of the Persons abus'd, nor the unhappiness to be unacquainted with the Temper and Honesty of the Libellers.

And as to the Bill for Confirmation of the Liberties[14] of the University – Whoever reads it will find a *Saving* to the Interest of all *Private* Persons; so that the Invasion of any *Private* Right of Copies can be no more compass'd thereby than 'twas design'd.

All Patents, granted to any Persons or Bodies are not secur'd but sav'd, in this Act of Parliament. They still rest upon their own Bottom, which was good in Law before the Act of Parliament, and is only left so by it.

All those Patents are not properly Monopolies whereby common Right is taken away, and lodg'd in particular Persons, but are Assignments only of the King's Interest in those Copies to private Purchasers that claim under him. For if those Patents were determin'd or vacated, *Common-Prayer Books, Bibles, Psalters* and *Testaments* would not, as is vainly imagined, be of Common Right, but the Ownership would remain in the King, not only as they are Books of publick Influence; and subjected to his Care; but as they were Translated and Printed at his Charge and by his Command, and cannot be claim'd by any other Proprietor whatsoever.

In short, these Effects will follow the Expiration or Discontinuance of this Act, *viz.*

I. A Necessity upon the Government to invent, contrive, and use strains of Law and Power for the Discovery and Suppression of Libels.

II. The Increase of numberless Law-suits, and Questions about Property in Copies, and Piracy thereupon. And

III. The Impoverishment and Ruine of Hundreds of *English* Families, and the enriching of the *Dutch* Printers and Booksellers, by the free Importation of their Prints.

*All which are humbly submitted to the Consideration of the* PARLIAMENT.

*Reasons Humbly Offered for the Liberty of Unlicens'd Printing. To which is Subjoin'd, The Just and True Character of Edmund Bohun, the Licenser of the Press* (London, *c.* 24 January 1693). Wing, B3313; ESTC, R17412.

# REASONS
Humbly offered for the
## LIBERTY
OF
## Unlicens'd Printing.
To which is Subjoin'd,
The Just and True CHARACTER
OF
## Edmund Bohun,
The Licenser of the Press.

# REASONS humbly offered for the Liberty of Unlicensed Printing, &c.

AT our Leisure-Minutes (*Honoured Sir*) we have entertained our selves with Discourses about the *Printing-Act*, wherein you having seemed to like the Restraint of the Press, and that Law being now expiring, I shall here present you with the Reasons, which incline me to wish that the Press may be open to all, and may not continue to be under the Spanish Gag.[1]

In the discharge of this Undertaking, I shall lay before you; First, *The Inventors of Licensing Books*. Next, *That this Law avails nothing to the suppressing of Scandalous, Seditious and Libellous Books, which were (or ought to be) mainly intended to be suppress'd*. Lastly, *That it highly tends to the discouragement of all Learning, and the stop of Truth; not only by blunting Mens Abilities in what they know already, but by hindring and stunting the Discovery that might be yet further made both in Religious and Civil Wisdom*.[2]

This Project of *Licensing* crept out of the *Inquisition*.[3] After the Emperors became Christian, the Books of those whom they took to be grand Hereticks, were examined, refuted and condemned in the General Councils; and not till then were prohibited or burnt by Authority of the Emperor.[4]

The Primitive Councils and Bishops were wont only to declare what Books were not commendable, passing no further, but leaving it to each one's Conscience to read or lay by; till after the Year 800, as was observed by *Padre Paolo*,[5] the great Unmasker of the *Trentine* Council. After which time the Popes of *Rome* engrossing what they pleased of Political Rule into their own Hands, extended their Dominion over Mens Eyes, as they had before over their Judgments; burning and prohibiting to be read, what they fancied not: Yet they were sparing in their Censures, and the Books not many which they so dealt with; till Pope *Martin* the 5*th* by his Bull,[6] not only prohibited, but was the first that excommunicated the reading / of Heretical Books; for about that time *Wickliff* and *Huss* growing terrible to the Roman Church, were they who first drave the Papal Court to a stricter Policy of prohibiting: which Course Pope *Leo* the 10*th* and his Successors followed, until the Council of *Trent*, and the *Spanish Inquisition*, engendring together, brought forth, or perfected those Catalogues and *Expurging Indexes*,[7] that rake through the Entrails of many an old good Author, with a Violation worse than any could be offered to his Tomb. Nor did they stay in Matters Heretical, but any Subject that was not to their Palat, they either condemned, or had it streight into the *New Purgatory* of an *Index*. To fill up the Measure of Encroachment, their last Invention was to ordain, That *no Book, Pamphlet or Paper* should be printed, (as if St. *Peter* had bequeath'd them the

Keys of the Press also out of Paradise)[8] unless it were approv'd and licens'd under the Hands of two or three Glutton-Friars.

And thus, *Sir*, you have the *Inventors*, and the Original of *Book-Licensing* ripp'd up: We have it not, that can be heard of, from any Ancient State, or Polity, or Church; nor by any Statute left us by our Ancestors elder or later; nor from the Modern Custom of any Reformed City, or Church abroad; but from the most Antichristian Council, and the most Tyrannous Inquisition that ever inquir'd. Till then, Books were ever as freely admitted into the World as any other Birth; the Issue of the Brain was no more stifled than the Issue of the Womb: No envious *Juncto*[9] sate cross-legg'd over the Nativity of any Man's Intellectual Offspring; but if it prov'd a Monster, who denies but that it was justly burnt?[10]

But some will say, What tho the Inventors were bad, the thing for all that may be good? It may be so; yet if that thing be no such deep Invention, but obvious and easy for any Man to light on, and yet the best and wisest Commonwealths through all Ages and Occasions, have forborn to use it; and the falsest Seducers and Oppressors of Men, were the first who took it up, and to no other purpose but to obstruct and hinder the first Approach of *Reformation*; I am of those who believe that it will be a harder *Alchymy* than *Lullius* ever knew, to sublimate any good Use out of such an Invention.[11] Yet this only is what I request to gain from this Reason, that it may be held a dangerous and suspicious Fruit, as certainly it deserves, from the Tree that bore it, until I can dissect one by one the Properties it has.[12] /

I am not able to unfold, how this cautelous Enterprize of *Licensing* can be exempted from the Number of vain and impossible Attempts. And he who were pleasantly dispos'd, could not well avoid to liken it to the Exploit of that Gallant Man, who thought to pound up the Crows by shutting his Park-gate.[13]

Besides, how shall *the Licencers* themselves be confided in, unless we can confer upon them, as they assume to themselves above all others in the Land, the Grace of Infallibility and Uncorruptedness? And again, *The Law of Licensing* conduces nothing to the End for which it was fram'd:[14] If we think to regulate Printing, thereby to rectify Manners, we must also regulate all Recreations and Pastimes, all that is delightful to Man. No Musick must be heard, no Song be set or sung, but what is Grave. There must be *Licensing Dancers*; that no Gesture, Motion, or Deportment be taught our Youth, but what by their Allowance shall be thought Honest. It will ask more than the Work of twenty Licencers, to examine all the Lutes, the Violins, and the Ghittars in every House; they must not be suffer'd to prattle as they do, but must be Licens'd what they may say. And who shall silence all the Airs and Madrigalls that whisper Softness in Chambers? Then, what more National Corruption, for which *England* hears Ill abroad, than houshold Gluttony? Who shall be the Rectors of our daily Rioting? Our Garments also should be referr'd to the Licensing of some more grave Taylors, to see them cut into a less wanton Garb.[15] And a *Licensing Office* should be erected over the Tire-Women, to check the tow'ring height of Topknots and Commodes.[16] Who shall regulate all the mixt Conversation of our Youth, Male and Female together? Who shall appoint what shall be discours'd, what presum'd, and no further? Lastly, Who shall forbid and separate all idle Resort, all evil Company? These things will be; but how they shall be least hurtful, herein consists the grave and governing Wisdom of a State. *Licensing of Books* necessarily pulls along with it so many other kinds of Licensing, as will make us all both ridiculous and weary, and yet frustrate.[17] But grant the thing to be prohibited were only Books, it appears that the Law is far insufficient to the End which it intends. Do we not see, not once or oftner, but weekly, nay daily, that continued *Jacobite Libels* against our present happy Establishment, are printed and dispersed amongst us, for all that *Licensing* can do? Yet this is the prime Service a Man / would think, wherein this Law should give proof of it self. If it were executed you'l say. But certain, if Execution be remiss or blindfold now, and in this Particular, what will it be hereafter?[18]

Another Reason, whereby to make it plain that this Law will miss the End it seeks, may be from the Consideration of the Quality which ought to be in every *Licenser*. It cannot be deny'd, but that he who is made a Judg, to sit upon the Birth or Death of Books, whether they may be wasted into this World, or not, had need to be a Man above the common Measure, both Studious, Learned and Judicious; there may be else no mean Mistakes in the Censure of what is passable, or not; which is also no mean Injury. If he be of such Worth as behooves him, there cannot be a more tedious and unpleasing Journey-work, a greater loss of time levied upon his Head, than to be made the perpetual Reader of unchosen Books and Pamphlets, ofttimes huge Volumes.[19] And I must, with the leave of *the present Licencer, Mr.* Bohun, say, that his short Trial hath wearied him out already, as I shall demonstrate before I close this Letter, and his own Expressions and Excuses to them who make so many Journeys to sollicite his Licence, are Testimony enough.[20] Seeing therefore he who now possesses the Imployment, by all evident Signs, wishes himself well rid of it; and that no Man of Worth, none that is not a plain Unthrift of his own Hours, is ever likely to succeed him, except he mean to put himself to the Salary of *a Press-Corrector*, we may easily foresee what kind of *Licencers* we are to expect hereafter; either Ignorant, Imperious and Remiss, or basely Mercenary. This is what I design'd, to shew wherein this Law cannot conduce to that End, whereof it bears the Intention.[21]

I lastly proceed from the *no Good* it can do, to the *manifest Hurt* it must cause, in being first the greatest Discouragement and Affront that can be offer'd to Learning and Learned Men; and I affirm, that so far to distrust the Judgment and the Honesty of one who hath but a common Repute in Learning, and never yet offended, as not to count him fit to print his Mind without a *Tutor* and

*Examiner*, is the greatest Displeasure and Indignity to a free and knowing Spirit, that can be put upon him. What Advantage is it to be a Man, over it is to be a Boy at School; if we have only scap'd the *Ferula*, to come under the *Fescue*[22] of an *Imprimatur*? If serious and elaborate Writings, as if they were no / more than the Theme of a Grammar-Lad under his Pedagogue, must not be utter'd without the Cursory Eyes of *a temporizing and extemporizing*[23] *Licencer*. He who is not trusted with his own Actions, his drift not being known to be evil, and standing to the Hazard of *Law and Penalty*, has no great Argument to think himself reputed in the Common-wealth wherein he was born, for other than a Fool or a Foreigner.[24]

When a Man writes to the World, he summons up all his Reason and Deliberation to assist him; he searches, meditates, is industrious, and likely consults and confers with his judicious Friends; after all which done, he takes himself to be inform'd in what he writes, as well as any that writ before him: If in this he must be still mistrusted and suspected, unless he carry all his considerate Diligence to the hasty View of *an unleasur'd Licenser*, perhaps much his younger, perhaps far his Inferiour in Judgment, perhaps one who never knew the Labour of Book-writing; and if he be not repuls'd or slighted, must appear in Print like a Puny with his *Guardian*, and his *Censor's* Hand on the back of his Title-Page, to be his *Bail* and *Surety*, that he is no *Idiot* or *Seducer*; it cannot be but a Dishonour and Derogation to the Author, to the Book, to the Privilege and Dignity of Learning.[25]

Further (Honored Sir) it seems to me an Undervaluing and Vilifying of our whole Nation; I cannot set so light by all the Invention, the Art, the Wit, the grave and solid Judgment which is in *England*, as that it can be comprehended in any twenty Capacities how good soever,[26] much less that it should not pass except their Superintendence be over it, except it be sifted and strain'd with their Strainers; that it should be uncurrant without their manual Stamp. We must not think to make a Staple Commodity of all the Knowledge in the Land, to mark and license it like our broad-Cloth, and our Wool-Packs: What is it but a Servitude like that imposed by the *Philistines*, not to be allowed the sharpening of our own Axes and Coulters, but we must repair from all Quarters to twenty *Licensing Forges*.[27]

There is yet behind of what I purposed to lay open, the incredible Loss and Detriment that this *Plot of Licensing* puts us to, more than if the *French* at Sea should stop up all our Havens, and Ports, and Creeks; it hinders and retards the Importation of our richest Merchandize, *Truth*: Nay it was first establish'd and put in Practice by *Antichristian Malice and Mystery*, on set Purpose to / extinguish, if it were possible, the Light of *Reformation*, and to settle Falshood, little differing from that Policy wherewith the *Turk* upholds his *Alcoran*, by the Prohibition of Printing.[28] Though all the Winds of Doctrine should be let loose to play upon the Earth, so *Truth* be in the Feild, we do injuriously, by Licensing and Prohibiting, to misdoubt her Strength: Let her and Falshood grapple. Whoever knew *Truth* put to the worst, in a free and open Encounter? Her confuting is the best and surest Suppressing.[29] What a Collusion is this, when as we are exhorted by the wise Man to use Diligence, *to seek for Wisdom as for hidden Treasure, early and late*, that another Law shall injoin us to know nothing but by Statute?[30]

When a Man hath been labouring the hardest Labour in the deep Mines of Knowledg, hath furnished out his Findings in all their Equipage, drawn forth his Reasons as it were a Battel rang'd, scatter'd and defeated all Objections in his way, calls out his Adversary into the Plain, offers him the Advantage of Wind and Sun, if he please; only that he may try the Matter by dint of Argument: for his Opponent then to sculk, to lay Ambushments, to keep a narrow Bridg of *Licensing* where the Challenger should pass. Though it be Policy in Souldiership, is but Weakness and Cowardize in the Wars of *Truth*: For who knows not that *Truth is strong next to the Almighty*? she needs no Policies, nor Stratagems, nor Licensings to make her victorious; those are the Shifts and the Defences that Error uses against her Power.

There were not a few Men of Note about the time of the late happy Revolution, who by their *unlicensed Books*, to the Contempt of an *Imprimatur*; first cured that *Cataract* that blinded our Eyes, and inabled the People to see Day. It may be reasonably hoped that none of those will be the Perswaders to renew upon us the Bondage which they themselves have wrought so much Good by contemning, and execute the most *Dominican* Part of the *Inquisition* over us: Should they be guilty in this Respect, I conclude that the Change of their Condition hath puffed them up more than their late Experience of *Tyrannous Practices* hath made them wise.[31]

And as for regulating the Press, surely no better Advice can be given, than that no Book be printed, unless the *Publisher* and the *Author's* Name, or at least the *Publisher's* be registred. Those which otherwise come forth, if they be found mischievous and libellous, the Fire and the Executioner will be the timeliest and the most effectual Remedy that Man's Prevention can use.[32] /

To conclude[33] (Sir) I shall lay before you some few of the ill Practices which have been used under the Pretence of *Licensing* Books. In the Beginning of the Reign of King *Charles* I. Bishop *Laud* was charged by a Petition of the *Printers* and *Booksellers* to the House of *Commons*, that the Licensing of Books being wholly restrained to him and his *Chaplains*, he allowed Books which favoured Popery, but denied to license such as were written against it.[34] And I remember that I have somewhere read a Remark which that great and good Man Archbishop *Abbot* made upon *Laud's* Licensing, and 'tis to this Effect, if not in his very Words; *To publish a good Book was made then a Sin, and an ill one a Vertue; and while one came out with Authority, the other could not have a Dispensation;*

so that we seem'd to have got an Expurgatory Press, *though not an* Index: *and the most religious Truth must be expung'd and suppressed in order to the false and secular Interest of some of the Clergy.*[35]

To come nearer to our Times. Mr. *Baxter* wrote his *Saints Rest*, about the Year 1651. and it was often printed before the Restoration; but the famous *LeStrange* having by his Solicitation procured the *Printing Act* to pass in 1662. this Book was then licensed to be printed by one Dr. *Gregg*, the Bishop of *London*'s Chaplain; nevertheless I am assured that it coming to be reprinted in the late King's Reign, it was stopp'd, the Sheets seized, and an Information brought against the Printers in the Crown-Office.[36] Also in the same Reign the Assemblies Catechism[37] being found Printing by one *Howe*, the poor Man was indicted for it at the *Old Baily*, and forc'd to leave his Trade, and fly the Kingdom. And yet at this time such Books as were wrote to promote *Popery and Tyranny*, were printed and published without Controul.

Sir, In a great Hurry I presume to hint these things to you, and I will hope that the Wisdom of this Parliament will provide against such wicked Practices.

January 17, 1693

I am
Your most humble Servant
J.M. /

## POSTSCRIPT.

Now (Sir) as you desired by your last, which I received just as I was going to seal this Letter, I proceed to give you something of the Character of *Edmund Bohun*,[38] the present *Licenser* at the Press, in the doing whereof I shall pursue this Method:

1. *Lay down his Principles as to the English Government.*
2. *His Notions about our Parliaments. And,*
3. *His Practices in the Late Reigns, and also under the present, and particularly in the Post of Licensing.*

To begin: As to the Government; take a Taste of this Gentleman from his Pamphlet, called, *A Defence of Sir* Robert Filmer, *against the Paper left by* Algernon Sidney, *Esq; before his Execution*, 7 *Dec.* 1683. (printed for *Walter Kettilby* in St. *Paul's-Church-Yard*.)[39]

(*Pag.* 6.) 'In Effect (saith he) the King doth swear to keep no Laws but such as in his Judgment are upright, and those not literally always, but according to the Equity of his Conscience joined with Mercy.'

'And if a King did strictly swear to observe all the Laws, he could not without Perjury give his Consent to the repealing or abrogating of any Statute by Act of Parliament.'

(*Pag.* 7.) 'If it please God for the Correction of the Prince, or Punishment of the People, to suffer Princes to be removed, and others to be placed in their Rooms, either by the Factions of the Nobility, or Rebellion of the People, in all such Cases, the Judgment of God, who hath Power to give and take away Kingdoms, is most just, yet the Ministry of Men, who execute God's Judgments without Commission, is sinful and damnable.'

(*Pag.* 8.) 'I will give the best Judgment I can (saith my Author), when and how far Subjects are bound to submit to an Usurper / I say, taking an Usurper in the right Notion, for one that hath no lawful or just Title, the Subjects are bound to resist him, and stand for the lawful Heir and his Posterity, as long as they are or can be known, as far as is possible, without apparent Destruction.

'But if the right Heir or Family fail, or is extinguish'd, then that Obligation fails, and the Event is to be taken as the Declaration of the Will of God; and the Heirs of the Usurper will have a good Title against any other Person or Family in the World. And that Injury which Usurpers do, is reserved to the Justice of a Righteous and Almighty God, who will punish them severely in the next World, if they escape in this.'

'I say (quoth he) that in every Society or Community under Heaven, that is perfect within it self, and doth not depend upon another, there must be an absolute and uncontroulable Power fixed some where, which may indispensably and irresistibly dispose of the Estates and Persons of the Subject within that Society or Community.'

(*Pag.* 12.) 'He (*Colonel SIDNEY*, saith my Author) has another odd Notion, That though a Prince, who hath no Title, puts by, or puts out one that hath an undoubted Title to an Hereditary Kingdom; yet if he have the Consent of the People (which he calls an Act of State) he is no Usurper, because he obtains the Crown by the Consent of a willing Nation. Than which (saith the Remarker) there can be nothing more injurious to Hereditary Kingdoms. Whereas the true Notion of an Usurper is, one that obtains the Possession of a Throne, to which he hath no rightful Title, whether he come in by the Consent of the People, or without it, by Force, Fraud, or Faction.'

In the next Place I lead you (Sir) to *Bohun's Preface to Sir* Robert Filmer's *Patriarcha; or the Natural Power of Kings*; printed for Mr. *Chiswel*, 1685.[40] whence I collect these ensuing Positions.

'*England* is under a Monarchy; and it is an Imperial Monarchy too, depending upon none but God Almighty. Nor can any Power upon Earth set the least

Limitation to it against the Consent of the proper Monarch for the time being, without Treason, and Rebellion, and Perjury; and if please Sacrilege too. /

'If a Prince breaks his Oath, and acts against his Laws, he is not responsible to his Subjects: For if by Tyranny he should forfeit his Crown, it does not Escheat[41] to the People, but to God, who is the sole Disposer of Kingdoms, and Punisher of Princes.'

☞ 'Now truly (*saith Bohun*) I would advise this Gentleman (*meaning the Author of* Patriarcha non Monarcha)[42] never to marry, for fear his Children turn Rebels against him, and teach him, by their Example, how dangerous a thing it is to read Lectures of Disobedience to Parents, in an Age in which Children, without such Lectures, are too apt to Rebel and Resist those to whom they owe both their Being and Well-being in the World.

'God extends his Judgments to the third and fourth Generation (*quoth he*). Now as no Usurpation can succeed without God's Permission, so much less can it establish it self, or continue long without his particular Blessing and Providence; who being the Sovereign Proprietor of Kingdoms, may, without Injury to any Man, dispose of them to whom he pleases: but this being no way to be known but by the Event, when a Family have enjoyed a Kingdom, or any thing else ABOVE FOUR DESCENTS, Men are not to look back to see how it was acquired, but to acquiesce in the Pleasure of God discovered by his Providence; and the Subjects of that Prince are THEN (*after four Descents*) bound to serve and defend him, as well as if he could derive his Pedigree from the eldest Son of *Noah*.

'Yet this is no Encouragement to Traitors to rebel and usurp upon their Princes; for they that first begin these Usurpations, are liable at once, both to the Wrath of God for rebelling against their lawful Princes, and to the Justice of those Princes too; and do very often pay dearly for it, and are disappointed in this World in the first Attempt, or after a short time in their Posterity, but however are certain never to escape the Justice of God in the World to come.' –

☞ '*Where there is no Right, there is no Usurpation*: As if *Lambert* had deposed *Cromwel*[43] and set up himself, he had not been an Usurper upon him or his Family, but upon the King who had the Right.

'O. Cromwel *was invested with the Power by the People* or Army, or who you please; but yet for all that, every Person that was / executed during his Reign, was murdered, *Oliver* not having any lawful Power of Life and Death, which the People could not give him, it does not appear God had, *his late Majesty, in whom that Right was, being all that while kept out by Violence.*' –

'Without doubt Princes ought not to abuse their Power; but if they do, their Subjects ought not to take Arms to revenge their Quarrel: for whether it be sooner or later, that will not mend the Matter, ☞ *they are Rebels whenever they do it, be the Cause what it will.*' –

'The Prince is the Minister of *God*, the only *unaccountable Person* to any but *God*; and *God is bound in Honour* to assert him against all that shall rise up against him. All violent and *undutiful Resistance is a Rebellion against God Almighty*, and can never go unpunished in this or the next World, *be the cause or Pretence what it will.*'

Take next (Sir) *Bohun*'s Positions about Government, as I transcribe them from his third Part of his *Address to the Freemen and Freeholders of the Nation*; printed for *George Wells* in St. *Paul*'s Church-Yard, 1683.[44]

*Two things* (saith he, *Pag.* 63. of that villanous Libel) *I will lay down as undoubted Rules or Maxims.*

'1. That the Kingdom of *England* is an Hereditary Kingdom or Monarchy, which for Ages hath gone to the next Heirs of the Blood-Royal, without any Election or Consent of the People, otherwise than by acknowledging their lawful Right derived from God, by their Blood to them.

'2. That this Hereditary Monarchy was set up at first, and hath been since upheld and maintained by the Providence of God.

'From which two I will infer this Conclusion; ☞ That *whoever shall attempt to alter this Right of Succession, without a manifest Revelation,* (which is not now to be expected) *is a notorious Usurper upon the Right of the Person who is to succeed, be the Pretence for it what it will*; and *a Rebel* against that Providence which gave him that Right.

'Nor will the Ancient Rebellions, Usurpations and Disorders, which have happen'd in this Kingdom, justify them that shall begin them again.

'Now if it should please God so to order it, that the Duke (*of York*)[45] should, at his Majesty's Death, be the next Heir to / his Crown; I cannot see how any Humane Power shall prevent his Succession to it, but by encroaching upon his Right, and by rebelling against the Divine Providence that gave it to him.'

(*Pag.* 64.) 'So that (saith my Author) *be the Inconveniences which shall follow upon such a Succession, what they will or can be, we must submit to them upon pain of Rebellion against both God and his Anointed, our lawful Prince.*' –

'So that *I conclude, neither the Church of* England, *nor any of her Children, will be guilty of a Rebellion against such a Prince, COME WHAT WILL COME.*'

My Author saith, (*Pag.* 78. of his second part of his *Address*) *I wonder in what part of the Gospel, Men learned to defend Christ's Religion by Rebellion: But we must know this is pure Scotch, Calvinistical, Jesuitical Doctrine.*' –

2. I come now (*Sir*) to observe to you this highly meriting *Licencer*'s Opinion of our Parliaments.

In his first part of his *Address to the Freemen and Freeholders of the Nation*, he thus declares himself, (*Pag.* 3.) *I was bred a Dissenter from the Religion now estab-*

*lished. A GREAT ADMIRER OF PARLIAMENTS,* &c. *– But I must confess I have seen great Reason to alter in part from what I was,* &c.

He saith, (Pag. 26.) 'The Dissenters shuffled such Members into *the Long Loyal Parliament,* (The *Pensionary Parliament*[46] he means) upon the several Deaths that happen'd during the many Years that Parliament was kept on Foot, that by this means *they have made Parliaments almost Impracticable,* and at last made that *Long Loyal Parliament* to act so much unlike it self, that his Majesty, who for many Years lived with it with all the Caresses of a happy Marriage, was yet at length forced to give her a Bill of Divorce, after she had lost that Loyalty and Affection, and dutiful Behaviour which she had before shewed towards him.'

He proceeds (*Pag.* 44.) 'By the Frauds of the *Jesuits* Abroad, and the Fury of the *Dissenters* within Doors, *this Long, Loyal, Healing, truly Protestant Parliament fell,* and with it the Terror of *France,* the Bulwark of our *Protestant Allies,* the Pillars of the Monarchy, the Peace and Prosperity of the *British Isles,* and the Glory of *England.* May my Reader pardon me, if I drop a few Tears at the Funeral of so great a Body, and which had deserved so well of his Majesty, the Church, the State, and / all *Europe*; and *I could almost say with* David, *Would God I had died for thee.*'[47]

In his second part of his *Address to Freemen and Freeholders,* Pag. 15. My Author giving an Account of the Parliament which met the 6*th* of *March,* 1678/9, proceeds thus.

'Friday, 4 *Apr. An Act for the better discovery and more speedy Conviction of Popish Recusants,* sent down from *the Lords,* was read the second time, and committed to a Committee; who were also to bring in a Clause to prevent any of the Royal Family from Matching with Popish Recusants.'

Upon which he thus interrogates that excellent House of Commons: *Was not this that Tacking of things of a different Nature together, which his Majesty had resolved against*?

He tells us, Pag. 20. '*The Commons* resolved Saturday the 26th of *March,* 1679, to sit the next Day to consider of the best means to secure and preserve the Kings Person, and also the Protestant Religion, against the Attempts of the Papists, both in the Reign of his Majesty and his Successors.

'And *accordingly they did sit and begun the Day very inauspiciously, &c.* – They voted that a Bill be brought in to banish all Papists, or reputed Papists, from *London,* &c.

'Then it was Resolved, *Nemine contradicente,* That the Duke of *York,* being a Papist, and the hopes of his coming such to the Crown, had given the greatest Countenance and Encouragement to the present Conspirators, and the designs of the Papists, the King and the Protestant Religion.

'*Nemine contradicente* (quoth he, Pag. 37.) *shews* the strength of the Party, and not the Consent of the whole House.'

Pag. 31. 'On Sunday, *May* 11, (quoth our present Licencer) The Commons voted that a Bill be brought in to disable the Duke of *Yorke* to inherit the Crown.'

This (as he affirms) proved the Occasion of breaking all the following Parliaments to this Day (1683),[48] and thereby to secure the Popish Lords[49] in the Tower from Trial, and to prevent all the excellent Laws that were then under Consideration. And finally, it proved an Obstacle of Union between the King and the Houses, to the great Advantage of our Enemies at Home and Abroad; to the great hazard of the Nation, and more especially of the Protestant-Religion, which was pretended to be secured by it.' /

My Author (*Pag.* 39, 40, 41.) remarking still upon this Parliament, puts down the particular Votes and Proceedings of *the Commons* (on the 23d of *May*, 1679) to discover *the Pensioners* of the last Parliament; and thus reflects upon them (Pag. 51). To conclude this matter, *As there was never any Law to prohibit Parliament-Men from taking the Liberality of our Princes in time of Parliament, so there was the greater reason for it in this Parliament, which LASTED TOO LONG to the Ruine of many Gentlemen of small Estates, who were Members of it.*

My Author here verifies our common Proverb, that *Liars should have good Memories*. He had now put off his Mourning, and wip'd away his Tears for the Dissolution of his *Long-Loyal-Parliament*, and forgot his Expression (*Pag.* 44) of his first part, I could almost say with David, *Would God I had died for Thee*. And yet here we have him of Opinion that this Parliament lasted too long, *&c.*

But not to interrupt him, see what follows (*Pag.* 47) On the 27*th* of *May*, the King Prorogued both Houses to the 14*th* day of *August.*

'The News of this Prorogation (*saith he*) was no sooner spread, but the Cry was taken up by the *zealous Impostors*, that it was done of purpose to hinder the Trial of the Popish Lords.'

My Author (*Pag.* 49) begins a long Relation of *a Scotish Rebellion* in 1679;[50] and (Pag. 74) saith, 'I cannot but admire the Providence of God in preventing this *Presbyterian Plot*, by a Prorogation in the very Nick of Time, without which this Rebellion would in all likelihood have had much countenance from some in *England* who encouraged it under-hand.'

My Author throughout his *third Part of his Address to the Freemen and Freeholders of the Nation*, most impudently slanders that highly meriting Parliament, which was summon'd to meet at *Westminster* the 17*th* of *Oct.* 1679, but by many Prorogations was kept off till *October* 1680. For Instance,

He tells us (*Pag.* 46) Mr. *Harbord*[51] reported an Address for the Support of the Kings Person and Government, and the Protestant Religion, *&c.*

'What Protestant Religion (*quoth the Remarker*) that by Law establish'd, or another as contrary to it as Popery?'

The effect saith he, (*Pag.* 47) of this *specious Address* was to possess the People what stout Champions the *Presbyterians* are / against *Popery*; and to let the World know what a horrid Opinion they had of *that silly impossible Meal-Tub-Plot.*'[52]

He proceeds (*Pag.* 49) saying, On the 30*th* of *Octob.* They (*the House of Commons*) passed a Vote, That *their Votes should be printed.*

*But for this Vote* (saith he) *it might have been difficult to have known what they had done, SO AS TO HAVE CHARG'D THEM. – This printing their Votes could be designed for nothing but to enable the People to pass a Judgment on their Actions; One of which Number I am,* (quoth he).

He proceeds (*Pag.* 50) saying, One Hardwich *being accused of some Misdemeanors against a Witness in the Popish Plot, was ordered to be sent for in Custody of the Serjeant at Arms, to answer the same.*

He now passes his Judgment upon them thus, ☞ *This was to punish a Man before they knew whether he were guilty or no, upon a bare Suggestion.*

*He* (Hardwich) *was continued in Custody during the Pleasure of the House* (Not one tittle, (saith *One of the Many*) being inserted concerning the Nature of his Misdemeanors). (Pag. 51) *Mr. Licencer* informs us, that it was *Resolved*, Nemine contradicente, *That a Bill be brought in for the better Uniting of Protestants.*

This also offended him, and he saith, *It was a New Name for a Toleration.*

Turn now, I pray you, Sir, to Pag. 53. and you will read thus; *Resolved, Nemine contradicente, That it is the Opinion of this House, That the Acts of Parliament made in the Reigns of Queen* Elizabeth *and King* James *against Popish Recusants, ought not to be, extended against Protestant Dissenters.*

But my Author is of another Mind; for he saith, *It would have been well if we had been told why they ought not to be extended to all that break them, one as well as another.*

Now he, who in his Day was (as a Justice of Peace in *Suffolk*)[53] as furious a Prosecutor of *Protestant Dissenters* as was to be found in *England*, would do well to tell us the Name of one *Papist* upon whom he executed these Laws.

He saith, (Pag. 54.) *A Bill to disable the Duke of* York *was read the second time.*

Upon which he gives this Opinion, (Pag. 55.) *This Bill perhaps may be made to appear to be of another Nature than was / pretended and rather against any thing than Popery.*

*I am sure* (saith he, *pag.* 58.) *that they* (the Commons) *became more hated than feared by their Proceedings.* –

And (*pag.* 60.) 'On the 15*th* of *November*, the Bill for disabling the Duke of York was read the first time in the House of Lords; and the Question being put,

Whether it should be read again? the House divided; No's, 63. Yea's, 30. So it was thrown out, THE BISHOPS ALL APPEARING AGAINST THE BILL, EXCEPT THREE.'

*Pag.* 71. 'To me it seems (*saith my Author*) the Reasons upon which the Bill of Exclusion is founded, are weak and unconcluding; and that no Malice could have contrived a more effectual way to hasten those Calamities upon us, which it pretends to prevent.'

Read him again, *pag.* 99. 'It (*the passing the Bill to exclude the Duke of* York) is so far from preventing our Calamities, that it will ascertain them at his Majesty's Death, with the Addition of a Civil War, &c.'

He proceeds (*pag.* 101.) 'On the 24*th* of *December,* they (*the Commons*) took occasion to chastise *Richard Thompson,*[54] Clerk, very severely; for he having been complained of by some of the Dissenters, who were now White-Boys,[55] and the Sober Loyal Protestants; The House remitted it to a Committee, &c.

'He was accused for several Expressions both in Preaching and Discourse: He said, it seems, the Presbyterians were such Persons as the Devil blush'd at. Accused *Hambden*[56] for choosing to rebel, rather than pay Ship-money, which he said was the King's Right by Law.

'He had said, There was great Noise of a Popish Plot, but there was nothing in it but a Presbyterian Plot.

'He was accused to have approved of the Doctrine of the Church of *Rome* in the Points of Justification, Auricular Confession, Penance, Extreme Unction, Chrism[57] in Baptism, &c.

'Upon inquiry I find (saith *Bohun*) notwithstanding all this Clamour, the Man hath a great and good Report for his Piety, Learning and Prudence; but his Zeal for the Religion establish'd, drew this Storm upon him from the exasperated Dissenters, who never stick thus to blast the Fame of Good Men, when it serves their ill Designs.' /

But what have we next? Why, *pag.* 103. 'It was Resolved, *Nemine contradicente,* That no Member of this House shall accept of any Office, or Place of Profit from the Crown, without leave of the House; or any Promise of any such Office or Place of Profit, during such time as he shall continue a Member of the House.

'It seems (*quoth the Remarker*) they had discovered that some of their zealous Men were selling themselves to the Court-Party for Preferment, and prepared this Vote to keep the Party together.'

*Pag.* 106. 'The House ordered Mr. *Thompson, Jan.* the 5*th,* to give Security to answer an Impeachment.

'I can see no reason (*saith Mr. Censurer*) why he should be prosecuted by an Impeachment:– He might much better have been proceeded against in the Spiritual or Civil Courts, but that his blaspheming *Calvin* and the Loyal Presbyterian Protestants, would have signified nothing there.'

*Pag.* 111. 'Having taken care (*saith he*) to chastise the Great Men, who as they (*the Commons*) believed had opposed them in the great business of the Bill of Exclusion. In the next place, they undertook to chastise his Majesty himself; and if their Design had taken effect, as it is to be hoped it never will, his Majesty and all his Successors should have known what it is to anger a House of Commons.'

*Pag.* 115. 'Had the King (*quoth the Babler*) but yielded to these Protestants at large, in the point of the Duke of *York*; they would soon have taught him, how little was to be gotten by complying with Men of their Temper; the only Service they did was to the French King.'

*Pag.* 117. 'The Bill for uniting Protestants, is a perfect Toleration of almost all other Religions except Popery.'

*Pag.* 119. ☞ 'So that the Day a Toleration, or, which is all one, an Union amongst Protestants, is settled, the Monarchy must be made Absolute, or it will not stand.'

*Pag.* 120. My Author coming to conclude, saith, 'My dearest Countrymen! I humbly beg you to reflect seriously on this in time, if it be not now too late, and unite heartily with his Majesty, our sweet-natur'd Sovereign, and the Religion Established, *&c.* – I AM A PRIVATE PERSON, and expect so to live and die. I HAVE NO AIM AT ANY PUBLICK IMPLOYMENT, or Place of Trust, nor any Means to attain it, if I had.

'As to those Gentlemen of the House of Commons (*saith he*) / who may possibly take offence at what I have written, I desire they would in cold Blood consider what they have done, and then let them think of me what they please: for IF EVER FACTION, ANGER, AND ILL DESIGNS were entertained by so great a Body of Men as the Major Part of this House was, it is apparent they were here.'

Allow me, *Sir*, in the next place to entertain you with a few Rarities, which I extract out of this degenerate Wretch's Libel, which he calls, *Reflections on a Pamphlet, stiled, A just and modest Defence of the Proceedings of the two last Parliaments*, (printed for *George Walls*, 1683.)[58]

I pass over many particular Instances of his notoriously scandalous Reflections, whereby he impudently traduces the Members of the *Westminster* and *Oxford* Parliaments; and intreat you to cast your Eye upon *pag.* 33. of this envenom'd Libel, where you will find him thus speaking.

'Though his Majesty hath given us the Opportunities of chusing three Parliaments one after another, we have not been able to send up one that has not fallen into those little Excesses, which have occasioned their Dissolution. And at length his Majesty is forced for some time to keep us without one, to try if Fasting will bring us into our Senses again: and in the mean time the Noise of the Popish Plot is drowned by new and more surprizing Attempts of the Whigs.'

*Pag.* 43. 'I believe (*saith the Incendiary*) all *Europe* will bear me witness, that all the great things the French King hath done, were in a great measure owing to the Disorders of our English Parliaments.' –

*Pag.* 44. Our Author proceeds, saying, '*France* feared the Long Loyal Parliament more than threescore such as have followed it.'

*Pag.* 95. 'No Act of Parliament can extinguish the Duke's Right, which God and Nature hath given him.'

*Pag.* 109. 'The Privileges of the House of Commons are not much unlike the Power claimed by the Pope, which is to judg all Men, and to be judged by no Man.'

*Pag.* 116, 'He (*King Charles the second*) connived so long at the Proceedings of the last Parliament of *Westminster*, that many Men wondred, and some murmured.' /

Having thus, Sir, given you some Touches of the Principles of this Libeller at the Press, I pass on to the last thing which I promised you, which is to give a few Instances of his Practices in the late Reigns, and also under the present, and particularly in his Licensing Post.

1. He was a vehement Stickler for the Surrender of Charters; and in the Dedication of his third Address to the *Abhorrers of Parliaments*, whom he stiles *the Loyal Persons* who addressed King *Charles* the Second for his Declaration,[59] (meaning that which was a Libel upon two Excellent Parliaments) you will find this lewd Expression; 'That which of all other things would the most speedily and effectually secure the Nation from a Relapse into Misery and Confusion, is, A SURRENDER OF THE CHARTERS of the Corporations into his Majesty's Hands, and the taking out of new ones, with such Restrictions as he and his Council think fit.'

And you may see a dainty Reason for so doing. (*pag.* 19. of that third Address) 'For all the World (his worst Enemies not excepted) acknowledg King *Charles* the Second to be A PRINCE OF A GODLIKE GOODNESS and Clemency, even to his Enemies.'

2. *Bohun*, as a Justice in *Suffolk*, was for many Years the common Disturber of the Peace of that County, in the time of King *Charles* the Second; and that not only by a rigorous Execution of the Laws against Protestant Dissenters, but by encouraging and upholding most villanous Informers in manifest Perjuries; particularly *Keeble* and *Barrell*, two vile Wretches, being upon a very fair Trial, and full Evidence, convicted of Perjury at the Assizes for that County. And a Motion being afterwards made for Judgment against him in the Court of *King's-Bench*, this Tory made a Swear for them, and by a written Affidavit made Oath, that they were *honest Sons of the Church*; by reason whereof Judgment could never

be obtained, though frequently moved for by Mr. Serjeant *Trenchard*, and Mr. Serjeant *Tremaine*, now Members of the present House of Commons.

3. The Law for Liberty to Dissenters, made since the happy Revolution, having put him out of Business in *Suffolk*, he (if his own / Word may be taken) was sent for to *London*, and made *Licenser of the Press*, and *Justice of the Peace* in *Middlesex*,[60] though, as I before told you, he had declared (*pag.* 120 of his third Address) That he expected to live and die a private Person, and had no Aim at any Publick Imployment or Place of Trust, nor any means to attain it, if he had. I will not pretend to guess by what means he attained his present Post, nor who invited him thereto, but am confident if he brought any Recommendation out of his *Native Country*, it must be from Dr. *Sancroft*.[61] Well, whoever sent for him, or whatever his Merit was, he is thrust into a Place beyond his Aim, and soon gave Evidence of his flaming Zeal: You may read his Opinion (*pag.* 10, of his first Address) 'Presbytery was hatch'd in Rebellion, and is totally inconsistent with Monarchy.'

Being now fix'd in his *Libelling Post*, he exerts himself according to his bigotted Principle, and licenses many Pamphlets on the side of the *suspended Bishops*, and other *Non-jurors*, and highly favouring the *Jacobite Interest*; when on the other hand he allows Libels to pass into the World, with the Face of Authority, to disparage and vilify *Protestant Dissenters* in this Kingdom; of whom he affirmed, *pag.* 12. of his second Address, That *they should be no more encouraged than Pyrates, and the common Enemies of Mankind*: and rests not there, but hath insolently fallen upon the Church of *Scotland*, and its present Establishment by Parliament, as is evident by the villanous Libels which *Blaspheming Hindmarsh*,[62] the *Cornhil* Bookseller, hath published under his Protection. And we are not to wonder at what he hath done in this Respect, for he lays it down as a *State-Maxim* (*pag.* 11. of his first Address) *Kings must be the irreconcilable Enemies of the Presbyterian Discipline, as long as they mean to be Masters of their Power.*

This *Apostatized Presbyterian*:[63] had asserted (*pag.* 9. of his first *Address*) 'That the Dissenters have mortal Feuds amongst themselves, and can no more agree one with another than with the Church of *England*.' But (*pag.* 44.) he complaining, says, 'They made up their own Breaches, and reconciled their own Differences. – And now (saith he) O my Country-men (of *Suffolk*) are these Vipers to be cherished in your Bosom any longer? Can you think a few fruitless Wishes can suppress them?' The Dissenters having been taught Wit, to the Grief of this Gentleman and others of his Complexion; those of them called *Presbyterian* and / *Congregational*, came to the dreaded *Union*; upon which out flies one *Davis*, in Print, with this Stately Allowance.

'You are hereby allowed to Print and Vend a certain Book, intituled, *Truth and Innocency vindicated, against Falshood and Malice*, &c. written by *Richard-Davis*;[64] and for so doing this shall be your sufficient Warrant.'
Novemb. 4. 1692.                                                      Edmund Bohun.

The Vindication of *Truth* and *Innocency* is indeed a very good, and oft-times an absolutely necessary Work, and that in Print too upon some Occasions. Now for the Rarity of this Vindication, I shall transcribe two or three Paragraphs out of this Book.

(*Pag.* 21.) 'He would be an happy Man that should break all the Churches in *England* to Pieces.'

(*Pag.* 33.) 'I conclude (saith my Author) this Union (of the Presbyterian and Congregational Churches) was untimely, because I observed that the greatest Numbers that were to make up this Union, were such as had forsook the *CAUSE* and *BANNER* of *Christ* (they had gone to Church and heard *COMMON-PRAYER*) in a Day of Adversity; and since had wip'd their Mouths clean, and justified themselves, and yet will be accounted great Dissenters still.'

'I (saith he, *pag.* 36.) dreaded the Design of this UNION, lest it should not be only a means framed for to jump into Benefices – but also a DEVICE OF SATAN to stop all the Dawnings of NEW LIGHT about Faith and Order.'

Sir, I shall not pretend to descant upon these Doctrines, because I am equally conscious that 'tis no more my Province to paraphrase upon them, than 'twas that *Schismatick Bohun*'s to license them. For I remember *the Act for preventing Abuses in Printing*, &c. 14 *Car.* 2. directs, that the Principal Secretaries of State, or one of them (it seems there were two in that Day)[65] *or some by their or one of their Appointments, should license all Books of History concerning the State of the Realm, or other Books concerning any Affairs of State.*

Indeed Sir *Roger Le Strange* extended this, to hook into his Commission, under the *Secretary*, the Licensing of the *Play-House-Bills*, for which there might then be some Reason, it being in that / Day *a grand Affair of State* to debauch the People. But it cannot enter my Head, that it is so in this happy Reign, to set *Protestants* together by the Ears; to break all the Churches in *England* to Pieces. To assert them to be *Renegades* from the *Banner* of *Christ*, who shall hear a Church-of-*England*-Minister; and that the honest and Christian Design of uniting Protestants, is a Device of Satan, to stop the Dawnings of *New Light*. And I humbly conceive that the Act did refer such high Points as these to the Judgment of *Divines*; for it saith expresly, (after it directs who shall license *Law-Books*; who, Books concerning *Heraldry*) *That all other Books, whether of Divinity, Physick, Philosophy, or whatsoever other Science or Art, shall be licensed and allowed by the Lord Archbishop of* Canterbury, *and Lord Bishop of* London, *or one of them, or by their, or one of their Appointments.*

But I leave *Bohun* to answer his Usurpation upon my Lord Archbishop of *Canterbury*, and my Lord of *London*, and shall only say that I do not believe that their Lordships, or any of their Chaplains would have suffered such Doctrines as fill the Book I mention, to have seen the Sun under their Allowance. But the *Dissenters* are *Vipers*; and Justice *Bohun* (their Plague in *Suffolk*, when in Power) grew pettish, when the Law delivered them from his Rage; and having leap'd into *London*, doth now persecute them at the Press; and lest their Breaches should be made up, he claps his Hands, and indeavours to excite them to worry one another. But, *Bonum est ab hoste doceri*.[66]

He stopp'd not in Church-Matters, but it being without doubt in his Opinion, a Matter of State, that Sir *Jonathan Raymond* should be Lord Mayor of *London*, he very pragmatically interposed in the Civil Government of the City, and to promote Sir *Jonathan*'s Election, licensed a Pamphlet, called, *A List of the Names of the Aldermen that will be put in Nomination for Lord Mayor*.[67] The Libeller pretended to a mighty Understanding in the Customs and Constitutions of the City, and by his Paper stuft with Lies, tells the Citizens that he hoped they would not be drawn aside from Voting and Polling for both *Raymond* and *Daniel*. This was stamp'd 26 Sept. 1692. Licens'd *Edmund Bohun*, and industriously spread about the City, as carrying a Badg of Authority with it; when at the same time *Bohun* himself in Person, went about (as if he had been a Magistrate of the City) to solicite against, and obstruct the Election of that well-deserving Magistrate Sir *John Fleete*, now happily Lord Mayor. /

*Sir*, Having thus shown you what sort of Pamphlets pass'd currently with this Censor at the Press; to make what speed I can towards a Conclusion, I proceed to shew you what Books he hath disallow'd and suppress'd.

That *Noble Peer*, the *Earl* of *Warrington*, having allowed a *Speech* which he made to the *Grand Jury* at *Chester*, in *April* 1692, to be printed; The Publisher carried an Advertisement thereof to be inserted in the Paper which comes out every *Munday*, intituled, *The City Mercury*:[68] But *this Press-Superintendant* disliking his *Lordship*'s excellent Positions, struck out the Advertisement, and forbad it to be printed. But humbly begging his *Lordship*'s Pardon for my presumption, I will (without *Mr. Hot-head*'s Licence) transcribe a Paragraph or two of this excellent Speech.

'The late King *James* his Administration (*saith his Lordship*) rendred him unmeet to sway the Scepter. And I am very well satisfied, that the Judgment upon him was Just; for unless a People are decreed to be miserable, which *God Almighty* will never do, except thereto very highly provoked by their Sins: certainly he will never so tie up their Hands, that they shall not be allowed to use them, when they have no other way to help themselves.

'Several Artifices were made use of in the two late Reigns, for the introducing *Arbitrary Power and Popery*; one of which was to insinuate into the Minds of the People, *that the Succession of the Crown was the chief Pillar of the Government*; and that the breaking into it, upon any Pretence whatsoever, was no less than a dissolution of the whole Constitution, and nothing but Disorder and Confusion would ensue.' –

'*Election was certainly the Original of Succession.*

'Succession is a very feeble Title, without something else to support it, and I think I may say Defective.

'I could never understand that *Divine Right* that was by some stampt upon the Title to the *Crown*, or that the *Succession* was preferable to the *Publick Good*. /

'I do not apprehend that a *King* that comes to the Crown by *Election*, should think worse of his Title, than if he had come in by *Succession*, but rather the more securely' –.

'Several Laws were put in execution against the *Dissenters*, which were plainly and directly made for other Purposes' – .

'I was always of Opinion that it would never go well with *England*, till every Man might worship *God* in his own way.' –

Thus was his *Lordship* pleased to express himself; and when you consider how vastly dissonant these his *true English Principles are* from the rotten Notions of our corrupt Statesman *Bohun*, you will cease to wonder at his Attempt to suppress them; but I hope will not forget his Impudence therein.

This *avowed Enemy* to the true Government of *England*, treated the Reverend and highly-meriting Mr. *Johnson's* late excellent *Argument upon the Abrogation of the late King* James *by the People of* England *from the Throne*,[69] which sets the Government upon its true Basis, as he did my *Lord* of *Warrington's*, and expung'd it out of the *Weekly City Mercury*.

Further, he refused to allow the printing of a Book called *A New Martyrology*, which gives an Account of the Cruelty and bloody Practices of *Jefferies* in the *West*; and told Mr. *Dunton*[70] the *Bookseller*, who carried it to him, that *he would not License it for its Weight in Gold.*

His Reason for this Denial may be seen in many places of his *three Addresses*, and particularly *Pag*. 58. of the third, whereby it appears how highly *Bohun* esteemed that grand Betrayer of our Liberties.

*Sir*, I would break off here, but that I remember the Promise I made you in my Letter, to give my Reasons why I thought *Bohun* weary of his Place. In short, they are these. /

1. I took notice that he published in the *City Mercury*, that *whosoever had business with Mr. Bohun Licencer at the Press, must during the Session of Parliament, attend him before eleven of the Clock in the Morning*. Now looking upon the List, and not finding him to be a Member of your House, and at the same time reading in his *three Addresses* how insolently he had arraigned former Parlia-

ments, and declared, (as *pag.* 49. of his third Address) That *the House of Commons printing their Votes, could be designed for nothing but to enable the People to pass a Judgment on their Actions; and that without printing, it might have been difficult to have known what they had done, so as to have charged them*: I began to suspect that he made it his daily work to attend in your Lobby, to gather Matter for an *Impeachment* against your House; or at least for *a fourth Address* to his *Freeholders* of *Suffolk* (for I am assured that the three former were mainly calculated for that County) to keep Sir *Samuel Barnardiston*, and Sir *Gervase Elwes*[71] out of the next Parliament. Now should this prove to be the Case, I conclude, that this Task, with that of *Licensing*, is too heavy for his Crazy Carcase, and that therefore he might choose to quit the trouble of watching the Press.

2. I observed, that in *the City Mercury*, he at another time advertised the World, That *his Affairs calling him into the Country, whoever had Business with Mr. Licencer, should repair to Mr.* Stevens,[72] *Messenger of the Press*. Upon which I thought that he who had such frequent Avocations, might be willing to surrender. If I mistake in this, I hope I do not, when I assert, that the man who is very fit to watch the Press, that Unlicens'd Books creep not out, may not be of a Capacity to judg what may, and what may not be printed; and if he be not, I am sure he is not qualified for the Place of *Deputy-Licencer*.

*Sir*, I hope you will pardon my Prolixity, when you consider that I have collected the accursed Principles of this vile Man out of many of his damnable Tracts, and that without being at the trouble of reading them, you have here before you the Quintessence of near 800 Pages; you here see the Sentiments of his Soul. He hath approved himself a very Evil Instrument, and taken great pains to poison the Kingdom with a Set of / Opinions, which have highly tended to the Ruin of the Peace of the Nation, and its Government: for he and his Accomplices who design'd to enslave us by *the base Doctrine of Passive Obedience*, involv'd us in the present Bloody War; and if We now behold a dreadful Cloud hanging over our Heads, and darkning that bright Sun-shine, of which we had a glimpse about four Years since, I will adventure to say, that it ought to be placed to the Account of these *Passive-Obedience-Men*, and to the rotten Principles to which they are forc'd to recur, for the support of their Darling Doctrine.

I have taken all this Pains to shew the World the right Spirit and Temper of a true *Tory*; and I crave leave to observe, that this Man cannot hide his Nature, the Erruptions of his Choler are ungovernable. I did before point at his Licensing a Pamphlet which traduces the Legal Establishment of the Church of *Scotland*, printed by *Hindmarsh*, to whom I gave the Epithet of *Blaspheming*; and upon second thoughts, I esteem my self accountable to give a Reason for so doing, and 'tis because about ten or twelve Years ago (to the best of my Remembrance) he publish'd a damnable Paper,[73] wherein the *Creed*, the *Lord's Prayer*, and *Ten Commandments* were turn'd Into *Burlesque* beginning thus, *I* believe in *John Calvin*, &c. This entitled him to *Bohun's* Favour; and his being *a Non-Juror* to their Majesties, with his old Service in furnishing their Enemies, *the Non-swearing Episcopal Clergy-men of Scotland*, with that grateful piece, gave him preference to all others to be their Bookseller. That Libel being come to my hand since I mention'd it to you, I find it is intituled *An Apology for the Clergy of Scotland, &c.*[74] and was Licens'd by *Bohun*, 24 Sept. 1692. and with your leave I will transcribe a few passages from it.

It *saith*, (Pag. 86) 'The whole Scheme of their (*the Presbyterian*) Religion (as they differ from the Episcopal Party) is nothing in it self but ungovernable Humour and Rebellion.'

And *pag*. 94. it very modestly asserts, That *the Presbyterian Preachments do more harm to Piety, than the most subtile Arguments of Ancient and Modern Atheists*. /

And *pag*. 96. *The Presbyterians began their Faction with Calumny, and they cannot now (if they would) lay it aside – When they forbear to breath, then it is that they forbear to slander and calumniate*. Pag. 99. *The more they lie, the more true they are to the Spirit of the Party*.

Behold here what a *Synagogue of Satan* their Majesties have established in their *ancient Kingdom*; the whole Scheme of their Religion (in *Hot-head*'s Judgment) is *Rebellion*; they are worse than *Atheists*.

I remember that in the latter End of *Charles* or *James* the Second (I am not certain in which) the French Ambassador made a Complaint, that our *dear and most Christian Brother and Ally*, his *Master*, had been rudely treated in a printed Pamphlet here; we immediately censur'd the Crime, and recanted it in the *Gazette*.

But here we see this *Scourge* of the *Scotish Nation*, who said, as I told you but now, that Presbytery was hatch'd in Rebellion, and that Kings must be their irreconcilable Enemies, as long as they mean to be Masters of their Power; he is set up not only to ridicule and revile that Kingdom, which not only began well in the Settlement of the Government, when they declared that *the late King, by breaking the Laws had forefaulted*, but hath signaliz'd it self in the Support of their *Majesties glorious Cause*, and particularly in the Battel of *Stenekirk*, where that noble and hopeful young Peer, the Earl of *Angus*, that excellent Commander General *Mackay*, with a great Number of gallant Officers and Souldiers of that Kingdom fell in their Service.[75]

But (which highly aggravates the Crime of this *Calunmiator*) that Nation and its Government is not only slander'd by him, but he tacitly and injuriously reflects, with the highest Impudence upon their Majesties, in saying, that the Religion which they have established there, is such as the Devil would blush at. And yet he is not made to blush for this Villany, but is a *White-Boy*[76] in the Opinion of some about *Whitehall*. /

Sir, 'Twas in my Purpose to have made more particular Remarks than I have done upon this Man's vile Principles, wherewith I believe I have nauseated you; but I have already ran out to a much greater length than I intended; however I would observe that he cannot be affectionate to the true English Government, that writes as he hath done; and his Loyalty to their Majesties, and Love to the present Establishment, may well be called into Question, who hath commended Parliaments, (and particularly those whose Members his Highness the Prince of *Orange* in his great Wisdom thought fit to assemble at *Westminster* in the *Interregnum*, to consult the Kingdom's Settlement)[77] at the rate which he hath done; but 'tis evident that it was his Practice and damnable Design to countenance and justify the highest Violations of our Liberties that ever were committed; to arraign one of the three Estates; and to delude a great part of the People into an *Abhorrence* of their own Representatives: And that such Practices as these should in this Reign recommend him to *a Place of Profit and Trust*; who when he wrote the pernicious Libels wherewith I have entertain'd you, in the time of *Charles* II, complained that he must live and die a private Person, for that *he had no means to attain any publick Imployment or Place of Trust*, is to me, I must confess, a Matter of Admiration.

I have done, Sir, when I have laid before you my humble Request, that you would oblige me in using your Interest at *White-hall*, to procure Answers to these following Queries, and that I may have them by the next Post conveyed to me.

Your Servant,<br>J.M. /

*Query* 1. IT is said that one Mr. *Fraser* was Mr. *Bohun's* Predecessor in the Place of *Licenser*.[78] I desire to be informed how he came to be removed, and wherefore; whether it were for allowing the late Reverend Dr. *Walker* to print his Book, intituled, *The true, modest and faithful Account of the Author of* Eicon Basilice, *&c*.[79] For that Book is made up of such unconquerable Truths, that I undertake not one of them will be gainsaid by any Minister of the Church of *England*, between *Whitehall* and *Aldgate*, upon the 30*th* of this Instant *January*, 1692/3?[80]

*Q*. 2. Who sent for *Bohun* out of *Suffolk* to put him into the Licensing Post?

*Q*. 3. Whether he deserves better than Mr. *Fraser*, and in what respect? Whether he hath not 100 or 200. *per Annum* Salary,[81] and who pays it? And what Salary Mr. *Fraser* had? I thus enquire, because I have heard he had none, but executed the Place for the Contingent Perquisites which accrued by Licensing Books.

*Q*. 4. Whether in case Mr. *Bohun* should have the Mishap to be removed, an Interest may not be made to restore Trusty Sir *Roger L*. to that Employment? for they are *Cronies*, and as 'tis well known have Acted by Concert; and I will undertake that he shall Article with *Bohun* to surrender and reinstate him at a Year's end; provided that they may take their turns in it.[82] What though *Sir Roger* be excepted in the Act of *Indemnity*, a Man may with little hazard take his place at *Pillory, Whipping-Post, or Tyburn* (tho' he deserv'd them all) for one Dish of Coffee at honest *Sam*'s.[83]

## ADVERTISEMENT.

Since I had taken a Resolution to publish these my Scriblings, I hear that *Bohun* is fallen under the displeasure of the Parliament; but that I may not be thought to insult over him, I have many Witnesses to attest that these Papers had been publish'd, though he had not fallen into Tribulation.[84]

I so detested the Title of the Book *King* William *and Queen* Mary *Conquerors*, &c.[85] for which he is it seems called into question, that I could not in some Days bring my self into Temper / to peruse it; but at length I have done it, and made these two Observations thereupon.

1. The Author hath (in my poor Opinion) raised as strong Objections against our present legal Establishment, as *Bohun* himself, in Conjunction with *Le-Strange* could have done; and answer'd them as weakly, as they, or the most malicious Enemy their *Majesties* have, can desire.

2. The Positions herein laid down smell so strong of *Bohun's* old Principles, that I almost suspect the thing to come out of his Mint: for Nature will be Nature: and therefore if he were not the Author, I wonder not that he usher'd it into the World. Now, seeing we are *Conquer'd*; I will put down our Duty, and what our Deportment is to be even under *Conquest*, tho' the highest *Tyranny* ensues upon it, as I find it laid down in his Preface, to *Filmer's Patriarcha; Conquer'd People* (saith he) *that are in some Countries treated as Slaves, and but a little better than Brutes, have certainly a very good Appeal to the Tribunal of God against their Princes; who will certainly right them in another World, if they suffer patiently in this.* O Wretched *Issachars*[86] that we are under this Enslaving Doctrine of *PASSIVE OBEDIENCE*!

To say no more, I cannot but esteem the whole Work weak, and as full of Errors as of Malice, against the English Government, and in truth against their Sacred Majesties. And I conclude, in the Words of the incomparable Mr. *Johnson*, in his Dedication to the present House of Commons; 'If we are a Conquer'd People; Then I am sure that all the boasted English Liberties amount to no more than this, that our Thoughts are Free, and their Post-Letters Frank.'[87]

*FINIS.*

*The Clauses chiefly Objected against in the Act 14o of Charles II. about Printing* ([London], [February 1693?]). Wing, C4597C; ESTC, R233924.

*The* CLAUSES *chiefly objected against in the Act* 14o. of Charles II. *about Printing*,[1] *are These*,

I. THAT which subjects the Houses of Peers to be searched for Unlicensed Books, by Warrant from a Secretary of State, upon the bare Suspicion and Suggestion of a Messenger of the Press, without Oath.[2]

II. (This other Clause) *And be it farther Enacted, by the Authority aforesaid, That no Person or Persons shall within this Kingdom, or elsewhere, Imprint or cause to be Imprinted*, &c. *any Copy or Copies, Book or Books, or part of any Book or Books, or Forms of blank Bills or Indentures, for any of his Majesties Islands, Printed beyond the Seas or elsewhere, which any Person or Persons, by Vertue of any Letters* Patents Granted *or Assigned to him or them*, or which shall hereafter be Granted or Assigned *to him or them, Or, (where the same are not Granted by any Letters Patents) by Force or Vertue of any Entry or Entries thereof duly made or to be made, in the Register-book of the said Company of Stationers*, &c. *have or shall have the right Priviledge, Authority or Allowance solely to Print*, &c. *upon the Penalty of Forfeiture, and also* 6 s. 8 d. *for every Book or Part*, &c. *and punishment of the Party as an Offender against the Act*. Whereby,

1. If any Man hath a Property in any Copy, which falls within a Patent Granted (*or to be Granted*) he is subject to the Penalties though his Book be Licensed.

2. If any Entry be made in the Register-book (in such Form as they count (*Duly*) no Man shall Print his own Copy, after it hath been Stoln from him and Entered as anothers; which has often happened in Fact: Whereby the right Owner is deprived of Remedy or Reparation by any other Law.

3. There being no sufficient Provision, for destroying the Forfeitures, it hath been an occasion, for the Company, to seize Foreign Books, and sell them again (to the prejudice of the English Printers and Booksellers, and Destruction of the English Manufacture) and to re-seize them, *toties quoties*,[3] in the Hands of those Persons, who have bought them of the Company or their Agents, which appears to have been their frequent Practice.

# SUPPRESSING JACOBITISM

William and Mary, *By the King and Queen, A Proclamation for the Better Discovery of Seditious Libellers* (London: printed by Charles Bill, and the Executrix of Thomas Newcomb deceas'd; Printers to the King and Queens most Excellent Majesties, 13 September 1692). Wing, W2605; ESTC, R23278.

*Animadversions upon that Proclamation of September 13. 1692. Entituled, for the Better Discovery of Seditious Libellers* ([London], '4 October 1692'). Wing, A3205; ESTC, R38496.

William Anderton, *True Copy of the Paper Delivered to the Sheriffs of London and Middlesex, by Mr. William Anderton, at the Place of Execution* ([London], after 16 June 1693). Wing, A3113; ESTC, R114.

*An Account of the Conversation, Behaviour and Execution of William Anderton Printer, who was Condemned at the Old Baily, on Thursday the 8th. Of June, for High Treason, and Executed for the same, at Tybourn on Friday the 16th of June 1693* ([London]: printed by John Wallis near the Green Dragon in Fleetstreet, [16–17 June] 1693). Wing, A266; ESTC, R4213.

The aftermath of the 'glorious' revolution of 1688–9 yielded greater scope for toleration and discussion of press freedom but little lessening of vigilance towards print by a new regime conscious of its vulnerability to Jacobitism and wider political criticism. This extended into 1692–3, as the Printing Act came up for renewal, against the background of the faltering prosecution of war with France and a Jacobite propaganda effort led by James's *Declaration* in April 1692, proposing renewed efforts to regain the throne. A government clampdown from the summer included proclamations against seditious libel, the renewal of the Printing Act (see The Printing Act in Question, above) and the pursuit of those running Jacobite presses, culminating in the execution of the printer William Anderton for two treasonable libels in mid-1693. The previous December had seen a proposal in the Commons to strengthen legislation by making it high treason to express or publish the view that William and Mary were not king and queen, or were usurpers, but this was narrowly defeated, in part over the extent to which words constituted treason.[1] However, existing legislation proved sufficient to convict and execute Anderton and send a warning to others. A clause confirming that it was treasonable to print, write or otherwise declare that James rather than William was rightful king would be duly included in the Treason Act of 7 & 8 Will. III, c. 27, which gained royal assent on 27 April 1696, alongside an Act reviving expiring laws from which Parliament had agreed to exclude the 1662 Printing Act (see Volume 4 of this edition).

The royal proclamation of 13 September 1692 followed its predecessors, notably that of January 1676, in urging in general terms the discovery and prosecution of seditious libellers, in print or manuscript. Although it did not attack Jacobitism by name, its drafting was ordered after the Privy Council considered the problem of Jacobite libels on 1 September and examined the earlier proclamation in determining a response.[2] Perceptions of its intended target were affirmed by the Jacobite *Animadversions* which appeared in response shortly afterwards.

The *Animadversions* on the 13 September proclamation, printed roughly and published anonymously, argued against Williamite control of the press on the basis that it suppressed the truth of Jacobite criticisms and purported to secure a peace that did not exist and could therefore not be 'seditiously' disturbed. The precise date of the tract is uncertain. On 4 October, Queen Mary seems to have requested the drafting of a further proclamation to prevent printed papers against the government.[3] The same date is given on the *Animadversions*, although the tract also alludes to the debate on the treason bill which occurred two months later.

The printer William Anderton, as the hostile *Account* of his treason trial conveys, was made an example after punishment of others involved in Jacobite publishing was thwarted by escape (Charles Leslie) or tempered by leniency (for example, the intermediary Anne Merryweather). Anderton had a press seized in 1692 and in May 1693 was again apprehended by Robert Stephens with copies of numerous Jacobite pamphlets, two of which were made the basis of his indictment: the anonymous *Remarks upon the Present Confederacy, and Late Revolution in England* and *A French Conquest, neither Desirable nor Practicable* (by Charlwood Lawton). Anderton's trial began on 13 June 1693 and the twenty-nine-year-old Yorkshireman was executed on 16 June at Tyburn. It was argued without success in court that Anderton was not responsible for the tracts, that a printer could not be proven to have the intent necessary for conviction under the treason act of Edward III, and that the recently-renewed Printing Act confirmed that alternative laws applied to printing. A critical account of the trial was written and published by the nonjuring pamphleteer Samuel Grascome (or Grascomb) under the title *An Appeal of Murther* (1693).

Anderton's farewell paper, signed on 15 June, was published by his supporters, probably including Grascome. The condemned man continued to deny having printed or published the offending pamphlet, nor having called William 'Hook-nose' as Stephens claimed, and appealed to the lesser punishments in the Printing Act. But he closed by expressing hopes for the restoration of James or his progeny.

Notes
1. *CJ*, 10, p. 730; E. Cruickshanks, S. Handley and D. W. Hayton (eds), *The House of Commons 1690–1715*, 5 vols (Cambridge: History of Parliament Trust, 2002), vol. 5, p. 524.
2. R. Astbury, 'The Renewal of the Licensing Act in 1693, and its Lapse in 1695', *Library*, 5th series, 33 (1978), pp. 296–322, on pp. 298–9.
3. *CSPD*, 4 October 1692.

William and Mary, *By the King and Queen, A Proclamation for the Better Discovery of Seditious Libellers* (London: printed by Charles Bill, and the Executrix of Thomas Newcomb deceas'd; Printers to the King and Queens most Excellent Majesties, 13 September 1692). Wing, W2605; ESTC, R23278.

## By the King and Queen,
## A PROCLAMATION
### For the better Discovery of Seditious Libellers.

MARIE R.

WE being sensible that divers Evil Disposed Persons being not Reformed or Wrought upon by Our Grace and Favour, not withstanding We have extended Our Royal Mercy and Clemency to Our Subjects, as well by Our General as Particular Pardons, since Our Accession to the Crown, do make it their business as well to Write and Print sundry False, Infamous, and Scandalous Libels, endeavouring thereby not only to Traduce and Reproach the Ecclesiastical and Temporal Government of this Kingdom, and the publick Ministers of the same, but also to stir up and dispose the minds of Our Subjects to Sedition and Rebellion: For the discovery of which wicked Offenders, and to the intent they may receive such Punishments as the Laws of this Our Realm in such Cases direct, We (with the Advice of Our Privy Council) do by this Our Royal Proclamation Publish and Declare, That if any Person or Persons shall discover or make known to either of Our Principal Secretaries of State,[1] or to any Justice of the Peace, the Person or Persons to whom any such Libel at any time since Our last General Pardon,[2] hath been, or shall hereafter be brought, and by him or them received, in order to Print, or Transcribe the same, or the place where such Libel shall be Printing, or Transcribing, whereby the same shall happen to be Seized, or the Person or Persons by whom any such Libel at any time since Our said General Pardon hath been or shall hereafter be Printed, Transcribed, or otherwise Published, or shall discover and make known to either of Our said Principal Secretaries of State, or to any Justice of Peace, any Press kept contrary to Law by any Person or Persons whatsoever, he or they making every such Discovery shall have and receive as a Reward from Us the Sum of Twenty Pounds.

And We do further hereby Publish and Declare, That if any Person or Persons shall Discover and make known to either of Our said Principal Secretaries of State, or to a Justice of the Peace, the Author of any such Libel, which at any time since Our said General Pardon has been or shall hereafter be devised and made, or the Person or Persons who at any time since Our said General Pardon have, or hath handed, or brought, or shall hereafter hand or bring any such Libel to the Press, or to any Person or Persons in order to Print the same, so that they may be brought to Punishment, he or they making such Discovery shall receive and have from Us the Sum of Fifty Pounds. And to the end that the Person or Persons making such Discovery may without any Charge or Attendance immediately after the same made, receive the respective Rewards hereby proposed, We do by this Our Royal Proclamation Require the Commissioners of Our Treasury, or Our High Treasurer of England for the time being, that upon a Certificate from either of Our Principal Secretaries of State, or any Justice of the Peace of any such Discovery made, he or they do satisfie and pay the said respective Sums to the Person or Persons making such Discovery without any Delay or Abatement whatsoever. And We do hereby strictly Charge and Command all and every Our Justices of the Peace, to whom such Discovery shall be made, that he or they with all possible speed do give Notice thereof to Us, or to one of Our Principal Secretaries of State, to the end that the said Libels may be Suppressed, and the Parties offending effectually prosecuted.

Given at Our Court at *Whitehall* the Thirteenth Day of *September*, 1692. In the Fourth Year of Our Reign.

God save King William and Queen Mary.

*Animadversions upon that Proclamation of September 13. 1692. Entituled, for the Better Discovery of Seditious Libellers* ([London], '4 October 1692'). Wing, A3205; ESTC, R38496.

*Animadversions upon that Proclamation of* September 13. 1692. Entitled *For the better discovery of Seditious Libellers.*

THE Observation is as true as it is common; That when any Breach or Alteration has been made upon the Antient and well Constituted Government of this Kingdom (which doth reside in an Uninterrupted Hereditary and Lineal Succession; This being Established and Confirmed by all the Statute and Common Laws, authentick Records and Right Precedents) either by wrong Invasion upon, and forcible Dispossession of it, or by subtle Intrusion or stepping in between, Hereupon the Tongues and Pens of People have been more open and enlarged than at other Times of righteous Settlement. The Reason whereof is so obvious, that there is no need to assign it; Because here is occasion given for it, but there is none then. For an Example hereof we need go no further back, than the Reign of *Oliver Cromwell,* and that eighteen Years of Confusion and Bloodshed which was then. What an exceeding deal of Work was for the Press in those days? When any Great and unusual thing is done in the World, if People should hold their peace, the Stones would immediately cry out[1] (according to that Rhetorical form of Speech) importing that the most dull and silent of Mankind must be affected with, and talk thereof. And tho' through the Evil and Depravation of our Nature, they do more consent unto, and are carried away with a corrupt and wrong Thing, especially where it gets Riches and Power, and the Multitude on its side; Yet the World was never so universally bad, That every without one exception should be led away with the Spreading, Prevailing, and contagious Error; But some have all along kept and preserved themselves in their Integrity, free and sound from the Disease and Corruption of the Times.

There have been a Remant,[2] and a few (as this is always the Lot and Portion of the Right and better Side) in whom hath appeared outwords[3] of Truth, and Principles of Righteousness and Honesty. So it will be (notwithstanding the utmost Opposition and Persecution) as long as God hath a Church in the World; Unless all Men should be transformed into wild Beasts or Devils; that is, until they come to lose all the Seeds and Tinctures of Reason and Religon, and they are made up of nothing but Violence and Evil. (Here it must be acknowledged that Pride, Revenge, Envy, Discontent, and the several Ingredients of Sin and Passion will be apt to creep in, and also intermingle with the Right side) so that if there should not be a word spoken or written; Yet as long as there is a Real and Essential Difference between Good and Evil, Truth and Falshood, Right and Wrong (which is so far ingrafted into the Nature of Men, that it cannot be utterly rooted out) Every one that hath but common understanding would discern the one from the other.

It hath been the constant Method, that when Iniquity hath been set up on High, and it hath intruded and Usurpt it self upon the Rightful Authority, They have also plaistered, and flourished it over with Goodly words:[4] But when on the other side Words of Truth do come forth, which make to see through, or under the Foundation thereof, and this doth it more and more, that the untempered Morter of the other can no longer Palliate,[5] or make it up again; Then the last Resort is to Gag the Mouth, Tye up the Hand, and Imprison the Body, to prevent and hinder all going forth of such True and right Words: *for every one that doth Evil, hateth the Light, neither cometh to the Light, lest his Deeds should be reproved,* John 3. Ver. 20. Or as it is in the Margin there, discovered.[6] Here if the upright in Heart (God being on their side, whilst they act and labour for him) would strive against these Devises of the Workers of Iniquity, their Foundation would be discovered, and at length fall, and be consumed. Surely their turning of things upside down *shall be esteemed as Potters Clay,*[7] which tho' they can or do fashion to this or that purpose, according to their own Will; yet it may be all broken into pieces, or dissolved into Dirt.

Here it comes to pass, *That the greatest Fool calls Fool first;*[8] for they do first throw out that Reproach of Sedition and Rebell on falsly upon others to ward off, and turn away that true imputation of both; which, as they are secretly and inwardly Conscious of, so it may be justly fastned upon themselves. Let them call it what they will, *Defence of the Parliament and Liberties of* England, *Preservation of Religion,* &c. It was six Years plain down Rebellion foregoing, that brought King *Charles* the First to the Block; And so notwithstanding it hath been termed Deliverance[9] (I believe they will not find it so at long run) It was plain invading this Realm by a Foreign Prince, bearing Arms, raising Tumults, (all which in *Ipsissimis verbis,*[10] was contrary to that Oath of Allegiance and Supremacy, which his Subjects had before taken) which caused our King to be Deposed. At which juncture of Time almost every Sermon from the Pulpit, and Paper from the Press was a false, Infamous, and Scandalous Libel: For as the Chief Justice *Coke* had long since Remarked that *Libelling is the fore-runner of Rebellion,*[11] so it did exactly prove; for, whereas the King had Emitted forth his Declaration for Liberty of Conscience; *That all people might worship God according to their several Opinions and Persuasions, and they might Preach all God's Word with this necessary Caution; Provided than there nothing should be delivered to alienate the Hearts of his Subjects, from Him or His Government; so as to make them withdraw, or cast off their Allegiance;*[12] for to do that, or to despise and falsifie a solemn Oath, there is not one Sentence in all the Old and New Testament, which can be truly alledged to justify that: Because such like a thing hath been done in former Generations, and in other Countries, therefore that it was lawfully done, is a fallacious and wrong Conclusion: But our People did abuse the favour of their King unto Evil surmisings and Rebellious Practices, as if He had granted this Universal Liberty only to bring in Popery: But supposing that should be granted (which perhaps was not so) for this is the most forcible / way of Reasoning, when admitting his Objection. we can certainly confute, if not convince, and actually bring over the Adversary; Yet God, who causeth Light to shine out of Darkness would have Established this to them, and to their Generations for ever more upon a righteous sure Foundation, what ever designs might lie hid in the Heart: All one as the Reformation was somewhat brought on, and furthered by the Lust and Revenge of *Henry* the VIII. By which may be seen that there is no such thing as Pure, Undefiled Religion among the Princes of this World: And tho now they have the same Liberty nevertheless, Yet God will judge whether it was not granted by the Political Methods of Iniquity (which trust do somewhat to oblige all Parties, and all sides, lest the seeming or called Godly should reprove it, as the Universally Righteous will nevertheless) as it is now retained by the Sinful silence of the first Sort, and by their Consenting with the Deeds of them. All the Churches are to know that the Almighty God could, and as he is Holy and True, so he would preserve, increase, and add to their Numbers, *if they did not overpass the Deeds of the Wicked; yet they prosper.* Jer. 5. Ver. 28. For they imagine that hereby they continue this their Priviledge, and therefore they have omitted. *Mar.* 23. 23. (from whence it appears, that omission of Duty is a Sin, and that Christ will enter into Judgment for the same) to speak forth all God's word against all manner of Sin and Transgression in all people from the greatest of them to the least of them for so indeed it ought to be spoken forth and declared.

But such is the untoward Nature of Men, who are weary of the best things, if they have them long, and they are desirous of Novelty and Variety, tho' it be unlawful, That as they will do ten times more in Loans and Gifts to an unjust Possessor, than to a rightful King; Even so the Religious also will hide their Eyes from the breach of almost all the other Commandments of God, as if the whole of Religion, and what he required of Man was to provide against, and keep out *Popery*. People are kept hoodwinkt or deluded with false Notions, or rather they do take up with half the thing, not understanding it throughly and wholly. Thus it is both as to serious and common Matters.

Suppose we give an instance in this last; When the *French* were moving upon the Waters the Summer before the Date hereof,[13] It was given out throughout all this Nation, to make the people more unanimous in Opposition of them, That they came to spoil and make a Conquest over this Country. They did not then come so near, as to send out their *Declarations*, and make their pretences known:

But if they had, and declared accordingly, That they came only to restore the deprived King; and that they did covet and design no more, but barely to effect this; and they would be contented only with the Charge of the Expedition paid, with some moderate Gratuities to the Soulders and Seamen. and henceforward these Nations should abide by one another in Unity, peace and Concord: If the usual Consultation, Treaty and Security was had hereupon, The people of *England* might credit and fully rely on these their so far seeming, reasonable and just demands, all one as they did take the *P.* of *O's*[14] Word to let him come in, when he had before declared, that he did not intend to make a Conquest over them. Indeed there is somewhat more to be considered in the disparity of the Numbers and *Power* which the one hath, over what the other had; But the Word and promise of the Princes and Potentates of the Earth are much alike, that there is no sure Trust or Reliance to be given to any of them. They were wont to speak in old time saying, *Thou shalt surely ask counsel at* Abel, and so they ended the Matter 2. *Sam.* 20. *Ver.* 18. As we are allow'd, yea, and commanded to search the Scriptures, so any one at his leisure may read the four following *Verses*, as they be open in the Bible. I am one of them that are peaceable and faithful in *England*. It seemeth hard and unequal to me, that a whole Nation should be endangered to be ruined and swallowed up by Strangers and Foreigners for the Ambition and Contention of two Men: Whereas Right might be done in a peaceable and prudent way (without their Aid or violent Interposure and Medling) upon the terms of universal Forgiveness, not one man excepted. But if one is so stiff as not to grant that; as I suppose he would with all his Heart be glad to be re-admitted in upon those mild and equitable Conditions, which will make him both revered and loved; for it is neither Duty, nor yet Wisdom to speak or behave ones self proudly in the day of distress. They are Adversarie to the King. 2 *Sam*, 19. *Ver.* 22. and hinder his Restauration, who dictate otherwise, notwithstanding their ignorant Zeal, and vain Talk for him; And if the Offenders are afraid to trust to this, as Wickedness and Guilt is Timerous and Suspicious, it being what is natural and usual, that they who have transgressed without a Cause should be also fearful without a Cause, that is, without a True Cause.) Then let all those that are indeed Criminals stand by themselves; for there is no reason why others who as yet are not so, should make themselves criminal also in defending them. And let him come singly to punish them, whilst all others stand perfectly Neuter, and disinterested as to that Cause, only in defence of their Country to stop the Incursion and Spoil of Strangers and Robbers. The right understanding and acting according to this Truth would go a great way towards the bringing and setling Peace again in our Borders. And though people now say the Righteous and Loyal party would bring the *French* in, Yet herein they say falsly, for if ever the *French* should come in (which, tho' at present unlikely, and that Word according to the Divine Method in *Psal.* 89. throughout, and *Jer.* 37.10.[15] seems to be falsified at first, to exercise the more our Faith therein nevertheless, Yet nothing is impossible with God, who knows which Side will have the worst of the War at long run:) Yet not we, but themselves would cause this breaking in of Foreigners and Strangers; For the original Cause, and first Occasion is to be lookt back into. Who invited another to come in, when all things were quiet, before he moved upon the Waters? To disturb quiet Things, that is properly Sedition, as Rebellion is the breaking out into the open Act of Hostility. And then they did drive their King out to seek his Bread in that Neighbour Country, where he supposed that he might sooner have it; And because he thought Himself not safe among the Children of them, who Murthered his Father; therefore He was forced to take Sanctuary among strangers. Here he should rather have abode quiet, and not sought to have Recovered his Kingdom again by Blood and Force of Arms. But yet he did, and doth still betake himself to those Methods which is usual for Sovereign / Princes, when they have been Dispossessed to do in like Cases. Which same Plea and Saying, tho it may seem a little allowable *in Foro Humano*,[16] Yet it will in no wise excuse or justifie him at the Bar of God for the Blood that hath been spilt on this Occasion. However they are much more inexcusable, who first Rebelled against him, and do still endeavour to keep him out with the Price of Blood, and with the loss of so many thousand Men's Lives, than Himself is, who seeks after this manner to be Re-instated again, They are sinners and Trangressors on both sides, Though his Rebellious Subjects are the greater.

From hence came those Wars and Fightings among us, So that after the way which they barely accuse others of Sedition and Rebellion, Themselves in very deed have been proved guilty of the same.

In the very same manner it may be Answered, as to what they call False, Infamous and Scandalous Libels:[17] A Libel signifies a little Book. Here again they are beforehand to term it so in these 3 Epithets, which herein are True, Proper, and Opposite: Because in what they call such Libels their own False, Infamous and Scandalous Doings are spoken and treated of: So that this Reproach offered by them must also cease, for it is truly turned upon themselves; and it doth not justly belong to the Authors of such Writings, but to themselves the Actors of such things. Wherein they have Erred, and are Deceived, and they do still go aside from the Way of Truth; whereby they are become a Shame and Infamy even to *Turks*, and to the other Nations, and they have made the Name of *Protestantism* to stink, *Gen.* 34. 30.[18] among the Superstitious Inhabitants of this and other Lands, whilst they have given occasion to both to say, *Those are the Disciples of Jesus Christ the Prince of Peace, and they call themselves of the Pure, Reformed Religion, who break and falsifie their Oaths, dishonour and disobey their Parents, they kill and murther one another.* I do hereby enter my Protestation against these Deeds of such Nuncupative *Protestants*.[19] They are become a Scandal, and Rock of Offence, not so much to them who call themselves so, but to all Real and

Universal Christians, such who have respect unto all the Commandments, and not keep some, and neglect others, as the manner of many is.

Every Libel (*see Coke's Report, Le Case de Libellis famosis*)[20] is to the Scandal of the Government, and to the Breach of the Peace. But when there is an Actual breach of the Peace already in this, and more especially in the Neighbour Nations; which hath so been for these four Years, Those Words of Truth and Soberness, which do exhort to fill and compose these troubled Waves ( - - - *Præstat motos componere fluctus*).[21] and which shew us the only good and right way, how it may be all retrieved and healed, and made up again without the farther Loss of so much as one Man's Life more. *viz*. By changing this New and wrong Constitution into the Antient and Rightful Government; This doth in no wise break the Peace, but would Establish it; Nor yet doth it widen, but it would repair the Breach: Only there is Strength and Will wanting to make it close and keep together. But then indeed it is a scandal to the present Governours (for Governour and Government are two distinct things; in that sometimes they take upon them to Govern, who have no Right so to do) that themselves should not be govern'd by the Law of God: That they should so long live, and act in the breach of sundry of God's Commandments; whereby they are in real danger of future Condemnation, and of going away into everlasting Punishment; that {one} would admire (unless they were deluded and deceived by Sathan, who holds them Captive at his Will), and it is to be fear'd, that after all the Warning which hath been given, they will at last fall into the hands of this Roaring Lion, {how} they can give sleep to their Eyes, and slumber to their Eyelids day after day, and night after night, as they do, until they throughly amend their ways, and their Doings, and until they throughly execute Judgment between a Man and his Neighbour. *Jer*. 7. *Ver* 5. *Lest they should Sleep the Sleep of Death and their Death should be gathered with the Sinners and Transgressors of former Generations*. By these Words, That ye thoroughly execute judgment between a Man and his Neighbour, is, or may be understood according to the Meaning and Requiring of the Spirit of God at his Day (for the Holy Ghost in the Penning and Giving forth of the Scriptures hath provided and ordained them for a Law to all Persons, Times and Places, Generations and Countries). That they do righten (See the Marginal Reading of {James} 4. *Ver*. 17.) Adjust and Determine the Matter between King *James* and the Prince of *Orange* according to the instruction of Wisdom justice judgment and Equity. *Prov*. 3. *Ver*. 3. But until they do this, How can they have any peace in their Conscience, unless they did act in the Deceivableness of Unrighteousness and had imbibed in strong Delutions?[22] But the Knowledge of the Truth would break this inward stupidity, in which sense it doth break the peace within, which is the most troublesome kind of any; nevertheless it is better so broken than kept. And as the same Truth doth barely recite, reprove, and discover their scandalous Doings, and as it doth lay open their Falshood and Hypocrisy, They do thus conceive Enmity against, and utter Error concerning it. Whatever they now do to prevent and hinder the goings forth of His Eternal Truth (because by the publication thereof some few Thoughts of their Hearts are revealed) *Herein they do provoke the Lord to jealousy. Are they stronger than he? Or how can they help when the Dead, small and great shall stand before God, That themselves shall not appear also?* And then all the Thoughts of all their Hearts will be Revealed, all the Words of every Tongue will be Declared, and all the Deeds of their past Life will be manifested and judged.

As to the Reward promised by the Workers of Iniquity, I have several times thought (as I have heard or read that Portion of Scripture, *When thou sawest a Thief, then thou consentest with him. Psal.* 50. *Ver.* 18.) That as there are three sorts of Thefts and Robberies, so they do use the like Methods: There is a little Degree, a middle Size, and the greatest of all. The first Sort is, when a Pocket is pickt, or any thing taken away privily, or when two or three or half a dozen do Rob upon the High-Way. These are Liberal and Bountiful to Oslers, Tapsters and Inn-keepers,[23] and the others will bribe it off to prevent their own Discovery; what they do easily come by, they do as frankly part withal. The middle size is, when a hundred or two do Rob together in a Company, as in some parts of *Italy*, the Desarts of *Arabia*, and Sea Pyrates. These do not see altogether so much because they do depend upon their Numbers, outward Strength and Force; and their Designs are open and Bare-faced to take violently away. But as the Pyrate told *Alexander*; The greatest Robbery of all is, *When Kings and Generals with their Armies {control} and dispossess whole Countries; Or when they do take a whole Kingdom or Principality away at once.*[24] Of this there are two sorts; either open Hostility, which seems fairest, because then Others can stand upon their Guard and Defence: The other is by the Close, Hidden and Hypocritical Methods of Usurpation. Like the turnings and windings of a River, which we know not presently whither it ends; Or like the glidings and insinuations of a Snake or Serpent, which may seem smooth or tickle[25] at first, but the end thereof is deadly. They commonly go this way to work, and scrue themselves in, then they cannot accomplish it by the other. But in the first sort of this great Violence or Robbery, They have some specious Reasons to Colour it over, Tho' at last they are forced to resort to the *French* King's *Motto* upon his great Guns *Ratio Ultima Regum*;[26] In which thing Another hath exactly imitated, and is like unto him; for though they seem to be at so great Enmity and Opposition, yet they do both agree and concern in the same Violent and Unrighteous Action; as appears by that inscription which as I have heard, was on the Cannon, that went over for the Reducing of *Ireland*; which was in the *Dutch* Language to this Signification; *I have got it, and I will maintain it*: Most opposite Word! and exactly agreeable to such a King. who is a King for that Womans Reason, because He is so, and only because He is in possession of a Kingdom.

This Proclamation (which gives occasion for these Remarks) in the *Gazette* is put in an opposite Column to that for High way men and Robbers[27] on purpose (as I suppose) to make Libellers more odious. But I do believe that God the / Judge of all men will rather judge themselves (by whose pretended Authority it is Emitted forth) to be of this sort, sooner than he will pronounce whom they call Libellers to be wicked Offenders; For in the mean while they do use the same Methods with High-way men and Robbers; for as these Fee Inn-Keepers, Oslers and Tapsters to hold their peace, so do they give forth the Wages of Iniquity to the several *Balaams*[28] among us; That whilst themselves have forsaken the Right way; and are gone astray, they may not be rebuked for their Iniquity. *The Prophets make my People Err That bite with their Teeth, and cry Peace, and He that putteth not into their Mouth, They even prepare War against them*: Mic 3. Ver. 5. *But seeing they are still fed, and Bread is put into their Mouths These Dogs are Dumb.* Isa. 56.10. as others are through fear and sloth whose Bread hath been taken away. However rough or harsh this may seem, it is the very {Phrase} of the Holy Ghost speaking on this wise, not out of Invidiousnes, or abusiveness of Expression, but to set forth the nature of this their Sin of Omission, with the aggravation thereof in the sight of God. And thus they stop the several Mouths, by giving a Livelihood or Preferment, which the Receivers consent unto for to get or keep the same. And then again exactly after the same Method of High-way men and Robbers, where Gifts and fair Means will not do, There they proceed to a Pistol or Sab,[29] so do these to Punishment and Severity. One may afford to lett good Bargains, where he hath Dispossessed the right Owner and be very Liberal of that which is not their own, but another Man's: But he that will *Judas*-like do any thing against the Word of God, and his Righteouness, Though it were covenanted for Twenty or Fifty pieces of Silver (which perhaps the Informer may be yet baulked of, notwithstanding such particular directions are here specified for the certain and speedy Payment thereof) may also meet with *Judas* his Doom; It would be good for him, if he had never been born: It would be better for him if he had never touched or meddled with such Money, which is the reward of Iniquity; The Consequence whereof will be Persecution and Oppression, if it be not the worst kind of direct Murder it self: This should make honest people have more care and engage them to a yet greater Faithfulness; as to whom ten or a hundred times as much would not be a prevailing Temptation to commit the Sins of Treachery and Unfaithfulness.

Another thing may be observed among High-Way men and Robbers; That they are commonly very Unanimous, and they do but seldom fall out; for if they should, then all the Gang would be in danger to be broken and ruined, This same is the very Reason, why there hath been such an universal Consent, Harmony and Agreement among the great Multitude of the Workers of Iniquity. There has been no such Clashing in their Parliamentary Consultations, nor confronting the Head thereof as in the Reign of former Rightful Kings; for indeed if it should be once so, This new erected *Babel* would endanger to fall, or at least it would not go forward as now it doth: For a rightful Government like an Oak well and deeprooted doth bear Winds and Storms, will stand amidst and against the Strivings and Divisions of the People; But a Constitution of Man's devising and Wisdom is like a Reed shaken with the Wind, which every Puff of contrary breath doth make to stagger, and if many Trees of the Wood should move against it, This would soon blow it quite away, or at least it would fall, and great would be the Fall thereof.

As Counterfeit Gold doth often shine and glister more than true, so Fiction and Falshood doth more Ape and Imitate what is true and real, than perhaps this doth exert it self forth: In like manner it is when the Wicked are joyned hand in hand (who shall not go unpunished as to the future, however they escape now) and they have got the Government lodged in them tho it be wrong. Yet nevertheless they will keep their hands inure,[30] and they will punctually, formally and continually practice the several acts of Administration thereof from time to time; for as the Life of a Law is in the Execution of it, so their ill-gotten Power (improperly called Authority, because this Word supposes what is lawful, which theirs is not) is kept up meerly by Use and Exercise thereof. As by taking the Royal Title, Signet and Arms, and by doing the several Regal Acts, Interlining their Names; into the Publick Established Liturgy, so that Prayers are said daily for them throughout the Realm, Conferring imaginary Titles of Honour, making seeming Laws, and a Multiplicity of them, whereby is shown forth a secret Consciousness, as if they were not altogether so Valid; Appointing *Judges*, and the Courts of *Judicature* go on, and are held in their Names: And then there must be Imprisonment and Punishment of Offenders, yea, and Executions for Treason, as if they were real Kings: For when an Intruder or Usurper steps up, He hath his Throne soaked, and cemented with Blood, whereby he doth imagine, that he makes it more sure and fast unto himself; not so much from the Conglutinating Nature thereof, but by the Victory, which with his vast Multitude, He doth get over the single Opposers: So that in all likelihood this Proclamation will be put into a vigorous and constant Execution; (If they do not get it confirmed into what is called an Act of Parliament at this their next meeting together) There was some Essay and Endeavour towards this in that their Sessions *on Nov.* 4.1692. in a Bill which was going forwards in the Lower-House, Entitled, *For the better Preservation of Their Majesties Persons and Government*, which same Bill proved Abortive, and was rejected,[31] or otherwise it will be as a nine days wonder, and vanish off again as meer Talk and waste Paper. But as I once heard Dr. *Patrick*,[32] the now Usurpt Bishop of *Ely* (as he was expounding the *Ten Commandments* in his then Parish Church at *Covent-Garden*) make a true Observation; That when Authority doth once begin to Command unlawful things, it doth thereupon grow and become weak and ridiculous. This he spake a little before the late Revolution, when there was a real Authority. So when that (which hath now the Name thereof) doth emit such kind of Edicts; tho' with their Armed Men and Multitudes, and by their diligent Execution thereof (for wrong is commonly more busie and active than right) They will take care, that it shall not hereupon become weaker; Yet there will not much heed and obedience be given to it from the Hearts and Conscience of Men; because for want of Lawfulness both in the Imposers, and also in the Matter it self, It hath not much; or rather no Obligation at all upon the Heart and Conscience.

## POSTSCRIPT

For my part I do not Vindicate all the Errors and Unjust Illegal Acts of the last Reign, as it is commonly called and understood, Though I do affirm Constantly, That all of them put together (taking in also the whole and utmost that Malice could invent, and Falshood Calumniate) will in no wise tantamount to justify a deprivation. There is a wide difference between Boasting and Reallity, between Self Commendation, and the Matter as indeed it is. Herein the present Rulers do wisely, if they do avoid that Severity, which was the miscarriage and overthrow of their immediate Predecessor. They do well herein for the Merciful *shall obtain Mercy*;[33] as themselves indeed have much need thereof from the hands of God for their Transgression of so many of his Commandments. But he knows not much in the Nature of Things, who doth not also understand, That for them, whose Title is Precarious, and meerly beholden to the Love and good Will; It is neither Prudent nor Safe for such to excercise Cruelty; This being deservedly odious to Mankind, as the contrary Virtue of *Mercy* is loved, and of good report: As on the one hand, *It is pity that Goodness should be abused and trampled upon* Soon the other, *We are not to be deluded with fair Words, and fine Phrases*. Among the several Writers concerning publick Affairs (as there hath been subject matter enough) it should considered *Quo Anime*,[34] and out of what principle they do it: Whether it the Zeal for, and Conscience towards God, or vain Humour, which their own several Books and Words will shew forth and manifest. I do in no wise Apologize, or make a Defence for every Scribler: If any has written indeed falsly, scurrilously and meer abusively against the present Governours, the Law is open that such may proceeded against, and also by the Word and judgment of God (*which requires to speak evil of no Man, to be no Brawlers*) if such should suffer, they would suffer as evil Doers.

Finished *October* 4. 1692.

**William Anderton,** *True Copy of the Paper Delivered to the Sheriffs of London and Middlesex, by Mr. William Anderton, at the Place of Execution* ([London], after 16 June 1693). Wing, A3113; ESTC, R114.

True Copy of the PAPER delivered to the SHERIFFS of *London* and *Middlesex*, by Mr. *William Anderton*, at the Place of Execution, which he designed there to have spoken, but being frequently interrupted by the Ordinary, Mr. *Samuel Smith*,[1] desired the said Sheriffs *to publish or dispose of it as they should think fit*, seeing a dying Man was not suffered to speak.

*To my Countrey-men.*
LIberty and Property hath for some Years made an hideous Cry in these Kingdoms, and nothing more than the Rights and Priviledges of the Subject is the Pretence of our present Deliverers; and doubtless it was for the sake of these that so many of my infatuated and blind Countrey men rebelled against their Lawful and Injured Monarch,[2] whilst Religion (Rebellions Umbrage) was made the Covert of the hidden Designs of those who have now demonstratively shewn, that they sought nothing less than our Ruine: And that these were only Pretences to gain their Ends, the very Blind, although they cannot see, yet most certainly feel it. Under the like Pretences do our Deliverers still continue to deliver us even from what they please, that they think will but in the least help to effect what they came for: Under the Notion of the Necessity of a War they deliver us from our Money, and from our Traffick and Commerce, by which so great a part of the Kingdom is sustained: Under the Notion of carrying it on, they kidnap our young Men, the Flower of our Kingdom, and directly contrary to Law transport them; and to save their own Foreigners, put them in the first Onsets of their Battles, as the Heathens did the Christians of Old, that their Enemies Swords might be blunted with killing them, before they came to encounter them: They exhaust all our Stores both for Sea and Land, and carry away all our Artillery; and if any Man seem but to disapprove of these their Proceedings, under the Notion of Law they murther him: Nay, if they do but so much as suppose him not to be on their Side, he must be a Traitor, and no matter what the Law says, they say he shall die.

Can any thing be more plain to demonstrate this than my present Case? My supposed Crime was Printing, and all that the Witnesses could personally say against me, was, That I was a Man against the Government, and had called the Prince of *Orange* Hook-nose,[3] though I protest I never did; not one of them could say, nor did they offer to say, that I ever printed the Books of which they accuse me, or procured them to be printed, or published any of them,[4] or that the Materials were mine, or that I hired the Room where they were found; but I was an ill Man, and that was sufficient: By which 'tis plain, that they were resolved right or wrong to have my Life.

That they designed not to *Try* but to *Convict* me is as plain; for they refused positively to allow me Counsel to such Matters of Law, as was never refused to any before; and though I caused several Statutes to be read, some to prove that there must be two Witnesses at least to the Fact, others, that though there had been two, as there was not one, yet positively declared that it was not Treason: Nay, the very last Session of Parliament was it enacted,[5] That the Printer of Seditious and Treasonable Books should for the *first* Offence be punished no otherwise than not to follow his Trade for three Years, and for the *second* Offence never to follow it more, and such farther Punishment as seemed fit to the Court, *not extending to Life or Limb*. Now though mine (had it been proved) had but been the *first*, yet you see contrary and in direct opposition to the Law,[6] they make it High-Treason: And when the Jury could not agree to find me Guilty, and came down to ask the Court whether the finding these Things there, and supposing them to be mine, since it could not be prov'd that I printed these Books, or had made any use of them, could affect my Life?[7] I say, when the Jury ask'd this Question, and the Lord Chief Justice *Treby*[8] told them positively, *No, it did not*; yet withal he told them, *That that was not their Business, their Business was to find me Guilty of Printing*:[9] And while they stayed, the Court frown'd upon them to that degree, that the Foreman told them, he was not to be frighted; upon which they publickly reviled them, calling them, *ill Men, ill Subjects, and a Pack of Knaves*; and so terrified them into a Compliance. That this is true, those who were near know too well, although the partial Writer of the Trials hath most perfidiously publish'd not only an unfair, imperfect, and lame Account,[10] but hath also stuff'd it with downright Untruths and Falsehoods, and left out whatsoever made for me; not so much as mentioning the Contradictions of the Witnesses in what they did swear, their swearing to some things that made for me, and when I took hold of them they denied them, nor hath he in the least told the World of the Judges[11] Over-ruling whatsoever I offered, without giving any other Answer than that *it should be so because they would have it so*; with many other such Things, which the conscientious Auditors can testify.

And now I pray consider where is this Liberty and Property? Where the Rights and Priviledges of the Subject? Nay, where the very Laws themselves? And consequently where is the Security of any Man? Why, even in the Deliverers Pockets, where your Money is, and where also without all doubt, if you look not well to your Selves, your Estates e're long will be there likewise. What are these Proceedings but Arbitrary in a Superlative manner, and such as no Reign ever produced before? These were they you were heretofore only afraid of, being jealous without just Cause; but now you see them actually come upon you. I hope you your selves will put a stop to them, by laying these Proceedings before the Parliament, for had it been sitting at this present these Proceedings durst not have been practised; and I pray God to put so speedy an end to them, that as I am the first, so I may be the last that may suffer by them.

I have hitherto lived a Member of the Orthodox Church of *England* as by Law Established, and I declare I now die in the Unity of the same: Therefore, according to its Discipline, I hold my self obliged to ask Pardon of the whole World, of every particular Person whom I have any ways offended; and I do freely and sincerely forgive every one that has offended me, particularly my most false and perjured Witnesses, and among them more particularly **Robin Stephens**,[12] my most unjust and unrighteous Judges, and my repenting Jury; and I pray God may not lay this their Sin of wilful Murther to their Charge at the General Bar, where they shall appear as Criminals, and not Judges.

M*Ay the Almighty bless, preserve, prosper, and* restore *our Sovereign Lord King* JAMES, *to the just Possesison of his indubitable lawful Crowns, strengthen him that he may vanquish and overcome all his Enemies here on Earth, and crown him with eternal Glory hereafter: And that he may never want Heirs to inherit his Crown, bless I beseech thee, O God, His Royal Highness the Prince of* Wales,[13] *and give him such a Numerable Issue, that there may never want one of his Loins to sway the Scepters of these Kingdoms so long as Sun or Moon endure* Amen. Amen.

June 15. 1693.  *William Anderton.*

*An Account of the Conversation, Behaviour and Execution of William Anderton Printer, who was Condemned at the Old Baily, on Thursday the 8th. Of June, for High Treason, and Executed for the same, at Tybourn on Friday the 16th of June 1693* ([London]: printed by John Wallis near the Green Dragon in Fleetstreet, [16–17 June] 1693). Wing, A266; ESTC, R4213.

An Account of the Conversation Behaviour and Execution of
## WILLIAM ANDERTON Printer,
Who was Condemned at the *Old Baily*, on *Thursday* the 8th. of *June*, For *High Treason*, and Executed for the same, at *Tybourn* on *Friday* the 16th of *June* 1693.

SUch has been Their Majesties Incomparable Clemency, since their Accession to the Throne, that among the many Lives Forfeited by the Law, on the account of Treasonable Books and Pamphlets, their boundless Mercy has taken but One: (as a great Lawyer has excellently observed) It was only Their Majesties Goodness toward many others, to call that a *Misdeamenor*, which the Law calls Treason.[1] The Treasonable Libels that this Man suffer'd, more particularly for, being but two,[2] of above two Score several sorts that have been disperst, since the Year 1691, in divers of which are contained as many and great Treasons as it was possible either for the Malice of the Devil or the Corrupt and Treasonable thought of Blood-thirsty Men to invent; *Containing Treasons against the King in his own Royal Person; against his Government, both Ecclesiastical and Civil, full of Treason against the Queen, Scandals against all manner of Professions both in Church and Kingdom, of Magistracy and Ministery*: It is therefore no more wonder to find those People *Distemper'd*, that are entertain'd with *Poyson*, instead of wholesome *Nourishment*, than to see the Sea Rage when the Winds blow.

Thus much said, may seem to give the Disaffected and Murmuring Party a greater Reputation then Convenient, were it not that their main Design, of shooting these *Paper Pellets*, (according to Old *Prines* Phrase),[3] has lately suffered so fatal a Disappointment, that many of them are at this Instant under a *Course of Justice*; Others in *Custody* and Expecting it:[4] And the *Residue* neither in *Humour*, nor *condition* to *Prosecute the Quarrel*; being so fully satisfied of the *Vigelance, Power* and *Activity* of their Majesties Friends, (which in Effect, are as many, as either, Love the Publique, or themselves) that they find it morally Impossible for them ever to bring any *Villany to perfection upon so desperate a*

*Bottome*: Besides they have Undeceived the World, and made appear to their Sacred Majesties, that all Mercy is lost upon them.

Mr. *Anderton*, The Subject of this Narrative was by Birth, a *North-Country Man*, and tho' but of Indifferent *Estated Parents*, yet he was well Educated as to Grammar Learning. From the School he was put Apprentice to a *Printer*, serving his time with one Mr. *Miles Fletcher*,[5] a Person of considerable Note of that Trade, after which for several Years: From a Printer, he became a Corrector of the Press, which Imploy he chiefly followed, till the late *Abdication* and *Revolution*, after which he took to his Printing again, but in Holes and by Corners only.

Mr. *Anderton* has been known to have been an *Old Offender against the Government*, in *Printing Seditious and Treasonable Libels* being generally thought to be concern'd in most of the most *Treasonable Pamphlets* that have been Dispersed for some Years past,[6] Notwithstanding he was Indicted and Convicted but of two of them; the manner of his Apprehending was as followeth.[7]

Mr. *Robert Stephens*, Messenger of the Press; having formerly taken many Private Presses,[8] wherein our Mr. *Anderton* was a Chief Manager, more particularly one at *Hogsdon* near *More Fields*, and another near *So-ho* Yet *Anderton* had the good Fortune always to Escape with his Person. But on the 2*d.* of *May* last, *Spying two Journey-Men Printers, whom he had missed from publick Printing Houses, for above six Months before; he followed them, and saw them go exactly into the house of one* Skudamore[9] (*where* Anderton *was found*) *and where he had reason to think he worked privately*: So having the *Beadle* and some other Persons to his assistance, he Apprehended *Anderton* there, but not without a great deal of trouble and abuse: Mr. *Stephens* and the others, made a particular Search, and in the Chamber where *Anderton* Lodged at the back of his Bed they found a private Door, which led them into a Room where Mr. *Stephens* found a *Printing Press, {chara}cters, &c* and searching farther, he found in an *Old Trunk* a great Quantity of *Libels*, and *Libellous Pamphlets*; one Entituled, *A Caution to the Navy*; a 2d *An Historical Romance on the Wars*; an other, *A Second Letter to the Bishop of Salisbury*; and there was an *Errata*, and an, *&c.* found set in the Press, the same that were in the Book called; *Remarks upon the Confederacy*. And in the Chamber where he lay, there was a *Desk* (which Mr. *Stephens* knew well to be the Prisoners, because he had seized it before, in which there was found the *Two Libels*, that he was afterwards tryed for, and divers others of the same sort, which *Desk the Prisoner owned to be his*; (these they seized and conveyed with the Prisoner to the *Lord Chief Justice Holts* Chamber:[10] He was Examined by my Lord, and committed to *Newgate* for *High Treason*.

On *Thursday* the 1 *June* in the Afternoon, Mr. *Anderton*, was brought to the *Bar*, where an Indictment of *High Treason* was read against him; for that he did *Compose, Print*, and *Publish Two Malicious* and *Treasonable Libels*. The First Entituled, *Remarks upon the present Confederacy, and late Revolution in England*.

The second Entituled, *A French Conquest neither desirable nor practicable*.[11] In which two Libels were contained the Rankest, Vilest, and most malicious Treasons that ever could be Imagined by any man to be put in Paper; in short the Design of them was merely to incite all the Kings Subjects to stir up and raise War and Rebellion against him, and to restore the late King *James*. After the Indictment was read, the Prisoner Pleaded *not Guilty*: And such was the tenderness of the Court towards him, not only in the large Allowances, of freedom, and favour while he was upon his *Tryal*, but upon his request, ordered him a Coppy of the Pannel,[12] and gave him time till *Saturday* to prepare for his *Tryal*, that he might want nothing for his Defence. Accordingly on *Saturday* morning about nine a Clock he was again brought to the Barr, where upon a full hearing and Evidence he was found Guilty of *High Treason*, and the last day[13] of the Sessions he Received his Sentence with the rest of the Malefactors. It was observed that his Countenance did not in the least change all the time of his being in Court, till just as the Sentence was Passing on him, at which moment of time, there was a visible appearance of his Countenance Changing very much.

And now Reader we come to the last Acts or Moments of *William Anderton*, who pursuant to the Sentence was this morning being *Friday* the 16 of *June*. conveyed on a Sledge from *Newgate* to *Tyburn*, the usual Place of Execution, Sir *T. Cooke*, Sir *T. Lane*, the Two Sheriffs, with Major *Richardson*, &c.[14] Riding by the Sledge to see the *Execution* done.

> At *Tyburn* he was attended on by Mr. *B.* and another Reverend Divine,[15] who assisted him with their Spiritual Comfort, and Advice at this last Moment of his life, he continued at the Place of Execution above an Hour, and having delivered, what he had to say, to the Sheriff, &c. the Divines often Praying with him, and he making several Ejaculations to himself very fervently, The Executioner did his Office.

# THE REJECTION OF LICENSING

John Locke's Comments on the 1662 Printing Act ([December 1694–January 1695]). NA, Shaftesbury Papers, 30/24/30/30, Part 1, ff. 88r–89v.

The Commons' Case against Renewing the Printing Act (17 April 1695), *CJ*, 11, pp. 305–6.

'A Bill for the Regulation of Printing and Printing Presses' ([December 1695]). Lambeth Palace Library, Cod. Tenison, MS 640, 17, pp. 207–35.

'Remarks upon the Act Read in the House of Commons for Regulating Printing and Printing Presses' ([?March 1695]). Lambeth Palace Library, Cod. Tenison, MS 640, 20, pp. 249–51.

'Oxford Objections against Scheme of Printing Act' (2 December 1695). Lambeth Palace Library, MS 939, 10.

The year 1695 has gone down in censorship history as the watershed year in which pre-publication licensing ended in England. The Printing Act formally expired with the prorogation of Parliament on 3 May, its fate sealed by waning support in the Commons and then the Lords. By 17 April the MP Edward Clarke was already speaking of it in the past tense. By the year's end, two substitute printing bills with less oppressive provisions had been put forward, their presence helping prevent a return to the original Act and their rejection confirming that England would end 1695 without a press law. Central to these events was the 'College' grouping involving Clarke, John Locke and John Freke, who together mounted a campaign against renewal guided in part by Locke's criticisms of the 1662 Act (see below). On 9 January 1695 a Commons committee recommended extending the Printing Act's term but on 11 February MPs chose instead to order a new bill, which was introduced on 2 March by Clarke and after a second reading on 30 March sent to committee. A version of this College-backed bill in Freke's hand survives in Locke's papers in the Bodleian Library (MS Locke b. 4, f. 77).[1] In the meantime the Lords had advanced a reviving bill whose clause A proposed renewing the existing Printing Act. The Commons accepted all but this one clause and advanced reasons for its exclusion, delivered by Clarke, which were accepted by the Lords on 19 April (see The Commons' Case against Renewing the Printing Act, below). The 'College' bill had not emerged from committee by the end of the session and when the next session proper commenced in November a further bill was ordered, to be prepared by Clarke and Robert Harley. The bill was first presented on 29 November and was an expanded and amended version of the bill copied by Freke for Locke in March. A copy is preserved in manuscript in Lambeth Palace Library, along with two sets of criticisms probably prepared by university heads for Archbishop Tenison, one appearing to refer to the March bill, the other referring to the November–December bill (all three reproduced below). The latter bill, like the March bill, failed to emerge from committee and although there was a further attempt to revive the Printing Act in March 1696 this was swiftly thrown out in the Commons (see Volume 4 of this edition). Effectively the 1662 Act was already dead by May 1695.

John Locke was instrumental in the end of pre-publication censorship in 1694–5, his written opinion contributing to the campaign led in Parliament by Edward Clarke against renewing the Printing Act and its licensing provisions. Locke's clause-by-clause critique of the 1662 Act is known from the manuscript in Locke's papers in the Bodleian Library.[2] Another copy of Locke's criticisms is held amongst the Shaftesbury papers in the National Archives at Kew and is presented here to make it more accessible to scholars, although the two versions do not differ substantially. The paper is badly damaged and missing sections have been supplied from the Bodleian version, as printed in De Beer's edition of Locke's *Correspondence*. It has been suggested that the Kew manuscript was a copy by Locke's amanuensis Sylvester Brounower but the handwriting appears to be Locke's, it is catalogued as such, and the sheet is endorsed on the reverse (in another hand) 'Promised ... [damage] Amendments to the Act ... An Act for preventing ... certain Libels in Mr Locke's hand writing'. The Bodleian manuscript was endorsed 'Printing 94' by the author and Locke's critical commentary probably dates from some weeks before the Commons ordered a new bill rather than renewal of the old Act on 11 February 1695. A few of the criticisms had been advanced as early as January 1693 in a letter from Locke to Clarke (an example Locke mentions in 1694–5 of importing Tully 'two or three years since' was in 1693 described as 'a very fresh instance').[3] Further letters passed between Locke, Clarke and Freke on the subject, particularly in February–March and December 1695. Locke objected to the legislation as a reader as much as a political activist, concerned not only that the Act infringed liberties and reflected ecclesiastical priorities but that it impeded learning by limiting the range and, through trade monopolies, the quality of books.

A reviving bill in the Lords which included the Printing Act as clause A was considered by the Commons on 9 April 1695 and a committee was given the task of drawing up reasons for its rejection to present to the upper house. Clarke duly delivered the Commons' Case against Renewing the Printing Act to the Commons and then the upper house on 18 April and the following day the Lords sent a message agreeing that clause A could be omitted.[4] Echoes of Locke appeared in several of the reasons given, which worked through the impracticalities of enforcing the legislation, as well as questioning the role of licenser, the identification of offensive books, the powers of search and seizure, and the degree of discretion over punishment.

The 'College' bill of March 1695 was followed by the similar bill introduced into the Commons, again by Clarke, on 29 November, 'A Bill for the Regulation of Printing and Printing Presses'. In both bills the most significant departure from the 1662 Act was the retreat from compulsory pre-publication licensing, along with the marginalizing of the Stationers' Company. However, whereas the College bill omitted all reference to licensing, the later bill restored the principle in diluted, voluntary form (see notes for a comparison). The version of this second bill presented here is held in Lambeth Palace Library in the papers of Archbishop Tenison, who took a close interest in press legislation during his tenure (see also Volume 4 of this edition). The manuscript carries no title or date but is catalogued under the title given here. It is accompanied in the Tenison papers by 'An Abstract of the Same' (MS 640, 18). Another copy of the bill is held in Cambridge University Library (MS Oo.6.93, item 6, ff. 39–47). This appears to be an early version copied for comment by the book trade as it has observations added in the same hand relating to copyright and the potential hardships faced by printers and others (see notes). The bill printed here incorporates changes that suggest a date later in December. One of the more notable is the addition of a provision for licensing by 'five or more persons of Credit of the Congregacon to which the said Author does in point of perswason belong'. This may have been added after a meeting Clarke was scheduled to have to hear nonconformists' concerns, which would have been after 14 December.[5] Comparing the March and December bills is not straightforward as Freke's copy of the former paraphrased and trimmed an original text (Locke refers to the distinction in his correspondence).[6] However, one change involved rewording a phrase that concerned Locke which forbade printing anything 'contrary to the Christian religion as it is establisht by law'; this became 'any thing contrary to Law or to the Christian Religion therein Contained'. Moreover, the word 'hereticall', about which Locke had also expressed concern, appeared in the March bill and first version of the November–December bill ('Treasonable Seditious Atheisticall or Hereticall ...') but had disappeared by the second version, Locke's disquiet having probably been seconded by nonconformist opinion in the meantime. This later version therefore represents a considerable easing of restraints on dissenting views, in tandem with the broader undermining of compulsory licensing, while the proposed legislation sought to retain a system of press registration, compulsory submission of printed sheets and printer's or publisher's details, and voluntary licensing to protect readers from sedition and atheism, and authors, printers and publishers from post-publication punishment. The bill nevertheless seems to have succumbed to a political context in which some desired more controls and others less, failing to make progress by the end of the session.

The manuscript 'Remarks' on the bill for regulating printing is also present in the papers of Archbishop Tenison in Lambeth Palace Library. The sheets are bound after an abortive printing bill of 1702-3 but clearly refer to the 'College' proposals of 1695, and the March rather than November-December bill. Tenison seems to have invited comment on the March bill from the universities but received Oxford's views only in December, making the 'Remarks' most likely the Cambridge counterpart. The 'Remarks' protested that the bill effectively removed pre-publication restrictions beyond registering an intention to print, since no provision was made for refusing permission. It also criticized ineffectual powers of search, inadequate penalties for erring printers and the loss of the universities' printing privileges.

Oxford University's views on the printing bills of 1695, dated 2 December, survive among the papers of Edmund Gibson, who became Tenison's librarian at Lambeth Palace in 1696 and was later Bishop of London. The manuscript is endorsed on the reverse in Tenison's hand 'Oxf. obj. ag. scheme of Printing Act'. As the text makes apparent, it was initially a belated response to the March bill, committed to paper amidst concern in November-December at the prospect of a similar bill, whose subsequent appearance is duly noted and its contents criticized. This latter bill was the slightly earlier version of 'A Bill for the Regulation of Printing and Printing Presses', since it lacked a proviso protecting the universities which was demanded by the 'Oxford Objections against Scheme of Printing Act' and adopted in the bill printed here.

Notes
1. The manuscript is printed in J. Locke, *The Correspondence of John Locke*, ed. E. S. De Beer, 8 vols (Oxford: Oxford University Press, 1976-89), vol. 5, pp. 791-5.
2. Printed in Locke, *Correspondence*, vol. 5, pp. 785-91; also in J. Locke, *Political Essays*, ed. M. Goldie (Cambridge: Cambridge University Press, 1997), pp. 330-7; and P. King, *The Life and Letters of John Locke* (London: Henry Bohn, 1858), pp. 202-8.
3. Locke, *Correspondence*, vol. 4, p. 614.
4. *CJ*, 11, pp. 305-6, 309.
5. Locke, *Correspondence*, vol. 5, pp. 482-3.
6. Ibid., vol. 5, p. 795.

# John Locke's Comments on the 1662 Printing Act ([December 1694–January 1695]). NA, Shaftesbury Papers, 30/24/30/30, Part 1, ff. 88r–89v.

## Anno 14. Car. 2. Cap XXXIII

An Act for preventing abuses in Printing Seditious, Treasonable & unlicensed Books & Pamphlets & for regulating printing and printing presses.

§. 2.[1] Heretical, Seditious, Schismatical [or Offensive][2] books, wherein any thing contrary to Xan[3] faith, or (y$^e$) Doctrine or Discipline of y$^e$ Church of England is asserted, or which may tend to y$^e$ scandal of Religion or y$^e$ Church or y$^e$ Government or Governors of y$^e$ Church, State, or of [any Corpora]tion or particular person are prohibited to be [printed imported or] sold.

[Some of these termes are so general and comprehensive or at least so submitted to y$^e$ sense and interpretation of y$^e$ Governors of Church or State for y$^e$ time being that it is impossible any book should passe but just what] suits their humors. And who knows but that y$^e$ motion of y$^e$ Earth may be found to be Heretical, &c., as asserting Antipodes once was?[4]

I know not why a man should not have liberty to print w$^t$ever he would speak, & to be answerable for y$^e$ one just as he is for y$^e$ oth$^r$: if he transgresses y$^e$ law in either.[5] But [gagging a] man for fear he should talk heresie or sedition has no other ground than such as will [make gives][6] necessary for fear a man should use violence if his hands were free and must at last end in y$^e$ imprisonm$^t$: of all whom you will suspect may be guilty of Treason or misdemeanour.

To prevent mens being undiscovered for w$^t$ they print you may prohibit any book to be printed, published or sold without y$^e$ printers or booksellers name under great penalties whatever be in it. And then let y$^e$ printer or bookseller whose name is to it be answerable for w$^t$ever is against law [in it as] if he were y$^e$ Author unless he can produce y$^e$ Author[7] which is all ye restraint ought to be upon printing.

§. 3. All books prohibited to be printed y$^{t8}$ are not first enterd in y$^e$ Regist$^r$: of y$^e$ Company of [Stationers] & licensed.

Whereby it comes to pass y$^t$ sometimes when a book is brought to be entered in y$^e$ Register of y$^e$ Company of Stationers, if they think it may turn to account they enter it there [as theirs], whereby y$^e$ oth$^r$: person is hinderd from printing & publishing it an Example whereof [can be given] by Mr. Awnsham Churchill.[9]

§. 6. No Books to be printed or imported w^ch: any [person or persons] by force or vertue of any Lett^r: patents [have y^e] right priviledg authority or allowance solely to print upon pain of forfeiture & being proceeded ag^t: as an offender against this present Act & upon y^e furth^r: penalty & forfeiture [of six] shillings eight pence for every such book [or books or part of such book or books]¹⁰ imported bound stitched or put to sale, a moiety¹¹ to y^e Kg & a moiety to y^e owner.

By this clause y^e Company of Stationers have a Monopoly of all y^e classick Authors & Schollars cannot but at excessive rate have ye fair & correct Editions of these books & ye comments on y^m:¹² printed beyond seas. For y^e Company of Stationers have obtaind from y^e Crown a patent to print all or at least y^e greatest part of ye Classick Authors, upon pretence as I hear, y^t they should be well & truely printed whereas they are by them scandalously ill printed, both for Lett^r: paper & correctnesse & scarce one tollerable edition made by them of any one of y^m: whenever any of these books of bett^r: editions are imported from beyond Seas y^e Company seize them & make y^e importer pay 6-8 for each book so imported or else they confiscate them, unlesse they are so bountifull as to let y^e importer compound w^th: them at a lower rate There are daily examples [of this: I] shall mention one w^ch: I had from y^e Sufferers own Mth. Mr. Sam Smith¹³ two [or three] / years since imported from Holland Tullys works of a very fine edition w^th new corrections made by Gronovius who had taken y^e pains to compare that w^ch: was thought ye best edition before with several ancient MSS & to correct his by them. These Tullys works upon pretence of their patent for their alone printing Tullys works, or any p^t:¹⁴ thereof & by vertue of this clause of this Act, y^e Company of Stationers seized and kept a good while in their custody demanding 6^s 8^d per book how at last he compounded with them I know not. But by this act schollars are subjected to y^e power of these dull wretches who do not so much as understand Latin whether they shall have any true or good copies or y^e [best ancient Latin] authors, unless they will pay them 6^s 8^d a book for that leave.

Another thing observable is y^t whatever money by vertue of this clause [they have levied] upon y^e subject either [as forfeiture or composition] I am apt to believe [not one farthing of it has ever been accounted for to y^e King or brought into y^e] Exchequer, [though this clause reserves a moiety to y^e King, and 'tis probable considerable sums have been raised.]

[Upon occasion of this] instance of ye Classick authors I demand whether [if another Act for printing] should be made it be not reasonable y^t nobody should have any [peculiar right in any] book w^ch has been in print fifty years but any one as well as anoth^r: might have [y^e liberty to] print it for by such Titles as these w^ch: lie dormant & hinder others many good books come quite to be lost.

But be yt determined as it will in regard to those Authors who now write & sell their copies to booksellers. This certain is very absurd at first sight yt any person or company should now have a Title to ye printing ye works of Tully Caesar or Livy[15] who lived so many [ages since, exclusive of] any oth{r}: nor can there be any reason in nature[16] why I might not print them as well as ye Company of Stationers if I thought fit. This liberty to anyone of printing them is certainly ye way to have ym: ye cheaper & ye better & 'tis this wch: in Holland has produced so many fair & excellent editions of them, whilst ye publishers and [publishers] printers all strive to outdo one anoth{r}: wch: has also brought in great sums to ye Trade of Holland. [Whilst our Company of Stationers,] having ye Monopoly here by this Act [& their patents, slubber[17] them] over as they can cheapest, so yt there is not a book of them vended beyond seas both for their badnesse & dearnesse nor will ye Schollars beyond Seas look upon a book of [them] now printed at London, so ill & false are they besides it would be hard to finde how a [restraint] of printing ye Classick Authors does any way prevent printing Seditious & Treasonable Pamphlets wch: is ye Title & pretence of this Act.

§. 9. No English book may be imprinted or imported from beyond [ye sea]. No foreigner or oth{r}: unless stationer of London[18] may import or sell any books of any language whatever.

This clause serves only to confirme & enlarge ye Stationers Monopoly.

§. 10. In this § besides a great [many other clauses to] secure ye Stationers' Monopoly of printing, [wch: are very] hard [upon ye subject,] ye Stationers [interest is so far preferred to all others yt a landlord who lets a house forfeits five] pounds [if he know yt] his tenant has a [printing press in it] & does not give notice of it to ye Master & Wardens of ye Stationers Company. Nor must a Joyner, [Carpenter or] Smith, &c., worke about a printing presse without giving ye like notice und{r} ye like penaltie.

Which is great{r} caution than I thinke is used about ye presses for coynage[19] to secure ye people from false Money.

By §.11. The Numbr of Mast{r} printers were reduced from a great{r} number to twenty & ye Numb{r} of Master found{rs} of Letts reduced to fower,[20] & upon vacancy ye Numb{r} to be filled by ye ArchBp of Canterbury [& Bishop of London] & to give security not to print any [unlicensed books.] /

This hindrs a man who has served out his time ye benefit of seting up his Trade, wch: whether it be not against ye right of ye subject as well as contrary to common equity deserves to be considerd.

§.12. The Numb{r}: of presses yt every one of ye twenty Master printers shall have are reduced to two only those [who have been] Masters or Upper

Wardens of ye Company may have three & as many more as ye ArchBP of Canterbury or BP of London will allow.

§.13. Everyone ~~Master~~ who has[21] been Master or Upper Warden of ye Company may have three, Every one of ye Livery two & every Master printer of ye Yeomanry[22] but one Apprentice at a time.

By wch: restraint of presses & taking of Apprentices & ye prohibition in §.14 of taking or useing any [Journeymen except Englishmen & Freemen][23] of ye trade is ye reason why o{r}:[24] printing is so very bad & yet so very dear [in England.] They who are hereby priviledged to ye Exclusion of others working & setting ye price as they please, whereby an advantage yt might be made to ye Realm by this manufacture is wholy lost to England & thrown into ye hands of o{r}: Neighbours. The Sole Manufacture of printing bringing into ye Low Countrys great sums every year. But o{r}: Ecclesiastical Laws seldom favour trade, & he yt reads this Act wth attention will finde it upse[25] Ecclesiastical. [The Nation] looses by this Act, for o{r}: books are so dear & ill printed yt they have very little vent amongst foreigners unlesse now & then by truck for theirs, wch: yet shews how much those who buy here books printed here are imposed on. Since a book printed at London may be bought cheap{r}: at Amsterdam than in Paul's Churchyard[26] notwithstanding all ye charge & hazard of transportation. For their printing being free & unrestrained they sell their books at so much a cheap{r} rate than our [booksellers] do ours, yt in truck valueing o{n}: proportionably to their own or their own [equally to o{n} wch:] is ye same thing they can afford books received from London upon such Exchanges [cheaper] in Holland than o{r}: Stationers sell them in England. By this Act England loses in General, [Schollars] in particular are ground & nobody gets but a lazy ignorant Company of Stationers to say no worse of them. But anything rather than let Mother church be disturbed in her opinions or impositions by any bold enquirer from ye presse.

§. 15. One or more of ye Messeng{rs}: of his Maties: Chamber by Warrant und{r} his Maties: Signe Manual,[27] or under ye hand of one of his Maties: principal Secretarys of State or ye Master & Wardens of ye Company of Stationers [taking with] him a Constable & such assistance as they shall think needfull has an unlimited power to search [all houses & to] seize upon all books wch: they shall but think fit to suspect.

How ye Gentlemen, much more how ye Peers of England[28] came thus to prostitute their houses to ye visitation & inspection of anybody, much less a messeng{r}: upon pretence of searching [for books] I cannot imagine. Indeed, ye houses of Peers & others not of ye Trades mentioned [in this Act are pretended to be exempted from this search, §. 18., where 'tis provided they shall not be searched but by special warrant under ye king's signe manual or under ye hands of one of yᵉ Secretaries of State.] But this is but yᵉ shadow of an exemption for they are still subject to be searchd every corner & coffer in them under pretence of unlicensed books, a mark of slavery wᶜʰ: I think their Ancestors would never have submitted to. Thus to lay their houses wᶜʰ: are their castles open not to yᵉ pursuit of yᵉ law agᵗ: a malefactor convicted of misdemeanour or accused upon oath but to yᵉ suspition of having unlicensed books, wᶜʰ: is whenever it is thought fit to search his house & see what is in it.

§.16. All printers offending any way agᵗ: this Act incapacitated to exercise their trade for 3 years. And for yᵉ second offence perpetual incapacity with any other punishmᵗ: not reaching to life or limb.

And thus a man is to be undone & starve for printing Dʳ: Bury's case or yᵉ History of Tom [Thumb unlicensed.]²⁹ /

§. 17. Three copies of every book printed are to be reservd whereof two to be sent to yᵉ two[Universities] by yᵉ Master of yᵉ Stationers' Company.

This clause upon examination I suppose will be found to be mightily if not wholy neglected, as all things yᵗ are good in this Act, yᵉ company of Stationers minding nothing in it but what makes for their Monopoly. I believe yᵗ if yᵉ publique Librarys of both Universities be looked into (wᶜʰ: this will give a fit occasion to do) there will not be found in them half pʳhaps not one in ten of yᵉ Copys of books printed since this Act. vid xxxxx³⁰ 17°. Car. 2. cap. 4.³¹

§. last. This Act though made in a time when everyone strove to be forwardest to make court to yᵉ Church & Court by giveing whatever was asked yet this was no manifest an invasion on yᵉ trade liberty & property of yᵉ subject yᵗ it was made to be in force only for two years. From wᶜʰ: 14ᵗʰ: Car. 2.³² it has by yᵉ joynt endeavour of [Church &] Court been from [time to time] revived & so continued to this day. Every one [being answer]able for books he [publishes prints or] sells conteining any thing seditious or agᵗ: Law makes this or any other act for yᵉ restraint of printing very needlesse in yᵗ part & so it may be left free in yᵗ part as it was before 14 Car. 2. That any person or company should have patents for yᵉ sole printing of antient Authors is very unreasonable & injurious to learning. And for those who purchase copies from Authors yᵗ now live & write it may be reasonable to limit their property to a certain number of years after yᵉ death of yᵉ Author or yᵉ first printing of yᵉ book as suppose 50 or 70 years. This I am sure 'tis very absurd & ridiculous yᵗ anyone now living should pretend to have a propriety in or a powʳ: to dispose of yᵉ proprietie of any copies or writeings of Authors who lived before printing was known & used in Europe.

## The Commons' Case against Renewing the Printing Act (17 April 1695), *CJ*, 11, pp. 305–6.

Mercurii, 17 die Aprilis ...

Mr. *Clark*[1] reported from the Committee, to whom it was referred to prepare Reasons, to be offered at a Conference with the Lords, for disagreeing to an Amendment, made by the Lords, to the Bill, intituled, An Act for continuing, and making perpetual, several Laws therein mentioned,[2] That they had prepared Reasons accordingly; which they had directed him to report to the House; and which he read in his Place; and afterwards [gave][3] in at the Clerk's Table: Where the same were twice read; and, upon the Question put thereupon, agreed unto by the House; and are as follow; *viz.*

The Commons cannot agree to the Clause marked A;[4]

1st, Because it revives, and re-enacts, a Law which in no-wise answered the End for which it was made; the Title and Preamble of that Act being to prevent printing seditious and treasonable Books, Pamphlets, and Papers: But there is no Penalty appointed for Offenders therein;[5] they being left to be punished at Common Law, as they may be without that Act; whereas there are great and grievous Penalties imposed by that Act for Matters wherein neither Church nor State is any ways concerned. /

2. Because that Act gives a Property in Books to such Persons, as such Books are, or shall be, granted to by Letters Patents, whether the Crown had, or shall have any Right to grant the same, or not, at the time of such Grant.

3. Because that Act prohibits printing any thing before Entry thereof in the Register of the Company of Stationers, except Proclamations, Acts of Parliament, and such Books as shall be appointed under the Sign Manual, or under the Hand of a principal Secretary of State; whereby both Houses of Parliament are disabled to order any thing to be printed; and the said Company are impowered to hinder the printing all innocent and useful Books; and have an Opportunity to enter a Title to themselves, and their Friends, for what belongs to, and is the Labour and Right of, others.

4. Because that Act prohibits any Books to be imported, without special Licence, into any Port in *England*, except *London*; by which Means the whole foreign Trade of Books is restrained to *London*, unless the Lord Archbishop of *Canterbury*, or the Lord Bishop of *London*, shall, in Interruption of their more important Affairs in governing the Church, bestow their time *gratis* in looking over Catalogues of Books, and granting Licences; whereas, the Commons think,

the other Ports of the Kingdom have as good Right as *London* to trade in Books, as well as other Merchandizes.

5. Because that Act leaves it in the Power either of the Company of Stationers, or of the Archbishop of *Canterbury*, and Bishop of *London*, to hinder any Books from being imported, even into the Port of *London*; for if one or more of the Company of Stationers will not come to the Custom-house, or that those Reverend Bishops shall not appoint any learned Man to go thither, and be present at the opening and viewing Books imported, the Custom-house Officer is obliged to detain them.

6. Because that Act appoints no Time wherein the Archbishop or Bishop of *London*, shall appoint a learned Man, or that one or more of the Company of Stationers shall go to the Custom-house to view imported Books; so that they or either of them, may delay it till the Importer may be undone, by having so great a Part of his Stock lie dead; or the Books, if wet, may rot and perish.

7. Because that Act prohibits any Custom-house Officer, under the Penalty of losing his Office, to open any Pacquet wherein are Books, until some or one of the Company of Stationers, and such learned Man, as shall be so appointed, are present: Which is impracticable; since he cannot know there are Books, until he has opened the Pacquet.

8. Because that Act confirms all Patents of Books granted, and to be granted; whereby the sole Printing of all, or most of, the Classick Authors are, and have been for many Years past, together with a great Number of the best Books, and of most general Use, monopolized by the Company of Stationers; and prohibits the importing any such Books from beyond Sea; whereby the Scholars in this Kingdom are forced not only to buy them at the extravagant Price they demand, but must be content with their ill and incorrect Editions; and cannot have the more correct Copies, which are published abroad, nor the useful Notes of Foreigners,[6] or other learned Men, upon them.

9. Because that Act prohibits any thing to be printed till licensed; and yet does not direct what shall be taken by the Licenser for such Licence; by colour whereof great Oppression may be, and has been, practised.

10. Because that Act restrains Men bred up in the Trade of Printing, and Founding of Letters, from exercising their Trade, even in an innocent and inoffensive Way, though they are Freemen of the Company of Stationers, either as Masters or Journeymen; the Number of Workmen, in each of those Trades, being limited by that Act.

11. Because that Act compels Master-Printers to take Journeymen into their Service, though they have no Work or Employment for them.

12. Because that Act restrains all Men, who are not licensed by the Bishop, from selling innocent and inoffensive Books, though never so useful, in any Part of *England*, except Freemen of the Company of Stationers, who may sell without

such Licence;[7] so that neither Church nor State is taken care of thereby; but the People compelled to buy their Freedom of Trade in all Parts of *England* from the Company of Stationers in *London*.

13. Because that Act prohibits any one not only to print Books, whereof another has entered a Claim of Property in the Register of the Company of Stationers, but to bind, stitch, or put them to Sale; and that under a great pecuniary Penalty; though it is impossible for a Bookbinder, Stitcher, or Seller, to know whether the Book brought to him, were printed by the Proprietor or another.

14. Because that Act prohibits Smiths to make any Ironwork for any Printing-Press, without giving Notice to [the] Company of *Stationers*, under the Penalty of 5*l*.; whereas he may not know to what Use the Iron bespoke of him, and forged by him, may be put.

15. Because that Act prohibits printing and importing not only heretical, seditious, and schismatical Books, but all offensive Books; and doth not determine what shall be adjudged offensive Books: So that, without Doubt, if the late King *James* had continued in the Throne till this time, Books against Popery would not[8] have been deemed offensive Books.

16. Because that Act subjects all Mens Houses, as well Peers as Commoners, to be searched at any time, either by Day or Night, by a Warrant[9] under the Sign Manual, or under the Hand of one of the Secretaries of State, directed to any Messenger, if such Messenger shall, upon probable Reason, suspect, that there are any unlicensed Books there; and the House[s] of all Persons free of the Company of Stationers are subject to the like Search, on a Warrant from the Master and Wardens of the said Company, or any one of them.

17. Because the Penalties for Offences against that Act are excessive; it being in the Power of the Judges, or Justices of the Peace, to inflict what Punishment they please, not extending to Life or Member.[10]

Lastly, There is a Proviso in that Act for *John Streater*,[11] That he may print what he pleases, as if the Act had never been made; when the Commons see no Cause to distinguish him from the rest of the Subjects of *England*.

*Ordered*, That a Message be sent to the Lords, to desire a Conference upon the Subject matter of the Amendments made by them to the said Bill.

*Ordered*, That Mr. *Clark* do carry the said Message.

## 'A Bill for the Regulation of Printing and Printing Presses'
([December 1695]). Lambeth Palace Library, Cod. Tenison, MS 640, 17, pp. 207–35.

Whereas[1] it has in all times been thought necessary that publick provision should be made for the Regulation of printing and printing presses to prevent the Mischeifes that might otherwise happen both in Church and State Be it Enacted by the Kings most Excellent Maj$^{tie}$ by and with the advise and consent of the Lords spirituall & temporall and Comons in parliament assembled and by authority of the same that noe printing press shall from and after the         Day of[2]         be erected used or Kept within the City of London or Westm$^r$ or suburbs of them untill notice hath been given[3] in writing to the Lord Chancellor or Lord Keeper of the Great Seale of England for the time being or to one of the principall Secretaryes of state for the time being or to one of their Chief Secretaryes to be Registered in their office or to the Lord Chiefe Justice of the Court of Kings Bench for the time being of the name of the person who is to use such printing press and the place where the same is to be Erected or Kept and that noe printing press shall be erected used or Kept after the         Day of         in Oxford or Cambridge[4] untill like notice hath been given to y$^e$ respective / Chancellor or Vice Chancellor for the time being of the Universityes of Oxford and Cambridge and that noe printing presse shall be Erected used or Kept in the Cityes of York Exeter Bristoll or Norwich[5] after the         Day of         untill like notice hath been given to the respective Lord Bishop of the Diocese and Mayor of the respective City[6] for the time being. And that noe printing press shall be Erected used or Kept in any part of England or the Dominion of Wales or Towne of Berwick upon Tweed Except within the Cityes of London and Westm$^r$ and suburbs of the same, or within Oxford Cambridge Yorke Bristoll Exeter or Norwich without the speciall License of his Maj$^{tie}$ his heirs or successors or the Bishop of the Diocese and every printing press that shall be erected used or Kept after the         Day of         whereof noe such notice is or shall be given or in any other place than London Westm$^r$ and the suburbs of the same or in Cambridge Oxford Yorke Exeter Bristoll or Norwich which shall not be Lycensed by his Maj$^{tie}$ his heires or successors or by the Bishop of the Diocese shall be adjudged and is hereby Declared and adjudged to be a private printing / presse and forfeited with all Letters & Utensills thereto belonging or therewith used and shall or may by vertue of this act be seized to the use of his Maj$^{tie}$ his heires & successors And whosoever shall Erect use or Keep such private printing presse shall be Disabled to use or Exercise the art Trade or Mistery of a printer for space of         under the penalty of         and shall forfeite alsoe the summe of         the one Moyety[7] thereof to the use of his Maj[tie] his heires & successors the other Moyety to such person as shall Informe & sue for the same. And be it further Enacted by the authority aforesaid that upon such Notice as abovesaid given to the Lord Chancellor or Lord Keeper of the Great seale of England or to either of the principall Secretaryes of State or their Cheife Secretaryes or to the said Lord Cheife Justice Chancellor or Vice Chancellor of either of the said Universityes or to the Bishop of the Diocese or Mayor of Yorke Bristoll Exeter or Norwich they shall respectively without fee or Reward Immediately Give a Certificate in writing of the Receipt of such notice. And Be it further Enacted by the authority aforesaid That any Books Concerning / the Comon Law of this Realme may be Licensed[8] to be printed by the Lord Chancellor or Lord Keeper of the Great Seale of England for the time being the Lord Chiefe Justices and the Lord Chiefe Baron for the time being or one or more of them or by the appointm[t] of one or more of them. And all Books of History Concerning the state of this Realme or other Books concerning any affaires of State may be Licensed to be printed by the principall Secretaryes of State for the time being or one of them or by their or one of their appointment and all Bookes Concerning Heraldry Honour and Armes or otherwise concerning the Office of Earle Marshall may be Licensed to be printed by the Earle Marshall for the time being or by his appointment or by the King at armes Garter or Clarenceux and Norroy[9] for the time being and all bookes concerning the Diseases or Cur of Diseases in Humane Bodyes may be Licensed to be printed by the president and Censors of the College of physitians[10] of London for the time being or one of them and all other Bookes whither of Divinity philosophy or other Science or art may be Licensed to be printed by the Arch Bishop of / Canterbury or Yorke for the time being or one of them or their or one of their appointm[t] or by the Bishop of the Diocese for the time being wherein the same shall be printed or by his appointment or by the Chancellor or Vice Chancellor for the time being of the University wherein the same shall be printed or by the appointm[t] of either of the said Chancellors or Vice Chancellors or by five or more persons of Credit of the Congregacon to which the said Author does in point of perswason belong[11] And it shall be lawfull for any printer to print any book soe Lycensed soe as the same be not printed in a Private presse without being accountable or answerable by Law for any Illegality Error or fault in the same But the Licensor or Licensors and author shall be answerable at Law for such Illegality Error or fault[12] Neverthelesse It shall be and it is hereby Declared and Enacted to be Lawfull to Print any booke not Containeing any thing therein Contrary to the Laws of God or Laws of this Realme without any such License soe as the Rules hereinafter prescribed by this act be pursued followed & performed by the printers thereof.[13] /

   And Be it further Enacted by the authority aforesaid that from and after the     Day of       every person who shall print any Book pamphlett portraiture or paper which was not before printed in England with License w^ch shall not be Licensed to be printed as above is Directed If the matter in such Book pamphlett portraiture or paper Concerne or relate to the Laws of England[14] then shall Carry or send or Cause to be Delivered One printed Coppy thereof sheet by sheet as the same is printed off and with the first sheet thereof A Note of the name of the printer[15] by whome and place where the same is printing to the Lord Chancellor or Lord Keeper or one of the Lord Chiefe Justices or Lord Chiefe Baron for the time being and if the matter in such book pamphlett or portraiture concern or relate to the History or State of this realme shall then carry or send and Cause to be Delivered one printed Coppy thereof sheete by sheete as the same is printed off and together with the first sheet thereof a Note of the name of / the printer by whome & place where the same is printing unto one of the Secretaryes of State or one of their Secretaryes in their respective office and if the matter of such book pamphlett Portraiture or paper Concerne or relate to Divinity philosophy or any other Science or art[16] shall Carry or send & cause to be Delivered one printed Copy thereof sheet by sheete as the same is printed off and together with the first sheete thereof and of the name of the printer by whome and place where the same is printing to the Arch Bishop of Canterbury or Yorke for the time being or such persons as they or one of them shall appoint or to the Bishop of the Diocese wherein the same shall be printed or such person as hee shall appoint or to the Vice Chancellor for the time being of the University where the same shall be printed if the same bee printed in Oxford or Cambridge under the penalty of being Disabled to use or Exercise the art or Mistery of a printer for the space of          from the time of Conviction of any such offense and the printing presse Letters and / Utensills Imployed in printing the same and the paper & books printed without such License as is in this Act Directed and not carryed & Delivered as is herein Directed are hereby Declared and adjudged forfeited[17] and shall or may by vertue of this Act be seized and Disposed of to the use of his Maj^tie his heires & successors And be it further Enacted by the authority afores^d that every person who shall hereafter print any Booke pamphlett portraiture or paper shall thereunto if the same be printed in one sheet of paper onely and in the page of Either page if the same Containe more than one sheete of paper print and Lett in words at Length the Christian name and Surname and the place of aboade of the Master printer or publisher[18] of the same or Else shall Incurr the penalty and forfeiture of          and of the whole Impression of the said Booke pamphlett portraiture or paper and of the printing presse Letters and Utensills Imployed in printing thereof and being further answerable for any thing contrary to Law or to / the Christian Religion therein Contained And be it further Enacted that whosoever shall print or order his name to be printed as printer or publisher of any matter or thing shall be answerable to the Law as if hee were the author of the same and the author shall be neverthelesse answ^erable and punishable for any thing Illegall therein if the author can be Discovered unlesse the same be Lycensed according as this act has allowed Bookes to be Lycensed and then the Lycensor and not the author publisher or printer shall be answerable & punishable for any thing Illegal therein Contained[19] And be it further Enacted by the authority aforesaid that noe person shall sell or publish or offer for sale any booke pamphlette pourtraiture or paper printed in England after the          Day of          whereon the printer or publishers name is not printed under the penalty of forfeiting          for every offence.

And be it further Enacted by the authority aforesaid / that noe person shall print the name of any person in any book pamphlett Portraiture or paper without such Printer or publishers Consent or without authority giveing in writeing for soe Doeing under the penalty of forfeiting the summe of          to the party whose name shall be without such Consent and authority soe printed as printer or publisher and the further summe of          the one Moyety thereof to his Maj$^{tie}$ his heires and successors the other Moyety to such person as will sue for the same and alsoe under the penalty of being Disabled to use or Exercise the art or mistery of a printer for the space of          after Conviction of any such offence.

And be it further Enacted by the authority aforesaid that every printer shall reserve three Coppyes of the largest paper whereon the same is printed of every new Book and Bookes reprinted with additions and shall before any publication or vending of such book carry / or send or Cause to be Delivered one of the said Coppyes to the Keeper of his Maj$^{ties}$ Library one other to such person as shall be appointed by the University or Vice Chancellor of Cambridge in the Towne or place where the same shall bee printed to Receive the same for the use of the publick Library of the University The other or third Copy to such person as the University or Vice Chancellor of Oxford shall appoint in the Towne or place where the same is or shall be printed to receive the same for the use of the publick Library of the said University And be it further Enacted by the authority aforesaid that either of the secretaryes of state and either of the Chiefe Justices of the Courts of Kings Bench or Comon pleas the Chancellor or Vice Chancellor of either of the Universityes and Cheife Magistrate of any City or Towne where any printing presse is or may be Erected or Kept and any Justice of peace in any place where noe printing presse is by this Act allowed to be erected or Kept shall or may by virtue of this act by their / respective Warrants Impower any person or persons from time to time and at all times within their respective Jurisdictions to enter into and search any printing house or place where any printing press is Kept and the Roomes warehouses and Cellars thereunto belonging or which are Imployed by any printer or any other place where any of the respective Magistrates shall be Informed upon Oath that there is any private printing press and in Case of Refusall of admittance with the assistance of a Constable who is hereby required to be aiding to any person soe Impowered to break open any Door Cupboard Box Trunk or

Chest or other place of Concealement[20] and to seize and take away all Coppies of prints of any Treasonable Seditious or Atheisticall[21] Booke pamphlett or paper and alsoe such private printing presse and the Letters and Utensills thereunto belonging and to apprehend and bring to Justice every person useing such private printing presse or Concerned in printing such Treasonable Seditious or Atheisticall Book pamphlett or paper And be / it further Enacted by the authority aforesaid that whosoever shall Import or bring into this Realme any book pamphlett or printed paper wherein is Contained any Treasonable Seditious or Atheisticall matter shall be Deemed and taken as author or printer of the same and shall be answereable and punishable as such   And Be it further Enacted by the authority aforesaid that after any Book has been adjudged to containe any Treasonable Seditious or Atheisticall matter by the author publisher printer or Importer of the same haveing been Convict and punished for writeing publishing printing or Importing the same It shall and may be lawfull for his Maj$^{tie}$ his heires and successors by proclamation to prohibite the selling Giveing or publishing such book pamphlett or paper and cause them to be seized and Burnt[22] wherever they shall be found and whosoever shall from thenceforth sell Give or publish the same shall Incurr the penalty and forfeite the summe of

And be it further Enacted by the authority aforesaid / that for the better preserveing of propertyes in the Coppies of Books whosoever shall print any Booke pamphlett portraiture or paper which has been before printed and the property thereof lawfully vested in any other person or persons without the Lycense of him or them in whome the lawfull property is or shall be vested shall Incurre the penalty and forfeite the summe of            to the person or persons in whome the property or sole right of Printing the same is or shall at that time be vested And be it further Enacted and Declared by the authority aforesaid that noe person or persons shall for the future have any sole property or sole right of printing any Book pamphlett pourtraiture or paper for any long or further time than             yeares to be accounted from and next ensueing the first printing of the same by such proprietor or proprietors any Law Statute Ordinance or Custome to the Contrary notw$^{th}$standing[23] And be it further Enacted by the authority aforesaid that all the penaltyes of this act for which noe particular / method is herein prescribed for the Levying & recovering the same shall or may be Recovered by Bills plaint Informations Indictment or Action of Debt in any of his Maj$^{ties}$ Courts of Record in which noe Essoigne protection privilege or wager of Law or more than one Imparlance[24] shal be allowed Provided alwayes And Be it further Enacted by the authority aforesaid that noe person shall be prosecuted or molested for any offence Committed ag$^t$ this act unlesse such prosecution be Commenced within            after the offence Committed and not Guilty or non {debet}[25] within            as the Case shall require shall be a good plea for the Def$^t$[26] & if found for him he shall be Discharged and if prosecuted at the suite of a subject shall have his Costs adjudged to him and such Remedy for recovery of the same as is usuall where the Def$^t$ by Law is to recover his Costs in other Cases  Provided alwyes that nothing in this act Contained shall be Construed to obtend to the prejudice or Infringing or any of the Just Rights and priviledges of either of the Two Universityes of this realme touching & Concerning the Lycensing or printing of books in either of the s$^d$ Universityes[27]  Provided that this act shall continue and be in force for          yeares to Commence from          Day of

## 'Remarks upon the Act Read in the House of Commons for Regulating Printing and Printing Presses' ([?March 1695]). Lambeth Palace Library, Cod. Tenison, MS 640, 20, pp. 249-51.

The design of the Bill for Regulating of Printing is manifestly to lay open the Press for all or any and who hath a mind to Print even without Lycence for Erecting such Press, for they are to give notice of such Intention, but no Person to whom they are to give such notice are authorised to refuse or deny it. And even to Print and Publish what they Please without any leave and Lycence.[1]

Now it has been found by Experience so difficult to prevent Scandalous Books, under such moderate restraint as now is how much more will it be so when such unlycensed Power is Granted.

How far this will be Consistant with the quiet and safty of Church or State we think well worthy of serious consideration before it be granted.

It hath been thought in this and other Kingdoms, a flower of the Crown to have an Inspection on the Press for restraining and regulating of the same as there is occasion, because of the manifold mischeifs that may otherwise ensue, and many Laws have been made to that purpose, which yet have been found Insufficient to prevent all such mischeifs, and how much more will it be so if all these Restraints be taken away.

The notice to be given to the Cheif Magistrate[2] of a Corporation of such intended Press, without any Power to hinder it is very Insignificant.

And the Power of searching for and seizing Treasonable Seditious Heretical or Atheistical Books when Printed Signifies not much more, for if this extend to whatever such searches shall think to, it will be liable to great Corruption by Bribing such persons to Connive or otherwise expose them to Suits of Law for justifying such seizures, when the issue at a Tryall shall be whether such Books be Treasonable &c and either the Printer Suffer great Loss by undue Seizures, or the Seizer condemned in great Damages in Case a Verdict go against them, and where shall there be found so many Trusty and Intelligent Persons to inspect so many Thousand Presses all England over.[3] /

And how many other Scandalous or Wicked Papers and Pamphlets may be thus printed, which will not directly fall under these Characters in a rigorous and Legall Sence.

The Seizures of such Papers or Utensils so Imployed will be as insignificant, for besides that the whole forfeiture of such obscure Printing house may be little worth, it will be hard to Prove how much that furniture was actually imployed in Printing that Book.

And the disabling such Person from Printing afterwards for a Certaine time, signifies nothing when another of his Confederates shall set up another Press for such Purposes the next day.

And all the Penalties not to be incurred till after Legall Conviction, which will seldom happen; and such Prosecution limitted to some short time.

As to the Printers or Publishers being Answerable for the matter contained in such Books, this is no more then what could be without this Law, upon an Indictment at Common Law[4] or an Action on the case or the like process.

As to what Concerns the Universities in particular Tis true this doth not make voyd their Liberty to Printing, but by thus leaving all in Common it makes it Cease to be a Priviledge or advantage to them.

For the design of such Grants intended for their advantage was to enable them to do what otherwise they might not.

And it will in the Consequence effectually destroy the ends of such Grants, For the declared designs of such Grants were to enable them to Print and Publish such usefull and Chargeable Books (out of Antient Manuscripts or otherwise) which would not turn to Acco[5] of themselves alone (and would therefore be lost) if not recompensed by some other more afordable and Beneficiall Books by Printing or which (or forbearing to Print upon some Composition) they may be enabled to sustain the Burden of such usefull / but Chargeable Books.

And it will in effect destroy the University Press for that Purpose. For what encouragement will it be to be at such Charges for Publishing a fair Edition of such usefull Books for the Honour of the Nation if every obscure Printer may Presently Print the same in a small Letter and on Worse paper, and thereby ruine those at whose charges such Books were prepared for the Press, and fairly Printed they (without such Preparative Charge which is done to their hand) being thereby able to undersell them.

And it is Considerable that this gives a Power to the Mayors of Oxford and Cambridge (as the cheif Officers of these Corporations) concurring to that of the Chancellors & Vice-Chancellors.

## 'Oxford Objections against Scheme of Printing Act' (2 December 1695). Lambeth Palace Library, MS 939, 10.

Dec. 2. 1695.

There was we understand in the last session of Parliam$^t$ a Bill brought into the house of Comons, and remitted, concerning the Regulation of the Presse;[1] (a Copy of w$^{ch}$ was sent down to the University to consider) but that Session ended before anything was determined upon it.

We do not know but that the same or a like bill may be brought in to the present session, and therefore have thought it our duty to represent our thoughts of it.

We do not presently remember all the particulars of the said Bill: But (so far as we do remember) the main drift of the Bill was to this purpose

That any one who will (and as many as will) may in any City or Town Corporate sett up one or more printing presses; first giving notice thereof to ye Mayor or other head Officer of the said corporations: wch the said Mayor or Head Officer is (under a {privity})[2] not to hinder, but permit it. And the Printer may then print what he thinks fit without any previous License.[3] Yet so that the said Mayor or Head Officer may (if he please) by himselfe or his Officer inspect the said Press or Presses, to see what is there printed; and may seize what he there finds of dangerous consequence, and the Press or other Utensils imployed in printing thereof; and such Printer, for the first time be disabled to print.

If any such Bill shall be now offered we humbly crave leave to suggest;

That if it have not been thought safe or prudent to allow such an Universal Liberty, as to selling of {Beer, Mo:},[4] or Wine, without restraint of number or persons; (for preventing of debauching and imoralitie) it will be much more dangerous to permit it as to printing in reference to morality, Religion, or the Governm$^t$.

In reference to moralities, how scandalous will it be (under a civiliz'd governm$^t$) to have papers dayly published in print in defense or excuse of all lewdness, Ribaldry, and debauchery.

In reference to Religion, how shall wee avoyd all [illeg.][5] Books or Pamphlets tending to the ruine or undermining not only of the Protestant Religion, as contradistinguished to the Papist and of the Orthodox, as opposite to Socinians, Anabaptists,[6] and other sects; but also of the Christian Religion, or then Revealed Religion in general, as opposite to Atheists, Anti-Scripturists, and such as deny the being or Providence of God, the soul's immortalitie, the Rewards and Punishment of heaven and hell, w$^{th}$ the like.

In reference to the Govermnᵗ: how easy will it be upon any discontent or sedition and treasonable designe, to scatter papers and pamphlets to that purpose and it cannot be thought reasonable there should be a like liberty to print against Religion and the Govermᵗ as for it.

If it be thought sufficient that such things may be afterwards punished if done how much better is it, that they be prevented. It is manifest (beside, the difficulty of a legal conviction) how little effect such punishmᵗ will have (in comparison to the mischief) by the daring boldness of clipping & coyning[7] notwithstanding the / strongest punishment in such case. And if permitted this doth not redress the mischief done by it. And if under such restraints of the press as hitherto it cannot be prevented but that such Books and pamphlets will (by stealth) get abroad; how much more if such Universall Liberty be allowed.

And it may be reasonably presumed that those who be forward to promote such liberty, do it with a prospect of publishing what would not be thought fitt to be published, for otherwise it is not hard to obtain a license for what is fit to be licensed. As to that of the Mayors or other head officers power of Inspections and seizing by themselves or their under officers:

On the one hand this may be very troublesome to innocent Printing, if such under officers may upon such pretense seize what they please (unless gratified under hand by the Printer to prevent such troubles) for wch he shall have nonsuch but by a tedious, chargeable, and uncertain tryal at Law; among wch he may loose all the advantage of publishing what he hath duly printed.

And on the other hand; how many Mayors or head Officers of Corporations throughout England, are not competent Judges of what is or is not fit to be printed; Or who will not trouble themselves (when nothing is to be got by it) to make such dilligent inspections as will be necessary to prevent such mischief.

And as to seizing the Press or Letters, by wch such are punished; it is very insignificant. For while such things are getting abroad, it will not be easy to find and prove by what man they were printed: or if so, what press or Letter was imployed in it: Unless under such pretense you will seize all the presses and Letters of such a man.

And as to the disabling that person to print for the future, it is less significant. For this cannot be done till after a legal conviction; so even then, what he may not do, shall be done by another of his complices the next day.

If it be further alleged that the Governmt may imploy Officers to inspect such presses: It will not be possible, or not without vast charge, for the Governmt to imploy so many all over England as shall be sufficient to reach all such presses, so dilligently as to prevent all such mischief. Now all this doth not particularly concern the two Universities as such; but the whole Church and Nation, and the Governmt in particular, and is of great concernmt to them all.

As to the Universities in particular; It may perhaps be said, that it is not intended to restrain them, but that they print as heretofore.

But when such power hath been granted to the Universitie as a priviledge, as Bodies fit to be intrusted in such matters: If every body else may so print as well as they; though it may yet remaine as a power, it will cease to be a priviledge; and they loose all favour and advantage intended them by such priviledge. And the / like for the Kings Printing and all other priviledged as to such and such Books; and those who have legal interest in such and such copies. And how far it will be thought adviseable to invade the rights of {regular} reform is a matter of serious consideration.

Thus far was written before I had seen the head of the New Bill.[8]

Upon sight of the head of the new bill, I thus Observe.

The design of this seems to be much the same with the former; but more covertly and under a disguise.

No press to be erected or kept in London, Westminster, Cambridge, Oxford, York, Exeter, Bristol, or Norwich,[9] without notice given as is directed. But then such notice being given, anyone that will (and as many as will) may sett up one or more Presse, that without restraint, and none is impowered to hinder it.

No press elsewhere without special License from his Majestie: But such License may (under some spurious pretense) be easily passed. And if not, it may be long concealed till mischief be done: and even then, the penalty (perhaps) not very considerable.

Books of such and such head, may be Licensed by such & such (if the Licenser will be answerable; which may be a hazard, in case the copy be allowed, after such License.) But (for ought appears) they may be printed without such License;[10] so that then the printer (if discoverd) may be answerable for the matter of it (not for printing without License).

That of delivering a Copy Sheet by Sheet &c: will be found impracticable and the penalty easily avoided. And the like for not printing his name.[11]

Thus far concerns the publike generally: not particularly the Universities.

For the Universities in particular

It is requisite that there be (as in several Acts of like nature) a proviso; to this purpose:

Provided always, and it is hereby enacted, that nothing in this Act confirmed shall be extended or interpreted to the prejudice or in derogation of the rights and priviledge of the two Universities of Oxford and Cambridge respectively;[12] but that they shall and may peaceably enjoy the same according to their ancient rights and {liberties} and the severall grants of his Ma[ties] Progenitors and Predecessors; And particularly according to the grants of King Charles the first, in his Letters Patents of the twelth of November in the Eighth year of his reigne, and of ye thirteenth day of March in the former year; and of the third day of March in the eleventh year of his reign, and according to the grants of king         the         of the         of         in the         year of his reign, to the University of Cambridge.¹³

Provided also that nothing herein confirmed shall obtend¹⁴ to the prejudice of the Royal Societies for the advancemt of national knowledge, as to the grant¹⁵ to them made concerning the Printing or Licensing of Books in the Letters Patents of King Charles the Second bearing date the         in the         year of his reign; and those of the         in the         year of his reign; but that they may peaceably and quietly enjoy the same.

# EDITORIAL NOTES

## Restoration Restraint

### *A Proclamation for Calling in, and Suppressing*
1. *Intituled ... Regiam*: John Milton, *Ioannis Miltoni, Angli Pro Popvlo Anglicano Defensio, Contra Clavdii Anonymi, aliàs Salmasii, Defensionem Regiam* ('London' [Leyden], 1650 [1651]). Milton's 'First Defence' was later published in English as *A Defence of the People of England, By John Milton: In Answer to Salmasius's Defence of the King* ([Amsterdam?], 1692). Salmasius, the French writer Claude de Saumaise, had published his defence of Charles I in 1649.
2. *And the other ... Sufferings*: John Milton, ΕΙΚΟΝΟΚΛΑΣΤΗΣ *in Answer to a Book Intitl'd* ΕΙΚΩΝ ΒΑΣΙΛΙΚΗ [*Eikonklastes* in Answer to *Eikon Basilike*] (London: printed by Matthew Simmons, 1649).
3. *Intituled ... Justice*: John Goodwin, *The Obstructours of Justice. Or A Defence of the Honourable Sentence Passed upon the late King, by the High Court of Justice* (London: Henry Cripps and Lodowick Lloyd, 1649).

### *Whereas Divers Scandalous Untruths and Treasonable Assertions*
1. *WHARTON*: George Wharton, royalist astrologer (1617–81); see headnote.
2. Edw. Nicholas: Sir Edward Nicholas (1593–1669), secretary of state under Charles I and Charles II.

### 'Impeachment against Drake'
1. William Drake: Little more is known of Drake. He was seemingly unconnected to the merchant William Drake involved in Love's plot in 1649–51, or to the MP Sir William Drake, sometimes wrongly identified as the author.

### *A Proclamation for the Re-Printing, Publishing, and Using of a Book*
1. *Intituled ... Allegiance*: Anon., *God and the King* (London, 1615); see headnote.

### 'Printing and Printers'
1. *dry-fats ... fardels*: types of containers and bundles.
2. *Primmers, Abcees*: primers and alphabet books.
3. John Streater *Stationer*: John Streater (c. 1620–77) was a printer, publisher and, during the Interregnum, a republican pamphleteer critical of Cromwell. He secretly printed James Harrington's *Oceana* in 1656 and was printer to the restored Rump, but in adapting to the Restoration regime somehow secured exemption from the 1662 Printing Act. Together

with Richard Atkyns (see headnote to Press Control and the Print Trade, above, p. 81) he campaigned in defence of royal printing patents, claiming a patent to print law books (see A. Johns, *The Nature of the Book* (Chicago, IL: University of Chicago Press, 1998)).

## L'Estrange Takes Control

### L'Estrange, *Considerations and Proposals*

1. Farewel-Sermons: sermons by ministers ejected under the terms of the 1662 Act of Uniformity.
2. *Obligation of the Covenant*: the Solemn League and Covenant, agreed in 1643 between the English Parliament and Scots Presbyterian leadership. The reference to obedience bringing damnation refers to obeying the King, not the Covenant.
3. *A Certain Gentleman*: the royalist Sir John Birkenhead (or Berkenhead), L'Estrange's predecessor as licenser, who had objected to *A Caveat for the Cavaliers* (London, 1661) (*CSPD*, 31 March 1663).
4. *lately Employ'd*: L'Estrange was first granted a warrant on 24 February 1662 (*CSPD*).
5. A Short Survey ... Ministry: Anon., *A Short Surveigh of the Grand Case of the Present Ministry* ([London], 1663). The work is signed M.D., S.C., I.F., O.R. and A.T., 'Some Conformable Non-Conformists'. L'Estrange later names the printer as Henry Bridges. The tract responded to Francis Fullwood, *The Grand Case of the Present Ministry* (London, 1663).
6. *the late Act for Printing*: the 1662 Printing Act (13 & 14 Car. II, c. 33).
7. *Ut Supra*: Latin, 'as specified above'.
8. *Leather-Guiders ... Quoyf-drawers*: tradesmen using equipment that L'Estrange feared could be adapted to presswork. 'Quoyf' is coif, the skullcap.
9. *Title, Marque, or Vinnet*: title, mark or vignette, i.e. distinctive printed ornament.
10. *The Speeches... Prodigies I* Part and 2: Thomas Harrison, et al., *The Speeches and Prayers of some of the late King's Judges* ([London]: [printed by Simon Dover and Thomas Creek], 1660); Henry Vane, *The Tryal of Sir Henry Vane* ([London], 1662); Anon., *Mirabilis Annus, or, The Year of Prodigies and Wonders* ([London]: [printed by Thomas Creek for Giles Calvert, Thomas Brewster and Elizabeth Calvert], 1661); Anon., *Mirabilis Annus Secundus: or, The Second Part of the Second Years Prodigies* ([London], 1662). The Vane tract included words Vane was prevented from speaking in court, hence L'Estrange inserting 'pretended'.
11. *Dry-Fatts ... Fardells*: various types of packages, bundles and cases.
12. Buchanan, *and* Knox ... Baxter, *and* Calamy: George Buchanan (1506–82), author of the resistance tract *De Jure Regni* (1579), and the religious reformer John Knox (c. 1514–72), compared to the Presbyterian ministers Richard Baxter (1615–91) and Edmund Calamy (1600–66), ejected under the Act of Uniformity.
13. The Armies Remonstrance ... 1648: *A Remonstrance of his Excellency Thomas Lord Fairfax, Lord Generall of the Parliaments Forces. And of the Generall Councell of Officers Held at St. Albans the 16. of November, 1648* (London: John Partridge and George Whittington, 1648). In the following notes, further details of titles are given where relevant, except when tracts are no longer extant.
14. Speeches and Prayers ... Judges: see note 10 above. 'Cook' (in margin) is John Cook (c. 1608–60), regicide solicitor-general for the Commonwealth.
15. Mercurius Politicus: newsbook authorized by the council of state in 1650 and edited over the next ten years by Marchamont Nedham (c. 1620–78), former and future roy-

alist. The printer was Thomas Newcombe (c. 1625–81), who at the Restoration was engaged to run the King's printing house.

16. Perkin Warbeck: French-born imposter who, posing as Richard, Duke of York, gained the support of James IV of Scotland in mounting failed attempts on the English throne in 1496–7.

17. The False Brother: [Cuthbert Sydenham], *The False Brother, or, A New Map of Scotland* (London: printed by R.W. for Francis Tyton, 1651). Sydenham (c. 1623–54) was an Independent minister employed as a writer by the council of state from 1649. The printer 'R.W.' was Robert White, who, together with Francis Tyton, the publisher, was involved in producing many of Richard Baxter's works. At the Restoration Tyton became printer-publisher to the House of Lords and also served Charles II.

18. Rise, Reign, and Ruine of the House of Stuarts: Sir Edward Peyton, *The Divine Catastrophe of the Kingly Family of the House of Stuarts: or, A Short History of the Rise, Reign, and Ruine Thereof* (London, 1652). Peyton (1587–1652) had been an MP and an officer in the parliamentary army. Giles Calvert and his wife Elizabeth were renowned radical publisher-booksellers: see note 15 to *An Exact Narrative of the Tryal and Condemnation of Twyn*, below, p. 444.

19. true Pourtraiture ... England: [?Henry Parker], *The True Portraiture of the Kings of England* (London: Giles Calvert, 1650). Parker (1604–52), the prominent parliamentarian political writer, claimed to have found rather than authored the book, in which Cuthbert Sydenham may also have been involved. It was printed by Robert White.

20. A Short Reply ... England: A. Kerr, *A Short Reply unto a Declaration Entituled, The Declaration of the Army of England, upon their March into Scotland. Together with a Vindication of the Declaration of the Army of England upon their March into Scotland* (London: printed by John Field for Francis Tyton, 1650). Field was printer for Parliament and the Protectorate in the 1650s and from 1655 until his death in 1668 printer to the University of Cambridge. The first part of the tract was also published separately in Edinburgh.

21. Plain English: Anon., *Plain English to his Excellencie Lord General Monck, and the Officers of his Army* (London, 1660). The pamphlet was published by the bookseller and Fifth Monarchist Livewell Chapman (fl. 1643–65). In the same month, March 1660, Chapman issued Milton's *Readie and Easie Way* and the council of state issued a proclamation demanding his arrest for seditious books. L'Estrange replied in *Treason Arraigned, in Answer to Plain English; being a Trayterous and Phanatique Pamphlet* (London, 1660).

22. Case of King Charles: John Cook, *King Charls his Case: or, An Appeal to all Rational Men, concerning his Tryal* (London: printed by Peter Cole for Giles Calvert, 1649). A warrant was issued by the council of state on 19 November 1649 for the arrest of Cole the printer, best known as printer-publisher of the herbalist Nicholas Culpeper's works.

23. English Translation ... Declaration: [Cuthbert Sydenham], *An English Translation of the Scottish Declaration against James Graham, alias Marquess of Montrosse* (London: printed by John Macock for Francis Tyton, 1650). Macock, who with Tyton became printer to the House of Lords at the Restoration, also printed the newsbooks of Henry Muddiman.

24. True State of the Case ... Common-Wealth: [Marchamont Nedham], *A True State of the Case of the Commonwealth* (London: printed by Tho. Newcomb, 1654).

25. Mercurius Britanicus: parliamentarian newsbook that appeared from 1643 to 1646, edited by Marchamont Nedham and printed by Robert White.

26. God's Loud Call: Edward Delamaine, *Gods Loud Call from Heaven* (London: printed by S. Dover, 1661). Delamaine was a leading Baptist imprisoned for his writings during

1661. Simon Dover, the printer, was prosecuted for another work in 1664: see below, pp. 59–60.

27. Smectymnuus Redivivus: *Smectymnuus Redivivus* (London: John Rothwell, 1660). This was a republication of the 1641 writings of the five Presbyterian churchmen whose initials provided the name Smectymnuus (Stephen Marshall, Edmund Calamy, Thomas Young, Matthew Newcomen, William Spurlow). Their fellow Presbyterian leader Thomas Manton (bap. 1620; d. 1677) contributed a preface to a further edition issued in 1654 under the title *Smectymnuus Redivivus* and this was reprinted at Manton's instigation in 1660 and again in 1661. The Presbyterian stationer John Rothwell published the 1654, 1660 and 1661 editions.

28. Sermon Preached ... Dec. 28. 1662: Edmund Calamy, *Eli Trembling for Fear of the Ark. A Sermon Preached at St. Mary Aldermanbury, Decemb. 28. 1662. By Edmund Calamy, B.D. Late Minister there. Upon the Preaching of which he was Committed Prisoner to the Gaol of Newgate, Jan. 6. 1662. And now through his Majesties Gracious Favour Released Jan. 12. 1662* (London, 1662 [1663]). An earlier version of the tract had been printed at Oxford prior to Calamy's release.

29. Animadversions ... Letter: Edward Bagshaw, *A Letter unto a Person of Honour and Quality, Containing some Animadversions upon the Bishop of Worcester's Letter* (London, 1662). Bagshaw (1629–71), an Independent, challenged Bishop George Morley's claims for episcopal authority, prompting a vitriolic printed exchange with L'Estrange, who contributed to Bagshaw's imprisonment in January 1663. The printer, identified by L'Estrange as John Hayes, succeeded John Field in 1669 as Cambridge University printer.

30. Year of Prodigies: see note 10 above. Creek was also involved in printing the *Speeches and Prayers* of the regicides but escaped punishment by incriminating his fellow printer Simon Dover and the bookseller Thomas Brewster. On that case, and on the Calverts, see section on The Trial and Execution of John Twyn, below.

31. Word of Comfort: Thomas Watson, ΠΑΡΑΜΥΘΙΝ [Paramuthion: 'Consolation']: *or A Word of Comfort for the Church of God* (London: Thomas Parkhurst, 1662). Watson (d. 1686) was rector of St Stephen Walbrook, London, from where he was ejected later in 1662. Parkhurst (c. 1632–1711) was a Presbyterian printer based in Cheapside. He remained in the trade until at least 1703. The regicides Miles Corbett (1594/5–1662) and John Barkstead (d. 1662) were captured in the Netherlands in 1661 and executed with seven others on 19 April 1662.

32. Dispute ... Ceremonies: George Gillespie, *A Dispute against the English-Popish Ceremonies Obtruded upon the Church of Scotland* ([Edinburgh], 1660). Gillespie (1613–48) was a Scots Presbyterian minister and writer. The first edition of his *Dispute*, printed in the Netherlands, was ordered burnt by the Privy Council at Edinburgh on its appearance in Scotland in 1637.

33. Parliament-Physick ... Nation: [Nathaniel Joceline], *Parliament Physick for a Sin-Sick Nation* (London: E[dmund] Blackmore, 1644). Joceline was pastor at Hardingham, Norfolk.

34. Ahabs Fall ... Fern: Charles Herle, *Ahab's Fall by his Prophets Flatteries* (London: printed by R.A. for J[ohn] Wright, 1644). Herle (1597/8–1659), a Presbyterian churchman and writer for Parliament, was made a licenser under the 1643 printing ordinance. Amongst other tracts he authorized the Independents' *An Apologeticall Narration*. From 1642 he was engaged in an extended pamphlet dispute with Henry Ferne (1602–62), Charles I's chaplain and later bishop of Chester. *Ahab's Fall* included three of Herle's sermons and a postscript 'Short Answer' to Ferne.

35. Peoples Cause ... *Vane*: 'The Peoples Cause Stated' (or 'The Peoples Case Stated') was a section of *The Tryal of Sir Henry Vane*, pp. 97–113: see note 10 above.
36. Observations ... *&c*.: Henry Parker, *Observations upon some of his Majesties late Answers and Expresses* ([London], [1642]). Robert White and George Bishop may have been the printers.
37. Right and Might well met: John Goodwin, *Right and Might well met* (London: printed by Matthew Simmons for Henry Crips, 1648). On Goodwin, see section on Restoration Restraint, above.
38. Jus Populi: Henry Parker, *Jus Populi. Or, A Discourse wherein Clear Satisfaction is Given, as well concerning the Right of Subjects, as the Right of Princes* (London: Robert Bostock, 1644).
39. Vindiciæ contra Tyrannos: Anon., *Vindiciæ contra Tyrannos: A Defence of Liberty against Tyrants* (London: printed by Matthew Simmons and Robert Wilson, 1648), a French Huguenot defence of resistance first published in 1579. The author is variously held to be Hubert Languet (1518–81) or Philippe du Plessis-Mornay (1549–1623).
40. Tenure ... Magistrates: J[ohn] M[ilton], *The Tenure of Kings and Magistrates* (London: printed by Matthew Simmons, 1649). Simmons (*c.* 1608–54) printed many of Milton's political tracts of the 1640s, as well as other radical works.
41. Declaration ... Four Bills: This appears to refer to *The Four Bills Sent to the King to the Isle of Wight to be Passed* (London: Edward Husband, 1647 [1648]).
42. De Monarchiâ Absolutâ: Edward Bagshaw, *De Monarchia Absoluta Dissertatio Politica* [A Political Dissertation on Absolute Monarchy] (Oxford: printed by Henry Hall for Thomas Robinson, 1659).
43. *Detrahere Indigno ... dubitabit*: Latin, 'although private men should not take magistracy from an unworthy man, nevertheless that the people all together are able, no one, I think, will doubt'.
44. Thorps Charge ... *1648*: Francis Thorpe, *Sergeant Thorpe Judge of Assize for the Northern Circuit his Charge, as it was Delivered to the Grand-Jury at Yorke Assizes the Twentieth of March, 1648* (London: printed by T.W. for Mathew Walbancke and Richard Best, 1649). Another edition was printed at York. Thorpe (*c.* 1594–1665) was a judge and MP whose charge to the York grand jury defended the Commonwealth. He faced calls for his execution at the Restoration.
45. Lex Rex: [Samuel Rutherford] *Lex, Rex: The Law and the Prince* (London: John Field, 1644). In the preface to the printed account of the trial and execution of the printer John Twyn, possibly written by L'Estrange, *Lex Rex* was claimed to be the 'Presbyterian Quiver' out of which was drawn the 'Arrow' of Twyn's fatal book *The Treatise of the Execution of Justice*.
46. The Great Question: Edward Bagshaw, *The Great Question Concerning things Indifferent in Religious Worship* (London, 1660).
47. Form and Order ... Second: Robert Douglas, *The Form and Order of the Coronation of Charles II. King of Scotland, together with the Sermon then Preached, by Mr. Robert Dowglas &c.* (Aberdeen: printed by James Brown, 1651; reprinted London, 1660). At least two editions appeared in London in 1660, and the contents were included in the *Phenix* in 1662 (see note 48 below).
48. Phoenix ... Covenant: Anon., *A Phenix, or, The Solemn League and Covenant* ('Edinburgh' [London], 'Printed in the year of Covenant-breaking' [1662]). The title and imprint refer to Parliament's 1661 order for the burning of the Solemn League and Covenant. L'Estrange elicited the names of those involved through investigations leading to

the trial and conviction of Brewster in 1664 (see section on The Trial and Execution of John Twyn, below). The book included Douglas's 1651 sermon (see note 47 above) and related material, which Brewster claimed to think was still covered by its original Scottish licence. It also contained Edmund Calamy's 1645 sermon on 'The Great Danger of Covenant-Breaking', originally published in 1646.

49. Two Papers of Proposals: *Two Papers of Proposals concerning the Discipline and Ceremonies of the Church of England* (London, 1661). Richard Baxter was the main author of the proposals.
50. Short Survey ... Case, &c.: see note 5 above.
51. *a King* Regis personam exuere: Latin, 'a king deprived of the person of a king', i.e. unfit for office.
52. se defendendo vim vi repellere: Latin, 'in defending himself to resist force with force'.
53. *Men of* Belial: followers of Belial, a biblical demon.
54. *Garter*: principal king of arms, the others being Clarenceux and Norroy.
55. *Pecuniary Mulcts*: financial penalties; fines.
56. Blew Bonnet: i.e. blue bonnet.

## 'L'Estrange to bee Surveyor of the Printing Presse'

1. *Imprimery ... aforesd*: i.e. printing establishments.
2. *Mercuries, Diurnalls ... Intelligence*: this provision gave L'Estrange a monopoly in printing news.
3. *Quacksalvers Bills*: bill-posters advertising medical services.
4. *Henry Bennet*: Sir Henry Bennet (bap. 1618; d. 1685) had become secretary of state in October 1662, giving him oversight of the Restoration censorship regime. He continued in office until 1674, being made Baron Arlington in 1665.

## L'Estrange, *Intelligencer*

1. Grant ... person: Charles II's appointment of L'Estrange; see above, p. 52.
2. Printed Intelligence: printed news.
3. *absolutely* Indifferent: undetermined, hence open to interpretation and decision.
4. Publick Mercury: i.e. a printed newspaper.
5. Pragmaticall: meddlesome, officious.
6. Colourable Right: pretended right.
7. *Menage*: management.
8. Gratefull: gratifying, pleasant.
9. Bruited: clamoured.
10. One Book a Week ... Printing it off: almost immediately, L'Estrange engaged in the weekly combination of *Intelligencer* and *Newes*, the former published on Monday, the latter on Thursday.
11. Mercuries: used here to denote a vendor of news, a hawker, rather than the newspaper itself.
12. Privity: collaboration.
13. *so good* a Husband, *as to* Vamp my Intelligence: i.e. so good a cultivator of words as to rework old news as if new.
14. Forreigners ... Separatists: foreigners, apprentices and those outside the Stationers' Company.
15. *ADVERTISEMENTS*: in the sense of public notices, rather than commercial propositions.

16. Private Place, Hole *or* Corner: i.e. a secret press.
17. Gun *in* Ivy Lane: also the premises of L'Estrange's publisher Henry Brome.
18. *Publique House*: i.e. an authorized printing house.
19. Vi: A typographical omission occurs at this point.
20. Quoyning: coining (i.e. creating his own news).
21. Count Ulefelts *horrid Conspiracy*: Corfits Ulfeldt, Danish statesman found guilty of plotting to raise rebellion and transfer the Danish crown to the elector of Brandenburg. He escaped before execution but died in February 1664.
22. Rampiers: ramparts.

## Letters from the Surveyor of the Press

1. *Willis*: Thomas Willis (1621–75), the renowned physician, anatomist and scientist, and like L'Estrange a high-church religionist. Willis published several influential medical texts in Latin during the 1660s, and a later work in English was licensed by L'Estrange: *Pharmaceutice Rationalis: or, An Excercitation of the Operations of Medicines in Humane Bodies* (London, 1679). The exact nature of L'Estrange's illness in 1668 is uncertain.
2. *those very Persons whom you have now in hold*: the radical printer John Darby (d. 1704) and bookseller Anne Brewster, widow of Thomas Brewster, were arrested and questioned over the publication of *The Poor Whores Petition* and other tracts at this time. Darby's wife Joan (d. 1708/9) and Brewster's son were also implicated. On 20 April the publisher Andrew Crooke, active in the Stationers' Company, and five others had been granted a warrant to search for illicit printing operations by Arlington (*CSPD*, 20 and 26 April).
3. *30 yeares assiduous, & unchangd able service*: In early 1639 L'Estrange had fought for Charles I in the first bishops' war.
4. *Mr Williamson*: Joseph Williamson, under-secretary of state.
5. *Felo de se. is undoubtedly Wallis his*: [Thomas Ford], *Felo De Se, or The Bishops Condemned out of their own Mouthes* ([London], 1668). Despite L'Estrange's confidence, the tract is generally attributed to the ejected Presbyterian minister Thomas Ford (1598–1674). 'Felo de se' means 'felon of oneself', i.e. self-destroyer, being a legal term for suicide but here referring to the bishops' purported self-condemnation.
6. *the Queryes*: Anon., *A Few Sober Queries upon the late Proclamation, for Enforcing the Laws and Conventicles, &c., and the late Vote of the House of Commons, for Renewing the said Act for Three Years More* (London, 1668). On 4 March the Commons had resolved to urge the King to publish his proclamation reinforcing the laws against conventicles. The proclamation was issued on 10 March and on 30 March a bill to continue the Conventicles Act was introduced in the Commons. The *Queries* claimed the nation wanted liberty of conscience, not repression. A handwritten note on the Huntington Library copy (see Early English Books Online) refers to John Darby being pilloried for his part in printing the tract.
7. *Omnia concessa in belo*: Anon., *Omnia Comesta a Belo. Or, An Answer out of the West to a Question out of the North* ([?London], 1667). An anti-episcopal tract, reprinted in 1679 and subsequently included in *State Tracts*. L'Estrange's rendering conveys 'All is allowed in war' rather than the title's meaning, 'All is consumed by war'.
8. *The Poor Whores petition*: Anon., *The Poor-Whores Petition. To the Most Splendid, Illustrious, Serene and Eminent Lady of Pleasure, the Countess of Castlemayne, &c. The Humble Petition of the Undone Company of Poore Distressed Whores, Bawds, Pimps, and Panders,*

&c (London, 1668), an anti-Catholic attack addressed to Charles II's mistress. John Darby was punished for his part in printing the tract.
9. *Liberty of Conscience*: by Charles Wolseley. See below, p. 129.
10. *saynts Freedom*: Anon., *The Saints Freedom from Tyranny Vindicated* (London, 1667).
11. *Roome for ye Cobbler*: R[alph] Wallis, *Room for the Cobler of Gloucester and his Wife: With several Cartloads of Abominable Irregular, Pitiful Stinking Priests* ([London]: for the author, 1668). Wallis (d. 1669) was a Gloucester cobbler turned ribald anti-clerical pamphleteer, first arrested by L'Estrange in 1664.

## The Trial and Execution of John Twyn

### *An Exact Narrative of the Tryal and Condemnation of Twyn*

1. John Twyn: On Twyn (bap. 1619; d. 1664), see headnote.
2. Lord Chief Just. Hide: Sir Robert Hyde (bap. 1596–1665), barrister from 1617, recorder from 1635, and an MP in 1640–2 before departing for royalist Oxford. He was knighted at the Restoration and in late 1663 became lord chief justice with the help of his cousin the Earl of Clarendon.
3. Simon Dover, Thomas Brewster, *and* Nathan Brooks: respectively printer, bookseller and bookbinder, tried for seditious libel in a parallel trial (see headnote). The laying of their indictments had been described in the preceding pages, omitted here.
4. *half the Jury are such*: The royalist publisher Richard Royston and printers Thomas Roycroft and James Flesher were prominent in the book trade, while Simon Waterson and John Williams had also been involved in the trade.
5. *Mr. Serjeant* Morton: Sir William Morton (bap. 1605; d. 1672), royalist officer in the civil war and Restoration MP, made king's sergeant in 1663.
6. before that day: 12 October 1663 was the date of the aborted Farnley Wood plot near Leeds, Yorkshire, which resulted in the execution of twenty-six alleged plotters.
7. *my Lord* Cooke ... Rebellion: Edward Coke (1552–1634), attorney-general, chief justice and legal writer. The phrase appears (in Latin) in Edward Coke, *The Second Part of the Institutes of the Lawes of England* (London, 1642), p. 226.
8. *Mr.* Le-Strange: Roger L'Estrange, surveyor of the press, the subject of the section L'Estrange Takes Control, above. See p. 21.
9. *Mr.* Secretary: the secretary of state Henry Bennet, later Lord Arlington.
10. Joseph Walker: Twyn's apprentice; little else is known about him.
11. Literals: literal errors, i.e. wrongly set letters.
12. *break the Form*: the form was the frame containing type.
13. Mr. *North*: Francis North (1637–85), then a barrister, later chief justice, lord keeper and Baron Guilford. North sat with Scroggs in the popish plot trials of 1679, and it was in his court that Stephen College was convicted (see headnote to The Tory Reaction I, above, p. 233).
14. Cloth fair: street in the Smithfield area of London, the meeting place of medieval cloth merchants and location of St Bartholomew-the-Great church. Benjamin Franklin worked as an apprentice in a Cloth Fair printing shop in 1725.
15. *Calverts* Maid: Elizabeth Evans, the servant of the bookseller Elizabeth Calvert (d. c. 1675). Elizabeth Calvert's husband Giles (bap. 1612) had died two months previously, leaving her in charge of their long-standing radical publishing business. The widow was

arrested in the Twyn case, along with her son Nathaniel and Elizabeth Evans, and was imprisoned from 2 February to 8 April.
16. J. Keeling: Sir John Kelyng (bap.1607; d. 1671), judge and from 1665 chief justice of King's Bench. John Bunyan, imprisoned by Kelyng in 1661, dubbed him 'Lord Hategood'.
17. Mr. *Dickenson*: the King's messenger.
18. *Mr.* Mabb: Thomas Mabb, a regular printer of stock works for the Company of Stationers as well as printing numerous tracts for Henry Brome, including this account of Twyn's trial.
19. *Joseph Williamson*: Joseph Williamson (1633–1701) was under-secretary to Arlington, later succeeding him as secretary of state.
20. *Serj.* Keeling: Kelyng had been made a sergeant-at-law at the Restoration.
21. *The* Rose *in* Smithfield: The rose was a commonly used sign, in this case presumably adorning a tavern.
22. *L.* Hide ... *alive*: At this point the court, and the account, turned to the case of Dover, Brewster and Brooks.
23. Weldon ... Newgate: the chaplain of Newgate jail.
24. *Sir* R. Ford: Sir Richard Ford, merchant, alderman and neighbour of Samuel Pepys, who recorded Ford 'beginning his shrievalty' on 28 September 1663. A few weeks before the Twyn trial Ford informed Pepys of the impending execution of the thief James Turner, which Pepys attended (*Diary*, 20–1 January 1664).

# Press Control and the Print Trade

## [Atkyns] *The Original and Growth of Printing*

1. Mr. Stow, *in his* Survey *of* London: Atkyns was not in fact drawing at this point on John Stow's *A Survay of London* (London, 1598; most recent edition 1633) but his *Annales, or A Generall Chronicle of England* (London, 1631), p. 404. Stow's annals had first appeared, as *The Chronicles of England*, in 1580. Stow gave the erroneous date 1471 for the arrival of printing in England.
2. John Guttenberg: Johannes Gutenberg (*c.* 1398–1468), credited with inventing the first printing press using movable type. After several years of experiment the press was in use by 1450 in Gutenberg's birthplace, Mainz in Germany (not Harlem, as Atkyns subsequently claims).
3. William Caxton ... *Mercer*: William Caxton (d. 1492), it is generally agreed, introduced the printing press to England, in 1476 or possibly 1475. A cloth merchant ('mercer'), he practised printing in Cologne and Bruges before establishing his press in the precincts of Westminster Abbey.
4. *Sir* Rich. Baker *in his Chronicle*: Richard Baker, *A Chronicle of the Kings of England* (London, 1643); republished in 1660.
5. Mr. *Howell* in his *Historical Discourse* ... Westminster: James Howell, *Londinopolis; An Historicall Discourse or Perlustration of the City of London* (London, 1657), p. 353. Howell's information derived from Stow's *Survey of London* (London, 1633), p. 525.

6. Islip *abbot of* Westminster ... England: The claim is erroneous. John Islip (1464–1532) was abbot, but only from 1500. Caxton had some dealings with Thomas Millyng, who was abbot from 1469 until his death in 1492.
7. Bernardus non videt omnia: Latin, '[even] Bernard sees not all', a reference to the story of St Bernard of Clairvaux being so deep in thought when walking on the shore of Lake Geneva that he did not notice the lake.
8. Mentz: Mainz, Germany.
9. *Printed at* Oxford, *in 1468*: A press was established at Oxford University in 1478. The book Atkyns refers to was the Latin commentary *Expositio in Symbolum Apostolorum*, wrongly dated 1468.
10. Lambeth-House: Lambeth Palace, London seat of the Archbishop of Canterbury. The manuscript Atkyns cites is not in Lambeth Palace Library and indeed has never been located.
11. Thomas Bourchier: Thomas Bourchier (c. 1411–86), archbishop of Canterbury from 1454. Henry VI held the throne until 1461 and again between October 1470 and April 1471.
12. Robert Turnour ... *Robes to the King*: Robert Turner, the king's master of the robes.
13. Frederick Corsellis: Corsellis and his role were the creation of Atkyns.
14. *Urben Moguntinam ... primam*: Latin, 'City of Mainz, first inventor of printing'. Moguntia was the city's Roman name.
15. *Aliens ... Strangers*: i.e. foreigners. The proviso in the 1484 Act was removed in 1534.
16. *Act of the 25* Hen. *8. cap. 15*: Act for Printers and Binders of Books (1534).
17. *Signiory*: seignory, the authority retained when granting usage rights.
18. minishment: diminishment.
19. Tottel ... Yestweirt: Richard Tottell and Charles Yetsweirt, printers and royal patent-holders in the latter part of the sixteenth century.
20. Weight *and* Norton: Thomas Wight and Bonham Norton, printers and briefly partners in holding the patent to print law books from 1597. Norton (d. 1635) later worked with his cousin John Norton and John Bill, the King's printers, exploiting further privileges.
21. More ... *Signet*: John More (d. 1638) gained a patent to publish common law books for forty years from 1629, which he left to his daughter Martha, whom Atkyns married in 1640. As a clerk of the signet, More would have been involved in processing royal patents.
22. *Primmer*: primer.

## The London Printers Lamentation

1. Strabo de situ Orbis: referring to the Greek writer Strabo's seventeen-volume *Geography*, first printed in Venice in 1510.
2. Lawrel ... crassie leaves: laurel; 'crassie' may refer to dense leaves (Latin: crassus, 'thick').
3. *Insculption*: inscription.
4. Facile ... addere: Latin, 'it is easy to add to an invention'.
5. *Antcessors*: antecessors, ancestors.
6. Cuthenburge: John Gutenburg.
7. Imprimit ... anno: rendered in English in the following lines.
8. 23. June ... Chamber: the Star Chamber decree of 23 June 1586.

9. *Kings-Bench Rules ... Justice*: The 'rules' referred to the area surrounding King's Bench prison in Southwark where certain prisoners were allowed to live. The boundaries were notoriously imprecise.
10. *last Decree*: the 1637 Star Chamber decree on printing.
11. O Tempora, O mores: Latin, 'oh the times, oh the customs' (Cicero).
12. Ca.2.v.15: Song of Solomon 2:15.
13. *gibbous excrescences*: bulging outgrowths.
14. Barker ... Bill: the King's printers. Barker's family connection to the title went back to 1577, Bill's to 1627, and their resumption of the role and its lucrative privileges at the Restoration was confirmed in 1662. Barker and Bill were primarily businessmen, assigning rights including the actual printing work to others.
15. Senex ... ferulam: Latin: 'the old parrot will not take the stick' (i.e. you cannot teach an old dog new tricks).
16. Thomas ... printers: On Newcombe and Field also see notes 15 and 20 to L'Estrange, *Considerations and Proposals*, above, pp. 438–9. Henry Hills (c. 1625–88/9) had acquired the Bible-printing monopoly under Cromwell in 1655, together with Field, then entered a mutually-beneficial arrangement with Barker and Bill at the Restoration. In 1674 he and Newcombe were formally made the King's printers.
17. young *Tarquin*: a reference to the son of the tyrannous last king of Rome before the republic, perpetrator of the rape of Lucretia.
18. *conjunctim* or *divisim*: together or apart.
19. Committee of Safety: set up by Army command in October 1659.
20. another of his name: his brother Matthew Barker.
21. obtained ... 1655: Field and Hills claimed to have bought the final manuscript of the King James Bible from Barker on acquiring the Bible privilege in 1655.
22. enforced entrance ... Registry: Oliver Cromwell ordered the Bible privilege of Field and Hills to be entered in the Stationers' Register in March 1655/6.
23. *Ludibrium*: object of scorn.
24. *1.Q. Elizabeth c.2*: the 1559 Act of Uniformity.
25. Impunitas ... peccandi: Latin: 'unpunished fault offers a hand to sin'.
26. *brazen Browes*: i.e. bare-faced cheek.
27. Anabaptist ... Adultery: Hills printed and preached for the Baptists in the 1650s but was estranged from the church for a time, during which he was also imprisoned, after setting up home with the wife of the tailor Thomas Hams. Hills later converted to Catholicism.
28. *Press at* New England: The first printing-press at Cambridge, Massachusetts, had been producing books since 1639 but controls were lacking until the 1660s.
29. Quod ... Deus: Latin: 'how unutterably evil to turn away from God'.
30. Donatist *and* Arian *Heresies*: Donatism and Arianism were early but enduring heresies, named after dissenting priests in the time of Emperor Constantine. Donatus and his followers questioned the sanctity and authority of the orthodox priesthood. Arius questioned the Trinitarian tenet that Christ the son was equal to, or of the same essence as, God the father.
31. transilire limites: Latin: 'to leap over its limits'.
32. Billa vera ... Ignoramus: in legal Latin, a 'billa vera' ('true bill') was a charge proven by evidence, whereas an 'ignoramus' verdict ('we are ignorant') declared it unproven.

## A Brief Discourse concerning Printing and Printers

1. *John Stow in his* Annals: see note 1 to [Atkyns] *The Original and Growth of Printing,* above, p. 445.
2. *S. Austins in Canterbury, S. Albans, and others*: S. Austins is St Augustine's. The source appears to be Stow's *Survey of London* (1633), p. 525.
3. *Act of Parliament*: 1 Rich. III, c. 9, protecting English merchants against competition from foreigners ('aliens').
4. *Act of 25 H. 8*: The 1534 Act for Printers and Binders of Books, 25 Hen. VIII, c. 15.
5. *con-corporated ... Stationers*: The Company of Stationers was incorporated at this time, receiving its royal charter in 1557.
6. *fear of losing a Work-Master*: i.e. fear of not being given printing work by the publisher-booksellers.
7. *whether a Printer ... Register*: The accusation is that the Stationers' Register was being manipulated to prevent printers securing textual property by registering copyright.
8. *If Protection and Subjection are reciprocal*: a phrase from Robert Filmer, *Observations upon Aristotles Politiques* (London, 1652), p. 49.
9. *Artists ... strangers*: 'Artists' are those practised in the art of printing, 'strangers' those outside the art.
10. *Chapmen*: hawkers, street sellers.
11. humble Remonstrance ... Parker *Esq*: [Henry Parker], *To the High Court of Parliament: The Humble Remonstrance of the Company of Stationers, London* ([London], [1643]).

## [Seymour] *The Case of Libels*

1. *Quo Warranto*: a requirement to justify one's legal warrant or authority; in this case a demand of King and Privy Council that the Stationers' Company justify the privileges conferred by its charter.
2. *certain By-Laws*: the main provision is outlined further down, being a formal undertaking by members not to print without licence, the penalty to be deprivation of any share in the printing and profit of the Company's stock (see F. Siebert, *Freedom of the Press in England, 1476–1776* (Urbana, IL: University of Illinois Press, 1952), pp. 258–9).
3. *Stationers Table*: a reference to decisions reached at the Court table, used for Stationers' Company meetings, notably those of the governing council, the Court of Assistants.
4. *Sollicitor General ... Pleas*: Sir Francis North (1637–85).
5. *Leading Man*: publisher, royal bookbinder and leading Stationers' Company figure Samuel Mearne (1624–83), warden of the Stationers' Company. The Lords committee on libels was told that Mearne was objecting to being made L'Estrange's slave (HL/PO/JO/10/1/363/g6: 6 April 1677). Mearne had been admitted to the company by royal request in 1668, as bookbinder to the King, and became closely involved in the policing of illegal presses. The antipathy between himself and L'Estrange was deepened by their competing claims to loyalty.
6. *One of their Members ... attend*: Mearne told the Lords committee he withheld the key as the Master was at a tavern and on his return was unfit to conduct business. The Master was Abel Roper (fl. 1638; d. 1680), uncle of Abel Roper the post-revolution political journalist and publisher.
7. *Rainsford*: Sir Richard Rainsford (1605–80), lord chief baron of the Court of Exchequer. On 3 March 1677 the House of Lords appointed Rainsford and North to prepare a new printing bill addressing defects in the 1662 Act (*LJ*, 13, p. 60).

8. *Case of a Journy-man-printer*: John Marlow had been indicted on 7 August 1676, along with Henry Bruges (or Bridges), for printing a pamphlet on a press at Bruges's house near Smithfield: *An Account of the Proceedings at Guildhall Relating to the City's Petitioning his Majesty for a New Parliament*. L'Estrange claimed Mearne forewarned Bruges of a warrant for his arrest. The tract featured a speech by the London Whig Francis Jenks; in June 1677 Bruges was indicted for printing a later Jenks speech.

## 'The Company of Stationers against Seymour'

1. *Gadbury's Almanacks*: the popular almanacs of the astrologer John Gadbury (1627–1704), produced annually between 1655 and 1703. The Stationers' Company claimed a monopoly in printing almanacs based on privileges antecedent to a grant by the King to Seymour in 1669.
2. *verbis & figuris*: Latin: 'word and form'.
3. *Common Prayer ... common Almanacks, &c.*: a distinction between the almanac as a calendar of saints' days and moveable feasts for the year ahead, and the more speculative predictive commentary directed at a popular audience.
4. *Pemberton*: Sir Francis Pemberton (bap. 1624; d. 1697), the King's sergeant-at-law. Pemberton was also involved in later press trials including that of Benjamin Harris.
5. *Judgment in the House of Peers*: On a writ of error brought by John Streater, the Lords reversed the judgement given in the King's Bench court in Streater v. Roper (1672), in favour of Streater's claim of a royal patent for printing law books.
6. *Orlando Bridgeman*: Sir Orlando Bridgeman (1609–74), presiding judge in the trial of the regicides and chief justice of common pleas 1660–8. The case referred to, however, appears to be that of Roper v. Streater.
7. *no certain Author*: almanacs were here being argued to be compiled rather than authored (by Gadbury, in this case), and moreover utilizing dates deriving from royal authority, as argued later in the case.
8. *Nicene Council*: ecumenical assembly of the early Church held in AD 325 in Nicaea.
9. *nisi causa*: Latin: 'unless just cause shown', i.e. the judgement may be open to reconsideration.

## *The Orders, Rules, and Ordinances of the Mystery or Art of Stationers*

1. *Demise or Lett*: grant by lease or let.
2. *Comminalty*: commonalty, i.e. the general membership of the Stationers' Company.
3. *Covenant-servants*: under-workers contracted under specific terms other than a full indentured apprenticeship.
4. *Chamberlain ... custom of the said City*: The Chamberlain of London was traditionally empowered to punish runaway or otherwise erring apprentices.
5. *Free-mans Oath*: the oath to abide by the company's rules, taken on being free of indentures, so completing one's apprenticeship, and accepted into the general membership.
6. *English Stock of this Company*: the joint-stock enterprise by which the Stationers' Company exploited its monopoly privileges in printing certain types of texts, such as almanacs.
7. *Finch ... North*: Heneage Finch (1621–82), lord chancellor; Sir Richard Rainsford (1605–80); Sir Francis North (1637–85). In 1677 Rainsford and North had been appointed by the House of Lords to investigate defects in the working of the existing printing legislation.

## An Ordinance Ordained by the Mystery or Art of Stationers

1. *Common Hall ... Ludgate*: Stationers' Hall was (and is) in Ave Maria Lane, having reopened in 1673 after the first hall on the site burned down in the 1666 Great Fire.
2. *said Act of Parliament ... Henry the Seventh*: 19 Hen. VII, c. 7, noted in the preface, which required any guild ordinance to be examined by three leading judicial figures.
3. *said Lord Keeper ... Benches*: mentioned in the preamble, repeated in conclusion.
4. *Tenth day of February ... 1682*: The preface records that the ordinance was submitted by the Stationers on this day in '1682' (i.e. 1683).
5. *North ... Pemberton*: Francis North had been made lord keeper on 20 December 1682; Edmund Saunders (d. 1683) had been rapidly elevated to chief justice of King's Bench in January, the same month that Francis Pemberton became chief justice of common pleas.

## A New Song in Praise of the Loyal Company of Stationers

1. *Charter ... June 1684*: The charters of the London corporation and the city's livery companies had been called in under quo warranto proceedings, requiring the companies to seek new grants. The Company of Stationers was the first to receive a new charter, dated 22 May rather than 'June' as Thompson suggests.
2. *Kit Arm'd ... Tender was for a surrender*: The song evokes the conflicting calls for resistance and quiescent self-interest in debates over charter forfeiture, through characters identifiable to contemporaries if not today.
3. *every Sea-man ... Guield*: a reference to the loss of chartered status opening the way for any man to enter the trade, or 'guild', and inviting a flood of cheap imports by sea.
4. *Ancesters Royal ... His Feet*: the Stationers' charter granted by Charles II's forebears now loyally delivered up to him without struggle, unlike some others (notably that of the London corporation).
5. *Bigot and Whig ... withdrew*: The new charter largely drew on the original charter, so the exclusion of 'Bigot and Whig' refers less to substantive provisions than to the process of listing anew the membership of the company, and more generally the ascendancy of loyal moderation over the 'rabble' opposing forfeiture. The ensuing lines convey the continuing disputes within the company between loyalists and dissentients.
6. *Bumper ... Armstrong's Fate*: a 'bumper' was a glass filled to the brim; 'Rumper' was a republican (supporter of the Rump Parliament); Sir Thomas Armstrong had been executed on 20 June 1684 for his part in the Rye House plot.

# Heresy, Orthodoxy and the Press, 1666-76

## The Catching of Hobbes

1. *Bill ... read the Second time*: The bill had received its first reading on 9 October. It emerged from committee with amendments and was read on 31 January 1667 but made no further progress before Parliament was prorogued on 8 February, although there were later attempts to advance the legislation (*CJ*, 8, pp. 636, 686).
2. *Long Robe ... have Voices*: The 'long robe' signified lawyers; 'have Voices' confirms that any member attending might speak.
3. *Book ... one White*: Thomas White (1593-1676), Catholic priest and prolific writer, was condemned by both English and Roman authorities for his unorthodoxy, his works being placed on the papal index of proscribed books. His alias 'Blacklo' lent the name

Blackloists to Catholics denying papal temporal power and infallibility in pursuit of toleration under Cromwell. An earlier work, *De Mundo* (1642), prompted a manuscript response by Hobbes, who suggested, rather ironically, that White's principles led to atheism. Parliament's concern may have been his views on the immortality of the soul, although offending passages were not specified.

4. *Hobbs ... Leviathan*: Thomas Hobbes, *Leviathan, or The Matter, Forme, and Power of a Common-Wealth Ecclesiasticall and Civill* (London: Andrew Crooke, 1651).
5. *bring in a Bill ... Defects*: There was little further progress before prorogation in February, with no bill emerging from committee.
6. *Williamson*: Joseph Williamson, under-secretary of state.
7. *book ... tract concerning Heresie*: The tract, denied a licence in 1668, was printed after Hobbes's death, with the contentious passage intact, as *An Historical Narration concerning Heresie, and the Punishment thereof* (London, 1680). The larger 'book' alluded to appeared in print as *An Answer to a Book Published by Dr. Bramhall, late Bishop of Derry; called The Catching of Leviathan. Together with an Historical Narration concerning Heresie* (London: William Crooke, 1682).
8. *Sam: Mearne*: see note 5 to [Seymour] *The Case of Libels*, above, p. 448.
9. *September 28$^{th}$, 1670*: the date of the raid, the date of the affidavit being 19 October, as subscribed by Mearne.
10. *Leak ... Roper ... Norton*: the booksellers William Leake and Abel Roper, and the printer Roger Norton.
11. *Thursday sennight*: the week after, so Thursday, 6 October. On 3 October the court of the Stationers' Company had followed up on the initial raid by ordering that Redmayne's press should be taken down and any remaining copies of *Leviathan* called in.
12. *Williams ... Crook*: the booksellers John Williams and Andrew Crooke. Crooke (c. 1605–74) was Hobbes's usual publisher and was master of the Stationers' Company in 1665–7. After his death, his nephew William published Hobbes's works.
13. *John Redmayne*: John Redmayne (fl. c. 1658–83) entered the printing trade in the 1650s under his father-in-law, the former Cambridge University printer Roger Daniel, and was a member of the Stationers' Company, probably from 1658. Despite the order that he lose his press he was again printing by 1672. The sheets he printed in 1670 appear to have been the basis for the second, 'Bear' edition of *Leviathan*, whose completion Noel Malcolm has dated to 1675–8 (for a detailed account, see 'The Printing of the "Bear"', in N. Malcolm, *Aspects of Hobbes* (Oxford: Clarendon Press, 2002) pp. 336–81).
14. *History of the Civill Wars ... in print*: T[homas] H[obbes], *The History of the Civil Wars of England* ([London], 1679). The work, written in the mid-1660s, was printed without Hobbes's authority. A second edition was published in 1679 and the book appeared under its best-known title, *Behemoth*, the following year.
15. *Mr. Hobbs about his Booke*: the response of Hobbes to the inquiry, as reported to the council.

## [Wolseley], *Liberty of Conscience*

1. *Magistrates Interest*: The two parts collected as the 'second edition' were published separately as [Charles Wolseley], *Liberty of Conscience upon its True and Proper Grounds Asserted and Vindicated* (London, 1668) and [Charles Wolseley], *Liberty of Conscience, the Magistrates Interest* (London, 1668). The first part argued that scripture and law

made it the magistrate's duty to allow toleration, the second part that it was in his interest to do so.
2. Sanguis Martyrum, semem Ecclesiæ: Latin: 'blood of the martyrs, seed of the church'.
3. *Cardinal* Woolsey: Thomas Wolsey (1470/1–1530) was cardinal from 1515. However, the 'letter' claimed by Wolseley did not exist, the words being Lord Herbert's supposition of what may have passed between Wolsey and the Pope in 1524. Moreover, Herbert's Wolsey was not arguing so much for censorship as for funds to pit 'Learning against Learning' because printing could not be suppressed: Edward Herbert, Baron Herbert of Cherbury, *The Life and Raigne of King Henry the Eighth* (London, 1649), p. 157.
4. Lord Herberts *Hist. of* Hen. *8*: See note 3 above. Herbert (c. 1582–1648) was commissioned to write the work by Charles I in the 1630s. It was reprinted in 1672 and in numerous editions thereafter.
5. Be wise ... Earth: Psalm 2:10.

## Cressy, *Fanaticism Fanatically Imputed to the Catholick Church*

1. *Doctour Stillingfleet* ... *against him*: Edward Stillingfleet, *A Discourse concerning the Idolatry Practised in the Church of Rome* (London: printed by Robert White for Henry Mortlock, 1671), 'Preface'. Two further editions appeared in 1671–2. Stillingfleet (1635–99) was a leading and still-rising star of the Church of England, commended for his writings in 1670 and appointed chaplain by Charles II and later made dean of St Paul's and bishop of Worcester. The *Discourse* and its reception prompted him to publish several more treatises on the same subject in the 1670s. A key adversary was Serenus (Henry) Cressy (1605–74), who, having been a member of the Tew Circle before the war, became a Benedictine monk in 1649 with a leading role in English Catholic circles in the 1660s and early 1670s.
2. *Prelats warning* ... *under their feet*: an accusation related to Stillingfleet's own latitudinarian leanings, which later gave way to the harsher view of *The Mischief of Separation* (1680). Cressy warns that preoccupation with Catholicism neglects the greater danger from protestant nonconformity, which oppressed the bishops in the civil war period.
3. *quondam friend*: former friend, referring to Stillingfleet's endeavours for comprehension, including Presbyterians in a broader Church.
4. Churches *are* meer Fanaticks: another allegation of Stillingfleet's embrace of multiple factions, as well as Cressy's further riposte to him 'lumping' Protestant dissenters and Catholics as fanatics.
5. *90*: paragraph numbering in original.
6. *New Faith* ... *Faith of New England*: a reference to the flourishing of nonconformist churches in the American colonies.
7. *Neophit*: neophyte, novice.
8. *wants an* Imprimatur: this jibe at lacking a licence was perhaps one reason for Stillingfleet's status as royal chaplain being added to the title page after the first edition. His *Answer* to his critics, published in 1673, carried the imprimatur of Samuel Parker for the archbishop of Canterbury.
9. Censor Librorum: censor of books.
10. *Book of Sermons*: This work has not been identified.
11. *Pouder Treason*: the gunpowder plot of 1605.

## [Clarendon], *Animadversions upon a Book*

1. Lord Bacon ... Advancement of Learning: Francis Bacon, *Of the Advancement and Proficience of Learning* (Oxford, 1640), first published in 1605. The point of Bacon's use of the biblical story of Moses and the serpents in book II was to argue that the answer to a surfeit of poor books is not fewer books but better books.
2. Martin Marprelate: the authorial name assumed for the anonymous anti-episcopal (hence mar-prelate) publishing campaign of the late 1580s (see Volume 1 of this edition).
3. *Classis*: class of citizens, although the word also connoted local governing bodies in reformed churches, such as a presbytery.
4. Thom. Nash: the writer Thomas Nashe (*c.* 1567–*c.* 1601) was associated with the loyalist and conformist 'anti-Martinist' publishing campaign sponsored by Archbishop Whitgift and others to answer the Marprelate tracts in similarly populist style.
5. Fanaticism ... by S.C.: Serenus Cressy's reply to Stillingfleet.
6. noisom Gall: foul bitterness.
7. *my name ... prejudice that is against it*: As arguably the most powerful Restoration figure below the King, now impeached and in exile, Clarendon's name was indeed unlikely to be greeted indifferently by readers. Following his death in 1674 his *Brief View and Survey* of Hobbes's *Leviathan* was published bearing his name but his other writings, notably the *History of the Rebellion*, were not published until the eighteenth century.
8. *Licensed by lawful Authority*: the tract was authorized by Thomas Tomkins, licenser to the archbishop of Canterbury, Gilbert Sheldon, an ally of Clarendon's, albeit an increasingly critical one.

## [Croft], *The Naked Truth*

1. Niti in Vetitum: Latin: 'to strive for what is forbidden'.
2. Naaman *did of* Elisha: 2 Kings 5:1–19.
3. *Papal Idolatry ... Stillingfleet*: Edward Stillingfleet's tracts against Catholic idolatry. See note 1 to Cressy, *Fanaticism Fanatically Imputed to the Catholick Church*, above, p. 452.

## [Marvell], *Mr. Smirke*

1. Arcanum *of their State*: secret of the clergy's status, position.
2. *stick*: illegible in first impression, supplied by Wing 873B (hereafter '*B*').
3. Ounce ... Clergy: or, 'an ounce of mother wit is worth a pound of school-wit'.
4. Effluvium: invisible vapour.
5. *Residentiary*: clergy member in residence.
6. *exquisite*: discriminating, fastidious.
7. *that is reposed in him*: B.
8. Omne ... Spirituale: Latin, 'his whole nature in every way, temporal as much as spiritual'.
9. *Easter Visitation*: the clergy's annual inspection of church and parish. The attack on Croft came at the end of February, at the start of Lent (Easter Sunday being 5 April), giving rise to Marvell's extended analogy.
10. Animadversions ... Primitive Church: [Francis Turner], *Animadversions upon a Late Pamphlet entituled The Naked Truth* (London, 1676). Turner (1637–1700), a well-connected young churchman and master of St John's College, Cambridge, probably wrote at

the instigation of Bishop Peter Gunning, whom he went on to succeed as bishop of Ely in 1684. Marvell makes much of his being a pen guided by patronage.
11. *Naked Truth*: by Herbert Croft; reproduced above, see pp. 141–2.
12. *rest*: B.
13. *Shrove-Tuesday ... sting at him*: Shrove Tuesday, as the last day before Lent, was traditionally a day when fairs and frivolity were enjoyed, farthings and pence being spent which during Lent would be given or received as alms. One customary piece of 'boys' play' was to hoist a cock in an earthenware vessel and throw stones, the thrower who broke the pot claiming the bird.
14. *close youth ... Preferment*: Turner is the 'close youth', his insinuating ways with the Church hierarchy a target for Marvell.
15. fluster: B.
16. *out*-boniface *an* Humble Moderator: Croft styled himself the 'humble moderator' in his anonymous tract; the ostentation of Pope Boniface VIII was often criticized.
17. Doriman: B.
18. Doriman ... Fopling Flutter: characters in George Etherege's play *The Man of Mode, or, Sir Fopling Flutter*, first performed on 2 March 1676 and printed in June. The foppish Sir Fopling seeks to emulate the rakish Dorimant.
19. *Tiring-Roome*: attiring room, dressing room.
20. *Borderers*: a play on the dwellers in Scottish (and Welsh) border country.
21. *Parliament ... more value*: Parliament had been prorogued on 22 November 1676, curtailing moves to make the Printing Act perpetual, amongst other things, and prompting Turner's conjectural punishment for *The Naked Truth*. An earlier bill 'for the ease of dissenters' had failed but the Earl of Shaftesbury and others had expressed hopes that a new Parliament would reverse this outcome.
22. *Epilogue ... represent them all*: lines from John Dryden's epilogue to Etherege's play.
23. *three are all of a piece*: the 1662 Act of Uniformity, 1662 Printing Act, and the 1670 Conventicles Act (successor to the 1664 Conventicles Act).
24. Parliamentum Indoctum: Latin: 'uninformed Parliament'.
25. Samaritan ... *Penalties*: referring to the parable of the Good Samaritan, Luke 10:30–7.
26. *last Session but one of Parliament*: the session ended 9 June 1675.
27. *Expurgatory ... Index*: a reference to the Catholic Church's *Index Expurgatorius* of censored books.
28. *Obsolete Apostle ... the Truth*: St Paul, 'obsolete' being ironical; 2 Corinthians 13:8.
29. *Mr.* Oldenburg: Henry Oldenburg (*c.* 1619–77), secretary of the Royal Society and editor of the *Philosophical Transactions*, and from February to May 1676 an official licenser of history books.
30. *Bishop of* London: Henry Compton (1631/2–1713), bishop since December 1675, whose imprimatur of 23 February authorized Turner's *Animadversions*.
31. Hooker ... Ecl. Policy: Richard Hooker, *Of the Lawes of Ecclesiastical Politie, Eight Bookes* (London, 1604), first published 1593 and reprinted regularly, either alone or in Hooker's *Works*, including in 1675 and 1676. Marvell's page reference tallies with the 1604 edition.
32. I trust ... Egypt: ibid., p. 43.

## News, Libels and the Crown, 1670–80

### *A Proclamation to Restrain the Spreading of False News* (1672)

1. *late Statute*: the 1661 Treason Act, 13 Car. II, c. 1.

### *A Proclamation to Restrain the Spreading of False News* (1674)

1. stir up dislike ... Government: the wording, like that of the 1672 proclamation, follows that of the 1661 Treason Act.

### 'Mr. Lestrange's Examination concerning "The Rehearsal Transposed"'

1. *Brome, a bookseller*: Henry Brome (d. 1681), closely associated with L'Estrange as his regular publisher and supporter.
2. *Ponder*: Nathaniel Ponder (1640–99), bookseller renowned for publishing nonconformist authors, notably John Bunyan and John Owen, as well as Marvell. Although he evaded punishment for *The Rehearsal Transpros'd*, in May 1676 he was briefly imprisoned for Marvell's *Mr Smirke*. His name is misspelled 'Pinder' in the manuscript account recorded in *HMC*, 7, pp. 517–18.
3. *Mr. Mearn*: see note 5 to [Seymour] *The Case of Libels*, above, p. 448.
4. *Earl of Anglesey*: Arthur Annesley (1614–86), lord privy seal from 1673–82 and nonconformist sympathizer. As well as protecting Marvell and Ponder he drafted a parliamentary bill in 1673 to ease penalties against dissenters.
5. *Parker*: Samuel Parker (1640–88), high-church controversialist, future bishop of Oxford, and an ecclesiastical licenser as chaplain to the archbishop of Canterbury. *The Rehearsal Transpros'd* was a response to Parker's *A Discourse of Ecclesiastical Polity* (London, 1670). Parker replied with *A Reproof to The Rehearsal Transprosed* (1673), in which he insisted that his opposition was not to the King's declaration of indulgence but to nonconformist demands for indulgence.
6. *printed from him*: 'printed *from* him' suggests how the concern was not only censorship but piracy, confirmed by Ponder in prefatory remarks to a further impression, which accepted L'Estrange's modifications and included Ponder's name on the title page.
7. *Bishop Laud*: William Laud (1573–1645), architect of Anglican Church policy during Charles I's personal rule, as bishop of London from 1628 and archbishop of Canterbury from 1633. He was impeached for treason by the Commons in December 1640 and held prisoner until his trial in 1644 and execution in January 1645.
8. *letter ... annexed to this examination*: the letter is lost.

### Charles II, in *London Gazette*

1. *Secretaries of State*: at this time, Joseph Williamson and Henry Coventry.
2. *Act of General Pardon*: the 1660 'Act of Free and General Pardon Indempnity and Oblivion' (Act of Oblivion, 12 Car. II, c. 11).

### *London Gazette*

1. *An Account ... Popery, &c.*: [Andrew Marvell], *An Account of the Growth of Popery, and Arbitrary Government in England* ('Amsterdam', 1677).
2. Seasonable Argument ... Juries, &c.: [Andrew Marvell], *A Seasonable Argument to Perswade all the Grand Juries in England, to Petition for a New Parliament* ('Amsterdam', 1677).

## 'Joseph Leigh'

1. *Joseph Leigh*: little more is known of Leigh or others involved; see headnote.
2. *Depon$^t$*: deponent, i.e. Leigh.
3. *Account of the Growth of Popery &c.*: by Andrew Marvell.
4. *Mathew Fowler's house*: a Dr Matthew Fowler was vicar of St Alphage in London, but the reference is obscure.
5. *for one ... wrought at ye Presse*: as one of those who had worked at the press.
6. *drunk ... fainedly soe*: pretending to be drunk.
7. *Bednal Greene*: old name for Bethnal Green.
8. *Dollaring ... Bibell and all*: presumably an accusation of producing counterfeit coinage (the term dollar being applied to foreign coins) and unauthorized bibles.
9. *corā me ... Miles Cooke*: in my presence, master of Chancery, (Sir) Miles Cooke.

## Restoration Crisis, 1679–81

### A Proclamation for Suppressing the Printing and Publishing

1. *Judges unanimously*: the judges' opinion solicited by the King; see headnote.
2. *12$^{th}$ day of May*: the proclamation was published on 17 May, as noted in the *London Gazette*, 1513 (17–20 May 1680).

### A Short, but Just Account of the Tryal of Harris

1. Scroggs: Sir William Scroggs (c. 1623–83), target and scourge of the press, had been a royalist officer in the civil war before enjoying the patronage of the Earl of Danby as a rising lawyer. He became lord chief justice of the court of King's Bench in 1678 and in 1678-9 presided over the popish plot trials which condemned fourteen defendants, before the non-conviction of Sir George Wakeman and others in July 1679 prompted attacks in newsbooks and pamphlets which Scroggs reciprocated by waging war on the press.
2. Benjamin Harris: Benjamin Harris (c. 1647–1720), bookseller and publisher of popish plot works, notably, from July 1679, the anti-Catholic newspaper the *Domestick Intelligence*. His clashes with authority led him in 1686 to leave for Boston, Massachusetts, and he is credited with publishing the first American newspaper, the *Publick Occurrences*, suppressed after a single issue on 25 September 1690. He returned to England and from 1695 again published newspapers, including the *London News* 1699–1705.
3. *An Appeal ... Religion*: attributed to Charles Blount. On Blount, see below, pp. 199–215.
4. Mr. Recorder: George Jeffreys (1645–89) became recorder of London on 22 October 1678, as the King's favoured candidate, and played a part in the popish plot trials, as well as those against the press. In 1683 he succeeded Scroggs as chief justice and presided at the trial of Algernon Sidney, and in 1685 he led the 'bloody assizes' that condemned to death 200 of the defeated Monmouth rebels. He was made Lord Chancellor by James II, whose demise in 1688 led to Jeffreys being held on treason charges in the Tower, where he died in April 1689.
5. a Printer's Wife: the wife of James Grover, a type-founder and printer mainly of almanacs and astrological works, including for the Stationers' Company.
6. Mary Darby: daughter of the printers John and Joan Darby.
7. Benjamin Tooke: Benjamin Tooke (fl. 1669–1716), King's printer in Dublin and London bookseller, who occupied posts with the Stationers' Company from 1677. His later claim to fame was as bookseller and publisher to Jonathan Swift, a role shared by his son, also Benjamin.

8. Serjeant Strode: Thomas Strode (d. 1698), sergeant-at-law.
9. Mr. Williams: William Williams (1633/4–1700), lawyer and MP, becoming an influential speaker of the Commons from 1680. He defended Harris and other print-trade defendants, contributing to animosity between himself and Jeffreys, although he subsequently departed from Whig loyalties sufficiently to be knighted and made solicitor-general by James II.
10. Mr. Ollibear: a bookselling colleague of Harris.
11. Smith: the bookseller Francis Smith; see note 1 to *An Impartial Account of the Tryals of Smith and Curtis*, below.
12. Domestick-Intelligences ... *Recognizance*: the *Domestick Intelligence; or, News both from City and Country*, which Harris had issued since the previous July. Just before the trial, on 16 January, the title had changed to the *Protestant (Domestick) Intelligence* due to the appearance of the competing *True Domestick Intelligence*.
13. *Robert Stephens*: Robert Stephens was the most enduring and notable of the 'messengers of the press', deputies responsible for investigating suspect printing and publishing. Officially the messengers served the secretary of state, although Stephens was employed by Scroggs to hunt down printers and publishers in 1679–80, bringing censure by the Commons on 23 December 1680 (*CJ*, 9, pp. 688–9). Known for his tenacity and Toryism, and known derisively as 'Robin Hog', Stephens's service stretched from the 1660s into the eighteenth century. Initially he assisted L'Estrange but, despite similarities in political outlook, their overlapping functions helped make them deadly enemies, particularly after Stephens targeted L'Estrange's *Observator* for suppression; see above, p. 249.
14. *all the Judges ... Account*: the judges' opinion of late October 1679, on which basis Scroggs had issued a warrant for search and arrest to Stephens on 29 November.
15. *Duke of* Monmouth: the tract was notable for openly proposing as Protestant successor James Scott, Duke of Monmouth (1649–85), Charles II's illegitimate son by Lucy Walter.
16. *Tippstaff ... Kings Bench*: the Tipstaff is an officer of the court. 'Kings Bench' here denotes King's Bench Prison in Southwark.

## *An Impartial Account of the Tryals of Smith and Curtis*

1. Francis Smith *Bookseller*: Francis Smith (d. 1691) combined the roles of bookseller-publisher and Baptist preacher and faced arrest for both, becoming a much-harried antagonist of government. Imprisoned for republican works in 1660 and arrested for preaching in the 1670s, Smith embarked in the wake of the popish plot on nearly three years of sustained activity against 'popery and arbitrary government'. This reached its height in the year after his 1680 trial with the condemned tracts *Vox Populi* and *A Ra-Ree Show*, arrest for treason, and the suppression of Smith's Whig newspaper the *Protestant Intelligence*. He fled but on returning in 1684 was imprisoned for his role in *A Ra-Ree Show* (reprinted below, see pp. 242–5), only being released in 1688.
2. Justice Jones: Sir Thomas Jones (1614–92), who escaped impeachment proceedings in the Commons later in 1680 and took part in the condemnation in 1681 of Stephen College for *A Ra-Ree Show*, which Smith was involved in publishing.
3. Holt: John Holt (1642–1710), knighted in 1686 and from 1689 chief justice of King's Bench and a privy councillor. In 1704, in the trial for seditious libel of John Tutchin, he would famously declare that no government could subsist without the power to call its critics to account (see Volume 4 of this edition).
4. *Sir* George Wakeman ... *1679*: Wakeman and his co-defendants, three Catholic monks, were acquitted, provoking outrage amidst the popish plot hysteria.

5. *Some Observations ... Tryal, &c.*: Anon., *Some Observations upon the Late Tryals of Sir George Wakeman, Corker and Marshal, &c. By Tom Tickle-Foot the Taborer, late Clerk to Justice Clodpate* (London: 'A. Brewster', 1679).
6. Mr. Recorder: the recorder of London, George Jeffreys; see note 4 to *A Short, but Just Account of the Tryal of Harris*, above, p. 456.
7. *two daies ago*: i.e. the trial of Benjamin Harris.
8. Lord Chief Justice *of the* King's Bench: judge William Scroggs, in whose court Wakeman and the others were acquitted. See note 1 to *A Short, but Just Account of the Tryal of Harris*, above, p. 456.
9. *render to Cæsar ... God's*: Matthew 22:21.
10. Mrs. Brewster: Anne Brewster, widow of the bookseller Thomas Brewster. Smith arranged the printing but only Brewster's name appeared on the imprint.
11. Williams: William Williams; see note 9 to *A Short, but Just Account of the Tryal of Harris*, above, p. 456.
12. *Rob. Stephens ... Margaret Clark*: Robert Stephens, messenger of the press (see note 13 to *A Short, but Just Account of the Tryal of Harris*, above, p. 457), and possibly Mary Clark, widow of the printer Andrew Clark and a printer in her own right.
13. Mrs. Smith: Eleanor Smith, who was used to standing in for her husband – she kept Smith's business going during his several periods of imprisonment and also after his death, until her own demise in 1696.
14. *Jane Curtis*: printer-publisher and wife of Langley Curtis (or Curtiss), the Whig printer and newspaper publisher whose punishment for a later tract is discussed in the section on The Tory Reaction I, below. Jane Curtis had been arrested and imprisoned on Scroggs's warrant in October 1679 for the same tract, *Satyr upon Injustice*. In 1679 she was also involved, with her husband and the writer Henry Care, in producing the Whig newspaper *A Weekly Pacquet of Advice from Rome*, and when Langley Curtis fled the authorities in 1681–2 she continued his *True Protestant Mercury* newspaper.
15. *A Satyr ... upon Scroggs*: Anon., *A Satyr Against In-Justice: or, Sc—gs upon Sc—gs* ([London: Jane Curtis, 1680]).
16. *Guilty*: The penalty is not recorded, although the unusually sympathetic tone of the judge confirms that Mrs Curtis avoided prison. Sutherland conjectures that her good looks may have been a factor, along with fears of a backlash (*The Restoration Newspaper and its Development* (Cambridge: Cambridge University Press, 1986), p. 199); Schwoerer points out that the earlier imprisonment had prompted protests to the Privy Council (*The Ingenious Mr. Henry Care, Restoration Publicist* (Baltimore, MD: Johns Hopkins University Press, 2001), p. 98).

## *The Triall of Carr*

1. *Recorder*: George Jeffreys, the London recorder. See note 4 to *A Short, but Just Account of the Tryal of Harris*, above, p. 456
2. *THIS Person*: Henry Care (1646/7–88), a previously obscure writer translated to the front rank of Whig polemic in the wake of the popish plot after he launched the paired periodicals *A Weekly Pacquet of Advice from Rome, or The History of Popery* and the *Popish Courant*. These ran from December 1678 to July 1683, with the involvement of the printer-publishers Langley and Jane Curtis until 1682. The *Weekly Pacquet* and other tracts made 'Harry' Care (or 'Carr') one of the most prolific author-publishers of the

period, and among the most pursued by the authorities (on Care, see Schwoerer, *The Ingenious Mr. Henry Care*).
3. *Weekly Pacquet of Advice from Rome*: the information against Care was for the 1 August 1679 issue of the *Weekly Pacquet of Advice from Rome* (actually the appended *Popish Courant*) which in the wake of the Wakeman acquittal accused justice of being deaf and blind, and entrusted to knaves.
4. *Judges ... met together*: the judges' meetings and collective opinions of October 1679 and May 1680, the latter having asserted the common law illegality of printing news without licence.
5. Winnington: Sir Francis Winnington (1634–1700), solicitor-general until removed in 1679, and a prominent Whig MP; after initial reservations he led demands to exclude James, Duke of York, from the throne.
6. L.C.J.: William Scroggs, lord chief justice (see note 1 to *A Short, but Just Account of the Tryal of Harris*, above, p. 456). His interjection refers to the murmurings of the public attending the trial.
7. *Disturbance ... public concern*: Scroggs is again interjecting to complain of disturbance from the public gallery.
8. *Case of Harris*: the trial of Benjamin Harris in February 1680.
9. *Five Hundred Pounds ... rott in Goal*: Harris had languished in jail since his trial, unable to pay his fines or surety.
10. *Printer himself*: the otherwise obscure printer 'Mr Stevens' had testified, rather circuitously, that Care and Langley Curtis were involved.
11. *guilty*: Care was ordered to discontinue the *Weekly Pacquet*, but the order was not heeded.

## 'Articles of Impeachment of Scroggs'

1. Henry Carr: Henry Care; see headnote to this section.
2. *in* haec verba: Latin: 'in these words'.
3. Dies Mercurii ... Per Cur: Latin: 'Wednesday next following the third week after Trinity, in the 32nd year of the reign of the King. It is ordered that the Book which is entitled *The Weekly Pacquet of Advice from Rome, or the History of Popery* not be further printed or published by any person whomsoever. By the court.'
4. *one* Jessop: nothing more is known of Jessop, nor his collaborator Hewett.
5. *Citizens of* London: all those listed were connected with printing and publishing.

# Arguments for Liberty of the Press, 1679–81

## [Blount], *A Just Vindication of Learning*

1. Session of Parliament: the session began on 18 March 1679.
2. *Tacitus ... Battavi*: The Batavians were a Germanic tribe inhabiting an area later forming part of the Dutch republic, which in the wake of the French Revolution would become briefly the Batavian Republic. Tacitus described their conspicuous bravery in the *Germania*.
3. *Omnes ... lacerantur*: Latin: 'For we are all of us either ravens that tear or corpses that are torn'. A version of the phrase, deriving from Petronius's *Satyricon*, occurs in Robert Burton's *Anatomy of Melancholy* (London, 1621), p. 32.
4. late Act ... near Expiring: 13 & 14 Car. II, c. 33, the 1662 Printing Act, as continued.

5. *Philopatris*: 'Patriot'. 'Philopatris' was Charles Blount (1654–93; see headnote). A number of writers utilized the name between 1679 and 1682.
6. Alexander ... *50 Talents*: Plutarch, *Life of Alexander*.
7. Candiots: Cretans.
8. Mr. Milton ... *Eye of God*: John Milton, *Areopagitica* (London, 1644), p. 4: 'who kills a Man kills a reasonable creature, Gods Image; but hee who destroyes a good Booke, kills reason it selfe, kills the Image of God, as it were in the eye'.
9. Plato ... Philolaus the Pythagorian: citing Gellius, *Attic Nights*.
10. Cardan ... par habet: Latin: 'Antiquity has nothing its equal': Cardanus (Girolamo Cardano), *De Subtilitate Rerum* (1550).
11. Thuanus ... unquam debuit: Latin: 'The Christian world is more indebted to them than any country ever was to the bravest generals for extending its territories': Thuanus (Jacques-Auguste de Thou), *Historia sui temporis* (History of his own Times) (1604–20).
12. *I shall here demonstrate* ... Imprimatur: Blount draws heavily from this point, without attribution, upon Milton's account of censorship history in *Areopagitica*, pp. 5 ff. For additional notes and commentary, see *Complete Prose Works of John Milton*, gen. ed. D. M. Wolfe, 8 vols (New Haven, CT: Yale University Press, 1953–82), vol. 2, ed. Ernest Sirluck.
13. Vetus Comædia: Latin: 'old comedy', such as that of Aristophanes.
14. Plato ... Dionysius: Plato was reputed to have recommended reading Aristophanes's work to Dionysius, the tyrant of Syracuse, who had asked about the workings of Athenian democracy.
15. Epicurus ... Cynick: The ancient Greek schools of thought represented by Epicureans, Cyreneans and Cynics all challenged conventional conceptions of virtue, the first two equating virtue with pleasure, the Cynics rejecting conventions of all kinds.
16. Lucretius ... Cicero: The first-century BC Roman orator and politician Gaius Memmius (not 'Memnius') was the addressee of the poet-philosopher Lucretius's *De rerum natura* (On the Nature of Things). The Roman statesman and writer Marcus Tullius Cicero is known to have read the work and praised the workmanship but the claim that he published the poem is doubtful. While largely following Milton's progression, Blount takes this example from later in *Areopagitica*: p. 16.
17. Lucilius, Catullus, *or* Flaccus: satirical writers of ancient Rome. Quintus Horatius Flaccus was the poet Horace.
18. Titus Livius ... Octavins Cæsar: Titus Livius was the historian Livy, whose inclination towards Pompey was said by Tacitus to appear in one of the many lost sections of Livy's monumental work. 'Octavins' (Octavian or Octavius) Caesar was Julius Caesar.
19. Porphyrius *and* Proclus: Neoplatonic writers of the third and fifth centuries AD respectively who were critical of Christianity. Porphyry's *Adversus Christianos* (Against the Christians) was ordered to be burned by Emperor Constantine.
20. Carthaginian *Council*: the fifth council of Carthage in AD 401.
21. *year 800* ... Trentine *Council*: 'Father Paul' is Paolo Sarpi (1552–1623), a major source for Milton, and therefore Blount, through his *The Historie of the Councel of Trent*, published in England in Latin in 1619 and in English translation in 1620, 1629 and 1639.
22. Martin *the* 5th ... Wicklif and Huss: Martin V's bull *Inter cunctas*, issued in 1418, ordered the suppression of writings spreading the heresies of the English religious reformer John Wyclif (d. 1384) and the Bohemian Jan Hus, who had been burned at the stake in 1415.

23. Leo the 10th: pope from 1513–21, Leo X faced the challenge of silencing Martin Luther, in person and by action against his writings, which circulated widely in print.
24. *Council of* Trent ... Licenser: great assembly of the Roman Catholic Church at Trento, now northern Italy, from 1545 to 1563, which authorized censorship measures including a system of press licensing and the *Index Librorum Prohibitorum*, a list of proscribed books. *Index Expurgatorius* referred to works that were determined to be allowable with deletions and corrections. The *Index* system was formally abolished in 1966.
25. Slavery ... Religion: the italics suggest a quotation but this does not derive from *Areopagitica*. Blount at this point moves from p. 8 to p. 20 of Milton's text, passing over Milton's discursive account of historical experience, scriptural and philosophical precedent, and the practical difficulties of licensing, and so passing 'from the no good it can do, to the manifest hurt it causes' (*Areopagitica*, p. 20).
26. *he should drop ... an* Imprimatur: a direct, unacknowledged, quotation from *Areopagitica*, p. 20. By 'drop a Scism' is implied the inadvertent writing of words deemed schismatic or heretical. A 'ferula' was a teacher's cane and a 'fescu' a teacher's pointer.
27. *When a man ... World*: Blount follows Milton almost word for word from here to 'Echyridion Unlicensed' in section 5, covering *Areopagitica* pp. 21–4.
28. Palladian *Oyl*: Pallas Athene, goddess of wisdom, was held to have taught men to extract oil from olives to light lamps for study.
29. *a Puny*: a schoolboy, a minor.
30. *Censors Hand on the back of his Title*: the imprimatur on the verso (although not necessarily on the reverse of the title page itself).
31. *Lord* Bacon ... Times: *Areopagitica*, p. 22. The quotation derives from a tract written by Francis Bacon in 1589, published anonymously in 1641 as *A Wise and Moderate Discourse concerning Church-Affaires*. Bacon was not condemning censorship in making the claim, which appears on p. 11, but recommending that authorized and unauthorized books were equally worthy of suppression.
32. *Vacuum, Motion, Air*: Blount here substitutes the contemporary interests of natural philosophy and the Royal Society for Milton's example of the religious reformer John Knox.
33. *20 Capacities*: a reference to the large number of licensers envisaged by the 1643 Ordinance on printing (actually thirty-two), not strictly relevant to Blount's case.
34. *Manual Stamp*: part of an extended analogy between censorship's control of the understanding and the checking and marking of general goods.
35. Philistines ... *Forges*: 1 Samuel 13:19–21. The Philistines denied Israelites their own forges to sharpen tools in case they were used to create weapons.
36. *Laick rabble*: an unreligious or irreligious mob.
37. *Enchyridion Unlicensed*: an unlicensed handbook, and possibly a pun on the similar Greek word for dagger (hand-knife).
38. *Pusillanimous*: timid. With this sentence Blount departs from Milton's words and over ensuing passages draws only selectively on *Areopagitica* pp. 25–35, sharing Milton's emphasis on truth but substituting contemporary concerns such as Catholic succession for Milton's focus on episcopacy and parliament.
39. *Fire and Faggot*: i.e. by burning of book or author, faggots being bundles of sticks.
40. Galileo: Galileo Galilei (1564–1642), condemned for heresy by the Roman Inquisition after publishing the claim that the Earth revolved around the Sun, rather than vice versa. In *Areopagitica*, Milton referred to having met Galileo, who spent his last years under house arrest (p. 24).

41. *evil Prince*: a fairly blatant reference to the prospect of James, Duke of York, succeeding as Catholic monarch, although the following sentences extend the warning by implication to include Charles II.
42. *freedom to write, as to speak*: echoed subsequently by John Locke, see below, p. 417.
43. *Wity Discourse ... Ingenuous Writing*: the contrast is still between the spoken and written/printed word, here between witty speech and artless writing.
44. *Thomas a Thumbis*: a composite of the combined inoffensiveness of the diminutive Tom Thumb and meditative Thomas à Kempis.
45. *Mahometans*: Muslims.
46. *the Turk ... Mufti and Conclave*: the Ottoman emperor ('the Great Turk') was taken as the pope's Islamic equivalent, 'Alcoran' is the Quran, 'Mufti' denotes the leading Islamic scholars, and the 'Conclave' the papal college of cardinals.
47. *Let her ... surest oppressing*: *Areopagitica*, p. 35, substituting 'oppressing' for 'suppressing'. The subsequent phrase, which is Blount's, probably should read 'to doubt' rather than 'no doubt'.
48. *The punishing ... tread it out*: Bacon, *A Wise and Moderate Discourse*, p. 11; Milton, *Areopagitica*, p. 26.
49. *When a man ... against her power*: *Areopagitica*, p. 36.
50. *Ephesian Books*: Acts 19:17–19; Christian converts in Ephesus burned scrolls they had previously used in sorcery. Blount paraphrases *Areopagitica*'s account, p. 12.
51. *Yet I cannot but wish ... unsafe*: Jeremy Taylor, *A Discourse of the Liberty of Prophesying* (London, 1647), p. 14.
52. *Chyrurgion*: surgeon. This sentence is also derived from ibid., p. 15.
53. *re alioqui non necessariâ*: Latin: 'in a matter otherwise indifferent'.
54. *I would fain know ... Idle Persons*: Taylor, *A Discourse of the Liberty of Prophesying*, p. 38.
55. *I am certain ... certainty*: ibid., pp. 38–9.
56. *increase of Interest ... worst of all*: ibid., p. 18.
57. *Tamberlain the Great*: Tamerlane (Timur the lame), the great central Asian military conqueror of the fourteenth century, subject of Christopher Marlowe's two-part *Tamburlaine the Great* (1587–8). His tolerance was attested in Richard Knolles, *The Generall Historie of the Turks* (London, 1603), p. 211, although Blount does not derive his quotation from Knolles.
58. *All Wise Princes ... publick Interest*: Taylor, *A Discourse of the Liberty of Prophesying*, p. 19.
59. *Scandala Magnatum*: in law, crimes of libel or slander against persons of high rank, considered a public and criminal rather than private and civil matter.
60. *3 and 4 of Ed. 6*: The 1549 'Act for the Abolishing and Putting Away of divers Books and Images', 3 & 4 Edw. VI, c. 10.

## Lawrence, *Marriage by the Morall Law of God Vindicated*

1. *Coke 3. part 40*: Lawrence uses the standard legal authority *The Institutes of the Lawes of England*, by Sir Edward Coke (1552–1634), published from 1628 in four parts and appearing in numerous editions. The reference here is to the *Third Part* (London, 1644), p. 40. The italicization suggests that only this sentence is quoted from Coke but in fact Lawrence takes from Coke everything down to his interjection 'What *English* Protestant can read this without horror?'; the italicized lines quote the statute.
2. *5. R. 2*: The Act against Heretical Preaching of 1382, spurred by the campaign to suppress John Wyclif and his followers. Coke's marginal note reads '5 R. 2. Stat. 2. cap. 5. repealed by 1 E. 6. c. 12. & 1 Eliz. ca. 1'.

3. Fautors: supporters.
4. *prefer'd*: raised, drew attention to.
5. *aniented*: destroyed, frustrated.
6. Ypleist au Roy: it pleases the King.
7. *Bailwick ... Liberties*: The sheriff's bailiwick was the area of his jurisdiction, 'liberties' referring to exempted parts supervised by another authorized bailiff.
8. 5. R. 2: in 1382.
9. John Braibrook: actually Robert Braybrooke (1336/7–1404), whose brief tenure as lord chancellor in 1382–3 ended after parliamentary anger at the events Coke describes.
10. *purclose*: ending, conclusion.
11. *Sheriff of N.*: Norwich. The duties implied by the writ were directed to the sheriff.
12. Nos volentes ... R. 2. 5: Latin: 'We, wishing the said agreements or ordinances to be inviolably observed in all their articles, enjoin you to ensure that the aforesaid agreements or ordinances be proclaimed publicly and held in those places in your bailiwick where you think it most expedient, as much within your liberties as without, according to the form noted above. Witness the King at Westminster, 26 May in the fifth year of the reign of King Richard the second.'
13. *kept from the Print*: Lawrence's extended borrowing from Coke ends at this point. Coke's account turns to 2 Hen. IV, c. 15, De Haeretico Comburendo.
14. fiery Furnaces: The Act was associated with the Marian persecutions, being revived in 1554, along with the statutes of 2 Hen. IV, c. 15 and 2 Hen. V, c. 7 (1414), by 1 & 2 Mary, c. 6, 'An Act for the Renewing of Three Statutes made for the Punishment of Heresies'.
15. Coke 2. Part. Fol. 584: Edward Coke, *The Second Part of the Institutes of the Lawes of England* (London, 1642), p. 584. Lawrence is quoting from Coke down to 'known of all men'.
16. *Statute of 35. E. 1*: the statute *De asportatis religiosorum*, 35 Edw. I, st. 1, c. 1, which in effect challenged ecclesiastical autonomy by restricting the exporting of charges and taxes for papal benefit by religious houses and heads.
17. *wholy omitted*: The claim is that the statute of Edward I originally addressed importing as well as exporting, with a clause preventing the promulgation of papal bulls and injunctions without due domestic authority. Coke held that this clause was revealed in being cited in the statute of Edward III, having been otherwise suppressed.
18. Provisors: papal nominees for posts, a subject of dispute between the Crown and Rome.
19. *known of all men*: Coke's words end here, and Lawrence's comment begins, blaming the bishops for the suppression of statutory limitations of Church authority.
20. Accipe ... Omnes: Latin: 'hear now the intrigues of these men, and from a single crime learn all their natures' (Virgil, *Aeneid*).
21. *prohibited to be Printed*: Coke's papers were seized after his death and printing of the final three parts of the *Institutes* prevented. In 1641 Parliament ordered the return of the papers and encouraged their publication.
22. obiter: by the way.
23. Canonical ... Apocryphal: as with the division between the books sanctioned for inclusion in the Bible and those deemed of lesser authenticity gathered in the *Apocrypha*.
24. *Transmarine Presses*: overseas presses.
25. pessimum ... Adulantes: Latin: 'flatterers are the worst kind of enemies' (Tacitus, *Agricola*).
26. Plutarch ... nothing: Plutarch, 'On how to Profit by one's Enemies', in *Moralia*.

27. *it was Enacted ... themselves*: the 1555 Peace of Augsburg.
28. *Pasquil*: a lampoon, satirical verses.
29. Alchoran: the Quran.
30. *dangerous way ... dark*: i.e. spreading heresy by spoken rumour.
31. *intelligence*: information, news.
32. *Gates of Princes*: Isaiah 13:2. The King James Bible has 'gates of the nobles'.
33. *pickt Sheriff*: Lawrence's supposed experience appears to be another borrowing, this time from Coke's life. On being named high sheriff of Buckinghamshire, Coke objected to the terms of the oath and in 1626 secured judicial, royal and parliamentary support for the removal of the clause complained of by Lawrence, which originally derived from the statute of 5 Ric. II. The events were recounted in John Rushworth's *Historical Collections* (London, 1659), p. 202. The licenser's comment reported by Lawrence was presumably invented.
34. Lollary: another term for Lollardry (or Lollardy). The oath-taker undertook to destroy 'all manner of Heresies and Error, commonly called Lollaries': Rushworth, *Historical Collections*, p. 202.
35. *Three Kingdoms*: England and Wales, Scotland, and Ireland.

## Denton, *An Apology for the Liberty of the Press*

1. sine permissu superiorum: Latin: 'without permission of superiors'.
2. *stealing a Nap*: napping, taking a quick sleep.
3. inter graviora delicta: Latin: 'among the more serious crimes'.
4. Canonical Slight: i.e. an act of disrespect to the truth.
5. Bible *it self* ... prohibited Books: Rome's prohibition of the vernacular Bible.
6. Theseus *his Ship*: According to Plutarch, when Theseus returned from slaying the Minotaur of Crete the Athenians preserved his ship as a memorial, replacing parts as they rotted. This gave rise to the long-standing philosophical paradox concerning identity suggested by Denton.
7. Indices ... extant: Strictly speaking, only one Roman *Index Expurgatorius*, listing books prohibited unless expurgated, had been published, in 1607. Denton includes the periodic updatings of the Roman Church's *Index Librorum Prohibitorum*, as well as the Spanish Inquisition's *Index*, published separately.
8. Chaldaick, Syriack, Aithiopick: languages of early Semitic peoples. 'Syriack' is Aramaic; 'Aithiopick' is Ethiopic or Ge'ez.
9. Index *printed at* Madrid, *1667*: the Spanish Inquisition's *Index*, updating that of 1612.
10. Cum experientia ... inseruntur: Latin: 'Since experience has taught that on account of the rashness, ignorance or wickedness of men, greater harm than good arises out of allowing a sacred Bible in a vulgar language, having the Bible exist in a vulgar language with all its parts printed or in manuscript is prohibited. Equally, summaries and compendia, however historical, of this same Bible or books of Sacred Scripture in dialects or a vulgar language: nevertheless, not the clauses, sentences, or chapter headings which are inserted in the books of the Catholics who explain and cite these things.'
11. reason of State Ecclesiastick: an application to the Church of 'ragion di stato' thinking which justified policy on the basis of the prince's or state's interest, rather than divine and moral law.
12. Ab initio non fuit sic: Latin: 'from the beginning it was not so'.
13. Heretical Books ... the Prince: cf. Sarpi, *The Historie of the Councel of Trent* (London, 1629), p. 472: 'The bookes of heretiques, containing doctrine condemned by Councels,

were often forbid by the Emperours for good gouernment'. Denton uses similar examples to Sarpi in what follows but supplements detail.

14. Council of Nice ... Imperial Law: The Nicaean Council of AD 325 condemned the Arian heresy, which denied the consubstantiality of God and Christ. Arius's writings, known under the title *Thalia*, were ordered to be burned by Emperor Constantine, who had summoned the council.

15. Second Council ... Theodosian Code: The council summoned by Emperor Theodosius I in AD 381 condemned Arianism, including the doctrine of the sect of the deposed bishop Eunomius. The 'Maniches', or Manicheans, were rationalizing critics of Christian belief whose dualism of good and evil posited God and Satan as co-eternal. Both groups suffered under anti-heresy laws enacted in AD 381 and afterwards by Theodosius and his son and co-ruler Flavius Arcadius. The Theodosian Code was the sixteen-book compilation of laws commissioned by Theodosius II.

16. third Council ... Civil Laws: Nestorius, patriarch of Constantinople, was condemned at the council in AD 430 for his heretical views on the incarnation, his writings ordered to be burned under Emperor Theodosius II. The 'body of the Civil Laws' is the Justinian Code, *Corpus Juris Civilis*, compiled under the sixth-century emperor Justinian.

17. fourth Council ... Martian: The heresies of Eutyches and his followers, relating to the nature of Christ, were condemned at Chalcedon in AD 451, its decrees given force by laws enacted by Emperor Marcian.

18. Spain ... Arrians: In AD 587 the ruler of the Iberian peninsula, Reccared I, suppressed previously dominant Arianism in favour of the Catholic Church.

19. *year 800* ... Conventicle of Trent: Denton, like Milton, drew on Sarpi's *History of the Council of Trent* for his 'watershed' date, implying that from AD 800 the punishments of Rome were applied to heresies confirmed as such by the sixteenth-century council.

20. Wickliff ... Praghe: the religious reformers John Wyclif and Jan Hus and their follower Jerome of Prague (Jeronym Prazsky). Hus was born in 1371, dying at the stake in 1415, Jerome sharing his fate the following year.

21. Pope Martin ... Bull: the bull *Inter cunctas*, of 1418. Denton follows Sarpi here, as did Milton, but adds the anachronistic reference to guardianship of the press.

22. *Council of Constance*: the Church council of 1414–18 that condemned as heretical the doctrines and writings of Wyclif, Hus and others.

23. Jo Cocleus ... Husitarum: Johannes Cochlaeus, *Historiae Hussitarum* [History of the Hussites] (1549).

24. *Bones*: Denton refers to the exhumation of Wyclif's remains for desecration after his condemnation by the Council of Constance, giving rise to the story of his bones being tried for heresy.

25. Index ... *1659*: the first *Index of Prohibited Books*, published by Pope Paul IV's authority in 1559 (not 1659).

26. Erasmus ... *eighteen*: Desiderius Erasmus, *In Novum Testamentum Annotationes* [Annotations on the New Testament] (1516). Pope Leo X extended his approval to the second edition. Denton takes this example, including the date, from Sarpi.

27. Hogen Mogen ... Mufty: using a phrase derived from the Dutch, the 'high and mighty' pope compared to the leader of Islam.

28. God in the Temple of God: 2 Thessalonians 2:4.

29. Judex ... mortuorum: Latin: 'judge of the living and of the dead'.

30. Cardinal Baronius: Cesare Baronius (1538–1607), whose *Annales Ecclesiastici* extended to twelve volumes by his death. His defence of the pope's authority over Sicily against

historic claims of a papal privilege granting spiritual powers to the Sicilian monarchy, by then in Spanish hands, led to the work being banned by Philip II of Spain, and in the controversy Baronius was passed over for the vacant see of Rome.
31. *King's Officers*: i.e. acting on behalf of Philip II.
32. *same year*: i.e. 1605.
33. *St. Peter's ... Keys*: Matthew 16:18–19.
34. *maugre*: 'notwithstanding'.
35. *Edict ... World over*: issued 3 October 1610.
36. *Rowland for his Oliver*: like for like; the saying seems to derive from the well-matched but disagreeing knights of Charlemagne in the *Song of Roland*.
37. *Deus bone!*: Latin: 'Good God!'
38. *per fas nefasq[ue]*: Latin: 'through what is allowed and what is forbidden'.
39. *Servite Padre Paulo*: Paolo Sarpi, of the Servants of Blessed Mary.
40. *Minorite*: subordinate; strictly, minor or Franciscan friars.
41. *Dan to Beersheba*: proverbially the northernmost and southernmost towns of the Holy Land.
42. *Trentine Creed or Mahumetan Alcoran*: the creed emerging from the Council of Trent and formalized in 1564, and the Quran.
43. *Sixtus Quintus ... Clement the 8th*: Sixtus V, pope 1585–90. Clement VIII was pope 1592–1605.
44. *Arminius ... Delf*: Jacobus Arminius (1560–1609) developed the theological view associated with his name after engaging to defend Calvinism against an anonymous pamphlet by two Delft ministers in 1589. The result was the critique of Calvinism expressed through the Dutch Remonstrant church and influential in England.
45. *Reignolds and his Brother*: The mutual proselytizing of the Oxford college head John Rainolds and his brother William in the late sixteenth century had been memorialized in Latin verse by William Alabaster.
46. *Veritas ... Artificers*: Latin: literally, 'truth seeks no corners'.
47. *Fable ... Park-Gate only*: cf. Milton, *Areopagitica*, p. 15.
48. *Deus ... Diabolo, &c.*: Latin: 'God ought to obey the devil'. This was among the heresies charged against Wyclif in 1682 and at the Council of Constance.
49. *Leo ... Books*: Pope Leo X's bull of 15 June 1520, which Luther burnt.
50. *Pope Paul ... Venetians*: In the Interdict crisis of 1606–7, Sarpi responded to Paul V's excommunication of the Doge and senate of Venice and banning of divine service by publishing the anti-papal opinions of Jean Gerson (1363–1429), spurring papal condemnation of Gerson's work and other tracts.
51. *Lydius lapis*: touchstone.
52. *Pithon*: Pythian Apollo, the prophetic god of the Oracle at Delphi.
53. *wise Republick*: the Venetian republic.
54. *Cardinals ... act*: Robert Bellarmine responded to the republication of Gerson in 1606, prompting a debate in print over the demands of papal allegiance that extended to France and England.
55. *Nitimur ... Adami*: i.e. we strive for the forbidden, books being like Adam's apple.
56. *fly in the faces ... alternate Fates*: cf. *Areopagitica*, p. 26; Milton derived the passage from Bacon.
57. *all Presses ... years past*: cf. ibid., p. 26. Denton paraphrases Milton from here to the end of the page.

58. *But no sooner ... old Barnacles again*: cf. ibid., p. 26. It is unclear what the marginal date refers to. A parliamentary committee to examine printing was convened before 2 March 1642 while the Printing Ordinance was passed after 2 March 1642/3 (14 June 1643).
59. Cimerian darkness of ignorance: Homer's *Odyssey* refers to Cimmerians inhabiting a far-off land where the sun never shone.
60. Magna ... prævalebit: Latin: 'for Truth is great and will prevail'.
61. Cornish Hug: a wrestling move.
62. Contraria ... obliqui: an approximate English rendering follows the Latin.
63. Go tell Judah ... the man: Jeremiah 3:12; 1 Kings 18:16–19; 2 Samuel 12:7.
64. *in the womb*: cf. *Areopagitica*, p. 9.
65. *behave themselves ... accordingly*: cf. ibid., p. 4.
66. Carter *a Printer*: The Catholic printer William Carter, after previous arrests and imprisonment, was executed in 1584 for printing Gregory Martin's *A Treatise of Schisme*. One passage proposed that Catholic women might destroy 'the master heretike', which was alleged to be an attempt to incite the assassination of the Queen.
67. *Jars*: disagreements.
68. *two Religious Orders ... Dominick*: The Franciscan and Dominican orders were founded around 1210.
69. *Inquisition ... Hereticks*: The papal inquisition was formalized by Gregory IX in 1231; Frederick II had established burning as the penalty for heretics by a law of 1224.
70. Limbus Patrum: Latin: 'limbo of the patriarchs', the conventional term for the *limbus*, the edge, of heaven (or hell).
71. Johannes Baptista Posa: the Basque Jesuit Juan Bautista Poza, whose own works had been placed on the Roman *Index* in 1628 in a dispute between the inquisitions of Spain and Rome.
72. Hurtado ... Escobar: the Jesuit writers Alberto Hurtado, Vincenzo Filliuci, Etienne Bauny, Leonard Leys and Antonio Escobar.
73. *Iliad*: i.e. as expansive as Homer's epic poem.
74. *days of* Luther ... Invention of Printing: Denton's information may derive from the supposed advice of Cardinal Wolsey to Clement VII in 1524, imaginatively reconstructed in Herbert of Cherbury's *The Life and Raigne of King Henry the Eighth* (London, 1649), p. 157, and repeated in Charles Wolseley's *Liberty of Conscience* in 1668 (reproduced above, see pp. 129–33). Denton's marginal note refers to Johann Gutenberg and Johann Fust, first founders of printing in Europe.
75. Arcana Imperii: Latin: 'state secrets'.
76. Centum gravamina: Latin: 'hundred grievances', the German complaints against Roman misrule that were submitted and published.
77. participes ... *Cheats*: the English glosses the Latin.
78. Myrmidon: base, mercenary functionary.
79. Cabala: Kabbalah, Judaic religious mysticism.
80. Mascarata: masquerade, a mask.

# The Tory Reaction I

## L'Estrange, *Observator in Question and Answer*

1. They are so: 'they' being the people, the masses.
2. *Hair'd and Juggled*: led and manipulated.

3. *the* Faction: generalized term for the disloyal and dissenting, assumed by L'Estrange to be united in opposition to Church and government.
4. oftner, or seldomer, *as I see Occasion*: The *Observator* was routinely published on Wednesday and Saturday, sometimes also appearing on Monday and Thursday, with six issues in one week in July 1682.
5. Turk: a Muslim.
6. Member ... Faction: i.e. a member of a unified political opposition.
7. *Protestation*, and the *Reformation*: L'Estrange distinguishes the initial protests against Rome's misrule by Luther (and others) and the separate reformed churches constructed thereafter.
8. Protestation ... Spires: the protest by the German princes against the decree passed at the imperial diet at Spires (Speyer, Germany) in April 1529, which had reaffirmed the 1521 Edict of Worms condemning Luther and banning his works. As this narrowly post-dated the beginnings of the English Reformation it contributes to L'Estrange's distinction between Protestants (or protestants) and Anglicans.
9. Smith ... Harris: the Whig nonconformist publishers Francis Smith and Benjamin Harris; see see note 1 to *An Impartial Account of the Tryals of Smith and Curtis*, and note 2 to *A Short, but Just Account of the Tryal of Harris*, above, pp. 457, 456.
10. Muncer ... Phifer: Thomas Müntzer and Heinrich Pfeiffer, radical reformers and leaders in the German peasant rising in 1524–5.
11. pretended Prophet: Smith was a Baptist preacher.
12. Sleidan ... Pagets Heresiography, *&c.*: L'Estrange lists English and European writers who attacked sectarian heresies, particularly Anabaptism. The English works, which drew on the earlier continental authors, are Daniel Featley, *The Dipper Dipt* (London, 1645); Ephraim Pagitt, *Heresiography* (London, 1645); Robert Baillie, *A Dissuasive from the Errours of the Time* (London, 1645). L'Estrange took his examples from these works.
13. Jack of Leydens Successor: Jan Bockelson, from Leiden, leader of the Anabaptist takeover of Münster in 1534–5 and installed as king before defeat and execution. His indirect 'successor' was Cornelis Appelman, also from Leiden, burned at the stake in 1545. An account appeared in Lambertus Hortensius, *Tumultuum anabaptistarum* [Tumults of the Anabaptists] (Basel, 1548).
14. Gastius ... lib. *I*. Pa *12*: John Gastio, *De anabaplismi exordio* [Rise of Anabaptism] (Basel, 1544).
15. Sleydans Comment. Lib. *10*: Johann Sleidan, *De statu religionis et rei publicae, Carrolo Quinto Caesare, commentarii* [Commentaries on Religion and the State in the Reign of Emperor Charles V] (Strasbourg, 1555).
16. *Protestant-Mercury*: The *True Protestant Mercury*, published by Langley Curtis, who was ordered to appear before King and Privy Council the day before the *Observator* appeared. Curtis fled, Henry Care helping publication resume before turning to writing his own *Impartial Protestant Mercury*.
17. *Smiths Prot. Int. N. 7*: [Francis] *Smith's Protestant Intelligence*, 18 February 1681.
18. *Stat. 35. Eliz. &c.*: Act against Popish Recusants, 35 Eliz. I, c. 2.
19. *Protestant-Mercury, N. 15*: *True Protestant Mercury*, 16 February 1681.
20. Smith ... Chuse: *Vox Populi: or The Peoples Claim* (London: Francis Smith, 1681). The tract was anonymous but L'Estrange held Smith to have authored its sentiments as publisher, if not writer.
21. Council: the Privy Council, accused of wrongly counselling the King.

## A Ra-Ree Show

1. Leviathan: Charles II, given the name of Thomas Hobbes's absolutist ruler.
2. Topham: John Topham, the King's sergeant at arms attending the Commons, here summoned to assist the transfer of Parliament to Oxford.
3. Houses Twain ... Cooper, Hughs and Snow: 'Houses Twain' is Parliament and Cooper, Hughs and Snow were officers of Parliament. In the accompanying illustration, Charles II heads west with a chest on his back and three attendants. On 2 May 1681 Topham was given funds to distribute as the King's reward for recent services to officers including the doorkeepers Thomas Hughs and Edward Cooper. An earlier payment for the same role had been made to John Snow and William Snow (*Calendar of Treasury Books*, 32 vols (London: HMSO, 1904–58), vol. 7).
4. Halifaxes Trap: George Savile, Marquess of Halifax, in leading efforts to forestall exclusion on behalf of the King, advanced compromise proposals to limit or temporarily exile the Duke of York.
5. Dom. Com.: the House of Commons.
6. Oxford, York, Carlile: Centres of royalism in the civil war and afterwards.
7. Tower Lords: the 'impeached lords' imprisoned in the Tower of London by Parliament in 1679 and afterwards for alleged treason in the popish interest.
8. Clifford ... Hallifax: privy councillors accused of counselling Charles against exclusion and for popery and arbitrary government. The Earl of Danby and Edward Hide, second Earl of Clarendon, were amongst those imprisoned in the Tower.
9. *Holy Ghost ... Rosamond in Bower*: lines linking Charles II with secrecy, popery and cowardice, the oak recalling his hiding place after the Battle of Worcester in 1651, and 'Rosamund' referring to the mistress of Henry II who, according to later romances, hid in a bower or maze from the vengeful Queen Eleanor.
10. *Popularity ... Displease*: a warning that popular addresses could not outweigh popular displeasure at stifling Parliament.
11. *Two States ... pent*: the two houses kept in the dark, held captive.
12. *Heathen* Hobbs: Thomas Hobbes.
13. Dry Bobbs: jests or blows, referring to past hurts by the Stuart monarchy and their outcome.
14. *Lecherous Loyns*: those of Charles II. From this verse a narratorial voice takes over from 'Leviathan', although the transition is not marked in the text.
15. *Swagger ... Fire*: in the accompanying engraving, Charles leads his 'rare show' westward only to fall into the mire under the weight of the chest on his back.
16. Gyant's down ... Pound: the King's fall frees the parliamentarians.
17. Convocation ... Rome: the freeing of Parliament allows the constraining instead of churchmen and royal pensioners.
18. six *and* Twenty ... Breda: the twenty-six bishops in the House of Lords, and the Lords who voted 'not guilty' in the recent trial of Lord Stafford, sent to Cologne and Breda, which hosted Charles II's court before the Restoration and its exiles afterwards.
19. Hunts *begun ... Like Son*: a call for a rising at Oxford, according to L'Estrange, with Charles II sharing the fate of his father.
20. French-*Lap ... Clap*: a jibe at Charles's kow-towing to France, and at the Duke of York's affliction since the 1660s, venereal disease.

## L'Estrange, *Notes upon College*

1. *Papers Charg'd*: *A Ra-Ree Show*, along with other papers.
2. *Edith College*: Stephen College's wife.
3. *the Castle*: Oxford Castle.
4. *the Design*: the original drawing on which the engraved illustration for *A Ra-Ree Show* was based.
5. *Graver*: the engraver.
6. *the Printer himself*: Langley Curtis; his wife Jane was also involved.
7. *Franck Smith*: the Whig publisher Francis Smith. See note 1 to *An Impartial Account of the Tryals of Smith and Curtis*, below p. 457.
8. *Staves*: the verses of the ballad.
9. *sung ... Oxford*: College was said at his trial to have sung the ballad in Oxford and at the home of Lord Lovelace.
10. *Sir Philip Matthews*: Matthews was not named in the trial report. A Whig election candidate in 1679, he was later a juryman in the trial of Titus Oates.
11. *Sculpture*: engraving.
12. *Vox Patriae*: Anon., *Vox Patriæ: or The Resentments and Indignation of the Free-Born Subjects of England* (London: Francis Peters, 1681).

## L'Estrange, *Observator*

1. *the Crack*: the talk, the gossip.
2. *Stephens*: Robert Stephens, the messenger of the press. See note 13 to *A Short, but Just Account of the Tryal of Harris*, above, p. 457.
3. *Represented ... Libell*: On 16 April charges were brought against Joanna Brome for publishing the *Observator*, the bill being found by the Grand Jury. Others before the court included Francis and Eleanor Smith, son and daughter of Francis Smith senior, for publishing *The Second Part of the Growth of Popery*, amongst other tracts.
4. *Secretary of State, Mr Attorney Generall*: Stephens reported to Sir Leoline Jenkins (1625–85), secretary of state since 1680. The attorney general was Sir Robert Sawyer (1633–92), who in April led the quo warranto proceedings to recall London's charter and later in the year prosecuted the accused Rye House plotters.
5. *Devill in the hoggs*: an allusion to the biblical story of the demons cast into a herd of swine (e.g. Mark 5:11–13) and to Stephens's nickname 'Robin Hog'.
6. *319th Observator*: Saturday, 14 April 1683. The content was indeed unremarkable, for the *Observator* at least, continuing an extended critique of Edward Pearse, *The Conformist's Plea for the Nonconformists* (London, 1683). L'Estrange rejected Pearse's claims that Catholics rather than nonconformists were authors of Charles I's downfall, and denied they were a present threat: 'for if they could Destroy Us, they would certainly Save Themselves; And not take possession of all our Jayls, and Hang, Draw, and Quarter, at the rate they do.'
7. *Dawbing*: false show.
8. *Propriety*: property.
9. *no Licensers appointed*: due to the non-renewal of the Printing Act in 1679.
10. *Mrs Brome*: Joanna Brome (d. 1684), publisher of L'Estrange's works following the death of her bookseller husband Henry in May 1681, a month after the *Observator* began. The couple had married in 1658. After Joanna's death their son Charles took over, aged twenty, and continued the family business until about 1712.

11. Kings Livery: messengers of the press carried the King's authority as Crown officers.
12. Care, Curtis, Starkey: the writer-publisher Henry Care (see note 2 to *The Triall of Carr*, above, p. 458); printer-publisher Langley Curtis; and the radical bookseller John Starkey (c. 1630–90), who fled to Holland later in 1683.
13. *the* Devil-a-bit: a mild curse, akin to 'the devil take it'.
14. *Treason in Grain* ... Sam. Harris *was* Arraign'd: [Edward Fitzharris], *Treason in Graine: That most Traiterous Libel of Fitz-Harris* ([London: printed by Samuel Harris, 1681]). Harris printed the manuscript libel against Charles II and the Duke of York which had contributed to the conviction and execution of Fitzharris in 1681. The printer faced trial in May 1682 but escaped punishment, the jury returning an ignoramus verdict.
15. Hunt: Thomas Hunt (1626/7–88), lawyer and author of *An Argument for the Bishops Right in Judging in Capital Causes in Parliament ... To which is added a Postscript, being a Letter to a Friend, for Vindicating the Clergy, and Rectifying some Mistakes that are Mischievous and Dangerous to our Government and Religion* (London: Thomas Fox, 1682). The *Postscript* attracted most attention, its criticisms of royalist sermonizing gaining Whig plaudits and L'Estrange's extended opposition across several issues of the *Observator*.
16. Seditious Leaven: seditious kind.
17. Breach ... *Instrument*: the breach in efficient censorship, and the breach between L'Estrange and Stephens.
18. Kings Proclamation: the proclamation against printed news of 12 May 1680; see above, p. 175.
19. *Ignoramus-Days are* gone: the curtailing of Whig juries returning ignoramus verdicts in the face of what, to loyalists like L'Estrange, was clear-cut evidence.
20. Kings Broad-Seal ... *Intelligence, &c.:* the warrant granted to L'Estrange in August 1663; see above, p. 50.
21. Consideration ... Gazette: the settlement agreed when L'Estrange's *Intelligencer* and *Newes* made way in January 1666 for the *Oxford Gazette*, subsequently the *London Gazette*.
22. *Secretaries of State*: Jenkins's counterpart as secretary of state for the north was Robert Spencer, Earl of Sunderland (1641–1702).
23. *Clark of the Peace*: the clerk of the peace was a legal officer supervising the operation of the courts, including framing charges and indictments.
24. Mr Recorder: Sir George Treby (c. 1644–1700), who lost the recordership later in the year but regained the post after the Glorious Revolution, one of his first tasks being to question L'Estrange about his writings as a suspected Jacobite.
25. Cross *or* Pile: heads or tails, the two sides of a coin.

## L–gley C—s His Lamentation in New-Gate

1. *Pacquet*: *A Weekly Pacquet of Advice from Rome, or The History of Popery*, the writer Henry Care's periodical chronicling the history of the Roman Church with appended news pages under the title the *Popish Courant*. The publication ran from December 1678 to July 1683, with Langley Curtis as publisher until August 1682, in conjunction with his wife Jane.
2. Chaplets: prayers.
3. *Courants*: The *Popish Courant*, partner paper to Curtis and Care's *Weekly Pacquet*.
4. *Tyburn ... Tapskie* below: the place of execution, and an encounter in hell with the lately deceased Earl of Shaftesbury, nicknamed 'Lord Tapski' by Tories because of a tap he bore

to drain fluid from an internal abscess and because of an alleged affinity with Polish elective monarchy.
5. *Charter ... Colledge the Martyr*: the calling in of London's charter in 1683, and the execution of Stephen College in the same year.
6. *lost* Ignoramus: the curtailing of Whig juries foiling Tory prosecutions by returning ignoramus verdicts.
7. Tony: Anthony Ashley Cooper, the Earl of Shaftesbury.
8. *Essex*: Arthur Capel, Earl of Essex, who after being arrested for involvement in the Rye House plot died on 13 July 1683 while imprisoned in the Tower, his throat cut by another's hand or his own.
9. *Wooden Ruff for a Saint of the Cause*: the wood of the stocks, and 'Saint' a derogatory term (to Tories) for nonconformists.
10. *flear*: sneer, laugh mockingly.
11. Raree Show: Curtis was involved in printing *A Ra-Ree Show*, for which Stephen College was executed in 1683.
12. *Russel*: William, Lord Russell (1639–83), executed on 21 July 1683 for his part in the Rye House plot. Curtis's arrest was for reflections in the aftermath of the plot, centring on the supposed appearance of Russell's ghost, in *The Night-Walker of Bloomsbury*.
13. Tory Rutland: a vintner named Rutland was questioned about the incident on which Curtis's offending tract was based (see P. Hinds, 'Roger L'Estrange, the Rye House plot, and the Regulation of Political Discourse in Late-Seventeenth-Century London', *Library*, 3:1 (2002), pp. 3–31).
14. Fountain-*Tavern*: the address of Mr Rutland (the original text has 'Founain').
15. *Gailed*: jailed, gaoled.
16. *Ketch ... Walcot*: John ('Jack') Ketch (d. 1686) was the public executioner, responsible for the deaths of Stephen College and the Rye House plotters in 1683, whose number included Colonel Thomas Walcot.
17. *save both my Ears*: loss of ears being a proverbial punishment for seditious libellers, most notoriously endured by William Prynne, John Bastwick and Henry Burton in 1637.
18. Prance: Miles Prance (d. 1688), a central figure in the popish plot's forging of accusations against Catholics.
19. Sidney: the republican political writer Algernon Sidney (1623–83), executed in the aftermath of the Rye House plot; see below, p. 268.
20. A—ld ... Giles: John Arnold (c. 1635–1702) led anti-Catholic activity in south Wales during the popish plot and became an exclusionist MP, claiming while in London to have been attacked by papists in Jackanapes Lane. John Giles was initially convicted but doubts were subsequently cast on whether the crime occurred. In November 1683 Arnold was charged with Scandalum magnatum for slandering his former patron the Marquess of Worcester, calling him a 'rank papist'.
21. Old *Rump*: the Rump Parliament, 1649–53, briefly revived in 1659.
22. Mowbery *and* Balderen ... *Whore*: In 1679 Lawrence Mowbray and Robert Bolron fabricated the existence of a papist plot to kill the King among Yorkshire gentry, led by their former employer Sir Thomas Gascoigne. Their claims resulted in several trials and the execution of the priest Thomas Thwing in 1680.
23. Dangerfield ... escaped: Thomas Dangerfield (1654–85), notorious informer and felon who attested to the spurious Meal-Tub plot, incriminating Presbyterians then Catholics and acting as witness in numerous cases. His credibility collapsed but he remained at liberty until convicted of misdemeanours in James II's reign.

24. Wildman ... Charlton: John Wildman (1622/3–93), John Trenchard (1649–95) and Francis Charlton (1639–98) were radical Whigs arrested and held in custody after the Rye House plot.
25. Jefferies: George Jeffreys, lord chief justice. See note 4 to *A Short, but Just Account of the Tryal of Harris*, above, p. 456

## An Account of the Proceedings against Thomson

1. House of ... Thompson: The printer, previously based in Fetter Lane, from 1684 gave the address 'at the entrance into the Old-Spring-Garden near Charing-Cross' in his imprint.
2. Prodigal returned home: E. L[ydiott], *The Prodigal Return'd Home; or, The Motives of the Conversion to the Catholick Faith of E.L. Master of Arts in the University of Cambridge* ([London: printed by Nathaniel Thompson,] 1684).
3. Stephens: Robert Stephens. See note 13 to *A Short, but Just Account of the Tryal of Harris*, above, p. 457.
4. Doleman *about Succession*: The Jesuit Robert Persons (or Parsons) (1546–1610) published, under the name 'R. Doleman', *A Conference about the Next Succession to the Crowne of Ingland* ([Antwerp], 1594). The tract created a stir, inclining to hereditary monarchy but within the limits of a partnership with the people that could justify resistance. Its relevance in the wake of the Rye House plot was reflected by William Assheton's *The Royal Apology: or, An Answer to the Rebels Plea* (London, 1684).
5. Habeas Corpus ... Corpus cum Causa: The Habeas Corpus Act had passed in 1679, in principle reducing the difficulties in petitioning for a prisoner's 'body and cause' to be brought to court and the case determined.
6. Nisi prius: Latin: 'unless first', meaning the original court, here the King's Bench.
7. Alexander Banks: The trial proceedings were printed for 'A. Banks', who had worked as a compositor for Thompson since at least the time of the Lords inquiry into libels in 1676, and by 1684 was also publishing ballads and short tracts.
8. *Books in Quires*: the books in sets of loose printed sheets.
9. *Appeal ... Noble Peers Speech, &c.*: [Charles Blount], *An Appeal from the Country to the City* (London, 1679); [Anthony Ashley Cooper, Earl of Shaftesbury], *A Speech lately Made by a Noble Peer of the Realm* (London: F[rancis] S[mith], 1681). Blount's book appeared in three editions in 1679 and another in 1680. In 1682 L'Estrange complained of Thompson having printed the *Appeal* (*Observator*, no. 163). Thompson also openly published Blount's *The Two First Books, of Philostratus* (London, 1680).
10. *Mr. Recorder*: Sir Thomas Jenner (1638–1707) was recorder of London 1683–6.
11. Mrs. Thompson: Mary Thompson (d. 1700), daughter of Nathaniel's former business partner, the printer Thomas Ratcliffe, and closely involved in her husband's trade. Stationers' Company records show that in 1688, after his death, she was called on to cease printing.
12. Gregory *the Great*: Gregory I, pope from 590 until his death in 604.
13. *St.* Augustine: Augustine (d. 604), first archbishop of Canterbury, rather than St Augustine of Hippo. He was sent by Pope Gregory the Great as leader of the founding Christian mission to Britain, arriving in 597 and becoming archbishop the following year.
14. *Lord Chief Justice*: Sir George Jeffreys. See note 4 to *A Short, but Just Account of the Tryal of Harris*, above, p. 456

## The Tory Reaction II

### The Judgment and Decree of the University of Oxford Past

1. *lately enterpriz'd*: the Rye House plot to assassinate Charles II and his brother James, exposed on and after 12 June.
2. *Proctors ... Regent*: proctors are university officers; 'Regent' Masters denoted those who on receiving their MA were resident and had teaching and administrative responsibilities.
3. Lex Rex: [Samuel Rutherford], *Lex, Rex: The Law and the Prince* (London: John Field, 1644).
4. de Jure Regni: George Buchanan, *De Iure Regni Apud Scotos* [The Rights of the Crown in Scotland] (Edinburgh: printed by John Ross for Henry Charters, 1579).
5. Vindiciae contra tyrannos: Anon., *Vindiciæ contra Tyrannos: A Defence of Liberty against Tyrants* (London: printed by Matthew Simmons and Robert Wilson, 1648), a French Huguenot defence of resistance first published in 1579. The author is variously held to be Hubert Languet (1518–81) or Philippe du Plessis-Mornay (1549–1623).
6. Bellarmine de Conciliis, de Pontifice: tracts by Cardinal Robert Bellarmine (1542–1621), viewed as Catholicism's leading defender of ecclesiastical (papal) authority over civil powers. *De Conciliis* and *De Summo Pontifice* formed parts of his *Disputationes*, published in three volumes in 1581, 1582 and 1593.
7. Milton, Goodwin: Although titles are not given, the targets included those works condemned by Charles II's proclamation in 1660: John Milton, *Angli Pro Populo Anglicano Defensio, Contra Claudii Anonymi, aliàs Salmasii, Defensionem Regiam* [A Defence of the People of England in Answer to Salmasius's Defence of the King] ('London' [Leyden], 1650 [1651]); John Milton, *EIKONOKΛΑΣΤΗΣ in Answer to a Book Intitl'd EIKΩN BAΣIΛIKH* [*Eikonklastes* in Answer to *Eikon Basilike*] (London: printed by Matthew Simmons, 1649); John Goodwin, *The Obstructours of Justice. Or A Defence of the Honourable Sentence Passed upon the late King, by the High Court of Justice* (London: Henry Cripps and Lodowick Lloyd, 1649).
8. Baxter H. C.: Richard Baxter, *A Holy Commonwealth, or Political Aphorisms, Opening the True Principles of Government* (London: Thomas Underhill and Francis Tyton, 1659).
9. Hunton ... Monarchy: [Philip Hunton], *A Treatise of Monarchy* (London, 1680). The work was first published in 1643, with Hunton's *Vindication* of it following in 1644. Hunton died in the months before the 1683 burning of his work at Oxford.
10. Polit. Catech.: [Henry Parker], *A Political Catechism* (London: Samuel Gellibrand, 1643). Parker's pamphlet, a response to Charles I's Nineteen Propositions, had been attacked by L'Estrange for its parallels to exclusion in 1679 in *The Case Put*, being labelled 'the most Audacious Libel (perhaps) that ever flew in the Face of any Government' (p. 24).
11. Hunt's Postscript: Thomas Hunt, *An Argument for the Bishops Right in Judging in Capital Causes in Parliament ... To which is added a Postscript, being a Letter to a Friend, for Vindicating the Clergy, and Rectifying some Mistakes that are Mischievous and Dangerous to our Government and Religion* (London: Thomas Fox, 1682). The *Postscript*'s criticisms of royalist sermonizing made the lawyer Hunt a Whig hero and Tory target.
12. Doleman: R. Doleman [Robert Persons], *A Conference about the Next Succession to the Crowne of Ingland* ([Antwerp], 1594). Parallels were drawn between the work's resistance arguments and the Rye House plot, most explicitly in William Assheton's linking of the Jesuit Persons and Algernon Sidney in *The Parallel* and *The Royal Apology* in 1684.

13. History of Succession: [John Somers], *A Brief History of the Succession* ([London], [1681]). Attributed to Somers, later Baron Somers, although never openly acknowledged.
14. Julian the Apostate: [Samuel Johnson], *Julian the Apostate* (London: Langley Curtis, 1682). On Johnson see also below, pp. 304–5.
15. Mene Tekel: 'Laophilus Misotyrannus', *Mene Tekel; ir, The Downfal of Tyranny* ([London], 1663). The tract is sometimes attributed to the Restoration conspirator Captain Roger Jones. 'Mene Tekel' derives from Aramaic words for currency, whose biblical appearance as 'writing on the wall' was interpreted as foretelling the doom of the kingdom of Belshazzar (Daniel 5:25–30).
16. Covenant: agreed in 1643 between the English Parliament and Scots Presbyterian leaderships, and published by Parliament as *A Solemn League and Covenant, for Reformation and Defence of Religion, the Honor and Happinesse of the King, and the Peace and Safety of the Three Kingdoms of England, Scotland, and Ireland* (London: Edward Husbands, 1643). It was burnt at the Restoration and its reprinting as *A Phenix* was punished in 1664 (see note 48 to *L'Estrange, Considerations and Proposals*, above, p. 441), but there were further illicit printings in 1676 and 1680 (as *The Scotch Covenant*), and a 1666 edition in Scotland was ordered burnt by the Privy Council at Edinburgh in January 1682.
17. Late Association: the draft document of association that formed part of alleged evidence of treason against the Earl of Shaftesbury in 1681–2. It appeared in print in the anonymously compiled *The History of the Association* (London: Richard Janeway, 1682), pp. 18–22.
18. de Cive. Leviathan: Thomas Hobbes, *Elementa Philosophica de Cive* [Philosophical Elements of the Citizen] (Amsterdam: Elzevir, 1646); Thomas Hobbes, *Leviathan, or The Matter, Forme, and Power of a Common-Wealth Ecclesiasticall and Civill* (London: Andrew Crooke, 1651). De Cive had also appeared in a very limited edition in 1641–2, and was reprinted in Hobbes's Latin works in 1668, as was a version of *Leviathan*. The English *Leviathan* seems to have been secretly reprinted in the late 1670s, although the edition appeared bearing the original date of 1651.
19. Apolog. Relat.: [John Brown], *An Apologeticall Relation, of the Particular Sufferings of the Faithfull Ministers and Professours of the Church of Scotland, since August. 1660* ([?Edinburgh], 1665). The tract was ordered to be burned by the Privy Council in Edinburgh early in 1666. The Presbyterian John Brown (c. 1610–79), ejected from his Church of Scotland ministry and exiled in 1662, had a second work condemned by the *Judgment and Decree*, his *History of the Indulgence* (1678).
20. Owen's Sermon: John Owen, *A Sermon Preached to the Honourable House of Commons in Parliament Assembled: On January 31. A Day of Solemne Humiliation* (London: Matthew Simmons, 1649). Having been chosen to preach to Parliament the day after Charles I's execution in 1648/9, Owen (1616–83) was subsequently Cromwell's appointment as Oxford vice-chancellor. He died a month after the university's condemnation in 1683.
21. Jenkin's Petition: William Jenkin, *The Humble Petition of William Jenkin* ([London], 1651). Jenkin (c. 1613–85), a London minister and writer, successfully petitioned Parliament after being arrested for involvement in the Presbyterian plot to restore Charles II in 1651. His *Petition* was reprinted in 1660.
22. Quakers: a generalized accusation rather than directed at a particular book.
23. Sheriffs case: Anon., *The Sheriffs Case. Whether, and How they may Lawfully Qualifie themselves for their Holding the Office, according to the Act for Corporations?* (London: Thomas Snowden, 1681).

24. Fifth-Monarchy men: a generalized accusation, recalling the rising by members of the Fifth Monarchist sect against the newly restored Charles II in the cause of Jesus's second coming as universal monarch, prophesied for around 1666.
25. Altare Damascenum: a Latin work of 1623 by the Scots minister David Calderwood (d. 1650), a shorter version of which had been published as *The Altar of Damascus or The Patern of the English Hierarchie, and Church-Policie obtruded upon the Church of Scotland* ([Amsterdam], 1621).
26. Hist. Indulgen: [John Brown], *The History of the Indulgence* ([Edinburgh], 1678).
27. Cartwright: the theologian Thomas Cartwright (1534/5–1603), forerunner of English Presbyterianism, whose published contributions to the Admonition controversy of the 1570s led to him having to go into exile, and whose subsequent writings and activities led to attempted prosecution in Star Chamber.
28. Travers: Walter Travers (c. 1548–1635), whose proto-Presbyterian 'Book of Discipline' led to Star Chamber prosecution for sedition, alongside Cartwright, in 1590–1. A first English version had been published by Cartwright in 1574 under the title *A Full and Plaine Declaration of Ecclesiastical Discipline*, and further editions appeared in 1588 and 1617.
29. Protestant Reconciler: [Daniel Whitby], *The Protestant Reconciler, Humbly Pleading for Condescention to Dissenting Brethren* (London: Awnsham Churchill, 1683). Whitby (1638–1726), a Church of England clergyman, made a public renunciation of the book later in 1683.
30. Knox, Goodman, Gilby: the religious reformers John Knox (c. 1514–72), Christopher Goodman (1521/2–1603) and Anthony Gilby (c. 1510–85).
31. Goodman: Christopher Goodman, *How Superior Powers Ought to be Obeyd* (Geneva: John Crispin, 1558). The offending sentiment is possibly that on pp. 96–7, although the doctrine in this form is expressed in John Ponet, *A Shorte Treatise of Politike Power* ([Strasbourg], 1556), sig. G8r–v. Ponet's tract was reprinted in 1642.
32. Phineas ... Napthali: James Stewart (1635–1713), *Naphtali, or The Wrestlings of the Church of Scotland* (n.p., 1667). On 12 December 1667 the Privy Council at Edinburgh ordered the burning of the book, which they noted had been imported. Stewart published *Jus Populi Vindicatum* (1669), then spent much of the next two decades in exile before enjoying high office in Scotland after the revolution. 'Naphtali' was the second son of Jacob and a tribe of Israel, the 'hind let loose' (Genesis 49:21). 'Phineas' (Phinehas) was a biblical priest who reversed a tide of heresy by peremptorily killing an Israelite prince who neglected his duty to do the same (Numbers 25:7–13).

## Sidney, *The Very Copy of a Paper Delivered to the Sheriffs*

1. *Age*: Sidney was 60, born in January 1623.
2. West, Rumsey, *and* Keyling: Robert West, John Rumsey and Josiah Keeling, conspirators and witnesses at Sidney's trial. Their second-hand testimony regarding Sidney's involvement, repeated in court, had led to his arrest on 26 June.
3. *Lord* Howard: William Howard, Baron Howard of Escrick (c. 1630–94). A Whig nonconformist and promoter of exclusion on entering the House of Lords in 1678, Howard was assisted by Sidney in 1681 in rebutting false charges of writing a seditious pamphlet, *The True Englishman* (London, 1680). In 1683 he gave evidence against Sidney and others in the Rye House plot trials and was pardoned for his own role later that year.

4. Papers ... in my Closet: The manuscript, now lost, of the work subsequently published as *Discourses concerning Government* (London, 1698). Sidney's implied admission of authorship was supplemented in his letters (see J. Scott, *Algernon Sidney and the Restoration Crisis, 1677–1683* (Cambridge: Cambridge University Press, 1991), pp. 314–15.)
5. Hand ... Lady Car's Case: At Sidney's trial, three witnesses – Sheppard, Cooke and Cary – attested that the handwriting of the *Discourses* approximated Sidney's handwritten endorsements on bills and invoices. In an earlier case, Lady Carr had been accused of perjury but incriminating letters said to be in her handwriting were discounted by the trial judge.
6. Filmer's Book: Sir Robert Filmer, *Patriarcha: or The Natural Power of Kings* (London, 1680). Filmer (1588–1653) wrote his classic work of patriarchal theory in the 1640s but its posthumous publication brought it wider attention, drawing major refutations by Sidney, John Locke (the first of the *Two Treatises*) and James Tyrrell.
7. France ... James: a reference to Louis XIV's assault on the Spanish Netherlands in 1667; and to James I, *The Kings Majesties Speech, as it was Delivered by him in Upper House of the Parliament ... On Munday the 19. Day of March 1603* (London, 1603).
8. long since: Sidney is believed to have started work on the *Discourses* in 1681.
9. Tarquin ... Innuendo *unto the King*: The *Discourses* overflows with references to past precedents, particularly to ancient Rome, Nero and Caligula featuring often in warning of arbitrary government (Scott, *Algernon Sidney*, p. 201). Pepin, the father of Charlemagne, seized control of France from the ruling Merovingian dynasty in 751, while Hugh Capet was crowned king of France in 987.
10. Pedigree ... Eldest Line: as Filmer's patriarchal theory proposed, monarchical power deriving by inheritance from God's initial gift.
11. Bench ... Blemishes to the Bar: Sidney's judges were the newly installed lord chief justice, Sir George Jeffreys, along with Sir Francis Wythens and Sir Thomas Walcott.
12. 46 Ed. 3: Jeffreys prevented Sidney reading the statute, saying he was indulging in 'discourses to captivate the people'.
13. 25 Ed. 3: the Treason Act of 1351.
14. OLD CAUSE: 'the good old cause', i.e. republicanism.
15. Daniel ... Dashwood: the Middlesex sheriffs.

## Northleigh, 'Introductory Remarks'

1. Expiration ... Act: the Printing Act, which had lapsed in 1679, and which was revived soon after Northleigh issued these lines in 1685.
2. gathering ... Waters: Isaiah 17:12.
3. *Westminster Parliament*: the 'Cavalier Parliament' of 1661–79.
4. Pensionary: the 1661–79 Parliament was dubbed the 'Pensionary Parliament' by those critical of the patronage conferred on its royalist membership.
5. the *long*: the Parliament of 1661–79, rather than the Long Parliament from 1640.
6. Oats: Titus Oates (1649–1705), whose purported revelations of a popish plot from 1678 had by the time of Northleigh's book ended in his trial for perjury, being sentenced in May 1685 to life imprisonment, although he was released at the end of 1688.
7. Lustrum: a five-year period, deriving from the term applied to the purificatory sacrifice offered for the people by the censors of ancient Rome after the five-yearly census.
8. *Nemine contradicente*: Latin: 'none opposed', unanimous.
9. State *Empericks*: political quack-doctors.

478                    *Notes to pages 273–5*

10. *vox Patriæ*: a general objection, but also the title of the anonymous Whig tract *Vox Patriæ: or The Resentments and Indignation of the Free-Born Subjects of England* (London: Francis Peters, 1681).
11. *Goliahs*: Goliaths.
12. Dagon: sea-monster deity of the ancient Philistines, mentioned by Milton in *Paradise Lost*.
13. The first ... noosed: The description, while rather grandiose, fits Roger L'Estrange, who indeed fought with sword and pen from the 1640s and by the early 1680s had gained the nickname Towzer the dog, being emblematically represented running for his life with a broken collar in *Strange's Case Strangly Altered* (London, 1680). Northleigh describes the *Observator* as 'that Learned piece of Loyalty' later in the book (p. 756).
14. *Des Cartes*: René Descartes (1596–1650), the French philosopher famed for his espousal of methodological doubt as a means to establishing truth.
15. *Protestant ... Papist*: L'Estrange's reservations about the popish plot evidence fuelled accusations that he was a 'papist' himself.
16. *Metamorphose ... Ovid*: the *Metamorphoses* of Ovid, poet of ancient Rome.
17. *Affidavit ... Babylon*: i.e. the sworn and repeated claims that L'Estrange was a Catholic were stronger in turning man to beast than the potions of the mythical enchantress Circe, the biblical beast and whore of Babylon of Revelations 17 being identified with Rome and the pope.
18. *Topham or a Tyburn*: John Topham was the Commons' sergeant-at-arms, charged with bringing the accused to the bar of the house; Tyburn was London's place of execution.
19. fly for his security: L'Estrange fled London and then England between October 1680 and February 1681 in the face of accusations of having attended mass and corrupted popish plot evidence, which persisted despite his successful defence before the Privy Council.
20. Another Worthy Person: the author of *Heraclitus Ridens: At a Dialogue between Jest and Earnest, concerning the Times*, which ran weekly from 1 February 1681 to 22 August 1682. It was printed by Benjamin Tooke but its authorship has remained uncertain, possibly being Edward Rawlins. Claims for the poet Thomas Flatman's role are undermined by Northleigh's seemingly genuine ignorance of the writer, despite Flatman being an avowed friend in supplying commendatory verses prefacing *The Triumph of Monarchy*.
21. Sermon of Separation: Edward Stillingfleet, *The Mischief of Separation* (London, 1680). The sermon was preached before the Lord Mayor of London on 11 May 1680. The 'Petulant Animadversions' prompted Stillingfleet to follow up with a larger work, *The Unreasonableness of Separation* (London, 1681).
22. virulent Scriblers ... Souldier: Thomas Hunt, *An Argument for the Bishops Right in Judging in Capital Causes in Parliament ... To which is added a Postscript, being a Letter to a Friend, for Vindicating the Clergy, and Rectifying some Mistakes that are Mischievous and Dangerous to our Government and Religion* (London, 1682).
23. Anonymous: [Vincent Alsop], *The Mischief of Impositions: or, An Antidote against a late Discourse* (London: Benj. Alsop, 1680). Alsop (c. 1630–1703) was an ejected Presbyterian minister. His writings were published by his son Benjamin (c. 1658–c. 1703), a notable nonconformist bookseller until fleeing into exile after taking part in the Monmouth rising in 1685.
24. *Association*: The draft document of association opposing a Catholic succession found amongst the Earl of Shaftesbury's papers and brought as evidence, unsuccessfully, of the treason he was accused of before the Middlesex grand jury in November 1681. The Asso-

ciation was excerpted in Northleigh's *Parallel* (see note 25 below) and printed in several accounts of the proceedings against Shaftesbury, and in *The History of the Association* (London: Richard Janeway, 1682), pp. 18–22.

25. my poor endeavours: Northleigh came to prominence as a Tory writer after penning a pamphlet comparing the Shaftesburian Association with the 1643 Solemn League and Covenant: *The Parallel: or, The New Specious Association an Old Rebellious Covenant* (London: B. Tooke, 1682). He then supported loyalists expressing their 'abhorrence' of the Association in messages to Charles II in *A Gentle Reflection on the Modest Account, and a Vindication of the Loyal Abhorrers* (London: Benj. Tooke, 1682).

26. *Sinon*: the Greek warrior who misled the defenders of Troy into taking the great wooden horse into the city.

27. Anonimus Scribbler: The anonymous *History of the Association* (London, 1682) included a postscript criticizing Northleigh's *Parallel*.

28. Evidence ... Rebellion: The playwright Elkanah Settle recanted his earlier Whig support, blaming it on misplaced pride after his play *The Empress of Morocco* met royal resistance, in *A Narrative Written by E. Settle* (London, 1683). In the preface he claimed that his 'Aldersgate-street patron' (Shaftesbury, who lived at Thanet House in Aldersgate Street) had urged him to speak more of rebellion in his pamphlet *The Character of a Popish Successour* (London, 1681).

29. *set me a work*: Northleigh denies he has been set to work for pay but rather has been set to work by the 'black' actions of rebels, particularly having in mind here the Association.

30. the wretch ... the Gentleman: the anonymous writer of the *History of the Association*'s postscript, and the Earl of Shaftesbury.

31. *Fauxes ... Fire*: his proxies failed to fire rebellion, the suggestion being that this caused Shaftesbury to flee abroad.

32. *Rebellious Republick*: the Dutch Republic.

33. the Jury: the grand jury, selected by the Whig sheriffs of London, which in November 1681 returned an ignoramus verdict on the treason accusations against Shaftesbury, including finding unproved the allegation that he had written the draft Association.

34. *the Peccant part*: the sinful or dangerous part, i.e. the compiler of the *History of the Association* published the Association without endorsing it.

35. *Bernardiston*: Sir Samuel Barnardiston (1620–1707), prominent exclusionist member of the House of Commons who served as foreman of the grand jury which rejected the treason allegations against Shaftesbury.

36. *Jigg by Joul*: cheek by jowl, adjacent. The Association's clauses were printed in Northleigh's *Parallel* for comparison with sections of the Solemn League and Covenant. The postscript to the *History of the Association* pointed to this irony, although Northleigh points out that the Association had already been printed in accounts of the proceedings against Shaftesbury.

37. the same ... Printed: the wording of the Association was read in court and appeared in several accounts of the legal proceedings against Shaftesbury, the official version being *The Proceedings at the Sessions House in the Old-Baily, London, on Thursday the 24th Day of November, 1681. Before his Majesties Commissioners of Oyer and Terminer, upon the Bill of Indictment for High-Treason against Anthony Earl of Shaftsbury* (London: Samuel Mearne and John Baker, 1681).

# Nonconformity as Sedition, 1683–5

## Delaune, *A Narrative of the Sufferings*

1. *SIR*: addressed to the Anglican churchman Benjamin Calamy, whose *A Discourse about a Scrupulous Conscience* (London, 1683) prompted the tract which led to Delaune's incarceration.
2. Scrupulous Consciences: a reference to the title of Calamy's attack on nonconformists' scruples against the doctrinal and ceremonial requirements of the Church of England.
3. November *last*: i.e. 1683.
4. *Compter in* Wood-street: the Wood Street compter, or 'counter', was a small prison used mainly for debtors and low-grade misdemeanours such as drunkenness.
5. *Plea for the Nonconformists*: Thomas Delaune, *A Plea for the Nonconformists* (London, 1683).
6. Anno ... 1683: Latin: 'the 35th year of Charles II, King of England, the year of our lord 1683'.
7. *A. Nicolas*: the signatory for Jenner.
8. *Press-yard*: an enclosed yard at Newgate prison.
9. Mittimus: warrant of custody.
10. *William Turner*: Sir William Turner, senior London alderman and former lord mayor.
11. *John How*: John How (*c.* 1657–1719), bookseller and printer, formerly apprenticed to Benjamin Harris, later printed John Tutchin's *Observator* and wrote a pamphlet defending printer's rights (see Volume 4 of this edition).
12. *Calamy ... Conscience*: Calamy, *A Discourse about a Scrupulous Conscience*.
13. *Fiat Justitia*: Latin: 'let justice be done'.
14. Stillingfleet: Edward Stillingfleet, dean of St Paul's and leading Anglican writer.
15. *Pruritus Disputandi*: Latin: 'itch of disputing'.
16. the Schools: the traditional methods of the scholastic philosophers and theologians, associated with orthodoxy, or with Catholicism.
17. Canonical Sleevs: i.e. orthodoxy, the Church hierarchy.
18. *Pomilian* or *Pontifical Canons*: Roman religion in ancient (pagan) and contemporary (popish) forms, the former describing the civil religion associated with Numa Pompilius, the legendary second king of Rome.
19. Pandects: bodies of law, from the compendium of Roman law.
20. Logick ... Al-a-mode: the logic of imprisonment growing fashionable.
21. *Bedlam*: the asylum hospital of St Mary of Bethlehem, resited in 1676 near London Wall; a by-word for the mentally deranged.
22. *Soveraign Legislator*: God, i.e. scripture precepts.
23. Meretricious Gawdery: false show, ornament.
24. *Rom. 14. 1*: 'Him that is weak in the faith receive ye, but not to doubtful disputations'.
25. Excentrick: eccentric, irregular.
26. *Negate*: negation, nullification.
27. *Letter ... Wife*: The letter follows in Latin (omitted), then in English.
28. *psalm 119. 105*: i.e. Psalm 119:105, 'Thy word is a lamp unto my feet, and a light unto my path'.
29. my Beloved Wife: Hanna, daughter of the Baptist minister Edward Hutchinson. She and the couple's children were to die with Delaune in prison.

30. Bampfield ... Ralphson: Francis Bampfield and 'Zachariah Ralphson' appeared for trial at the Old Bailey on 17 January, the same day as Delaune. Bampfield was convicted with three other nonconformist ministers of refusing to take the oaths of allegiance and further detained. Ralphson was found guilty of publishing a seditious libel, *An Apology for God Worship and Worshippers*, but not guilty of writing and printing the book, which was held to contain reflections against the King and government. His punishment was the same as Delaune's: fined 100 marks, required to find sureties, and the books burnt. Delaune records that he died soon afterwards. According to Edmund Calamy, all three men died in Newgate in 1684, and he adds that 'Ralphson' was the alias of Jeremiah Marsden, a dissenting minister who fled to London from Yorkshire after involvement in the Farnley Wood plot of 1663 (*The Nonconformists Memorial*, 2nd edn, 2 vols (London, 1777), vol. 1, p. 64, vol. 2, pp. 552–4).
31. forgive us ... indebted to us: Luke 11:4.
32. Sessions-House: the court of the Old Bailey.
33. Bale-Docks: the dock of the court.
34. *Attorney General*: Sir Robert Sawyer (1633–92), attorney general since 1681, and recently prosecutor in the Rye House plot trials.
35. *Modo et forma*: in manner and form.
36. *vi et Armis*: with force and arms; the standard wording in an indictment for seditious libel.
37. *chief Justice*: Sir George Jeffreys. See note 4 to *A Short, but Just Account of the Tryal of Harris*, above, p. 456.
38. *As 'tis recorded*: the sentence in Latin (omitted) is then rendered in English.
39. *Supersedeas*: term for a legal writ enjoining a stay of proceedings. On Ralphson see note 30 above.
40. Gorge Jefferies: George Jeffreys; the spelling is repeated a few lines later.
41. *opheilemata*: transliterated Greek term for debts.
42. houto's: Greek: 'this'.
43. Grotius: the Dutch religious and political writer Hugo Grotius (1583–1645). His 1622 work *On the Truth of the Christian Religion*, published in English in 1633, had been issued in a new translation by Simon Patrick in 1683.
44. Tertullian ... Austin: early Church fathers; Austin is St Augustine.
45. Aliis atque aliis verbis: Latin: 'there is freedom to use different words'.
46. *Pater-noster*: Latin: 'our father', the Lord's prayer, which churchmen were enjoined to use by a decree emerging from third Church council at Toledo, Spain.
47. And ... *Lords prayer*: The paragraph is presented as it appears in the original, with unclosed quotation and parentheses.
48. *Petty Jury*: the jury empanelled to try the case after the grand jury has found a true bill of indictment against the accused.
49. *Wormwood and Hemlock*: poisonous plants mentioned in the Bible, and in hemlock's case, famous as the poison taken by Socrates in fulfilment of his death sentence.

## 'Mr Baxter's Tryal'

1. *Paraphrase ... before*: Richard Baxter, *A Paraphrase on the New Testament, with Notes, Doctrinal and Practical* (London: B. Simmons and Tho. Simmons, 1685). The book's appearance was remarked by L'Estrange in the *Observator* of 25 February.
2. Westminster *Hall*: The site of the present Houses of Parliament was the location of law courts until the nineteenth century, Westminster Hall then being incorporated into the new Palace of Westminster.

3. OATS ... *Palace-Yard*: Titus Oates (1649–1705), the disgraced informer of the popish plot, had been tried ten days previously for perjury and, as part of his punishment, was placed in the pillory in Palace Yard. The following day he was whipped through the streets to Newgate prison.
4. *Sir* Henry Ashhurst: Henry Ashurst (1645–1711) was from a Lancashire puritan family and became acquainted with Baxter in his youth. Later a merchant and Whig stalwart, briefly sitting as an MP in 1681, Ashurst remained a committed Presbyterian whose assistance to Baxter at his trial extended to legal, financial and moral support.
5. *Sir* Roger L'Estrange: L'Estrange, who had been knighted on 30 April, was still two months away from full restoration of his powers as licenser with the revival of the Printing Act, but he had attacked the *Paraphrase* in the *Observator* in February and Baxter and his supporters were justified in claiming he had urged prosecution and furnished textual evidence.
6. Wallop: Richard Wallop (bap. 1616; d. 1697), leading Whig lawyer.
7. Bishops ... *speaks of*: Baxter's *Paraphrase* was indeed fairly careful to identify unworthy prelates as those of Rome and the pope, past and present, although L'Estrange and Jeffreys clearly agreed that the innuendo remained.
8. Swear him: i.e. have Baxter answer the charge.
9. Latin *or* English: a reference to the Latin indictment, as well as, possibly, the reading of Church history.
10. Rotheram: John Rotherham (bap. 1630; d. 1708), later a judge and knighted under James II, his connections with nonconformity proving useful for James's religious policies.
11. Kidderminster: well known as Baxter's place of ministry, so a 'Kidderminster bishop' would be a Presbyterian one.
12. Tithe Pig Metropolitan: The phrase appears in Samuel Butler's *Hudibras*, first published in 1663 and reprinted in 1684 (p. 195). Butler's point was that Presbyterianism effectively creates an archbishop in each village, sustained by the distinctly rustic method of taking pigs as tithes.
13. Old Fellow: Baxter was 69; Jeffreys had just turned 40.
14. Egg ... Meat: egg full of yolk.
15. Donne: a don, head of the Presbyterian 'party'.
16. *Bates*: William Bates (1625–99), leading Presbyterian and a friend of Baxter's since the 1650s. He was ejected from his ministry in 1662 and had been fined for preaching in a private house in 1682. In 1667 Bates had urged Charles II to suppress pernicious doctrines and 'licentiousness of the press' (*ODNB*).
17. Attwood: William Atwood (d. 1712), lawyer (later the chief justice of New York) and writer on legal history and on politics and religion, supporting the Whig and nonconformist causes.
18. Roswell's *Case*: the trial for treason of the Presbyterian Thomas Rosewell (1630–92), who had come before Jeffreys on 25 October 1684 and been found guilty of declaring in a sermon that Charles I and II had introduced popery and such enemies should be overthrown. The questionable evidence, supplied in large part by paid informers, led to the King granting a pardon on 28 January 1685.
19. Attwood ... *Written*: Atwood had published a number of works espousing an ancient constitutionalist position, stressing the antiquity of the rights of the English people, notably *Jani Anglorum Facies Nova* (London, 1680) and *Argumentum Anti-Normannicum* (London, 1682), as well as publishing *A Letter of Remarks upon Jovian* (London,

1682) in defence of Samuel Johnson's *Julian the Apostate* and *A Seasonable Vindication of the Truly Catholick Doctrine of the Church of England* (London, 1683). The works were issued anonymously but Atwood's authorship of the constitutional histories was well known and he received high praise by name from the republican writer Henry Neville in *Plato Redivivus* (London, 1681), p. 110.

20. *to your Tents O Israel*: 1 Kings 12:16; biblical passage associated with the civil war, not least as the title of a pamphlet thrown into the carriage of Charles I as he left Parliament following the failed attempt to arrest MPs in January 1642.

## Censorship and Punishment under James II

### A Proclamation against Spreading of a Traiterous Declaration

1. *Duke of Monmouth*: James (1649–85), illegitimate son of Charles II and Lucy Walter (d. 1658), who was knighted as Sir James Scott on his marriage in 1663 and was created Duke of Monmouth in the same year. Rising to high place in Charles II's armed forces, the alarms of the popish plot and rivalry with the Duke of York led to him becoming favoured as a Protestant successor through exclusion. His openness to the possibility led to estrangement from court and involvement with the Rye House plotters, after confessing to which he fled to the Continent in early 1684. On 11 June the following year he landed at Lyme Regis with a small invasion force, expecting to gather support on arrival, and issued the declaration made subject to this proclamation.
2. *Declaration ... York*: the extended title of Monmouth's *Declaration*. Copies reached London on 13 June. A bill of attainder was introduced in the Commons on 15 June and the *Declaration* ordered to be burnt.
3. *Headboroughs ... Petty-Constables*: officers of the law, headboroughs and petty constables both operating at parish level.

### The True Account of the Behaviour and Confession of Disney

1. *Indited of High Treason*: Disney's trial was held at a special sessions at Marshalsea prison on the south bank of the Thames.
2. *Musqueteers*: i.e. a troop armed with muskets.
3. *Hanger ... Scymeter*: i.e. a belt-hanging sword shaped like a scimitar.
4. *His Daughter*: Little is known of Disney's family, but three children were granted pensions after the revolution for the sufferings of their father (*ODNB*).
5. *perfect*: complete, i.e. printed on both sides. The *Declaration* was eight pages quarto, so four printed pages on each side of the sheet.
6. *Minister of St. George*: Andrew Weston, whose account follows. St George the Martyr was the neighbouring church in Southwark, the churchyard abutting the Marshalsea prison walls.
7. *Ordinary*: the prison chaplain or minister appointed to accompany a prisoner at his execution.
8. *Christ ... chief*: 1 Timothy 1:15. The non-italicized words to 'chief' are also part of the scripture passage.
9. *If the Wicked ... alive, &c.*: Ezekiel 18:27.
10. *dolour*: suffering, distress.
11. *were*: i.e. which.

## An Account of the Proceedings against Johnson

1. *A Humble ... Invaded*: The two tracts were effectively suppressed at the time but appeared in print after the revolution of 1688–9 and were reprinted in *The Works of the Late Reverend Mr. Samuel Johnson* (London, 1710), pp. 160–8. The titles were given there as *An Humble and Hearty Address to all the English Protestants in this present Army* (pp. 160–1), and *The Opinion is This: That Resistance may be us'd, in case our Religion and Rights shou'd be Invaded* (pp. 161–8).
2. *Both ... Rebellion, &c.*: The two works had the same final aim but differed markedly in tone, one being a short polemical message to troops stationed on Hounslow Heath to the west of London, the other a lengthier disquisition into politics, religion and history, partly in Latin and said to represent the opinion of Lord Russell.
3. *Three Brushes*: an inn near the White Lion prison off High Street, Southwark.
4. *took it up in* Spittle-fields: collected it in Spitalfields.
5. *Earl ... Warrant*: Robert Spencer, Earl of Sunderland (1641–1702), was secretary of state from 1679 to 1688, therefore having oversight of press control.
6. *John Darby ... Wife*: John Darby (d. 1704) and his wife Joan (d. 1708/9), printers of numerous radical works over the previous twenty-five years, had been involved in the printing of Johnson's *Julian the Apostate*.
7. *Acquittance*: a receipt.

## The Sentence of Johnson

1. *Sentence*: delivered at the court of King's Bench at Westminster, 16 November 1686.
2. *Attorney-General*: Sir Richard Nagle (1635/6–99), an Irish Catholic lawyer, who had been knighted and made attorney general in February.
3. *degraded ... Preferment*: degradation, as well as itself being punishment, was necessary for the imposition of punishments not appropriate to the dignity of clergy, such as pillorying and whipping.

## A Proclamation for Suppressing and Preventing Seditious and Unlicenced Books

1. *An Act ... Continued*: The 1662 Printing Act, 13 & 14 Car. II, c. 33, renewed for seven years from 24 June 1685 by 1 Jac. II, c. 17.

## An Account of the Proceedings at Westminster-Hall

1. *Kings*: one of several words in the initial lines partly illegible in the copy of the London printing used but checked against the edition printed at Edinburgh (Wing A364). Other affected words are, in the first sentence, 'prayer', 'which', 'invalidate'; in the second sentence, 'not be', 'presented'; in the third sentence, 'Original', 'which', 'the proof'.
2. *Council*: counsel.
3. *Court*: 'Corut' in the original.
4. *Lord Chief Justice*: Sir Robert Wright (c. 1634–89), chief justice since early 1687 and a close colleague of Judge Jeffreys, now Baron Jeffreys and lord chancellor. He died while held in Newgate after the revolution.
5. *Arch-Bishop*: George Sancroft (1617–93), archbishop of Canterbury since January 1678. On receiving the King's order to read the declaration of indulgence of 4 May 1688, Sancroft agonized, consulted and decided to disobey on the grounds that the monarch did

not have power to dispense with laws at pleasure On delivery of the petition to this effect to James II, he and the six other bishops subscribing their names were initially committed to the Tower then released on bail before their trial and exoneration. Despite his conflicts with James, Sancroft refused to transfer allegiance at the revolution and was formally deprived on 1 February 1690 (see *ODNB*).

6. Lambeth: Lambeth Palace, the London seat of the archbishop of Canterbury, south of the river Thames and so formally in Surrey rather than London or Westminster.
7. Finch: Heneage Finch (1648/9–1719), made solicitor general in 1679 but dismissed in 1686 for opposition to James II's Catholicizing moves. As counsel for the bishops he prolonged the case and altered the grounds of the bishops' exoneration, not least to the view of posterity, by presenting new matters when the question of publication appeared to be sufficient to curtail the prosecution. An extended account of the debate on the publication issue appears in *State Trials*, vol. 12, pp. 183–524, on pp. 326–52.
8. *Lord President*: Robert Spencer, Earl of Sunderland (1641–1702), formerly secretary of state from 1679.
9. *Sollicitor*: Sir William Williams; see note 9 to *A Short, but Just Account of the Tryal of Harris*, above, p. 457.
10. *home*: pertinent.
11. W. Williams: William Williams.
12. *Attorny General ... Shores*: the attorney general was Sir Thomas Powys (1649–1719); Sir Bartholomew Shower (1658–1701) was briefly recorder of London in 1688, with a minor part in prosecuting the seven bishops.
13. *Baldock's Argument*: Sir Robert Baldock (1624/5–91), made a sergeant-at-law by James II in 1685 and after the bishops' trial appointed a judge. His argument here was that the King's printed declaration required only promulgation by circulation, rather than reading aloud by each bishop personally.
14. *Judg* Holloway: Sir Richard Holloway (c. 1627–99), a prosecutor of Stephen College in 1681, became a judge in 1683 and convicted Algernon Sidney. As a result of opining that the bishops had no seditious intent he was later removed from the bench.
15. *Judg*-Powel: Sir John Powell (1632/3–96), rapidly elevated to judge of King's Bench under James II, but removed from his post after siding with the bishops.
16. *Judg* Allibon: Sir Richard Allibone (1636–88) was another lawyer who enjoyed rapid promotion under James II, assisted by his Catholicism. His refusal to follow his colleagues in finding for the bishops ensured he remained on the bench after the trial but he died two months later.
17. *Petition ... Government*: Allibone also argued that petitions on such issues were rightly directed to Parliament.
18. Chester ... Rochester: Thomas Cartwright (1634–89), bishop of Chester, and Thomas Sprat (bap. 1635; d. 1713), bishop of Rochester, had supported reading the declaration of indulgence, giving rise to their unpopularity with the crowd and this writer. They acquiesced with differing degrees of enthusiasm, the Tory Cartwright later departing the country with James II while Sprat, long-time leading light of the Royal Society, embraced the revolution.
19. Summers: John, later Lord, Somers.

## A Proclamation Discharging the Importing, Vending, Dispersing, or Keeping

1. *Macers*: a term for mace-bearers in Scottish law and elsewhere, their duties including involvement in promulgating proclamations. In the original text a space appears before 'Macers' for specifying further addressees.
2. *Buchanan ... Nephtali*: titles also condemned by the Oxford *Judgment and Decree* of 1683, as were *The Apologeticall Relation* and *Mene Tekel*: see above, pp. 263–7.
3. *The Cup ... Mist*: [Robert McWard], *The Poor Man's Cup of Cold Water, Ministred to the Saints and Sufferers for Christ. In Scotland* (n.p., 1678); Anon., *The Scots Mist, yet Gathering to Wet English-Men to the Skinne* ([London, 1648]). McWard (*c.* 1625–81) was a Presbyterian minister, in exile from 1661, mainly in Rotterdam. A further printing of his condemned tract appeared in 1681.
4. *Hynd set loose*: [Alexander Sheilds], *A Hind let Loose, or An Historical Representation of the Testimonies of the Church of Scotland* ([Edinburgh], 1687). Sheilds (d. 1700) was a young Scots Presbyterian minister who preached in London in the early 1680s but was arrested for refusing to take the oath of allegiance. Committed to the Privy Council at Edinburgh for punishment he was subsequently imprisoned but escaped and forged a bond with James Renwick, setting out their position in *A Hind let Loose*. Sheilds's book was burnt and Renwick was executed for treason in February 1688.
5. *Proclamations ... Argile*: the published declarations renouncing Stuart rule, firstly the Covenanter declarations issued in 1680 and 1685 from the southern Scottish town of Sanquhar, and second those in defence of the Monmouth rising in England in 1685 and its Scottish arm, led by the Earl of Argyll, Archibald Campbell (1629–85).
6. *Baillie ... Burrows*: Scottish legal offices.
7. *Dyets*: days; 'betwixt' refers to the period between the proclamation's promulgation and the date given.
8. *incontinent ... Mercat-Crosses*: without delay, to go to the remaining market-crosses of the Scottish boroughs (to publish the proclamation).
9. *Per Actum ... Concilii*: Latin: 'enacted by the authority of the Privy Council'.
10. *Will. ... Concilii*: Latin: 'William Paterson, clerk to the Privy Council'.

## A Proclamation to Restrain the Spreading of False News

1. *lately Published*: James II, *His Majesties most Gracious and General Pardon* (London, 1688), issued on 27 September.

## A Proclamation. Whereas the Prince of Orange and his Adherents

1. *Papers and Declarations*: the first, and most notable, was *The Declaration of His Highnes William Henry, by the Grace of God Prince of Orange, &c. Of the reasons inducing him, to Appear in Armes in the Kingdome of England, for Preserving of the Protestant Religion, and for Restoring the Lawes and Liberties of England, Scotland and Ireland*. This was dated 10 October, with an 'Additional Declaration' of 24 October appended. The declaration was printed initially at The Hague by Arnout Leers but was reprinted in numerous versions almost immediately. *The Prince of Orange's Third Declaration*, a radical Whig forgery, was dated 28 November, after James II's proclamation.

## Arguments against Censorship, 1689–90

### [Spinoza], 'In a Free Commonwealth it should be Lawful'

1. *beginning ... 17th Chapter*: Spinoza argued there that no man can transfer all his power and right, because the most powerful ruler 'cannot enter into any Mans thoughts', it being 'vain for Supreme Power to command a Subject to hate his Friend and love his Enemy; or to command a Man not to be provoked with Reproach and Contempt, or not to desire to be freed from fear, and other things of the like kind, which necessarily follow from the Laws of Nature' (pp. 353–4).
2. *Palats*: palates, i.e. differing tastes.
3. *we have proved ... Power*: chapters 16–19.
4. *Piety ... Commonwealth*: 'I will first shew, *That Religion hath the Force of a Law, only from their Decrees who have the Supream Power; and that all External Religious Worship, and Outward Practice of Piety, ought to be suited and accommodated to the Peace of the Commonwealth*; ... But that I may not be mistaken, I speak only of the outward Worship and Exercise of Religion and Piety, and not of Piety it self, and the inward Worship of God, or of the Means whereby the Mind is internally disposed to worship God in sincerity: for the inward Worship of God, and Piety it self, is in every man's own power' (p. 413).
5. *a Baffle*: a check, a confutation.
6. *Remonstrants and Contra-remonstrants*: The split within Dutch Protestantism between Arminians and strict Calvinists, stemming from the 1610 'Remonstrance' by followers of the theologian Jacobus Arminius and confirmed by the expulsion of Remonstrants from the Church at the Synod of Dort in 1618–19. Along with more narrowly theological issues the Arminians favoured greater separation of matters of conscience from political intervention, although they benefited from the protection of powerful allies and the support of the States-General of Holland, ensuring the conflict was political as much as religious.

### Hickeringill, 'Of the Restraint of the Printing-Press'

1. *Sir Roger ... Chaplain*: licensing powers were exercised by Sir Roger L'Estrange and by the chaplains of the bishops, mainly the archbishop of Canterbury and bishop of London, both having authority in London.
2. *Act of Parliament*: the 1662 Printing Act, renewed for seven years in 1685.
3. *Laws of the Medes and Persians*: Daniel 6:15, 'the law of the Medes and Persians is, That no decree nor statute which the king establishes can be changed'. The Medes and Persians were ancient Iranian peoples, whose empires and wars were the subject of Herodotus, the Greek historian of the fifth century BC.
4. *Priests told Herodotus ... as since*: In the second book of his *History*, Herodotus recounted how during his visit to Egypt he was told by priests that over 341 generations the sun had changed course to rise twice in the west and set twice in the east.
5. *change their Acts*: referring to the statutes on religion of Edward VI, Mary I and Elizabeth I, which Hickeringill had discussed on p. 30.
6. *White Powder*: white gunpowder had less slow-burning charcoal than 'black' gunpowder, in combination with sulphur and saltpetre (potassium nitrate), increasing its violence but also the effective shooting range.
7. *By-Law ... Company*: the Ordinance of 1683; reproduced above, see pp. 114–16.

8. Diana of Mr. Licenser: the profit of L'Estrange; an allusion to the silversmith whose shrines for the goddess Diana were a source of gain (Acts 16:24).
9. Index Expurgatorius: the generic term for the Roman Catholic Church's lists of prohibited books and books allowable if expurgated, the *Index Librorum Prohibitorum* and *Index Librorum Expurgatorius*.
10. *Great Duke of* Buckingham: Henry Stafford, second Duke of Buckingham (1455–83).
11. Cock stands: the weathercock; i.e. the lower clergy follow the lead of the bishops.
12. *Haggards*: wild-caught hawks, usually female and mature, notoriously intractable when used for hunting (also extended to intractable women).
13. *Mathematicks ... Synodals, &c.*: the claim is that the clergy obediently follow and fund their superiors, as if instructed by synod, in spite of what reason and financial acumen dictates. Hickeringill also alludes to convocation, which met in 1689 and whose lower house allowed the inferior clergy a semi-independent voice.
14. let their Light so shine ... Heaven: Matthew 5:16.
15. Talent in a Napkin: Matthew 25.
16. Light under a Bushel: Matthew 5:15; Luke 11:33.
17. *Goaler*: jailer.
18. quench the Spirit: 1 Thessalonians 5:19.
19. *give to* Cæsar ... Cæsars: Matthew 22:21; Luke 20:25; Mark 12:17.

## [Parkinson], *The Fire's Continued at Oxford*

1. *Controversy ... Exeter-Colledg at* Oxford: The controversial college rector Arthur Bury (1623–1713) had expelled a college fellow, James Colmer, for 'incontinence' (fornication) in late 1689, the ensuing feud leading to a visitation in July 1690 by the bishop of Exeter, Jonathan Trelawney (1650–1721), which was obstructed by college fellows. In the preceding months Bury had published his criticisms of the doctrine of the Trinity in *The Naked Gospel*, adding fuel to Colmer's accusations of heresy and resulting in the Oxford University convocation condemning the book.
2. Gazette ... *Decree*: The *London Gazette* no. 2586 advertised the printing of 'The Censure and Decree of the University of Oxford, Published in Convocation, Aug. 19. 1690. against several Heretical and Impious Propositions, Published in a Book, Intituled, The Naked Gospel, Printed at the Theatre in Oxford; together with the said Propositions. Sold by Thomas Bennet at the Half-Moon in St. Pauls Church-yard, London'. The extant printed version, bearing the title *Judicum et Decretum Universitatis Oxoniensis*, retains the Oxford convocation's Latin, with the offending propositions in the English of Bury's original.
3. Naked Gospel: [Arthur Bury] *The Naked Gospel* ([Oxford], '1690').
4. *Convocation ... Work*: the Church of England convocation for the Canterbury diocese, as distinct from the University of Oxford convocation, which had first assembled on 21 November 1689 but did not meet after 13 December, and was dissolved in January 1690.
5. *stolen Impression*: Wing lists the Oxford impression as B6198A and the London printing as B6199. The latter is readily distinguished, the text being double column.
6. *Convocation*: Church of England convocation.
7. *famous Judgment ... State*: The *Judgment and Decree* of 1683; reproduced above, see pp. 263–7.
8. *Lady of* Loretto's *Heirs*: Roman church's name for Mary, mother of Jesus, hence implying Catholic heirs.

9. N.G.: *Naked Gospel*.
10. *Convocation ... Decree*: the Oxford University convocation and its decree of 1683; see above, pp. 263–7.
11. Parkinson: the author, James Parkinson. See headnote.
12. *Vice-Chancellor ... Bristol*: Gilbert Ironside (1631/2–1701), who at the revolution was given his father's former bishopric at Bristol, and later became bishop of Hereford.
13. *Dr. H—'s*: Dr Timothy Halton (bap. 1633; d. 1704), provost of Queen's College and university pro-vice-chancellor, who expelled Parkinson on 4 September 1683. Having been vice-chancellor in 1684–5, he continued as provost at Queen's, remaining at the college until his death.
14. *Explusion!*: From this point, Parkinson considers and rebuts the evidence used in the Oxford *Censure and Decree* to condemn Bury's alleged heresy.

## The Printing Act in Question, 1692–3

### *Reasons Humbly Offered to be Considered before the Act for Printing be Renewed*

1. *that Act*: the 1662 Printing Act, 13 & 14 Car. II, c. 33.
2. *inhauncing*: enhancing, i.e. increasing.
3. *generality ... Apprenticeship*: the meaning suggests 'apprenticeship' in a general sense as subservience, and 'haberdashers' as general traders with some interest in printed books, their number including John Jekyll, mentioned below.
4. *James I ... Prohibition to all others*: In March 1616 James I reaffirmed an initial grant of 1603, and this formed the basis of the lucrative English Stock monopolized by the Stationers' Company and controlled by its officers.
5. *Solicitation of Sir R. Lestrange*: This overstates the influence of Roger L'Estrange in 1662, and invents a confederacy with the Stationers, but certainly they shared a common interest for differing ends in having the 1662 Printing Act regulate the press.
6. Preventing ... Books &c.: the terms in the title and preamble of the 1662 Act.
7. *Corporations Inheritance*: the Stationers' Company's reserves, accrued from previous profits.
8. cent. per cent: 100 per cent.
9. *Seditious ... Act*: the complaint that seditious books were charged only for being unlicensed and breaching the monopoly, rather than for their actual criminal content.
10. *Messenger ... aforesaid*: Robert Stephens, the messenger of the press (see note 13 to *A Short, but Just Account of the Tryal of Harris*, above, p. 457), who became a member of the Company in 1683, although he left subsequently. He continued in employment as messenger after the revolution, his work including prosecuting breaches of copyright, one known case being that involving the play *Sodom or the Quintessence of Debauchery* in early 1690. He was still active in the early eighteenth century: see Volume 4 of this edition.
11. John Jekil *stood Trial*: John Jekyll (1611–90), merchant haberdasher, Whig activist and sometime printer. He was amongst those put on trial for riot following the London sheriff elections in 1682 but evidence concerning his trial for printing is scant. It must have taken place before 1676, the year in which the judge Sir Mathew Hale died. In 1685 Jekyll and his son John were named in a royal proclamation demanding that those involved in printing adopt the livery of the Stationers' Company, but the Jekylls appear to have withdrawn from the trade rather than apply (*ODNB*).

12. Athias *a Jew*: Joseph Athias (d. 1700), who at Amsterdam printed highly praised editions of the Bible dated 1660 and 1677.
13. *farmed ... Cambridg*: The Cambridge University printers John Hayes and George Sawbridge entered covert agreements not to undermine the Stationers' patent interests, despite the University's attempts to break with earlier deals with the Company in appointing Hayes in 1670.
14. *petition ... Quo Warranto*: The petition of 29 April 1688 was the work of Henry Hills (c. 1625–89), who as King's printer and master of the Stationers' Company combined the interests of the two main Bible printers in opposition to Oxford's revived printing of books previously foregone in return for payment by agreement with the Stationers. Although the Catholic Hills was ousted at the revolution, dying soon after, the Company pursued its case against the University's counter-claims of privilege enshrined in its 1636 royal charter.
15. *Father Peters*: Sir Edward Petre (d. 1699), Jesuit confessor to James II, appointed to the Privy Council in 1687. He fled to France in December 1688.
16. *Edwards ... Printers*: Jonathan Edwards (1638–1712) was vice-chancellor until October 1692, when he was succeeded by the dean of Christ Church College, Henry Aldrich (1648–1710). In October 1691 Edwards led acceptance of a controversial new agreement with the Stationers, and he and Aldrich physically intervened to halt printing in December–January 1691–2 (Harry Carter, *History of the Oxford University Press, vol. 1* (Oxford: Oxford University Press, 1975), pp. 106–7).
17. *Dr. Hammond, Mr. Pool*: Henry Hammond (1605–60) and Matthew Poole (d. 1679). Poole had been required to pay the bookseller Cornelius Bee a quarter share in the proceeds of his 1669 *Synopsis* of Bible commentaries, some of which had previously been included in a work issued by Bee in 1660.
18. *Regula Placitandi*: Anon., *Regula Placitandi: A Collection of Special Rules for Pleading* (London: printed by the assigns of Richard and Edward Atkyns for Thomas Basset and Thomas Bever, 1691).
19. *Charter ... Parliament*: The royal charter of 1636 had granted a privilege of printing that included the types of books within the Stationers' English Stock, giving rise to later agreements reserving these to the Company in return for payment.
20. *discontinued*: The Act lapsed in May 1679.
21. *Lestrange ... renewed*: L'Estrange had become MP for Winchester in the Parliament which commenced in May 1685 and renewed the Printing Act.
22. *Chaplains ... Studies*: The chaplains exercised licensing powers on behalf of their bishops.

## [Bohun], 'Reasons for Reviving the Act for Regulating the Press & Printing'

1. *Plato's Laws*: Plato, *De Legibus* [The Laws]. In book seven's delineation of laws applying to the poets, Plato asserts that no-one should be allowed to expose his work to others without the approval of the guardians.
2. *celerity*: speed, swiftness.
3. *1517*: the year of Luther's posting of the 95 Theses.
4. *holy League*: the Catholic League against Protestantism. Bohun dates this to the purported secret agreement between France and Spain at Bayonne in 1565 in his historical work *The Character of Queen Elizabeth* (London, 1693), p. 203.

5. *Decree ... Star Chamber*: the Star Chamber decree of 1586, presumably also embracing the decree of 1637.
6. *Ordinances of Parliament*: first and foremost the Printing Ordinance of 14 June 1643, to which Milton's *Areopagitica* responded. The ordinance appointed press licensers but Bohun adds the label 'Surveyor' based on Restoration experience.
7. *this Act ... Preamble*: the 1662 Printing Act, 13 & 14 Car. II, c. 33. For the preamble, see above, pp. 3–4.
8. *Invasion ... Insurrection at home*: the fear of French invasion following defeats for William III's army in Flanders in 1692, and internally the continuing fear of Jacobitism, as well as renewed tensions between Crown and Parliament.
9. *Common Law ... Papers*: press licensing did not directly punish content, a point also made in the printers' petition at this time, see above, p. 352.
10. *the Book at Station: hall*: the Stationers' Register at Stationers' Hall, into which proposed printed books were required to be entered to secure copyright, as well as allowing oversight for censorship purposes. The complaint of the register being cut and abused is expressed in *Reasons Humbly Offered* (see above, p. 355).
11. *Rasures*: erasures.
12. *supposed to be paid ... saved money*: The author's apparent ignorance of the licenser's pay casts some doubt on authorship, but the next sentence suggests he knew the messenger was paid £50, and Bohun was indeed offered the remaining £200 a year as licenser (*The Diary and Autobiography of Edmund Bohun* (Beccles: privately printed, 1853), p. 98.)
13. *They move ... book*: the proposal by the authors of *Reasons Humbly Offered*.

[Harrington], *Reasons for Reviving the Act for the Regulation of Printing*

1. *the Act*: the 1662 Printing Act.
2. *near 100 Years past*: in fact, over 100 years, if the reference is to the 1586 Star Chamber decree.
3. *Provision ... Published*: i.e. the pamphlets, not the legal provisions, were deemed in contempt of the King.
4. *Publick Register*: the Stationers' Register.
5. *Act ... 1649*: the 1649 Printing Act, actually dated 20 September.
6. *Charge of the Crown*: the tract follows the historical claim of Richard Atkyns, see above, pp. 85–8.
7. *4 or 5 per Cent*: a claim rather contrary to that of *Reasons Humbly Offered to be Considered*, see above, pp. 352–4.
8. Object: objection, followed by answer.
9. *Jekyl ... since*: John Jekyll (see note 11 to *Reasons Humbly Offered*, above, p. 489).
10. *Stat. ... price of Books*: the 1534 Act for Printers and Binders of Books, 25 Hen. VIII, c. 15.
11. *Two Mercenary Fellows*: Peter Parker and Thomas Guy, the Oxford University printers who were forced to cease operations in 1692 after the university agreed to take payment from the Stationers' Company in return for not exercising its Bible-printing privilege. Guy's 'mercenary' endeavours laid the basis for the foundation of Guy's Hospital, London, after his death in 1724. Harrington's legal expertise was employed by Oxford University in the disputes over the press.
12. *Licence*: the licence to print Bibles and other works enjoyed by Parker and Guy.
13. *granting ... Stationers*: the agreement between University and the Stationers was made in October 1681. See Carter, *History of the Oxford University Press*, pp. 106–8, where it is

also noted that the quality of Parker and Guy's work was not as poor as was claimed at the time.

14. *Bill ... Liberties*: a bill was introduced in Parliament in 1689–90 to confirm Oxford University's Laudian 'Great Charter' of 1636, which included a liberty to print 'all manner' of books.

## Reasons Humbly Offered for the Liberty of Unlicens'd Printing

1. Printing-Act ... *Spanish Gag*: the 1662 Printing Act, 13 & 14 Car. II, c. 33, likened to the Spanish inquisition and papal censorship.
2. *First ... Wisdom*: Milton, *Areopagitica*, pp. 3–4.
3. *This Project ... Inquisition*: ibid., p. 4.
4. *After ... Emperor*: ibid., pp. 6–7. The *Reasons* lacks the discussion of pre-Christian times found in Charles Blount's *Just Vindication of Learning*, which derived in part from *Areopagitica*.
5. *Padre Paolo*: Paolo Sarpi, whose *History of the Council of Trent* was Milton's source. This sentence, and all down to 'Glutton-Friars', is taken from *Areopagitica*, p. 7.
6. *Pope ... Bull*: The bull *Inter cunctas* of 1418 suppressed writings spreading the heresies of the reformers John Wyclif (d. 1384) and Jan Hus (d. 1415).
7. *Council of Trent ... Indexes*: The counter-reformation Council of Trent, 1545–63, authorized censorship measures including the *Index Librorum Prohibitorum*, the list of prohibited books, to which the *Index Expurgatorius* was a supplement.
8. *St. Peter ... Paradise*: *Areopagitica*, p. 7. Christ promised his disciple Peter 'the keys to the kingdom of heaven' (Matthew 16:19) in building the Christian Church. The reference was omitted in *A Just Vindication*.
9. *Juncto*: Juno, queen of the Roman gods, who sought to prevent the birth of Hercules. The use of 'Juncto' rather than Milton's 'Juno' could be an error but equally could play on the increasingly common use, from the 1640s, of 'juncto' or 'junto' to describe a powerful cabal or coterie. The passage is omitted in *A Just Vindication*.
10. *And thus ... burnt*: This paragraph is taken from *Areopagitica*, pp. 8–9.
11. *Alchymy ... Invention*: Lullius was the Spanish writer and alchemist Ramon Lull (d. 1315). The passage is omitted in *A Just Vindication*.
12. *But some ... it has*: This paragraph is taken from *Areopagitica*, p. 9.
13. *I am not ... Park-gate*: ibid., p. 14. The passage does not appear in the *Just Vindication* but was used by Denton in his *Apology for the Liberty of the Press*, with 'crows' becoming 'rooks'.
14. *how shall ... fram'd*: a paraphrase of *Areopagitica*, pp. 14–15.
15. *If we think ... Garb*: ibid., pp. 16–17.
16. *Licensing ... Commodes*: Here the author interjects with his (or her) own observations on current fashions. A tire-woman (attire woman) was a dressmaker or costumier, or a lady's maid.
17. *Who shall ... frustrate*: *Areopagitica*, p. 17.
18. *But grant ... hereafter*: from ibid., p. 18, substituting 'Jacobite Libels' for Milton's 'Court-Libell'.
19. *Another Reason ... Volumes*: ibid., p. 19.
20. *And I must ... Testimony enough*: an interjection slighting Edmund Bohun, appointed licenser in late September 1692. See headnote.
21. *Seeing therefore ... Intention*: *Areopagitica*, p. 20.

22. Ferula ... Fescue: see note 26 to *A Just Vindication*, above, p. 461.
23. temporizing and extemporizing: indecisive and unprepared or arbitrary.
24. *I lastly proceed ... Foreigner*: This paragraph is taken from *Areopagitica*, pp. 20–1, but omits Milton's criticisms of the clergy.
25. *When a man ... Learning*: This draws heavily on ibid., p. 21, but omits Milton's passage referring to Palladian oil, included in *A Just Vindication*. A 'puny' is a child, a schoolboy. 'Censor's Hand' refers to the imprimatur, subscribed with the licenser's name.
26. *Undervaluing ... soever*: This reworks *Areopagitica*, pp. 22–3. Like the *Just Vindication* the author retains the anachronistic reference to the large number of licensers envisaged by the 1643 Printing Ordinance (up to 32).
27. Philistines ... Forges: see note 35 to [Blount], *A Just Vindication*, above, p. 461. 'Coulter' denotes a blade used on a plough.
28. *There is yet ... Prohibition of Printing*: *Areopagitica*, p. 29, substituting 'the French' for 'som enemy'. 'Alcoran' is the Quran.
29. *Winds ... Suppressing*: *Areopagitica*, p. 35.
30. *What a Collusion ... Statute*: ibid., p. 36. The paragraph which follows continues the passage from Milton. The italicized passage is from Proverbs 2:4–6; it does not appear in *A Just Vindication*.
31. *Men of Note ... wise*: *Areopagitica*, p. 39, updated with references to the 'late happy Revolution'.
32. *regulating ... Prevention can use*: ibid., p. 39, with publisher substituted for printer.
33. *To conclude*: Here the text departs from *Areopagitica* and presents claims drawn from elsewhere.
34. Laud *was charged ... against it*: The claim is taken from the recently published *A Letter from Major General Ludlow to Sir E.S.* ('Amsterdam', 1691), p. 8. In 1640–1 the ninth article of impeachment against William Laud (1573–1645), archbishop of Canterbury, charged that as bishop of London in 1628–33 he employed licensing chaplains who were disaffected to the reformed religion and allowed books of superstition.
35. Abbot ... Clergy: The quotation originally derives from Andrew Marvell's *Mr Smirke* (see above, p. 149). This author takes it from *A Letter from Major General Ludlow*, p. 8, where the words appear as a marginal addition to criticisms of Laud's licensing regime, with the contrary policy of his predecessor as archbishop, George Abbot (1562–1633), described on the following page.
36. Saints Rest ... Crown-Office: Richard Baxter (1615–91), *The Saints Everlasting Rest* (London, 1650). One of the great Presbyterian writer's most successful works, the ninth edition appeared in 1662 and further editions in 1669, 1676 and 1688. The chaplain Thomas Grigg (d. 1670) was sympathetic to Baxter, although he withheld licences to other works on at least two occasions. Baxter recalled that a subsequent chaplain, William Jane, complained in a sermon before the lord mayor in 1676 of the book having the civil war parliamentarians Lord Brooke (Robert Greville), John Pym and John Hampden meeting in 'the Blessed Parliament' in heaven, despite Baxter having excised these references in editions after the Restoration (*Reliquae Baxterianae* (London, 1696), p. 177).
37. *Assemblies Catechism*: the catechisms (shorter and longer) devised by the Presbyterian-led Westminster Assembly of divines in 1646–7 and published with difficulty, mainly through secondary exposition, after the Restoration.
38. Edmund Bohun: press licenser from 7 September 1692 to 21 January 1693. See headnote.

39. A Defence ... Church-Yard: Edmund Bohun, *A Defence of Sir Robert Filmer* (London, 1684). Sidney was executed on 7 December 1683. The quotations taken from the *Defence* adopt Bohun's wording, but that from p. 7 has Bohun directly quoting Sir Robert Filmer, *Patriarcha: or The Natural Power of Kings* (London: Walter Davis, 1680), p. 22.
40. Preface ... Chiswel, *1685: Patriarcha: or The Natural Power of Kings. By the Learned Sir Robert Filmer Baronet. The second edition ... To which is added ... A Conclusion or Postscript, by Edmund Bohun* (London, 1685). Bohun's 'conclusion' actually appeared as a 101-page unpaginated preface to the reader.
41. *Escheat*: revert by confiscation.
42. Author ... *Monarcha*: James Tyrrell (1642–1718). Tyrrell's *Patriarcha non Monarcha* (London, 1681) was one of three notable responses to the 1680 first printed edition of Filmer's *Patriarcha*, the others being John Locke's *Two Treatises of Government* and Algernon Sidney's *Discourses concerning Government*. It was the only one published in its entirety when Bohun wrote his preface. Tyrrell's sister Eleanor was married to Charles Blount.
43. Lambert ... Cromwel: John Lambert (*c.* 1619–84) and Oliver Cromwell (1599–1658), comrades and subsequently adversaries in leading the military and political construction and operation of the Protectorate.
44. Bohun's *Positions ... 1683*: Edmund Bohun, *An Address to the Free-Men and Free-Holders of the Nation* (London, 1683). The *Address* was printed in three parts in 1682–3. The initial quotations derive from *The Third and Last Part*.
45. *Duke* (of York): James II from 1685.
46. Loyal Parliament ... Pensionary Parliament: the first Parliament of Charles II, which ran from 1661 to 1679.
47. Would God ... thee: 2 Samuel 18:33.
48. *1683*: i.e. the time of writing the *Address*.
49. *Popish Lords*: the peers arrested by order of the House of Commons in 1678 and held in the Tower of London awaiting impeachment for treason.
50. Scotish Rebellion *in 1679*: the rebellion ended with the defeat of 6,000 Scottish covenanters at Bothwell Bridge in June 1679.
51. Harbord: William Harbord (1635–92), Whig MP active in opposing the Duke of York. He fled England on James II's accession, returning with William of Orange's fleet in 1688.
52. Meal-Tub-Plot: spurious plot alleged against Presbyterians in 1679, then claimed as a cover for papist plotting, with incriminating papers forged by the informer Thomas Dangerfield hidden in a meal tub at the home of the Catholic midwife Elizabeth Cellier.
53. *Justice of Peace in* Suffolk: Bohun became a Suffolk Justice of the Peace in 1675. He was removed from the commission of peace in 1687, attributing this to disfavour towards his anti-Catholicism, was restored in 1689, then in 1694 was again removed, this time blaming the 'republican party' (*ODNB*).
54. Richard Thompson: The Commons ordered the Bristol cleric Richard Thompson to be impeached after voting him guilty of promoting popery and sedition, having heard how, amongst other things, he preached in January 1679 that the popish plot was a ruse in the service of a Presbyterian plot empowering Parliament to act against the King: *CJ*, 9, pp. 693–4. The proceedings ended with the dissolution of Parliament in 1681.
55. *White-Boys*: favourites; also applied to Monmouth's supporters (*OED*).
56. Hambden: John Hampden (d. 1643), leader of parliamentary opposition to Charles I's attempts to revive 'ship-money' taxes for military use.
57. *Chrism*: anointing.

58. Reflections ... *1683*: [Edmund Bohun], *Reflections on a Pamphlet, stiled, A Just and Modest Defence of the Proceedings of the Two last Parliaments* (London, 1683). *A Just and Modest Vindication* (London, 1682) is attributed to Algernon Sidney and Sir William Jones (1631–82).
59. *third Address ... Declaration*: i.e. the third part of Bohun's *Address to the Free-men and Free-Holders*. Charles II's declaration was *His Majesties Declaration to all his Loving Subjects, touching the Causes and Reasons that moved him to Dissolve the Two last Parliaments* (London, 1683).
60. Justice ... Middlesex: Bohun was in fact restored to the Suffolk commission of peace in June 1689.
61. Sancroft: William Sancroft (1617–93), archbishop of Canterbury from 1678, came from a farming family in the Diss area of Suffolk. While Bohun saw him as a great friend, the immediate encouragement to apply for the licenser's post came from John Moore (1646–1714), bishop of Norwich.
62. Blaspheming Hindmarsh: Joseph Hindmarsh, publisher of mainly Tory authors who was 'bookseller to his Royal Highness' in the last two years of Charles II's reign. In 1692–3 he published several pamphlets on ecclesiastical affairs in Scotland, including the one in note 74 below, as well as tracts defending Charles I's authorship of *Eikon Basilike* and works by John Dryden, Aphra Behn and Roger L'Estrange.
63. Apostatized Presbyterian: In the *Address*, Bohun had recalled coming from a dissenting family background.
64. Truth ... Davis: Richard Davis, *Truth and Innocency Vindicated against Falshood and Malice* (London: Nath. and Robert Ponder, [1692]). Davis (1658–1714) was an Independent (Congregational) minister in Northamptonshire whose intransigent opposition undermined moves towards a union between Presbyterians and Independents. *Truth and Innocency Vindicated*, a reply to an earlier attack on Davis, was licensed by Bohun on 4 November.
65. the Act ... *two in that Day*: the 1662 Printing Act, 13 & 14 Car. II, c. 33. There were still two posts of secretary of state, for the northern and southern departments, although at this time both roles were occupied by Daniel Finch, Earl of Nottingham.
66. Bonum ... doceri: Latin: 'it is a blessing to learn even from an enemy'.
67. Raymond ... Mayor: Sir Jonathan Raymond was one of two Tory mayoral candidates but public criticism of their role under Charles II led to the election of their Whig opponent Sir John Fleet.
68. Earl of Warrington ... Mercury: The *City Mercury* was a free weekly paper of advertisements, including book notices. Henry Booth, Baron Delamere (1652–94), was a prominent Whig exclusionist MP who had been arrested in the Rye House plot investigations and again in connection with the Monmouth rebellion, eventually being tried for treason. He was created Earl of Warrington in 1690. His speech was printed as *The Speech of the Right Honourable Henry Earl of Warrington, Lord Delamere, to the Grand Jury at Chester. April 13. 1692* (London: Richard Baldwin, 1692).
69. Johnson's ... Throne: Samuel Johnson, *An Argument Proving, that the Abrogation of King James by the People of England from the Regal Throne, and the Promotion of the Prince of Orange, one of the Royal Family, to the Throne of the Kingdom in his Stead, was According to the Constitution of the English Government, and Prescribed by it* (London: for the author, 1692). On Johnson see above, pp. 304–5. The *Argument* reached its fifth edition within a year.

70. *Martyrology ... Dunton*: 'Thomas Pitts' [John Tutchin], *A New Martyrology: or, The Bloody Assizes* (London: John Dunton, 1693). The book, detailing the Monmouth rebels' treatment by lord chief justice Sir George Jeffreys, had first been published in 1689. Tutchin (*c*. 1660–1707), who took part in the rebellion, was later author of the early eighteenth-century periodical the *Observator* (see Volume 4 of this edition). The bookseller John Dunton (1659–1732) subsequently penned the invaluable source of print trade lore, *The Life and Errors of John Dunton* (London, 1705). Bohun admitted giving him 'kind usage' (*The Diary and Autobiography*, p. 115).
71. *Barnardiston ... Elwes*: the Whig county MPs returned for Suffolk in 1690 and 1695. Barnardiston had been convicted of seditious libel in 1684 for letters sympathetic to the Rye House plotters, a conviction reversed after the revolution.
72. *Stevens*: Robert Stephens, the long-serving messenger of the press. See note 13 to *A Short, but Just Account of the Tryal of Harris*, above, p. 457.
73. *damnable Paper*: Hindmarsh had been indicted in February 1681 for publishing [Thomas Ashenden], *The Presbyterian Pater Noster, Creed, and Ten Commandments* ([London, 1681]).
74. *Apology ... Scotland*, &c.: [Alexander Munro], *An Apology for the Clergy of Scotland* (London: Jos. Hindmarsh, 1693). Bohun's imprimatur appeared on the title page. Hindmarsh published several tracts by Munro (d. 1698), a nonjuring Scots episcopalian.
75. *Stenekirk ... Service*: In August 1692 William III's multi-national army had been defeated by the French at Steenkerque in the low countries. William's trusted Scottish general Hugh Mackay was killed, along with James Douglas, the 20-year-old Earl of Angus.
76. *White-Boy*: see note 55 above.
77. *Parliaments ... Settlement*: the Convention Parliament of 1689.
78. *Fraser ... Licenser*: James Fraser (1645–1731), a Scots-born dealer in books, supplying several high-placed customers, who served as licenser from the revolution to August 1692. Bohun complained that under him 'the whigg party had golden days' (*The Diary and Autobiography*, p. 110).
79. *Walker ... Basilice*, &c.: [Anthony Walker], *A True Account of the Author of a Book entitled Eikon Basilike* (London: Nathanael Ranew, 1692). Only some copies carried the title-page affirmation of having been licensed. The Essex clergyman Walker (bap. 1622; d. 1692) argued for John Gauden's authorship of the *Eikon Basilike* attributed to Charles I, fuelling a long-running debate over the book's status.
80. *30th ... January, 1692/3*: the anniversary of Charles I's execution.
81. *Salary*: Bohun was offered £200 a year. The secretary of state, the Earl of Nottingham, also gave him £25 for new clothes (*The Diary and Autobiography*, p. 98).
82. *Sir Roger L. ... turns in it*: Bohun shared Sir Roger L'Estrange's politics and, in Charles Brome, his publisher, but the two do not seem to have been particularly close. Bohun first inquired about the licenser's post in 1688–9 when it became clear L'Estrange's incumbency would end.
83. *honest* Sam's: Sam's coffee-house, in Ave Maria Lane, also the location of Stationers' Hall. L'Estrange was often said to hold court there.
84. *displeasure .. Tribulation*: Bohun was arrested on 23 January and removed from his post by order of the Commons on 24 January; see headnote.
85. *Book ... Conquerors*, &c.: [Charles Blount], *King William and Queen Mary Conquerors* (London: Richard Baldwin, 1693). The book carried Bohun's licence, dated 11 January 1693.

86. Issachars: ancient tribe of Israel, named after Issachar, characterized in Genesis 49:14–15 as a stolid ass between two burdens, who 'bowed his shoulder to bear, and became a servant unto tribute'. The term was used to satirize passive obedience and non-resistance (the two burdens) in the anonymous poem *The Tribe of Issachar: or, The Ass Couchant* (London, 1691).
87. Johnson ... *Frank*: Samuel Johnson, *An Argument Proving*, p. 23.

## *The Clauses chiefly Objected against in the Act 14o of Charles II*

1. *Act ... about Printing*: the 1662 Printing Act, 13 & 14 Car. II, c. 33.
2. *Houses of Peers ... without Oath*: The requirement of a warrant from the secretary of state for searches of peers' houses was originally intended as a special exemption from ordinary searches in the Act.
3. toties quoties: 'so often as often', i.e. time after time, repeatedly.

# Suppressing Jacobitism

## *A Proclamation for the Better Discovery of Seditious Libellers*

1. *Secretaries of State*: both secretarial positions were at this time occupied by Daniel Finch, Earl of Nottingham.
2. *General Pardon*: 1690 had seen an act for a free and general pardon, 2 Wm. & Mar., c. 10.

## *Animadversions upon that Proclamation*

1. *Stones ... cry out*: Luke 19:40.
2. *Remant*: error or variant on remnant, or on the obsolete spelling 'remanent'.
3. *outwords*: an error or possibly a play on 'outworks', i.e. words as the defence of truth.
4. *Plaistered ... Goodly words*: plastered and obscured with florid language.
5. *Foundation ... Palliate*: i.e. the ill-made mortar of falsehood cannot sustain the foundation of truth.
6. *Margin ... discovered*: The alternatives of 'reproved' or 'discovered' are offered in the translators' notes to the King James version.
7. esteemed as Potters Clay: a paraphrase of Isaiah 29:16.
8. greatest Fool ... first: proverbial.
9. *Deliverance*: i.e. the revolution of 1688–9.
10. Ipssisimis verbis: Latin: 'in the words themselves', verbatim.
11. Coke ... Rebellion: see note 7 to *An Exact Narrative of the Tryal and Condemnation of Twyn*, above, p. 444.
12. Declaration for Liberty of Conscience ... Allegiance: the title of James II's 1687 Indulgence, which indeed required 'that nothing be preached or taught amongst them which may any ways tend to alienate the hearts of our people from us or our government'.
13. French ... *Date hereof*: the early summer of 1692, when plans for an invasion to restore James II were halted by the defeat suffered by the French fleet at La Hogue.
14. P. *of O's*: Prince of Orange's.
15. Divine Method ... Jer. *37.10*: The references concern defeated or demoralized forces rising again.
16. in Foro Humano: Latin: 'in the court of humanity'.

17. *False, Infamous and Scandalous Libels*: the epithets used in the royal *Proclamation* being criticized.
18. *Gen. 34. 30*: 'And Jacob said to Simeon and Levi, Ye have troubled me to make me to stink among the inhabitants of the land, among the Canaanites and the Perizzites: and I being few in number, they shall gather themselves together against me, and slay me; and I shall be destroyed, I and my house'.
19. *Nuncupative* Protestants: nominal, so-called Protestants.
20. Coke's ... famosis: The case *De Libellis famosis*, in Coke, Reports, vol. 5, p. 125, first printed 1605 as *The Fift Part of the Reports of Sr. Edward Coke Knight, the Kings Attorney General*.
21. Præstat motos componere fluctus: Latin: 'let me still the raging waves' (Virgil, *Aeneid*).
22. *Delutions*: dilutions.
23. *Oslers, Tapsters and Inn-keepers*: all terms for innkeepers or tavern keepers (osler = ostler).
24. *Pyrate told* Alexander ... at once: a story told of Alexander the Great by St Augustine in *City of God*.
25. *tickle*: connoting supple and delicate, presumably.
26. Ratio Ultima Regum: Latin: 'the final resort of kings', or 'the ultimate reason of kings'.
27. Gazette ... *Robbers*: The Proclamation, as well as being printed and posted separately, was also published in the *London Gazette*, 2802 (15 September 1692), dominating the front page alongside a proclamation for apprehending highwaymen and robbers.
28. Balaams: 'Which have forsaken the right way, and are gone astray, following the way of Balaam the son of Bosor, who loved the wages of unrighteousness' (2 Peter 2:15).
29. *Sab*: possibly sabre, or 'stab'.
30. *inure*: inured, accustomed.
31. Nov. 4.1692 ... *was rejected*: There was no such treason bill on 4 November 1692, a date which also contradicts that of 4 October 1692 which is given as the date of writing at the end of the tract. A bill with this title was only introduced on 1 December 1692, making it unclear what actions of the Commons are being referred to. It would be 1695–6 before a new treason Act passed into law, by which time the beneficiary was William alone (7 & 8 Will. III, c. 27).
32. Patrick: Simon Patrick (1626–1707), bishop of Ely from April 1691. The non-juring bishop Patrick 'usurped' was Francis Turner (1637–1700), earlier the target of Andrew Marvell's *Mr Smirke* (reproduced above, see pp. 143–50).
33. *Merciful* ... Mercy: Matthew 5:7.
34. Quo Anime: Latin: 'what animates [their writings]', what are their motives.

## Anderton, *True Copy of the Paper Delivered to the Sheriffs*

1. Smith: Samuel Smith (1620–98), chaplain-in-ordinary of Newgate prison, who supplied his own version in *A True Account of the Behaviour, Confession, and Last Dying Speeches of the Criminals that were Executed at Tyburn, on Friday the 16th, of June, 1693* (London, 1693), reporting that Anderton declined to repent before the crowd, instead protesting at his conviction.
2. *Monarch*: James II.
3. *Hook-nose*: Anderton was alleged to have uttered the insult at the time of his arrest.
4. *Books ... any of them*: The books Anderton was accused of printing were Anon., *Remarks upon the Present Confederacy, and late Revolution in England* (London, 1693), and [Charlwood Lawton], *A French Conquest, neither Desirable nor Practicable* (London: printed 'by His Majesty's Servants', 1693). Lawton (1660–1721) was also author at this

time of *The Jacobite Principles Vindicated* (London, 1693). The printers William Newbolt and Edward Butler, tried for printing James II's *Declaration* later in 1693, had printed the *French Conquest*.

5. *last Session ... enacted*: the bill to revive and continue expiring laws, including the 1662 Printing Act, had been enacted on 14 March.
6. first *Offence ... Law*: The Printing Act set limits to punishment for the avoidance of licensing, including by seditious and treasonable books, but not to punishment under other law for seditious libel and treason. It was contrary to normal practice and probably justice to punish Anderton for treason, but not contrary to law in terms of the Printing Act.
7. *Jury ... my Life*: Jacobite pamphlets were found in Anderton's rooms, which also housed a press. He could not be connected to the pamphlets but the prosecution claimed that a sheet of errata and additional material for *Remarks upon the Present Confederacy* had also been found and was printed on the press.
8. Treby: Sir George Treby (bap. 1644; d. 1700), Whig lawyer and MP who at the revolution regained the recordership of London, previously held in 1681–3, and in April 1692 became chief justice of common pleas.
9. *Business ... Printing*: Treby acknowledged that the mere presence of Jacobite pamphlets did not prove guilt but directed the jury to the recently printed errata sheet to the *Remarks* and the presence of a press (*State Trials*, vol. 12, pp. 1258–9).
10. *partial Writer ... Account*: the account in *Proceedings of the Old Bailey*, session beginning 31 May, which provided the basis for the trial information in *An Account of the Conversation, Behaviour and Execution of William Anderton*, reproduced below.
11. *Judges*: the trial was before lord chief justice Sir George Treby, Sir John Powell, baron of the exchequer, Sir John Fleet, the lord mayor, and Sir Salathiel Lovell, the recorder of London.
12. *Robin Stephens*: Robert Stephens, the messenger of the press (see note 13 to *A Short, but Just Account of the Tryal of Harris*, above, p. 357), who apprehended Anderton, searched his premises, and was the main prosecution witness at his trial.
13. Prince of *Wales*: James II's son James Francis Edward Stuart (1688–1766), subsequently James III to Jacobites and the 'Old Pretender' to their opponents.

## An Account of the Conversation, Behaviour and Execution of Anderton

1. *Clemency ... Treason*: The identities of the 'many lives' are unclear. Anne Merryweather had been convicted of treason on 16 January 1693 for helping print and publish James II's *Declaration* but was reprieved. William Newbolt and Edward Butler were similarly convicted and reprieved but only in September 1693. Another five or six defendants were punished for seditious libel as a misdemeanour at the Old Bailey between 1689 and June 1693 (*Proceedings of the Old Bailey*).
2. *Libels ... but two*: see note 4 to Anderton, *True Copy*, above, p. 498.
3. *Old* Prines *Phrase*: William Prynne (1600–69), prolific puritan writer tried in Star Chamber for seditious libel in 1633 and again in 1637. Attribution of 'paper pellets' to Prynne is also found in the 1664 edition of Richard Atkyns's *Original and Growth of Printing*, although the phrase occurs at least as early as 1597 and fairly frequently thereafter.

Notes to pages 410–17

4. *in* Custody *and Expecting it*: William Newbolt and Edward Butler had been apprehended in the previous fortnight for their part in printing James II's *Declaration*. Their trial for treason followed on 8 September, at which they were sentenced to death but they were reprieved on the eve of execution.
5. Fletcher: Miles Fletcher, or Flesher, was a member of a print trade family that also included James Flesher, a jury member in John Twyn's treason trial in 1664. The name first appeared on imprints in 1632, a forebear if not the same Miles Flesher to whom Anderton was apprenticed, the latter being active until 1688.
6. Old Offender ... *Years past*: The trial was told that Anderton had been printing Jacobite literature since 1691.
7. *as followeth*: The information which follows in the text is mainly drawn from the trial account in the *Proceedings of the Old Bailey* for the session commencing 31 May. The latter forms the basis of the *State Trials* account, along with the contrasting version provided by Anderton's supporter Samuel Grascome in *An Appeal of Murther* (London, 1693).
8. *Private Presses*: Anderton seems to have been the 'Thomas Topham' whose press was seized by Robert Stephens in June 1692 (*ODNB*).
9. *Skudamore*: Scudamore, a carpenter based in St James' Street, in whose premises Anderton had rooms.
10. Holts *Chamber*: Sir John Holt (1642–1710), who was made chief justice of King's Bench shortly after the revolution.
11. Libels ... practicable: see note 2 above.
12. *Pannel*: the list of jurors.
13. *last day*: Thursday, 8 June.
14. Richardson, &c.: Anderton's brother and a minister, who was a friend, also accompanied him (Smith, *A True Account*).
15. *another Reverend Divine*: see note 1 to Anderton, *True Copy*, above, p. 498.

# The Rejection of Licensing

## Locke's Comments on the 1662 Printing Act

1. *§. 2.*: Locke proceeds clause by clause, providing a more or less accurate rendering of each clause before advancing his criticisms.
2. *[or Offensive]*: The manuscript at NA, PRO 30/24/30, is badly damaged. Missing and illegible sections are indicated between square brackets. Missing words have been supplied by comparison with MS Locke b. 4, ff. 75–6, in the Bodleian Library, as transcribed in *The Correspondence of John Locke*, ed. E. S. De Beer, 8 vols (Oxford: Clarendon Press, 1976–89), vol. 5, Appendix, pp. 785–91. Orthography has occasionally been adjusted to follow the style of the NA manuscript. Selected variants are indicated in notes, with the Bodleian manuscript designated *B*.
3. *Xan*: Christian.
4. *Earth ... Antipodes once was*: a reference to the suppression of Copernican cosmology, most notably the Roman inquisition's condemnation of Galileo in 1636. Thomas Hobbes uses the same example in *Leviathan* (London, 1651), p. 380: 'Our own Navigations make manifest, and all men learned in humane Sciences, now acknowledge there are Antipodes ... Neverthelesse, men that have in their Writings but supposed such Doc-

trine, as an occasion to lay open the reasons for, and against it, have been punished for it by Authority Ecclesiasticall.'

5. *liberty to print ... either*: Locke's case is against pre-publication censorship, not post-publication punishment under other laws. Compare Charles Blount's *Just Vindication of Learning*: 'Why should I not have the same freedom to write, as to speak? If I speak any thing that is evil, I am lyable to be punish'd, but yet I am never examined before I speak what I am about to say' (above, p. 211).

6. *gives*: gyves, shackles.

7. *Author*: 'Author person he had it from' *B*.

8. *y*: that.

9. *Awnsham Churchill*: Awnsham Churchill (1658–1728), bookseller and Locke's regular publisher. He worked in partnership with his brother William until 1690, then with another brother, John, from that time.

10. *or books or part of such book or books*: 'or books or part of such book or books' *B*; these words are not interlined. In NA there is no space for the phrase to be other than an interlinear insertion, although only a trace is visible.

11. *moiety*: half share.

12. *y^m*: them.

13. *Sam Smith*: Samuel Smith (1658–1707), bookseller, specializing particularly in the importation of Latin works, including Locke's *Epistola de Tolerantia* in 1689. The instance Locke gives, relating to Jacob Gronovius's edition of Cicero published at Leiden in 1692, was described as a recent event in a letter Locke wrote in January 1693 (Locke, *Correspondence*, vol. 4, p. 614).

14. *p^t*: part.

15. *to y^e printing y^e works of Tully Caesar or Livy*: 'of printing the works of Tully's, Caesar's or Livy's' *B*.

16. *in nature*: *B* interlines these words.

17. *slubber*: go over carelessly.

18. *unless stationer of London*: *B* does not interline these words.

19. *presses for coynage*: the presses used to mint coins. Counterfeiting and 'clipping' of coins was a major contemporary concern, about which Locke also wrote.

20. *Master found^rs ... fower*: master founders of letter-type reduced to four.

21. *Everyone Master who has*: 'Everyone who hath' *B*.

22. *Livery ... Yeomanry*: Stationers' Company membership below the officers was divided between those of the livery, considered the elite, and the yeomanry. The clause established the maximum number of apprentices allowed to printers in each category.

23. *Journeymen ... Freemen*: the constraints on taking on freelance workers, requiring they be English and be free of indentured apprenticeship.

24. *o^r*: our.

25. *upse*: in its essence (from the Dutch, literally 'in his' or 'in its').

26. *Paul's Churchyard*: St Paul's churchyard was traditionally the centre of the London book trade, the location of booksellers including Locke's publisher Awnsham Churchill.

27. *Mat^ies: Signe Manual*: his Majesty's signature, which on a royal order was sufficient authority for preparing warrants 'under the sign manual', hence differing from the special warrants required to search peers' homes.

28. *Peers of England*: The extension of the Printing Act's search provisions to the houses of peers was the subject of an objection in the House of Lords when the Act was renewed in 1693. See above, p. 347.

29. *Dʳ: Bury's case ... unlicensed*: a reference to the furore over Arthur Bury's *The Naked Gospel* in 1690; see above, pp. 330–1. The *History of Tom Thumb* was taken to typify harmless entertainment.
30. *vid ⁓⁓⁓⁓*: 'vid' *B*; the illegible word presumably gave erroneous statute details.
31. *17°. Car. 2. cap. 4.*: The 1665 'Act for continuance of a former Act for Regulateing the Presse', which in renewing the 1662 Act added two clauses relating to copies of books to be delivered to the universities.
32. *14ᵗʰ: Car. 2.*: 13 & 14 Car. II, c. 33, the 1662 Printing Act.

## The Commons' Case against Renewing the Printing Act

1. Clark: Edward Clarke (*c.* 1650–1710), MP and political ally of John Locke. Having entered Whig politics in the milieu of the Earl of Shaftesbury and Locke, Clarke maintained a correspondence with the latter through Locke's exile after 1683 and until his death in 1704. On becoming MP for Taunton in 1690, Clarke provided the main parliamentary voice for 'the College' grouping around Locke, the ending of pre-publication censorship being one of their several reform projects during the 1690s.
2. *Amendment ... mentioned*: The House of Lords had agreed an amendment that added the renewal of the Printing Act to the bill for continuing several other expiring laws.
3. *gave*: this word is missing.
4. *Clause marked A*: the amendment continuing the Printing Act.
5. *no Penalty ... therein*: The penalties in the Act were for failing to acquire due licence, not the content of the tract per se.
6. *Notes of Foreigners*: the commentary and supplementary notes of continental scholars, an issue particularly pressed by Locke with his example of Gronovius's edition of Cicero.
7. *Bishop ... Licence*: i.e. a licence to sell, rather than without an imprimatur. The Act required traders in books outside London to have permission from the bishop of the relevant diocese but Stationers' Company members were exempt.
8. *would not*: 'would' – the addition of 'not' is an error.
9. *Peers ... Warrant*: The Act used the term 'special warrant' in relation to searches of peers' homes but the uncertain distinction between this and normal warrants had been a source of concern for the Lords.
10. *Life or Member*: the Act's phrasing is 'life or limb'.
11. John Streater: The printer-publisher Streater curiously gained a personal exemption in 1662 (see note 2 to 'Printing and Printers', above, p. 437). This was no longer relevant, not least because Streater had died in 1677.

## 'A Bill for the Regulation of Printing and Printing Presses'

1. *Whereas*: The opening and subsequent text differs from the earlier 'College' bill as transcribed by John Freke, held in the Bodleian Library and printed in Locke, *Correspondence*, vol. 5, pp. 791–5. Selected variants are given or indicated in the notes, with Freke's version designated *B*. Some variation derives from Freke paraphrasing (see note 3 for an example) but there are also substantive differences, not least that this later bill restores the principle of licensing. A small number of variations from the version earlier in December, now in Cambridge University Library, are also indicated, designated *C*.
2. *after the ... Day of*: Spaces were left for the insertion of dates and penalties.
3. *Whereas ... hath been given*: 'For preventing the mischiefs that may happen in church or State for want of a due Regulation of Printing and Printing Presses Be it Enacted etc.

That from and after the day of Noe Printing Press shall be erected used or kept within the City of London or Suburbs thereof untill notice hath been given ...' *B*.
4. *erected used or Kept ... Oxford or Cambridge*: 'erected used or kept in either of the universitys' *B*.
5. *in the Cityes ... Norwich*: 'in any other City or Town' *B*. The names of specific cities are absent, here and below, in *B*; Exeter is omitted in *C*.
6. *respective Lord Bishop ... City*: 'chief Magistrate of the same City or Town' *B*. The 'College' version, here and below, does not include the requirement that the bishop of the relevant diocese be notified; *C* requires the bishop *or* mayor, rather than bishop *and* mayor.
7. *Moyety*: moiety, half-share.
8. *And Be it further Enacted ... may be Licensed*: This and all down to 'such Illegality Error or fault' (at note marker 12) is absent in *B*. That is to say, the College bill omits mention of licensing altogether, while the later bill restores the principle but in a much-diluted, voluntary form ('may' be licensed).
9. *Earl Marshall ... Norroy*: royal officers concerned with heraldry and ceremony, there being three kings-at-arms designated Garter, Clarenceux and Norroy.
10. *Censors ... physitians*: officers of the College of Physicians whose normal duties centred on administrative and disciplinary matters more than 'censorship' as such.
11. *or by five ... belong*: omitted in *B* and *C*. This was a notable change, allowing for licensing on the part of dissenting congregations, and along with the following provision may have been the compromise required to have the principle of licensing restored to the legislation.
12. *And it shall ... fault*: omitted in *B*, since the College bill did not require licensing. The provision represents a considerable shift in responsibility from printer to licenser. From this point in the text, the end of the section on licensing, the themes of the two bills converge once more.
13. *Neverthelesse ... printers thereof*: 'And be it further Enacted that noe person shall Print any thing Contrary to the Laws of this Realm or Contrary to the Christian Religion as it is Establisht by Law in this Realm' *B*. Compare also the 1662 Printing Act: 'no person or persons whatsoever shall presume to print or cause to be printed ... any heretical seditious schismatical or offensive Bookes or Pamphlets wherein any Doctrine or Opinion shall be asserted or maintained which is contrary to Christian Faith or the Doctrine or Discipline of the Church of England or which shall or may tend to be to the scandal of Religion or the Church or the Government or Governors of the Church State or Commonwealth or of any Corporation or particular person or persons whatsoever'.
14. *And Be it further Enacted ... Laws of England*: The passage echoes *B* but the latter begins the provisions for legal deposit with books of divinity rather than law, and omits reference to books 'Licensed to be printed as above'.
15. *One printed Coppy ... printer*: *B* requires only the delivery of one printed copy, not 'sheet by sheet'. This difference is repeated with other categories of books. *C* has an extended marginal note, as follows: 'It is impossible for the printer to observe this clause wth security to himselfe for the printer is made the person who is to print at his perrill Except he can {produce} the Booke to be Licensed which now will be difficult if not an impossible thing to be done by reason the Licenser is by this Bill left at his liberty whether hee will Lycence or no And therefore it will be very hard upon the printer who cannot be supposed to be a person who understands all the Language wch hee prints neither if hee did can hee be thought a fitt judge of the matter neither doth it give the Arch-Bpps or Bispps

Lord Keeper or Judges power to make any Alteration in or Lycence to the sheetes carryed to them And if the Arch-Bpps should be out of London and other Bps should be out of their dioceses or in their Visitations or at Parliamt And the Judges in their Circuits the process must all stand still wch will be the ruine of many familyes who cannot subsist wthout a daily maintenance'.

16. *Divinity philosophy or any other Science or art*: 'Divinity' B. Books of divinity are the first category treated in B.
17. *without such License ... forfeited*: Absent in B, the clause complicates if not contradicts the earlier undertaking of voluntary licensing, but presumably implies that books are forfeit if not *either* licensed or delivered sheet by sheet.
18. *printer or publisher*: 'printer and publisher' B.
19. *unlesse the same be Lycensed ... Contained*: omitted in B.
20. *and in Case ... Concealement*: omitted in B.
21. *Treasonable Seditious or Atheisticall*: 'Treasonable Seditious Atheisticall or hereticall' B and C. The same change occurs a few words later, and in further iterations in C.
22. *whosoever shall Import ... Burnt*: All this section relating to importing and burning is omitted in B.
23. *Burnt wherever ... notw<sup>th</sup>standing*: All this section dealing with property is omitted in B. At 'notwithstanding', C has an additional clause inserted: 'Provided alwayes And be it further Enacted That any person and persons who now have propriety in any Coppyes or the sole Right of printing any Booke pamphlett pourtraiture or paper shall have and enjoy the same to them and their Assignes for the terme and space of          yeares onely to be accounted from and next ensueing the last day of this session of parliament and no longer'.
24. *Bills plaint ... Imparlance*: legal terms relating to the recovery of fines or damages, essoin connoting an excuse for non-compliance, and imparlance an extension of time pending negotiation.
25. *non {debet}*: not in debt, not liable. The word is unclear and does not occur in B, where the discussion of this area is less thorough.
26. *Def*: defendant.
27. *Two ... Universityes*: clause omitted in B and C. An additional comment appears in C, as follows: 'That if the Importation of Bookes whose property belongs to Traders be not prohibited our Coppyes will be corruptly printed in Holland (as the Bible and Statute Bookes were in the tyme of King Charles the Second) and brought in upon us by reason paper and servants wages are much cheaper there then here which will be the ruine of many familyes who have beene bred upp in the Trade of printing and are fitt for no other Imployment It will likewise be the destruction of the paper trade sett upp here in England and Encouraged by an Act made the last parliament'.

## 'Remarks upon the Act for Regulating Printing and Printing Presses'

1. *leave and Lycence*: The College bill in March avoided even the word 'licence'.
2. *Cheif Magistrate*: the College bill used this term, the November–December bill employing 'mayor'. The inclusion of 'Heretical' in the next sentence also indicates that the earlier bill was being criticized.
3. *where ... England over*: The phrase is intended as a question.
4. *Answerable ... Common Law*: ironically, the same objection advanced by Edward Clarke in the Commons for the abolition of the Printing Act rather than its strengthening.
5. *Acco<sup>t</sup>*: account, i.e. be financially viable.

## 'Oxford Objections against Scheme of Printing Act'

1. *Bill ... Presse*: the 'College' bill introduced in March.
2. *privity*: an unspoken agreement. The word is unclear.
3. *without ... License*: The bill removed any reference to licensing, but retained provisions for searching for objectionable books and pamphlets.
4. *Beer, Mo*: The intended word is uncertain.
5. *illeg.*: The word resembles 'sophistry'.
6. *Socinians, Anabaptists*: religious schools of thought and practice, although also catch-all terms of opprobrium for the heterodox. Socinians were those influenced by ideas of rational religion associated with the theologian Faustus Socinus. Anabaptists were Baptists, practising adult baptism, the term Anabaptists recalling the violent theocracy in sixteenth-century Munster.
7. *clipping & coyning*: a major contemporary concern was criminal 'clipping' of coin edges to melt and make further coins, devaluing the currency, despite it being accounted treason and punishable with death.
8. *New Bill*: the revised bill tabled in Parliament on 29 November; see above, pp. 413–16.
9. *York ... Norwich*: cities specified in the version of the bill held by Tenison and printed above, pp. 425–30 (the Cambridge University Library version omits Exeter).
10. *printed without such License*: The bill provided that printed works 'may be licensed', so while the printer could be punished for the content under other laws, or could request a licence, he was not acting illegally in printing without licence.
11. *delivering ... name*: The alternative to requesting a licence was to deliver the work as the sheets were printed, with the printer's or publisher's name indicated.
12. *proviso ... Cambridge respectively*: such a clause was added to the bill.
13. *grants ... Cambridge*: The grants to Oxford University are listed, including the Great Charter of 1636, with spaces left for insertion of comparable details for Cambridge.
14. *obtend*: obtain, tend.
15. *Royal Societies ... grant*: Beginning with its founding charter in 1662, the Royal Society was given self-governing powers relating to the publication of scientific discoveries, most notably in the society's *Philosophical Transactions*.